Using C-Kermit
Communication Software

Second Edition

Using C-Kermit
Communication Software

Second Edition

Frank da Cruz
and
Christine M. Gianone

Digital Press
Boston • Oxford • Johannesburg • Melbourne • New Delhi • Singapore

Library of Congress Cataloging-in-Publication Data
Da Cruz, Frank, 1944–
      Using C-Kermit / Frank da Cruz, Christine M. Gianone. — 2nd ed.
            p.   cm.
      Includes bibliographical references and index.
      ISBN 1-55558-164-1
      1. C-Kermit. 2. Communications software. I. Gianone, Christine
M. II. Title.
      TK5105.9.D33   1997
      005.7'13—dc20   96-38354
                                                    CIP

British Library Cataloguing-in-Publication Data
A catalogue record for this book is available from the British Library.

The publisher offers special discounts on bulk orders of this book.
For information, please contact:
Manager of Special Sales
Butterworth-Heinemann
225 Wildwood Avenue
Woburn, MA 01801-2041
Tel: 781-904-2500
Fax: 781-904-2620
For information on all Butterworth-Heinemann publications
available, contact our World Wide Web home page at:
http://www.bh.com

10 9

Printed in the United States of America

Contents

Illustrations

Tables

Preface

"Who Is Kermit and Why Is He in My Computer?" asked a (now not so) recent headline [60].[1] Kermit is not a "he" at all, but rather an inanimate, genderless, yet friendly computer software package that lets just about any two computers in the world communicate effectively with each other, no matter how they may differ in size, age, appearance, location, power, architecture, manufacture, or nationality.

This book describes *C-Kermit*, quite possibly the world's most portable communications software program, for UNIX computer systems (hundreds of different ones); Digital Equipment Corporation (Open)VMS on both VAX and Alpha; PCs with Windows 95, Windows NT, or OS/2; Data General AOS/VS, Stratus VOS, the Commodore Amiga, the Atari ST, and computers with the QNX and OS-9 realtime operating systems. The UNIX version of C-Kermit runs on all known implementations of UNIX (see page 16) and on computers ranging from PCs to large mainframes and supercomputers.

C-Kermit software offers you terminal connection, error-free file transfer and management, script programming, and comprehensive support for national and international character sets, over a wide variety of communication methods including direct and dialed serial connections and (in most versions) TCP/IP, X.25, or other networks. C-Kermit's full-featured script programming language operates consistently across all of C-Kermit's platforms and over all types of connections. It allows routine, complex, or time-consuming communications tasks to be executed for you automatically.

---

[1]Numbers in brackets refer to entries in the References on page 595.

C-Kermit transfers text and binary files faithfully and efficiently with any other kind of computer. The Kermit file transfer protocol takes care of synchronization, error detection and correction, file format and character set conversion, and myriad details you should never have to worry about. It was designed to work in even the most hostile communication environments, where other protocols fail. C-Kermit's Kermit implementation, along with that of MS-DOS Kermit, with which it was codeveloped, is the premiere and definitive rendition of the Kermit protocol.

The Kermit file transfer protocol was originally designed in 1981 by Frank da Cruz and Bill Catchings at Columbia University, which has been "Kermit headquarters" ever since, and extended over the years by the authors and others — principally Joe Doupnik of Utah State University and John Chandler of the Harvard / Smithsonian Astronomical Observatory — to meet the evolving needs of the people who depend on it. Because the Kermit protocol is well documented [21], easy to implement, robust, extensible, and adaptable to almost any style of communication and any computer architecture, it has long since taken its place as a worldwide de facto standard for reliable data transfer.

Acknowledgments

C-Kermit was written by Frank da Cruz of Columbia University with contributions from hundreds of other developers and testers, all of whom have our deepest thanks, with our sincere apologies to anyone else we might have overlooked (U = University, locations are in the USA unless otherwise indicated, and note that affiliations or locations might have changed since the contribution was made):

Chris Adie (Edinburgh U, Scotland); Robert Adsett (U of Waterloo, Canada); Larry Afrin (Clemson U); Jeffrey Altman (Columbia U); Greg Andrews (Telebit Corp); Barry Archer (U of Missouri); Bengt Andersson (ABC-Klubben, Sweden); Robert Andersson (International Systems A/S, Oslo, Norway); Chris Armstrong (Brookhaven National Laboratory); William Bader (Software Consulting Services, Nazareth, PA); Fuat Baran (Columbia U); Stan Barber (Rice U); Jim Barbour (U of Colorado); Donn Baumgartner (Dell Computer Corp); Nelson Beebe (U of Utah); Karl Berry (UMB); Mark Berryman (SAIC); Dean W Bettinger (State U of New York); Gary Bilkus; Peter Binderup (Denmark); David Bolen (Advanced Networks and Services, Inc.) Marc Boucher (U of Montreal, Canada); Charles Brooks (EDN); Bob Brown; Mike Brown (Purdue U); Rodney Brown (COCAM, Australia); Jack Bryans (California State U at Long Beach); Mark Buda (DEC); A. Butrimenko (ICSTI, Moscow); Fernando Cabral (Padrão IX, Brasília, Brazil); Björn Carlsson (Stockholm U Computer Centre QZ, Sweden); Bill Catchings (formerly of Columbia U); Bob Cattani (formerly of Columbia U); Davide Cervone (Rochester U, NY); Seth Chaiklin (Denmark); John Chandler (Harvard U/Smithsonian Astronomical Observatory, Cambridge, MA); Bernard Chen (UCLA); Andrew A Chernov (RELCOM

Team, Moscow); John L Chmielewski (AT&T, Lisle, IL); Howard Chu (U of Michigan); Bill Coalson (McDonnell Douglas); Kenneth Cochran; Bertie Coopersmith (London, England); Chet Creider (U of Western Ontario, Canada); Alan Crosswell (Columbia U); Jeff Damens (formerly of Columbia U); Mark Davies (Bath U, England); Sin-itirou Dezawa (Fujifilm, Japan); Clarence Dold (Pope Valley & Napa, CA); Joe R. Doupnik (Utah State U); Frank Dreano (US Navy); John Dunlap (U of Washington); Alex Dupuy (SMART.COM), Jean Dutertre (DEC France and *Club Kermit*); David Dyck (John Fluke Mfg Co.); Stefaan Eeckels (Statistical Office of the European Community, CEC, Luxembourg); Paul Eggert (Twin Sun, Inc.); Bernie Eiben (DEC); Peter Eichhorn (assyst, Gesellschaft für Automatisierung, Software und Systeme mbH, Kirchheim bei München, Germany); Kristoffer Eriksson (Peridot Konsult AB, Örebro, Sweden); John Evans (IRS, Kansas City); Glenn Everhart (DEC); Vincent Fatica (Syracuse U); Charlie Finan (Cray Research, Darien, CT); Herm Fischer (Encino, CA); Carl Fongheiser (CWRU); Mike Freeman (Bonneville Power Authority); Marcello Frutig (Catholic U, São Pãulo, Brazil); Hirofumi Fujii (Japan National Laboratory for High Energy Physics, Tokyo); Chuck Fuller (Westinghouse); Andy Fyfe (Caltech); Christine M. Gianone (Columbia U); Joseph (Yossi) Gil (Technion, Haifa, Israel); John Gilmore (UC Berkeley); Madhusudan Giyyarpuram (HP France); Rainer Glaschick (Siemens AG, Paderborn); William H. Glass; Hunter Goatley (Western Kentucky U); Malka Gold (Columbia U); German Goldszmidt (IBM); Chuck Goodheart (NASA); Alistair Gorman (New Zealand); Juri Gonastaev (ICSTI, Moscow); Richard Gration (Australian Defence Force Academy); Chris Green (Essex U, England); Alan Grieg (Dundee Tech, Scotland); Volkmar Grote (Hamburg, Germany); Valdemar Gunnarson (Iceland); Yekta Gursel (MIT); Jim Guyton (Rand Corp); Vesa Gynther (Finland); Michael Haertel; Marion Hakanson (ORST); John Hamilston (Iowa State U); Steen Hammerum (U of Kobnhavn, Denmark); Simon Hania (Netherlands); Darryl Hankerson (Auburn University); Stan Hanks (Rice U); Ken Harrenstein (SRI); Eugenia Harris (Data General); David Harrison (Kingston Warren Corporation); James Harvey (Indiana/Purdue U); Rob Healey; Chuck Hedrick (Rutgers U); Ron Heiby (Motorola Computer Group); Steve Hemminger (Tektronix); Christian Hemsing (Rheinisch-Westfälisch Technische Hochschule, Aachen, Germany); Andrew Herbert (Monash U, Australia); Mike Hickey (ITI); Dan Hildebrand (QNX Software Systems Inc., Ontario); R.E. Hill; Bill Homer (Cray Research); Ray Hunter (The ex-Wollongong Group); Randy Huntziger (US National Library of Medicine); Larry Jacobs (Transarc); Xander Jansen (SURFnet, Utrecht, Netherlands); Graham Jenkins (TABCORP, Melbourne, Australia); Steve Jenkins (Lancaster U, England); Bo Johansson (Sweden); Dave Johnson (Gradient Technologies); Mark Johnson (Apple Computer); Jyke Jokinen (Tampere U of Technology, Finland); Eric Jones (AT&T); Luke Jones (AT&T); Peter Jones (U of Quebec, Montreal, Canada); Phil Julian (SAS Institute); Peter Kabal (U of Quebec); Mic Kaczmarczik (U of Texas at Austin); Sergey Kartashoff (Institute of Precise Mechanics & Computer Equipment, Moscow); Howie Kaye (Columbia U); Rob Kedoin (Linotype Co., Hauppauge, NY); Phil Keegstra; Mark Kennedy (IBM); Terry Kennedy (St Peter's College, Jersey City, NJ); Carlo Kid (Technical U of Delft, Netherlands); Tim

Kientzle; Ted Kilgore (Auburn U); Paul Kimoto (Cornell U); Douglas Kingston; Lawrence Kirby (Wiltshire, England); John Klensin (United Nations University); Kurt Klingbeil (Province of Alberta); Tom Kloos (Sequent Computer Systems); Jim Knutson (U of Texas at Austin); John T. Kohl (BSDI); Scott Kramer (SRI International); John Kraynack (US Postal Service); David Kricker (Encore Computer); Thomas Krueger (U of Wisconsin at Milwaukee); Bo Kullmar (Central Bank of Sweden, Kista, and ABC-Klubben, Stockholm); R. Brad Kummer (AT&T Bell Labs, Atlanta, GA); John Kunze (UC Berkeley); David Lane (Stratus Computer Inc); Russell Lang (Monash U, Australia); Bob Larson (USC); Bert Laverman (Groningen U, Netherlands); Steve Layton; David Lawyer (UC Irvine); David LeVine (National Semiconductor Corp.); Daniel S. Lewart (UIUC); S.O. Lidie (Lehigh U); Tor Lillqvist (Helsinki U, Finland); Robert Lipe (Arnet Corp); Benny Löfgren (DIAB, Sweden); Dean Long; Mike Long (Analog Devices); Kevin Lowey (U of Saskatchewan, Canada); Andy Lowry (Columbia U); James Lummel (Caprica Telecomputing Resources); David MacKenzie (Environmental Defense Fund, U of Maryland); John Mackin (U of Sidney, Australia); Martin Maclaren (Bath U, England); Chris Maio (formerly of Columbia U); Montserrat Mané (HP France); Fulvio Marino (Olivetti, Ivrea, Italy); Arthur Marsh (DIRCSA, Australia); Peter Mauzey (AT&T); Tye McQueen (Utah State U); Ted Medin (NOSC); Ajay Mehta (DEC); Melissa Metz (Columbia U); Hellmuth Michaelis (Hanseatischer Computerservice GmbH, Hamburg, Germany); Leslie Mikesell (American Farm Bureau); Gary Mills (U of Manitoba, Canada); Martin Minow (DEC); Pawan Misra (Bellcore); Ken Mizialko (IBM, Manassas, VA); Ray Moody (Purdue U); Bruce J. Moore (Allen-Bradley Co); Steve Morley (Convex); Peter Mossel (Columbia U); Tony Movshon (NYU); Lou Muccioli (Swanson Analysis Systems); Dan Murphy; Neal P. Murphy (Harsof Systems, Wonder Lake, IL); Gary Mussar (Bell Northern Research); John Nall (Florida State U); Jack Nelson (U of Pittsburgh); Jim Noble (PRC, Inc.); Ian O'Brien (Bath U, England); John Owens; Michael Pins (Iowa Computer Aided Engineering Network); André Pirard (U of Liège, Belgium); Paul Placeway (Ohio State U); Piet Plomp (Groningen U, Netherlands); Ken Poulton (HP Labs); Manfred Prange (Oakland U); Christopher Pratt (APV Baker, UK); Frank Prindle (NADC); Tony Querubin (U of Hawaii); Phil Race (ICL, Manchester, England); Jean-Pierre Radley; Anton Rang; Ruth Raphaeli (Columbia U); Scott Ribe; Alan Robiette (Oxford U, England); Michel Robitaille (U of Montreal, Canada); Huw Rogers (Schweizerische Kreditanstalt, Zürich); Kai Uwe Rommel (Technische Universität München, Germany); Judith Rosenhouse (Technion, Haifa, Israel); Larry Rosenman (Irving, TX); Jay Rouman (U of Michigan); Jack Rouse (SAS Institute); Stew Rubenstein (Harvard U); Cory Sane (Medical U of SC); Bill Schilit (Columbia U); Ulli Schlüter (RWTH Aachen, Germany); Michael Schmidt (U of Paderborn, Germany); Eric Schnoebelen (Convex); Benn Schreiber (DEC); Dan Schullman (DEC); John Schultz (3M); Steven Schultz (GTE Government Systems Corp); APPP Scorer (Leeds Polytechnic, England); Gordon Scott (Micro Focus, Newbury, England); Jay Sekora (Princeton U); Gisbert W. Selke (Wissenschaftliches Institut der Ortskrankenkassen, Bonn, Germany); David Singer (IBM Almaden Research Labs); David Sizeland (U of London Medical

School, England); Friðrik Skulason (Iceland); Rick Sladkey; Dave Slate; Bradley Smith (UCLA); Fred Smith (Merk); Richard Smith (California State U); Ryan Stanisfer (UNT); Bertil Stenström (Stockholm U Computer Centre QZ, Sweden); James Sturdevant (CAP GEMINI AMERICA, Minneapolis, MN, and Medtronic, Inc., Fridley, MN); Margarita Suarez (Columbia U); Peter Svanberg (Kungl. Tekniska Högskolan, Sweden); James Swenson (Accu-Weather, Inc., State College, PA); Chris Sylvain (U of Maryland); Andy Tanenbaum (Vrije U, Amsterdam, Netherlands); Tim Theisen (U of Wisconsin); Glen Thobe; Lee Tibbert (DEC); Markku Toijala (Helsinki U of Technology, Finland); Teemu Torma (Helsinki U of Technology, Finland); Linus Torvalds (Helsinki, Finland); Rick Troxel (US National Institutes of Health); Warren Tucker (Tridom Corp, Mountain Park, GA); Dave Tweten (NASA); G. Uddeborg (Sweden); Walter Underwood (Ford Aerospace); Pieter Van Der Linden (Centre Mondial, Paris, France); Ge van Geldorp (Netherlands); Fred van Kempen (MINIX User Group, Voorhout, Netherlands); Johan van Wingen (Leiden, Netherlands); Wayne Van Pelt (General Electric Corporate Research and Development); Mark Vasoll (Oklahoma State U); Don Vickers (DECUS); Konstantin Vinogradov (ICSTI, Moscow); Paul Vixie (DEC); Bernie Volz (Process Software); Eduard Vopicka (Prague School of Economics, Czech Republic); Dimitri Vulis (D&M Consulting Services, NYC); Roger Wallace (Raytheon); Stephen Walton (California State U at Northridge); Jamie Watson (Adasoft, Switzerland); Rick Watson (U of Texas); Robert Weiner (Programming Plus, New York City); Lauren Weinstein (Vortex Technology); Clark Wierda (Illuminati Online, Austin TX); David Wexelblat (AT&T Bell Labs); Bill Whitney (DEC); Joachim Wiesel (U of Karlsruhe, Germany); Lon Willett (U of Utah); Michael Williams (UCLA); Nate Williams (U of Montana); David Wilson; Joellen Windsor (U of Arizona); Patrick Wolfe (Kuck & Associates, Inc.); Gregg Wonderly (Oklahoma State U); Farrell Woods (Concurrent); David Woolley (London, England); Jack Woolley (SCT Corp); Frank Wortner; Ken Yap (U of Rochester, NY); John Zeeff (Ann Arbor, MI); Martin Zinser (Gesellschaft für Schwerionenforschung GSI, Darmstadt).

The second edition brings *Using C-Kermit* up to date with C-Kermit 6.0. The changes are too numerous to list, but noteworthy among them is the new "intelligent and portable" dialing directory (Chapter 5), whose design required an education in the art of dialing telephones. For their help with this work, grateful thanks to Pat Townsend for moderating the comp.dcom.telecom newsgroup, a goldmine of telephony information and expertise, and to those who assisted directly, especially: Toby Nixon (Program Manager, Windows Telephony, Microsoft Corporation); Dave Kramer (Head of International Consumer Markets, Sprint International); Bernard Lyons (IS Specialist, Claris Ireland); Ken Levitt (Informed Computer Solutions, Wayland, MA); Mark Brader (SoftQuad Inc., Toronto); Martin Kealey (Auckland, New Zealand); and David Woolley (London, England).

Big thanks, as always, to the "Kermites," who do such an amazing job of technical and customer support while running our day-to-day production operations so smoothly: Max Evarts, Andy Newcomb, and the generations who came before, especially Bob Tschudi, Peter Howard, Lucy Lee, and Ken Suh.

A special note of appreciation to Jeffrey Altman, for some years a (prodigious) volunteer contributor to the Kermit Project, and now a full-time developer on the Kermit team, for massive contributions to C-Kermit 6.0 — and not just code, but energy, enthusiasm, and great ideas too.

Thanks to everyone who helped in the production of this book: Liz McCarthy, Karen Pratt, and Mike Cash at Digital Press / Butterworth Heinemann / Reed Elsevier; to the former team of the original Digital Press, wherever they are now, who produced the first edition of this book as well as our other Kermit books; to Marjan Baće and Lee Fitzpatrick of Manning Software, the publisher of Kermit 95, for which this book serves as technical reference; and to Guy Steele of Sun Microsystems for permission to reproduce his *Telnet Song* and to Deborah Cotton of the ACM for the right to do so.

And finally, thanks to our management and colleagues at Columbia University for their encouragement and support, especially Vaçe Kundakçı, Deputy Vice President for Academic Information Systems, and Elaine Sloan, Vice President for Information Services and University Librarian; to Bruce Gilchrist and Howard Eskin, directors of our organization during the early days of Kermit; to Alan Crosswell and the AcIS Systems Group for taking care of our well-known server, kermit.columbia.edu, and for help in many other forms; and to Lee Lidofsky, a Great Teacher, for a timely push in a good direction, a long time ago.

Frank da Cruz and Christine M. Gianone
The Kermit Project, Columbia University
New York City, September 1996

fdc@columbia.edu, cmg@columbia.edu

IMPORTANT:

This edition of *Using C-Kermit* is current as of C-Kermit version 6.0.192. Any changes made after this edition was published, but before the next edition is published, are listed in an online file that accompanies the C-Kermit software. The name of the file depends on the operating system and distribution method, but will generally begin or end with the characters "UPD" — CKERMIT.UPD, CKCKER.UPD, UPDATES.DOC. Be sure to consult this file to learn about new features.

Other supplemental online documentation files include "beware" files, whose names end with ".BWR", which contain current information about bugs and restrictions, with suggested workarounds, for C-Kermit in general (CKCKER.BWR), and for particular implementations (ckuker.bwr for UNIX, CKVKER.BWR for VMS, etc). There are also files containing detailed installation instructions for each operating system (CK*INS.DOC), plus a configuration guide (CKCCFG.DOC) and a program logic manual (CKCPLM.DOC).

Chapter 1

Introduction

An ever-increasing amount of communication is electronic and digital: computers talking to computers — directly, over the telephone system, through networks. When you want two computers to communicate, it is usually for one of two reasons: to interact directly with another computer or to transfer data between the two computers. Kermit software gives you both these capabilities, and a lot more too.

C-Kermit is a communications software program written in the C language. It is available for many different kinds of computers and operating systems, including literally hundreds of UNIX varieties (HP-UX, AIX, Solaris, IRIX, SCO, Linux, . . .), Digital Equipment Corporation (Open)VMS, Microsoft Windows NT and 95, IBM OS/2, Stratus VOS, Data General AOS/VS, Microware OS-9, the Apple Macintosh, the Commodore Amiga, and the Atari ST. On all these platforms, C-Kermit's services include:

- *Connection establishment.* This means making dialup modem connections or (in most cases) network connections, including TCP/IP Telnet or Rlogin, X.25, LAT, NET-BIOS, or other types of networks. For dialup connections, C-Kermit supports a wide range of modems and an extremely sophisticated yet easy-to-use dialing directory. And C-Kermit accepts incoming connections from other computers too.

- *Terminal sessions.* An interactive terminal connection can be made to another computer via modem or network. The Windows 95, Windows NT, and OS/2 versions of C-Kermit also emulate specific types of terminals, such as the Digital Equipment Corporation VT320, the Wyse 60, or the ANSI terminal types used for accessing BBSs or PC UNIX consoles, with lots of extras such as scrollback, key mapping, printer control, colors, and mouse shortcuts.

- *File transfer.* Transferring either text or binary files from your computer to the other one, or vice versa, free of errors, using the most advanced and high-performance implementation of Columbia University's Kermit file transfer protocol available anywhere. On some platforms, other protocols such as ZMODEM are also included.

- *Client / server features.* These allow uniform and convenient access from your desktop computer to the wide variety of other computers and services for which Kermit servers are available, in which you may initiate all sorts of file transfer and management functions from your client software.

- *International character-set conversion.* Kermit software stands alone among communications protocols and software in its ability to reconcile the differences among incompatible character sets used to represent text in many languages.

- *Automation.* C-Kermit's command language is also a script programming language that is both powerful and easy to use, as well as portable across hundreds of platforms *and* diverse communication methods. Use it to automate all your routine communication tasks, ranging from paging, to simple data exchange, to complex update operations, to network monitoring and reporting.

All of C-Kermit's features are configurable and customizable, giving you an unprecedented and unparalleled degree of control over your connections.

This book is the technical reference manual for C-Kermit in its many incarnations. It concentrates on what all the versions have in common: the communications functions, the command language, file transfer, the character-set conversion features, and the scripting language. The specifics of each version are covered either in a separate publication such as the Kermit 95 manual, in an appendix to this book, or in an online file.

Why Kermit?

In the present age of graphical user interfaces, Web browsers, and near-universal Internet access, what use is a text-mode serial communications program like C-Kermit? Let's clear up two misconceptions right away. First, C-Kermit is not just a serial communications program any more; it is also both a network client and a network server. And second, its text-mode user interface can be (and often is) concealed behind a graphical interface but can still brought bear on the hard problems when real power is needed.

The world of computing and data communications is still surprisingly heterogeneous. To this day there remains a vast diversity of computers large and small, as well as devices that most of us might not think of as computers — laboratory equipment, cash registers, bar-code scanners, you name it — that do not fit the Internet-connected, multimedia, Web-browsing model, yet still need to exchange data with other computers. Minis and mainframes still exist despite all attempts to kill them off, not to mention countless discontinued "legacy" systems ranging from CP/M microcomputers to Soviet-era supercomputers, still in good service, that would be powerless to communicate without Kermit.

Kermit conforms to well-established open standards. It gives you freedom of choice. It does not lock you into a particular brand of hardware or operating system, or a particular or proprietary communication method. Learn it once, use it everywhere.

- Kermit software is universal. Kermit programs have been written for hundreds of different kinds of computers (see page 11). Kermit software is available for just about any computer and operating system you can think of.

- Kermit software communicates not only over dialup connections, but also over direct serial connections, local area networks, and wide area networks, so you can use the same software for practically any kind of connection.

- Kermit software is flexible. It is adaptable to the styles and formats of the many computer manufacturers and communication service providers.

- Kermit software is easy to use. The commands are ordinary words, rather than cryptic codes. Menus are available upon demand. Some Kermit programs, such as Kermit 95 and Kermit/2, have a graphical user interface in addition to the traditional command interface described in this book.

- Kermit software is powerful. Procedures can be automated using a script programming language composed of ordinary Kermit commands.

- Kermit scripts are portable. The same scripting language is usable on hundreds of different platforms.

- Kermit file transfer is robust. It works in hostile or restrictive communication environments where other protocols and software fail.

- Kermit file transfer — perhaps contrary to popular belief — can be *fast*.

- Kermit file transfer is international. It can transfer text in many languages and character sets without scrambling the special characters.

- Kermit software is accessible. Because it offers a character-mode user interface, it is compatible with speech, Braille, and other enabling devices.

One software package for practically all your communication needs: no switching from package to package to access different kinds of computers or services or to use different communication methods; no need to learn or support multiple packages. And as an added benefit, most Kermit software programs have the same basic set of commands and procedures — once you've learned one Kermit program, you've learned them all.

The Other Computer
(REMOTE)

YOU ARE NOT HERE

Your Computer
(LOCAL)

YOU ARE HERE

Figure 1-1 Remote and Local Computers

How Kermit Works

Picture two computers, like the ones in Figure 1-1. You are using one of them directly: it is a PC or workstation on your desk, or it is a timesharing system connected to a terminal (or terminal emulator) on your desk. Let's call this the *local* computer. You want to connect your local computer to a more distant, *remote* computer or service and transfer data.

> *IMPORTANT:* Remember the terms *local* and *remote*. They are used throughout this book. The local computer is the one you are making the connection *from*. The remote computer is the one you are making the connection *to*.

Let's say you are connecting the two computers by telephone. First be sure that each computer has a modem. Then you must know the name of the device on your local computer that the modem is connected to, the transmission speed to use, and the telephone number to call. Let's look at Figure 1-2. We start the local Kermit program simply by typing the word *kermit*.

> *IMPORTANT:* In the figures, and in all examples used in this book, the text you type is underlined. When you are typing commands to your operating system or to a Kermit program, you must terminate them by pressing the Return or Enter key at the point where the underlining ends (unless otherwise indicated).

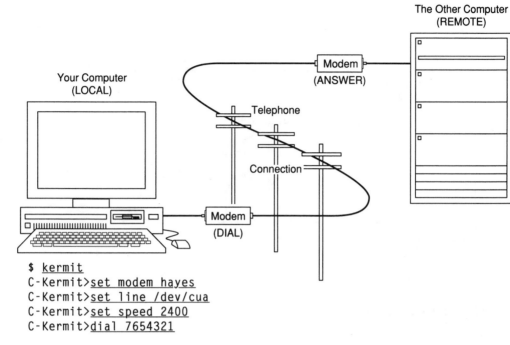

```
$ kermit
C-Kermit>set modem hayes
C-Kermit>set line /dev/cua
C-Kermit>set speed 2400
C-Kermit>dial 7654321
```

Figure 1-2 Connecting the Local and Remote Computers

When the local Kermit's prompt appears, tell it the modem type and the communication device name and speed, and then tell it to dial the other computer's phone number. When the other computer answers the phone, give your local Kermit the CONNECT command[2] and now you are talking to the remote computer just as if you were using it directly. Log in as shown in Figure 1-3 and carry on a dialog to conduct your business. Eventually you might decide that you want to move a file from one computer to the other.

To transfer a file, both computers must be running Kermit programs. Your local computer already is. Simply type "kermit" on the remote computer to start the remote Kermit program.[3] Now you must tell *each* Kermit program what to do: one of them must be told to send a file of a certain name and the other must be told to receive the file. The basic rule is: (1) tell the remote computer what to do first (SEND or RECEIVE), then (2) get back to the local computer and tell it the opposite (RECEIVE or SEND)[4], as shown in Figure 1-4.

---

[2]If you give the DIAL command at the C-Kermit prompt and the call is answered successfully, C-Kermit CONNECTs automatically, so in this case no CONNECT command is needed.

[3]If there is no Kermit software on the remote computer, other file transfer methods are available.

[4]Some versions of C-Kermit have an "autodownload" feature that simplifies this process.

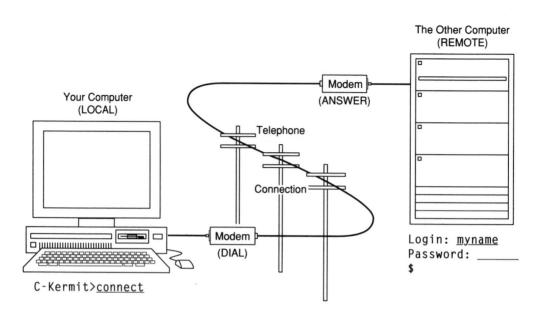

The Other Computer
(REMOTE)

Your Computer
(LOCAL)

Modem
(ANSWER)

Telephone

Connection

Modem
(DIAL)

Login: myname
Password: _____
$

C-Kermit>connect

Figure 1-3 Logging in to the Remote Computer

How do you get back to the local computer? After you CONNECT to the remote computer, the local Kermit sends all the characters you type straight to the remote computer, without paying any attention to them itself. But one character is special during a CONNECT session. C-Kermit notices when you type this special character (usually a control character such as Ctrl-Backslash) and interprets the next character that you type as a command; for example, the letter *C* to Come back to the prompt. This two-character sequence is shown in the figure as *Ctrl-\c*, and entering it is referred to as "escaping back." (In the Windows and OS/2 versions, you can use Alt-key combinations or the mouse for this.)

Here is an example of the basic procedure, in which you are transferring the file OOFA.TXT from the remote computer to the local one, Your local computer is a UNIX workstation with C-Kermit and the remote computer is running VMS, also with C-Kermit:

1. Start Kermit on your local computer:

```
$ kermit
C-Kermit 6.0.192, 6 Sep 96, Solaris 2.5
Type ? or HELP for help
C-Kermit>
```

2. Tell it the modem type and the name and speed of the communication device:

```
C-Kermit>set modem type mwave
C-Kermit>set line /dev/cua
C-Kermit>set speed 57600
```

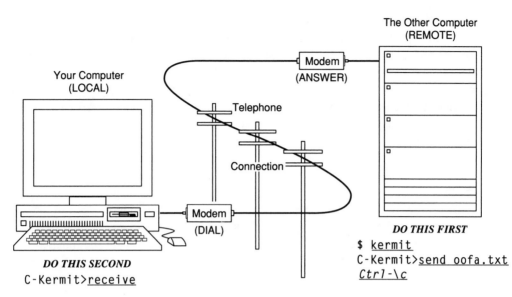

Figure 1-4 Transferring a File

3. Have it dial the telephone number of the remote computer:

   ```
   C-Kermit>dial 7654321
   ```

4. Enter terminal mode:

   ```
   C-Kermit>connect
   ```

5. Log in to the remote computer and start Kermit there:

   ```
   Welcome to the Remote Computer
   Username: myusername
   Password: _____
   $
   $ kermit
   C-Kermit 6.0.192, 6 Sep 96, OpenVMS VAX
   Type ? or HELP for help
   C-Kermit>
   ```

6. Tell the remote Kermit program to send the file:

   ```
   C-Kermit>send oofa.txt
   Return to your local Kermit and give a RECEIVE command.

   KERMIT READY TO SEND...
   ```

7. Enter the key sequence to escape back from terminal mode to your local Kermit program and tell it to receive the file:

   ```
   Ctrl-\c
   C-Kermit>receive
   ```

Now the two Kermit programs begin talking to each other using specially formatted messages called packets, which contain not only data from your files, but also control information, such as "here is the file name," "here is the first piece of data from the file," "here is the second piece," "that was the last piece," "please send the second piece again," and so on. The data in each packet is encoded to contain only printable characters to ensure that it will pass through sensitive communication devices. All packets include error checking and sequencing information to prevent your data from being lost, duplicated, or damaged.

This is the basic scenario for file transfer. There are many variations: you can send files in the other direction (by exchanging the SEND and RECEIVE commands), you can transfer a group of files in a single operation, you can operate the remote Kermit as a fully protocol-driven file server, and you can automate the process to any desired degree using C-Kermit's script programming language. The details of the Kermit file transfer protocol are given in a separate book [21, Chapters 8–12].

Capabilities of C-Kermit

C-Kermit is among the most advanced and powerful of all the Kermit programs. These are some of its features (the terminology will be explained more fully as we go along):

- Support for nearly all known varieties of UNIX (see page 16), for Digital Equipment Corporation (Open)VMS, IBM OS/2, Microsoft Windows NT and Windows 95, Stratus VOS, Data General Corporation AOS/VS, Microware OS-9, Commodore AmigaDOS, and Atari ST GEMDOS.

- Error-correcting, efficient file transfer using the Kermit protocol. Text or binary files may be transferred singly or in groups.

- Operation at a full range of speeds using standard serial communication ports.

- Ability to make network connections on TCP/IP, X.25, DECnet, NETBIOS, and Named Pipe networks, depending on the platform.

- On TCP/IP networks, ability to act as a Telnet client or an Rlogin client, and the ability to accept incoming TCP connections.

- Communication settings that can be matched to virtually any other computer.

- Automatic dialing with built-in knowledge of a wide variety of modems, plus easy configurability for additional modem types.

- The ability to accept incoming modem calls.

- Terminal connection to remote computers, including character set translation, key mapping, keyboard macros, and session logging capabilities.

- In the Windows and OS/2 versions, also high-quality, fast emulation of VT320/220/102/100/52, terminals, as well as Wyse, Data General, Televideo, Heath, and other models.

- A simple, consistent, and intuitive command language with built-in help, in most ways compatible with MS-DOS Kermit and other Kermit programs.

- Command and initialization files.

- Command macros and a powerful script programming language, including built-in and user-definable variables and functions; FOR, WHILE, SWITCH, IF-ELSE, and GOTO, string and arithmetic processing, file I/O and management, and of course communications input, output, and triggering.

- Logging, security, and debugging features.

- Kermit protocol capabilities including long packets, sliding windows, international text character-set conversion, checksum and CRC error correction, the ability to transfer 8-bit data through a 7-bit communications channel using both single and locking shifts, automatic parity detection, transmission of file attributes, server mode, run-length data compression, control-character unprefixing, file transfer recovery, file transfer interruption, dynamic packet lengths, dynamic packet timers, file management functions, and more. C-Kermit also has the ability to transmit and receive files without error checking when the other computer doesn't have a Kermit program, as well as to execute built-in or external implementations of other protocols such as XMODEM, YMODEM, and ZMODEM.

On the Internet, C-Kermit is widely known as the "scriptable Telnet that can transfer files," the Telnet client of choice. It is also perfectly suited for use as the Telnet application for your Web browser, offering numerous advantages over a traditional Telnet program:

- Automation of Telnet sessions via C-Kermit's script programming language.

- The ability to upload or download text or binary files over the Telnet connection itself.

- The ability to log (record) the session.

- The ability to translate among a wide variety of otherwise incompatible character sets.

In addition, of course, the Windows and OS/2 versions of C-Kermit offer countless terminal emulation features lacking from traditional Telnet programs, including comprehensive key mapping, a Compose key, scrollback, a wider selection of terminal emulations, mouse shortcuts, colors, printer control, and so on.

Capabilities of Popular Kermit Programs

C-Kermit's capabilities are compared with other popular Kermit programs in Table 1-1. C-K is C-Kermit; K-95 is the Windows 95 and NT version; K/2 is the OS/2 version. MS-K is MS-DOS Kermit, McK is Macintosh Kermit, K-370 is IBM Mainframe Kermit, K-11 is PDP-11 Kermit, K-80 is CP/M-80 Kermit, and K-65 is Apple II Kermit.

Table 1-1   Kermit Software Features

Feature	C-K	K95	K/2	MS-K	McK	K-370	K-11	K-80	K-65
Local operation	Yes	Yes	Yes	Yes	Yes	No	Yes	Yes	Yes
Remote operation	Yes	No	No	Yes	No	Yes	Yes	No	No
Terminal connection	Yes	Yes	Yes	Yes	Yes	N/A	Yes	Yes	Yes
Terminal emulation	No	Yes	Yes	Yes	Yes	N/A	No	Yes	Yes
Automatic modem dialing	Yes	Yes	Yes	Yes	Yes	N/A	Yes	No	Yes
Can make network connections	Yes	Yes	Yes	Yes	No	N/A	No	No	No
Automatic feature negotiation	Yes	Yes	Yes	Yes	Yes	Yes	Yes	Yes	Yes
Character-set translation	Yes	Yes	Yes	Yes	Yes	Yes	No	No	No
File transfer recovery	Yes	Yes	Yes	Yes	No	Yes	No	No	No
File transfer interruption	Yes	Yes	Yes	Yes	Yes	Yes	Yes	Yes	Yes
Filename collision actions	Yes	Yes	Yes	Yes	Yes	Yes	Yes	Yes	Yes
Single shifts	Yes	Yes	Yes	Yes	Yes	Yes	Yes	Yes	Yes
Locking shifts	Yes	Yes	Yes	Yes	Yes	Yes	No	No	No
Run-length compression	Yes	Yes	Yes	Yes	Yes	Yes	Yes	No	No
Control-character unprefixing	Yes	Yes	Yes	Yes	Yes	No	No	No	No
Alternate block checks	Yes	Yes	Yes	Yes	Yes	Yes	Yes	Yes	No
Automatic parity detection	Yes	Yes	Yes	Yes	No	No	No	No	No
Dynamic packet length	Yes	Yes	Yes	Yes	Yes	Yes	No	No	No
Dynamic packet timers	Yes	Yes	Yes	Yes	Yes	No	No	No	No
Act as server	Yes	Yes	Yes	Yes	Yes	Yes	Yes	No	No
Act as client of server	Yes	Yes	Yes	Yes	Yes	Yes	Yes	Yes	Yes
Client/server "whatami"	Yes	Yes	Yes	Yes	Yes	Yes	No	No	No
Advanced server functions	Yes	Yes	Yes	Yes	Yes	Yes	Yes	Yes	Yes
Security for server	Yes	Yes	Yes	Yes	Yes	No	No	N/A	N/A
Local file management	Yes	Yes	Yes	Yes	Yes	Yes	Yes	Yes	Yes
Command/Init files	Yes	Yes	Yes	Yes	Yes	Yes	Yes	Yes	Yes
Long packets	Yes	Yes	Yes	Yes	Yes	Yes	Yes	No	No
Sliding windows	Yes	Yes	Yes	Yes	Yes	No	No	No	No
Attribute packets	Yes	Yes	Yes	Yes	Yes	Yes	Yes	No	No
Command macros	Yes	Yes	Yes	Yes	Yes	No	No	No	No
Script programming language	Yes	Yes	Yes	Yes	Yes	No	No	No	No
Auto up/download	Yes	Yes	Yes	Yes	No	N/A	No	No	No
Application Program Command	Yes	Yes	Yes	Yes	No	N/A	No	No	No
Auto transfer mode "whoami"	Yes	Yes	Yes	Yes	Yes	Yes	No	No	No
Raw file transmit and capture	Yes	Yes	Yes	Yes	Yes	N/A	Yes	Yes	Yes

Kermit Software Versions

C-Kermit is only one of many Kermit software programs. As you can see from Table 1-2, which begins on the next page, Kermit is available for almost any kind of computer you can think of. Kermit software is written in a wide variety of programming languages, and source code is available for most versions.

The table does not show the hundreds of makes of computers and variations of operating systems for which C-Kermit, MS-DOS Kermit, and CP/M Kermit have been adapted. MS-DOS Kermit runs on countless IBM-compatible PCs and quite a few non-compatible models too. The CP/M versions have been adapted to about 70 different machines. The UNIX version of C-Kermit has been built successfully on about 500 *different* platforms. Some of them are listed beginning on page 16, after Table 1-2.

How to Get Kermit Software and Information

Kermit software is available in computer book and software stores, or can be ordered from Columbia University on 3.5-inch DOS-format diskettes, on 9-track magnetic tape in TAR, ANSI, or OS format, on various kinds of tape cartridges in TAR format, on DEC TK50 tape cartridge in VMS BACKUP format, and others. Use the tear-out discount order form in the back of this book.

For an up-to-date catalog and mail-order instructions, and to be placed on the subscriber list for the free journal, *Kermit News*, contact:

> The Kermit Project
> Columbia University
> 612 West 115th Street
> New York NY 10025-7799, USA
> Voice: +1 212 854-3703
> Fax: +1 212 662-6442 *or* +1 212 663-8202
> Email: kermit-orders@columbia.edu

Various shipping and payment methods are available, and overseas orders are accepted.

If you have access to the Internet, point your World Wide Web browser at:

    http://www.columbia.edu/kermit/

or use anonymous FTP to IP host kermit.columbia.edu to get and read the file `kermit/READ.ME`. Our FAQ — Frequently Asked Questions (and answers) — is available by FTP as `kermit/FAQ.TXT`, and also on the Web site. If you have access to Usenet newsgroups (netnews), read our newsgroups: comp.protocols.kermit.announce and comp.protocols.kermit.misc.

Users of Kermit software are requested to purchase the appropriate published manuals (such as this one). Sales of these manuals are the primary source of funding for the non-profit Kermit project, and they are also a good investment — they show you how to use the software to best advantage and they answer your questions, saving wear and tear on both you and your organization's or service provider's help desk, thus keeping costs down and productivity up.

Kermit software is *not in the public domain* and there are restrictions on its redistribution. Be sure to read all relevant copyright notices and policy statements. For up-to-date information, contact Columbia University as shown on the previous page.

Table 1-2 Kermit Software Listed by Computer Type

Implementation	Computer	OS	Language
C-Kermit	*many*	UNIX	C
Kermit 95	*many*	Windows 95	C
Kermit 95	*many*	Windows NT	C
MS-DOS Kermit	*many*	MS-DOS	8088 Assembler, C
MS-DOS Kermit	*many*	Windows 3.x	8088 Assembler
Kermit-80	*many*	CP/M-80	8080 Assembler
Kermit-86	*many*	CP/M-86	8088 Assembler
Kermit-TD	*various*	TurboDos	8080 Assembler
EMACS-Kermit	*various*	GNU EMACS	EMACS LISP
PICK-Kermit	*various*	PICK	DATA/BASIC
Kermit-UCSD	*various*	UCSD p-System	UCSD Pascal
BBC-Kermit	Acorn BBC	Acorn OS	6502 Assembler
Kermit-65	Apple II	DOS, PRODOS	6502 Assembler
Mac-Kermit	Apple Macintosh	Mac OS	C
Atari-Kermit	Atari 800	DOS	Action
C-Kermit	Atari ST	GEMDOS	C
C-Kermit	BeBox	BeOS	C

Table 1-2   Kermit Software Listed by Computer Type (continued)

Implementation	Computer	OS	Language
Kermit-CT	Burroughs B20	BTOS	C
Kermit-B78	Burroughs A-Series	MCS/AS	Algol
Kermit-B68	Burroughs B6800	Burroughs	Algol
Kermit-B78	Burroughs B7800	Burroughs	Algol
Kermit-B79	Burroughs B7900	Burroughs	Algol
Kermit-CD3	CDC Cyber	NOS	Fortran-5
Kermit-CDC	CDC Cyber	NOS, NOS/BE	Fortran-77
Kermit-CYB	CDC Cyber	NOS 2.2	Compass
Kermit-NOS	CDC Cyber	NOS 2.4	Compass
CC-Kermit	Chinese PCs	CC-DOS	8088 Assembler
Kermit-C64	Commodore 64	DOS	6510A Assembler
Kermit-C64	Commodore 128	DOS	6510A Assembler
C-Kermit	Commodore Amiga	AmigaDOS	C
Kermit-CT	Convergent NGEN	CTOS	C
Cray Kermit	Cray-1	CTSS	Fortran-77
Cray Kermit	Cray-XMP	CTSS	Fortran-77
C-Kermit	DEC Alpha	OpenVMS	C
C-Kermit	DEC Alpha	Digital UNIX	C
C-Kermit	DEC Alpha	Windows NT	C
Kermit-12	DEC PDP-8	OS/8	PAL-8 Assembler
Kermit-11	DEC PDP-11	IAX	Macro-11 Assembler
Kermit-11	DEC PDP-11	RSTS/E	Macro-11 Assembler
Kermit-11	DEC PDP-11	RSX-11	Macro-11 Assembler
Kermit-11	DEC PDP-11	RT-11	Macro-11 Assembler
Kermit-11	DEC PDP-11	TSX+	Macro-11 Assembler
MUMPS Kermit	DEC PDP-11	MUMPS	MUMPS-82
Kermit-12	DEC PDP-12	OS/12	PAL-8 Assembler
Kermit-11	DEC Pro-3xx	P/OS	Macro-11 Assembler
Kermit-11	DEC Pro-3xx	Pro/RT	Macro-11 Assembler
C-Kermit	DEC VAX	ULTRIX	C

Table 1-2   Kermit Software Listed by Computer Type (continued)

Implementation	Computer	OS	Language
C-Kermit	DEC VAX	VMS, (Open)VMS	C
Kermit-12	DECmate I, II, III	OS/278	PAL-8 Assembler
C-Kermit	DECstation	ULTRIX, OSF/1	C
Kermit-10	DECsystem-10	TOPS-10	MACRO-10 Assembler
Kermit-20	DECSYSTEM-20	TOPS-20	MACRO-20 Assembler
C-Kermit	Data General AViiON	DG/UX	C
C-Kermit	Data General MV	AOS/VS	C
Kermit-RDOS	Data General Nova	RDOS	BASIC or Fortran-5
GEC-Kermit	GEC 4000	OS4000	MUM/SERC
Gould Kermit	Gould/SEL 32	MPX-32	Fortran-77+
HPM-Kermit	HP 1000	RTE	Fortran-77, Assembler
Rover-Kermit	HP 264x	ROM	8080 Assembler
HP3-Kermit	HP 3000	MPE	SPL
C-Kermit	HP 9000	HP-UX	C
HPB-Kermit	HP 9xxx	HP BASIC	HP BASIC
HPP-Kermit	HP 9xxx	HP Pascal	HP Pascal
Aegis Kermit	HP/Apollo	Aegis	Pascal
HP8-Kermit	HP86, HP87	HP BASIC	HP BASIC
Kermit-H100	Harris 100	VOS	Fortran-77
Kermit-H800	Harris 800	VOS	Pascal, Assembler
MULTICS-Kermit	Honeywell	MULTICS	PL/I
HG-Kermit	Honeywell DPS6	GCOS	C
HB-Kermit	Honeywell DPS8	GCOS	B
HC-Kermit	Honeywell DPS8	CP-6	PL/6
CS9-Kermit	IBM CS9000	CSOS	Pascal
MS-DOS Kermit	IBM PC family	MS-DOS	C, 8088 Assembler
Kermit/2	IBM PC family	OS/2	C
C-Kermit	IBM PC family	QNX	C
C-Kermit	IBM PC family	SCO, Linux, etc	C
MS-DOS Kermit	IBM PC family	Windows 2.x, 3.x	C, 8088 Assembler

Table 1-2   Kermit Software Listed by Computer Type (continued)

Implementation	Computer	OS	Language
Kermit 95	IBM PC family	Windows NT, 95	C
Kermit-370	IBM mainframe	CICS	370 Assembler
Kermit-370	IBM mainframe	MUSIC	370 Assembler
Kermit-370	IBM mainframe	MVS/ROSCOE	370 Assembler
Kermit-370	IBM mainframe	MVS/TSO	370 Assembler
Kermit-370	IBM mainframe	VM/CMS	370 Assembler
GUTS-Kermit	IBM mainframe	MVS/GUTS	370 Assembler
MTS-Kermit	IBM mainframe	MTS	PLUS, Pascal, Assembler
C-Kermit	IBM RS/6000 or PPC	AIX	C
VME-Kermit	ICL 2900	VME	S3
Perq-Kermit	ICL/Perq	Perq OS	Pascal
Kermit-8051	Intel 8051	–	Assembler
Kermit-ISIS	Intel MDS	ISIS	PL/M
Kermit-MDS	Intel MDS	iRMX	8088 Assembler
Kermit-RMX	Intel MDS	RMX	PL/M
Kermit-LMI	LMI LISP Machine	LMI-LAMBDA	ZETALISP
Kermit-Lilith	Lilith Workstation	MEDOS	Modula-2
ABC-Kermit-80	Luxor ABC-80	ABC-DOS	Z80 Assembler
ABC-Kermit	Luxor ABC-800	ABC-DOS	ABC-BASIC-II
Kermit-B4	MAI Basic Four	BOSS/VS	BASIC BB86
Kermit-MODCOMP	MODCOMP Classic	MAX IV	Fortran, Assembler
Flex-Kermit	Motorola 6809	Flex	C or Assembler
C-Kermit	Motorola 680x0	OS-9	C
Kermit-9800	NCR 9800	VE	C
MS-DOS Kermit	NEC PC9801	MS-DOS	C, Assembler
Kermit-ND	Norsk Data	Intran III	ND-Pascal
Kermit-PE	Perkin-Elmer 3200	OS/32	Fortran
Kermit-PE7	Perkin-Elmer 7000	IDRIS	C
C-Kermit	PowerPC	Windows NT	C
Prime-Kermit	Prime	PRIMOS	PL/P

Table 1-2   Kermit Software Listed by Computer Type (continued)

Implementation	Computer	OS	Language
Kermit-RML	RML 480Z	ROS	C
C-Kermit	SGI	IRIX	C
Kermit-QL	Sinclair QL	QDOS	C or BCPL
Kermit-1100	Sperry 1100	Exec	Assembler or Pascal
Kermit-VS9	Sperry 90/60	VS9	Assembler
C-Kermit	Stratus	VOS	C
C-Kermit	Sun	SunOS or Solaris	C
Kermit-LMS	Symbolics 36xx	Symbolics	ZETALISP
Kermit-TI990	TI 990	DX10	Pascal
Kermit-TIX	TI Explorer	LISP	Common LISP
Kermit-CoCo	TRS-80 CoCo	DOS	EDTASM Assembler
Kermit-TRS80	TRS-80 I, II, III	TRSDOS	8080 Assembler
Kermit-M4	TRS-80 Model 4	TRSDOS	8080 Assembler
Tandem-Kermit	Tandem Nonstop	Guardian	TAL
Kermit-T100	Tandy 100	Tandy 100	BASIC
C-Kermit	Tandy 1600	Xenix	C

UNIX C-Kermit Versions

As of this writing, C-Kermit 6.0.192 has been tested successfully on 16-bit, 32-bit, and 64-bit architectures under portable UNIX versions including 4.2 and 4.3BSD, 4.4BSD, AT&T UNIX System III, AT&T UNIX System V Releases 2, 3, and 4; Mach and Mach-Ten; POSIX, Linux, NeXTSTEP, OSF/1, AIX, and Solaris versions. C-Kermit version 5 or 6 has also been built and tested successfully on the following specific platforms:

Acorn RISCiX; Altos ACS68000 with UNIX System III R2; Amdahl mainframes with UTS 2.4 and UTSV 5.2.6b; Amdahl mainframes with UNIX System V R5.2.6; Apollo workstations with Aegis 9.7 and with DomainOS SR10.0 and 10.4; Apple Macintosh with A/UX; AT&T 3B2 and 3B20 systems with UNIX System V R2; AT&T 6300 PLUS with UNIX System V R2; AT&T 6386 WGS UNIX PC with UNIX System V/386 3.2; AT&T PC 7300 UNIXPC (3B1) System V R3.51m; Atari Falcon with MiNT; Atari ST with MINIX ST 1.5; BeBox with BeOS DR7 and 8; Bull DPX/2 with BOS/X; Charles River Data Systems Universe with UNOX 9.2; Commodore Amiga with UNIX System V R4; Concurrent (Masscomp) computers with RTU 4.0 through 6.0; Concurrent (Perkin-Elmer) computers with Xelos System V R02; Convergent Technologies MiniFrame with CTIX

System V R3; Convex C1 and C2 with Convex/OS 8.x and 9.x; Convex 3240, C220, and C240 with ConvexOS V10.x; Cray supercomputers with UNICOS 6.1 through 8.0and with CSOS 1.0; DEC Alpha and DECstation with OSF/1 versions 1 through 3 and Digital UNIX 3.2 through 4.0; DEC PDP-11 with 2.11BSD; DEC VAX with 4.2BSD, 4.3BSD, 4.3BSD-Reno, 4.3BSD-Networking/2; DEC VAX with AT&T Bell Labs Research UNIX 10th Edition; DEC VAX with ULTRIX 1.0, 2.0, 3.0, 4.0, 4.2, and 4.3; DEC VAX with AT&T System V R3; DECstation with MACH 2.6; DECstation with ULTRIX 4.2 and 4.3; Data General AViiON with DG/UX 4.3 through 5.4.3; DIAB DS90 with DNIX 5.2 and 5.3; Dolphin Server Technology Triton 88/17 with Dolphin UNIX System V/88 R3.2; Encore Multimax with UMAX 4.3; Encore 88K with UMAX V 5.2; Fortune 32:16 with For:Pro 2.1; FPS 500 with FPX 4.1; Harris HCX-2900; Harris Night Hawk 68K and 88K with CX/UX; HP-9000 with HP-UX 5.21 through 10.0; IBM 370-series mainframes with AIX/370 1.2; IBM PS/2 with AIX 1.2; IBM RS/6000 AIX 3.1 through 4.1.1; IBM RT PC with AIX 2.x and 4.3BSD-Reno; ICL DRS400 and 400E with System V R3; ICL DRS3000 and DRS6000 with DRS/NX UNIX System V R4; Integrated Solutions VS8 with ISI 4.2BSD; Intergraph Clipper with CLIX; MIPS Computer Systems with RISC/OS UMIPS 4.52; Modcomp Realstar 1000 with REAL/IX D.1; Motorola VME Delta Series with System V/68 R3 and System V/88 R32 and R40; NCR Tower 32 with OS 2.01; NCR System 3000 and MP-RAS with System V R4 V2.0x and NCR UNIX 02.02.01; NeXT workstations with Mach 1.0 through 3.1; Nixdorf Targon/31 M15 with TOS 4.0.13; Norsk Data Uniline 88/17 with System V/88 R3.2; OkiStation 7300 Series with System V R4; Olivetti CP 486 with UNIX System V R4; Olivetti LSX 3005 through 3045 with X/OS UNIX 2.3 through 3.0; Olivetti LSX 5020 with SCO UNIX 3.2.2; PCs with 386BSD (Jolix); PCs with AT&T UNIX System V R3.2; PCs with BSDI/386; PCs with Dell UNIX System V/386 R4.04 issue 2.2; PCs with DG/UX; PCs with ESIX System V R3 and R4; PCs with FreeBSD; PCs with Interactive Systems Corporation System V/386 3.x; PCs with Linux; PCs with Lynx/386; PCs with Mark Williams COHERENT/386 4.0; PCs with MINIX/386; PCs with Microport 3.0U3 and SVR4.0 V4.1; PCs with NetBSD; PCs with NeXTSTEP/486; PCs with QNX 4.1 thour 4.23; PCs with SCO ODT 1.1 through 3.0; PCs with SCO Open Server R5.0; PCs with SCO UNIX/386 3.2.x; PCs with SCO Xenix/286 2.3.3; PCs with SCO Xenix/386 2.2.x and 2.3.x; PCs with SunSoft Solaris 1.0 through 2.4; PCs with Trusted Xenix; PCs with UnixWare 1.0 through 2.10; Pyramid MIS T Series with OSx 4.4 through 5.1a; Pyramid MIS S and ES Series with DataCenter/OSx; Sequent Balance or Symmetry with DYNIX 3.x and DYNIX/ptx 1.3, 1.4, and 4.0; Siemens SINIX; Silicon Graphics with IRIX 3.3 through 6.01; Solbourne 5E/900 with OS/MP 4.1A; Sony NEWS with NEWS-OS 4.x; Sperry 5000 with UTS V and System V R3; Stardent 1520 UNIX System V R3 2.2; Stratus computers with FTX 2.x; Sun workstations, computers, and servers with SunOS 3.2 through 5.1 or Solaris 1.0 through 2.5; Tandy Model 6000 with XENIX 3.2; Tektronix 6130 with UTek OS; UNISYS S/4040 with CTIX SVR3.2; UNISYS U6000/65 MP with UNIX System V R4.

## Chapter 2

Running C-Kermit

C-Kermit is a large program with many features, designed to be used on a wide variety of hardware and software platforms. If your computer does not have enough memory or does not offer certain capabilities, some of the C-Kermit features described in this book might not be available. C-Kermit's SHOW FEATURES command lists the features that are included and those that are missing. See the appendix particular to your operating system, such as Appendix III for UNIX, or the relevant supplementary manual or file.

This book describes C-Kermit version 6.0.192. If you are running an earlier version, you should get the latest release (see page 11). If you have a later version, see the online updates file for changes that were made since this book was published.

Starting C-Kermit

Remember, in the examples used throughout this book, the characters that you type are underlined. The characters that are not underlined are prompts or messages from the computer.

If the C-Kermit program is correctly installed on your computer, you should be able to run it simply by typing its name at the system prompt (which is shown as dollar sign in this example, but might be some other character or text):

```
$ kermit
```

In Windows, type "k95"; in OS/2 type "k2". In response, you should see a herald and a prompt looking something like this:[5]

```
C-Kermit 6.0.192, 6 Sep 96, OpenVMS Alpha
Type ? or HELP for help
C-Kermit>
```

What do the herald and prompt tell us? "C-Kermit" is the name of the program. "6.0.192" is the version number: the major release number is "6", the minor release, or level, is "0", the edit number is "192", and the program release date is "6 Sep 96". "OpenVMS Alpha" is an identifier for the type of computer and operating system that C-Kermit was configured for.

The prompt, C-Kermit>, means that C-Kermit is ready for a command. The line above the prompt, Type ? or HELP for help, means just what it says. If you type a question mark at the prompt, you get a list, or menu, of commands available at that point. These are C-Kermit's "top-level" commands. If you type the word *help*, you get a brief introduction to C-Kermit with pointers to additional information.

C-Kermit's command style should be familiar to anyone who has used MS-DOS Kermit or other popular Kermit programs.[6] A Kermit command is like an English sentence, usually consisting of a verb followed by objects or adverbs. When the C-Kermit prompt appears, you can type a command. Commands are entered using ordinary letters, numbers, and punctuation, plus the special characters that are summarized in Table 2-1 on page 30. A command is executed only after you press the Return or Enter key. When the command has finished executing, the prompt appears again and you can type another command, and so on:

```
C-Kermit>version
C-Kermit 6.0.192, 6 Sep 96, OpenVMS Alpha
 Numeric: 600192
C-Kermit>echo Hello
Hello
C-Kermit>check character-sets
 Available
C-Kermit>
```

---

[5]If you see an error message such as "not found", "permission denied", or "unrecognized command verb", the program has not been installed or wasn't installed correctly. Or maybe it was installed with some other name, perhaps "ckermit" or "wermit." If you see a "Usage" message, beginning something like:

```
Usage: kermit [-x arg [-x arg]...[-yyy]...]
```

then you have either a very, very old version of C-Kermit, or else your version of C-Kermit has been installed without an interactive command parser.

[6]Or the late, lamented DECSYSTEM-20, which inspired the Kermit command style.

This style of operation is called *interactive command mode*, and it gives you full access to all of C-Kermit's features.

By the way, if you don't like C-Kermit's prompt, you can change it to suit your tastes, for example:

```
C-Kermit>set prompt VAX-Kermit>
VAX-Kermit>
```

to remind you that you are using Kermit on a VAX. Later when you start to use Kermit to talk to two computers at once, this will help you keep track of which one you're talking to.

Exiting from C-Kermit

When you are finished using C-Kermit, type the command EXIT or QUIT (the two are the same) and then press the Return or Enter key to return to the system prompt:

```
C-Kermit>exit
$
```

The system prompt varies with your operating system and other circumstances. When C-Kermit exits, it closes any files it might have had open, restores your command terminal to normal, and generally cleans up after itself. See page 463 for a complete description of the EXIT command.

Entering Interactive Commands

Kermit's interactive command language is easy for users of all levels. For novices, it is intuitive and nonthreatening. Commands are normal English words rather than cryptic codes. Help is available when you need it; but unlike a menu system, it does not force itself on you when you don't want it. Later, when you become familiar with Kermit's commands, you can enter them more quickly by using abbreviations or even by grouping multiple commands into short "macros," described in Chapter 17.

A command consists of one or more words separated by spaces, like a sentence. The words are called *fields*. In a Kermit command, a field can be a *keyword*, a *file name*, a *number*, or some other quantity. A keyword is a word chosen from a particular list; all words on that list are valid, other words are not.

Commands begin with a keyword, normally an English verb like SEND, RECEIVE, or SET. Keywords can be entered in uppercase or lowercase, or any combination. We show command keywords within running text in UPPERCASE for clarity (for example, the SEND command) but in lowercase in examples:

```
C-Kermit>send oofa.txt
```

because that is how people normally type them.

Getting Help within a Command

A question mark (?), typed at any point in a command, produces a message explaining what is possible or expected at that point. Depending on the context, the message can be a brief explanatory phrase, a menu of valid keywords, or a list of files.

If you type a question mark at the prompt, you'll see a list of all C-Kermit's top-level commands. If you type a letter *s* at the prompt and then question mark, you'll see a list of the commands that start with *s*:

```
C-Kermit>s?
Command, one of the following:
 script       server       show        statistics  suspend
 send         set          space       stop        switch
C-Kermit>s
```

After the help message is displayed, you can continue the command from where you left off. The *s* is still there, and now you can type a letter *e* and another question mark to see which commands start with *se*:

```
C-Kermit>se?
Command, one of the following:
 send     server     set
C-Kermit>set
```

You can continue this process to the next field of the command by typing a space and then another question mark:

```
C-Kermit>set ? Parameter, one of the following:
 alarm             escape-character output          speed
 attributes        exit             parity          suspend
 background        file             printer         take
 block-check       flow-control     prefixing       tcp
 buffers           handshake        prompt          telnet
 carrier-watch     host             protocol        temp-directory
 case              input            quiet           terminal
 command           key              receive         transfer
 control-character language         repeat          transmit
 count             line             retry-limit     unknown-char-set
 delay             login            script          wildcard-expansion
 destination       macro            send            window-size
 dial              modem            server
 duplex            network          session-log
C-Kermit>set
```

This tells you that Kermit wants you to type another keyword, a parameter to be SET, and then Kermit lists all the possibilities for you, such as SET FILE. Let's see how far we can go with the SET FILE command.

```
C-Kermit>set file ? File parameter, one of the following:
 bytesize          destination      end-of-line          type
 character-set     display          incomplete
 collision         download-directory names
```

```
C-Kermit>set file type ? type of file, one of the following:
 binary   text
C-Kermit>set file type binary ?
 Type a carriage return to confirm the command
C-Kermit>set file type binary <CR>
```

At the end of the command, press the Return, Carriage Return, or Enter key (shown above, for emphasis, as <CR>) to have C-Kermit actually execute the command. Linefeed, Ctrl-J, Formfeed, and Ctrl-L also serve the same purpose.

When a command fails, for example because a keyword was misspelled, an error message is usually printed:

```
C-Kermit>set file type biiiinary
?No keywords match - biiiinary
C-Kermit>
```

In addition, a "status variable" is set that can be queried in various ways, including by the SHOW STATUS command:

```
C-Kermit>set file type biiiinary
?No keywords match - biiiinary
C-Kermit>show status
FAILURE
C-Kermit>set file type binary
C-Kermit>show status
SUCCESS
C-Kermit>
```

(The status variable is a key ingredient in C-Kermit's script programming language, which is covered in Chapters 17 through 19.)

We seem to have prepared C-Kermit for transferring binary files. Let's look at the command that actually sends the file, which is SEND followed by the filename. See how question mark also produces an alpabetized filename list:

```
C-Kermit>send ? File(s) to send, one of the following:
 ckcasc.h  ckcmai.c  ckcxla.h  ckuscr.c  ckuus4.c  ckuusx.c  makefile
 ckcdeb.h  ckcnet.c  ckucmd.c  ckusig.c  ckuus5.c  ckuusy.c  oofa.bin
 ckcfn2.c  ckcnet.h  ckucmd.h  ckustr.c  ckuus6.c  ckuver.h  oofa.doc
 ckcfn3.c  ckcpro.w  ckucon.c  ckutio.c  ckuus7.c  ckuxla.c  oofa.hlp
 ckcfns.c  ckcsig.h  ckudia.c  ckuus2.c  ckuusr.c  ckuxla.h  oofa.txt
 ckcker.h  ckcsym.h  ckufio.c  ckuus3.c  ckuusr.h  ckwart.c
C-Kermit>send
```

If you type the question mark after one or more characters of the filename, Kermit lists the matching files:

```
C-Kermit>send oo? File(s) to send, one of the following:
 oofa.bin  oofa.doc  oofa.hlp  oofa.txt
C-Kermit>send oofa.txt
Return to your local Kermit and give a RECEIVE command.

KERMIT READY TO SEND...
```

If your command doesn't make sense or it contains spelling or grammatical errors, Kermit gives you a brief error message and a new prompt:

```
C-Kermit>sned ?No keywords match: sned
C-Kermit>
```

No harm is done by spelling errors in keywords (unless your error results in another valid keyword). An invalid command is not executed, and it has no side effects. But watch out for spelling errors in filenames or numbers, where Kermit usually has no way to tell the difference between what you typed and what you meant to type.

If you enter a command that is partially correct, you are given an error message and then you are reprompted with the correct part of the command:

```
C-Kermit>set block head
?No keywords match - head
C-Kermit>set block
```

At this point, you can type a question mark to see which keywords are legal, or you can cancel or edit the command (explained shortly).

Abbreviating Keywords

You don't always have to spell keywords out in full; you can abbreviate them as much as you want, as long as the result isn't ambiguous within its field. For example, the shortest way to enter the SET FILE TYPE BINARY command would be:

```
C-Kermit>set fi t b
```

If you abbreviate a keyword too much, Kermit complains that your command is "?Ambiguous." No harm is done, and the command is not executed:

```
C-Kermit>se ?Ambiguous - se
C-Kermit>se? Command, one of the following:
 send    server    set
C-Kermit>
```

Some command keywords are used so frequently that they have special one-letter abbreviations, even though more than one command begins with that letter. These include C for CONNECT, S for SEND, R for RECEIVE, and H for HELP. For example, the command:

```
C-Kermit>s oofa.doc
```

sends the file oofa.doc. Note, however, that filenames *cannot* be abbreviated.

Any abbreviation that is valid in a regular command is also valid in a HELP command; for example:

```
C-Kermit>h s
```

prints the help text for the SEND command.

Correcting Mistakes in Commands

If you make typographical errors or change your mind about a command before you enter it, you can alter or cancel it using the following special characters:

DEL   (The Delete, Rubout, or Backspace key, or Ctrl-H) Deletes the rightmost character from the command.

^W   (Ctrl-W) Erases the rightmost word from the command.

^U   (Ctrl-U) Erases the entire command.

^R   (Ctrl-R) Redisplays the current command.

The notation ^X or Ctrl-X means press the key marked X while holding down the key marked Ctrl or Control. X can be any letter A–Z, and also certain punctuation characters such as underscore (_), backslash (\), circumflex (^), or right bracket (])[7]. The Ctrl key is used like the Shift key. Characters entered in conjunction with the Ctrl key are called *control characters*. You can type the editing characters DEL and ^W repeatedly to delete all the way back to the prompt.

C-Kermit tries to keep your command line looking right: deleted characters, words, and lines "disappear" but the prompt stays where it was. But there are ways for the command line to become jumbled (for example, if someone sends you a message while you're in the middle of typing a command). That's what Ctrl-R is for; it redisplays the prompt and the current command, properly formatted:

```
C-Kermit>set fi
<BEEP>From olaf: What do you want on your pizza?
le type^R
C-Kermit>set file type
```

Keyword and Filename Completion

C-Kermit has a special reinforcement mechanism to help you make sure you have not abbreviated a keyword too much, or that the abbreviation you have used really stands for what you think it does, or to finish typing a filename for you.

This mechanism is called *completion*, and you invoke it by pressing the Esc (Escape) or Tab key, or Ctrl-I, whichever is more convenient for you. If the keyword or filename characters you have typed so far are sufficient, Kermit fills in the rest of the characters for you and positions you for the next field of the command:

```
C-Kermit>sen<ESC>d oofa.t<ESC>xt
```

---

[7]See Table VII-1 on page 557 for a listing of all the control characters.

If not, Kermit beeps and waits for you to supply more characters:

```
C-Kermit>se<ESC><BEEP>n<ESC>d oofa.<ESC><BEEP>t<ESC>xt
```

In these examples, <ESC> signifies the Escape (Esc) key, and <BEEP> shows where you would hear a beep. If you are deaf, you can still tell when a beep occurs: whenever you press <ESC> and the cursor does not move. Some versions of Kermit, such as MS-DOS Kermit, Kermit 95, and Kermit/2 also offer a "visual bell", which flashes the screen instead of making a sound.

When you use the completion feature in a filename, C-Kermit completes as much of the name as it can, and if more characters are required from you after that, C-Kermit beeps and waits for you to supply them. For example, suppose you have two files, oofa.txt and oofa.new, and they are the only two files whose names start with the letter O. If you type an O and then an Esc or Tab, Kermit supplies the characters "ofa." and then waits for you to finish the filename:

```
C-Kermit>send o<ESC>ofa.<BEEP>t<ESC>xt
```

The completion feature also can be used to fill in *default* values for fields that have them. If you press the Esc or Tab key at the beginning of a field, before typing any other characters, and if that field has a default value, Kermit fills it in:

```
C-Kermit>set block-check <ESC> 3
```

Here Kermit supplies the default block-check value, namely 3. If there is no default value for a field, Kermit beeps:

```
C-Kermit>send <ESC><BEEP>
```

When the final field of a command has a default value, you can enter the command without specifying a value:

```
C-Kermit>set block-check
```

This sets the block-check parameter to its default value of 3.

Including Special Characters in Commands

Characters like question mark and Ctrl-U have special meanings within C-Kermit commands. What if you need to include them as part of the command itself without triggering their usual functions (help and erase)? You can enter such a character into a C-Kermit command literally by preceding it with the backslash character (\), for example:

```
\?
```

enters a question mark. To enter a backslash literally, type two of them:

```
\\
```

Certain characters, however, such as Ctrl-C or Ctrl-Z (depending on your computer's operating system), cannot be quoted this way because they send a signal to the operating system to interrupt Kermit.

You can include problem characters in Kermit commands by using a backslash followed by the character's numeric ASCII code value; for example \3 for Ctrl-C, \26 for Ctrl-Z, \10 for linefeed, or \13 for carriage return (Table VII-1 on page 557 lists these codes). Example:

```
C-Kermit>echo Hello!\13\10How are you\?
Hello!
How are you?
C-Kermit>
```

A common use for backslash is to include "?" as a wildcard[8] in a file specification:

```
C-Kermit>send oofa.? File(s) to send, one of the following:
  oofa.c    oofa.h    oofa.txt    oofa.hlp
C-Kermit>send oofa.\?
```

Without the backslash, the question mark gives you a list of filenames that match what you have typed so far. With the backslash, it is used to match any single character, so the SEND command in the example sends the files oofa.c and oofa.h.

In Windows, OS/2, and Atari GEMDOS the directory separator is backslash, the same as C-Kermit's quoting character. On these systems, C-Kermit goes to unbelievable lengths to figure out whether a backslash in a filename is a directory separator or the quoting character, and it usually guesses right.

However, some situations are intrinsically ambiguous. For example, suppose you have defined a variable "\%a" (explained in Chapter 17) to be the name of some directory, and you also have an actual top-level directory called %a. What should the following command do?

```
C-Kermit>send \%a\oofa.txt
```

In this case, C-Kermit will decide to expand the variable. In such cases, you can *force* C-Kermit to treat backslashes as part of the filename by doubling them:

```
C-Kermit>send c:\\%a\\oofa.txt
C-Kermit>send c:\\dos\\autoexec.bat
```

This also applies when using C-Kermit to transfer files with MS-DOS Kermit. But fortunately, in Windows 95 and NT, and in OS/2, forward slash (/) is also recognized as a directory separator:

```
C-Kermit>get c:/%a/oofa.txt
C-Kermit>get c:/dos/autoexec.bat
```

---

[8]A "wildcard" is a character used in a filename to indicate a group of files. Wildcard characters differ from system to system. See Table 9-1 on page 173.

Spaces and Braces in Commands

As noted, a C-Kermit command is a series of "words" from left to right, each in its own position. Words are separated by "whitespace;" that is, one or more spaces or tabs. For example, in the command:

```
rename oofa.txt oofa.old
```

the first word is "rename", the second is "oofa.txt" and the third is "oofa.old".

Now suppose you want to rename a file whose name contains a space, such as "oofa txt". If you try to use the RENAME command in the normal way:

```
C-Kermit> rename oofa ?No files match - oofa
C-Kermit>
```

As soon as you type the space after "oofa" C-Kermit thinks you have entered the first filename, and so looks it up. But you don't have a file called "oofa" by itself, so this results in an error. To force multiple words together into a single word, use braces (the curly ones, not brackets or parentheses):

```
C-Kermit> rename {oofa txt} {My new name has even more words}
C-Kermit>
```

Words and text strings have leading and trailing whitespace stripped by C-Kermit as a normal part of command processing. Use braces to force the whitespace to be kept:

```
C-Kermit> echo    I am indented.
I am indented.
C-Kermit> echo {   I am indented.}
   I am indented.
C-Kermit> echo {{   I am indented.}}
{   I am indented.}
C-Kermit> rename oofa.txt { oofa.txt}
```

The final command creates a file whose name starts with a space (if your operating system allows it), making it difficult or impossible for most system commands or applications (other than C-Kermit) to access. But of course, you can use C-Kermit to fix its name:

```
C-Kermit> rename { oofa.txt} oofa.txt
```

Finally, braces are used in script programs for grouping lists of commands in a way described in Chapter 18, but that might surprise you if you stumble upon in accidentally at this stage. If a command *ends* with an *opening* brace ({), this tells Kermit to keep reading more lines until it comes to a line that *starts* with a *closing* brace (}):

```
C-Kermit> echo {
one
two
three
}
one, two, three
C-Kermit>
```

Interrupting a Command

After you have entered a C-Kermit command by pressing the Return or Enter key, the command begins to execute. You can interrupt most commands during their execution by typing Ctrl-C (hold down the Ctrl key and press the C key).[9] This returns you to the C-Kermit prompt immediately, so you can enter another command. Example:

```
C-Kermit>type moon.doc
No celestial body has required as much labor for the study of its
motion as the moon.  Since Clairault (1747), who indicated a way
of constructing a theory containing all the properties of ^C...
C-Kermit>
```

Note: ^C indicates a real Control-C character, not a circumflex followed by the letter C.

Recalling Commands

C-Kermit saves your commands in a command recall (history) buffer, which, by default, holds your last 10 commands. To recall your previous command, type Ctrl-B (that is, hold down the Control or Ctrl key and press the B or b key) or Ctrl-P. Type Ctrl-B (or Ctrl-P) again to recall the command before that, and so on. If you try to go back too far, C-Kermit beeps at you. (Note: Ctrl-P should not be used in Windows or OS/2 because those operating systems intercept it as a printer command.)

Each time you recall a command, it appears before you as if you had typed it up to, but not including, the Enter (Return) that actually causes it to execute. If you want to execute the command, press the Enter (Return) key. If you want to edit it, use the editing keys, including Ctrl-U to erase it.

When you are viewing recalled commands, you can also go forward in the command recall buffer by typing Ctrl-N. This is handy in case (for example) you typed too many Ctrl-Bs and went back too far.

In Windows 95, Windows NT, OS/2, and possibly some other versions, you may also use the up- and down-arrow keys for command recall.

Use the SET COMMAND RECALL-BUFFER-SIZE command to change the size of the command history buffer:

```
C-Kermit> set command recall 0        (Disable command recall)
C-Kermit> set command recall 100      (Make the buffer bigger)
C-Kermit> set command recall 1000     (Make bigger still)
```

---

[9]The interrupt character might be something other than Ctrl-C; for example, in some versions of UNIX it is your "intr" character, which is often Delete or Rubout, in which case you can change it with a UNIX "stty" command, or else use it as the interrupt character and use Ctrl-H to erase characters in C-Kermit commands.

Table 2-1 Special Characters in C-Kermit Commands

Character	Function
<SPACE>	(the space bar) Separates fields.
?	(question mark) Requests a menu or help message for the current field.
–	(dash) At the end of a line only (after removal of any trailing comment and/or whitespace): this command is continued on the next line.
\	(backslash) Introduces a backslash code or quotes the following character. Backslash codes are summarized in Table 2-4 on page 49.
;	(semicolon) At the beginning of a command, or within a command preceded by at least one space or tab: introduces a comment.
#	(number sign) Same as semicolon: introduces a comment.
,	(comma) Separates commands in macro definitions, function arguments.
{ }	(braces) Used for grouping, preserving leading/trailing blanks.
<ESC>	(Esc or Escape key, or Ctrl-[) Attempt to complete the current field.
<TAB>	(or Ctrl-I) Within a field, same as <ESC>. Between fields, same as <SPACE> (but only in command files).
<DEL>	(or Backspace, or Rubout, or Ctrl-H) Deletes the rightmost character from the command.
Ctrl-H	Same as <DEL>.
Ctrl-I	Same as <TAB>.
Ctrl-W	Deletes the rightmost word.
Ctrl-U	Deletes the entire command, back to the prompt.
Ctrl-R	Redisplays the command.
Ctrl-B	Recall previous command. Also, Ctrl-P or (OS/2 and Windows only), gray up-arrow.
Ctrl-N	Next command. Also (OS/2 and Windows only) gray down-arrow.
Ctrl-C	Interrupts a command in execution, returns to the prompt. On some UNIX systems, this purpose is served by your interrupt character, which might be something other than Ctrl-C. Use stty all or stty -a to find out what your interrupt (intr) character is.
Ctrl-S	Stops screen output, if Xon/Xoff flow control is in effect.
Ctrl-Q	Resumes screen output, if Xon/Xoff flow control is in effect.
Ctrl-Z	(or whatever your suspend character is) Suspends Kermit so it can be continued later (UNIX only). See UNIX appendix.
Ctrl-Y	VMS interruption character. See VMS appendix.
<RETURN>	(Carriage Return, Return, Enter, Ctrl-M) Terminate and enter the command. Also written as <CR>.
<LINEFEED>	(Ctrl-J) Same as <RETURN>. Also written as <LF>.
<FORMFEED>	(Ctrl-L) Same as <RETURN>. Also written as <FF>.

Command Files

If you issue the same sequence of commands to Kermit every time you run it, that can add up to a lot of typing over the years. Better to enter the commands just once and let the computer remember them for you. Use your favorite text editor to record the commands in a *Kermit command file* and you won't ever have to type them again.

Kermit commands are lines composed of plain text characters. The text editor used to create or modify Kermit commands should be set up to handle these simple, unadorned lines of text. Editors like EDIT or NotePad can be used in Windows. ED, EX, VI, and EMACS are appropriate for UNIX. EDT, EVE, and EMACS can be used in VMS. SED or SPEED can be used in AOS/VS. Similar editors can be used in other operating systems. If you use a word processor or desktop publishing software that is concerned with fonts, boldface, italics, underscore, and similar effects, please be sure to save (or "export") your Kermit command file in plain-text (ASCII) format.

To execute commands from a file, use the TAKE command:

TAKE *filename*

> Executes C-Kermit commands from the specified file. C-Kermit reads and executes the commands in order, from top to bottom, until the end of the file is encountered or until a command is executed that tells C-Kermit to stop, change direction, or to execute another command file. In this example, C-Kermit is told to execute commands from a file called COMPUSERVE.KSC:

```
C-Kermit>take compuserve.ksc
```

If Kermit can't find the command file and if the filename that you gave was not "absolute" — that is, it did not include a full path (device and/or directory information) — then Kermit looks in either your home directory or your Kermit software installation area, depending on the operating system. For example, in OS/2, Windows NT, or Windows 95, it looks in the SCRIPTS subdirectory of the Kermit directory; in UNIX or VMS it looks in your home (login) directory.

Kermit command files can have any name at all. A file type of .ksc ("Kermit SCript") is recommended for easy identification.

Execution of a command file can be interrupted by typing Control-C (or whatever your system's interrupt character is) at any time during its execution. If the TAKE command was given from the C-Kermit prompt, the interruption returns you directly to the prompt.

The following sections describe features commonly used in command files, but you can also use them interactively at the program prompt.

Adding Comments to Commands

Kermit's commands can be annotated with comments. A full-line comment can begin with the word COMMENT or the single character semicolon (;) or number sign (#):

```
COMMENT - This is a C-Kermit command file.
; I copied it from "Using C-Kermit".
# And I put lots of comments in it.
```

Commands can also have trailing comments. These are introduced by a semicolon or number-sign preceded by at least one space or tab:

```
echo Hi there!      ; Print a friendly greeting.
space               ; Let's see how much disk space is free.
log transactions    ; I always want to keep a log of what I do.
```

Because ; and # are recognized as trailing comment indicators only at the beginning of a line or when preceded by whitespace, you can include these characters literally in commands by preceding them with printing characters:

```
get oofa.txt;3                  ; Fetch file from VMS Kermit server.
remote host lpr -#4 oofa.txt # Print 4 copies of remote file.
```

In this example, `oofa.txt;3` is a VMS filename, and `lpr -#4` is the UNIX command to print 4 copies of a file.

If you need to include ; or # preceded by a space as part of a command, then prefix it with backslash or, in certain contexts, use braces:

```
C-Kermit>echo Text ; with a comment
Text
C-Kermit>echo Text \; with a comment
Text ; with a comment
C-Kermit>echo {Text ; with a comment}
Text ; with a comment
C-Kermit>
```

Continuing a Command

Kermit commands are by nature one line long. Some Kermit commands, however, can be quite lengthy — even wider than your screen. There is nothing to prevent you from typing past the end of your screen, and if your terminal emulator or console driver "wraps" your lines for you, you can even see what you're doing.

But the compulsive among us may wish to break long commands at nice places, so as to have a neat-looking screen or readable command files. C-Kermit commands can be continued by ending them with a dash (–) as the last character in the line:

```
C-Kermit>set -
file -
type -
binary
C-Kermit>
```

Note that the prompt doesn't come back until you (a) finish entering the command, (b) request a menu with ?, or (c) make a mistake. In command files only (not at the prompt), you may add trailing comments after the continuation character:

```
set -                           ; This is a SET command
file -                          ; related to files
type -                          ; in particular the file type
binary                          ; which is to be binary.
```

The command editing characters <DEL>, Ctrl-W, and Ctrl-U may be used with continued commands, but their effects are shown only on the current line. Use Ctrl-R to show the overall effect when you delete back into previous lines.

If you need to enter a command that actually ends in a dash, you can encode the final dash as \45 (the ASCII code for dash) or you can use braces:

```
C-Kermit> echo Ends in dash \45
C-Kermit> echo {Ends in dash -}
```

Describing Kermit's Commands

Before we start explaining C-Kermit's commands, we need some notational conventions for describing their *syntax*, or form. We use special punctuation and typography to show what fields are required, what fields are optional, and what type of data goes into a field, as in this typical command syntax description:

SET *{* **RECEIVE, SEND** *}* **END-OF-PACKET** *[number]*

This example illustrates the use of boldface to represent keywords literally, italic braces to enclose a list of alternatives, italic square brackets to show an optional field, and a word in italics to show a substitutable parameter.

Here is a complete listing of the notation used in this book:

WORD

An uppercase word in **BOLDFACE** means that the word should be typed literally. If it is a keyword (and it usually is), letters can be omitted from the end as long as what remains is enough to distinguish the word you have abbreviated from any other word that is valid in the same context. Letters may be typed in either lowercase or uppercase. For example, in:

SET FILE TYPE BINARY

all four words are keywords, and the command can be entered as "SET FILE TYPE BINARY", "set file type binary", "Set File Type Binary", and so on, and abbreviated as "set fil typ bin", "set fi ty bi", or "set fi t b". (Of course, many other combinations are possible.)

word

> A word in *italics* is a *parameter*, which is to be replaced by an actual value of your choice. The word in italics indicates what sort of quantity is expected: a *number*, a *filename*, a *directory-name*, a *variable-name*, and so forth. For example, in:
>
> **SET WINDOW** *number*
>
> the word *number* is to be replaced by an actual number, like 4 or 10.

underlining

> In examples, underlined characters, words, or phrases show text that you should type. The text should normally be terminated by pressing the Return or Enter key at the point where the underlining ends.

[anything=value]

> Any word enclosed in italicized (slanted) square brackets is optional, meaning you don't have to include it in the command. If you see square brackets that are not italicized, they should be taken as literal brackets that you should type. The *=value* portion, if any, shows the value that is used if you don't specify one for this field, that is, the *default* value. Example:
>
> **SET BLOCK-CHECK** *[number=3]*
>
> This means that the SET BLOCK-CHECK command takes an optional number. If you enter the command without specifying a number, then 3 is used:

```
C-Kermit>set block-check 2
C-Kermit>set block-check 1
C-Kermit>set block-check
```

{ something, something, something }

> Within italicized curly braces, a list of items separated by commas means that you should pick one of the items from the list. This notation is usually used for a list of keywords:
>
> **SET FILE TYPE** *{* **TEXT, BINARY** *}*
>
> This shows that the possible file types are TEXT and BINARY. If you see braces that are not italic, { such as the ones around this phrase }, these are actually part of the command.

. . .

> An ellipsis (three dots) means that the preceding item can be repeated. Example:
>
> **MSEND** *file [file [file [. . .]]]*
>
> or, more compactly:
>
> **MSEND** *file* . . .
>
> This means the MSEND (multiple send) command can be given with one or more file-names separated by spaces.

The most common C-Kermit command parameters are:

number

A decimal (base 10) number, like 31 or 9024. You also can enter small positive numbers (0–255) in octal (base 8) or hexadecimal (base 16) using backslash notation. If you don't know what octal or hexadecimal notation is, skip the rest of this paragraph. Use \onnn for an octal number; that is, backslash followed by the letter *O* (upper- or lowercase) followed by one to three octal digits (which are 0 through 7). For a hexadecimal number, use \xnn; that is, backslash followed by the letter *X* (upper or lower), followed by exactly two hexadecimal digits, which are 0 through 9 and A through F. The letters A–F can be in uppercase or lowercase. Example:

SET RETRY *number*

means you can type commands such as:

```
C-Kermit>set retry 13         (A decimal number)
C-Kermit>set retry \13        (A decimal number)
C-Kermit>set retry \d13       (A decimal number)
C-Kermit>set retry \o15       (An octal number)
C-Kermit>set retry \x0D       (A hexadecimal number)
```

The allowable range for the number depends on the command. If you enter a number that is out of range, an error message is given and the command has no effect:

```
C-Kermit>set window 793
?Sorry, 32 is the maximum
C-Kermit>
```

In most contexts where a *number* is expected, you can also enter an expression, provided it does not contain any spaces:

```
C-Kermit>set window (10+10)/4
```

More about expressions in Chapter 18.

control-character

Whenever you see this in a command syntax description, it means you can enter a control character in any of several ways. First, you can enter its ASCII code value (listed Table VII-2 on page 558) as a *number* in any of the formats listed above. The value must be between 0 and 31, or else 127 (decimal). You can also enter most (but not all) control characters literally if you precede them with a backslash (\). Finally, you can enter them in circumflex notation; for example, ^C (circumflex followed by the letter C) stands for Control-C (ASCII code 3). The following examples all select Control-X (ASCII code 24) as the CONNECT-mode escape character (explained in Chapter 8):

```
C-Kermit>set escape 24        (As a decimal number)
C-Kermit>set escape \24       (As a decimal number)
C-Kermit>set escape \o30      (As an octal number)
C-Kermit>set escape \x18      (As a hexadecimal number)
C-Kermit>set escape ^X        (In circumflex notation)
C-Kermit>set escape \Ctrl-X   (Literally after backslash)
```

hh:mm:ss

A time of day in 24-hour clock notation. *hh* is the hour, 0 through 23; *mm* are the minutes past the hour, 0 through 59; *ss* the seconds past the minute, 0 through 59. In most contexts, the time is understood to be in the current day if it is equal to or later than the current time, otherwise in the next day. Example:

```
C-Kermit>pause 23:23:00   (Pause until 11:23 pm)
```

filename

The name of a file on the computer where you are running C-Kermit. The name can, but need not, include device and/or directory information. Upper- and lowercase letters are treated differently in UNIX, VOS, and OS-9 filenames, but case does not matter in VMS, Windows, OS/2, AOS/VS, and most other operating systems. The filename may not contain wildcard characters. For example:

TAKE *filename*

means that the TAKE command needs the name of a file on your computer:

```
C-Kermit>take oofa.*
?Wildcards not allowed in command file name
C-Kermit>take oofa.ksc
C-Kermit>take $disk2:[olga]oofa.ksc      (A VMS file)
C-Kermit>take hd80:test:folder:oofa.ksc  (A Macintosh file)
C-Kermit>take /usr/ivan/kermit/oofa.ksc  (A UNIX file)
C-Kermit>take b:/usr/ivan/kermit/oofa.ksc (An Amiga file)
C-Kermit>take f:\olaf\kermit\oofa.ksc    (OS/2 or Windows file)
C-Kermit>take :udd:olga:sunday.ksc       (AOS/VS files)
C-Kermit>send %ssi#m1_do3>usr>david>pm.c (Stratus VOS files)
```

Note how file names can also include device, directory, or other identifying fields meaningful to your operating system. Again, ksc stands for Kermit Script File, which is the preferred filetype (extension) for Kermit command files.

filespec

A file specification applying to the computer where you are running C-Kermit. Just like a *filename*, except it is allowed to (but need not) contain wildcard characters to indicate a group of files. Example:

SEND *filespec*

means you can give commands like:

```
C-Kermit>send oofa.txt                (A single file)
C-Kermit>send oofa.*                  (A group of files)
C-Kermit>send *.*                     (A big group of files)
C-Kermit>send $disk2:[olga]*.ksc      (VMS files)
C-Kermit>send :udd:eugenia:ckd+       (AOS/VS files)
C-Kermit>send /usr/ivan/kermit/*.ini  (UNIX, OS-9)
C-Kermit>send a:/usr/ivan/kermit/*.ini (Amiga files)
C-Kermit>send f:\olaf\kermit\*.*      (OS/2 or Windows files)
C-Kermit>send %ssi#m1_do3>usr>david>*.c (Stratus VOS files)
```

remote-filename

The name of a file on another computer, in whatever form the other computer requires. If it contains any backslashes, such as directory separators, they must be doubled. It should not contain wildcard characters. Example:

REMOTE TYPE *remote-filename*

lets us give commands like:

```
C-Kermit>remote type oofa txt a                (A VM/CMS file)
C-Kermit>remote type f:\\olaf\\oofa.txt        (DOS or Windows)
C-Kermit>remote type $disk2:[olaf]oofa.txt;17  (VMS)
C-Kermit>remote type :udd:olaf:oofa.txt        (AOS/VS)
C-Kermit>remote type ~olaf/oofa.txt            (UNIX or OS-9)
C-Kermit>remote type diska:/olaf/oofa.txt      (Amiga)
```

remote-filespec

Just like *remote-filename*, but wildcard characters may (but need not) be included. Wildcards, if used, should be in a format acceptable to the other computer. Example:

GET *remote-filespec*

allows:

```
C-Kermit>get * exec                        (Files from VM/CMS)
C-Kermit>get f:\\olaf\\oofa.*              (From DOS)
C-Kermit>get $disk2:[olaf]oofa.*;0         (From VMS)
C-Kermit>remote type :udd:olaf:oofa.-      (From AOS/VS)
```

directory-name

The name of a directory on the computer where C-Kermit is running. Upper- and lowercase letters are distinct in UNIX and OS-9 directory names, but case does not matter in most other operating systems. Example:

CD *[directory-name]*

allows:

```
C-Kermit>cd                    (Everywhere)
C-Kermit>cd /usr/olga/         (UNIX)
C-Kermit>cd c:\usr\olga        (Windows or OS/2)
C-Kermit>cd sys$help:          (VMS)
C-Kermit>cd :udd:olga          (AOS/VS)
```

remote-directory-name

The name of a directory on another computer, in whatever form the other computer requires. Backslashes must be doubled. Example:

REMOTE CD *[remote-directory-name]*

allows:

```
C-Kermit>remote cd             (Everywhere)
C-Kermit>remote cd c1          (VM/CMS)
C-Kermit>remote cd f:\\public  (Windows, OS/2, or MS-DOS)
```

command

Usually, a system command on the computer where C-Kermit is running, such as you would type to the UNIX shell, to DCL in VMS, or to the AOS/VS CLI. Alphabetic case matters in UNIX and OS-9, but not in most other operating systems. Example:

RUN *command*

allows:

```
C-Kermit>run diff oofa.old oofa.new    (A UNIX command)
C-Kermit>run purge/log oofa.*          (A VMS command)
C-Kermit>run more < ckermit.ini        (A Windows command)
C-Kermit>run help/v copy               (An AOS/VS command)
C-Kermit>run status                    (An Amiga command)
C-Kermit>run deldir test               (An OS-9 command)
```

In other contexts, *command* stands for a C-Kermit command.

remote-command

The name of a command or program on another computer, in the form required by the other computer. Example:

REMOTE HOST *remote-command*

allows:

```
C-Kermit>remote host lf oofa * (date   (A command for VM/CMS)
C-Kermit>remote host mkdir hw2         (A command for UNIX)
```

text

Any old text. Zero or more words, everything you type up to the end of the command. As in all C-Kermit commands, trailing comments are ignored. Enclose in braces if leading or trailing spaces are to be preserved or if the text ends with a hyphen that should not be taken as a continuation character. Example:

ECHO *text*

allows:

```
C-Kermit>echo                          (No words)
                                       (A blank line appears)
C-Kermit>echo Hi ; This is a comment   (One word, with comment)
Hi
C-Kermit>echo Time to go home          (Several words)
Time to go home
C-Kermit>echo {  Indented text }       (Spaces around)
  Indented text
C-Kermit>
```

device

The name of a device on your computer. For example:

SET LINE *device*

allows /dev/cua (UNIX), TXA0: (VMS), and so on.

Some Basic C-Kermit Commands

You already know Kermit's EXIT command. C-Kermit also includes a few other commands that you can experiment with right now, before you learn how to use the program for data communication and file transfer. These commands, listed below and summarized in Table 2-3 on page 49, give you access to file management and other functions of your computer's operating system. Use these commands to practice the features you've read about in this chapter: question mark to get help, completion, abbreviation, recall, correction, continuation, and comments. Within a few minutes you should be comfortable with C-Kermit's command style and an expert navigator of Kermit commands.

CD *[directory-name]*

Changes your default directory (CD stands for Change Directory). If you specify a directory name, it becomes your new default directory for all file-related Kermit commands. The directory name can be fully specified or it can be relative to your current directory. If you omit the directory name, most versions of C-Kermit put you back in your login or home directory. Examples:

```
C-Kermit>cd $disk1:[olga.letters]    (Fully specified, VMS)
C-Kermit>cd [.letters]               (Relative directory, VMS)
C-Kermit>cd /usr/olga/letters        (Fully specified, UNIX)
C-Kermit>cd :udd:olga:letters        (Fully specified, AOS/VS)
C-Kermit>cd c:\olga\letters          (Fully specified, Windows)
C-Kermit>cd c:\\olga\\letters        (Alternate form, Windows)
C-Kermit>cd c:/olga/letters          (Alternate form, Windows)
C-Kermit>cd c:\\olga\\letters        (Fully specified, Atari)
C-Kermit>cd c:/olga/letters          (Fully specified, Amiga)
C-Kermit>cd ~olaf                    (User's home directory, UNIX)
C-Kermit>cd letters                  (Relative directory)
C-Kermit>cd                          (Login (home) directory)
```

The CD command applies only within Kermit itself and any programs that Kermit runs. When you EXIT from Kermit, you should find yourself back where you started. Synonyms: **CWD** (Change Working Directory), **SET DEFAULT** (for VMS).

DELETE *filespec*

Deletes (removes, erases, destroys) all files whose names match the *filespec*, which may contain wildcards, directory names, and/or device designators. Successful execution of this command requires that you have appropriate access rights to the specified file or files. Synonym: **RM**. UNIX examples:

```
C-Kermit>delete oofa.txt          (One file in current directory)
C-Kermit>del *                    (All files in current directory)
C-Kermit>del /usr/olaf/a.txt      (Fully specified UNIX file)
```

VMS examples:

```
C-Kermit>delete oofa.txt;0          (One file in current directory)
C-Kermit>del *.*;*                  (All files in current directory)
C-Kermit>del $disk1:[olaf]a.txt;7   (Fully specified VMS file)
```

DIRECTORY *[[filespec, directory-name]]*

Lists files. If no filespec or directory name is given, lists all files in the current directory. If a directory name is given, lists all files in the specified directory. If a filespec is given, lists all files that match it. Examples for UNIX:

```
C-Kermit>directory       (List all files in current directory)
C-Kermit>dir ~olga       (All files in olga's login directory)
C-Kermit>dir ~/kermit    (All files in my kermit directory)
C-Kermit>dir kermit      (All files in kermit subdirectory)
C-Kermit>dir ck*.*       (Files whose names match)
C-Kermit>dir ..          (All files in superior directory)
C-Kermit>dir ../a*.*     (Matching files in superior directory)
```

Corresponding VMS examples:

```
C-Kermit>dir             (List all files in current directory)
C-Kermit>dir $disk:[olga]  (All files in olga's login directory)
C-Kermit>dir [olga.kermit] (and in olga's kermit subdirectory)
C-Kermit>dir [.kermit]   (All files in my kermit subdirectory)
C-Kermit>dir ck*.*       (Files whose names match)
C-Kermit>dir [-]         (All files in superior directory)
C-Kermit>dir [-]a*.*     ("a" files in superior directory)
```

Corresponding AOS/VS examples:

```
C-Kermit>dir             (List all files in current directory)
C-Kermit>dir :udd:olga:+   (All files in olga's login directory)
C-Kermit>dir :udd:olga:kermit:+  (in olga's kermit subdirectory)
C-Kermit>dir kermit:+    (All files in my kermit subdirectory)
C-Kermit>dir ck-.-       (Files whose names match)
C-Kermit>dir ^+          (All files in superior directory)
C-Kermit>dir ^:a+        ("a" files in superior directory)
```

Synonym: **LS**.

ECHO *[text]*

Displays the *text* on the screen. The text may contain imbedded backslash codes to be interpreted. If the *text* is omitted, an empty line is displayed. Examples:

```
C-Kermit>echo Good morning.
Good morning.
C-Kermit>echo \7Wake up!\7   ; Comment won't echo
<BEEP>Wake up!<BEEP>
C-Kermit> echo {  This text is indented.}
  This text is indented.
C-Kermit>
```

Synonym: **WRITE SYS$OUTPUT**. Related: **WRITE SCREEN, XECHO**.

BEEP

Sounds a beep without printing anything. Example:

```
C-Kermit>beep
<BEEP!>C-Kermit>
```

HELP *[command]*

Displays a help message. The *command* is a C-Kermit command, one or two words at most, such as COMMENT, ECHO, or SET DUPLEX. Example:

```
C-Kermit>help set parity
Syntax: SET PARITY name
Parity to use during terminal connection and file transfer:
EVEN, ODD, MARK, SPACE, or NONE.  The default is NONE.
C-Kermit>
```

If you do not include any text after the word HELP, a brief overview is displayed. Use question mark to get menus within the HELP command. Synonym: **MAN**.

MKDIR *directory-name*

Tells Kermit to create a directory. You may supply either a relative or an absolute directory name.

PAUSE *[number=1]*

Tells Kermit to do nothing for the given number of seconds. The prompt returns after the time has expired or if you type anything in the meantime. Examples:

```
C-Kermit>pause          (Pause for 1 second)
C-Kermit>pau 30         (Pause for 30 seconds)
```

Related: **MSLEEP**, like PAUSE but the number is in milliseconds.

SET PRINTER *[{ devicename, filename, command }]*

Tells C-Kermit where print material should be sent. If "set printer" is entered by itself, your default printer is used, which depends on your operating system and configuration. On systems such as VMS and Windows, where a printer has a device name, you can specify a device name such as LPT:, LPT1:, PRN, or NUL, using the syntax of your operating system for device names to specify a real printer or other device, or the "null" device in case you want all printer output to be discarded.

If you specify a *filename*, then printer output is appended to the given file, if it exists, or if not, a new file is created.

To specify a command, use the "pipe" symbol, vertical bar (|), for example:

```
C-Kermit> set printer |lpr               (UNIX)
C-Kermit> set printer |textps.exe>\dev\lpt1   (Windows or OS/2)
```

If you need to include spaces, enclose the command in curly braces:

```
C-Kermit>  set printer { | lpr -Pmyprintername }
```

PRINT *filename [options]*

Prints the local file on your SET PRINTER device. Options can be included after the filename for your computer's printing command. Examples:

```
C-Kermit>print oofa.txt          (Print a file)
C-Kermit>print oofa.txt -#2      (UNIX, 2 copies)
```

PUSH

Invokes your system's command processor "underneath" Kermit interactively in such a way that you can return to Kermit later.

```
C-Kermit>push
% send ivan Hi there!
% exit
C-Kermit>
```

To return from the lower command processor to C-Kermit, use the `exit` or `Ctrl-D` command in UNIX or OS-9, the EXIT command in OS/2, LOGOUT in VMS, POP in AOS/VS, ENDCLI on the Amiga. Synonyms: **!**, **@**, **RUN**.

PWD

Stands for Print Working Directory. It displays the name of your current default (working) directory; that is, the one you are CD'd to. Examples:

```
C-Kermit>pwd
/usr/olga/letters          (UNIX, OS-9, or Amiga)
$DISK1:[OLGA.LETTERS]      (VMS)
:UDD:OLGA:LETTERS          (AOS/VS)
C:\OLGA                    (OS/2, Windows, or Atari ST)
```

Synonym: **SHOW DEFAULT**.

RMDIR *directory-name*

Removes the specified directory. On most systems, this is allowed only if the directory contains no files. Synonym: **RD**.

RENAME *filename1 filename2*

Changes the name of the file whose name is *filename1* to *filename2*, for example:

```
C-Kermit>ren space-adventure.exe spreadsheet.exe
```

In most C-Kermit versions, *filename2* can be a device or directory name, in which case *filename1* is simply moved. The ability of the RENAME command to operate across directories or devices depends on the capabilities of the underlying operating system. Synonym: **MV**.

RUN *[command]*

Runs the named system command or program and returns to the C-Kermit prompt automatically when the command or program is finished. If no command name is given, the RUN command is exactly like the PUSH command. Examples:

```
C-Kermit>run fortune
Who messed with my anti-paranoia shot?
C-Kermit>
```

Synonyms: **PUSH**, **!**, **@**. Examples:

```
C-Kermit>@search area-codes.txt Chicago      (VMS)
C-Kermit>!grep Chicago area-codes.txt        (UNIX or OS-9)
C-Kermit>!find "Chicago" areacode.txt        (OS/2 or Windows)
```

The C-Kermit Initialization File

The initialization file is a command file that C-Kermit executes automatically when it starts. Its name and location depend on which type of computer system you have (see Table 2-2 on the next page), normally CKERMIT.INI; .kermrc in UNIX and OS-9.

On multiuser computers, the standard initialization file might be kept in a common central location — for example /usr/share/lib/kermit/ckermit.ini in HP-UX 10.0, or pointed to by the system logical name CKERMIT_INI: in VMS — to avoid unnecessary replication. On others, it is kept in each user's home or login directory, or on systems such as OS/2 and Windows that do not (necessarily) have "users," it is kept in the directory where the C-Kermit program is installed, or in a common place on a file server.

The initialization file contains commands that should be executed every time you start the C-Kermit program. C-Kermit is distributed with a *standard* initialization file that sets up your dialing and services directory and defines several handy "macros" (groups of commands, described in Chapter 17). The standard initialization file also issues a command to execute your personal "customization file," described later.

The Standard Initialization File

Like all other C-Kermit command files, the standard C-Kermit initialization file is a plain-text file that you can read or print. Most of its contents are explained in Chapters 7 and 17 through 19. The initialization file itself is thoroughly commented and is a good place to look for examples of how to use various script-programming constructs.

The standard initialization file does the following things for you. We recommend that you not alter it or replace it unless (a) you do not care about any of the services it provides, and (b) you know what you are doing.

- Prints a greeting message such as "Executing CKERMIT.INI for VMS" . . . If you do not see this message, then C-Kermit probably did not find its initialization file.

- Sets up system-dependent definitions for your C-Kermit customization file, your default editor, and your dialing and network directories, plus login and access macros for various types of hosts and services (explained in Chapter 7).

- Executes your personal customization file.

If there are settings or definitions in the standard initialization file that you don't like, it is better to undo them in your customization file than to edit or replace the standard initialization file.

Table 2-2 C-Kermit Initialization File Name

System	File Name	Remarks
Atari ST	CKERMIT.INI	C-Kermit looks first in the current directory, then in your home directory, then in the root directory.
Commodore Amiga	CKERMIT.INI	C-Kermit looks first in the s: directory, then in the current directory.
Data General AOS/VS	CKERMIT.INI	C-Kermit looks in your home directory.
IBM OS/2	K2.INI	The file K2.INI in your Kermit/2 directory.
Microware OS-9	.kermrc	C-Kermit looks in your home directory first, then in the current directory.
Stratus VOS	ckermit.ini	A specially designated common system directory, or else your home directory.
UNIX (all versions)	.kermrc	A specially designated common system directory, or else your home directory, depending on how C-Kermit was installed.
Windows 95	K95.INI	The file K95.INI in your Kermit 95 directory.
Windows NT	K95.INI	The file K95.INI in your Kermit 95 directory.
Digital (Open)VMS	CKERMIT.INI	C-Kermit looks for CKERMIT_INI:, then for the file defined by the symbol CKERMIT_INIT, and finally in your home directory, SYS$LOGIN, for CKERMIT.INI.

The Customization File

Your customization file is for commands or settings that customize C-Kermit to your own personal requirements. It is called .mykermrc on UNIX and OS-9, ckermod.ini on Stratus VOS, and CKERMOD.INI elsewhere. It is generally in your home or login directory or, in systems like Windows and OS/2 that do not have login directories, in the same directory as as initialization file.

To illustrate the use of the customization file, suppose you have a UNIX workstation whose serial communication device is connected to a US Robotics high-speed modem and you always use C-Kermit to dial out on this device. Your customization file might contain commands like these:

```
echo Olga's customizations...
set modem type usr                   ; So DIAL command works right
set line /dev/ttyb                   ; Use ttyb for communication
set speed 57600                      ; Modem's highest speed
echo Ready for USR dialing at 57600 bps on /dev/ttyb.
echo Remember to turn on the modem!
```

(The SET commands are explained in the next chapter.) Note the use of trailing comments for documentation.

With this customization file, the only command you need to give Kermit to dial up another computer is DIAL (also explained in the next chapter):

```
$ kermit                            (Start Kermit)
Ready for USR dialing at 57600 bps on /dev/ttyb.
Remember to turn on your modem!
C-Kermit>show communications        (Check effect of init file)

Communications Parameters:
 Line: /dev/ttyb, speed: 57600, mode: local, modem: usr
 ...
C-Kermit>dial 9876543               (Dial another computer)
Call completed.                     (So easy!)
```

As you progress through this book, other likely candidates will suggest themselves for inclusion in your customization file — terminal settings (Chapter 8), file transfer protocol settings (Chapters 9–11), character-set selections (Chapter 16), macro definitions (Chapters 17–19). A *sample* customization file is distributed with C-Kermit; you can use this as a starting point. Just edit it to suit your needs and preferences.

Alternative Initialization Files

If you want Kermit to use a specific command file for initialization instead of the default command file shown in Table 2-2, you can specify a different initialization-file name on the command line, using the -y (lowercase) command-line option:

```
$ kermit -y special.ksc
```

If you want to run C-Kermit without any initialization file at all, use the -Y (uppercase) command-line option:

```
$ kermit -Y                         (UNIX, Windows, OS/2, etc.)
$ kermit "-Y"                       (VMS, quotes required)
```

(if necessary, replace "kermit" by the appropriate program name, such as "k95" for Kermit 95, "k2" for Kermit/2, etc).

If you want C-Kermit to execute a particular command file *after* it executes the initialization file but before it issues its first prompt, include the filename as the first word after *kermit* (or *k95*, or *k2*, etc) when you invoke C-Kermit from the system prompt:

```
$ kermit tuesday.ksc
```

A C-Kermit command file whose name is given as the first command-line argument, such as tuesday.ksc in the example, is called a C-Kermit application file. If you want C-Kermit to exit after executing an application file, include an EXIT command in the application file itself.

Commands for Controlling Commands

The commands in this section influence how other commands behave.

SET SUSPEND { **OFF**, **ON** }

On systems such as UNIX that allow programs to be stopped and continued, this command controls whether C-Kermit will allow this. For example, on UNIX systems with "job control" you can type Ctrl-Z (or other character) to "suspend" a program, and then use the UNIX "bg" or "fg" command to have it continue executing in the background or foreground. If you want to disallow this sort of thing in C-Kermit for any reason, use SET SUSPEND OFF. See examples in Appendix III.

SET TAKE { **ECHO**, **ERROR** } { **OFF**, **ON** }

This command controls the execution of command files by the TAKE command. Normally commands that are read and executed from command files are not displayed on the screen. If you would like to watch the commands as they are executed, use SET TAKE ECHO ON; commands are echoed (printed) on your screen, showing the line number of each command, which is handy for debugging command files.

Errors in command files are not fatal to the execution of the command file. If you want C-Kermit to stop executing a command file immediately when an error is encountered, use SET TAKE ERROR ON.

SET PROMPT [*text*]

Even though we don't show this in all our examples (less is more), C-Kermit's normal prompt shows your current directory, plus the program name and a right angle bracket:

```
[/users/home/olga] C-Kermit>
```

You can use the SET PROMPT command to change the prompt to something else (either a constant string or a string containing variables — described in Chapter 17 — that are re-evaluated every time the prompt is issued), for example:

```
[/users/home/olga] C-Kermit> set prompt K>
K> ; I like a short prompt.
K> set prompt [\v(time)] K>
[16:35:27] K> set prompt [\v(host)] K>
[hp.olga.com] K>
```

If you give the SET PROMPT command without any *text*, the default prompt is restored. This is equivalent to:

```
C-Kermit> set prompt [\v(directory)] C-Kermit>
```

If you want to have a null (empty, zero-length) prompt:

```
[/users/home/olga] C-Kermit> set prompt {}
```

CHECK *feature*

Checks if a particular feature is present, e.g. CHECK KANJI. Fails if the given feature is not present. Type "check ?" for a list of things you can check.

The SET COMMAND Command

SET COMMAND BYTESIZE { 7, 8 }

This command defines the character size, 7 or 8 bits, used by the command processor. The default is 8 bits in Windows and OS/2, 7 bits elsewhere. If you need to use 8-bit characters (such as accented or non-Roman letters), *and* you have a clear 8-bit connection between your terminal or display and C-Kermit, then tell C-Kermit to SET COMMAND BYTESIZE 8.

SET COMMAND RETRY { OFF, ON }

This command controls whether you are automatically reprompted with the "good part" of a failing command. Normally ON, meaning that you are reprompted.

SET COMMAND RECALL-BUFFER-SIZE *number*

Use this command to change the size of C-Kermit's command history buffer. It can be any reasonable size.

Screen Size and More-Prompting

In displays produced by C-Kermit commands, such as the keyword or file lists that are shown when you type a question mark in a command, as well as the output of HELP and similar commands, C-Kermit does its best to pause at the end of each screenful, ask "More?" and wait for you to type something before displaying the next screen.

The place where C-Kermit pauses is based on its idea of your screen dimensions, which it obtains by asking the operating system. If the operating system doesn't know, then 24 lines by 80 columns is assumed. You can change C-Kermit's idea of your command-screen dimensions with the commands:

SET COMMAND HEIGHT *number*

This command tells C-Kermit the number of rows (lines) on the command screen.

SET COMMAND WIDTH *number*

This command tells C-Kermit the number of columns (characters) across the command screen.

In OS/2 and Windows, these commands actually change the size of your command window. In UNIX, VMS, and elsewhere, they simply inform C-Kermit what the screen size actually is so it can format messages appropriately.

The "More?" prompt gives you time to read the material on the screen before it scrolls away. At the "More?" prompt you can reply "y" (for "yes," or press the space bar) to see the next screen, or "n" (for "no"), or "q" (for "quit") to cancel the display and return to the prompt.

You can turn more-prompting on and off with the command:

SET COMMAND MORE-PROMPTING *{ ON, OFF }*

If you turn it off, long reports — such as file lists produced by typing a question mark in a filename field (such as "send ?" in a directory that has many files) will scroll past without pausing. This behavior might be preferred by those using command windows that can be scrolled back with the mouse or special keys like Page Up.

Taming the Wild Backslash

If you are using C-Kermit on Windows 95 or NT or in OS/2, or you are using C-Kermit to transfer files with another system that is running DOS, Windows, or OS/2, and you find C-Kermit's treatment of the backslash character confusing or annoying, you can use the following command to tell C-Kermit to treat backslash just like any other character:

SET COMMAND QUOTING *{ ON, OFF }*

If you SET COMMAND QUOTING OFF, you enter DOS pathnames in the natural way in all commands, but you can't use backslash codes for special characters or variables:

```
C-Kermit> set command quoting off
C-Kermit> get c:\users\olaf\letter.txt
```

If you SET COMMAND QUOTING ON, you can use backslash codes, but you might have to enter DOS pathnames with double backslashes, as in:

```
C-Kermit> set command quoting on
C-Kermit> get c:\\users\\olaf\\letter.txt
```

All of your SET COMMAND settings are displayed for you when you command Kermit with the SHOW COMMAND command:

```
C-Kermit> show command
 Command bytesize: 7 bits
 Command recall-buffer-size: 10
 Command retry: on
 Command quoting: on
 Command more-prompting: on
 Command height: 24
 Command width:  72
 Maximum command length: 4072
 Maximum number of macros: 256
 Macros defined: 9
 ...
C-Kermit>
```

Finally, in case you are growing weary of the word "command," let it now be noted that you may abbreviate this overused word to CMD in both the SET and SHOW cmds.

Summary Tables

Table 2-3 lists many of the commands discussed in this chapter, and shows the equivalent system commands in UNIX, VMS, and AOS/VS. Table 2-4 summarizes the backslash codes used in C-Kermit commands.

Table 2-3 Basic C-Kermit Commands

Kermit	UNIX	VMS	AOS/VS	Description
cd	cd	set default	directory	Change directory
delete	rm	delete	delete	Delete files
directory	ls -l	directory	filestatus	List files
echo	echo	write	write	Display text on screen
help	man	help	help	Display help messages
mkdir	mkdir	create/dir	create/dir	Create a directory
pause	sleep	wait	pause	Sleep for some seconds
print	lp, lpr	print	print	Print files on a printer
push	sh, csh, ksh	spawn, @	push	Enter system
pwd	pwd	show default	directory	Show current directory
rename	mv	rename	rename	Rename files
rmdir	rmdir	delete/dir	delete	Remove a directory
run	*command*	[run] *command*	[xeq]	Run a command or program
space	df	show quota	space	Show disk space
type	cat	type	type	Display contents of a text file

Table 2-4 Summary of Backslash Codes

Code	Example	Meaning
\		(at end of command) Line continuation
\{	\{27}3	Braces are used for grouping
\%	\%a	A user-defined simple variable
\&	\&a[4]	An array reference
\$	\$(TERM)	An environment variable
\b	\b	The BREAK signal (OUTPUT command only)
\d	\d123	A decimal number
\f	\feval(2+2)	A built-in function
\l	\l	The LONG BREAK signal (OUTPUT command only)
\m	\m(oofa)	A macro used as a variable
\o	\o123	An octal number
\v	\v(time)	A built-in variable
\x	\x0f	A hexadecimal number
\\	\\	The backslash character itself
	\123	Decimal digit: a 1- to 3-digit decimal number
	\?	Anything else: quote the next character

Chapter 3

Making the Connection

In Chapter 2 you learned how to operate C-Kermit within the safe and circumscribed environment of a single computer, much like you would use most other computer software applications. But unlike those applications, the purpose of Kermit software is to let you use *two* computers at once, such as the PC on your desk and a BBS, a timesharing computer, or an information service located elsewhere.

Before we proceed, let's refresh our memories about *remote* and *local*. A Kermit program is in local mode if you are using it to establish a connection to another computer. Otherwise, it is in remote mode. For example, if you are using an MS-DOS PC on your desk to access a remote UNIX computer where C-Kermit resides, you will be using MS-DOS Kermit in *local mode* and C-Kermit in *remote mode*, as illustrated in Figure 3-1 on the next page. The PC establishes the connection, so it's the local computer. The UNIX system receives the connection, so it's the remote computer.

○ ○ ○ ○ ←——*(Stepping stones)*
If you will be using C-Kermit *only* in remote mode, you can skip ahead to Chapter 9, page 171, to learn how to transfer files. If necessary, also consult the "Getting Online" section of the documentation for your local Kermit program, for example, Chapter 7 of *Using MS-DOS Kermit* [35].

There are two ways to use C-Kermit in local mode, depending on what kind of computer you have. The first method is used when you have a PC or workstation on your desk from which you establish a connection to a remote computer. Figure 3-2 shows your local computer as a Sun SPARCstation, with a modem connection to a remote IBM mainframe.

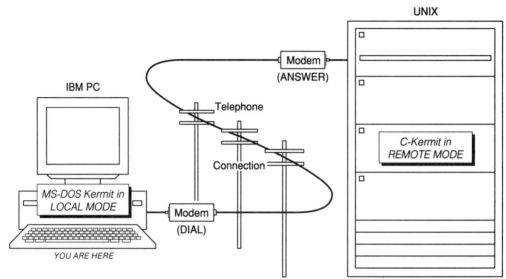

Figure 3-1 C-Kermit in Remote Mode

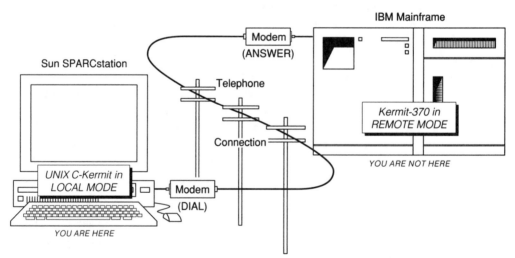

Figure 3-2 C-Kermit in Local Mode

The workstation could be any UNIX or OS-9 workstation, a VAXstation, a PC with OS/2 or Windows NT or Windows 95 or UNIX, a Macintosh, an Amiga, or an Atari ST. Any of these computers could use C-Kermit to establish a connection to a remote computer or service.

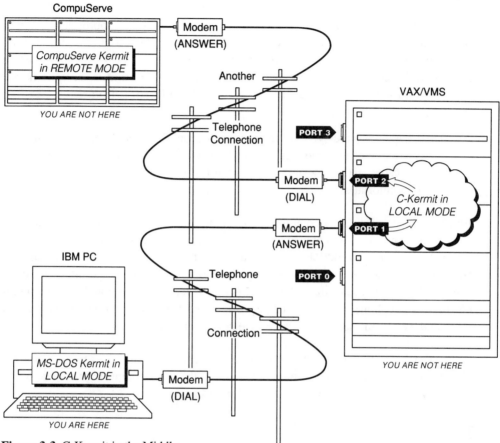

Figure 3-3 C-Kermit in the Middle

In the second scenario, illustrated in Figure 3-3, you are accessing a multiuser UNIX, VMS, VOS, or AOS/VS timesharing system from a PC, Macintosh, workstation, or terminal on your desk, and you are using C-Kermit on the multiuser computer to connect to a third computer. You would use this method if the multiuser computer has a connection method not available to your desktop computer, or if the multiuser computer is where you do most of your work.

Figure 3-3 shows an IBM PC with MS-DOS Kermit calling a VAX/VMS computer and using C-Kermit on the VAX to place a call to CompuServe. As you can see, you are using two communication ports on the VAX: the first for logging in and the second for dialing out. This illustrates how a *local* Kermit program uses a *separate device*, having nothing to do with your keyboard and screen, to communicate with the remote computer.

Using C-Kermit in Local Mode

Local-mode operation of C-Kermit has four phases: setting the appropriate communication parameters, making the connection, using the connection, and releasing the connection. The process can be easy or difficult, depending on your local computer, the connection method used, and the remote computer or service. C-Kermit is set up to handle the easy cases automatically, but the hard cases require a little extra effort.

○ ○ ○ ○
This chapter assumes you are familiar with serial data communication concepts such as modem, null modem, interface speed, modulation speed, parity, flow control, cable, and connector. If you aren't, please turn to Appendix II on page 479 for a tutorial.

Before you can make two computers communicate, you have to learn certain essential facts about them and the connection between them. What is the connection method — dialup, direct, or network? For dialup and direct connections, what is the name of the communication device on the local computer and what speeds are permitted? For dialup connections, what type of dialout modem is on the local computer and what is the remote computer's telephone number? For network connections, which type of network are we using and what is the address of the remote computer on the network?

Use C-Kermit's SET command to supply these facts. C-Kermit tries to give you reasonable defaults when possible; if your connection to the other computer fits the defaults, you need just a few SET commands and connecting is easy.

A Test Drive

To show you just how easy a connection can be, let's use C-Kermit to dial the Digital Equipment Corporation Electronic Store. In this example, we're running C-Kermit on a DEC 3000 Alpha workstation in a terminal window, which provides VT terminal emulation. We dial out using a US Robotics Sportster V.34 modem at an interface speed of 57600 bits per second. This same example should work on practically any other computer where C-Kermit runs, but probably you will have to substitute a different modem type and a different device name in the SET LINE or SET PORT command.[10]

How do you know the name of the communication device? If you have a desktop workstation, look in your workstation's user manual. Some sample workstation dialout

---

[10]If your version of C-Kermit is running on a computer that is connected to the Internet, you can tell C-Kermit to "telnet orders.sales.digital.com" instead of dialing a modem.

device names are listed in Table 3-1 on the next page, in which the modem is assumed to be attached to the first serial device on each computer.[11] If you are dialing out from a multiuser computer, consult your site-specific documentation or ask the system support staff.

This demonstration is available only in the North American calling area, and it works only if C-Kermit is running in an environment that supports DEC VT100, VT200, VT300, or higher VT terminal emulation, such as a true VT terminal or emulator connected to the system where C-Kermit is running, a DECterm or xterm window on a workstation, the console driver on a PC-based UNIX system, or you are using MS-DOS Kermit, Kermit/2, or Kermit 95, which provide their own VT terminal emulation.

```
$ kermit                          (Start Kermit on the DEC3000)
C-Kermit 6.0.192, 6 Sep 96, Digital UNIX 4.0
Type ? or HELP for help
C-Kermit>set modem type usr       (What kind of modem you have)
C-Kermit>set line /dev/ttyp00     (Communication device to use)
C-Kermit>set speed 57600          (Dialing speed)
C-Kermit>dial 1-800-234-1998      (Place the call)
 Number: 1-800-234-1998           (Messages from C-Kermit...)
 Device=/dev/ttyp00, modem=usr, speed=57600
 Call completed.<BEEP>


Connecting to /dev/ttyp0, speed 57600.
The escape character is Ctrl-\ (ASCII 28, FS).
Type the escape character followed by C to get back,
or followed by ? to see other options.

Welcome to Digital's Electronic Store.  Please wait a moment ...

  (Follow the directions,
    browse around for a while, and then...)
```

To get back to C-Kermit at any time after connecting to the remote service, type Ctrl-Backslash and then the letter C. That is, hold down the Ctrl (or Control) key and press the backslash key,[12] then let go of the control key and press the C key.

```
Ctrl-\C                           (Escape back to C-Kermit)
C-Kermit>exit                     (All done, exit to UNIX)
$
```

Wasn't that easy? Here's hoping that all your connections are so easy! In this case, all

---

[11]If your workstation has a serial mouse, the modem might be attached to the *second* serial device.

[12]On the NeXT workstation, substitute the right bracket key for the backslash key. Most NeXT keyboards do not support the Control-Backslash key combination. On PCs running OS/2 or Windows NT or 95, use either Control-Rightbracket C or Alt-x (hold down the Alt key and press the x key).

Table 3-1 Sample Dialout Device Names

System	Default Device	Dialout Device Name
Apple A/UX	*console*	/dev/modem
AmigaDOS	serial.device/0	serial.device/0
Amiga UNIX	*console*	/dev/term/ser or /dev/term/ql00
AT&T 6300 PLUS	*console*	/dev/tty1
AT&T 7300 UNIX PC	*console*	/dev/ph0
Atari ST GEMDOS	AUX:	AUX:
BeBox	*console*	/dev/serial1
Data General AViiON	*console*	/dev/tty00
Data General AOS/VS	*console*	@con1
DECstation ULTRIX	*console*	/dev/tty00
Dell UNIX	*console*	/dev/tty01 (if mouse on /dev/tty00). For RTS/CTS, use /dev/tty01h.
HP-9000 HP-UX	*console*	/dev/cua00 or /dev/cua0p0
IBM RS/6000 AIX	*console*	/dev/tty0
Interactive UNIX/386	*console*	/dev/tty0 or /dev/acu0
NeXTstation	*console*	/dev/cua. Use /dev/cufa for RTS/CTS.
OS/2	*console*	COM1
OS-9	*console*	/t1
QNX	*console*	/dev/ser1
SCO UNIX/ODT/OpenServer	*console*	/dev/tty1A (uppercase A selects modem control)
SCO Xenix	*console*	/dev/tty1a
Silicon Graphics	*console*	/dev/ttym0. Use /dev/ttyf0 for RTS/CTS.
Sun SPARCstation	*console*	/dev/cua0 or /dev/cua/a
UnixWare 1.*x*, 2.*x*	*console*	/dev/term/01s or use /dev/term/01h for RTS/CTS.
Windows 95 or NT	*none*	COM1
VMS, OpenVMS	*console*	TXA0:, TTA0:, or LTA0:

you had to do was tell C-Kermit what kind of modem to use, the name of the communication device that the modem was connected to, and the speed to use for dialing. Then you dialed the phone number, connected, did some window shopping, got back to C-Kermit, and then returned to your operating system.

Overview of Connection Establishment

C-Kermit supports three types of connections: direct serial, dialed serial, and network. Direct serial connections are a special case, since they don't really need to be established — they are "hardwired," they are "just there." Dialed serial and network connections are similar, however, in that both types need to be established by you. You have to tell Kermit what sort of modem or network you have, perhaps along with some related configuration details, and then you have to give Kermit the telephone number or network address you are trying to reach. The procedures are summarized in the following chart:

	Direct Serial	*Dialed Serial*	*Network*
Select method:		SET MODEM TYPE *name*	SET NETWORK *name*
Select device:	SET LINE *device*	SET LINE *device*	
Specify speed:	SET SPEED *number*	SET SPEED *number*	
Set flow control:	SET FLOW *type*	SET FLOW *type*	SET FLOW NONE
Make connection:		DIAL *number*	SET HOST *address*
Go online:	CONNECT	CONNECT	CONNECT
Close connection:	HANGUP	HANGUP	HANGUP

Examples:

	Direct Serial	*Dialed Serial*	*Network*
Select method:		SET MODEM TYPE USR	SET NETWORK TCP/IP
Select device:	SET LINE COM1	SET LINE COM1	
Specify speed:	SET SPEED 57600	SET SPEED 57600	
Set flow control:	SET FLOW RTS/CTS	SET FLOW RTS/CTS	SET FLOW NONE
Make connection:		DIAL 7654321	SET HOST IBM.COM
Go online:	CONNECT	CONNECT	CONNECT
Close connection:	HANGUP	HANGUP	HANGUP

○ ○ ○ ○

This chapter and the next two cover serial connections; networks are discussed in Chapter 6. If you are only going to be using C-Kermit on network connections, by all means skip ahead to Chapter 6.

Making a Serial Connection

A serial connection is made over an asynchronous serial communication device (what a mouthful!), also called a serial port, terminal port, tty port, RS-232 port, V.24 device, EIA port, UART, or asynchronous adapter. If the port is connected directly to another computer, which would normally be done with a null modem cable, the connection is *direct*. If it is connected to a modem (or it *is* a modem) that is, in turn, connected to a telephone line that must be dialed, the connection is *dialed*.

Selecting the Communication Device

For any type of serial connection, you must tell Kermit the name of the serial device, since most computers have more than one of them to choose from. The command is SET LINE or SET PORT:

SET LINE [*device*]

Opens the serial communication device through which you will be communicating. If you give the SET LINE command without including a device name, C-Kermit closes any currently open communication device and returns to the default communication device, which in most cases is your controlling terminal (*console*) and remote mode, or to the default dialout device, as shown in Table 3-1. Synonym: **SET PORT**. Examples:

```
C-Kermit>set line /dev/cua          (UNIX)
C-Kermit>set line txa4:             (VMS)
C-Kermit>set line @con2:            (AOS/VS)
C-Kermit>set line com2              (Windows or OS/2)
C-Kermit>set line 2                 (Same as line com2)
C-Kermit>set port 2                 (Same as line 2)
C-Kermit>set line                   (All, select default device)
```

Whenever you give a SET LINE (or SET PORT) command, C-Kermit closes any currently open communication device before attempting to open the new one. The SET LINE command can fail for any of the following reasons, which are printed as error messages on your screen:

Sorry, access to device denied

The communication device is protected against you. Contact your system administrator to see if you can get the required access (or if you *are* the system administrator, change the device's permission or the way in which Kermit is installed).

Sorry, access to lock denied

(UNIX only) The lock mechanism that prevents more than one person from using the same communication device at the same time is protected against you; contact your system administrator or change the way Kermit is installed (see Appendix III).

Sorry, device is in use

Somebody else is currently using the communication device you have specified. If you get the "device is in use" message in UNIX, C-Kermit attempts to let you know who is using it by showing a directory listing of the lock file:

```
C-Kermit>set line /dev/ttyh6
-r--r--r--  1 olga  11  Feb 8 15:17 /var/spool/locks/LCK..ttyh6
pid = 15688
/dev/ttyh6: Sorry, device is in use
C-Kermit>
```

The file owner, "olga", is the user who created the lock. The "pid" is the process ID of the program that created the lockfile. If you know where Olga is, you can ask her when she will be finished with the device you need.

Sorry, can't open connection
    Kermit encountered some other kind of error or difficulty when trying to open the device. The appropriate system error message is also printed, for example:

```
No such file or directory
```

Timed out, no carrier
    You have given a SET CARRIER-WATCH ON command (see page 61) that specified a time limit for SET LINE to wait for the carrier signal, but carrier did not appear within the time limit.

If a SET LINE command appears to be stuck, it means that the operating system is having difficulty opening the device, or is waiting for the carrier signal to appear. You should be able to get back to the C-Kermit prompt by typing Ctrl-C.

If a new prompt appears and there is no error message, C-Kermit has opened the serial communication device successfully.

Specifying the Communication Speed

Before using the serial communication device that you specified in your SET LINE or SET PORT command, you should specify the transmission speed. This should be the same speed as the remote computer or service uses or, if a modem is involved, the interface speed to be used between C-Kermit and the modem (which, for a data-compressing modem, should be two to four times higher than the modulation speed; see Appendix II). In general, on any given connection, you should use the highest speed that works.

SET SPEED *number*
    Specifies the transmission speed, in bits per second, to use on the serial communication device specified in your most recent SET LINE or SET PORT command. If you don't give a SET SPEED command, Kermit tries to learn the device's current speed and use it. Only certain speeds are available; type SET SPEED ? to find out what they are. The list can vary from computer to computer. Here is a typical example:

```
C-Kermit>set speed ?
Transmission rate in bits per second, one of the following:
 110      19200     300      4800     7200       9600
 1200     200       3600     50       75
 150      2400      38400    600      75/1200
C-Kermit>set speed 19200
```

Notice that the speeds are arranged in "alphabetical" rather than numeric order (reading by columns, top to bottom, left to right). Because they are keywords, you can use abbreviation and completion with them, and you cannot enter an illegal value by mistake. Examples:

```
C-Kermit>set speed 9600        (9600 bits per second)
C-Kermit>set sp 9              (9600 bits per second)
C-Kermit>set sp 9500           (Not in the list)
?No keywords match - 9500
C-Kermit>
```

If you see a 75/1200 entry, it is for use with split-speed modems, found mostly in Europe. Split speed operation is supported only in C-Kermit versions where the underlying operating system and hardware also support it. 75/1200 means C-Kermit transmits at 75 bps and receives at 1200 bps.

Remember, SET SPEED applies to the device given in the most recent SET LINE or SET PORT command. Kermit must know which device's speed you are setting. So the rule is: SET LINE (or SET PORT) first, then SET SPEED.

You can't use C-Kermit's SET SPEED command to change your login terminal's speed. If you issue the SET SPEED command while Kermit is in remote mode, you'll get an error message:

```
C-Kermit>set speed 57600
?Sorry, you must SET LINE first
```

More About Communication Speeds

The common serial interface speeds are 300, 600, 1200, 2400, 4800, 9600, 19200, 38400, 57600, 115200, and 203400. But not all speeds are supported on all platforms. In UNIX, for example, only those speeds that are supported by the underlying operating system and application program interface (API) can be set. Even today, it is common to find UNIX systems that do not support speeds above 19200 or 38400 bps, even though the hardware itself might be capable of going much faster. On the other hand, a certain speed might be "legal" to the software but not supported by the underlying hardware.

With the appearance of the V.32*bis* and V.34 modem standards (see Appendix II), we also have a number of new "in-between" speeds: 7200, 12000, 14400, 16800, 21600, 24000, 26400, and 28800. These are modulation speeds that, in general, are not intended to be used as serial interface speeds.

Instead, because most modern modems support error correction and data compression, you are expected to set the interface speed between the modem and the computer *higher* than the modem's modulation speed and to keep the interface speed fixed. This is especially important with V.34 modems, which can change modulation speeds many times during a session by negotiating "speed shifts" with the other modem, according to observed fluctuations in line quality.

The Carrier Signal

Serial communication devices might not allow themselves to be opened if the software and hardware don't agree about how to treat the RS-232 Carrier Detect (CD, DCD, RLSI) signal (see Appendix II), a signal from the modem to the computer. Most versions of C-Kermit assume that CD is off during dialing, that it is on when the connection has been made and is in use, and that it goes off again when the connection is broken. But your modem might be configured to keep CD on (or off) all the time, or the cable connecting the modem to your serial port might not convey the CD signal correctly. The SET CARRIER-WATCH command lets you adjust Kermit to such situations:

SET CARRIER-WATCH { AUTO, OFF, ON *[number]* **}**

Successful operation of SET CARRIER-WATCH depends on the capabilities of the operating system and version, and Kermit's knowledge of them, as well as the configuration of your serial port, the port device driver, the modem, and the cable. The SET CARRIER-WATCH command takes effect on the next communications-oriented command. Synonym: **SET MODEM CARRIER-WATCH**. Here are the SET CARRIER-WATCH options:

SET CARRIER-WATCH AUTO

Requires carrier during CONNECT, TRANSMIT, INPUT, OUTPUT, and SCRIPT commands, and during file transfer, but not during DIAL operations. AUTO is the default.

SET CARRIER-WATCH OFF

C-Kermit is to ignore CD at all times. This is useful for direct connections, misbehaving modem connections, miswired or misconfigured modems, or buggy serial device drivers. It is also usually needed when you want to CONNECT to the modem and type commands to it yourself. SET CARRIER-WATCH OFF should be used only when necessary because it takes away Kermit's ability to detect a broken connection.

SET CARRIER-WATCH ON *[number]*

C-Kermit is to require carrier for all communication. An error is diagnosed if carrier disappears; C-Kermit should give an error message and pop back to its prompt automatically. When SET CARRIER-WATCH ON is in effect, CD must be present when you give the SET LINE or SET PORT command. If not, Kermit waits for the carrier signal to appear. This provides a way to wait for an incoming telephone call (but the ANSWER command is an even better way; see page 73).

If you want to set a limit on how long SET LINE should wait for carrier, you can include an optional number after SET CARRIER-WATCH ON that indicates how many seconds to wait before timing out and returning to the prompt, for example:

```
C-Kermit>SET CARRIER-WATCH ON 30
```

You can also type Ctrl-C to interrupt a SET LINE command that is taking too long. In both cases (timeout and Ctrl-C interruption), the device is not assigned.

Flow Control

Flow control is how two independently functioning computers (or other devices) that are sending data to each other prevent data loss by controlling the rate at which the data flows. Flow control is covered in greater detail in Appendix II and in Chapter 10.

The C-Kermit command to select the flow control method is:

SET FLOW-CONTROL { AUTO, KEEP, NONE, RTS/CTS, XON/XOFF }

The options are:

AUTO

This tells C-Kermit to pick the type of flow control most appropriate for the connection. This is the default and recommended setting. Use the other settings when you know better.

KEEP

Use whatever type of flow control the device was configured with at the time that C-Kermit first opened it.

NONE

Don't use any method of flow control. Use this option when the two computers or devices do not share a flow control method in common, or when flow control is provided in some other way not known to or controllable by Kermit, or when the connection is not serial at all, for example a TCP/IP network connection, in which case the underlying network protocol should provide the flow control.

RTS/CTS

Hardware flow control using the RTS and CTS wires. This option is not available in all versions of C-Kermit because some operating systems do not support it. If it is available, it will show up in the keyword menu if you type "SET FLOW ?". Use this option with high-speed modems, terminal servers, or other devices that also support it, and on direct serial connections when the two serial devices and their driver software also support it and the null modem cable is properly wired to convey these signals (Model B in Figure II-6, Appendix II, page 494).

XON/XOFF

Software flow control using Ctrl-S and Ctrl-Q characters. This method may be used end-to-end, transparently through intermediate communication devices such as modems and terminal servers, or it may be used between C-Kermit and the device it is immediately connected to, depending on how the various devices are configured. Use this method when both parties support it and RTS/CTS is not available.

RTS/CTS flow control is sometimes available to you even when C-Kermit's SET FLOW command does not offer it. For example, in certain UNIX versions, such SGI IRIX, it can be selected by using special device names (see Table 3-1 on page 56). On other systems it can be enabled by giving a system command before starting C-Kermit, for example:

```
% stty crtscts < /dev/ttyh4
```

on certain UNIX systems (but, of course, not others), or:

```
) characteristics /on/ifc/ofc
```

in AOS/VS. Consult your system documentation for further information.

Certain versions of C-Kermit might also support less common hardware flow-control options, such as DTR/CD or DTR/CTS. If your version of C-Kermit, and the underlying device and driver software, and the directly connected communication device, support these options, then you can use them in place of RTS/CTS. Use them with caution, however; the CD signal normally tells C-Kermit the connection is broken, so you must SET CARRIER-WATCH OFF before attempting to use DTR/CD flow control. Also, when using either DTR/CD or DTR/CTS, make sure your communication device is configured not to hang up the connection if your computer turns off the DTR signal!

Displaying Communication Settings

To find out your current communication device, speed, carrier, flow control, and other settings, use the SHOW COMMUNICATIONS command, as in this example for UNIX:

```
C-Kermit>sho comm

Communications Parameters:
 Line: /dev/ttyh4, speed: 9600, mode: local, modem: none
 Terminal bits: 7, parity: none, duplex: full, flow: xon/xoff
 Carrier: auto, lockfile: /var/spool/locks/LCK..ttyh4
 Escape character: 28 (^\)

Carrier Detect       (CD):  On
Dataset Ready        (DSR): On
Clear To Send        (CTS): On
Ring Indicator       (RI):  Off
Data Terminal Ready  (DTR): On
Request To Send      (RTS): Off

Type SHOW DIAL to see DIAL-related items
```

Direct Serial Connections

Figure 3-4 shows a direct serial connection from a DEC VAXstation to a remote computer using a null modem cable. The VAXstation could also be any other kind of computer where you are running C-Kermit in local mode. This kind of connection is relatively easy to use because no modems are involved and dialing is not required. All you have to do is

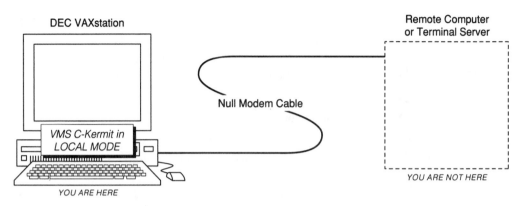

DEC VAXstation

Remote Computer
or Terminal Server

Null Modem Cable

VMS C-Kermit in
LOCAL MODE

YOU ARE HERE

YOU ARE NOT HERE

Figure 3-4 A Direct Connection

tell C-Kermit the name of the communication device that the cable is connected to and the communication speed to use. The other end of the cable should be connected to a port on the remote computer that has been set up to let you log in. The remote computer in the figure also can be a terminal server or similar device with which you have a brief dialog to select a computer or service and which then connects you to it. It can also be any other DTE (see Appendix II) that is prepared to communicate.

The only commands C-Kermit should need to establish a direct connection are SET LINE, SET SPEED, and perhaps SET FLOW (if SET FLOW AUTO does not produce the best result). Here is an example of setting C-Kermit up for a local-mode direct connection, showing the order in which you should give the commands:

```
C-Kermit>set speed 9600            (Set the speed)
?Sorry, you must SET LINE first    (Oops)
C-Kermit>set line txa5             (Select communication device)
C-Kermit>set speed 9600            (Now set the speed)
C-Kermit>                          (No complaint)
```

If you have trouble establishing a direct connection:

• If you were expecting a login prompt but see nothing at all, make sure the port on the remote computer is set up to allow logins.

• Make sure the serial devices on the two computers are configured to use the same communication speed.

• Watch out for flow-control deadlocks. Try SET FLOW NONE or the equivalent operating-system command.

• Make sure you have used a null modem cable rather than a modem cable (see Figure II-6 on page 494), and that each computer's serial port asserts the DTR signal and receives all the signals it requires, usually DSR, CTS, and CD (Model B in the figure), or else that the appropriate signals are cross-wired or looped back (Model A).

- Make sure the total length of the cable does not exceed 15 meters or 50 feet. For longer distances, use powered line drivers or limited distance modems at each end of the cable, or use a shielded low-capacitance cable.

- Try SET CARRIER-WATCH OFF before SET LINE.

REMEMBER: SET CARRIER-WATCH first (only if necessary), then SET LINE, then SET SPEED. In that order.

If your direct connection is wired with a true null modem cable (such as the one shown in Figure II-6, Model B), Kermit should notice when you log out from the remote computer crashes or when it crashes, and return you automatically to the local C-Kermit prompt with a message like "communications disconnect". If you have used a "fakeout" cable (like Model A in the figure), Kermit does not notice, and the connection remains open.

○ ○ ○ ○
The rest of this chapter tells how to make dialed connections. If you will not be making dialed connections, but you will be making network connections, turn to Chapter 6 on page 117. If you will not be making dialed or network connections, turn to Chapter 8 to learn how to go online.

Dialed Serial Connections

When you can't connect two computers with a direct cable (or with a network), you can do it with modems and telephone lines, as illustrated in Figure 3-5. With C-Kermit and an appropriate modem, your computer can call any other computer or data service in the world that accepts modem calls and has a modem compatible with yours. C-Kermit sends dialing commands to the modem, the modem places the call and tells Kermit whether there was an answer, and then Kermit tells you whether the call was placed successfully.

Let's demonstrate the simple steps that should work in most situations. Find out what kind of modem you will be dialing with, the name of the communication device it is attached to, and the phone number of the computer or service you will be dialing. Follow this example, substituting your own particulars for the ones shown, but issue the given commands in exactly this order:[13]

---

[13]All telephone numbers shown in this book are fictitious unless noted otherwise.

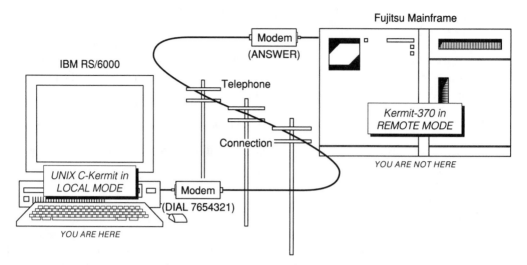

Figure 3-5 A Dialed Connection

```
C-Kermit>set modem type ppi        (Identify the modem type)
C-Kermit>set line /dev/cua         (Identify the communication device)
C-Kermit>set speed 57600           (Select the dialing speed)
C-Kermit>dial 93,1-800-555-1234    (Dial the phone number)
```

REMEMBER: SET MODEM TYPE first, SET LINE second, SET SPEED and other communications parameters third, and then DIAL.

USING MODEM SERVERS: A different technique is used for dialing a modem that is connected to a TCP/IP modem server. It is described on page 126 in the networks chapter.

The SET MODEM TYPE Command

The SET MODEM TYPE command lets you tell C-Kermit what type of modem you will be using so the appropriate commands can be given to the modem to configure it and make it dial, and so the modem's responses can be interpreted correctly to let you know whether the call was completed successfully. You should give the SET MODEM TYPE command *before* the SET LINE or SET PORT command so the operating system doesn't block waiting for the CD signal when trying to open the device.

There are three categories of modem types:

NONE (or DIRECT)

This is the default modem type. Use NONE when there is no modem and therefore no modem signals and no dialing, as on a directly wired connection, or to cancel a previously established modem type. Examples:

```
C-Kermit>set modem type none       (Direct connection)
C-Kermit>set modem type direct     (Same as above)
C-Kermit>set modem type            (Same as above)
```

UNKNOWN

This means that there is a modem, but it is of a type unknown to C-Kermit (or to you). You must specify the modem's entire dialing sequence in C-Kermit's DIAL command. Modem signals are ignored while dialing, but Kermit, after dialing, waits for the CD signal for a certain amount of time (usually between one and two minutes) to see whether the call was succesfully completed. Example (in which the modem is actually Hayes compatible):

```
C-Kermit>set modem type unknown
C-Kermit>dial ATDT7654321
```

USR, HAYES, ROLM, . . .

If you name a specific type of modem, Kermit uses its built-in knowledge of the dialing language and conventions for that modem when you issue a DIAL command, and it declares the connection complete or failed based upon responses from the modem. Some of the modems known to C-Kermit are listed in Table 3-2 (older ones are omitted). To see a complete list, type "SET MODEM TYPE ?":

```
C-Kermit>set modem type ?          (See what's available)
  att-dataport      digitel-dt22       microlink         rockwell-v34
  att-dtdm          gateway-telepath   motorola-fastalk  rolm-dcm
  att-isn           gdc-212a/ed        multitech         supra
  att-switched-net  hayes-1200         mwave             telebit
  att-7300          hayes-2400         none              unknown
  boca              hayes-high-speed   old-telebit       user-defined
  cermetek          intel              penril            usrobotics
  concord           itu-t-v25bis       ppi               ventel
  df03-ac           maxtech            racalvadic        zoltrix
  df100-series      microcom-at-mode   rockwell-v32      zoom
  df200-series      microcom-sx-mode   rockwell-v32bis   zyxel
C-Kermit>set modem type ppi      (Practical Peripherals Inc.)
```

When you select a modem type, many characteristics of the modem are automatically filled in from C-Kermit's modem database. Some of these characteristics are listed in Table 3-2; here is what the abbreviations mean:

AT   Uses Hayes AT command set.
ITU Uses ITU-T V.25bis command set.
EC   Capable of error correction.
DC   Capable of data compression.
LF   Capable of local flow control.
KS   Implements "Kermit Spoof" (modem executes Kermit protocol).
TB   Made by Telebit (used internally for simplification).

Table 3-2 Modem Types Known to C-Kermit

Name	Characteristics							Description
ATT-DATAPORT	AT	EC	DC	LF	SB			AT&T / Paradyne DataPort.
ATT-DTDM								AT&T Digital Terminal Data Module
ATT-ISN								AT&T ISN Network
ATT-SWITCHED-NET	AT							AT&T switched network modems
ATT-7300								AT&T 7300 (3B1) internal modem
BOCA	AT	EC	DC	LF	SB			Various BOCA models
DIGITEL-DT22	ITU							Digitel DT-22 (Brazil)
GATEWAY-TELEPATH	AT	EC	DC	LF	SB			Gateway 2000 Telepath II
HAYES-1200	AT							Hayes Smartmodem 1200
HAYES-2400	AT							Hayes Smartmodem 2400
HAYES-HIGH-SPEED	AT	EC	DC	LF	SB			Hayes Ultra, Optima, or Accura
INTEL	AT	EC	DC	LF	SB			Intel High-Speed Faxmodem
ITU-T-V25BIS	ITU							ITU-T (CCITT) V.25*bis*, async only
MAXTECH	AT	EC	DC	LF	SB			MaxTech XM or GVC Faxmodem
MICROCOM-AT	AT	EC	DC	LF	SB			Microcom AX, QX, SX in AT mode
MICROCOM-SX		EC	DC	LF	SB	KS		Microcom AX, QX, SX in SX mode
MICROLINK	AT	EC	DC	LF	SB			ELSA GmbH MicroLink 14.4 / 28.8
MOTOROLA-FASTALK	AT	EC	DC	LF	SB			Motorola FasTalk II
MULTITECH	AT	EC	DC	LF	SB			Multitech MT Series MultiModem
MWAVE	AT	EC	DC	LF	SB			IBM Mwave
NONE								*Default* direct connection (= DIRECT)
OLD-TELEBIT	AT	EC	DC	LF	SB	KS	TB	TrailBlazer,T1000/1500/2000/2500
PPI	AT	EC	DC	LF	SB			Practical Peripherals, V.22*bis*–V.34
ROCKWELL-V32	AT	EC	DC	LF	SB			RC96ATi and RC144ATi family
ROCKWELL-V32BIS	AT	EC	DC	LF	SB			RCV144ACi and ACL V.32*bis* family
ROCKWELL-V34	AT	EC	DC	LF	SB			RC288 ACi and ACL V.34 family
ROLM-DCM								Rolm (Siemens) CBX DCM
SUPRA	AT	EC	DC	LF	SB			Supra Corporation SupraFAXModems
TELEBIT	AT	EC	DC	LF	SB	KS	TB	T1600/3000, Q/Fast/WorldBlazer...
UNKNOWN								Unknown (generic) modem type
USER-DEFINED								Characteristics filled in by the user
USR	AT	EC	DC	LF	SB			US Robotics Courier or Sportster
ZOLTRIX	AT	EC	DC	LF	SB			Zoltrix V.32*bis* or V.34
ZOOM	AT	EC	DC	LF	SB			Zoom V.32*bis* or V.34
ZYXEL	AT	EC	DC	LF	SB			ZyXEL V.32*bis* or V.34

Now you can SET LINE (or SET PORT) to choose a communication device. If the SET LINE command succeeds, the DTR signal of the computer's communication device is (or should be) turned on to enable communication with the modem. If SET LINE fails, you'll get an informative error message (see page 58 for a list of them).

Now choose a communications interface speed using Kermit's SET SPEED command. Normally this would be the highest speed supported by C-Kermit and the modem. If you don't give a SET SPEED command, the device's current speed is used, which might not be the speed you want. Remember that if your modem is capable of data compression, you should choose an interface speed that is at least twice the modem's modulation speed.

The rest — error correction, data compression, flow control, and other capabilities and the modem-specific commands that enable them — are filled in automatically from Kermit's modem database so the modem will be configured as you desire automatically. Of course, there are also ways to override every little detail (explained in Chapter 4).

Here is an example showing how to set up Kermit for dialing with a high-speed modem:

```
C-Kermit>set modem type zyxel     (Modem type first)
C-Kermit>set line /dev/cua        (Then device)
C-Kermit>set speed 115200         (Then speed)
```

Those are usually all the commands you need to set up your modem.

The DIAL and REDIAL Commands

Now you are ready to dial:

DIAL *text*
> Dials the given *text* (telephone number) using C-Kermit's built-in method for operating the type of modem you identified in your last SET MODEM TYPE command.

If a particular modem type is set, just include the phone number and C-Kermit issues the appropriate configuration and dialing instructions and reads the responses:

```
C-Kermit>dial 7654321
```

If the modem type is UNKNOWN, you must include the modem's dialing command in the phone number, for example:

```
C-Kermit>dial at&c1dp7654321
```

The *text* is a number or access code expressed in the syntax of your telephone system or PBX, possibly including other characters meaningful to the modem or PBX. Example:

```
C-Kermit>dial 93W1 (212) 555-4321
```

In this example, for a Hayes or compatible modem, parentheses, spaces, and hyphens are ignored and may be included for clarity. 93 is a PBX code to get an outside line, the W is a Hayes command to wait for the secondary dialtone, and the 1 requests a long distance call in the North American dialing region. Consult Table II-2 on page 487 for details about the special characters allowed in Hayes modem dial strings, or read your modem manual. The "phone number" can also be the name of an entry in your dialing directory. C-Kermit's dialing directory is the topic of Chapter 5.

REDIAL

Dial the number specified in your most recent DIAL command again. Example:

```
C-Kermit>dial 7654321          (Dial the number)
Failed ("BUSY")                (Get a busy signal)
C-Kermit>redial                (A few minutes later...)
```

Tone versus Pulse Dialing

To select tone or pulse dialing, type the following command (or put it in your C-Kermit customization file, or execute it in any other desired way):

SET DIAL METHOD { DEFAULT, PULSE, TONE }

Specifies pulse or tone dialing. The default is DEFAULT, meaning don't tell the modem which method to use, i.e. the modem should use its default dialing method.

Tone dialing is not available everywhere, which is why it is not the default method. Pulse dialing is not the default method either, because the extra telephone keys "*" and "#" cannot be dialed on a rotary telephone line, and also because pulse dialing is slow and annoying to people who are accustomed to tone dialing. So we expect the modem to be configured for the appropriate type of dialing.

Dialing Repeatedly

Computers are said to be good at repetitive, boring, mechanical tasks. Unlike people, who become aggravated when a telephone number is busy or doesn't answer, the computer can dial repetively, as many times as you like, until the call succeeds. Normally, Kermit dials only once, but you can tell it to keep trying with the following commands:

SET DIAL RETRIES *number*

Tells Kermit how many times to dial the number again if there is no answer or the number is busy. The default is 0. When multiple numbers for the same name have been fetched from the dialing directory, the entire sequence is retried the given number of times. Retries are not done if there is an unrecoverable error (modem is not turned on, no dialtone, etc).

SET DIAL INTERVAL *seconds*

How many seconds to pause between dial retries. The default interval is 10 seconds. This interval applies when retrying the same number or group, but not between multiple entries in a group.

IMPORTANT: AUTOMATIC REDIALING IS PROHIBITED BY LAW IN SOME COUNTRIES, and the intervals at which and/or the number of times a call can be redialed may be restricted. Be sure not use Kermit's automatic redial feature in any way that is against the your local laws.

You can cancel an automatic redialing sequence by typing your system's interrupt character, which is usually Ctrl-C.

When Dialing Is Complete

If the DIAL command succeeds and the connection is made, C-Kermit can either issue a new prompt and wait for you to enter another command, or it can "go online" so you can "see" and interact directly with the computer or service you have called. Like all other things in C-Kermit, there is a command to control this:

SET DIAL CONNECT { ON, OFF, AUTO }

Instructs C-Kermit what to do when a DIAL or REDIAL command succeeds. ON means that Kermit should immediately enter terminal, or "CONNECT," mode, explained in Chapter 8. OFF means it should await another command. AUTO, which is the default, means it should CONNECT automatically if the DIAL command came from the keyboard — i.e. you typed it — but if the DIAL command came from a command file or macro (explained in Chapter 17), it should keep executing commands from the command file or macro.

The default setting of AUTO should do the right thing in almost every case. Use ON or OFF to force C-Kermit to do exactly what you want if the AUTO setting does not.

Closing the Connection

To terminate a connection, use the HANGUP command:

HANGUP

If you are using a modem, the HANGUP command attempts to put your modem in command mode and then issue the modem command to hang up the phone, such as ATH0 for Hayes and compatible modems. If this doesn't work, or if you have a direct serial connection, C-Kermit lowers the Data Terminal Ready (DTR) signal for half a second. If that doesn't work, C-Kermit closes and reopens the communications device.

Normally, the HANGUP command need not be used. When you log out from a remote computer or service, it hangs up its end of the connection, and C-Kermit should notice and automatically pop back to its prompt. Use the HANGUP command in situations where this does not happen, or it takes too long, or when you want to be doubly sure that the connection is broken and the telephone is hung up.

Manual Dialing

You can also dial a modem by hand. This might be necessary if you have a modem that C-Kermit doesn't know about or if you want to change or query the modem's configuration. Here is an example, using a Hayes modem:

```
C-Kermit>set carrier-watch off    (Ignore the carrier signal)
C-Kermit>set modem type none      (Pretend there is no modem)
C-Kermit>set line /dev/cua        (Select communication device)
C-Kermit>set speed 2400           (Set the communication speed)
C-Kermit>connect                  (Begin terminal connection)
Connecting to /dev/cua, speed 2400.
The escape character is Ctrl-\ (ASCII 28, FS).
Type the escape character followed by C to get back,
or followed by ? to see other options.
AT                                (Make sure it's there)
OK                                (Modem responds OK)
ATDT7654321                       (Type the dialing command)
CONNECT 2400                      (Modem confirms the connection)

    (Conduct a session with the remote computer or service)

Ctrl-\C                           (Escape back to the prompt)
C-Kermit>
```

Partial and Multistage Dialing

Some types of modems can be told to return to command mode immediately after being given a dial command, without waiting for carrier. For Hayes and compatible modems, this is done by including a semicolon (;) as the last character of the phone number. This is useful in several circumstances, including:

1. The number you are calling is not a modem and it will never send carrier. For example, it is a voice number, a beeper, or a numeric pager.

2. The dial string is too long for the modem and needs to be broken into pieces.

So, to dial a numeric pager, whose number is 555-1234, from a Hayes or compatible modem, you might:

```
C-Kermit>dial 5551234@nnnnnnnnn#;
```

where "@" is the Hayes "wait for quiet answer" code, *nnnnnnnnn* is the pager message, "#" is an end-of-message signal to the pager (this can vary), and ";" is the Hayes "return-to-command-mode" indicator. This way, Kermit returns to its prompt immediately rather than waiting a long time only to get a timeout or a NO CARRIER message.

To dial a credit-card call that is too long for your modem, you might expect to be able to use the semicolon trick and then issue two DIAL commands (a comma in the dial string tells a Hayes or compatible modem to pause for a couple seconds):

```
C-Kermit>dial 10288,0,212,5551234,,,;
C-Kermit>dial 4114 9999 9999 9999
```

This would be fine, except that the second DIAL command hangs up the phone and reinitializes the modem, so this technique is guaranteed to fail. Therefore we need a special command for partial dialing:

PDIAL *number*

> Like DIAL, but issues the dialing command in the modem-specific way that causes the modem to return to command state immediately after dialing the number, rather than waiting for carrier, and instructs Kermit not to expect a call completion code. Furthermore, Kermit remembers that this call was partial, and so does not reinitialize or hang up the modem when the next DIAL or PDIAL command is issued.

If your modem is Hayes or compatible, C-Kermit automatically appends a semicolon to the number so you need not (and should not) include it yourself, and it looks for an OK response rather than CONNECT or BUSY (etc.).

Now we can call that long telephone number:

```
C-Kermit>pdial 10288,0,212,5551234,,,
C-Kermit>dial 4114 9999 9999 9999
```

Finally, suppose you issue a partial dialing command but then wish to cancel the partially-dialed status, so that the next DIAL or PDIAL command does not skip the modem hangup or initialization stages. To accomplish this, either:

HANGUP

> Which hangs up any open connection and also clears the dial status.

or:

CLEAR DIAL-STATUS

> Which clears Kermit's dial status without hanging up the modem.

CLEAR DIAL-STATUS also sets the \v(dialstatus) variable (variables are explained in Chapter 17) to its default value, -1, meaning "no calls have been placed yet."

Answering Incoming Calls

You can have C-Kermit not only place calls, you can also have C-Kermit answer them. The command is:

ANSWER *[timeout]*

> Wait for a telephone call to come in. If a *timeout* value is included, wait up to the given number of seconds and then give up. If no *timeout* value is included, or a *timeout* value of 0 is given, wait indefinitely or until interrupted from the keyboard with Ctrl-C.

To answer an incoming call, give the following sequence of commands:

```
C-Kermit>set modem type telepath   (Choose modem type)
C-Kermit>set line /dev/cua         (and communication port)
C-Kermit>set speed 57600           (and interface speed)
C-Kermit>answer                    (Wait for a call to come in)
```

In subsequent chapters, we'll see what sorts of services C-Kermit can offer to incoming callers: interactive chatting, callback, file transfer and management, "host mode," and so on, and we will see how automate operations like those above so you don't have to type lots of commands.

Troubleshooting Dialed Connections

When you encounter problems with dialing, C-Kermit has some commands that can help you diagnose and overcome them. Use the SHOW DIAL command first. It gives you a quick summary of all the settings that are likely to affect dialing, including the current LINE, MODEM, and SPEED values:

```
C-Kermit>set modem type telebit  (First select a modem type)
C-Kermit>set line /dev/cua       (Then a serial device)
C-Kermit>set speed 2400          (Then the speed)
C-Kermit>show dial               (Now let's take a look...)
 Line: /dev/cua, Modem type: telebit, speed: 38400, carrier: auto
 Dial status:  -1 = (none)
 Dial directory: /w/u/si/fdc/.kdd
 Dial method:   tone      Dial display: on
 Dial hangup:   on        Dial interval: 10
 Dial retries:  0         Redial number: (none)
 Dial timeout:  0 (auto)  Dial connect: auto
C-Kermit>
```

This is the first place to look for something obviously wrong: wrong line, wrong speed, wrong modem type. If any of these are incorrect, use SET commands to fix them and try dialing again (hint: use the REDIAL command).

If dialing still doesn't work, we'll have to dig deeper. The next command to use is SET DIAL DISPLAY ON. It doesn't fix anything, but it lets you watch what goes on between Kermit and the modem and might give you an idea of what needs to be changed.

SET DIAL DISPLAY *{ OFF, ON }*

Tells whether C-Kermit should display its dialog with the modem on your screen during the dialing process. Normally DIAL DISPLAY is OFF. When it is ON, you can watch Kermit's commands to the modem and the modem's responses.

Let's continue our example with the Telebit modem. We have already SET MODEM TYPE, SET LINE, and SET SPEED. Now let's watch a successful DIAL command in action:

```
C-Kermit>set dial method tone        (Use Tone dialing)
C-Kermit>set dial display on         (Watch dialing actions)
C-Kermit>dial 741-8100               (Dial the number)
 Dialing 741-8100
 Device=/dev/cua, modem=telebit, speed=2400
 The timeout for completing the call is 68 seconds.
 To cancel: type Ctrl-C (hold down Ctrl, press C).

+++ATQ0H0                             (Kermit sends)
OK                                    (Modem responds)
 Modem hangup OK                      (Message from Kermit)
 Initializing: 13:18:37...            (Message from Kermit)
ATQ0X2&S0&C1&D2S12=50S50=0S61=1S63=0  (Kermit sends)
OK                                    (Modem responds)
ATS7=58                               (Kermit sends)
OK                                    (Modem responds)
...                                   (Some stuff omitted)
 Dialing: 13:18:48...                 (Message from Kermit)
ATD741-8100                           (Kermit sends)
DIALING                               (Message from modem)
RING                                  (Message from modem)
CONNECT 1200                          (Modem responds)
 Speed changed to 1200               (Message from Kermit)
 Call completed.                      (Message from Kermit)
C-Kermit>                             (Prompt returns)
```

There are many items of interest here, each of which can affect the success of the DIAL command. First, Kermit tells us that it will allow 68 seconds for the call to be completed. If the modem has not responded by that time, Kermit closes the call and gives an error message: "Timed out." What if more time is needed to dial?

SET DIAL TIMEOUT *number [differential]*

When you give a DIAL command, C-Kermit waits a certain number of seconds for a report from the modem telling whether the call succeeded or failed. The time limit is computed automatically based on the length of the phone number, the type of modem, and other factors. In some cases, the timeout might not be long enough, for example for an international call or for an advanced type of modem that must go through protracted negotiations with a different type of remote modem. Use this command to make Kermit skip its dial timeout calculation and use your value instead. Example:

```
C-Kermit>set dial timeout 200    (200 seconds)
```

When you have SET MODEM TYPE to HAYES or any other type that uses the AT command set, C-Kermit also sets modem register S7 correspondingly, so the modem waits slightly less long than C-Kermit for the call to be completed. The difference is normally 10 seconds, but you can change this by including an appropriate *differential* in the SET DIAL TIMEOUT command.

Returning to our Telebit dialing example, SET DIAL DISPLAY ON now shows how Kermit sends a series of commands to the modem, and how the modem responds to each one.

Modem commands are either settings, to which the normal response is OK, or action commands, such as the one to dial, to which the modem responds with some sort of call completion status, such as CONNECT, BUSY, NO DIALTONE, NO CARRIER, and so on.

One common source of dialing trouble is that you are using a modem whose command set is different from what Kermit thinks it is. This can happen, for example, when the modem manufacturer issues a new model that is slightly incompatible with a previous model Kermit knows about. The easiest way to find out if this is the case is to watch the SET DIAL DISPLAY ON dialog and see if the modem responds with the word ERROR, or similar message, to any of the commands. If this happens, you'll need to adjust the commands that Kermit sends, as explained in Chapter 4.

The message "Hangup OK" means that Kermit hung up the phone connection as a first step. This ensures that the modem is in command mode rather than still online from a previous connection; otherwise, the modem might totally ignore Kermit's dialing commands. Unfortunately, this seemingly proper and innocent measure sometimes can result in unwanted problems caused by improper configuration or wiring or by the inability of the underlying operating system to handle the hangup request correctly, in which case you will see a "Hangup failed" message, or worse. Here are two commands to work around such situations:

SET DIAL HANGUP *[{ OFF, ON }]*

Tells Kermit whether to hang up the phone at the beginning of the dialing process. Use SET DIAL HANGUP OFF only if you get hangup-related error messages during the DIAL command or if dialing doesn't work with DIAL HANGUP ON.

SET MODEM HANGUP-METHOD *{ MODEM-COMMAND, RS232-SIGNAL }*

Applies only when DIAL HANGUP is ON. When MODEM HANGUP-METHOD is RS232-SIGNAL, C-Kermit hangs up by turning off the DTR signal to the modem for about half a second. When MODEM HANGUP-METHOD is MODEM-COMMAND, C-Kermit attempts to return the modem to command mode (e.g. by sending "+++" to it) and then uses a modem-specific command (such as Hayes ATH0), and then turns off DTR only if a confirmation (such as OK) fails to appear from the modem. The MODEM HANGUP-METHOD is MODEM-COMMAND by default.

After we get past the preliminaries, Kermit sends the modem's "initialization string." That's the long cryptic one that starts with ATQ0X2&S0&C1&D2... This is a modem-specific command that sets basic operating parameters for the modem: how to issue result codes, how to handle modem signals, how to handle modulation negotiations, and so on. After that, Kermit sets the modem's variable parameters according to Kermit's own settings for flow control and so on. Finally Kermit dials the number:

```
ATDT741-8100
```

The modem response, CONNECT 1200, tells Kermit that the remote modem answered the call, but at a lower speed than the one we used for dialing. Kermit noticed this and changed its own transmission speed to 1200 by doing a SET SPEED 1200 command internally and informed you with a message, "Speed changed to 1200." Very nice!

Or maybe not so nice. Most newer-model modems have a feature called *speed buffering*, lacking from Hayes 1200 and 2400, which keeps the interface speed constant even when the connection speed changes. Speed-buffering modems might report the *connection* speed in the CONNECT message, rather than the *interface* speed. Furthermore, they might or might not have their speed-buffering feature disabled. So how does Kermit know how to react to the speed given in the modem's CONNECT message? You must tell it:

SET MODEM SPEED-MATCHING { OFF, ON }
This command tells C-Kermit whether to treat the connection speed reported by your modem as a signal to change its interface speed. The default setting is OFF if your modem can do speed buffering, which tells Kermit that the modem's interface speed is locked, so C-Kermit should ignore the CONNECT speed reported by the modem. SET MODEM SPEED-MATCHING ON tells Kermit to match its interface speed to the one in the modem's CONNECT message.

Troubleshooting Summary

For dialing to work, you must ensure proper setup and configuration of Kermit, your computer, the modem, the modem cable, and the telephone line. And it doesn't hurt if all the stars and planets are in perfect alignment too. If you can't complete a dialed call, just follow these sixteen easy steps (some of which apply only to external modems):

1. Make sure your modem is turned on and connected to the phone line.

2. Make sure your modem is connected to your computer with a straight-through modem cable (not with a null modem cable, see Appendix II), and that the cable has not wiggled loose at one or both ends, *and* that you have told Kermit which port the modem is connected to. Use SHOW MODEM or SHOW DIAL to check C-Kermit's settings and the modem signals.

3. Make sure your modem cable conveys (has wires for) all the necessary signals, including SG, TD, RD, DSR, RTS, CTS, CD, and DTR (see Appendix II).

4. Make sure the wires in the cable and the pins in the connector are not broken and that the pins are all sticking straight out.

5. SET CARRIER-WATCH OFF and CONNECT. Type a command at the modem and see if you get a response. For Hayes and compatible modems, type the letters AT and then press the Enter or Return key. You should see OK or the digit 0. If not, you probably have a basic connection problem: wrong port or wrong speed.

- Or perhaps the computer is not asserting the DTR signal or the wire is not conducting it. If you are sure you have the right port and speed, try configuring your modem to ignore DTR and always assert carrier. Read your modem manual to find out how to do this.

- Or maybe Kermit is set for RTS/CTS flow control, but the modem is not asserting the CTS signal. Either tell Kermit to SET FLOW NONE or else reconfigure the modem to behave properly (see your modem manual).

6. Make sure your modem supports at least one modulation technique (Bell 103, Bell 212, ITU-T V.21, V.22, V.32, V.32*bis*, V.34, Telebit PEP, etc.) in common with the modem you are calling.

7. Make sure you give the appropriate SET MODEM TYPE command *first*, then a SET LINE command for the device the modem is actually connected to, and then a SET SPEED command for a speed that your modem's dialer can handle. These commands must be given in that order.

8. Use SET DIAL DISPLAY ON to watch the dialog between Kermit and the modem and see if you can find any commands that cause errors.

9. If dialing fails with a "Timed out" message, increase the DIAL TIMEOUT interval.

10. The hangup operation might be causing problems. Try SET DIAL HANGUP OFF or SET MODEM HANGUP-METHOD RS232 before dialing.

11. Make sure your modem's escape sequence is not a character or sequence that you would need to send to the remote computer during terminal emulation or that Kermit would send in a file transfer packet. The default Hayes sequence, for example, is safe: +++ preceded and followed by at least one full second of silence. Other modems have been known to use unsafe sequences like a single Ctrl-A (which happens to be Kermit's start-of-packet character) and/or to not require any guard time; in cases like this, change your modem's escape character or disable it entirely (or change Kermit's start-of-packet character; see Chapter 10).

12. If your modem has error-correcting or compression protocols enabled, try turning them off. In particular, MNP modems send characters to each other *after* carrier has been established to negotiate protocol level and features. These characters can pass through the remote modem and interfere with the host's speed detection or login procedures if the answering modem doesn't support MNP. In general, take your modem down to its least sophisticated level and work up from there one feature at a time. See the next chapter for details.

13. On the other hand, if you are experiencing lots of noise, make sure your modem's error-correction protocol, if any, *is* enabled. (Again, see the next chapter.)

14. Read your modem manual carefully in search of clues. Pay special attention to modulation, error-correction, and data compression selection and fallback.

15. If all else fails, SET CARRIER-WATCH OFF, CONNECT to the modem, and try to dial manually by typing dialing commands in the modem's own syntax directly at it (see your modem manual). Make sure the speaker is turned on so you can listen for dial-tone, ringing, busy signals, etc. If it is an external modem, look at the lights. If you still can't dial, check your modem's configuration and then repeat the previous steps.

16. Consult the documentation or "beware" file for your particular Kermit program for additional hints, tips, and late-breaking news.

This wraps up our discussion of the basics of making serial connections. The next chapter goes into more detail about modems, Chapter 5 presents the dialing directory.

A summary list of commands appears on the next page.

Command Summary

If you are making a dialed connection, first tell Kermit the type of modem you are using, and then give any desired SET MODEM commands (defaults are bold):

```
SET MODEM TYPE    { NONE, name }
SET MODEM HANGUP-METHOD { MODEM-COMMAND, RS232-SIGNAL }
SET MODEM SPEED-MATCHING { ON, OFF }
```

Use the SET CARRIER-WATCH OFF command, if necessary, to allow any communications with the modem prior to dialing, or for using any serial device that does not present a carrier signal; otherwise the default setting of AUTO is normally best:

```
SET CARRIER-WATCH { AUTO, ON, OFF }
```

Now choose the serial communication device and make the appropriate settings:

```
SET LINE device
SET PORT device   (Same as SET LINE)
SET SPEED number
SET FLOW-CONTROL { AUTO, KEEP, NONE, RTS/CTS, XON/XOFF }
```

If you are dialing a modem, make any desired DIAL settings and then give one of the dialing commands. Use CLEAR DIAL-STATUS to cancel the effects of any previous DIAL or PDIAL operation.

```
SET DIAL CONNECT { ON, OFF }
SET DIAL DISPLAY { ON, OFF }
SET DIAL HANGUP { ON, OFF }
SET DIAL INTERVAL seconds
SET DIAL RETRIES number
SET DIAL TIMEOUT seconds [ differential ]
DIAL phone-number
PDIAL phone-number
REDIAL
CLEAR DIAL-STATUS
```

To hang up the connection, use HANGUP. To close the communication device, which might be necessary on direct connection where hanging up might not be noticed by the other computer, use SET LINE without a device name:

```
HANGUP
SET LINE
```

And to display your communications-related settings:

```
SHOW COMMUNICATIONS
SHOW DIAL
SHOW MODEM
```

Chapter 4

Configuring Modems

○ ○ ○ ○

This chapter thoroughly covers Kermit's features for controlling and configuring modems. If you are already operating your modem to your satisfaction, feel free to skip ahead to the next chapter and learn more about dialing, and come back here for reference when you need to.

When you give Kermit a DIAL, REDIAL, PDIAL, or ANSWER command, C-Kermit operates your modem using built-in knowledge of its commands and capabilities, or an external driver for the modem (such as Microsoft TAPI), or else information that you have supplied for a "user-defined" modem type. It's important that you give Kermit the best possible information about the modem. Usually, all that's needed is to tell Kermit what type of modem you have, and Kermit does the rest automatically. As explained in Chapter 3, the command:

SET MODEM TYPE *name*

Selects a modem type (or NONE for direct serial connections) from Kermit's built-in database of modems. The default modem type is NONE.

Kermit's built-in knowledge applies to many types of modems. Table 3-2 in Chapter 3 shows the list as of this writing. "SET MODEM TYPE ?" might display additional names if you have a C-Kermit version that postdates this edition of *Using C-Kermit*.

When you give a SET MODEM TYPE command, Kermit fetches all the modem-specific information from its built-in database and also sets many of its own communication parameters accordingly. You can see how this works by giving a SET MODEM TYPE command and then viewing the information with the SHOW MODEM command. Example:

```
[/usr/olga] C-Kermit>set modem type ppi        (Specify modem type)
[/usr/olga] C-Kermit>show modem                (View modem info)

Modem type: ppi
Practical Peripherals V.22bis or higher with V.42 and V.42bis

Modem carrier-watch:      auto
Modem capabilities:       AT SB EC DC HWFC SWFC
Modem maximum-speed:      115200 bps
Modem error-correction:   on
Modem compression:        on
Modem speed-matching:     off (interface speed is locked)
Modem flow-control:       auto
Modem kermit-spoof:       off
Modem escape-character:   43 (= "+")

MODEM COMMANDs (* = set automatically by SET MODEM TYPE):

  * Init-string:          ATQ0X4N1S37=0S82=128\{13}
  * Dial-command:         ATD%s\{13}
  * Compression on:       ATS46=2\{13}
  * Compression off:      ATS46=0\{13}
  * Error-correction on:  AT&Q5S36=7S48=7\{13}
  * Error-correction off: AT&Q0S36=0S48=128\{13}
  * Autoanswer on:        ATS0=1\{13}
  * Autoanswer off:       ATS0=0\{13}
  * Hangup-command:       ATQ0H0\{13}
  * Hardware-flow:        AT&K3\{13}
  * Software-flow:        AT&K4\{13}
  * No-flow-control:      AT&K0\{13}
  * Pulse:                ATP\{13}
  * Tone:                 ATT\{13}
```

Each of these items is explained in this chapter, and each of them can be changed by you if necessary with the appropriate commands. The SHOW MODEM command (and Table 3-2) include a compact listing of the modem's capabilities; the capability codes are explained in Table 4-1.

As you read this chapter, remember that C-Kermit commands need not always be typed at the prompt. They can also be collected into files that you tell C-Kermit to TAKE, or even put into your initialization or customization file, which is executed automatically when you start Kermit. Also remember that the backslash (\) character is special in Kermit commands; it is used to introduce a "backslash code" that stands for a control character or a variable. In this chapter, you can see examples such as "\13" and "\{13}", which represent the ASCII carriage return character (ASCII character number 13), and "\\", which represents backslash itself; that is, a literal backslash.

Table 4-1 Modem Capabilities

Code	Description
AT	Modem uses Hayes AT command set and responses
ITU	Modem uses ITU-T (CCITT) V.25*bis* command set and responses
SB	Modem can do speed buffering (interface speed can be locked)
EC	Modem can do error correction (MNP or V.42/LAPM)
DC	Modem can do data compression (MNP or V.42*bis*)
HWFC	Modem can do local hardware flow control (RTS/CTS) (listed in Table 3-2 as LF)
SWFC	Modem can do local software flow control (Xon/Xoff) (also listed in Table 3-2 as LF)
KS	Modem has "Kermit spoof" (modem itself runs Kermit protocol)
TB	Made by Telebit (used internally for simplification)

What If My Modem Is Not on Kermit's List?

Remember, just because a modem is said to be "Hayes compatible," that does not mean it uses the same commands other brands of modems, other models of the same brand, or in fact, any other modem on the planet. All it means is that it has commands that start with the letters AT and *perhaps* also has some of the basic commands listed in Table II-2 in Appendix II. Beyond that, all bets are off. The command to, say, enable hardware flow control on one modem might cause an ERROR response on a second modem and might do something entirely unexpected on a third.

If your modem is not directly supported by C-Kermit, perhaps it is compatible with one that is. But how would you know? Only detailed and laborious poring through your modem manual and comparing each modem command with the corresponding commands for every facet of modem operation of each of Kermit's built-in models could turn up a match. In a case like this, you are probably better off starting from scratch and defining your own new modem type.

However, two common cases are easy to handle. First, your modem might already be configured exactly the way you want it, in which case Kermit does not need to give it lots of commands.

Second, you have a new model of a modem that Kermit already supports, and it differs only slightly from the one Kermit knows about. In that case, you can use the commands described later in this chapter to make the necessary modifications to a built-in type. All of these methods are described in this chapter; keep reading.

Important Settings

Look again at the following portion of the SHOW MODEM listing (line numbers have been added for reference):

```
1. Modem error-correction: on
2. Modem compression:      on
3. Modem speed-matching:   off (interface speed is locked)
4. Modem flow-control:     auto
```

When you give a SET MODEM TYPE command:

1. If Kermit knows that the modem is capable of error correction, Kermit will tell the modem to use it.

2. If Kermit knows that the modem is capable of data compression, Kermit will tell the modem to use it.

3. If Kermit knows that the modem is capable of speed buffering, Kermit will *assume* the modem has been configured to use it and will, therefore, not change its own interface speed in response to CONNECT speed reports from the modem.

4. If the modem is capable of local flow control, Kermit will configure it to use the same kind of flow as Kermit itself is set to use. If Kermit's FLOW-CONTROL is set to AUTO, and your version of C-Kermit supports RTS/CTS flow control, and the modem does too (SHOW MODEM lists HWFC capability), then Kermit switches to RTS/CTS and also configures the modem for RTS/CTS. Otherwise Kermit will configure itself for Xon/Xoff flow control, and if the modem supports *local* Xon/Xoff, Kermit will configure the modem to use it; otherwise Xon/Xoff is used end-to-end.

Kermit does *not*, however, set any of the following automatically:

1. Communication device.

2. Speed of the communication device.

3. Parity or bytesize.

4. Duplex.

So you should take care to ensure they are set appropriately. Kermit does its best to catch mistakes or possible mismatches, however. For example, you can't DIAL or CONNECT until after you have chosen a communication device with SET PORT or SET LINE (or, in the case of network modem servers, SET HOST). You also can't DIAL without first specifying a modem type. Furthermore, if you try to DIAL on a modem whose maximum speed (according to Kermit's database) is less that the current speed of the device, Kermit prints a warning message.

Changing Things

The next set of commands lets you turn selected features of your modem on and off (if it has them). Give these commands *after* the SET MODEM TYPE command to override the values that are picked up from the database.

SET MODEM SPEED-MATCHING { ON, OFF }

Kermit assumes that if your modem is capable of speed buffering, it is configured to do so, and therefore keeps its interface speed constant, no matter what connection speed is negotiated. On the other hand, Kermit assumes that if your modem (according to Kermit's database) is *not* capable of speed buffering, then its interface speed will change according to the connection speed, and so therefore Kermit will also have to change its own interface speed to match. When these assumptions prove incorrect, Kermit's speed will not match the modem's, and you will see only garbage. Give this command to adapt Kermit to how the modem actually behaves.

SET MODEM ERROR-CORRECTION { ON, OFF }

When this is ON and the modem has EC capability, Kermit sends the MODEM COMMAND ERROR-CORRECTION ON string to the modem as part of the dialing process, to enable its error correction feature. When this is OFF and the modem has EC capability, Kermit sends the MODEM COMMAND ERROR-CORRECTION OFF string. Sometimes when an error-correcting modem dials another modem that can't do error correction, the negotiations confuse the other modem so badly that the connection can't be made. Use SET MODEM ERROR-CORRECTION OFF to disable your modem's error correction feature prior to dialing. Note: This also disables compression and (depending on the modem) sometimes also speed buffering.

SET MODEM COMPRESSION { ON, OFF }

Works similarly to MODEM ERROR-CORRECTION. Data compression is almost always beneficial when it is done by the modem, at least as long as you have an effective means of local flow control (preferably RTS/CTS) between your computer and the modem. If adequate flow control is lacking, or if the compression negotiations confuse the other modem, use this command to disable data compression.

WARNING: Certain modems that claim to supply error correction and data compression require external software drivers for these functions. Such modems are usually marketed as "Windows" modems, and the drivers are available only for Microsoft Windows. These modems usually include the abbreviation "RPI" or the word "controllerless" in the technical specifications, often buried in the fine print. If you try to use such a modem "bare" without its driver, and Kermit's database does not know this, then dialing will fail when Kermit tries to enable error correction or compression. SET DIAL DISPLAY ON to see this happen. In such cases, you will have to tell Kermit to SET MODEM ERROR-CORRECTION OFF, SET MODEM COMPRESSION OFF, and possibly also SET MODEM SPEED-MATCHING ON. Expect extremely poor results.

The next group of commands lets you help C-Kermit over various sorts of obstacles that are likely to be thrown in its path:

SET MODEM FLOW-CONTROL { AUTO, NONE, RTS/CTS, XON/XOFF }

This tells Kermit how to configure the modem's local flow-control feature, if any. AUTO, the default, tries to "do the right thing" based on a combination of the modem's capabilities (from Kermit's modem database) and Kermit's FLOW-CONTROL setting. The other options let you override the automatic procedure, for example, when you have a version of UNIX that does not let Kermit SET FLOW RTS/CTS, but which nevertheless lets you have RTS/CTS flow control by using a "special" device name, e.g. "set line /dev/cufa". So, for example, if Kermit's FLOW-CONTROL is NONE but you tell Kermit to SET MODEM FLOW-CONTROL RTS/CTS, then Kermit will still configure the modem for hardware flow control.

SET MODEM HANGUP-METHOD { MODEM-COMMAND, RS232-SIGNAL }

Tells Kermit how to tell the modem to hang up: the appropriate modem command (e.g. ATH0) or by manipulating RS-232 signals (turning off DTR). MODEM-COMMAND is the default when the modem database includes a command for hanging up, otherwise the RS232-SIGNAL method is used. If one gives you trouble, try the other.

SET MODEM ESCAPE-CHARACTER *number*

For Hayes compatibles, Kermit normally uses "+++" as the escape sequence in the MODEM-COMMAND sent to hang up the modem. The escape sequence brings you back to the modem's command processor, and then you give the modem-specific hangup command, such as ATH0. However, if the local modem has the same escape character as the remote modem, then when you use the escape sequence, the connection will become unusable if the answering modem improperly pops back to command mode, too. In such cases, use this command to change your modem's escape character; *number* is the numeric ASCII value of the character to be used, e.g. 43 for the customary "plus" character, "+". For Hayes compatibles, we use a one-second guard time, three copies of the escape character, and guard time again. For others (e.g. Microcom in native mode) we just send the escape character. This command is also handy for disabling the escape character altogether, e.g. SET MODEM ESC 128, in case your modem does not use a guard time around the escape character and you need to make it transparent to all character sequences.

SET MODEM KERMIT-SPOOF { ON, OFF }

Some modems have a *Kermit spoof*, in which the modem actually executes the Kermit protocol itself. A matching modem (e.g. Telebit) is required on the other end. Kermit can usually transfers files faster without the modem's help (see Chapter 12) so the modem's Kermit spoof (if any) is disabled by default. Use SET MODEM KERMIT-SPOOF ON to enable it.

Modifying Modem Commands

During the dialing process, as many as eight separate interactions might take place between C-Kermit and the modem, each involving one or more modem commands. These commands are normally taken from Kermit's internal database, but you can replace each one with any other modem-specific command of your choice using Kermit's SET MODEM COMMAND command:

SET MODEM COMMAND *feature [string]*

Tells Kermit the modem-specific command *string* for the specifed *feature*. If the *string* is omitted, the associated command is not sent to the modem.

Of course, you will need to work from your modem manual. The the SET MODEM COMMAND commands are described on this and the next two pages. When using most modern modems, alphabetic case does not matter, but in some older ones, uppercase is required. When in doubt, use only uppercase letters in modem commands. For Hayes and compatible moderms, remember that each command must begin with the letters AT, and end with carriage return, represented in Kermit commands by using backslash notation, \13 (carriage return is ASCII character 13).

SET MODEM COMMAND INIT-STRING *string*

The command string that should be used to initialize the modem. This string should contain the modem commands to enable result codes and to select the desired level of result codes (so Kermit can read and process them), plus any other commands that would apply regardless of Kermit's settings, such as: the commands to enable modulation fallback, to allow the BREAK signal to pass through transparently, and perhaps the commands to tell the modem what to do about the CD, DSR, and DTR signals (see Appendix II if you don't understand these terms).

As a fictitious example, let's say you've just bought a new-model Hayes modem. It works just like the Hayes Ultra, Accura, and Optima, except that the S82 register (which controls how BREAK is handled in the earlier models) is not supported in the new model, and so the built-in "init-string" —

```
ATQ0X4N1Y0&S0&C1&D2S37=0S82=128\{13}
```

(which you can see by telling Kermit to SET MODEM TYPE HAYES-HIGH-SPEED and then SHOW MODEM) — causes an ERROR response from the modem, which, in turn, makes the DIAL command fail. In real life, this sort of thing happens all the time and is easily discovered by using SET DIAL DISPLAY ON.

Further suppose that late-night dialing noises from your modem's speaker drive your spouse crazy and so you need to turn the speaker off. The Hayes command for this is M0 (M zero; see Table II-2).

In this case, you would choose the HAYES-HIGH-SPEED modem type, but then use the SET MODEM COMMAND INIT-STRING to construct a new "init-string" without the offending S82 reference and with M0 added:

```
set modem command init-string ATQ0X4M0N1Y0&S0&C1&D2S37=0\13
```

Remember, \13 is used to represent carriage return.

Obviously you can also make any other changes here you like.

Here are the rest of the SET MODEM COMMAND commands:

SET MODEM COMMAND AUTOANSWER ON *string*

The command string that puts the modem into autoanswer mode, i.e. that makes it wait for an incoming call; used by the ANSWER command. Example:

```
set modem command autoanswer on ats0=1\13
```

SET MODEM COMMAND AUTOANSWER OFF *string*

The command string that takes the modem out of autoanswer mode, i.e. that puts it in originate mode for making calls. Example:

```
set modem command autoanswer off ats0=0\13
```

SET MODEM COMMAND COMPRESSION ON *string*

The command string that instructs the modem to negotiate data compression with the other modem. These vary wildly from one modem model to the next. Example:

```
set modem command compression on at&k4\13
```

SET MODEM COMMAND COMPRESSION OFF *string*

The command string that turns off the modem's data compression feature and disables data-compression negotiation with the other modem. Example:

```
set modem command compression on at&k3\13
```

SET MODEM COMMAND DIAL-MODE-STRING *string*

Command (if any) used to put the modem into dialing mode (normally does not apply to Hayes compatibles).

SET MODEM COMMAND DIAL-MODE-PROMPT *string*

The prompt (if any, normally none) issued by the modem when it is in dialing mode (normally does not apply to Hayes compatibles).

SET MODEM COMMAND ERROR-CORRECTION ON *string*

The command string that enables the modem to negotiate error correction with the other modem. Example (for Hayes Ultra):

```
set modem command error-correction on at&Q5S36=7S48=7\13
```

SET MODEM COMMAND ERROR-CORRECTION OFF *string*

The command string that turns off the modem's error correction feature and disables error-correction negotiation with the other modem. Example (for Hayes Ultra):

```
set modem command error-correction off at&Q0\13
```

SET MODEM COMMAND HANGUP-COMMAND *string*

The command string that tells the modem to hang up the telephone connection. Example (for most Hayes compatibles):

```
set modem command hangup-command ath0\13
```

SET MODEM COMMAND HARDWARE-FLOW *string*

The command string that enables local hardware (RTS/CTS) flow control in the modem. Example (for Microcom Deskporte in Hayes mode):

```
set modem command hardware-flow at\\q3\13
```

Note the double backslash, which must be used to send a single backslash to the modem.

SET MODEM COMMAND SOFTWARE-FLOW *string*

The command string that enables local software (Xon/Xoff) flow control in the modem. Example (for Microcom Deskporte in Hayes mode):

```
set modem command hardware-flow at\\q1\13
```

SET MODEM COMMAND NO-FLOW-CONTROL *string*

The command string to disable local flow control in the modem. Example (for Microcom Deskporte in Hayes mode):

```
set modem command hardware-flow at\\h0\\q0\13
```

If Kermit is using Xon/Xoff flow control, then this will be effective end to end (if the other end cooperates) rather than locally.

SET MODEM COMMAND PULSE *string*

The command string that instructs the modem to use pulse (or rotary) dialing. Note that certain characters (such as "*" and "#") cannot be dialed with pulse dialing. For Hayes compatible modems, the command is:

```
set modem command pulse atp\13
```

SET MODEM COMMAND TONE *string*

The command string that sets the modem's dialing method to tone. Note that tone dialing is not available in all areas. For Hayes compatible modems, this command is:

```
set modem command tone att\13
```

Adding a New Modem Type

We introduced the previous section with an example of how to use the SET MODEM COMMAND command to adapt C-Kermit to a minor variation on a modem it already knew about. Now let's look at another case, in which we have a new modem that is "Hayes compatible" but whose commands are totally different from anything else in Kermit's database, but which has various "configuration profiles" that you can select with a single command. For example, suppose your modem uses the AT command set and has a hardware flow-control profile. Your modem manual says that issuing the command AT&F1 to the modem enables not only hardware flow control but also error correction, data compression, speed buffering, and all available fallback options, and this is exactly how you want your modem to be set up. Further suppose that you always want to use tone dialing. In that case can set up the modem as follows:

```
set dial method default
set modem type hayes
set modem speed-matching off
set modem command init-string ATQ0V1T&F1\13
```

The first command tells Kermit to skip sending the pulse-versus-tone command. The second command chooses the HAYES modem type, meaning Hayes 1200 or 2400, so this enables the Hayes AT command set and simultaneously disables all the commands that would normally be sent to configure flow control, error correction, and data compression. SET MODEM SPEED-MATCHING OFF overrides the normal setting of ON for the low-speed Hayes modems. The init-string includes Q0 to enable dialing result codes and V1 to request them in word (rather than digit) format, T to enable tone dialing, and &F1 to load the desired profile. Word-format result codes are relatively consistent among all Hayes-compatible modems, whereas digit codes tend to be different for each make and model of modem.

The User-Defined Modem Type

The commands in this section let you define a new modem type for Kermit, so it can be used just like any of the built-in types.

SET MODEM TYPE USER-DEFINED [name]

The optional *name* identifies one of the built-in modem types. The default *name* is UNKNOWN, which has no commands. If you give a *name* (other than UNKNOWN or NONE), all the characteristics of that modem type are copied to the user-defined type. For example, if you are adding a high-speed modem that uses the Hayes command set, you can choose a modem of that sort (e.g. HAYES-HIGH-SPEED, PPI, etc).

Then you can define its basic characteristics with SET MODEM NAME, SET MODEM CAPABILITIES, and SET MODEM MAXIMUM-SPEED; then use the SET MODEM DIAL-COMMAND and SET MODEM COMMAND commands to change any of its commands that differ from those of the built-in modem, if any, that you chose as a model. Of course, you can use any of these commands to change the definition of a built-in modem type, too.

SET MODEM NAME *text*

Changes the descriptive name of the modem (effects SHOW MODEM only).

SET MODEM MAXIMUM-SPEED *bits-per-second*

Tells Kermit what the modem's maximum *interface* speed is. Note: currently, the only effect of this command is to cause a warning message if Kermit's speed is higher than the modem's maximum speed when you give a DIAL command. Example:

```
set modem maximum-speed 38400
```

SET MODEM DIAL-COMMAND *string*

This is the command used by the modem to dial a call. The *string* must contain "%s" (without the quotes) to show where the phone number must be placed, and remember to include "\13" on the end if the command should be terminated by a carriage return, as is usually the case. For example, for a Hayes modem, you would use:

```
set modem dial-command ATD%s\13
```

SET MODEM CAPABILITIES *[item [item [...]]]*

Tells Kermit the modem's capabilities. The *items* may be entered as as the code shown in Table 4-1, or with their full names ("error-correction", etc), which will be listed for you if you type "set modem capabilities ?". AT must be set for any modem that uses the Hayes AT command set and responses; otherwise, Kermit won't be able to read the responses. Similarly ITU must be set for for V.25*bis* modems.

If your user-defined modem does not use Hayes word-result, Hayes digit-result, or V.25*bis* completion codes, then Kermit decides whether a call has completed or failed based on whether the carrier signal comes on within the DIAL TIMEOUT interval.

Now you must tell Kermit the modem-specific commands to use for each modem function it must control. This is done with the SET MODEM COMMAND command, described in the previous section. For Hayes compatibles, the "init-string" should contain Q0 to ensure the modem gives result codes for commands. They can be either numeric or word result codes; Kermit handles both automatically; however, word codes are recommended because they are more consistent from modem to modem. To ensure that word codes are used, also include V1. You can also make the modem echo (E1) or not echo (E0) its commands — Kermit should work either way.

The init string should contain all commands that are not affected by other SET MODEM settings, particularly the command to enable BREAK transparency, the command to enable modulation negotiation, a command to enable a fairly high level of dial result codes (for example, X4).

Example 1: Best Data 14400 bps Fax Modem V.32*bis*/V.17

```
SET MODEM USER-DEFINED PPI      ; Use PPI as the template
SHOW MODEM                      ; To see what you've got
```

Now make any needed changes:

```
SET MODEM NAME Best Data 1442FTX
SET MODEM MAXIMUM-SPEED 57600
SET MODEM COMMAND INIT ATF1N1W1Y0X4S37=0\13
SET MODEM COMMAND HARD AT&K3\\G1\13
SET MODEM COMMAND SOFT AT&K4\\G1\13
SET MODEM COMMAND NO-F AT&K0\\G0\13
SET MODEM COMMAND ERROR ON  AT&Q6\\N3\13
SET MODEM COMMAND ERROR OFF AT&Q0\\N1\13
SET MODEM COMMAND COMPRESS ON  AT%C3\13
SET MODEM COMMAND COMPRESS OFF AT%C0\13
```

SET MODEM CAPABILITIES was omitted, since the PPI has the same ones. Notice how each command begins with AT and ends with carriage return (\13). Also notice that a double backslash is used wherever a single backslash must be sent to the modem. And notice how command words can be abbreviated. Use SHOW MODEM to verify that these commands have taken effect.

Example 2: SupraExpress 144i Fax/Modem

This one is an RPI model, and so lacks error correction and data compression, but the commands and other features are the same as the built-in Supra type:

```
SET MODEM-TYPE USER-DEFINED SUPRA
SET MODEM NAME SupraExpress 144i Fax/Modem RPI
SET MODEM CAPABILITIES AT SB HWFC SWFC
```

or if speed buffering doesn't work (since, in general, it depends on an error-correcting protocol between the modems):

```
SET MODEM CAPABILITIES AT HWFC SWFC
```

By removing the EC and DC capabilities, we prevent Kermit from sending any EC- or DC-related commands to the modem, which, in this model, would cause an error.

Where to Put Modem Commands

You probably don't want to type all these commands every time you use Kermit. If you always use the same modem, you would want your modem-related commands executed automatically every time you start Kermit. In that case, you would add them to your C-Kermit customization file (see Chapter 2). If you need more flexibility, all sorts of options are open to you, which are covered in Chapter 17, *Command Files, Macros, and Variables*. But remember, there is nothing magic about where the commands come from. You can type them at the prompt, execute them automatically at startup, execute them explicitly from a file or from a macro — it makes no difference, the result is the same.

Modem Command List

Here is a concise list of all C-Kermit's SET MODEM commands. Recall that each keyword can be abbreviated as long as the abbreviation still distinguishes the keyword from any other keyword that can appear in the same position.

Note that SET CARRIER-WATCH is a synonym for SET MODEM CARRIER-WATCH. Also, for compatibility with earlier releases of C-Kermit, SET DIAL is accepted as a substitute for SET MODEM in most commands; for example, SET DIAL SPEED-MATCHING OFF.

The first group must be set by the user. If not, the defaults shown in boldface are used:

```
SET MODEM TYPE name
SET MODEM CARRIER-WATCH { AUTO, ON, OFF }
SET MODEM HANGUP-METHOD { MODEM-COMMAND, RS232-SIGNAL }
SET MODEM KERMIT-SPOOF { ON, OFF }
SET MODEM FLOW-CONTROL { AUTO, NONE, RTS/CTS, XON/XOFF }
```

The rest are loaded from the modem database when a SET MODEM TYPE command is given. Use these commands *after* SET MODEM TYPE to to override the values that are loaded from C-Kermit's database:

```
SET MODEM NAME string
SET MODEM CAPABILITIES { AT, DC, EC, HWFC, ITU, KS, SB, SWFC, TB }
SET MODEM MAXIMUM-SPEED { ..., 1200, ..., 57600, 115200, ... }
SET MODEM SPEED-MATCHING { ON, OFF }
SET MODEM ESCAPE-CHARACTER number
SET MODEM DIAL-COMMAND string
SET MODEM ERROR-CORRECTION { ON, OFF }
SET MODEM COMPRESSION { ON, OFF }

SET MODEM COMMAND AUTOANSWER ON string
SET MODEM COMMAND AUTOANSWER OFF string
SET MODEM COMMAND COMPRESSION ON string
SET MODEM COMMAND COMPRESSION OFF string
SET MODEM COMMAND DIAL-MODE-PROMPT string
SET MODEM COMMAND DIAL-MODE-STRING string
SET MODEM COMMAND ERROR-CORRECTION ON string
SET MODEM COMMAND ERROR-CORRECTION OFF string
SET MODEM COMMAND HANGUP-COMMAND string
SET MODEM COMMAND HARDWARE-FLOW string
SET MODEM COMMAND SOFTWARE-FLOW string
SET MODEM COMMAND NO-FLOW-CONTROL string
SET MODEM COMMAND INIT-STRING string
SET MODEM COMMAND PULSE string
SET MODEM COMMAND TONE string
```

Modem-Related Variables

Even though you don't know what a variable is unless you've been peeking at Chapter 17, a list of modem-related variables is shown in Table 4-2 for reference. They refer to the modem selected in the most recent SET MODEM TYPE command, if any; otherwise they are empty. You can use these variables in Kermit commands, where there are replaced by their actual values. For example:

```
C-Kermit> set modem type telebit
C-Kermit> echo My modem type is "\v(modem)".
My modem type is "telebit".
C-Kermit> echo My modem's dialing command is "\v(m_dial)".
My modem's dial command is "ATD%s\{13}".
C-Kermit>
```

You can use the SHOW VARIABLES to see the current values:

```
C-Kermit> sho var
  ...
 \v(modem) = telebit
 \v(m_aa_off) = ATS180=0\{13}
 \v(m_aa_on) = ATS0=1\{13}
  ...
C-Kermit>
```

Table 4-2 Modem Variables

Variable	Description
\v(modem)	Current modem type (SET MODEM TYPE value).
\v(m_aa_off)	Modem command to turn Auto Answer Off.
\v(m_aa_on)	Modem command to turn Auto Answer On.
\v(m_dc_off)	Modem command to turn Data Compression Off.
\v(m_dc_on)	Modem command to turn Data Compression On.
\v(m_dial)	Modem command to dial a telephone number.
\v(m_ec_off)	Modem command to turn Error Correction Off.
\v(m_ec_on)	Modem command to turn Error Correction On.
\v(m_fc_hw)	Modem command to select Hardware Flow Control.
\v(m_fc_no)	Modem command to select No Flow Control.
\v(m_fc_sw)	Modem command to select Software Flow Control.
\v(m_hup)	Modem command to hang up the phone.
\v(m_init)	Modem initialization command.
\v(m_pulse)	Modem command to enable pulse Dialing.
\v(m_tone)	Modem command to enable tone Dialing.

## Chapter 5

Using the Dialing Directory

C-Kermit's dialing directory is a collection of one or more plain-text files that associate names with phone numbers, allowing you to dial by name so you don't have to remember specific numbers. For example, you can type "dial mcimail" rather than "dial 18004566245". Dialing directory files can be maintained by a text editor that reads and saves files in plain-text (ASCII) format, such as EMACS, VI, or Windows EDIT or NotePad. Recall the syntax of the DIAL command:

DIAL *text*

The *text* can be either a telephone number or the "name" of a telephone number. If you give a name instead of a number, the name is automatically looked up in your dialing directory (if you have one). Before C-Kermit can use a dialing directory, it must be told where to find it. The command is:

SET DIAL DIRECTORY *[file1 [file2 [file3 [...]]]]*
>   Selects zero, one, or more dialing directories. If you do not include any filenames, the dialing directory feature is disabled and the DIAL command expects and handles only real telephone numbers. If you include one or more filenames, then Kermit searches the given files when you DIAL a "number" that starts with a letter (the exact rules are spelled out in more detail shortly).

Examples:
```
C-Kermit> set dial directory                          (None)
C-Kermit> set dia direct ckermit.kdd                  (One file)
C-Kermit> set di dir ckermit.kdd bbslist.kdd cis.kdd  (3 files)
```

If you installed C-Kermit according to instructions and you are using the standard initialization file, then the default dialing directory is:

```
.kdd                    (UNIX, OS-9)
ckermit.kdd             (VOS)
CKERMIT.KDD             (OS/2, Windows, VMS, AOS/VS, etc)
```

and if such a file exists, it it used. In the absence of an initialization file (or of a SET DIAL DIRECTORY command in your initialization or customization file), C-Kermit uses the file(s) given by the environment variable K_DIAL_DIRECTORY, if it is defined, for example (in UNIX ksh):

```
export K_DIAL_DIRECTORY="/usr/local/ckermit.kdd  $HOME/.kdd"
```

In this example, which might be added to the system-wide login profile on a multiuser UNIX computer, two dialing directory files are set up: the first is a system-wide directory, centrally administered and shared by everyone, and the second is a personal dialing directory in each user's home directory. A similar technique might be useful on a corporate PC-based LAN, where the corporate-wide directory would be placed on the file server, and the user's directory on her or his own disk; the LAN login procedure would then set up the environment variable.

Dialing Directory Format

Each dialing directory entry consists of a name followed by a telephone number, optionally followed by a comment. The name is a "word" that does not contain any spaces[14]; alphabetic case distinctions in names are ignored. The number can be in any format at all that is acceptable to your dialout modem, meaning, in most cases, it can include spaces and/or certain punctuation. The comment, if any, begins with a semicolon preceded by at least one space or tab.

Full-line comments may also be entered. These begin with a semicolon. Blank lines in the dialing directory are ignored.

Here is a short sample dialing directory:

```
; Olga's dialing directory - Last update: 11 June 1996
IBM        +1 (800) 874 2881  ; IBM BBS
Hayes       1 800 874-2937    ; Hayes Online BBS
NYCSprint 1 212 7418100       ; New York City Sprint
DECstore  18002341998         ; Digital Equipment Corporation store
Heise       011 49 511 5352301 ; Verlag Heinz Heise c't BBS, Germany
```

---

[14]A name may contain spaces if it is surrounded by braces, for example:

```
{Heise MailBox} 011 49 511 5352301
```

Each entry is either "portable" or "literal". In portable entries, phone numbers start with a plus sign (+), as in the IBM entry in the example. Literal entries do not start with a plus sign, so the Hayes, NYCSprint, DECstore, and Heise entries above are literal.

The advantage a literal entry is its ease of use. Just enter the number exactly as you would dial it (possibly inserting spaces for clarity) and you need not be concerned with any of the locale-related features that occupy the rest of this chapter. The drawback is that literal entries can not be dialed from other locations (different area codes or countries) than the one for which they were created. But literal entries are perfectly adequate for directories that are always used from the same place.

Portable entries, on the other hand, can be used from any location, but before you can create and use portable entries, you'll need to read the rest of this chapter.

The Trouble with Literal Entries

Suppose you live and work in New York City, and you call the local Sprint number to access Dow Jones News/Retrieval (DJNR). Your dialing directory entry for DJNR might look like this:

```
DJNR          741 8100                 ; Dow Jones News/Retrieval
```

To place the call, you simply tell Kermit to DIAL DJNR. But now suppose you are traveling with your laptop to another city. DIAL DJNR doesn't work any more because the number lacks the necessary long-distance dialing prefix and the area code. Of course, you could change the entry to read:

```
DJNR          1 212 741 8100           ; Dow Jones News/Retrieval
```

but this would not work when you returned to New York City, where local calls cannot be dialed as if they were long distance.

If you made two entries:

```
DJNR          741 8100                 ; Dow Jones News/Retrieval
DJNR          1 212 741 8100           ; Dow Jones News/Retrieval
```

then Kermit would try the first one, and if that didn't work, it would try the second. But this is a poor solution, because if you are outside New York City, the first number is very likely to be someone's home telephone. Of course, you could avoid this problem by giving each entry a different name. But if you travel to many different places, you'll need lots of different entry names for calling the same place:

```
DJNR          741 8100                ; From within NYC
DJNRNYCPBX    9,741 8100              ; From a PBX in NYC
DJNRNA        1 212 741 8100          ; From elsewhere in North America
DJNRNAPBX     93,1 212 741 8100       ; From a different PBX outside NYC
DJNRUK        00 1 212 741 8100       ; From the UK
DJNRUKHR      102 00 1 212 741 8100 ; From a hotel room in the UK
```

As the list grows, you will begin having as much trouble remembering the names of the entries as you would remembering the numbers themselves. And this approach also complicates directory maintenance; if a phone number changes, you must change your directory in many places.

Portable Entries

You can solve all these problems by using portable directory entries. Portable entries are for people who travel, or for dialing directories that are to be distributed to and used from diverse locations, such as the sample dialing directory that you received with your Kermit software. By entering the phone number in a specific format and providing some additional "locale" information, you enable Kermit to figure out, in most cases, whether a call is internal, local, toll-free, long-distance, or international, and then dial it in the appropriate way automatically.

Portable entries are in ITU-T (CCITT) E.234 [8] format:

```
+ country-code ( area-code ) local-number
```

Here are some examples:

```
IBM         +1 (800) 874 2881 ; IBM BBS
Hayes       +1 (800) 874 2937 ; Hayes Online BBS
DJNR        +1 (212) 741 8100 ; Dow Jones News Retrieval NYC
DECstore    +1 (800) 234 1998 ; Digital Equipment Corporation store
Heise       +49 (511) 535 2301 ; Verlag Heinz Heise c't BBS, Germany
```

The plus sign (+) means two things. First, it means that the phone number is in the standard format that Kermit understands. Second, it means that the digits between the plus sign and the opening parenthesis are a country code. And then:

- The number in parentheses is the area or city code within the country.

- The number following the number in parentheses is the local number within the area.

- The plus sign and parentheses are discarded before passing the number to the modem.

Characters other than plus sign, digits, parentheses, and space are allowed, but are not truly portable. Such characters are passed to the modem literally, so the result depends on your modem. For example, most Hayes and compatible modems ignore hyphens and periods in phone numbers, so the following notation works with Hayes modems but might not work with other kinds:

```
+1 (212) 555-1212  ; Phone number contains hyphen
+1 (212) 555.1212  ; Phone number contains period
```

Note that letters included in a phone number are *not* translated to dialing digits. If you want Kermit to dial 1 800 COLLECT, you must give the phone number as 1 800 2655326.

Table 5-1 Telephone Number Modifiers for Hayes Modems

Character	Description
,	(comma) Pause (usually 2 seconds)
W	Wait for secondary dialtone, e.g. when getting an outside line
@	Wait for quiet answer, i.e. phone is answered, but not by a modem
!	(exclamation mark) Flash (try to get dialtone)
;	(semicolon) Return to command state immediately after dialing
$	(dollar sign) Wait for "bong", e.g. to enter calling-card number

Certain phone-number modifiers, shown in Table 5-1, apply to Hayes and compatible modems, and are also widely used even by non-Hayes compatibles, so you can include them in phone numbers when you know your modem handles them appropriately. But this makes your dialing directory nonportable to modems that don't understand them, and so it is better to assign these characters to the dialing prefixes and suffixes described later in this chapter.

Mixed-Mode Directories

You can mix literal and portable entries in the same directory. Each entry is treated individually, depending on whether the telephone number starts with a plus sign.

Multiple Entries

If you have multiple entries with the same name, Kermit builds up a list of all the numbers for that name. Each number is dialed until the phone is answered successfully or until no more entries remain. These entries need not be adjacent, or even in the same file, thus the directory can be arranged any way you like.

Multiple Directories

If you specify multiple dialing directory files, Kermit searches through all of them, in the order given in the SET DIAL DIRECTORY command, looking for matching entries when building up its list of telephone numbers.

Order of Dialing

After Kermit builds up its list of numbers, it sorts them into the six categories shown in Table 5-2, which are supposed to be (but obviously cannot be guaranteed to be[15]) "cheapest first," and dials them in order of category (the category numbers are displayed

---

[15]Example: dialup information services that charge a premium when accessed from a toll-free number.

Table 5-2 Dialing Category Codes

Code	Description
0	Internal PBX
1	Toll free
2	Local
3	Literal
4	Long distance
5	International

by Kermit when you give a LOOKUP command). No sorting is done within each category. Literal numbers are those that do not begin with "+" in the dialing directory, and therefore can't be categorized.

In some cases, this sorting might produce unwanted effects, as when a toll-free number actually results in higher charges to you than (say) a local call, or when literal numbers (whose "geography" can't be recognized by Kermit) don't fall where you want them to, or when a long-distance call is actually cheaper than a local call. In such cases, you can inhibit sorting and force Kermit to dial the numbers in the same order in which they are encountered with the command:

SET DIAL SORT { OFF, ON }

OFF inhibits "cheapest-first" sorting, ON (the default) enables it.

Use the LOOKUP command to check the sort order to see whether you might want to SET DIAL SORT OFF before calling a particular destination from a particular location.

You also have another control. When the numbers for a particular entry range from local to international, you can put a cap on how "far" Kermit is allowed to dial:

SET DIAL RESTRICT { INTERNATIONAL,LOCAL,LONG-DISTANCE,NONE }

INTERNATIONAL means international calls are restricted, i.e. not allowed.
LONG-DISTANCE means that long-distance and international calls are restricted.
LOCAL means all calls except internal PBX calls are restricted. NONE, the default, means all calls are allowed. *Note:* This command has nothing to do with your phone — telephones may have their own restrictions, which are independent of Kermit's.

Suppose, for example, you have a dialing directory that contains 500 different worldwide Sprint access numbers, and all the entries are called "sprint". If the toll-free numbers are all busy, and the local access numbers are also busy, and all the long-distance numbers in your entire country are also busy, you might not want to pay for a call to Scotland or Venezuela (unless you happen to live there). So SET DIAL RESTRICT INTERNATIONAL would be appropriate for such a call.

Looking up and Dialing Numbers

There are two ways to look things up in the dialing directory: one, the LOOKUP command, just does the looking up part; the other, DIAL looks up *and* dials:

LOOKUP *name*

> Looks up the *name* in your dialing directory or directories, and displays the entries, if any, that match. If any matching entries are found, then the *name* becomes the default name for the next DIAL command.

Entry names can be abbreviated, provided no entries start with the same abbreviation but are different from each other. For example, if your directory has entries with the following names:

```
acorn  aardvark  abba  abccorp  aa  abdicate  abccorp
```

then "abc" would select the two "abccorp" entries, but "ab" would be ambiguous and the lookup would fail. Note, however, that if you spell out the name in full, then all exact matches are used, even if other entries start the same way; for example "aa" matches only the "aa" entry and not the "aardvark" entry.

DIAL *[text]*

> Dials a phone call. If the *text* is omitted, the name, if any, from the most recent DIAL command or successful LOOKUP command is used. Then:

- If the *text* does not begin with a letter, it is not looked up in the dialing directory or directories.

- If the *text* begins with an equals sign ("="), the equals sign is discarded (the *text* becomes the part after the equals sign) and the name is not looked up in the dialing directory, even if it begins with a letter.

- If the original *text* began with a letter and a dialing directory is active, the *text* is looked up. If it is found, it is replaced by one or more phone numbers; if the *text* is not found, then the text itself is used as the phone number.

- If the phone number (as given, or as found in the dialing directory) does not start with "+", it is sent as-is to the modem.

- If the phone number starts with "+", it is converted to the appropriate form for dialing, based on your dialing location.

If the same *text* is found more than once in the dialing directory, each number listed under *text* is dialed until one answers. If none of them answers, then the entire process is repeated automatically according to your DIAL RETRIES setting until there is an answer, or the maximum number of retries is exceeded, or the police come.

Adding Prefixes and Suffixes

The following two commands give you a simple and straightforward way to modify phone numbers — a prefix and a suffix that are blindly added to all phone numbers prior to dialing, no matter whether the number was obtained from the dialing directory or whether it is internal, local, long-distance, or international. (If you are dialing out from a PBX, however, the PBX outside-line prefix precedes the dial prefix.)

SET DIAL PREFIX *[text]*
> An item to precede the phone number, for example, to get a tie-line or to disable call waiting. This goes before anything else in the phone number except the PBX-OUTSIDE-PREFIX (if any). Example:
>
> ```
> SET DIAL PREFIX *70,
> ```
>
> which is used in many parts of North America to disable call-waiting for the duration of the call, generally desirable when making modem calls.

SET DIAL SUFFIX *[text]*
> An item to follow the phone number.

There is no default prefix or suffix. Use these commands to create prefixes and suffixes; give these commands without any *text* to remove them, once created.

About Country and Area Codes

Every country has a country code — a short number, presently one to three digits long, that identifies your country to the worldwide telephone system. Most countries have their own country code, such as 39 for Italy, 47 for Norway, 351 for Portugal. Some countries share a country code; for example, country code 1 is shared under the North American Numbering Plan (NANP) by the USA, Canada, and various Carribean and Pacific islands. Likewise, country code 7 is presently (or was recently) shared among Russia and some of the other former Soviet Republics.

A list of the world's country codes appears in Appendix VIII-1 (according to our best knowledge at this writing). In case you don't know what your (or somebody else's) country code is, you can probably find it there.

Just as the world is divided into countries, most countries are divided into calling areas, identified by area codes or city codes. For example, in North America, 212 is the area code for the Borough of Manhattan in New York City; 416 is the area code for Toronto, Ontario; 808 is the area code for Hawaii (all of these are subject to change due to area-code splits). In other countries area codes might be longer or shorter, while some countries, such as Costa Rica, Luxembourg, and Singapore, do not have area codes at all.

Be careful not to confuse your country code or area code with your long-distance dialing prefix. For example, in the NANP dialing area, the country code is 1 and the normal long-distance dialing prefix is also 1, whereas in most other places, the long-distance dialing prefix is different from the local country code. In most West European countries, the long-distance dialing prefix is 0; it is not part of the area code. So, for example, in Central London, the country code is 44 and the area code is 171 (not 0171). Only a few countries have area codes that begin with 0; examples include Australia, Finland, and Russia (this information is also subject to change).

Using Portable Entries

To use portable dialing directory entries, Kermit must know the country code and area code you are dialing from. If it doesn't have this information, portable ("+") entries can't be dialed. The commands are:

SET DIAL COUNTRY-CODE *number*
> The numeric country code of the country you are dialing *from*. Examples: 1 for USA and Canada (etc), 44 for the UK, 33 for France, 49 for Germany. This command tells Kermit what your local country code is, so it can compare it with the country codes given in portable dialing directory entries to tell whether a call is national or international. If you have not set a long-distance or international dialing prefix at the time you give this command, Kermit sets default ones for you: for country code 1, these are 1 and 011, respectively, and for all others they are 0 and 00. If these are not correct (as they will not be for many countries), use the SET DIAL LD-PREFIX and SET DIAL INTL-PREFIX commands, described shortly, to specify the right prefixes.

SET DIAL AREA-CODE *[number]*
> The numeric area or city code you are dialing *from*. If your country does not have area codes, give this command but omit the *number*. Be careful not to include your long-distance dialing prefix as part of the area code (e.g. 0 in England or Germany, 9 in Finland). Here are some examples:

0	for Helsinki, Finland (prior to 12 October 1996)
9	for Helsinki, Finland (beginning 12 October 1996)
69	for Frankfurt, Germany
171	for central London, England (note: not 0171)
212	for Manhattan, New York City, USA
516	for Long Island, New York, USA
511	for Hannover, Germany
6431	for Marburg, Germany
38427	for Blowatz, Germany
(blank)	for Singapore, no area codes

The reason Kermit needs to know your area code is so it can distinguish between local calls and long-distance calls. In most countries, local calls are dialed without a long-distance prefix and without an area code. Of course there are exceptions, and we will discuss them shortly.

SET DIAL LD-PREFIX *number*
> The prefix for dialing long-distance (non-local) calls from where you are. This is the access code you must dial in order to place a call outside your own dialing area, but inside your country code. Examples: 1 for USA and Canada (etc), 0 for Germany, England, and most others. Strictly speaking, this item need not be a number; it may contain commas or other dial modifiers if needed (see Table 5-1 on page 99) that are sent to the modem literally. It also can be a long-distance-carrier access code, such as 10288 for "10-ATT" or 10652 for "10-NJB".

SET DIAL INTL-PREFIX *number*
> The prefix for dialing international calls from where you are. Examples: 011 for USA and Canada (etc), 00 for many other countries, with many notable exceptions (reportedly, 0061 for Japan, 810 for Russia, 98 for Mexico, etc). This one, too, might also contain non-numeric characters if necessary, and can also be an international-carrier access code.

Versions of C-Kermit that come with installation programs collect this information from you at installation time. Otherwise, you will have to add this information to your C-Kermit customization file yourself.

Kermit has no built-in defaults for these items, but it will pick up initial values for them from the environment, if they are defined there. The environment variable names are K_AREACODE, K_COUNTRYCODE, K_INTL_PREFIX, K_LD_PREFIX.

Kermit also makes these values available to you in variables (see Chapter 17 to learn how to use them):

\v(d$ac)	DIAL AREA-CODE
\v(d$cc)	DIAL COUNTRY-CODE
\v(d$lp)	DIAL LD-PREFIX
\v(d$ip)	DIAL INTL-PREFIX

Example: France

Beginning 18 October 1996, France, like Germany, England, and other European Union countries, will have "0" as its long-distance prefix and "00" as its international dialing prefix, but with a difference.

All calls within France, even local ones, *must* be dialed with an area code. Thus all calls within France will start with "01", "02", . . . "06".

In fact, the area code consists of a one-digit "long-distance" prefix ("0") and a one-digit area code ("1"–"6"). This is a subtle distinction inside France, because it makes no difference what the digits are called. When calling into France from outside, however, the leading zero must be dropped.

So for new French numbers to entered portably in the dialing directory, the leading zero must be dropped (according to our usual rule):

```
paris   +33 (1) 55 55 55 55
```

Kermit users within France, beginning 18 October 1996, should configure their dialing setup as follows:

```
SET DIAL COUNTRY-CODE 33
SET DIAL AREA-CODE 999
SET DIAL LD-PREFIX 0
SET DIAL INTL-PREFIX 00
```

The use of an area code, "999", that will never occur in a real phone number forces all calls to be dialed with the long-distance prefix and the area code.

Toll-Free Calls

The following command allows Kermit to recognize toll-free calls in your dialing directory and dial toll-free numbers in preference to (presumably) more expensive calls when you have multiple dialing directory entries with the same name:

SET DIAL TOLL-FREE-AREA-CODE *[number [number [...]]]*
Specify zero, one, or more toll-free area codes in your country, such as 800 and 888 in the North American dialing area. If one or more toll-free area codes are specified, then dialing-directory entries with these area codes within your country are considered toll-free, rather than long-distance, for purposes of "cheapest-first" sorting. Synonym: **SET DIAL TF-AREA-CODE**.

The following command can be used to specify a dialing prefix for toll-free calls that is different from your long-distance dialing prefix:

SET DIAL TOLL-FREE-PREFIX *[number]*
Prefix to be used when making toll-free calls. If not set, then your long-distance prefix (DIAL LD-PREFIX) is used. Synonym: **SET DIAL TF-PREFIX**.

These items will also be picked up by Kermit at startup from the environment variables K_TF_PREFIX and K_TF_AREACODE. The latter can include multiple area codes separated by spaces.

How a Portable Number Is Dialed

When a dialing-directory entry is in portable format or you give a portable-format number directly in your DIAL command, Kermit chooses the dialing method as follows:

1. If your local COUNTRY-CODE is unknown, then Kermit prints a warning message and stops dialing. Otherwise:

2. If your COUNTRY-CODE is different from the number's country code, then Kermit makes an international call using its INTL-PREFIX, the country code, area code (if any), and subscriber number. Otherwise:

3. If the country codes match, but your AREA-CODE is not blank and it differs from the number's area code, Kermit makes a long-distance call: the country code is ignored and the call is placed using the LD-PREFIX, the area code, and the subscriber number (toll-free calls fall into this category too). Otherwise;

4. Kermit makes a local call. The country code and area code are ignored, and Kermit dials the subscriber number directly.

Alternative Notations

It is permissible to omit parentheses from around the area code in a portable dialing directory entry, for example:

```
+1 212 555 1212
```

or:

```
+12125551212
```

(Remember, spaces are ignored.) If you do this, Kermit treats the entry a bit differently. Since it can't "parse" this type of phone number (i.e. separate its country code, area code, and subscriber number), it tries to match the concatenated DIAL COUNTRY-CODE and DIAL AREA-CODE (if any) with the beginning of the phone number, ignoring the initial "+", as well as any "/", ".", and spaces. Thus permissive entries can also look like this:

```
+1 / 212 / 555-1212
+1/212/555-1212
+1.212.555.1212
```

(This notation is not recommended, but it does agree with notation commonly used in some parts of the world, and might aid in importing dialing directories from other applications or databases.)

This type of entry can be used in parts of the world where the distinction between area code and subscriber number are blurry. By setting different length DIAL AREA-CODEs, you can "move" digits between the area code and subscriber number for matching. For example, suppose you have this dialing directory entry:

```
Some-Name   +9876543210
```

If you:

```
SET DIAL COUNTRY-CODE 9
SET DIAL AREA-CODE 87
```

then Kermit dials "6543210". But if you:

```
SET DIAL COUNTRY-CODE 9
SET DIAL AREA-CODE 8765
```

then Kermit dials "43210".

Dialing from Private Branch Exchanges

A private branch exchange (PBX) is a private telephone system installed within a building, company, hotel, organization, or other thing, that is also connected to the public telephone network. For our purposes, a PBX has the following properties:

1. If you are dialing out from the PBX to the public telephone network, you must dial a special prefix, such as "9", to get an outside line (the prefix could be anything at all, and there might be more than one of them, and it might include some kind of account code for internal charging purposes).

2. If you are dialing from your PBX phone to another phone on the same PBX, the dialing method is different from what it would be if you were making a local call into the PBX from outside. For example, if your local phone number (as seen from outside) is 987-6543, it might be dialed internally as 6543, or 7-6543.

The following commands allow you to use the same dialing directory entry for internal calls within the PBX, calls to the outside from within the PBX, and calls into the PBX from outside:

SET DIAL PBX-OUTSIDE-PREFIX *[number]*
> Tells the prefix you must dial in order to get an outside line. Issue this command to specify the prefix when you are using a PBX phone. And be sure that no PBX-OUTSIDE-PREFIX is defined when you are dialing on the public telephone network (issuing this command without a *number* removes the prefix).

SET DIAL PBX-EXCHANGE *[number]*
> Tells the leading digits of a subscriber number within the AREA-CODE that identify it as belonging to the PBX, typically a 3- or 4-digit number. (Kermit does not presently handle PBXs with multiple exchanges.)

SET DIAL PBX-INSIDE-PREFIX *[number]*
> Specifies the prefix, if any, that must be used to dial an internal number.

If a PBX-OUTSIDE-PREFIX is defined and a call is determined to be local (same area code), the PBX-EXCHANGE (if any) is compared with the beginning of the local phone number. If they match, then those digits are removed from the local phone number before dialing. In addition, if a PBX-INSIDE-PREFIX is specified, it is added to the beginning of the phone number before dialing.

Here's an example. Suppose we have the following dialing directory entries:

```
MARKETING  +1 (617) 555 1234
BOONDOCKS  +1 (617) 444 6789
```

and suppose we have given the following commands:

```
SET DIAL COUNTRY-CODE 1
SET DIAL AREA-CODE 617
SET DIAL PBX-OUTSIDE-PREFIX 9
SET DIAL PBX-EXCHANGE 555
SET DIAL PBX-INSIDE-PREFIX 4
```

Then, if we "dial boondocks", the number that is actually dialed is 94446789 because, since our PBX exchange does not match the beginning of the "boondocks" subscriber number, we treat it as an external call (which happens to be local, since the country code and area code match our own). So the outside-line prefix is dialed, followed by the local number.

But if we "dial marketing", we note that the exchange "555" matches our PBX-EXCHANGE, so we strip the "555" and replace it by our PBX-INSIDE-PREFIX, which is "4", resulting in an internal PBX call, "41234".

On the other hand, if we are dialing from outside (e.g. from home), we use:

```
SET PBX-OUTSIDE-PREFIX
```

(no prefix) to indicate we are not using a PBX (the normal case), and then "dial marketing" is just like dialing any other number; it is dialed as a local, long-distance, or international call, depending on our location.

On LANs or multiuser computers that use PBXs for dialing out, the following environment variables can be set to ensure that Kermit does the right thing for all users by default:

Environment Variable	*SET DIAL Parameter*
K_PBX_INSIDE	PBX-INSIDE-PREFIX
K_PBX_OUTSIDE	PBX-OUTSIDE-PREFIX
K_PBX_EXCHANGE	PBX-EXCHANGE

Having the Final Word

When obtaining a phone number from the directory, Kermit performs various transformations prior to dialing, which you have just read about. But the result might not be exactly what is needed. In cases where Kermit is likely to err, you can ask it to display the phone number before it dials, and give you a chance to change it:

SET DIAL CONFIRMATION { ON, OFF }

Requests confirmation of the phone number before dialing. Normally OFF. When ON, Kermit displays the number, exactly as it is about to be dialed, and you may respond Yes or No. If you respond No, Kermit prompts you for a replacement number. You may also enter Ctrl-C to cancel dialing altogether and return to the C-Kermit prompt.

Checking Portable Entries

If you want to see the effect that the various SET DIAL settings have on telephone numbers, make a test dialing directory containing many entries with the same name (say "test"), but with different country and area codes.

Set different DIAL COUNTRY-CODEs and DIAL AREA-CODEs (and PREFIXes, and SUFFIXes, and PBX items, and TOLL-FREE items, etc etc), then issue a LOOKUP command on the test name.

Here's an example in which we have set our country code to 1 and our area code to 212 (all phone numbers are fictional):

```
7 telephone numbers found for "test":
   1. Test          +1 (212) 555 1234   =>  7 1234              (0)
   2. Test          +1 (800) 555 4321   =>  1800555 4321        (1)
   3. Test          +1 (888) 555 4321   =>  1888555 4321        (1)
   4. Test          +1 (212) 555 5432   =>  555 5432            (2)
   5. Test          5559924             =>  5559924             (3)
   6. Test          +1 (201) 555-6543   =>  1201555-6543        (4)
   7. Test          +49 (551) 7654321   =>  011495517654321     (5)
```

All the matching entries are listed in the order they will be dialed, showing the name, the number from the directory entry and then, after the arrow (=>), the number that actually will be dialed, and finally the type of call (local, long-distance, international, etc; see Table 5-2 on page 100).

If the ordering is not what you desire, tell Kermit to SET DIAL SORT OFF and do the LOOKUP again. This forces Kermit to dial the numbers in the same order they were encountered in the directory or directories. Or else rearrange the order of the entries in your dialing directories.

Exceptions to the Rules and How to Handle Them

The rules and procedures presented in the foregoing sections are adequate in many cases, but the world's telephone systems are not always so well-ordered:

"San Marino is country code 378, and Italy is country code 39. If you're dialing from Italy to any other country code except San Marino, you dial 00 country-code city-code local-number, but if you're dialing San Marino, you must dial it as 0549 local-number (instead of 00-378 local-number).

"Likewise, if you dial from San Marino to any country except Italy, you dial 00 country-code city-code local-number, but if you're dialing Italy, you dial 0 city-code local-number (instead of 00-39 city-code local-number).

"Such special arrangements also exist between Singapore and Malaysia, Mexico to US/Canada/Carribean, Ireland and Northern Ireland, Estonia and Russia, Switzerland/Austria/France/Germany/Italy (often between just pairs of cities across the border from each other), Uganda/Kenya/Tanzania/Rwanda/Burundi, etc."

– *Toby Nixon, Program Manager, Windows Telephony, Microsoft Corp.*

Meanwhile, in Canada:

"Here in Toronto, we're in area code 416. If I want to call 416-488-*xxxx*, that's a local call, and it's in my area code, so I dial 7 digits, 488-*xxxx*. If I want to call 905-276-*xxxx*, that's a local call, and it's outside my area code, so I dial 10 digits: 905-276-*xxxx*. And if I want to call 905-528-*xxxx*, that's long distance, so I dial 11 digits: 1-905-528-*xxxx*. Finally, if I want to dial 976-*xxxx*, that's a premium call, which is like long distance, so I have to dial 1-416-976-*xxxx*, using the 416 even though that's my own area code.

"Ottawa is in area code 613. If they dial 232-*xxxx*, that's a local call and reaches 613-232-*xxxx*. But if they dial 778-*xxxx*, they reach 819-778-*xxxx*. Why? Because that number is in their local calling area, while 613-778-*xxxx* either would be long distance, or doesn't exist. When the call *is* long distance (or premium), they dial it the same as in Toronto: 11 digits. (Historically, until quite recently they would have dialed long distance calls within their area code as 8 digits: 1-778-*xxxx* to reach 613-778-*xxxx*. This had to change when area codes 334, 360, 630, etc, were introduced in 1995.)"

– *Mark Brader, SoftQuad Inc., Toronto*

And then in Massachusetts:

> "There are 400–500 active exchanges in area code 508. Of those, 27 are in what NYNEX[16] has defined as my local area. I am not permitted to dial 1-508 before any of those 27 exchanges, but I am *required* to dial 1-508 to reach any of the remaining exchanges in area code 508.

> "I could put these in as fixed numbers, but all I would have to do would be to take my laptop computer 1.5 miles north from here and then I would be in a different local area where some of my old local area would still be local, but some would now require a 1-508, and some that previously needed 1-508 would now only be able to be dialed without the 1-508."

> – *Ken Levitt, Informed Computer Solutions, Wayland, MA.*

Rather than build error-prone and inadequate knowledge-based "intelligence" into the software, we draw the line at this point and recommend that such pathological cases be handled by:

- Inserting literal entries into the directory, even if that means different entries are needed for dialing the same number from different locations, or:

- By using SET DIAL CONFIRMATION ON to give you a chance to change the number manually at the last minute, or:

- Bypassing the dialing directory and dialing such numbers literally, i.e. "dial 987654321" (Hint: Use LOOKUP to look it up first, then enter it correctly in the DIAL command), or:

- Sneaky tricks.

Here are some sneaky tricks that can be used to handle certain common cases:

1. North American 10-digit dialing to a different area code:

   Just SET DIAL LD-PREFIX to nothing prior to dialing the number. Then set it back to your normal long-distance prefix before dialing any numbers that need it.

2. North American 10-digit dialing to same area code:

---

[16]Note that information in these anecdotes is very likely to change with little or no notice, as companies are merged and acquired, area codes split or changed, and dialing plans are altered to accommodate the rapid demand for telephone numbers brought on by fax machines, pagers, and cellular phones. For example, the reference to NYNEX — New York New England Telephone — might already be obsolete.

Normally, Kermit removes the area code if it is the same as your local one prior to dialing. To force Kermit to keep it on, SET DIAL AREA-CODE to nothing prior to dialing the number. Then Kermit will treat it as a "long" local number. This is the same technique that is used in countries that do not have area codes (such as Singapore).

3. North American 11-digit dialing to same area code:

Set your area code to one that does not exist, e.g. SET DIAL AREA-CODE 000 prior to dialing and then put it back to normal afterwards. This is the same technique that is used in countries in which all calls must be dialed with an area code, such as France beginning 18 October 1996.

Use your imagination to extend these examples to other difficult situations. Tricks such as these can be accomplished conveniently by defining macros (Chapter 17) that save and restore your long-distance prefix or area code around dialing, for example:

```
DEFINE ST1 {                    ; Sneaky Trick 1
    LOCAL \%a \%x
    ASSIGN \%a \v(d$lp)         ; Save current LD-PREFIX
    SET DIAL LD-PREFIX          ; Set LD-PREFIX to nothing
    DIAL \%1                    ; DIAL the given number
    ASSIGN \%x \v(status)       ; Save DIAL command status
    SET DIAL LD-PREFIX \%a      ; Restore LD-PREFIX
    END \%x                     ; Return with DIAL's status
}
```

If you added this macro definition to your C-Kermit customization file, then you would type "st1 oofa" to force 10-digit dialing for the dialing directory entry named "oofa".

Long-Distance Carriers and Calling-Card Numbers

Thanks, at least in the USA, to deregulation, it is now possible to use different companies to make long-distance and international calls from the same telephone. Each phone has a default long-distance company, which is used if you make these calls in the normal way, but you can also choose a different long-distance company on a per-call basis by dialing the phone number in a different way. Furthermore, you can charge calls made on other phones to your own account by dialing in perhaps another special way and then specifying your account number.

The easy case involves specification of an alternative long-distance prefix. For example, to use New Jersey Bell in the USA, the prefix is "10-NJB" (i.e. "10652") rather than the customary "1". Everything works exactly as described previously, except your long-distance bill comes from a different company:

```
SET DIAL LD-PREFIX 10652
```

Now suppose you also need to supply a credit-card number, but only on long-distance calls. We assume that this must come either before the area code or after the phone number (rather than imbedded in the phone number), so therefore it can be part of the LD-PREFIX or it can be a suffix. Not the DIAL SUFFIX, which is always applied (if defined), but rather:

SET DIAL LD-SUFFIX *[text]*

> The *text*, if any, is appended to the phone number prior to dialing if Kermit has determined the call is long distance and not toll free.

For example, suppose that to have a long-distance call billed to your credit card, you must dial 0, the area code, the number, and then pause for several seconds, and then enter your credit-card number:

```
SET DIAL LD-PREFIX 0
SET DIAL LD-SUFFIX ,,xxxxxxxxxxxxxxxxxx
```

where the *x*'s represent your card number, possibly followed by "#". Depending on the capabilities of your modem and the behavior of the long-distance carrier, you might be able to replace the comma(s) by a "wait for bong" character (normally "$").

In another scenario, you might be using your default long-distance carrier to call another long-distance carrier, and then calling the desired number from there, also supplying a credit- or calling-card number. Here you are really making a phone-call-within-a-phone-call. For example, you dial:

```
1 800 nnnnnnn
```

(where the *n*'s are replaced by the second carrier's number), wait for a "quiet answer" (no carrier), then enter 0, the area code, the subscriber number, then wait for a bong, then enter the credit card number. The appropriate commands would be:

```
SET LD-PREFIX 1,800,nnnnnnn@0
SET LD-SUFFIX $xxxxxxxxxxxxxxxxxx
```

Finally, allowing for the possibility that the billing method for international calls might be different from long-distance calls within one's country, we also have:

SET DIAL INTL-PREFIX *[text]*
SET DIAL INTL-SUFFIX *[text]*

OBVIOUSLY, you *do not* want to put credit-card or account information in the dialing directory or any other file, as that is a classic security risk. Therefore, you are going to have to provide this information to Kermit each time you run it and you know that you will be making toll calls. In Chapters 17 through 19, you can find out how to do this easily with command files, macros, or script programs.

Traveling Tips

If you've read this far, you know that to have a portable dialing directory, it's important to separate the concepts related to the number to be dialed from those relating to the location where dialing occurs and the method of dialing. So the dialing directory contains no information at all about your locale. You have also learned the commands for setting up your dialing locale and method. All that's left to be said is that the process need not be painful and laborious. Kermit's command-file and macro capabilities, explained in Chapter 17, let you assign complicated configurations to friendly words of your choice. For example, suppose you carry a laptop around to various locations:

```
DEFINE USA {
    SET DIAL COUNTRY-CODE 1
    SET DIAL LD-PREFIX 1
    SET DIAL INTL-PREFIX 011
}

DEFINE GERMANY {
    SET DIAL COUNTRY-CODE 49
    SET DIAL LD-PREFIX 0
    SET DIAL INTL-PREFIX 00
}

DEFINE MANHATTAN    USA,     SET DIAL AREA-CODE 212
DEFINE LONG-ISLAND USA,     SET DIAL AREA-CODE 516
DEFINE HANNOVER    GERMANY, SET DIAL AREA-CODE 511
DEFINE MARBURG     GERMANY, SET DIAL AREA-CODE 6421
```

And when at work in Manhattan where you have a PBX:

```
DEFINE WORK {
    MANHATTAN
    SET DIAL PBX-OUT 93, SET DIAL PBX-EXT 987, SET DIAL PBX-IN 7
}
```

And then for Hoboken, New Jersey, where you need to dial using a particular long-distance carrier:

```
DEFINE HOBOKEN {
    USA
    SET DIAL AREA-CODE 201
    SET DIAL LD-PREFIX 10652
}
```

These macro definitions would be kept in your Kermit customization file. And then, whenever you start up Kermit to make a call, just enter one word: MANHATTAN, HOBOKEN, HANNOVER, WORK, etc, to declare your location. Then DIAL away.

A macro library of such "rule sets" can be built up over time and included in your Kermit customization file, so these macros will be available to you whenever you use Kermit. You can create and modify macro definitions easily, since they are plain text and not part of the binary executable Kermit program or any particular kind of database.

Old-Format Directories

Previous releases of C-Kermit used a dialing directory with a slightly different format. Here's what happens if you use an old-format directory with C-Kermit 6.0 or later:

```
C-Kermit> set dial directory olga.kdd
C-Kermit> dial office
WARNING: Old-style dialing directory detected: /usr/olga/olga.kdd
 Shall I convert it for you?
```

You may reply "yes" or "no". If you say yes, the old directory is backed up and a converted directory is produced that has the same name as the original directory. You can use the following command to control whether or how this happens:

SET DIAL CONVERT-DIRECTORY *{ ASK, OFF, ON }*

> ASK (the default) behaves as described above. OFF means try to use old-format directories and don't convert them. ON means convert old-format directories silently.

Command Summary

The following commands and variables are used with C-Kermit's dialing directory:

```
DIAL [ text ]
LOOKUP name
SET DIAL AREA-CODE [ text ]
SET DIAL CONFIRMATION { ON, OFF }
SET DIAL CONVERT-DIRECTORY { ASK, OFF, ON }
SET DIAL COUNTRY-CODE number
SET DIAL DIRECTORY [ file1 [ file2 [ file3 [ ... ] ] ] ]
SET DIAL INTL-PREFIX [ text ]
SET DIAL INTL-SUFFIX [ text ]
SET DIAL LD-SUFFIX [ text ]
SET DIAL PBX-EXCHANGE [ number ]
SET DIAL PBX-INSIDE-PREFIX [ number ]
SET DIAL PBX-OUTSIDE-PREFIX [ number ]
SET DIAL PREFIX [ text ]
SET DIAL RESTRICT { INTERNATIONAL, LOCAL, LONG-DISTANCE, NONE }
SET DIAL SORT { OFF, ON }
SET DIAL SUFFIX [ text ]
SET DIAL TOLL-FREE-AREA-CODE [ number [ number [ ... ] ] ]
SET DIAL TOLL-FREE-PREFIX [ number ]
```

Variables:

\v(d$ac)	DIAL AREA-CODE value
\v(d$cc)	DIAL COUNTRY-CODE value
\v(d$lp)	DIAL LD-PREFIX value
\v(d$ip)	DIAL INTL-PREFIX value
\v(dialnumber)	Number or name most recently dialed
\v(dialresult)	Dial result message or code from modem
\v(dialstatus)	Numeric code expressing dial result, Table 5-3, next page

Table 5-3 C-Kermit Dial Status Codes

Code	Meaning
-1	No DIAL command given yet
0	DIAL succeeded
1	Modem type not specified
2	Communication device not specified
3	Device can't be opened
4	Communication speed not specified
5	Hangup failure
6	Internal error (memory allocation, etc)
7	Device input/output error
8	DIAL TIMEOUT expired
9	Dialing interrupted by user
10	Modem not ready
11	through 19 (reserved)
20	Modem command error
21	Failure to initialize modem
22	Busy
23	No carrier
24	No dialtone
25	Ring (incoming call)
26	No answer
27	Disconnected
28	Answered by voice
29	Access denied, forbidden call
30	Blacklisted
31	Delayed
32	Fax connection
98	Unknown error
99	Unspecified failure detected by modem

Chapter 6

Using Networks

Almost any version of Kermit can be used on the "far end" of a network connection, and many versions of Kermit — C-Kermit included — can also make network connections themselves. When you use Kermit software on a network connection, the underlying network protocol and services take the place of a serial connection.

While it is beyond the scope of this book to explain computer networks in any depth, it is important to note that, in the context of Kermit software, network connections differ from serial connections in several important ways:

- Network connections are *usually* inherently error free; the underlying network protocol includes error detection and correction. This means that all communication, even terminal sessions, should be free of noise and data loss.

- Network protocols include their own flow control methods. You rarely have to worry about buffer overflows on a network connection.

- Network protocols are sometimes more reliable than RS-232 signals as indicators of whether a connection is open or closed.

Network connections might be faster than serial connections or they might be slower. Large shared networks, such as the worldwide Internet, can become bogged down and sluggish during periods of heavy traffic. Serial connections, by contrast, are point-to-point, dedicated connections that never become overloaded except when error-correcting or compressing modems are involved, or the end systems (or the local nets they are on) become overloaded.

C-Kermit can be used in several ways in a computer network. You can use a network to access C-Kermit on a remote host and transfer files or you can have C-Kermit establish network connections itself. C-Kermit has certain advantages over other network virtual terminal and file transfer software, such as TCP/IP Telnet and FTP, including:

- Files can be transferred over Telnet, Rlogin, X.25, DECnet, LAT, and other network terminal connections.

- The Kermit file transfer protocol can be more flexible than network file transfer. It includes update and recovery features not usually found in network FTP programs. It is more adept at converting text files into useful form when transferring them between unlike computers. In particular, Kermit protocol is unique in its ability to translate national and international character sets during file transfer (Chapter 16).

- C-Kermit's terminal connection includes features not found in most network virtual terminal programs, including character-set translation, key mapping, session logging, and support for Shift-In/Shift-Out for transmitting 8-bit characters across 7-bit connections (Chapters 8 and 16), as well as VT320, ANSI, Wyse, and other terminal emulations in the Windows and OS/2 versions.

- Kermit's built-in script programming language can be used to automate network file transfers and to set up unattended or repeated operations (Chapters 17–19).

- Kermit's logging facilities can be used in combination with its script programming language for network monitoring and reporting.

- If you have already learned Kermit for serial communications, then you already know it for network connections too, and vice versa.

Making Network Connections

Setting up a network connection from C-Kermit to another network host is similar to setting up a dialed connection, but with different commands. C-Kermit presently supports several network types, TCP/IP [20], X.25 [14], NETBIOS, DECnet (PATHWORKS), Meridian Technology SuperLAT, and Named Pipes. Other networking methods might also have been added since this writing. The selection of networking methods available on your particular version of C-Kermit might include none, one, or several of these. To find out which ones are available to you, use the SHOW NETWORK command:

```
C-Kermit> show network
...
Supported networks:
 SunLink X.25
 TCP/IP
...
```

As of this writing, TCP/IP support is available in the UNIX, VMS, VOS, OS/2, Windows NT, Windows 95, OS-9, and AOS/VS II versions that have TCP/IP installed. X.25 support is currently available for Stratus VOS and for Sun computers equipped with the Sun-Link X.25 product. DECnet, NETBIOS, and Named Pipe support is available only for suitably equipped OS/2 systems; SuperLAT is available for Windows 95 and NT systems that have this product installed. The list is sure to grow.

SET CARRIER-WATCH, SET SPEED, and other serial-device commands have no effect on network connections. The basic commands needed to set up a network connection are:

SET NETWORK TYPE *{ TCP/IP, X.25, NETBIOS, . . . }*

This command tells C-Kermit which type of network to use when making subsequent SET HOST connections. SET NETWORK TYPE is analogous to SET MODEM TYPE, which is used on dialed serial connections to tell Kermit which kind of modem to use for the next DIAL command. The available network types depend on your computer, operating system, and which, if any, networking protocols or products are installed, and of course, whether your computer is attached to a network at all:

```
C-Kermit>set network type ? One of the following:
 tcp/ip     x.25
C-Kermit>set network type tcp
```

The SHOW NETWORK command shows the types of network connections and protocols available, plus information about the currently active network type and connection, if any.

SET HOST *[host [network-specific-info]]*

This command tells C-Kermit to make a network connection to the given *host* name or address, on the type of network specified in the most recent SET NETWORK command. When making network connections, SET HOST takes the place of SET LINE and DIAL on serial connections. The SET HOST command closes any currently open connection (network or serial) and then attempts to open a connection to the specified host immediately. If the connection cannot be established, an error message is printed and the command fails. If no host name is given, the currently open network connection (if any) is simply closed and Kermit reverts to its default communication device.

If you give a SET HOST command without a prior SET NETWORK command, the default network type is used, which is usually TCP/IP — use SHOW NETWORK to display the current network type if you are in doubt.

HANGUP

When the current connection is via TCP/IP, X.25, or some other type of network, the HANGUP command closes the network connection.

The remainder of this chapter discusses the considerations for each type of network and then introduces the network directory — a simplified way of making network connections.

TCP/IP Networks

TCP/IP is the protocol used by the worldwide Internet. TCP/IP network hosts address each other using a protocol called IP (Internet Protocol). Each computer on a TCP/IP network has a 32-bit IP address, written as four decimal numbers separated by periods, with each number between 0 and 255 (inclusive), for example:

```
128.59.39.2
```

The IP address is like the address on a letter; it lets an IP message travel through a complicated network to its destination.

People aren't particularly good at remembering long numbers, so IP hosts can also have names that stand for their numeric addresses. An IP hostname is usually a series of words separated by periods, for example:

```
watsun.cc.columbia.edu
```

The fields in the name don't have any particular relationship to the fields in the numeric address. The dotted name fields represent a hierarchy from left to right, called a domain name. The example identifies the computer called "watsun" on the Computer Center (cc) network, which has many computers; at Columbia University (columbia), which has many local area networks; on the educational portion of the Internet (edu), which also includes many other educational institutions. The Internet has other major subdivisions besides "edu," including "com" for the commercial portion, "gov" for the government portion, "it" for the Italian portion, and so on.

Host names are translated to numeric IP addresses by network servers called domain name servers, or, more simply, name servers. The name server can be on your own computer, on some other computer on your network, or even on a distant computer outside your organization.

People tend to prefer short names to long ones. Therefore IP hosts can have nicknames, like "watsun" or "w" for watsun.cc.columbia.edu. Nicknames are generally valid only within an organization's local network and are translated to IP numbers by a local name server from a local host table.

C-Kermit's SET HOST command accepts any of these forms, and it also can look up addresses in its network directory, discussed later in this chapter.

If you give a host name (or a host name is fetched from the network directory), C-Kermit attempts to find a name server that will supply the corresponding address. If you give a numeric address, C-Kermit uses it directly, without attempting to contact a name server. So, if you have trouble making a TCP/IP connection to a host by name, try its IP address instead if you know it. Here are some examples showing how to establish connections with the SET HOST command:

```
C-Kermit>set net type tcp                    (Choose network type)
C-Kermit>set host ? IP host name or number,
 or carriage return to close an open connection
C-Kermit>set host watsun                      (Unknown nickname)
 Can't get address for watsun
C-Kermit>set host watsun.cc.columbia.edu      (Full domain name)
C-Kermit>set host 128.59.39.2                 (IP address)
C-Kermit>set host                             (Close the connection)
 Closing Connection
C-Kermit>
```

You should use names rather than numbers when possible, because numbers can change without your knowledge. The name server, however, is supposed to have a current number for each name.

TCP Service Ports

C-Kermit connects to the TELNET server (TCP port 23) on the remote host by default, but you can specify any desired TCP port or service after the IP host name or address (see Table 6-1 for a sampling):

SET HOST *host service*

or you can append it to the *host* field with a colon (no spaces):

SET HOST *host:service*

As with addresses, Kermit asks the operating system to translate a service name (like telnet) into a TCP port number. If you give a port number, it is used as is. Examples:

```
C-Kermit>set host watsun                      (Default port is 23)
C-Kermit>set host watsun 23                   (Port 23 specified)
C-Kermit>set host 128.59.39.2 telnet          (TELNET is port 23)
C-Kermit>set host federal.bbs.gpo.gov 3001    (Port 3001)
C-Kermit>set host martini.eecs.umich.edu:3000 (Port 3000)
```

Table 6-1 Commonly Used Assigned TCP Port Numbers

Port	Name	Description
7	ECHO	Echoes back whatever is sent to it.
13	DAYTIME	Prints time of day.
19	CHARGEN	Character generator, sends characters continuously.
23	TELNET	Telnet server.
37	TIME	Time server.
70	GOPHER	Information retrieval.
79	FINGER	Shows who is logged in.
513	LOGIN	Rlogin server.

The SET HOST command displays the translation from IP host name to numeric IP address:

```
C-Kermit>set host callsign.cs.buffalo.edu:2000
 Trying 128.205.32.4...
```

and then tries to establish the connection. If the connection cannot be made, you are given an informative error message. Examples:

```
C-Kermit>set host 123.123.123.123
 Trying 123.123.123.123...
Sorry, can't open connection: Network is unreachable
C-Kermit>set host watsun oofa
 Trying 128.59.39.2...
Sorry, can't open connection: Cannot find port for service oofa
C-Kermit>set host watsun 2345
 Trying 128.59.39.2...
Sorry, can't open connection: Connection refused
```

The first message means that either there is no such IP address or the network implied by the IP address cannot be located or reached. The second message means that the TCP service-name database did not contain an entry for a service called *oofa*. The last message indicates that there is no server on TCP port 2345 at host watsun.

Use the SHOW NETWORK command to display the name, address, service, network, and protocol of an active connection:

```
C-Kermit>sho net
...
Active network connection:
 callsign.cs.buffalo.edu:3000 [128.205.32.2] via: tcp/ip
 TELNET protocol
 Echoing is currently remote

C-Kermit>
```

Fine-Tuning the TCP Connection

C-Kermit's SET TCP command lets you tune TCP networking performance on a per-connection basis by adjusting parameters that you normally would not have access to. You should use these commands only if you feel that the TCP/IP protocol stack that Kermit is using is giving you inadequate performance, and then only if you understand the concepts (see, for example, [20]), and then at your own risk. The SET TCP settings are displayed by SHOW NETWORK. Not all SET TCP options are necessarily available in all C-Kermit versions; they depend on the underlying TCP/IP services.

SET TCP { RECVBUF, SENDBUF } *number*
Overrides the system default TCP receive and send buffer sizes.

SET TCP KEEPALIVE { ON, OFF }
Setting this ON might help to detect broken connections more quickly. It works when both ends of the TCP connection support the TCP Keepalive feature. Default is ON.

SET TCP LINGER *{* **ON** *[timeout],* **OFF** *}*

Setting this ON ensures that a connection doesn't close before all outstanding data has been transferred and acknowledged. The optional *timeout* specifies how many 10ths of a millisecond TCP should wait for a "close" to succeed. 0 means no timeout, wait forever. Default is OFF, meaning don't wait — just assume that no data will be lost.

SET TCP NODELAY *{* **ON, OFF** *}*

ON means send short TCP packets immediately rather than waiting to accumulate a bunch of them before transmitting (Nagle algorithm). Default is OFF. Turning this ON can significantly degrade overall network performance, but might be necessary if you experience slow echoing on TELNET connections.

The RLOGIN Command

The RLOGIN command combines the functions of SET NETWORK TYPE TCP/IP, SET HOST, and CONNECT (explained in Chapter 8), as well as automatically specifying the special "login" (513) service port. The RLOGIN command might not be available in your version of C-Kermit, especially on systems (including most variations of UNIX) where RLOGIN is a privileged service.

Rlogin is like Telnet (next page), but simpler and less widely available. It is supposed to always provides a transparent 8-bit communication path, and it automatically and transparently communicates any change in screen dimensions.

Rlogin protocol [52] also sends your user ID as part of the login sequence, so C-Kermit's RLOGIN command lets you include it:

RLOGIN *[host [user-ID]]*

Closes any currently open connection. If a *host* is included, a connection is opened to port 513 on the the specified IP host. If a user ID is included, it is sent in advance to the host so you won't have to type it as part of the login process.

If a user ID is included, it also becomes the value of the \v(userid) variable (Chapter 17). If a user ID is not included but you have previously used a SET LOGIN USERID command to specify a user ID, then that is used; otherwise if a your local username, if any, is used; if you don't have a local username, the USER environment variable is used. If none of these is fruitful, you are asked to supply a user ID, since the Rlogin server requires one.

Typically when you give a successful RLOGIN command, C-Kermit enters its terminal screen (Chapter 8) and you see a Password: prompt. Just type in your password and you're online.

On the other hand, if the host does not support RLOGIN protocol, or your client process lacks the needed privilege, then your connection will not be accepted.

The TELNET Command

The TELNET command combines the functions of SET NETWORK TYPE TCP/IP, SET HOST, and CONNECT (explained in Chapter 8) into one convenient command:

TELNET *[host [service]]*

Opens a connection to the specified IP host on the designated TCP port (23 = TELNET by default). If successful, C-Kermit enters CONNECT mode automatically, otherwise it issues an appropriate error message and remains at the prompt. If a host is not specified, the currently active TCP/IP connection, if any, is resumed. Examples:

```
C-Kermit>telnet ? IP host name or number,
 or carriage return to resume an open connection
C-Kermit>telnet watsun ? TCP service name or number,
 or carriage return for telnet (23)
C-Kermit>telnet watsun 2000      (Specify port 2000)
C-Kermit>telnet watsun:2000      (Ditto)
C-Kermit>telnet                  (Resume an open connection)
```

TELNET Protocol Negotiations

C-Kermit performs TELNET option negotiation protocol [59] automatically. These negotiations are used primarily to inform the remote host of your terminal type and to determine which side does the echoing. If the TCP service port is TELNET (23), Kermit sends the initial negotiations. Otherwise, Kermit sends no TELNET negotiations but is prepared to handle them should they arrive from the remote host. Negotiations can take place at any time during the connection: in CONNECT mode (for example, to turn echoing off and on around password entry), during script program execution, and so on. The SET TELNET command can be used to alter C-Kermit's initial TELNET configuration:

SET TELNET ECHO { REMOTE, LOCAL }

In accordance with the TELNET Network Virtual Terminal (NVT) specification [59], C-Kermit begins a TELNET connection in local-echo mode, meaning C-Kermit itself echoes the characters that you type on the keyboard. In the rare cases where this causes problems (for example with a remote server that does its own echoing without negotiating this first, contrary to the TELNET protocol), you can use this command to change C-Kermit's initial echoing state for TELNET connections.

SET TELNET BINARY-MODE { ACCEPTED, REFUSED, REQUESTED }

TELNET connections are normally in NVT (ASCII) mode, but there is also a binary mode that can or should be used for certain purposes. Unfortunately, TELNET server implementations are inconsistent in this area, and so you might have to use this command to adapt. Normally, Kermit refuses to enter binary mode. If you find that you can't display or send 8-bit characters or you experience other kinds of strange behavior, try disconnecting, telling Kermit to SET TELNET BINARY ACCEPTED or REQUESTED, and then starting a new connection.

SET TELNET NEWLINE-MODE { BINARY, NVT } { ON, OFF, RAW }

The TELNET specification also states that while the connection is in NVT mode, the Return or Enter key should normally be transmitted to the TELNET server as a carriage-return and linefeed pair (CRLF). If the connection is in binary mode, then carriage return is sent as-is. This is how C-Kermit behaves unless you use this command to change things. You can control Kermit's behavior separately for NVT and binary mode. The options for each mode are: ON (send CR as CRLF), OFF (send CR as CR followed by NUL), and RAW (send CR by itself, the default for binary mode). Use this command if your TELNET session doesn't behave as expected without it.

SET TELNET TERMINAL-TYPE *text*

The remote TELNET server might request C-Kermit to send your local terminal type. Unless you say otherwise, C-Kermit sends what it believes your terminal type to be, based, for example, on the value of the TERM environment variable, in uppercase (as required by the TELNET specification). In OS/2 and Windows, it is your actual terminal emulation type. But if the remote system does not support your terminal type or recognize its name, it won't be able to set your terminal type automatically. Use this command to tell C-Kermit the terminal name to use in TELNET negotiations; case is preserved. Example:

```
C-Kermit>set telnet term VT100
```

This command does not affect your local terminal type.

Here is an example showing how to use C-Kermit to connect from a TCP/IP host to the Internet Network Information Center, a source of information about the Internet.

```
$ kermit                                (Start Kermit)
C-Kermit 6.0.192 6 Sep 96, Solaris 2.5
Type ? or HELP for help
C-Kermit>telnet internic.net           (Connect to host)
 Trying 198.41.0.5...
Connecting to host internic.net:23
The escape character is Ctrl-\ (ASCII 28, FS).
Type the escape character followed by C to get back,
or followed by ? to see other options.

SunOS UNIX 4.1 (rs0) (ttyp9)

Please be advised that use constitutes consent to monitoring
(Elec Comm Priv Act, 18 USC 2701-2711)

[vt320] InterNIC > ?
Command, one of the following
  DATE         FINGER       HELP         KERMIT        LOGOUT
  STATUS       WHOIS        GOPHER       WAIS          X500WHOIS
[vt320] InterNIC > logout
Communication disconnect (Back at Local System)
C-Kermit>exit                          (Leave Kermit)
$                                      (Back where we started)
```

Testing and Managing Your TCP/IP Connection

Several special features are available for testing and managing your TCP/IP connection. At the C-Kermit prompt, you can use the PING command:

PING *[host]*

to send an IP message to see if the host is reachable and responsive. If a host is not specified, the message is sent to the current SET HOST or TELNET host, if any. This command simply runs your system's PING command, so the response depends on your system:

```
C-Kermit>set host spacelink.msfc.nasa.gov
C-Kermit>ping
spacelink.msfc.nasa.gov is alive
C-Kermit>
```

The other special features are available as CONNECT-mode escape commands and are described in Chapter 8, but they are also listed here for completeness:

A Send a TELNET "Are You There?" command.

B Send a TELNET Break command.

I Send a TELNET Interrupt Process command.

For example, typing Ctrl-\ (hold down the Ctrl key and press the backslash key, C-Kermit's normal CONNECT-mode escape character) followed by the letter A sends a Telnet "Are You There?" protocol message, to which the Telnet server should respond with something like "[yes]" if you have a working Telnet connection.

How to Dial Using a TCP/IP Modem Server

If your site maintains a pool of dialout modems on a "reverse terminal server" that is on your TCP/IP network, you can use C-Kermit to dial out by following these steps *in the order given:*

1. Give a SET HOST (not TELNET) command, specifying the IP host name or numeric address of the terminal server. In most cases, a special port number is also required, such as 2000.

2. Give a SET MODEM TYPE command to specify the type of modem.

3. Issue any necessary SET DIAL or SET MODEM commands.

4. Give a DIAL command for the desired phone number.

If the connection succeeds but echoing is incorrect, you can try giving a SET TELNET ECHO REMOTE (or LOCAL) command as a first step, or else give a SET TERMINAL ECHO REMOTE (or LOCAL) command after the connection is made.

Receiving TCP/IP Connections

Some versions of C-Kermit can not only make TCP/IP connections, but also can receive them. To receive TCP/IP connections, give the following commands:

```
C-Kermit>set network type tcp/ip
C-Kermit>set host *:2000
```

That is, use "*" in place of the hostname, and specify a non-TELNET non-privileged port. C-Kermit waits until a connection comes in, or until you interrupt it with Ctrl-C, before giving its next prompt and accepting another command.

Once a connection comes in, you can enter CONNECT mode for a chat session, or SERVER mode to be a Kermit file transfer and management server, or you can run a custom script to conduct an interactive dialog with the client (as explained in subsequent chapters).

It is important to note that when receiving incoming connections, C-Kermit is *not* a TEL-NET server. It does not give the client a login prompt, an interactive shell, or even a Kermit prompt. Sometimes, however, especially when executing scripts, it is desirable — even necessary — to control certain TELNET protocol options. This requires a basic understanding of the TELNET protocol, which is beyond the scope of this publication (see, for example, [20], or the TELNET RFCs).

Very briefly, however, the TELNET protocol calls for control messages to be mixed in with ordinary data. TELNET messages begin with the special character IAC (Interpret As Command), which is a byte consisting of eight 1's; that is, a decimal value of 255. The messages determine which side echoes characters, how various characters are interpreted, and so on.

As a TELNET client, C-Kermit takes care of this for you automatically, using built-in defaults, or else the values you have given in any SET TELNET commands. But when receiving a connection, it might sometimes be necessary to initiate TELNET negotiations explicitly.

Forcing TELNET Options

The following command can be used to send TELNET negotations to force, or attempt to force, certain known or desired states:

TELOPT *{DO, DONT, WILL, WONT }* *{BINARY, ECHO, NAWS, SGA, TTYPE }*
    Sends the TELNET command, DO, DONT, WILL, or WONT, for the given protocol option, BINARY, ECHO, NAWS, SGA, or TTYPE.

DO requests that the TELNET client or server on the other end of the connection do the given option; DONT requests it *not* to do the option. WILL informs it that C-Kermit will do the option; WONT tells it that C-Kermit will *not* do the option.

The options are:

BINARY

Binary mode, in which all data except IAC may be sent "raw" without any form of quoting or escaping.

ECHO

This parameter determines which party performs the echoing of characters.

NAWS

Negotiate About Window Size. If both parties agree to this option, then they can send messages to inform each other of their screen dimensions.

SGA

Suppress Go Ahead. This one is also used in echo control, and generally must be negotiated for remote echoing.

TTYPE

Terminal Type. If both parties agree to this option, they can inform each other of their terminal type.

Making LAT Connections

Digital Equipment Corporation LAT (Local Area Transport) is a protocol designed for use on local area networks and, when VAX or Alpha computers are involved, is similar to TELNET in that it allows logging in to the VMS or UNIX computer and having an interactive terminal session.

LAT networking is provided either by Digital as part of its PATHWORKS product or by its licensee, Meridian Technology, as SuperLAT. As of this writing, PATHWORKS is supported by Kermit/2 on OS/2 and SuperLAT is supported by Kermit 95 on Windows 95 and NT. For PATHWORKS, the commands are:

SET NETWORK TYPE DECNET
Specifies DECnet PATHWORKS LAT as the networking method.

SET HOST *nodename*
Makes a LAT connection to the specified DECnet node on the local network.

Once these two commands are executed successfully, you can use all of Kermit's communication features — terminal emulation, file transfer, scripting, etc — in the same way you would on a serial or TCP/IP connection. Similarly, for SuperLAT:

SET NETWORK TYPE SUPERLAT
Specifies Meridian Technology SuperLAT as the networking method.

SET HOST *service-name [password]*

Makes a LAT connection to the specified DECnet node on the local network. *service-name* is normally the DECnet host (node) name of the system you are connecting to. It can also be a node/port combination (no spaces), with a a (forward) slash separating the node and port designations, for example to access a specific modem port on a DECserver. If the service is password-protected, you must also include a password after the service-name or node/port. Examples:

```
C-Kermit> set network type superlat  (Network type)
C-Kermit> set host myvax              (Service name)
C-Kermit> set host myvax secret       (Service name with password)
C-Kermit> set host latbox/3           (Serial Port 3 on LATBOX)
C-Kermit> set host latbox/3 secret    (Ditto, with password)
```

Note: Uploading files (see Chapter 9) on a LAT connection is problematic due to intrinsic limitations of LAT buffering. Using 90-byte packets and 1 window slot seems to work in most cases (tell the host Kermit to "set receive packet-length 90"); greater lengths tend to hang the VMS session. Downloads can usually use any packet length or window size.

Warning: When accessing a VMS host, do *not* tell VMS or VMS C-Kermit to disable flow control. VMS C-Kermit *must* have "set flow xon/xoff".

X.25 Networks

X.25 is a wide-area networking method predating TCP/IP by some years, typically used for terminal-to-host connections (similar to TELNET) or host-to-host connections. As of this writing, X.25 connections are supported for Stratus VOS and for Sun computers that have the SunLink X.25 package and a connection to an X.25 network, such as the public data networks found in many countries (SprintNet or Tymnet in the US, Datapac in Canada, for example). Use the SHOW NETWORK command to find out if X.25 support is available in your version of C-Kermit.

For X.25 connections, an X.121 [17] address is used in the SET HOST command; this is a many-digit number usually consisting of a 1-digit prefix, a 4-digit DNIC (Data Network Identification Code) followed by an NTN (Network Terminal Number) up to 10 digits in length, or a 3-digit DCC (Data Country Code) followed by a country-dependent NN (National Number) up to 11 digits in length. For example, the following sequence might set up a connection to a hypothetical host in Brazil (Country Code 724):

```
C-Kermit>set parity mark
C-Kermit>set net type x.25
C-Kermit>set host 07240987654321
```

In most cases, you should SET PARITY to MARK (or some other value besides NONE) before attempting to transfer files over an X.25 connection.

Before giving a SET HOST command for an X.25 connection, you can issue the following commands to specify how the connection is to be made:

SET X.25 CALL-USER-DATA { OFF, ON *text* **}**

Lets you specify up to 12 characters of "call user data," usually an identifier or password required by the host you are calling. Consult the instructions from your service provider to see if you need to send call user data and what it should be.

SET X.25 CLOSED-USER-GROUP { OFF, ON *n* **}**

Membership in a closed user group gives you access to addresses that otherwise might be off limits. C-Kermit assumes no user group. If you need to access a service that is in a closed user group, use SET X.25 CLOSED-USER-GROUP ON *n* to specify a closed user group number, 0 to 99.

SET X.25 REVERSE-CHARGE { OFF, ON }

Normally, the caller pays for an X.25 call. If the remote host or service is willing to pay for your call, use SET X.25 REVERSE-CHARGE ON. The default is OFF.

An X.25 terminal connection goes through a PAD (Packet Assembler Disassembler), which is something like an autodial modem or a terminal server. You can converse with it directly (in *command mode*) or have it pass your data through to the selected host (*data mode*). When your local host is connected directly to the X.25 network (as opposed to dialing up a PAD), it takes the place of the PAD, and you have to use C-Kermit commands to control the simulated PAD:

PAD CLEAR

Clears the X.25 virtual circuit. Discards any information that might be in transit.

PAD INTERRUPT

Sends an X.25 interrupt packet.

PAD RESET

Resets the X.25 virtual circuit.

PAD STATUS

Requests a status report from the PAD.

C-Kermit also sets the PAD parameters itself. Each of these commands controls a different PAD parameter. The numbers correspond to CCITT X.3 parameters [13]. X.3 parameter numbers higher than 12 are not necessarily available on all X.25 networks.

SET PAD BREAK-ACTION *n*

X.3 Parameter 7, or what the PAD should do if it receives a BREAK signal (escape-character followed by B) from C-Kermit. *n* is the sum of the following digits: 0 means nothing, 1 means send an X.25 Interrupt packet, 2 means reset the connection, 4 means send an Indication of Break message, 8 means escape back to the PAD, 16 means discard pending output. The default is 21 (= 16 + 4 + 1).

SET PAD CHARACTER-DELETE *n*

X.3 Parameter 16. $n = 0–127$, the ASCII value of the character to be used for erasing a character during terminal emulation. The default is 8 (Ctrl-H, Backspace).

SET PAD CR-PADDING *n*

X.3 Parameter 9, Padding After Carriage Return (CR). $n = 0–255$, the number of padding characters the PAD should send to C-Kermit after sending a CR, default 0.

SET PAD DISCARD-OUTPUT { 0, 1 }

X.3 Parameter 8. 0 means normal data delivery, 1 means discard output, default 0.

SET PAD ECHO { 0, 1 }

X.3 Parameter 2. 0 means the PAD will not echo, 1 means the PAD will echo. The default is 1 (Kermit assumes the PAD will echo). This command also changes Kermit's DUPLEX setting.

SET PAD EDITING { 0, 1 }

X.3 Parameter 15. 0 means you can't edit the lines you type at the PAD before it sends them to the host, 1 means editing is allowed. The default is 1.

SET PAD ESCAPE { 0, 1 }

X.3 Parameter 1. 0 means escaping back to the PAD is not possible, 1 means you can use (DLE) Ctrl-P to escape to the PAD. 32–126 is the ASCII value of a character to use as the escape character. The default is 1.

SET PAD FORWARD *n*

X.3 Parameter 3, Data Forwarding Characters. The PAD forwards the characters it has received to the remote host as soon as it sees the packet forwarding character. $n = 0$ means none, 2 means carriage return. The default is 2, to make X.25 packets correspond as much as possible with Kermit packets. Other possible values are 1 (any alphanumeric character); 4 (ESC, BEL, ENQ, ACK); 8 (DEL, CAN, DC2); 16 (EXT, EOT); 32 (HT, LF, VT, FF); 64 (any other control character).

SET PAD LF-PADDING *n*

X.3 Parameter 14. $n = 0–255$, the number of padding characters to be sent by the PAD after it sends a linefeed. The default is 0.

SET PAD LF-INSERT *n*

X.3 Parameter 13, Linefeed (LF) Insertion after Carriage Return (CR). $n = 0$ means no LF insertion, 1 means the PAD inserts a LF after each CR sent to C-Kermit, 2 means the PAD inserts a LF after each CR received from C-Kermit, 4 means the PAD echoes LF as CRLF. The default is 0.

SET PAD LINE-DELETE *n*

X.3 Parameter 17. $n = 0–127$, the ASCII value of the character to be used for erasing a line when PAD EDIT is 1. The default is 21 (Ctrl-U).

SET PAD LINE-DISPLAY *n*

X.3 Parameter 18. $n = 0–127$, the ASCII value of the character you can type to redisplay an edited line when PAD EDIT is 1. The default is 18 (Ctrl-R).

SET PAD LINE-FOLD *n*

X.3 Parameter 10, Line Folding, or what to do when a line is too long to fit on your screen. $n = 0$ means no line folding, 1–255 specifies the number of graphic characters per line after which the PAD should insert folding characters. The default is 0, and should be kept at 0 during file transfer to prevent damage to Kermit's file transfer packets.

SET PAD PAD-FLOW-CONTROL *{ 0, 1 }*

X.3 Parameter 5. 0 means no flow control by the PAD, 1 means the PAD may send Xon/Xoff flow control to C-Kermit during data transfer; 2 means the PAD may send Xon/Xoff flow control to C-Kermit during data transfer and in PAD command mode. The default is 0, which allows Xon/Xoff flow control to work end-to-end.

SET PAD SERVICE-SIGNALS *{ 0, 1 }*

X.3 Parameter 6, PAD Service and Command Signals. 0 means PAD service signals are not sent to C-Kermit, 1 means PAD service signals sent. The default is 1. Other options, 4–48, select different classes of service signals.

SET PAD TIMEOUT *n*

X.3 Parameter 4, Data Forwarding Timeout. $n = 0–255$ (twentieths of a second), how long the PAD should wait for its packet buffer to fill up or for a forwarding character to appear before it times out and transmits what it has so far. The default is 0, no data forwarding on timeout is required.

SET PAD USER-FLOW-CONTROL *{ 0, 1 }*

X.3 Parameter 12. 0 means the PAD should ignore any flow control characters sent by C-Kermit, 1 means the PAD should pay attention to them. The default is 0.

During CONNECT mode, the following X.25-specific keyboard escape options are available. Type these letters in after typing the CONNECT-mode escape character (normally Control-Backslash):

I   Send an X.25 Interrupt packet. Equivalent to PAD INTERRUPT.

R   (X.25 only) Reset the X.25 connection. Equivalent to PAD RESET.

Named Pipes

Named pipes, normally used as an interprocess communication mechanism, can also be used on a LAN as a networking method. Unlike TCP/IP, LAT, and X.25 networking, however, one cannot normally use named pipe connections for interactive login sessions to UNIX, VMS, or other hosts. Rather, it is a "peer-to-peer" protocol, in this case used directly between two Kermit programs. As of this writing, Named Pipe sessions are available in the OS/2 version of C-Kermit.

In order to use named pipes to communicate across a local area network, both computers must have installed named pipe network support software. Each computer may be a client, a server or both. Each server on a particular network has a unique named pipe server name assigned as part of the Named Pipe software installation.

To have a named pipe connection between two Kermit programs, one of the Kermit programs must the "server" and the other must be the "client". The server is the one that is started first, and that waits for a connection to come in from the client. The server is started this way:

```
C-Kermit> set network type named-pipe pipename
C-Kermit> set host *
```

If the pipename is omitted, "kermit" is used. "SET HOST *" means to wait for a connection to come in from another Kermit program.

Then the client makes a connection to the server:

```
C-Kermit> set network type named-pipe pipename
C-Kermit> set host servername
```

where *pipename* is the pipename used by the server you want to communicate with (default "kermit"), and *servername* is the name of the server on the network. If you specify a servername of "." (period), this means your own computer; e.g. between two copies of C-Kermit running in different windows. Both *pipename* and *servername* are case-independent, and can contain spaces.

Here are some useful scenarios for named-pipe connections:

1. The named-pipe server is in Kermit SERVER mode (Chapter 11). Clients can perform SEND, GET, REMOTE, FINISH, and similar commands.

2. Both Kermit programs are in CONNECT mode, allowing two network users to "chat" interactively with each other. Each user should give the following commands:

```
C-Kermit> set terminal echo local
C-Kermit> set terminal cr-display crlf
C-Kermit> connect
```

To close a named-pipe connection, give the HANGUP command (or the SET HOST command, specifying no hostname) to either the client or the server.

After the client disconnects, the connection will be reset to await the next client. This allows for the use of kermit server as a pseudo-FTP site for those without TCP/IP.

Note: when using named pipes with LAN Server or LAN Manager, only the machine which has the Network Server software is capable of successfully using the SET HOST * command. This is because the client network requesters do not implement the server side of the named-pipe network redirection.

NETBIOS

NETBIOS connections are similar to named pipe connections but use a different underlying networking method. As with named pipes, usually only peer-to-peer connections are available, meaning no login sessions to UNIX, VMS, or similar hosts. However, NETBIOS connections are sometimes available to IBM SNA LU6.2 mainframe systems.

Just as with named pipes, to have a NETBIOS connection connection between two Kermit programs, one Kermit program must the "server" and the other must be the "client." The server is the one that is started first and that waits for a connection to come in from the client. The server is started this way:

```
C-Kermit> set network type netbios localname
C-Kermit> set host *
```

If the *localname* is omitted from the SET TYPE NETWORK NETBIOS command and a HOSTNAME environment variable is defined, that is used; otherwise if a SYSTEMNAME environment variable is defined, that is used; otherwise "kermit" is used. The *localname* must be unique on the NETBIOS network; if not, the SET NETWORK command will fail.

"SET HOST *" means to wait for a connection to come in from another Kermit program.

Then the client makes a connection to the server:

```
C-Kermit> set network type netbios localname
C-Kermit> set host servername
```

where *localname* is the new name used to identify the client Kermit session, and *servername* is the localname of the server's Kermit session. The *localname* and *servername* are case-dependent (alphabetic case matters) and can contain spaces, and can be up to 16 characters in length.

Using the Network Directory

C-Kermit's network directory works like the dialing directory described in Chapter 5, but for networks. You can have zero, one, or more network directory files, and the rules are the same as for dialing directories. For example, you can have multiple entries with the same name, and so on. Please review Chapter 5 for details.

The command to tell Kermit what your network directory files are is:

SET NETWORK DIRECTORY *[file1 [file2 [file3 [. . .]]]]*
   Selects zero, one, or more network directories. If you do not include any filenames, then the network directory feature is disabled and host names or addresses must be given directly to the SET HOST or TELNET command. If you include one or more file-names, then SET HOST and TELNET commands look in each network directory file and collect all the matching entries, if any, prior to dialing.

If you installed C-Kermit according to instructions and you are using the standard initialization file, then the default network directory name is:

```
.knd                          (UNIX, OS-9)
CKERMIT.KND                   (Elsewhere)
```

and if such a file exists, it it used. In the absence of an initialization file, C-Kermit uses the file(s) given by the environment variable K_NET_DIRECTORY, if it is defined, for example (in UNIX ksh):

```
export K_NET_DIRECTORY="/usr/local/ckermit.knd  $HOME/.knd"
```

As with the dialing directory, you can use the LOOKUP command to look things up in the network directory, without actually making a connection, and you can force a name to be used literally, without directory lookup, by prefixing it with an equals sign (=).

Then to actually make a connection, just use the name of a directory entry in place of a host name or address in your SET HOST or TELNET command. The advantages include:

- For TCP/IP hosts, you can make up your own abbreviations that the name servers might not know about.

- For X.25 hosts, you can use names instead of numbers.

- If your version of Kermit supports multiple networks, you don't have to remember to give a SET NETWORK TYPE command when switching network types, because the network type is recorded in the directory.

- Additional information, like the TCP socket number, can also be picked up from the network directory.

The format of the network directory is:

```
entry-name  network-type hostname-or-address other-stuff ; comment
```

where:

entry-name
> Is the name of the entry. It must start with a letter and contain no spaces or tabs.

network-type
> Is one of the network-type keywords acceptable to the SET NETWORK TYPE command, such as TCP/IP, X.25, NETBIOS, etc.

host-name-or-address
> Is the host name or address for this entry, in the format acceptable to the SET HOST command when used with the indicated network type.

other-stuff
> Is optional additional material specific to the network type, described in the following sections.

comment
> Trailing comments are optional. When present, they must begin with a semicolon that is preceded by at least one space or tab. Full-line comments are also allowed, in which case the semicolon is the first non-space, non-tab character on the line.

TCP/IP Entries

For TCP/IP networks, you can follow the *host-name-or-address* with a TCP port (service) name or number, and you can follow that with a user ID. If you include a user ID, it sets the \v(userid) variable (Chapter 17) and, if the service is "login" or 513, the RLOGIN port, it is also automatically sent as part of the contact information. Examples:

```
internic   tcp/ip   internic.net
weather    tcp/ip   madlab.sprl.umich.edu   3000
myhost     tcp/ip   myhost.cmgcorp.com      513      olga
```

Field 4 is the service port, TELNET (23) by default, and so 23 is used for the "internic" entry, 3000 for the "weather" entry, and 513 for the "myhost" entry. Field 5 is the user-name field, used only by the "myhost" entry because the service port is 513 (rlogin).

LAT and SuperLAT Entries

DECNET (PATHWORKS) entries have only the required three fields, but SuperLAT entries can also include a password as the fourth field. Of course, this is not recommended, since it is a security risk to record passwords in a file:

```
myvax      decnet     myvax
dialout3   superlat   latbox/3   secret
```

Table 6-2 X.3 Numeric PAD Parameters and Values

Parameter	SET PAD Command, Values
1	ESCAPE, 0 (none), 1 (DLE), or ASCII value 32–126.
2	ECHO, 0 (PAD doesn't echo) or 1 (PAD echoes).
3	FORWARD, bit-masked option, 0–63, normally 2 (CR).
4	TIMEOUT, twentieths of seconds, 0–255, normally 0.
5	FLOW-CONTROL (by PAD), 0 (none), 1 (online), or 2 (online and command), normally 0.
6	SERVICE-SIGNALS, 0–48, normally 1.
7	BREAK-ACTION, 0–31, normally 21.
8	DISCARD-OUTPUT, 0 (don't discard) or 1 (discard), normally 0.
9	CR-PADDING, 0–255, normally 0 (none).
10	LINE-FOLD, 0–255, normally 0 (don't).
11	Binary speed, not used by Kermit.
12	USER-FLOW-CONTROL, 0 (none) or 1 (Xon/Xoff), normally 0.
13	LF-INSERT, 0–4, normally 0.
14	LF-PADDING, 0–255, normally 0.
15	EDITING, 0 (no editing) or 1 (editing allowed).
16	CHARACTER-DELETE, ASCII value, 0–127, normally 8 (BS).
17	LINE-DELETE, ASCII value, 0–127, normally 21 (Ctrl-U).
18	LINE-DISPLAY, 0–127, normally 18 (Ctrl-R).

X.25 Entries

After the third field (host address), X.25 entries have "keyword parameters" to allow you to supply any combination of parameters without being forced to supply others that are irrelevant or inappropriate. The form of a keyword parameter is *keyword=value* (no spaces). The parameters available for X.25 entries are:

cug   Closed User Group number (0 through 99), if any.

rev   Reverse Call. Values are ON (to reverse the charges) or OFF (to pay for the call).

cud   Call User Data, a string up to 12 characters long to be supplied with the call.

pad   PAD profile, a series of X.3 parameter-number : value combinations separated by commas, containing no spaces, such as 12:1,15:0,16:127,1:1,3:2,5:1. Include any PAD parameters that you want to change from their defaults or from your normal SET PAD configuration. Refer to Table 6-2 and to the SET PAD command.

Here are some sample X.25 entries:

```
myhost        x.25    012345678
yourhost      x.25    876543210   rev=on
privatehost   x.25    987654321   cug=21 cud=secret
pickyhost     x.25    123456789   pad=5:1,12:1,0:33,39:0
```

The first entry simply lets you use a name instead of a long number. The second entry includes the reverse-call parameter. The third specifies a closed user group and some "call user data" to go along with it, and the fourth sets a series of PAD parameters.

NETBIOS and Named Pipe Entries

NETBIOS entries consist of just the three required fields: entry name, network type, and address. Named Pipe entries also need the pipename field: Here are some examples:

```
hosta     netbios      aristotle
hostx     named-pipe   archimedes   whocares
```

Command-Line Options for Network Connections

C-Kermit command-line options provide a way to set certain parameters or initiate certain actions as part of the system command that starts C-Kermit. For example:

```
$ kermit -l /dev/tty04 -b 38400
```

starts C-Kermit with "/dev/tty04" as its communication device ("-l"), with the speed ("-b") set to 38400 bits per second. Alphabetic case is significant in command-line options: −a is not the same as −A. C-Kermit's command-line options are described in Appendix I, but for completeness, those used for network connections are listed here too:

-j *host [service]*

Equivalent to SET NETWORK TYPE TCP/IP, SET HOST *host*. The HOST is an IP host name or address. The default *service* is 23 (Telnet). The *service* name or number can be separated from the *host* by a space, or appended to the *host* with a colon. Examples:

```
$ kermit -j 128.59.39.2
$ kermit -j kermit.columbia.edu
$ kermit -j kermit.columbia.edu 2000
$ kermit -j kermit.columbia.edu:2000
```

-J *host [service]*

Similar to −j. Equivalent to SET NETWORK TCP/IP, TELNET *host*; allows repeated escaping back and reconnecting, and causes C-Kermit to exit automatically when the connection is closed. Just like a Telnet program.

-F *number*

Like −j, but interprets the number as the numeric file descriptor of an already-open TCP/IP connection.

-M *username*

Equivalent to SET LOGIN USERID, primarily for use with RLOGIN connections, e.g.:

```
$ kermit -j kermit.columbia.edu 513 -M olga
```

-X *address*

Equivalent to SET NETWORK TYPE X.25, SET HOST *address*.

-Z *number*

Like -X, but interprets the number as the numeric file descriptor of a connection that is already open, rather than as a numeric X.25 address.

-U *text*

Call User Data for an X.25 connection.

-o *number*

X.25 closed user group.

-u X.25 reverse charge call

-N *number*

NETBIOS adapter number, 0–4.

For example, suppose you want to use Kermit 95 as the Telnet program in Netscape. Fill in the Netscape's blank for "Telnet application" (in the Options menu) like so:

```
c:\k95\k95 -J
```

where "c:\k95\" is Kermit 95's disk and directory.

Command Summary

The following network-related commands were discussed in this chapter:

```
HANGUP
LOOKUP name
PAD { CLEAR, INTERRUPT, RESET, STATUS }
PING [ host ]
RLOGIN [ host [ user-id ] ]
SET HOST [ host [ additional-data ] ]
SET NETWORK DIRECTORY [ file1 [ file2 [ ... ] ] ]
SET NETWORK TYPE { DECNET,NAMED-PIPE,NETBIOS,SUPERLAT,TCP/IP,X.25 }
SET PAD many-things
SET TCP { KEEPALIVE, LINGER, NODELAY, RECVBUF, SENDBUF } ...
SET TELNET { ECHO, BINARY-MODE, NEWLINE-MODE, TERMINAL-TYPE } ...
SET X.25 { CALL-USER-DATA, CLOSED-USER-GROUP, REVERSE-CHARGE } ...
SHOW NETWORK
TELNET [ host [ port ] ]
TELOPT { DO, DONT, WILL, WONT } { BINARY, ECHO, NAWS, SGA, TTYPE }
```

Variable: \v(connection) shows the network type.

## Chapter 7

Using The Services Directory

○ ○ ○ ○
This chapter can be skipped by users of Kermit for Windows 95, Windows NT, or OS/2, since these programs include their own built-in graphical connections database, explained in the appropriate user manual.

The services directory is a step up from the dialing and network directories. Like them, it makes the physical connection, but unlike them it can use any of C-Kermit's communication methods — direct serial, dialed serial, TCP/IP, X.25, LAT, and so on — which is why we have postponed discussion of it until this point. And having made the connection, it also can log you in to the host or service it has connected you to automatically.

The services directory is a plain-text file containing one line, or "entry," for each service that you want to access. The name of the services directory file is `.ksd` in UNIX and OS-9, `ckermit.ksd` in Stratus VOS, and `CKERMIT.KSD` in Windows, OS/2, VMS, AOS/VS, and elsewhere. It can be used only if you are also using the standard C-Kermit initialization file, because that is where the relevant macros are defined (macros, and the mechanisms underlying the services directory, are presented in Chapters 17 through 19).

Each line in the services directory has the following parts:

name-of-entry   login-macro-name   username   connection-details

For example:

```
HP9000 unixlogin olga net tcp/ip hp.xyzcorp.com
```

where HP9000 is the entry name, "unixlogin" is the login macro name, "olga" is the username, and "net tcp/ip hp.xyzcorp.com" are the connection details.

To use this entry, you would give the following command at the C-Kermit prompt:

C-Kermit>access hp9000

or:

C-Kermit>access hp9000 xxxxxx

where "xxxxxx" is your password on the computer you will be accessing. C-Kermit's ACCESS macro handles the connection details: "net" means it's a network connection; "tcp/ip" tells which type of network, and "hp.xyzcorp.com" tells the name or address (in this case, the name) of the computer or service on the network. If you don't supply a password to the ACCESS command, you are prompted for it. You do not (can not, and should not) include passwords in your services directory file.

Here's another example, in which the connection is made by dialing a modem:

COMPUSERVE cislogin 765,4321 call usr /dev/cua 38400 compuserve

Here, "COMPUSERVE" is the entry name, "cislogin" is the name of the login macro, "765,4321" is your CompuServe user ID, and the connection details are: "call usr /dev/cua 38400 compuserve". "Call" means we will be making a phone call; "usr" is the modem type (US Robotics), "/dev/cua" is the name of the SET LINE device, "38400" is the communication speed, and "compuserve" is the name of a dialing directory entry. Of course an actual telephone number could also be used.

Login Macros

Each login macro looks for the appropriate prompts and responds accordingly with your username, password, and/or other information, and then waits until it sees the main prompt of the host or service, or other indication that you have been logged in success-fully. The following login macros are included in the standard C-Kermit initialization file:

UNIXLOGIN

For logging in to all types of UNIX systems: Solaris, HP-UX, Linux, IRIX, DG/UX, NeXTSTEP, OSF/1, SunOS, etc etc. The default system prompt (explained on the next page) is "\10$\32"; that is, linefeed, dollar sign, space.

VMSLOGIN

For logging in to DEC VAX or Alpha VMS systems. The default system prompt is "\13$\32"; that is, carriage return, dollar sign, space. This macro can also be used for logging in to DG AOS/VS systems if you specify a different prompt ("\10)\32").

VMLINELOGIN

For logging into IBM mainframes with VM/CMS over linemode connections.

VMFULLOGIN

For logging into IBM mainframes with VM/CMS over fullscreen connections.

CISLOGIN

For logging in to CompuServe.

DOWLOGIN

For logging in to Dow Jones News/Retrieval.

DJNRSPRINT

For logging in to Dow Jones News/Retrieval over SprintNet.

NOLOGIN

For accessing computers or services that do not require logging in.

Each login macro name must be followed by a username, even NOLOGIN. For NOLOGIN, just include a fake name, like "xxxx", as a place-filler that will not be used. Other login macros can be easily constructed, modeled on those above, as described in Chapters 17–19. If you add or modify login macros, you should put their definitions in your C-Kermit customization file.

Suppose the main prompt of the system or service you are logging in to does not match the default prompt assumed by the login macro? You can override the default with the SET LOGIN PROMPT command:

```
C-Kermit>set login prompt {\10%\32}
C-Kermit>access cshell
```

or you can include a specific prompt in your services directory by grouping it together in curly braces with the login macro name:

```
{macroname prompt}
```

For example:

```
CSHELL     {unixlogin \10%\32}    olga net tcp/ip bsd.xyzcorp.com
CHEMISTRY  {vmslogin \13CHEM$}     OLGA net tcp/ip chem.xyzcorp.com
DG         {vmslogin \13\10)\32}   olga net tcp/ip aos.xyzcorp.com
```

The first example specifies the C-Shell prompt, "% ", rather than the default UNIX (Bourne Shell, K-Shell) prompt of "$ ". The second example accesses a system that has a custom prompt. The third uses the VMSLOGIN macro to access an AOS/VS system by specifying the AOS/VS prompt, ") ", since otherwise the Username: and Password: prompts are the same as for VMS. The "backslash-number" notation is a way of including special (usually nonprintable) characters in C-Kermit commands and files, explained back on page 26. The number is the ASCII character number, such as 10 for linefeed, 13 for carriage return, 32 for space (ASCII codes are listed in Table VII-1 on page 557).

Connection Details

The connection details part of a services directory entry starts with one of the following words, which are names of macros defined in the C-Kermit initialization file:

CALL   The connection is made with a phone call through a modem.

SERIAL   The connection is a direct (dedicated) serial connection.

NET   The connection is made on a network.

TCPCALL   The connection is made by dialing a modem that is connected to a TCP/IP "reverse terminal server."

The subsequent information depends on the type of connection.

CALL must be followed by the following information, in this order:

1. The modem type (a valid SET MODEM TYPE value).

2. The name of the device on your computer to which the modem is connected.

3. The speed, in bits per second, at which to use the device.

4. The telephone number to dial. This can also be the name of an entry in your dialing directory.

SERIAL must be followed by the following information, in this order:

1. The serial device name.

2. The communication speed.

NET must be followed by:

1. The network type: TCP/IP, X.25, DECNET, etc (a valid SET NET value).

2. The name or address of the host or service you want to connect to, or the name of a network directory entry.

3. Additional network-specific information, like a service or socket number. This same information is also obtained from the network directory, so if you include it here too, it takes precedence over whatever was found in the directory.

TCPCALL is followed by the terminal server IP host name or address, the modem type, and the phone number. If a special TCP port number is to be used, it is appended to the IP name or address by a colon, e.g. "dialout.xyzcorp.com:2000".

For TCP/IP network connections, you can include a socket number by appending it to the IP name or address with a colon, for example:

```
WEATHER  nologin  xxxx  net tcp/ip madlab.sprl.umich.edu:3000
```

Create your services directory file with a text editor as a plain-text (ASCII) file. If you are using a word processor, be sure to save your services directory as a plain text file.

To use your services directory, just type "access" and the service name at the C-Kermit prompt, for example:

```
C-Kermit>access hp9000
 olga's password: secret
```

(The password does not actually echo when you type it in response to a password prompt.)

To list your services directory, type "list" at the C-Kermit prompt. To look up a particular services directory entry, type "list" and then the name, for example "list hp9000".

Sample Services Directory

Here is a short example of a services directory. The first entry is for a straightforward TCP/IP connection. The next two show how to specify nonstandard system prompts to the login macro.

The next two, GEOGRAPHY and WEATHER, illustrate public Telnet services on the Internet that are on special TCP service ports, and that do not require a login.

The last one is for a direct null-modem connection between two computers, and the two before that are for modem calls. The CIS entry references a dialing directory entry called "compuserve".

```
KERMIT    unixlogin             olaf   net   tcp/ip kermit.columbia.edu
DG        {vmslogin \10)}       olaf   net   tcp/ip dg.xyzcorp.com
NETBSD    {unixlogin %}         olaf   net   tcp/ip foo.bar.gov
GEOGRAPHY nologin               xxxx   net   tcp/ip martini.eecs.umich.edu:3000
WEATHER   nologin               xxxx   net   tcp/ip madlab.sprl.umich.edu:3000
CONGRESS  nologin               xxxx   net   tcp/ip dra.com
CIS       cislogin     000,0000 call  hayes  /dev/cua  2400 compuserve
DJNR      djnr                  xxxx   call  rolm   /dev/rolm 9600 93,741-8100
DIRECT    unixlogin             olaf   serial        /dev/tty0 19200
```

The formatting is arbitrary. The only requirements are: one entry per line, and at least one space or tab between each field.

To use the services directory, remember that the standard C-Kermit initialization file must have been executed; otherwise the ACCESS, UNIXLOGIN, LIST, and other necessary macros will not have been defined. To check:

```
C-Kermit> access                        (Try it)
?No keywords match - "access"           (Not defined)
C-Kermit> access
Access what?                            (ACCESS is defined)
C-Kermit>
```

Now let's try one of the entries:

```
C-Kermit> list geography
GEOGRAPHY nologin xxxx net tcp/ip martini.eecs.umich.edu:3000

C-Kermit> access geography
Opening /w/u/si/fdc/.knd...
 Trying 141.213.11.44...
Connection successful.
Connecting to host martini.eecs.umich.edu:3000.
The escape character is Ctrl-\ (ASCII 28, FS)
Type the escape character followed by C to get back,
or followed by ? to see other options.
# Geographic Name Server,
# Copyright 1992 Regents of the University of Michigan.
# Version 8/19/92.  Use "help" or "?" for assistance.
.
. New York, NY
0 New York
1 36061 New York
2 NY New York
3 US United States
R County Seat
F 45 Populated place
L 40 42 51 N   74 00 23 W
P 7071639
.quit
C-Kermit>
```

If you type the ACCESS command at the C-Kermit prompt and the connection is made successfully, C-Kermit goes online automatically as shown in the example. If the ACCESS command is executed from a command file or macro, C-Kermit does not go online automatically but, rather, continues executing commands from the command file or macro. This allows easy construction of scripts that automatically make connections and then transfer information, unattended. More about scripts in Chapter 19.

Please note that you do not *have* to have or use a services directory, a dialing directory, or a network directory. They are conveniences that you can use if you want to, but C-Kermit functions perfectly well without any of them.

Finally, if you are using the standard initialization file, which defines the macros described in this chapter, but you don't plan to use the ACCESS macro in a particular session, you can use the "-R" (uppercase) command-line option to have C-Kermit skip over all the directory-related material, and this makes the program start up faster.

## Chapter 8

Terminal Connection

○ ○ ○ ○

If you will not be using C-Kermit in local mode to establish connections to other computers, skip this chapter and proceed to Chapter 9 on page 171 to learn how to transfer files.

Most versions of C-Kermit — UNIX, VMS, AOS/VS, VOS, etc. — provide terminal connection without emulation. These versions act as a "semitransparent pipe" between the remote computer and your terminal, terminal emulator, console driver, or window, which in turn emulates (or is) a specific kind of terminal.

Other versions, such the ones for Windows NT, Windows 95, or OS/2, include full-featured terminal emulators with numerous special features that are covered in separate user manuals.

This chapter covers the fundamentals of terminal connection as they apply to all C-Kermit versions — UNIX, VMS, AOS/VS, VOS, and the rest.

C-Kermit's CONNECT command lets you carry on an interactive dialog with a remote computer or service. It works in both the 7-bit and 8-bit communication environments, on both full and half duplex connections. It includes a mechanism for shifting back and forth between the remote and local computer, a way to record the remote session, various mechanisms for automated host control of your session, character-set conversion, and a key mapping feature.

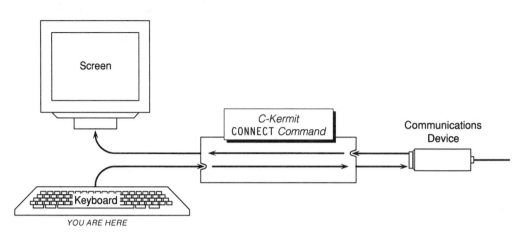

Figure 8-1 Terminal Connection

When you use C-Kermit in local mode, no matter what your connection method—dialup, direct, or network—the method of shifting back and forth between the two computers is the same: use the CONNECT command at the C-Kermit prompt to go to the remote computer, and type a special key sequence to get back to C-Kermit.

The CONNECT Command

CONNECT [/QUIETLY]

The CONNECT command makes C-Kermit act like a terminal to the remote computer. The characters you type on your keyboard are sent to the remote computer, and the characters that arrive from the remote computer are sent to your screen, as shown in Figure 8-1. Once the CONNECT command is given, C-Kermit remains CONNECTed until you "escape back", or the connection is broken, or under certain other conditions explained later. Note:

- The CONNECT command can be abbreviated by a single letter, C, even though it is not the only C-Kermit command begins with C.

- Whenever Kermit enters CONNECT mode, it prints a message several lines long informing you about the connection and telling you how to get back to the C-Kermit prompt. You can surpress this message by including the "QUIETLY" switch:

  C-Kermit> <u>connect /quietly</u>

  or simply "c /q".

- If you type a successful DIAL or ACCESS command at the C-Kermit prompt, C-Kermit goes into CONNECT mode automatically.

Remember: In UNIX, (Open)VMS, VOS, AOS/VS, OS-9, AmigaDOS, and GEMDOS, C-Kermit is *not* a terminal emulator — it is a communications conduit between the remote host and your console, terminal, or emulator. In particular, this means:

- C-Kermit does not interpret (most) escape sequences sent by the host. This includes any kind of terminal identification or status query. When C-Kermit is in CONNECT mode, these sequence are passed through to your terminal or emulator, which should react accordingly.

- C-Kermit does not know anything about the special keys on your keyboard. It can't even "see" them — F-keys, arrow keys, editing keys, and so on, are visible to C-Kermit only insofar as your terminal or emulator has programmed them to send characters or character sequences. If, for example, your up-arrow key sends <ESC>[O, C-Kermit can not tell whether this sequence of characters came from an arrow key or three separate keystrokes.

The Escape Character

Typing the escape character regains the attention of the local C-Kermit program during a CONNECT session. When you give the CONNECT command, C-Kermit tells you what its escape character is:

```
C-Kermit>connect                        (Begin terminal connection)
Connecting to TXA0:, speed 19200.       (Messages from C-Kermit...)
The escape character is Ctrl-\ (ASCII 28, FS).
Type the escape character followed by C to get back,
or followed by ? to see other options.
```

Ctrl-\ (Control-Backslash) is C-Kermit's normal escape character. It is produced by holding down the Ctrl (or Control) key and pressing the backslash (\) key.[17] When C-Kermit reads the escape character from the keyboard, then instead of sending it to the other computer, it waits for you to type a second "command" character, such as the letter *C* to return to the C-Kermit prompt without breaking the connection. You can change the escape character with the SET ESCAPE command:

SET ESCAPE *control-character*

Changes the escape character to the control character of your choice; see page 35 for how to enter a control character in a command. Example:

```
C-Kermit>set esc 2
C-Kermit>show escape
  CONNECT-mode escape character: Ctrl-B (ASCII 2, STX)
```

---

[17]The keyboards on most NeXT workstations do not generate the Control-Backslash character. The NeXT version of C-Kermit uses Control-Rightbracket as its escape character. The OS/2 and Windows versions also use Ctrl-Rightbracket, and they also allow Alt-key equivalents, such as Alt-X.

This changes your CONNECT-mode escape characer to Control-B (ASCII character number 2, called STX). Only 7-bit control characters (codes 0 through 31 and 127) may be used for this purpose. You should select a character that you are unlikely to use at the remote host and that you can generate on your local keyboard. You can use SHOW ESCAPE or SHOW TERMINAL to find out the current escape character.

The mechanics of terminal connection are easy after a few minutes of practice. Use CONNECT to go to the remote host and use Ctrl-Backslash C (hold down the Ctrl key, press the backslash (\) key, then let go of both these keys, then press the C key) to escape back to C-Kermit. If your escape character isn't Ctrl-Backslash, make the appropriate substitution. Now practice going back and forth a few times. In this example, we have a direct connection from a VAX workstation to a central computer:

```
C-Kermit>set line txa0:            (Direct connection)
C-Kermit>set speed 19200           (Set the speed)
C-Kermit>connect                   (Begin terminal connection)
Connecting to ttxa0:, speed 19200.
The escape character is Ctrl-\ (ASCII 28, FS).
Type the escape character followed by C to get back,
or followed by ? to see other options.

WELCOME TO RALPH'S ACADEMY OF BRAIN SURGERY
EARN WHILE YOU LEARN!

Username: olaf                     (Log in)
Password: _____                   (Supply your password)
$ Ctrl-\c                          (Escape back)
C-Kermit>pwd                       (Give a C-Kermit command)
   $DUA0:[OLAF]
C-Kermit>set esc 22                (Change the escape character)
C-Kermit>c                         (Connect again)
Connecting to ttxa0:, speed 19200.
The escape character is Ctrl-V (ASCII 22, SYN).
Type the escape character followed by C to get back,
or followed by ? to see other options.
$                                  (Back at Ralph's)
$ show time                        (Give a command)
   11-JUN-86 11:44:00
$ Ctrl-Vc                          (Escape back again)
C-Kermit>run fortune               (Give a C-Kermit command)
The brain is a wonderful organ; it starts working the moment you
get up in the morning and does not stop until you get to school.
C-Kermit>c                         (Connect again)
```

You can connect and escape back as often as you like. Escaping back does not break the connection. If characters arrive from the remote computer or service while you are not CONNECTed, they are buffered to the capacity of the underlying operating system and displayed next time you CONNECT. If the operating system's buffer becomes too full, flow control, if in effect, should prevent any loss of characters.

Before we leave this topic, let us emphasize that C-Kermit's escape character is the *only* keyboard character that is treated specially in CONNECT mode. Every other character is simply passed on to the remote computer or service.

Suppose, however, that for some reason you did not want *any* characters to be treated specially, and you wanted *all* keyboard characters transmitted immediately, exactly as typed. There is a command for this:

SET TERMINAL ESCAPE { DISABLED, ENABLED }
> SET TERMINAL ESCAPE DISABLED makes C-Kermit totally transparent to all characters that are entered at the keyboard, sending them straight to the host without further ado. In the Windows and OS/2 versions, you can still get back to the C-Kermit prompt with Alt-key combinations such as Alt-X. In the other versions, there is no way to get back to the prompt except (maybe) by logging out from the remote host or service and hoping that C-Kermit notices that the connection dropped and returns to its prompt.

More about this in a few pages . . .

Closing the Connection

When you're finished using the remote computer, you should close the connection. There are several ways to do this. You should try them in this order:

1. If you were logged in to the remote computer or service, log out from it. This should pop you back to the C-Kermit prompt automatically. Example:

```
$ logout
Communications disconnect (Back at local system)
C-Kermit>
```

2. If you're not back at the C-Kermit prompt yet, type *Ctrl-\U* (your CONNECT-mode escape character followed by the letter *U*) to hang "Up" the connection:

```
Ctrl-\u
Communications disconnect (Back at local system)
C-Kermit>
```

3. If you're still not back at the C-Kermit prompt yet, type *Ctrl-\C* to return to the C-Kermit prompt and give the SET LINE command to close the communication device:

```
Ctrl-\c
(Back at local system)
C-Kermit>set line
C-Kermit>
```

If you EXIT or QUIT from C-Kermit, that will also close the communication device and any other open devices or files.

CONNECT-Mode Keyboard Escape Commands

When the CONNECT command is active and TERMINAL ESCAPE is ENABLED, C-Kermit monitors the keyboard for its CONNECT-mode escape character. When you type the escape character, C-Kermit interprets the next character from the keyboard as a CONNECT-mode command. If you press a key that is not a valid CONNECT-mode command, Kermit beeps, ignores the key, and remains in CONNECT mode.

If you type the escape character and then decide you didn't mean to do it, just press the space bar. C-Kermit ignores the escape character and the space bar, and does not beep at you. No characters are transmitted to the remote computer, and Kermit remains in CONNECT mode.

Table 8-1 C-Kermit CONNECT-Mode Escapes

Character	Description
? *or* H	Help—prints the available CONNECT-mode escape options.
! *or* @	Enters the local system command processor. EXIT (DOS, UNIX), LOGOUT (VMS), BYE (AOS/VS) to return to C-Kermit CONNECT mode.
0	(the digit zero) Transmits a NUL (ASCII 0).
A	Sends "Are You There?" (TELNET only).
B	Transmits a BREAK signal.
C	Returns to the C-Kermit prompt without breaking the connection.
I	Sends a network Interrupt request.
L	Transmits a Long BREAK signal.
Q	Hangs up, closes the connection, and Quits from C-Kermit.
R	(X.25 only) Resets an X.25 connection.
S	Shows the status of the connection: device name, speed, parity, etc.
U	Hangs Up the phone or network connection.
Z	(UNIX only) Suspends Kermit. Use the UNIX fg command to continue Kermit's CONNECT session.
SP	(Space) Sends nothing, stays in CONNECT mode.
\	(Backslash) Introduces a backslash code that translates into a single character, for example \127 or \xff.
Ctrl-\	(or whatever your escape character is) Type the escape character twice to send one copy of it to the remote computer.

C-Kermit's escape-character commands are listed in Table 8-1. and are described in the following sections. Letters are shown in uppercase, but they may be entered in either upper- or lowercase. Each command must be preceded by Kermit's CONNECT-mode escape character.

Getting Help: ?, H

Typing the escape character followed by question mark or the letter *H* lists the available CONNECT-mode escape options. These can vary depending on the C-Kermit version and the features it was built with. This message tells you which ones are available in your version. Example:

```
Ctrl-\?
Press C to return to the C-Kermit prompt, or:
 ? for this message
 0 (zero) to send a null
 B to send a BREAK
 L to send a Long BREAK
 U to hangup and close the connection
 Q to hangup and quit Kermit
 S for status
 ! to push to local shell
 Z to suspend
 \ backslash code:
    \nnn  decimal character code
    \Onnn octal character code
    \Xhh  hexadecimal character code
    terminate with carriage return.
 Type the escape character again to send the escape character, or
 press the space-bar to resume the CONNECT command.
Command>
```

After printing the help text, C-Kermit prints a prompt, Command>, and waits for you to enter one of the options just listed.

Returning to the C-Kermit Prompt: C

Typing the escape character followed by the letter *C* returns you to the C-Kermit prompt without breaking the connection to the remote computer. This is called escaping back. After escaping back, you can give commands to C-Kermit to change its settings, transfer files, and so forth. Give another CONNECT command to get back to the remote computer. Example:

```
C-Kermit>connect          (Connect to remote computer)
$                         (Remote computer's prompt)
$ ^\c                     (Escape back to C-Kermit)
C-Kermit>                 (C-Kermit's prompt)
C-Kermit>connect          (Return to remote computer)
$                         (Remote computer's prompt)
```

Here we start out at the local C-Kermit prompt, CONNECT to the remote computer, escape back to the C-Kermit prompt, and CONNECT again.

Status Inquiry: S

Typing the escape character followed by the letter *S* tells Kermit to print a brief message showing the status of the connection and then resume the CONNECT session. Example:

```
C-Kermit>connect
$
$ ^\s
Connected through /dev/ttyh8, speed 9600
Terminal bytesize: 7, Command bytesize: 7, Parity: none
Terminal echo: remote
 Carrier Detect       (CD):  On
 Dataset Ready        (DSR): Off
 Clear To Send        (CTS): Off
 Ring Indicator       (RI):  Off
 Data Terminal Ready  (DTR): On
 Request to Send      (RTS): On
$
```

The report includes the communication device name and relevant parameters, plus (for serial devices only, and only if your system supports it) a report of the RS-232 modem signals (listed and explained briefly in Table II-1 on page 484). The status report is useful if you have trouble communicating during CONNECT mode. The information shown here might indicate the cause: wrong device, wrong speed, a missing modem signal, and so on.

Escape to Local System: !, @, Z

Typing the escape character followed by an exclamation mark (!) or at-sign (@) tells C-Kermit to start an "inferior" copy of your system's command processor, such as the UNIX shell or VMS or AOS/VS command line interpreter, leaving your Kermit connection open.[18] This is similar to putting a telephone call on hold. You can have an interactive dialog with your system for as long as you like without disturbing your Kermit connection. To return to your Kermit CONNECT session, use the appropriate command to exit from the system command processor (EXIT in UNIX, Windows, or OS/2; LOGOUT in VMS; POP in AOS/VS, and so on). Example:

```
$ kermit                           (Start Kermit)
C-Kermit>set line /dev/tty1        (Select communication device)
C-Kermit>set speed 19200           (and speed)
C-Kermit>connect                   (Start CONNECT session)
Connecting to /dev/tty1:, speed 19200, etc...

login: olga                        (Log in)
Password: _____                 (Enter password)
%
% send ivan Hi, are you ordering pizza today?
```

---

[18]If this feature is missing from your version of C-Kermit, then it has been built with the NOPUSH option to prevent users from directly accessing the system from within Kermit.

```
% message from ivan: Yes, but I need the phone number.
% send ivan OK, wait a second...
%
% ^\!                                (Escape to local shell)
$                                    (Note different prompt)
$ grep "Yummy Pizza" phones.txt      (Look up phone number)
Yummy Pizza: 765-4321
$ exit                               (Exit local shell)
%                                    (Resume CONNECT session)
% send ivan It's 765-4321.
%
```

In UNIX only, you can also follow the escape character by the letter Z to suspend Kermit, if SUSPEND is SET to ON. See Appendix III for details.

While Kermit is "pushed from" or suspended, any data that arrives on the communication connection is saved for you in an operating-system buffer. If the buffer becomes full, C-Kermit's flow-control option (if not NONE) should prevent any data loss; on network connections, the network protocols serve the same function.

Sending BREAK Signals: B and L

Typing the escape character followed by the letter *B* tells C-Kermit to transmit a BREAK signal. On serial (terminal device or modem) connections, BREAK is a spacing (0) condition lasting about 275 milliseconds (slightly more than a quarter of a second), required by some hosts, services, and communication processors for transmission speed recognition, to get their attention, or to interrupt a runaway or stuck process. Here's an example showing how to log in to an IBM VM/CMS mainframe over a linemode connection, in which you are instructed to "press BREAK key." The setup and connection details are omitted.

```
C-Kermit>connect
Connecting to /dev/cua, speed 9600...

VIRTUAL MACHINE/SYSTEM PRODUCT--CUVMB    --PRESS BREAK KEY
^\b
!
Enter one of the following commands:
   LOGON userid               (Example:  LOGON VMUSER1)
   LOGOFF
.logon olga
Enter password: _____
.
```

Typing the letter *L* instead of *B* after the escape character tells C-Kermit to transmit a Long BREAK signal. On serial connections, this is a spacing condition lasting about 1.5 seconds that is used to get the attention of certain communication devices.

Network Functions

On network connections, some of the CONNECT-mode escapes behave differently and some additional ones are available. Type the escape character followed by:

A (TELNET only) Send a TELNET "Are You There" message. If the remote TELNET server is active, it will send back a message like "[Yes]." This usually works only on true port-23 TELNET connections, not when you TELNET to non-TELNET ports.

I Send an Interrupt message (X.25 Interrupt or TELNET Interrupt Process). The action taken depends on the network and the remote host. Sending a TELNET interrupt is usually equivalent to typing the remote host's interrupt character.

B Send a network BREAK. Again, the interpretation depends on the network and the remote host. On TELNET connections, a TELNET protocol Break message is sent, which might be interpreted by the remote TELNET server as a stand-in for the BREAK signal as it is used on serial connections, or as an interruption command.

L On network connections, L is treated exactly like B.

Sending Special Characters

Several methods are provided for sending special characters to the remote host during a CONNECT session. Type the CONNECT-mode escape character followed by:

0 (the digit zero) Transmit a NUL (ASCII 0). This is useful if your remote computer or application wants you to send a NUL character, but your keyboard doesn't give you a way to type it.

^ (Ctrl-Backslash, or whatever you have set the escape character to be) Type the escape character twice in a row to send one copy of it to the remote computer. (This is not necessary if you SET TERMINAL ESCAPE DISABLED.)

A more general technique lets you transmit any character at all. If you follow the CONNECT-mode escape character with a Backslash (\) (not Control-Backslash) character, then you can enter a number representing any 7- or 8-bit code for Kermit to send.

The backslash is followed by an optional base indicator: *d* for decimal, *o* for octal, or *x* for hexadecimal, and then a 1-, 2-, or 3-digit number in the indicated base (hexadecimal numbers must be exactly two characters long), which Kermit interprets as a character code between 0 and 255 inclusive. If there is no base indicator, base 10 is assumed.

Terminate the code by pressing the Return or Enter key, and Kermit sends the character represented by the code. The carriage return itself is not sent. If you type an ungrammatical backslash code, Kermit beeps and sends nothing. In all cases, Kermit leaves you in CONNECT mode after processing the backslash code.

Suppose your keyboard has a broken A key. The ASCII code for uppercase A is 65 decimal, 101 octal, or 41 hexadecimal (see Table VII-1). During a CONNECT session, you can transmit it in any of these ways:

```
^\\65     ^\\d65     ^\\o101     ^\\x41
```

For example:

```
I wish my ^\\65
 key worked.
```

The host will receive:

```
I wish my A key worked.
```

Hanging Up and Quitting: U and Q

Typing the escape character followed by the letter *U* tells C-Kermit to hang up. On dialed serial connections when DIAL MODEM-HANGUP is ON, Kermit attempts to put the modem in command mode and then gives it the command to hang up the phone. If MODEM-HANGUP is OFF, or if it doesn't work, or if the modem type is DIRECT, Kermit turns off the Data Terminal Ready (DTR) signal for about half a second. If your serial communication device is connected to a modem, this is supposed to signal the modem to hang up the phone connection. Network connections are simply closed. If you are running C-Kermit in interactive mode, a successful hangup should return you automatically to the C-Kermit prompt. If you started C-Kermit with the -c, -n, or -j command-line option, hanging up should return you to the system prompt (see Appendix I). Typing *Q* instead of *U* after the escape character tells C-Kermit to hang up and then quit (exit), returning you to the system prompt no matter how you started C-Kermit.

Setting Terminal Parameters

The following commands control the number of data bits used during C-Kermit's CONNECT command and other terminal-oriented operations.

SET COMMAND BYTESIZE { 7, 8 }

Tells whether to use 7 or 8 data bits per character on the connection between C-Kermit and your keyboard and screen, shown in Figure 8-2 (next page) as (A). In Windows and OS/2, the default is to use 8 data bits; in UNIX, VMS, and the other versions, it is to use 7 data bits and ignore the 8th bit. This setting applies to both command mode (when you see the C-Kermit prompt) and CONNECT mode.

SET TERMINAL BYTESIZE { 7, 8 }

Tells whether the CONNECT command should use 7 or 8 data bits per character on the connection between C-Kermit and the other computer, (B) in Figure 8-2. The default in all C-Kermit versions is to use 7 data bits. If you give a value of 8, then 8-bit characters are used if PARITY is set to NONE, otherwise 7-bit characters are still used.

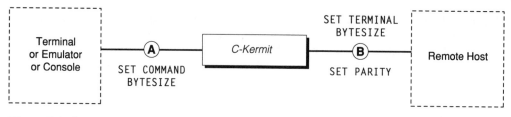

Figure 8-2 Command and Terminal Bytesize

SET PARITY { EVEN, ODD, MARK, SPACE, NONE }

Tells which kind of parity to use on the connection between C-Kermit and the remote computer, (B). The default parity is NONE. A PARITY setting of EVEN, ODD, MARK, or SPACE causes C-Kermit to use 7 data bits per character, regardless of the TERMINAL BYTESIZE setting. A PARITY setting of NONE allows the TERMINAL BYTESIZE setting to determine the number of data bits per character.

Remember, the default setting for PARITY is NONE, and the default setting for TERMINAL BYTESIZE is 7. This is because it is common for remote hosts or services, or the devices that connect you to them, to use (add or strip) parity bits. And it is just as common for users to be unaware of it.

If the terminal bytesize bytesize were set to 8 rather than 7 by default, parity bits on characters arriving from the remote host or service would change them into other characters and you would see gibberish on your screen. If C-Kermit's default parity was not NONE, this could prevent non-parity connections from working.

The default settings allow the initial connection to be made successfully in most cases. If your connection needs parity, then SET the appropriate kind. If you are using a VT220 or higher emulator to access a VMS system, you must either tell Kermit to SET TERM BYTE 8 or tell VMS to SET TERM /NOEIGHT. If you need to use 8-bit accented or non-Roman characters, be sure to read Chapter 16.

SET TERMINAL CHARACTER-SET *remote-cset [local-cset]*

Specifies the remote and local character sets so C-Kermit can translate between them during CONNECT sessions. The default terminal character-set is TRANSPARENT, which means that characters are not translated during terminal connection. This command and character sets in general are discussed in Chapter 16.

SET TERMINAL ECHO { LOCAL, REMOTE }

Tells whether C-Kermit should echo the characters you type locally (LOCAL) or let the remote computer echo them (REMOTE). The default is REMOTE except for TELNET network connections, where it is LOCAL until and unless renegotiated by TELNET protocol or overriden by a SET TELNET ECHO command (see Chapter 3). If characters don't echo when you type them, you should SET TERMINAL ECHO LOCAL. If characters echo twice when you type them, then SET TERMINAL ECHO REMOTE. The SET DUPLEX and SET LOCAL-ECHO commands perform the same functions as this command.

SET TERMINAL LOCKING-SHIFT { ON, OFF }

Tells whether C-Kermit should use Shift-In and Shift-Out control characters (Ctrl-N and Ctrl-O) for transmitting 8-bit characters on a 7-bit connection between C-Kermit and the remote computer during a CONNECT session (see Chapter 16 for a fuller discussion of this feature). This setting applies in both directions: to characters you type at the keyboard and to characters arriving from the remote computer or service.

SET TERMINAL NEWLINE-MODE { ON, OFF }

Tells whether C-Kermit should automatically convert carriage return (CR, ASCII 13) characters typed at the keyboard into carriage-return-linefeed combinations (CRLF, ASCII 13 and ASCII 10) before transmission. Normally OFF. Don't use this one unless the remote host or service seems to ignore your commands, or your commands seem to overwrite one another or stay on the same line.

SET TERMINAL CR-DISPLAY { CRLF, NORMAL }

This is like SET TERMINAL NEWLINE-MODE, but in the opposite direction. It tells whether carriage return characters received from the communication device should be displayed as carriage return only (NORMAL, the default) or as carriage return and linefeed (CRLF). Use the CRLF option when connected to a device that terminates its output lines with bare carriage returns.

SHOW TERMINAL

Displays your current terminal settings:

```
C-Kermit>sho term
Terminal parameters:
    Bytesize: Command: 7 bits          Terminal: 7 bits
                Type: vt320
                Echo: remote      Locking-shift: off
        Newline-mode: off           Cr-display: normal
                 APC: off         Autodownload: off
              Height: 24                 Width: 80
               Debug: off          Session log: (none)

    CONNECT-mode escape character: 28 (Ctrl-\, FS): enabled
    Terminal character-set: transparent
```

In the Windows and OS/2 versions (which also have a much longer SHOW TERMINAL display), the "Type:" is your current terminal emulation. In the UNIX, VMS, and other versions that do not include terminal emulators, the terminal type is obtained by asking the underlying operating system system what it thinks your terminal type is.

Coordinating Screen Dimensions

The SHOW TERMINAL display includes C-Kermit's idea of your screen size:

```
Height: 24     Width: 80
```

When using C-Kermit's CONNECT command to access full-screen applications on the host, it is important that the host and C-Kermit (or the terminal or emulator from which you are controlling C-Kermit) agree about your screen dimensions, especially when your screen is not the standard 24×80 size. If SHOW TERMINAL displays an incorrect number of rows or columns (including -1, which means "I don't know"), that means that C-Kermit was unable to obtain the correct information from the underlying operating system. In that case, you can use the following commands to inform C-Kermit about your terminal dimensions:

SET TERMINAL HEIGHT *number*

This command tells C-Kermit the number of rows (lines) on the command screen.

SET TERMINAL WIDTH *number*

This command tells C-Kermit the number of columns (characters) across the command screen. *NOTE:* In Kermit 95 and Kermit/2, these commands also *change* the size of your terminal screen.

C-Kermit uses this information to inform the remote host about your screen size during TELNET or Rlogin negotiations, and it to set its built-in \v(cols) and \v(rows) variables so you can use them in scripts.

Nevertheless, there are still numerous ways in which the remote host or service can fail to learn your true screen dimensions automatically. In such cases, there is usually a command you can use to inform the system of your screen dimensions. For example, most UNIX systems allow something like:

```
stty rows 55 cols 80
```

In VMS it would be:

```
set term /page=55 /width=80
```

Once you have entered CONNECT mode and logged into the remote computer, you should use the appropriate command to check its idea of your screen dimensions, such as the `stty -a` (or similar) command in UNIX, SHOW TERMINAL in VMS, etc.

Some hosts offer commands that send escape sequences to query your terminal emulator about its dimensions. In UNIX it is usually:

```
`eval resize`
```

(*with* the "backquotes") and in recent VMS versions the SET TERMINAL /INQUIRE command has incorporated this function.

Key Mapping

C-Kermit can substitute any character or character string for keys that you press during a CONNECT session. For keys that produce 7- or 8-bit codes, the default assignment for each key is itself, that is, the key transmits the code that it produces when you press it. You can use the following commands to change the default assignments.

SHOW KEY

Tells Kermit to ask you to press a key. When you do, Kermit shows you the code value of the key and the key's current definition. Here is an example using a NeXT workstation:

```
C-Kermit>set command bytesize 8
C-Kermit>show key
 Press key: Alt-s
 Key code \251 => Character: ß \251 (self, no translation)
```

The user types Alt-s (holds down the Alternate key and presses the s key). On the NeXT, this produces "German sharp s" (ß, Ess-Zet). 251 is the key code. It is shown in decimal. In most C-Kermit versions, only 7-bit or 8-bit code values are accessible. In the Windows and OS/2 versions, any key or key combination can be mapped.

SET KEY *key-code [definition]*

Assigns the given definition to any (and all) key(s) that produce the given key code. The *key-code* may be a simple decimal number or a backslash code used to express the number in decimal, octal, or hexadecimal notation (Table 2-4). Normally you would use the same notation for the key as SHOW KEY displays for it. The *definition* can be a single character, expressed literally (if possible) or in backslash notation, or a string of characters (possibly containing backslash codes). If the definition is omitted, the key's default definition is restored. Here are some examples, in which we assign various values to the NeXT Alt-s key:

```
C-Kermit>set key \251 \28            (Ctrl-Backslash)
C-Kermit>set key \251 x              (The single character 'x')
C-Kermit>set key \251 ss             (Double 's')
C-Kermit>set key \251 Oh my, this is a wordy keystroke!\13
C-Kermit>set key \251                (Restore default value)
```

SET KEY CLEAR

This command erases all key definitions.

SAVE KEYMAP *filename*

Saves the current key settings in a file that can be TAKEn.

C-Kermit's SET KEY command has several restrictions:

• If you use SET KEY to assign CONNECT-mode escape commands to single keys, the characters assigned to the key are transmitted, rather than treated as escapes.

- If you include a NUL (ASCII 0, \0) value in a key definition, it terminates the definition, and the NUL character itself is not transmitted when you press the key.

- In C-Kermit versions that do not include built-in terminal emulation, you can't use SET KEY with function, arrow, editing, or other special keys that produce a multibyte value or a scan code greater than 255.

- To use 8-bit key codes, you must first SET COMMAND BYTESIZE 8. The method for entering 8-bit characters depends on your computer, operating system, terminal emulator (if any), keyboard, and keyboard driver.

A common use for the SET KEY command is to relocate inconveniently placed keys for easy typing. For example, some keyboards have the Esc (Escape) key far off in right field, out of reach, and the accent-grave (backquote) key where you want the Esc key to be. Use SET KEY to swap them:

```
C-Kermit>set key \96 \27
C-Kermit>set key \27 \96
```

Another common use of SET KEY is to change what is sent by your BACKSPACE key. Some hosts expect DEL (Delete, ASCII 127), others expect BS (Backspace, Ctrl-H, ASCII 8). This example assigns ASCII BS to the NeXT's backspace key, whose key code (and therefore default assignment) is 127:

```
C-Kermit>set key \127 \8
C-Kermit>set key \8 \127
```

In the non-terminal emulating versions of C-Kermit (for UNIX, VMS, etc), SET KEY assignments are effective only while the CONNECT command is active. When you press a key that has been given a definition with SET KEY, all terminal and communication settings are applied to the characters in its definition before they are sent, just as if you had typed the definition characters on the keyboard during CONNECT mode.

C-Kermit in the Middle

Let's say you have a PC at home with Windows 95, and you use Kermit 95 to dial up the VMS (or UNIX, etc) computer at your job, and from there you use C-Kermit to dial or TELNET out to some distant place — the situation shown in Figure 3-3 back in Chapter 3. Let's call your home PC Computer A, the computer you have dialed Computer B, and the most distant one Computer C. C-Kermit on Computer B is *in the middle*.

There are several interesting wrinkles to this situation. First, let's assume that Kermit's escape character on both computers A and B is the same, Ctrl-Backslash, and that the Kermits on both A and B are in CONNECT mode, so you are having an online dialog with

Computer C. What happens when you type Ctrl-Backslash C? (Try it and see.) Right, you come back to Computer A's Kermit prompt. But what if you want to come back to Computer B's Kermit prompt? Hint: Look at the last item in Table 8-1, page 152. So you have to type *two* Ctrl-Backslashes. Why? Because Computer B's Kermit needs to see *one* Ctrl-Backslash, and typing *two* Ctrl-Backslashes to Computer A is the way to send *one* of them to Computer B.

Now suppose you use C-Kermit on Computer C to make make a connection to a fourth host, Computer D, and again, the escape character for C-Kermit on Computer C is Ctrl-Backslash. How would you escape back to Computer C?

> Optional exercise for the mathematically inclined: If Computer X_n is n hops away, how would you escape back to Computer X_{n-1}? *(To find the answer, turn to page 169 at the end of this chapter* :-)

(To find the answer, turn to page 169 at the end of this chapter :-)

Knowing the answer to this question might be important some day when you need to transfer a file between two different computers at arbitrary points along the chain. You need to escape back to the right one!

But that's not all you need to know. There is also the issue of transparency. By default, when C-Kermit is in CONNECT mode, it gives you a seven-bit connection, so 8-bit data will not pass through it. This includes 8-bit character sets as well as binary data, and so can prevent all sorts of operations that require a clear 8-bit path, including VT320 emulation, XYZMODEM (but not Kermit) file transfer, and the use of Latin-1, Latin-2, Russian, Hebrew, Japanese, or other character sets that use the 8th bit. To make the connection transparent to all eight bits, give these commands to C-Kermit on Computer B prior to entering CONNECT mode:

```
C-Kermit> set parity none
C-Kermit> set command bytesize 8
C-Kermit> set terminal bytesize 8
```

Now suppose Computer C offers only the XMODEM protocol for transferring files. Kermit 95 supports XMODEM too, but all attempts at using it between computers A and C fail, because there is *another* component to transparency: transparency to all control characters. Protocols such as XMODEM use every possible bit pattern, including all control characters. But C-Kermit on computer B has reserved one control character, Ctrl-Backslash in our example, as its escape character. As soon as XMODEM on Computer A sends its first Ctrl-Backslash character, this causes C-Kermit on Computer B to enter its escape-character processing procedure, and what it does next depends entirely on the next character to arrive. In any case, it will *not* do what is needed, namely pass the escape character through as ordinary data. To achieve transparency to the escape character, give the following command to C-Kermit on Computer B prior to entering CONNECT mode:

```
C-Kermit> set terminal escape off
```

(Remember that you never will be able to escape back to Computer B's Kermit prompt after giving this command, so you should test first whether the automatic pop-back on loss of connection works here.)

But there's more. If C-Kermit on Computer B is using Xon/Xoff flow control, it won't be transparent to Ctrl-Q and Xoff Ctrl-S characters. So:

```
C-Kermit> set flow none
```

(or SET FLOW RTS/CTS, as appropriate). Also, if C-Kermit on Computer B had been told to SET TERMINAL LOCKING-SHIFT ON, it will not be transparent to Ctrl-N and Ctrl-O characters, so:

```
C-Kermit> set terminal locking-shift off
```

Finally, C-Kermit on Computer B will not be not transparent even to ordinary printable characters if you have instructed it to do character-set translation. So also be sure to:

```
C-Kermit> set terminal character-set transparent
```

Now, with just two more commands, explained in the next section, we can achieve total transparency:

```
C-Kermit> set terminal autodownload off
C-Kermit> set terminal apc off
```

Let's find out what these are . . .

Automatic Actions While in CONNECT Mode

We haven't explained file transfer yet, but in the spirit of collecting all the information about CONNECT mode in one place, this might be a good time to mention that most versions of C-Kermit, when in CONNECT mode, can detect when a Kermit (and in some cases also ZMODEM) file transfer has been been initiated by the remote host or service; C-Kermit automatically activates the appropriate file-transfer protocol, transfers the file, and then automatically puts you back in CONNECT mode when the transfer is done. More about this in Chapter 13, after we have discussed file transfer.

If you are using a version of C-Kermit, such as Kermit 95, that is at the local end of the connection — not "in the middle," as described in the previous section — then automatic transfer is usually a convenient and desirable feature. But if you are also going through a copy of C-Kermit that is in the middle, you would not want automatic transfers enabled in both your local Kermit program and the one in the middle; if they were, then both Kermits would go into protocol mode at the same time, Very Confusing!

To minimize the confusion, the Windows and OS/2 versions, and any other version that is used only in local mode, have automatic transfers permitted by default, but in the other versions (VMS, UNIX, VOS, AOS/VS — the ones that can find themselves in the middle), automatic transfers are disabled unless you enable them. The command to control automatic transfers is:

SET TERMINAL AUTODOWNLOAD *{* **ON**, **OFF** *}*

If you are using Kermit software to make a multihop connection, use the SET TERMINAL AUTODOWNLOAD command to enable automatic transfers on the desired computer and to disable it on the other(s).

Similarly, the remote computer can send an escape sequence that causes your local Kermit program to execute commands. This is called the Application Program Command (APC) sequence; it is discussed in Chapter 13. For purposes of this chapter, you should know the command for enabling and disabling APCs:

SET TERMINAL APC *{* **ON, OFF, UNCHECKED** *}*

The default setting is OFF, and should remain so until you have read Chapter 13.

Logging and Debugging Your Terminal Session

You can have C-Kermit copy all the characters that appear on your screen during a CONNECT session to a file called the session log. You can also make C-Kermit display control and 8-bit characters graphically rather than passing them directly to your terminal emulator or console driver. Here are the commands:

LOG SESSION *[filename [{* **APPEND, NEW** *}]]*
This command tells C-Kermit to copy the characters that are sent to your screen into the file whose name is given, as well as displaying them on the screen in the normal way. If no filename is given, Kermit creates a new file called SESSION.LOG in your current directory. The trailing keyword, APPEND or NEW, tells whether to append the session log to the end of an existing file or to create a new file. The default is NEW.

Characters are recorded in their 8-bit form if PARITY is NONE and TERMINAL BYTESIZE is 8. Otherwise only 7-bit characters are logged. If the terminal character set is not TRANSPARENT, the characters are recorded after translation.

The SHOW FILE command displays the name of your current session log file. It is also shown in the CONNECT message and by the CONNECT-mode status-display request:

```
C-Kermit>log ses            (Start a session log)
C-Kermit>connect            (Begin terminal connection)
Connecting to /dev/ttyh8, speed 9600
```

```
...
(Session logged to /usr/olga/session.log, text)
login: Ctrl-\S                    (Status request)
...
Logging to: /usr/olga/session.log
```

CLOSE SESSION

Terminates session logging and closes your session log file. The log file is also closed automatically when you EXIT from C-Kermit.

SET SESSION-LOG { BINARY, TEXT }

(UNIX, AOS/VS, and OS-9 only) A binary-mode session log contains every character that is received from the remote computer, including NUL and DEL padding characters, Xon and Xoff (if they are passed through by the terminal driver), as well as carriage returns.

When the session-log type is TEXT, C-Kermit discards NUL, DEL, and CR characters, so the result is more likely to be usable as a UNIX or AOS/VS text file; in OS-9, carriage returns are kept and linefeeds are discarded. This command has no effect in VMS, Windows, OS/2, or C-Kermit's other operating systems. TEXT is the default type of session log.

SET TERMINAL DEBUG { ON, OFF }

This command changes your CONNECT-mode screen into a kind of data analyzer. Control and 8-bit characters are displayed graphically[19]. For example, Ctrl-A is displayed as ^A, ESC is displayed as ^[, etc. (see Table VII-2). An 8-bit character is shown as a tilde (~) followed by the 7-bit version of the character, for example the bit pattern 11000001 is displayed as ~A. On a TELNET connection, TELNET protocol negotiations are displayed on the screen.

Terminal character sets are not translated when TERMINAL DEBUG is ON. The 8-bit character indication (~) is not shown if PARITY is anything besides NONE or if the TERMINAL BYTESIZE is 7.

TERMINAL DEBUG is OFF by default.

Here is an example of a debugging display on a TELNET connection, in which both TELNET negotiations and control characters are displayed symbolically:

```
C-Kermit>set terminal debug on
C-Kermit>telnet kermit
```

---

[19]The OS/2 and Windows versions use a more sophisticated debugging display; see the appropriate manuals for further information.

```
[WILL TERMINAL TYPE][DO SUPPRESS GO AHEAD]<DO TERMINAL TYPE><WIL
L SUPPRESS GO AHEAD><SB TERMINAL TYPE 01 IAC SE>[SB TERMINAL TYP
E 00 VT300 IAC SE]<WILL ECHO>[DO ECHO]<DO ECHO>^M^J^M^JSunOS UNI
X (kermit)^M^J^M^@^M^J^M^@login: olaf^M^JPassword:^M^JLast login
: Sat Jul  4 16:20:45 from thorn.^M^JSunOS Release 4.1.1 (KERMIT
) #1: Mon Sep 23 20:11:19 EDT 1994^M^J^M^J^[[1;24r^[[24;1H^M^@We
lcome to /dev/ttyp6^M^J$ exit^M^J[WONT ECHO]<DONT ECHO>
```

The TELNET options that Kermit sends are enclosed in square brackets and the ones it receives are enclosed in angle brackets. `^[[1;24r^[[24;1H` is a screen setup command for a VT terminal. `^M^J` is a carriage return and linefeed sequence, and `^@` is a NUL.

Using the terminal debug display, you can pinpoint misbehaving TELNET negotiotions so you can correct them with the appropriate SET TELNET commands, as explained in Chapter 6. You can also use it to find control characters or escape sequences that might be causing trouble, so you can get an idea of what sort of remedy needs to be applied.

Finally, the debugging display lets you see exactly what characters arrive — including ones that you normally could not see — which might be that essential bit of information needed to get a script program working. More about scripts in Chapters 17–19.

Command Summary

Here is a concise list of C-Kermit's CONNECT-related commands. Recall that each keyword can be shortened to any length that still distinguishes the keyword from any other keyword that can appear in the same position. Also note that the Windows and OS/2 versions have numerous additional SET TERMINAL commands affecting their specific terminal emulation features.

CLOSE SESSION
CONNECT *[/QUIETLY]*
LOG SESSION *[filename [{* APPEND, NEW *}]]*
SET COMMAND BYTESIZE *{* 7, 8 *}*
SET ESCAPE *number*
SET KEY *key-code [definition]*
SET PARITY *{* EVEN, ODD, MARK, SPACE, NONE *}*
SET SESSION-LOG *{* BINARY, TEXT *}*
SET TERMINAL APC *{* ON, OFF, UNCHECKED *}*
SET TERMINAL AUTODOWNLOAD *{* ON, OFF *}*
SET TERMINAL BYTESIZE *{* 7, 8 *}*
SET TERMINAL CHARACTER-SET *remote-cset [local-cset]*
SET TERMINAL CR-DISPLAY *{* CRLF, NORMAL *}*
SET TERMINAL DEBUG *{* ON, OFF *}*
SET TERMINAL ECHO *{* LOCAL, REMOTE *}*
SET TERMINAL ESCAPE *{* DISABLED, ENABLED *}*
SET TERMINAL HEIGHT *number*
SET TERMINAL LOCKING-SHIFT *{* ON, OFF *}*
SET TERMINAL NEWLINE-MODE *{* ON, OFF *}*
SET TERMINAL WIDTH *number*
SHOW KEY
SHOW TERMINAL

To make a CONNECT session totally transparent:

SET PARITY NONE
SET FLOW NONE *or* RTS/CTS
SET COMMAND BYTESIZE 8
SET TERMINAL APC OFF
SET TERMINAL AUTODOWNLOAD OFF
SET TERMINAL BYTESIZE 8
SET TERMINAL CHARACTER-SET TRANSPARENT
SET TERMINAL ESCAPE OFF
SET TERMINAL LOCKING-SHIFT OFF

Variables:

\v(cols)	Number of columns (characters) across the screen.
\v(rows)	Number of rows (lines) on the screen.
\v(terminal)	Terminal type.

THE TELNET SONG
("Control–Uparrow Q.")

A function of N.
N = 4 is recommended.

Words and music by
The Great Quux

There is a pro—gram called TEL-NET that gets to a— noth-er C—P— U. Con—trol up— ar— row is the es—cape; it's dou-bled to send it through, and "quit" is con—trol up— ar— row Q. A hack—er once used TEL-NET to get to a—noth—er C— P— U. He knew he could quit when—ev—er he want-ed to: all he had to do was type con— trol up— ar— row Q. In—stead the hack-er used TEL-NET to get to a— noth—er C— P— U. He knew he could quit when— ev—er he want—ed to: all he had to do was type con—trol up—ar—row, con— trol up—ar—row Q. In— Q. The hack—er soon grew bored with this, and want—ed to get back. He sighed, and start-ed the ex—po— nen—tial pop—ping of the stack: The hack—er flushed the TEL-NET to the most dis—tant C— P— U; He

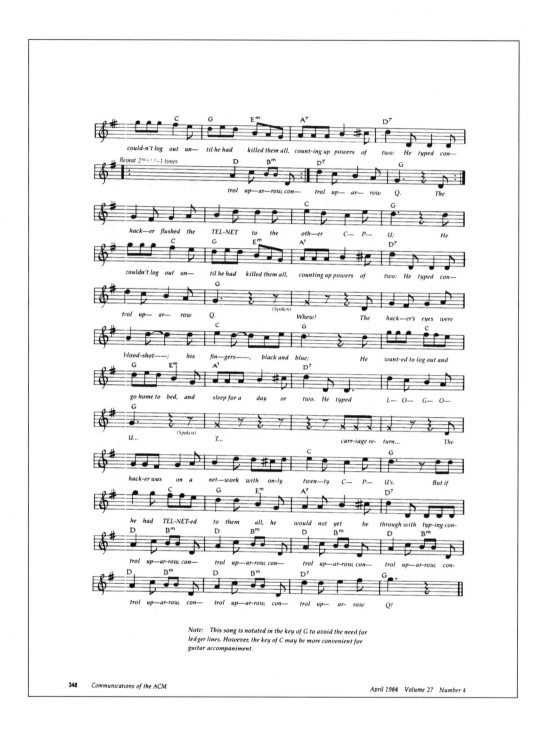

Note: This song is notated in the key of G to avoid the need for ledger lines. However, the key of C may be more convenient for guitar accompaniment.

Chapter 9

The Basics of File Transfer

○ ○ ○ ○
This chapter explains the basic method for transferring files from one computer to another using the Kermit protocol. The next several chapters discuss selected aspects of file transfer in greater depth: how to solve file-transfer problems, how to use Kermit software in a client/server setting, how to maximize file-transfer performance, and how to incorporate character-set translation into the file transfer process. VMS users should also read Appendix IV for special procedures used for VMS file transfer.

Getting Started

The Kermit protocol transfers files from one computer to another and it requires Kermit software on both computers. Kermit programs communicate with each other using formatted messages called packets (see Chapter 12 for more detail about packets). If packets are lost, duplicated, or damaged during transmission, the receiving Kermit notifies the sending Kermit and corrective action is taken automatically to ensure your files are transferred without error. For a detailed description of the Kermit protocol, see the book *Kermit, A File Transfer Protocol* [21].

We assume you understand the terms "local computer" and "remote computer," and you are able to connect your local computer to the remote one with Kermit communications software. If necessary, please review Chapter 3 or consult the documentation for your local Kermit program if it is not C-Kermit.

Automation and How to Stifle It

Kermit file transfers can be done The Old Fashioned Way, in which you instruct each Kermit program what to do, or using the more convenient "client/server" arrangement presented in Chapter 11, or in most modern Kermit programs, automatically when the terminal emulator recognizes a Kermit packet. We have already alluded to the latter method in Chapter 8, a few pages back.

To recapitulate, if C-Kermit (or MS-DOS Kermit, or Kermit 95, or Kermit/2) is in CONNECT mode and it "sees" a Kermit protocol packet on its screen and if its TERMINAL AUTODOWNLOAD setting is ON, it automatically engages the other Kermit program in the type of file transfer indicated by the observed packet — no hands!

But before you can use the ultra-convenient automatic method without mishap, you need to understand the basics, so until we say otherwise, please issue the following command to your local Kermit program (the one whose CONNECT command you are using) before following any of the examples in this chapter:

SET TERMINAL AUTODOWNLOAD OFF

This is like learning to drive with a manual transmission before being allowed to use an automatic one. It helps you understand what is going on under the hood so you can make better use of your car. But perhaps more important, some day you might really *have* to drive a stick-shift. Not all Kermit implementations are automatic!

Basic File Transfer Commands

The basic file transfer commands are SEND and RECEIVE. One computer's Kermit must be told to send a file and the other computer's Kermit program must be told to receive it.

The SEND Command

SEND *filespec*
    Sends the file or files denoted by *filespec* to the Kermit program on the other computer, which must be given a RECEIVE command.

The *filespec* is allowed to contain "wildcard" characters, allowing multiple files to be sent. A wildcard is a special character used in a filename to denote a group of files whose names match a given pattern. Wildcards are also called *metacharacters* (in UNIX) or *templates* (in AOS/VS).

Wildcard syntax varies from system to system. Table 9-1 gives a summary of special characters that can be used in filenames on systems where C-Kermit runs (the DOS

Table 9-1 Special Characters in C-Kermit File Specifications

Field or Pattern	UNIX	VMS	AOS/VS	DOS	OS-9	Amiga	Atari
Username	~				~		~
The directory separator	/	[.]	:	\ or /	/	/	\
The current directory	.	[]	=	.	.		.
The superior directory	..	–	^	..	..	/	..
* Inferior directories		...	#				
* Any string of characters	*		+		*	*	
* Any string not containing "."		*	–	*			*
* Any single character	?				?	?	
* Any character but "."		%	*	?			?
* Any character from a set	[abc] [a-z]						
* Any string from a set	{foo,bar}						
* Exception string			\				

column is for all DOS-like operating systems, including OS/2 and Windows); the items marked by asterisk (*) in the first column are considered wildcards. Consult the system-specific appendices of this book, or the supplemental manuals, or the online notes, for details.

The name of each file is transmitted to the receiving Kermit program so the file can be stored with its own name automatically when it arrives. SEND can be abbreviated to the single letter S, even though other C-Kermit commands begin with S. Examples:

```
C-Kermit>send oofa.txt          (A single file)
C-Kermit>sen oofa.+             (All AOS/VS oofa files)
C-Kermit>sen oofa.*             (All oofa files, other systems)
C-Kermit>s \?\?                 (UNIX files with 2-char names)
C-Kermit>s %%                   (VMS files with 2-char names)
```

The default directory for filenames is the one where you started C-Kermit or the one given in the most recent CD command. You can include disk and/or directory information in the *filespec* for files that are not in your current directory. During transmission, filenames are stripped of any device, directory, or version information (unless you say otherwise). For example, when the following file is sent by VMS C-Kermit:

```
C-Kermit>send $disk1:[olga]login.com;5
```

the receiver is told that its name is simply LOGIN.COM.

The RECEIVE Command

RECEIVE *[as-name]*

Tells C-Kermit to wait for one or more files to arrive from the other Kermit program, which must be given a SEND command. By default, incoming files are stored in the current directory.

Incoming filenames are converted to the format of C-Kermit's underlying operating system; for example, UNIX C-Kermit converts all-uppercase names to lowercase. The RECEIVE command can be abbreviated by the single letter R. Examples:

```
C-Kermit>receive                  (Receive one or more files)
C-Kermit>r                        (Receive one or more files)
```

If the optional *as-name* is included, the arriving file is stored under that name rather than the name it arrived with:

```
C-Kermit>receive oofa.txt         (Store incoming file as oofa.txt)
```

The "as-name" can include disk and directory information so you can store the incoming file somewhere other than your current directory, and it can also denote a device such as a printer if your operating system allows.

The as-name may not contain wildcard characters. If the as-name is a filename, as opposed to a device or directory name, and more than one file arrives, then only the first file is renamed; the subsequent files are stored under their own names. The as-name is converted to uppercase if the underlying file system does not support lowercase letters in filenames.

The RECEIVE command requires that you have write access to the device and directory in which the arriving file is to be stored. C-Kermit will not create files for you that you could not otherwise create yourself.

Most versions of C-Kermit (UNIX, VMS, OS/2, Windows, OS-9, etc.[20]) accept a device or directory name in place of the *as-name* to specify that *all* incoming files (not just the first one) should go into the specified device or directory under the names they were sent with. Here is an example in which Kermit/2 is downloading files from an IBM mainframe:

```
Kermit-CMS>send oofa * c          (Send all oofa files from C disk)
Alt-x                             (Escape back to OS/2)
C-Kermit>receive d:               (Receive all files onto disk D:)
```

---

[20]You can check yours with C-Kermit's SHOW FEATURES command. Look for CK_TMPDIR in the list of compilation options.

Other Commands for Sending Files

A variation on the SEND command lets you send a single file under an assumed name:

SEND *filename [remote-filename]*

Sends the file specified by *filename*, which must not contain wildcards, transmitting it under the name *remote-filename* ("as-name"). Example:

```
C-Kermit>send night.txt day.txt
```

This sends the file `night.txt` but tells the receiving Kermit that its name is `day.txt`. The *remote-filename* field should be a filename in the syntax of the remote computer. It can contain any printable characters, even spaces. C-Kermit does not (and can not) check it for syntax, and does not convert it in any way. If you do not supply a *remote-filename* field, the file is sent with its own name.

Another variation on the SEND command lets you supply a list of files to be sent, rather than just one file specification:

MSEND *filespec [filespec [...]]*

Multiple Send. This command sends all the files in the list in a single operation, so you have to give only one RECEIVE command to the other Kermit. The names are separated by spaces (*not* commas). The maximum length of this command is the same as for any C-Kermit command, usually about 4000 characters (use SHOW COMMAND to obtain a precise figure). Each file is sent under its own name. Each item in the list can be the name of a single file or a wildcard file-group specification. The files can be on different devices and in different directories. Note that there is no way to give "as-names" in the MSEND command (but keep reading). Examples:

```
C-Kermit>msend oofa.txt oofa.new      (Two files or...)
C-Kermit>mse ~olga/*.c ~olaf/*.h      (from different directories)
C-Kermit>ms [olga]*.c [ivan]*.h       (Ditto, VMS)
C-Kermit>ms ckc*.c cku*.c ckw*.c ck*.h makefile
```

The MSEND command is equivalent to the `-s` command-line option (Appendix I).

Sometimes it is desirable to delete files after they have been successfully sent, in effect *moving*, rather than *copying*, them from one computer to another. The commands are:

MOVE *filespec [remote-filename]*

This command is exactly like the SEND command, except it automatically deletes (removes, erases) each file that is sent successfully. Any files that are not sent successfully are preserved.

MMOVE *filespec [filespec [...]]*

Multiple Move. This command is exactly like the MSEND except it automatically deletes each file that is sent successfully.

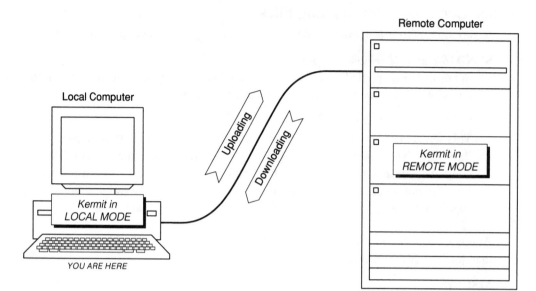

Figure 9-1 Upload and Download

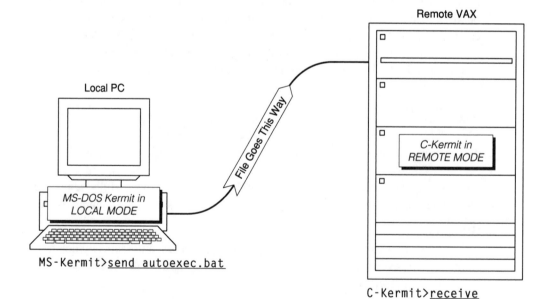

`MS-Kermit>`<u>`send autoexec.bat`</u>

`C-Kermit>`<u>`receive`</u>

Figure 9-2 Uploading a File

Easy File Transfer Examples

Let's introduce two new words, illustrated in Figure 9-1: upload and download. *Upload* means to send a file from your local computer to the remote computer. *Download* means to transfer a file from the remote computer to your local computer.

Most Kermit programs are set up to transfer ordinary 7-bit US ASCII text files unless you say otherwise, so let's begin by doing that. The procedure for *uploading* is:

1. Start Kermit on your local computer.

2. Make a connection to the remote computer.

3. CONNECT to the remote computer and log in.

4. Start Kermit on the remote computer and tell it to RECEIVE the desired file.

5. If necessary, escape back to Kermit on the local computer.

6. Tell the local Kermit to SEND the file.

7. Watch the file transfer display.

8. Wait for the beep or message that says the transfer is complete.

9. CONNECT back to the remote computer, conduct any further business you might have there, and then log out from it when you're finished.

10. Escape back to your local Kermit (if necessary) and exit from it.

In our first example, shown in Figure 9-2, you are sitting at a PC equipped with MS-DOS Kermit. You will connect to a VAX computer over a direct line and upload a file to C-Kermit on the VAX.

```
C:\>kermit                          (Start Kermit on the PC)
MS-Kermit>set port com1             (Select the communication port)
MS-Kermit>set speed 19200           (Set the desired speed)
MS-Kermit>connect                   (Begin terminal emulation)

Username: olga                      (Log in on the VAX)
Password: _____                     (Type your password)

$ kermit                            (Start Kermit on the VAX)
C-Kermit 6.0.192, 6 Sep 96, for OpenVMS VAX
Type ? or HELP for help
C-Kermit>receive                    (C-Kermit receives the file)
Return to your local Kermit and give a SEND command.

KERMIT READY TO RECEIVE...
Alt-X                               (Escape back to the PC)
                                    (Hold down Alt key and press X)
MS-Kermit>send autoexec.bat         (Tell the PC to send the file)
```

```
        (The file is transferred...)
MS-Kermit>                              (Beep, all done)
```

Presto, the file is transferred. Notice that the name of the file to be send is given only to the Kermit program that is sending the file. The sending Kermit sends the filename to the receiving Kermit so the file is automatically stored with the right name. For completeness, let's go back to the VAX and properly finish our session:

```
MS-Kermit>connect                       (Connect back to the VAX)
C-Kermit>dir /size/date autoexec        (Is the file really there?)
Directory $DISK1:[OLGA]
AUTOEXEC.BAT;1   3   22-DEC-95 11:23:02
C-Kermit>exit                           (Exit from C-Kermit on the VAX)
$ logout                                (Log out from the VAX)
Alt-X                                   (Escape back to the PC)
MS-Kermit>exit                          (Exit from MS-DOS Kermit)
C:\>                                    (Back to the DOS prompt)
```

Now you're back where you started.

> *HINT:* If the file transfer didn't work, it's probably because of a communication parameter called *parity* (defined in Appendix II). Try giving the command:
>
> ```
> C-Kermit>set parity space
> ```
>
> (or, if that didn't help, SET PARITY EVEN) to C-Kermit before you give the RECEIVE command, escape back, and give the same SET command to your local Kermit before giving the SEND command. We'll cover parity and other difficulties in Chapter 10.

Downloading

Downloading is just like uploading, except with the SEND and RECEIVE commands exchanged. In this example, illustrated in Figure 9-3, we connect from a desktop CP/M microcomputer (remember CP/M?) to a remote Data General MV AOS/VS system. The micro is the local computer, the MV is the remote, and they have a direct connection:

```
B>a:kermit                              (Start Kermit on the micro)
Kermit-80 v4.11
Kermit-80>set speed 9600                (Set the desired speed)
Kermit-80>connect          ·            (Begin terminal emulation)
Username: ivan                          (Log in to the MV system)
Password: _____                         (Type your password)
) kermit                                (Start Kermit on the MV system)
C-Kermit 6.0.192, 6 Sep 96, for AOS/VS
Type ? or HELP for help
C-Kermit>                               (AOS/VS C-Kermit prompt)
C-Kermit>send login.cli                 (C-Kermit sends the file)
Return to your local Kermit and give a RECEIVE command.

KERMIT READY TO SEND...
```

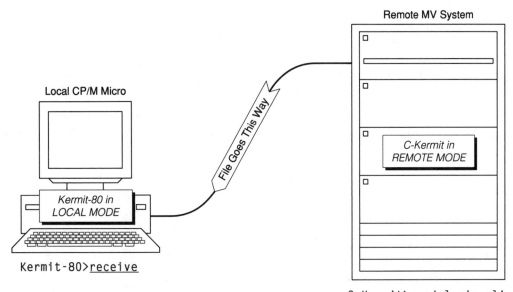

Remote MV System

Local CP/M Micro

C-Kermit in
REMOTE MODE

File Goes This Way

Kermit-80 in
LOCAL MODE

Kermit-80>receive

Figure 9-3 Downloading a File

C-Kermit>send login.cli

```
Ctrl-]C                              (Escape back to the micro)
Kermit-80>rec                        (The micro receives the file)

  (The file is transferred...)

Kermit-80>                           (Beep, finished)
Kermit-80>dir login                  (Check it)
LOGIN  CLI   3
Kermit-80>
```

See, the file is really on your micro's disk, stored automatically under the correct name.
Now connect back to the remote computer, finish your session, and log out:

```
Kermit-80>c                          (Connect back)
C-Kermit>exit                        (Exit from C-Kermit)
) bye                                (Log out from AOS/VS)
Ctrl-]C                              (Escape back)
Kermit-80>
```

What Are Those Squiggles?

When you give the SEND command to the remote Kermit, as in the previous example, it
waits for a few seconds to give you time to escape back to the local Kermit program and
issue a RECEIVE command. Then it sends its first file transfer packet. The normal waiting
time is about 5 seconds. If you fail to escape back quickly enough, you will see the first

packet on your screen, as in the following example:[21]

```
C-Kermit>send oofa.txt
Return to your local Kermit and give a RECEIVE command.

KERMIT READY TO SEND...
^A8 S~* @-#Y3~^4K*0___D"U1.
```

No harm is done; you have about a full minute to escape back and engage the receiving Kermit before the remote Kermit loses patience and returns to its prompt. But if you are disconcerted by the appearance of this packet on your screen, you may lengthen the delay:

SET DELAY *number*

Tells C-Kermit how many seconds to wait before sending its first packet after it has been given a SEND command, when it is in remote mode. Example:

```
C-Kermit>set delay 5
```

Once you have become highly dextrous and proficient at escaping back and typing RECEIVE, the normal 5-second delay can be surprisingly annoying, so you can also shorten the waiting time:

```
C-Kermit>set delay 1
```

Or even SET DELAY 0 for no delay at all (which is appropriate when you have TERMINAL AUTODOWNLOAD enabled; explained in Chapter 13). The SET DELAY command has no effect on C-Kermit when it is receiving files or when you are uploading files from C-Kermit on your local computer.

Regaining Control of Your Keyboard

When you put the remote C-Kermit program into packet mode by giving it a file transfer command like SEND or RECEIVE, it is no longer responsive to your keystrokes. It wants to see valid only Kermit protocol packets. But suppose (for example) you have mistakenly put C-Kermit into protocol mode, and you want to get back to the prompt?

Just type three Ctrl-C characters in a row: hold down the Ctrl key and press the *C* key three times:

```
$ kermit
C-Kermit> receive
Ctrl-c Ctrl-c Ctrl-c ^C...
C-Kermit>
```

When Kermit's packet reader sees the three Ctrl-C's, it echoes "^C...", breaks C-Kermit out of protocol mode, and returns you to the C-Kermit prompt or the system prompt, depending on how C-Kermit was started.

---

[21]If you have given a RECEIVE command and did not escape back fast enough, you will see a packet that looks like this: "# N3".

The danger of this escape mechanism is that three Ctrl-C's might appear as noise on the connection. So of course there is a command to let you change the sequence to anything you like, or disable it altogether:

SET TRANSFER CANCELLATION *{ OFF*, **ON** *[code [number]] }*

OFF turns off the protocol-mode cancellation feature, preventing escape from packet mode except by normal protocol operations: completion, timeout, error packet, etc. Use with caution. ON (the default) enables this feature. The optional *code* is the ASCII code for the control character (0 through 31 or 127) to be used for interruption (the default is 3 = Ctrl-C), and the optional *number* is the number of consecutive copies of the character required to cause interruption; we recommend you never use a *number* less than 3. Synonym: **SET XFER CANCELLATION**.

For example, SET XFER CANCEL ON 6 5 tells C-Kermit to break out of protocol mode upon receipt of 5 consecutive Ctrl-F (ASCII 6) characters. Note that the parity bit is ignored for this purpose, so (for example) 3 and 131 are treated the same.

If you SET TRANSFER CANCELLATION OFF, you might still need a manual method of getting remote-mode C-Kermit out of packet mode. This can be accomplished by escaping back to your local Kermit and giving a RECEIVE command, then typing E (or Ctrl-E) to send an error packet.

Network File Transfer

If you are accessing the remote computer with a true high-speed network connection, C-Kermit works the same as in the previous examples but (usually) much faster. In this example we access a UNIX host computer via a TCP/IP Ethernet connection from MS-DOS Kermit on a PC and *download* a file:

```
MS-Kermit>set port tcp kermit.columbia.edu
MS-Kermit>connect

login: olaf
Password: _____

$ kermit                          (Start UNIX Kermit)
C-Kermit 6.0.192, 6 Sep 96, for SunOS 4.1
Type ? or HELP for help
C-Kermit>send mailing.lst         (Send a file)
Alt-X                             (Escape back to the PC)
MS-Kermit>r                       (Receive the file)

  (The file is transferred...)

MS-Kermit>c                       (Connect back to UNIX)
C-Kermit>exit                     (Exit from C-Kermit)
$ exit                            (Log out from UNIX)
```

If the file transfer failed, SET PARITY to SPACE and start the file transfer again.

Local-Mode File Transfer

In this example, you are running C-Kermit on your *local* computer, a UNIX workstation or timesharing system, and you are dialing up a remote computer to download some files. Note the use of the wildcard character * to denote a file group.

```
$ kermit                                (Start Kermit on UNIX)
C-Kermit 6.0.192, 6 Sep 96, for SunOS 4.1
Type ? or HELP for help
C-Kermit>set modem type usrobotics     (Specify modem type)
C-Kermit>set line /dev/ttyh8           (and communication device)
C-Kermit>set speed 57600               (and speed)
C-Kermit>dial 5551234                  (Dial the number)
Connection completed.                   (Call completed)
C-Kermit>connect                        (Begin terminal emulation)

Connecting through /dev/ttyh8, speed 57600.
The escape character is Ctrl-\ (ASCII 28, FS).
Type the escape character followed by C to get back,
or followed by ? to see other options.

ELECTRO-BRAIN 9000
LOGIN: olaf                             (Type your username)
PASSWORD: _____                      (and your password)

WELCOME. CHOOSE:
1. Chess
2. World Domination
3. Kermit
4. Logout

YOUR CHOICE? 3                          (Kermit, of course)
Electro-Kermit>send plan*.txt          (Send some files)
Ctrl-\c                                 (Escape back to C-Kermit)
C-Kermit>receive                        (Receive the files)

   (The files are transferred...)

C-Kermit>connect                        (Go back to remote computer)
Electro-Kermit>exit                    (Exit from the remote Kermit)
YOUR CHOICE? 4                          (Log out)
ELECTRO-BRAIN 9000 HAS TERMINATED YOUR SESSION.
GOOD BYE.
Communications disconnect (back at local system)
C-Kermit>dir plan*.txt                 (List the received files)

-rw-rw----  1 olaf          42378 Aug  8 19:21 plan1.txt
-rw-rw----  1 olaf           5986 Aug  8 19:21 plan2.txt
-rw-rw----  1 olaf          12873 Aug  8 19:21 plan3.txt

C-Kermit>exit                           (Exit from C-Kermit)
$
```

Here is another example, in which you use C-Kermit to make a TCP/IP TELNET connection to an Internet host and upload some files to it (something you can't do with a regular TELNET program). Both computers have C-Kermit, so you take advantage of the SET PROMPT command to keep yourself oriented:

```
C-Kermit>set prompt Local>        (Prompt for local Kermit)
Local>telnet hq                   (Go to the remote host)

login: olaf                       (Log in)
Password: _____                 (Enter your password)

$ kermit                          (Start Kermit on remote computer)
C-Kermit 6.0.192, 6 Sep 96, for HP-UX 10.0
Type ? or HELP for help
C-Kermit>set prompt Remote>       (Prompt for remote Kermit)
Remote>r                          (Receive some files)
Ctrl-\c                           (Escape back to local C-Kermit)
Local>s /usr/include/t*.h         (Send some files)

   (The files are transferred...)

Local>c                           (Connect back to remote computer)
Remote>exit                       (Exit from remote Kermit)
$ exit                            (Log out from remote computer)
Communications disconnect (back at local system)
Local>
```

The File Transfer Display

When C-Kermit is used in local mode, it displays the progress of the file transfer on your screen in one of several formats: fullscreen, serial, crt, or none at all. The command to select the display style is:

SET TRANSFER DISPLAY *{ CRT, FULLSCREEN, NONE, SERIAL }*

The default type of display is FULLSCREEN if your version of C-Kermit supports it, otherwise it is CRT. The SHOW FILE command displays the current transfer display type; use SET TRANSFER DISPLAY to change it.

The FULLSCREEN display, available in VMS, OS/2, Windows, OS-9, Amiga, and most UNIX C-Kermit versions, produces a formatted report on a 24-line by 80-column screen as shown in Figure 9-4. The fields on the right are updated continuously to keep you informed of the progress of the transfer. The top line shows the Kermit version number, release date, and the name of your local computer (if known). The estimated time remaining to transfer the current file is updated continuously and can fluctuate as the speed of the transfer changes. "CPS" means characters per second, an indication of the efficiency of the file transfer (discussed more fully in Chapter 12).

```
C-Kermit 6.0.192, 6 Sep 96, MYVAX

     Current Directory: $DISK1:[OLAF.TMP]
         Network Host: XYZCORP.COM:23 (UNIX)
         Network Type: TCP/IP
               Parity: none
          RTT/Timeout: 03/04
              Sending: OOFA.TMP;6 => OOFA.TMP => /usr/olaf/oofa.tmp
            File Type: TEXT (no translation)
            File Size: 5608489
         Percent Done: 25  ////////////-
                           ..10..20..30..40..50..60..70..80..90..100
  Estimated Time Left: 00:01:39
   Transfer Rate, CPS: 39664
         Window Slots: 3 of 4
          Packet Type: D
         Packet Count: 731
        Packet Length: 2000
          Error Count: 0
           Last Error:
         Last Message:

X to cancel file, Z to cancel group, <CR> to resend last packet,
E to send Error packet, ^C to quit immediately, ^L to refresh screen.
```

Figure 9-4 C-Kermit's Fullscreen File Transfer Display

The "Sending" line shows the local filename, the name used in the packet, and the name used on the remote computer. Various other interesting facts are displayed to reassure you that the desired file is being transfered in the desired mode to the desired place. The type, size, and number of each packet is shown, along with some protocol information like the current window size (explained in Chapter 12) and the current round-trip time (RTT) and timeout. At the end of a successful transfer, the Last Message field changes to a summary report, a beep is sounded (unless you have told C-Kermit to SET TRANSFER BELL OFF), and the C-Kermit prompt reappears:

```
           Last Error:
         Last Message: Files: 4, Bytes: 18529024, 43520 CPS
C-Kermit>
```

To check whether the FULLSCREEN display is available:

```
C-Kermit>check fullscreen
 Available
C-Kermit>
```

Even when available, the fullscreen display won't work right in UNIX or VMS if your ter-minal type is set incorrectly or is not supported.

The SERIAL file transfer display, works with all kinds of display devices, including video and hardcopy terminals as well as Braille and speech units. It looks like this:

```
SF
X to cancel file,  CR to resend current packet
Z to cancel group, A for status report
E to send Error packet, Ctrl-C to quit immediately:
A
Receiving: PLAN1.TXT => plan1.txt
Size: 8113, Type: text
........Z [OK]
F A
Receiving: PLAN2.TXT => plan2.txt
Size: 12341, Type: text
..........T%..N%..Z [OK]
F A
Receiving: PLAN3.TXT => plan3.txt
Size: 10001, Type: text
..........Z [OK]
B
```

The single letters like S, F, A, Z, and B are Kermit protocol packet types, listed in Table 9-2 on the next page. If there is any information to report, it is shown after the packet letter. For example, after the A packet, C-Kermit reports the file name, such as PLAN1.TXT, and its size. => plan1.txt shows the local name for file.

When the file's contents start to arrive, C-Kermit prints a period for every K (1024 characters) of data successfully received. If an expected packet does not arrive within a given timeout interval, a T is printed. If a negative acknowledgment is sent or received, an N is printed. If a packet is retransmitted, a percent sign (%) is displayed.

If TRANSFER DISPLAY is set to CRT, the dots are replaced by a line continuously showing the bytes (characters) transferred so far, the percentage done, the current transfer rate in characters per second (CPS), and the length of the current packet. This line is refreshed by simple overstriking, and so should work on any CRT (video) terminal:

```
Sending: ckuxla.h => CKUXLA.H
Size: 2875, Type: text
    File     Percent           Packet
    Bytes    Done      CPS     Length
    2599     89%       229     998
```

When TRANSFER DISPLAY is OFF, C-Kermit skips the display and transfers files silently. The file-transfer interruption characters (X, Z, E) are disabled, but you can still get back to the C-Kermit prompt by typing Ctrl-C. The file transfer display is turned off automatically if C-Kermit is transferring files in the background.

Table 9-2 Kermit Packet Types

Type	Name	Function
A	Attributes	Attributes of file.
B	Break	End of transmission.
C	Command	Host command for a server.
D	Data	Data from file.
E	Error	Fatal error, contains message.
F	File Header	Start of file, contains filename.
G	Client	Client command for a server.
H	Retrieve	Move a file from server to client.
I	Information	Protocol parameters sent to a server.
J	Reget	Asks server to recover a file.
N	NAK	Negative acknowledgment, requests retransmission.
R	Get	Asks server to send a file.
S	Send	Negotiates parameters and starts sending.
T	Timeout	(Pseudopacket) Indicates a timeout waiting for a packet.
Y	ACK	Acknowledgment.
X	Text Header	Precedes screen data.
Z	End of File	Tells receiver to close the file.
%	Retransmission	(Pseudopacket) Indicates that a packet was retransmitted.

Interrupting a File Transfer

While files are being transferred, you can interrupt the transfer or query its progress. This is done from the *local* Kermit program by pressing a key, a key combination, a sequence of keys, or in some cases a mouse button.

When C-Kermit is the local Kermit program, you usually need type only a single key, such as X. However, if C-Kermit is running on an older version of AT&T System V UNIX, you might have to type the CONNECT-mode escape character (normally Ctrl-Backslash) before you type the interruption key. C-Kermit's file transfer interruption keys are available to you when its file transfer display is active. When the transfer begins, C-Kermit tells you what the available interruption keys are, for example in the legend at the bottom of the file-transfer display.

The same interruptions can be sent to a *remote* C-Kermit program from your local PC, Macintosh, or other Kermit program. They work the same way, but you might have to enter them differently; for example, programs with graphical file transfer displays have interruption buttons that you can click on with your mouse. Consult the documentation for your local Kermit program.

Canceling a Single File: X

The X key (or, if required, escape-character followed by X) cancels the file currently being transferred. If a group of files is being sent, Kermit skips ahead to the next one.

```
C-Kermit>s ckuusr.*
SF
X to cancel file,  CR to resend current packet
Z to cancel group, A for status report
E to send Error packet, Ctrl-C to quit immediately:
A
Sending: ckuusr.c => CKUUSR.C,
Size: 98353, Type: text
.......X
Canceling File  [incomplete]
F A
Sending: ckuusr.h => CKUUSR.H
Size: 45973, Type: text
.............Z [OK]
C-Kermit>
```

If C-Kermit is sending a file, it tells the remote receiver that this file is finished, but incomplete. If C-Kermit is receiving a file, it tells the sender to cancel the transfer, then disposes of the partially received file appropriately (discussed later).

Canceling a Group of Files: Z

If you type Z instead of X and more than one file is being transferred, the entire file group is canceled and C-Kermit should return to its prompt. If only one file is being transferred, Z works exactly like X.

Retransmitting a Packet: Carriage Return

If the file transfer appears to be stuck, you can type a carriage return (press the Return or Enter key) to resend the most recent packet. This does no harm because packets are numbered and duplicates are automatically discarded.

Requesting a Status Report: S

If you type the letter S, C-Kermit prints a brief summary of how the transfer has progressed so far, then continues with the transfer:

```
..................S
Status report:
  file type: text            block check: 1
  file number: 1             compression: 1
  size: 50532                8th-bit prefixing: 0
  characters so far: 20761   packet length: 89
  percent done: 41           window slots: 1
.............................. [OK]
```

The A command is ignored if you are using the FULLSCREEN file transfer display, since most of this information is already on the screen.

Suspending C-Kermit: Ctrl-Z

On UNIX computers with job control, you can type Ctrl-Z to suspend Kermit during local-mode file transfer in such a way that the file transfer can be continued in either the foreground or the background. See Appendix III for details.

Interrupting C-Kermit: Ctrl-C

You can always type Ctrl-C to interrupt any file transfer. In local mode you only need to type one Ctrl-C to get back to the prompt immediately. A remote-mode C-Kermit can be returned to its prompt by typing three Ctrl-C's in a row:

```
C-Kermit>send me.away          (Send a file)
^A0 Sz* @-#Y1~*  yE            (See the Kermit packet)
Ctrl-C Ctrl-C Ctrl-C           (Type three Control-C's)
^C...                          (Kermit confirms that it got them)
C-Kermit>                      (and returns to its prompt)
```

When you interrupt a local-mode file transfer with Ctrl-C, no protocol messages are sent to the remote Kermit (if any), so it remains in packet mode, possibly spewing many K of packets onto your screen. Therefore, use this method only as a last resort or if you forgot to start the Kermit program on the other end.

Sending an Error Packet: E

You can cancel any kind of transfer and put the remote Kermit back into a known state by typing the letter *E* (or the escape character followed by E) while your file transfer display screen is active. This makes C-Kermit send an error (E) packet.

This is useful, for example, if the remote Kermit does not respond to the X or Z cancellation messages; most popular Kermit programs do (see Table 1-1 on page 10). If the remote Kermit was started interactively and was given a SEND or RECEIVE command, the error packet should make it return to its prompt. If the remote Kermit is in server mode (explained in Chapter 11), the error packet makes it ready to receive a new command.

You can also send an error packet by issuing the following command at the C-Kermit prompt or from a command file:

E-PACKET

Send an Error packet to the other Kermit. Example:

```
C-Kermit>e-packet             (Send an error packet)
```

This command can be used to get the local and remote Kermit programs back "in sync" when one is command mode and the other in packet mode. If C-Kermit is not in local mode, the error packet appears on your screen containing the text "User canceled." It does no harm.

Transferring Text Files

○ ○ ○ ○

Techniques for transferring text files that contain accented letters, non-Roman letters, or other national or international characters are presented in Chapter 16. But please don't skip ahead; the material from here through Chapter 12 apply to all types of file transfer.

○ ○ ○ ○

The VMS file system is far more complex than the simple model presented here, and VMS C-Kermit's handling of the VMS file system is quite different. VMS C-Kermit users should be sure to read Appendix IV in addition to this and the next few chapters.

A text file is one that you can read on your screen without using any special kind of formatting software such as a word processor or electronic publishing package. If you can display a file with your computer's TYPE (or equivalent) command and it looks right, then it's most likely a text file.

Text files are made up of lines containing ordinary printable characters such as letters, digits, spaces, and punctuation marks, without special effects like boldface and italics. Different computers have different ways of representing text files: different codes to represent the characters (the character set) and different ways of separating the lines (the record format). On an ASCII-stream-based file system, for example, text files are generally made up of ASCII (or national or international) printing characters, with lines separated by carriage return, linefeed, or both, and containing no other control characters or formatting codes except perhaps for tab, and maybe backspace or formfeed.

Kermit automatically converts ordinary text files into a useful and appropriate format when you transfer them between unlike computers, just as you would expect. It uses a

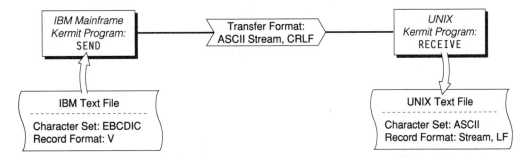

Figure 9-5 Kermit Text File Conversion

standard representation for text within its file transfer packets, which is normally ASCII (ISO 646 USA version) character codes (listed in Table VII-1 on page 557) with Carriage-Return Linefeed (CRLF) line terminators. The sending Kermit translates from the local computer's text file conventions to this form, and the receiving Kermit converts back to its own local conventions, as in the example shown in Figure 9-5.

Some C-Kermit versions transfer in text mode by default, others in binary mode. The default transfer mode is announced when C-Kermit starts. To be certain that Kermit will transfer files in text mode, use this command:

SET FILE TYPE TEXT
> Tells Kermit to perform character set and record format conversions during file transfer, storing files in conventional and useful text format on the receiving computer. This is Kermit's default file transfer mode. Synonyms: **TEXT, ASCII**.

Transferring Binary Files

Files that are not text files are called *binary files*. Our own peculiar definition of a binary file is a file that is not to be converted in any way during transfer. A good example would be an executable program image. Kermit does not know and cannot guess (except on VMS) which files you want converted and which ones you don't. You must tell it. The command is:

SET FILE TYPE BINARY
> Tells Kermit that no conversions of any kind are to be performed on the file during transfer. Synonym: **BINARY**.

Let's look at an example of binary file transfer in which we upload a copy of a PC ZIP archive to a UNIX computer, making it available for other people to download to their PCs:

```
C>kermit                            (Start Kermit on the PC)
MS-DOS Kermit 3.15
Type ? or HELP for help
MS-Kermit>dir oofa.zip              (Check the file's size)
 OOFA     ZIP      192488   2-08-95  3:28p
MS-Kermit>set modem pp14400         (Specify the modem type)
MS-Kermit>set port com2             (Select the communications port)
MS-Kermit>dial 555-1234             (Dial the UNIX computer)
MS-Kermit>connect                   (Begin terminal emulation)
                                    (Press Enter to begin)
login: olaf                         (Type your username)
Password: _____                   (and password)

Welcome to UNIX.

$ kermit                            (Start C-Kermit)
C-Kermit 6.0.192, 6 Sep 96, for UNIX System V R4
```

```
Type ? or HELP for help
C-Kermit>set file type binary    (Use BINARY mode)
C-Kermit>receive                 (Tell C-Kermit to receive the file)
Alt-x                            (Escape back to MS-DOS Kermit)
MS-Kermit>set file type binary   (Use BINARY mode)
MS-Kermit>send oofa.zip          (Send the file)

    (The file is transferred...)

MS-Kermit>connect               (Connect back to UNIX)
C-Kermit>dir oofa.zip            (Check file file's size)
-rw-rw-r--  1 olaf        192488 Feb  8 15:28 oofa.zip
C-Kermit>
```

The two directory listings show that the received file on UNIX is exactly the same size as the original, which is a good indication that no conversions have taken place.

To download the file from UNIX, follow the same procedure, but give a SEND command to UNIX C-Kermit first and then a RECEIVE command to MS-DOS Kermit:

```
C-Kermit>set file type binary   (Use binary mode)
C-Kermit>send oofa.zip          (Tell C-Kermit to send the file)
Alt-x                           (Escape back to the PC)
MS-Kermit>set file type binary  (Binary mode here too)
MS-Kermit>receive               (Tell MS-DOS Kermit to receive)
```

> **VMS USERS PLEASE NOTE:** Special procedures are required for transferring ZIP files to and from VMS. Please refer to page 535 in Appendix IV.

It is not always necessary to give the SET FILE TYPE command to both Kermit programs. It is often sufficient to give it only to the file sender, or to the client of a server, and then the sender (or client) informs the receiver (or server) of the file type automatically by means of a special protocol message. However, since advanced features such as this are usually not supported in non-Columbia Kermit protocol implementations, it is often necessary to put *both* Kermit programs into binary mode prior to transferring a binary file. (The precise rules for determining text or binary mode transfer are listed on page 236 in Chapter 11.)

Building a Send List

Now that you know about text and binary transfer mode, it might have occurred to you that — except in VMS, in which file types can be recognized from their directory entries — none of the commands discussed so far (SEND, MOVE, MSEND, MMOVE) allow a mixture of text and binary files to be transferred together in the same group. You also might have noticed that when sending a list of files with MSEND or MMOVE, there is no provision for applying "as-names" to them.

Requirements such as these are met with the "send list," a list of files to be sent, with separate transfer modes and optional as-names for each, that you give to C-Kermit in the form of a series of commands. All the files in the list are sent in a single transaction; thus the other Kermit can receive them all with a single RECEIVE command.

The commands for building and using a send list are:

CLEAR SEND-LIST

Clear the send list, remove all entries, make it empty.

ADD SEND-LIST *filespec* [{ **TEXT**, **BINARY** } [*as-name*]]

Places the file or files denoted by *filespec* on the send list. A transfer mode, text or binary, may be specified; if no transfer mode is specified, the current FILE TYPE setting is used. If a transfer mode is specified, and if the *filespec* is not wild, an as-name may follow the transfer mode. If no as-name is given, the file is sent under its own name. If the *filespec is* wild, all files in the group are sent under their own names. Examples:

```
C-Kermit>clear send-list        (Start a new send list)
C-Kermit>set file type text     (Set global mode)
C-Kermit>add send-list oofa.txt (Global mode, no as-name)
C-Kermit>add send oofa.exe binary (Binary mode, no as-name)

C-Kermit>add send *.obj binary   (Binary mode, no as-name)
C-Kermit>add s oofa.c text source.c (Text mode, with as-name)
```

SHOW SEND-LIST

Display the current contents of the send list; example:

```
oofa.txt, mode: text, alias: (none)
oofa.exe, mode: binary, alias: (none)
*.obj, mode: binary, alias: (none)
oofa.c, mode: text, alias: source.c
```

SEND

The SEND command, when given without any filenames, sends all the files from the send list. If there is no send list, an error message is printed:

```
C-Kermit> send
?No send list - use ADD to make one.
```

To start a new send list, use CLEAR-SEND LIST. Use ADD to add files or file groups to it, and SEND (by itself) to send all the files from the list.

The send list stays put after the SEND command, in case you want to send it again. To get rid of it, use CLEAR SEND-LIST. Even when a send list is defined, you can still SEND files in the regular ways, by specifying their name(s) in a SEND or MSEND command, etc, without disturbing the send list.

File Names

Kermit transfers not just a file's contents, but also its name. By default, file names are converted to a simple standard form on the assumption that the file is being transferred to a computer that has different file naming conventions. Kermit's normal form for names should be inoffensive enough to agree with all kinds of computers. You can alter Kermit's treatment of file names with the SET FILE NAMES command:

SET FILE NAMES CONVERTED

When sending files, C-Kermit converts the file name to uppercase if necessary and ensures that there is no more than one dot (period) in it. Extra dots or unusual characters like spaces or punctuation are translated to X or underscore (_) and if a dot is the first character, an X is placed in front of it. In addition, all device, directory, and path names, as well as version numbers, are removed. For example:

The file:	Is sent as:
oofa.txt	OOFA.TXT
/usr/olga/oofa.txt	OOFA.TXT
$DISK1:[OLGA]OOFA.TXT;3	OOFA.TXT
oofa.tar.Z	OOFA_TAR.Z
oofa.txt.~3~	OOFA_TXT.X3X
.login	X.LOGIN

When receiving a file whose name contains all uppercase letters, UNIX C-Kermit converts the name to lowercase. If the incoming name is mixed case or lowercase, the case is preserved. Other C-Kermit implementations have similar rules for converting incoming names to normal and legal local form.

SET FILE NAMES LITERAL

Do not change the case of letters, do not remove extra dots, do not strip version numbers. Device and directory specifications are handled according to SET SEND/RECEIVE PATHNAMES, discussed in the next section. This option should be used only between like operating systems whose file specifications follow the same format.

No matter what your FILE NAMES setting, the other computer still might have to make some changes in the name. For example, MS-DOS restricts a file name to eight characters before the dot and three after, so, if necessary, MS-DOS Kermit shortens the incoming name. For example, FILEWITHLONGNAME.ANDLONGTYPE becomes FILEWITH.AND.

Thus a file can have up to three names in its passage: its original name, the name it is sent with, and the name it is stored under on the receiving system. Hence the three names shown in the fullscreen file transfer display:

```
Sending: OOFA.TMP;6 => OOFA.TMP => /usr/olga/oofa.tmp
```

To accomplish effects not possible with SET FILE NAMES, use the "as-name" option of the SEND or RECEIVE command.

Transferring Files between Similar Systems

When Kermit programs begin a file transfer, they exchange some information with each other, possibly including the type of system they are running on. This lets them know whether they are on systems that have the same kind of file structure and naming conventions. For example, any two versions of UNIX (such as HP-UX and Solaris) would be considered the same; DOS and OS/2 or Windows would be considered the same; any two versions of VMS or OpenVMS on VAX or Alpha would be the same. But UNIX and Windows would be different (because the file specifications and file records are in different formats); VMS and AOS/VS would be different, and so on.

When the two Kermits recognize each other's file systems as "the same," they automatically enter binary file-transfer mode using literal filenames, just as if they each had been told to SET FILE TYPE BINARY and SET FILE NAMES LITERAL; no filename or record format conversion is needed, and indeed could prove harmful (e.g. if a binary file were sent in text mode by mistake). In OS/2 and VMS, labeled mode is used instead of binary mode for like-to-like transfers (see the VMS or OS/2 Kermit documentation).

In case you need to inhibit automatic transfer-mode switching — for example, when transferring text files between like systems when the character set needs to be translated (as explained in Chapter 16) — you can use this command:

SET TRANSFER MODE *{ AUTOMATIC, MANUAL }*
> AUTOMATIC enables automatic transfer-mode switching based on system type; MANUAL disables automatic transfer-mode switching.

Figure 9-4 on page 184 illustrates how C-Kermit's fullscreen file transfer display shows the other computer's system type if it known, "UNIX" in this case.

Directory Names

If files are sent to C-Kermit whose names include recognizable device or directory specifications, you can use the following command to tell C-Kermit how to handle them:

SET RECEIVE PATHNAMES *{ ON, OFF }*
> Applies to incoming filenames; ON means to leave the name alone and attempt to use it as is, OFF means to attempt to remove the path (device and/or directory) information, and pay attention only to the filename itself.

SET RECEIVE PATHNAMES ON works only if the pathname (disk/directory) information in the incoming file name is in the notation of the local file system, and therefore recognizable. If not, the results are unpredictable; for example, if a file called:

```
MYVAX::DUA0:[OLAF.PICS]MONA_LISA.GIF;17
```

is sent to a UNIX system, UNIX C-Kermit can not be expected to distinguish the path information from the file name itself and will treat the entire string as the filename.

In VMS, UNIX, OS-9, OS/2, Windows, and VOS, SET RECEIVE PATHNAMES has an additional meaning: If the incoming file name contains recognizable directory information, such as [.KERMIT]OOFA.TXT in VMS, kermit/oofa.txt in UNIX, or:

```
C:\TEXT\LETTERS\ANGRY\OOFA.TXT
```

in Windows or OS/2 — either absolute or relative — then if the named directory or any of its ancestors do not exist, Kermit attempts to create it (or them), and then creates the output file in the new directory.

For example, suppose your current directory (in UNIX) is /usr/olga/budget, and a file arrives under the name:

```
aaa/bbb/ccc/ddd/bankrupt.txt
```

and that the /usr/olga/budget/aaa directory already exists, but it does not have a bbb subdirectory. Then Kermit creates the bbb subdirectory, and then the ccc subdirectory under bbb, and then the ddd subdirectory under ccc, and then stores the bankrupt.txt file in the directory:

```
/usr/olga/budget/aaa/bbb/ccc/ddd
```

In UNIX, tilde notation for usernames (like "~olga") is recognized, and any directories that are created inherit the permissions of their parents, and the owner and group of the user who is running the Kermit program. Naturally, directory creation fails if the user lacks the appropriate permissions. Directory creation fails in OS/2 and Windows if a disk letter is included for a nonexistent or non-writable disk.

You can also control pathnames when sending files. The command is:

SET SEND PATHNAMES *{ ON, OFF }*
> This command is effective only when FILE NAMES are LITERAL. OFF, the default, means to strip path information "OFF" the outbound filename, leaving only the name itself. ON means to leave pathnames "ON" outbound file names, except they are always stripped from outbound filenames when FILE NAMES are CONVERTED, and in OS/2 and Windows, disk letters are always stripped, no matter what.

SET SEND PATHNAMES applies only to the file specification given directly to a SEND (or MSEND, MOVE, MMOVE, or ADD SEND-LIST) command and not to the *as-name*, which is always sent literally, regardless of SEND PATHNAMES or FILE NAMES settings.

Use SHOW FILE to display the SEND / RECEIVE PATHNAMES settings.

Filename Collisions

What should C-Kermit do if it receives a file that has the same name as an existing file? Should it silently overwrite the existing file? Should it make an effort to preserve the existing file? Should it reject the incoming file? These are called file collision actions, and you have six to choose from:

SET FILE COLLISION BACKUP

This setting, which is C-Kermit's default file collision action, allows the file to arrive and to be stored under the name it was sent with, without destroying any previously existing file that has the same name. The existing file is given a new, unique name that fits within the operating system's file naming conventions, generally by adding digits to the name; for example, in UNIX `oofa.txt` becomes `oofa.txt.~1~`. See the appropriate appendix for details.

SET FILE COLLISION OVERWRITE

Overwrites (replaces) the existing file. Use this setting with caution.

SET FILE COLLISION APPEND

Adds the incoming file to the end of the existing file. This option is useful for appending information to a log file, but it should be used with caution to avoid, for example, joining two files of different types (like text and binary).

SET FILE COLLISION DISCARD

Refuses and/or discards the incoming file and preserves the existing file. This option is handy for resuming multi-file transmissions that were broken. Only those files that do not have a counterpart on the receiving system are transferred.

SET FILE COLLISION RENAME

This is just like the BACKUP option, except that the *incoming* file gets the new name, rather than the existing file. Not recommended.

SET FILE COLLISION UPDATE

Accepts the incoming file only if it is newer than the existing file, in which case the existing file is overwritten. This feature depends on the file creation date field in the attribute packet (explained in Chapter 12), and requires the other Kermit to support attribute packets (Table 1-1, p. 10). The UPDATE option is handy for keeping a parallel collection of files up to date on another computer; only those that have changed since the last update are sent.

The SET FILE COLLISION command is effective only when given to the file *receiver*. The VMS version of C-Kermit always creates a new version of any incoming file that is not rejected, preserving earlier versions according to the file's version limit, which makes the BACKUP, OVERWRITE, and RENAME options identical in VMS.

Incomplete File Transfers

If a file transfer fails in the middle of a file for any reason — the connection is broken or a disk write fails — Kermit can react in one of two ways: it can discard the partially received file (so you won't be misled into thinking it was fully received in case you happened to miss the error message), or it can keep it so you can resume the transfer later. Unless you say otherwise, incompletely received files are kept, to allow subsequent resumption. You can control this behavior with the following command:

SET FILE INCOMPLETE *{* **KEEP, DISCARD** *}*

Tells whether a partially received file is to be kept if the transfer is interrupted for any reason, including intentional cancellation. To discard incomplete files:

```
C-Kermit>set file incomplete discard
```

The SET FILE INCOMPLETE command is effective only when given to the file *receiver*; it has no effect when given to the file sender. Synonym: **SET INCOMPLETE**.

Recovering from Interrupted File Transfers

If you were transferring a file in binary mode — using Kermit or any other method (such as XMODEM, ZMODEM, or FTP) — and the transfer was interrupted, and the partially received file was kept, you can use Kermit's RESEND command to complete the transfer from the point at which it was interrupted provided the other Kermit program also supports the recovery feature[22].

Imagine, for example, transferring a 10-megabyte file over a 2400-bps modem connection when, after 9 megabytes have been sent, your call-waiting feature kicks in and drops the modem connection. Transferring 9 megabytes at 240 cps takes about 11 hours. The remaining megabyte would take about 1.2 hours. The recovery feature lets you complete the failed transfer in the amount of time it takes to send the as-yet-untransmitted part of the file, rather than sending the entire file again from the beginning — in this example, a savings of 11 hours.

Before seeing how to use this feature, let's look at the restrictions:

1. Recovery works only for binary-mode transfers between computers that have Kermit programs that support this feature. It does not work with any other transfer modes, including text, because it depends on a byte-for-byte correspondence between the source

---

[22]At this writing, recovery is supported by MS-DOS Kermit for DOS and Windows 3.x; IBM Mainframe Kermit for VM/CMS, MVS/TSO, CICS, and MUSIC; and C-Kermit for UNIX, VMS, OS/2, Windows, AOS/VS, Stratus VOS, OS-9, and the Commodore Amiga.

and destination files; in text-mode transfers, files often change contents or formats because of system differences[23]. In other words, if you want to be able to use the recovery feature, you must tell the file sender to SET FILE TYPE BINARY.

2. The original transfer, if done by Kermit software, must have had SET FILE INCOMPLETE KEEP in effect at the receiver, meaning that incompletely received files are kept rather than discarded (this is the default).

3. You should never use SET FILE COLLISION RENAME if you intend to use the recovery feature, because this will prevent proper identification of the destination file during recovery (unless you rename it yourself by hand prior to recovery).

To recover a failed upload use the RESEND command:

RESEND *filename [remote-filename]*
Sends the file to the other Kermit in recovery mode. C-Kermit's FILE TYPE must be BINARY. If the other Kermit does not support the recovery feature (as determined in protocol negotiations), the command fails. Otherwise, if a file of the name that the file was sent with (*filename* or *remote-filename*) exists on the other computer, transmission is resumed at the point at which it was interrupted, except that if the file on the remote computer is the same size as the local file, the file is not sent. If such a file does not exist on the other computer, then the file is sent in its entirety.

To recover a failed upload: re-establish the connection, access the same account and directory to which you were sending the file previously, start Kermit there, and put it in RECEIVE mode. Then escape back to the local Kermit program, SET FILE TYPE BINARY, and give it a RESEND command that uses exactly the same name(s) as the SEND command that failed. For example:

```
C-Kermit> set file type binary
C-Kermit> send oofa.zip

(Connection is broken -- make a new one, log in again and...)

C-Kermit> set file type binary
C-Kermit> resend oofa.zip
```

You can recover a failed download in the same way, but give the RESEND command to the remote Kermit and the RECEIVE command to the local one. Again, make sure you are accessing the same directories as before and the files have (or are being sent with) the same names as before.

---

[23]In fact, text-mode transfers can also be recovered when done between two systems that use exactly the same record format and character set for text files, but the recovery must still be done in binary mode.

The RESEND command ignores your SET FILE COLLISION setting; thus you need not change your FILE COLLISION setting when RESENDing, and you will not find it altered afterwards either. (But please do not use SET FILE COLLISION RENAME if you ever intend to use the RESEND command.)

Since the RESEND command does not retransmit a file that does not need to be retransmitted, and it transmits a file in its entirety if it does not exist on the other end, it can also be used to resume the interrupted transfer of a group of files. Suppose you originally had done the following (sending from DOS to VMS):

Receiver	*Sender*
`CD DUA0:[OLGA.ZIPS]`	`CD C:\ZIPFILES`
`SET FILE INCOMPLETE KEEP`	`SET FILE TYPE BINARY`
`RECEIVE` (or `SERVER`)	`SEND *.ZIP`

and the phone hung up in the middle of one of the ZIP files. Just re-establish the connection, and recover by issuing all the same commands again:

Receiver	*Sender*
`CD DUA0:[OLGA.ZIPS]`	`CD C:\ZIPFILES`
`SET FILE INCOMPLETE KEEP`	`SET FILE TYPE BINARY`
`RECEIVE` (or `SERVER`)	`RESEND *.ZIP`

except the file sender is told to RESEND rather than SEND.

The files that were already sent are skipped, the file that was partially sent is recovered, and the files that were not sent yet are sent.

Manual Recovery: The PSEND Command

The PSEND ("partial send") command is like the SEND command, but it begins sending from a specified position in the file:

PSEND *filename position [as-name]*

The *filename* must refer to a single file, not a file group. The *position* is the byte position in (offset into) the file; 0 means the beginning (i.e. just before the first byte); 1000 means the 1001st byte (i.e. start just after the 1000th byte). As with the SEND command, the file is sent under its own name unless you specify an AS-NAME. Unlike RESEND, PSEND can be used for both text and binary transfers, and no special capabilities are required of the Kermit program on the receiving end. The PSEND command can be viewed as part of a "do-it-yourself" recovery feature to be used when the other Kermit program does not support recovery.

For example, suppose you were sending a file called CUSTOMERS when the connection was broken, and that the receiving Kermit program had been instructed to keep incompletely received files (SET FILE INCOMPLETE KEEP). If the transfer was in binary mode, you could note the length of the partial file on the receiving end by getting a directory listing; let's say it was 123456. Then tell the file receiver to:

```
set file collision append
receive
```

and tell the sender to:

```
set file type binary
psend customers 123456
```

If the receiver does not support SET FILE COLLISION APPEND, you could use PSEND to create a new file:

```
set file type binary
psend customers 123456 customers.2
```

and then, after the transfer is complete, join the two pieces together on the receiving end, using a system command or utility.

With a bit more effort, you can use the same techniques to recover a broken text-mode transfer, even when it occured between computers that have different record formats. You'll have to identify the location in the source file that corresponds to the end of the partially transferred file "by inspection" and use this in your PSEND command.

File Attributes

The Kermit protocol has the ability to convey and process information about a file, called the file's *attributes*, along with the file's name and contents, if both Kermit programs support this option and agree to use it. The attributes are sent in a special *attribute packet* (A-packet). Attribute information includes the file's character set (see Chapter 16), the file's creation date, length, type (i.e. transfer mode, text or binary), disposition, and an identifier for the sending system. Attribute packets are supported by (at least) C-Kermit, MS-DOS Kermit, Macintosh Kermit, IBM Mainframe Kermit, and PDP-11 Kermit for RSX-11, RT-11, and RSTS/E (see Table 1-1 on page 10).

When the file arrives at the other Kermit, it introduces itself with a capsule biography: "Hello, I am a text file with carriage return and linefeed at the end of each line; I was born in MS-DOS on January 9, 1986, at 10:28:00am, I am 12345 bytes long, I am encoded in Latin Alphabet 1, and I would like you to print me," or, translated into Attribute-packet language:

```
A.#AMJ"U8#1119860109 10:28:00!!11%12345*'CI6/100"+!P@
```

Based on this information, the receiver can decide whether to accept or refuse the file, how to interpret it, and what to do with it. Here are the attributes supported by C-Kermit:

TYPE

The sending Kermit tells the receiving Kermit whether the file is being sent in text (A) or binary (B) mode. This allows the receiving Kermit to switch between text and binary modes automatically on a per-file basis. UNIX and most other C-Kermit versions send the text or binary file type attribute according to the sender's prevailing transfer mode, established by the most recent SET FILE TYPE command, or by automatic transfer mode determination. When receiving a file, the incoming file type attribute takes precedence over the receiver's FILE TYPE setting (but in VMS, not always; see Appendix IV).

DATE

When sending a file, C-Kermit includes its creation or last modification date and time (given in local time) in the attribute packet. When receiving a file whose creation date and time is given in the Attribute packet, C-Kermit stores the file with the given creation date and time (or refuses to accept it if FILE COLLISION is set to UPDATE and the arriving file is not newer than an existing file of the same name). Time zone information is not conveyed.

LENGTH

When sending a file, C-Kermit includes its length in the attribute packet. If the receiving computer notices that the file is bigger than its available disk space or the user's disk quota, it may refuse the file, which can save you a lot of wasted time and phone charges. When the file is accepted, this information allows the receiving Kermit (if it is in local mode) to continuously display the percent done while the file is being transferred. When receiving a file, the Windows, OS/2, VMS, Commodore Amiga, and Atari ST versions of C-Kermit reject a file that is too large to fit in the available disk space (in VMS, the user's quota is not checked). The UNIX, AOS/VS, and OS-9 versions of C-Kermit currently do not check the reported file size against available disk space, and always accept the file.

CHARACTER-SET

This is the TRANSFER CHARACTER-SET (explained in Chapter 16). When sending a file in text mode and when the TRANSFER CHARACTER-SET is not TRANSPARENT (which is the default), C-Kermit translates from the current FILE CHARACTER-SET to the TRANSFER CHARACTER-SET and includes a code to identify the TRANSFER CHARACTER-SET in the Attribute packet. Codes contain registration numbers from the ISO Register of character sets [48]. They include:

I6/100	ISO 8859-1 Latin Alphabet 1
I6/101	ISO 8859-2 Latin Alphabet 2
I6/138	ISO 8859-8 Latin/Hebrew Alphabet
I6/144	ISO 8859-5 Latin/Cyrillic Alphabet
I14/13/87	Japanese EUC

When receiving a text file, C-Kermit learns the TRANSFER CHARACTER-SET from the Attribute packet and translates from it into the current FILE CHARACTER-SET.

DISPOSITION

What to do with the file. Normally, transferred files are simply stored on disk. This attribute is used by the MAIL and REMOTE PRINT commands, presented in Chapter 11, to request that a file be sent as electronic mail or that it be printed, rather than stored on disk, and also by RESEND.

SYSTEM-ID

The file sender includes a code identifying its computer and operating system, in case the file receiver wants to use this information in any way. C-Kermit sends this item when sending files and ignores it when receiving files. System IDs are listed in [21], pages 275–278.

If the other Kermit does not support, or want to receive, attribute packets, C-Kermit does not send them. This is settled automatically when the two Kermits first say hello to each other with the S or I packet.

But when the two Kermits agree to exchange attribute information, you might find that the effects are not what you desire. For example, you might not want arriving files stored with their original dates because this causes your backup system to skip over them. Or you may find that Kermit's estimate of available disk space is too conservative and it refuses a file that you believe will fit. So C-Kermit gives you the ability to turn each attribute on or off:

SET ATTRIBUTE { CHARACTER-SET, DATE, DISPOSITION, LENGTH, SYSTEM-ID, TYPE } { ON, OFF }

Turns a particular attribute on or off, leaving the others undisturbed. The individual settings are used only if the entire attribute mechanism is on.

And if the attribute mechanism itself — as opposed to one or more particular attributes — is causing problems, you can disable and enable it with this command:

SET ATTRIBUTE { ON, OFF }

Turns the entire attribute mechanism on or off. When it is off, C-Kermit will not engage in attribute packet exchange with the other Kermit.

You can also use SET ATTRIBUTE ALL ON or OFF to turn all individual attributes on or off at once without affecting whether the attribute mechanism itself is enabled or disabled. For example, to turn off all attributes except type, you could:

```
C-Kermit>set attr all off       (Turn 'em all off)
C-Kermit>set attr type on        (Turn this one back on)
```

The SHOW ATTRIBUTES command displays C-Kermit's current attribute-related settings.

Odds and Ends

Before we finish with basic file transfer techniques, let's complete the list of SET FILE commands:

SET FILE BYTESIZE *{ 7, 8 }*

Normally, 8-bit input and output is used when sending and receiving files. If, for some reason, you want to remove the 8th bit from each byte of a file that you are sending or receiving, use SET FILE BYTESIZE 7.

SET FILE DESTINATION *{ DISK, PRINTER, SCREEN }*

This applies when receiving files. Normally incoming files are stored on disk. You can use this command to route them to the default printer (or whatever other printer, file, or process you have specified in your most recent SET PRINTER command, if any) or to your screen instead. If you choose SCREEN, this replaces the file transfer display. If you choose PRINTER or SCREEN, then your FILE NAMES and PATHNAMES settings are ignored. Synonym: **SET DESTINATION**.

SET FILE DOWNLOAD-DIRECTORY *[directory-name]*

Use this command to specify whether Kermit should place received files into a special *download directory* rather than into its current directory. If you specify a directory name, then all received files will go into that directory, no matter what your current directory is, unless you have given a pathname in your RECEIVE command, or the file arrives with a pathname and you have SET RECEIVE PATHNAMES ON. If you omit the *directory-name*, then incoming files are placed in Kermit's current directory in the absence of any other instructions.

SET FILE END-OF-LINE *{ CR, CRLF, LF }*

This command applies when sending files in text mode. C-Kermit converts from the local text-file format to the standard one, so if you are sending from UNIX or AOS/VS, C-Kermit expects lines to be terminated by a single linefeed (LF); if you are sending from OS-9 or a Macintosh, C-Kermit expects lines to end with a single carriage return (CR); if you are sending from OS/2, Windows, or GEMDOS, C-Kermit expects lines to end with carriage return and linefeed (CRLF). However, if you have a text file on your computer that has been stored in the wrong format (e.g. because it was transferred to your computer from an unlike system in binary mode), you can use this command to tell C-Kermit what the line terminator is, so it can still send the file correctly in text mode. Synonym: **SET FILE EOL**.

Use the SHOW FILE command to display all your current file-related settings.

Keeping a Record of Your File Transfers

During a long multi-file transfer, you probably have better things to do than keep your eyes glued to the screen. But then how will you know what happened? Perhaps a file was skipped for some reason, or transferred in the wrong mode, or some other error occurred. You can ask C-Kermit to keep a record for you in a file called the *transaction log*:

LOG TRANSACTIONS *[filename [{* **APPEND, NEW** *}]]*

Records information about the file transfer in the given file. The default filename is TRANSACT.LOG (lowercase on UNIX) in the current directory. C-Kermit creates a new log file, overwriting any existing file of the same name, unless you include the keyword APPEND after the filename. Examples:

```
C-Kermit>log trans               (transact.log, new)
C-Kermit>log t tuesday.log new    (A new daily log)
C-Kermit>log t february.log append (Add to a monthly log)
```

CLOSE TRANSACTIONS

Closes the current transaction log file, if any. The transaction log is also closed automatically when you EXIT from C-Kermit.

Here is a sample transaction log:

```
Transaction Log: C-Kermit 6.0.192
 Solaris 2.x

Transaction begins Fri Sep  6 23:23:00 1996
Global file mode: text
Remote system type: MS-DOS
Sending /usr/olga/mupeen.txt
 as MUPEEN.TXT
 mode: text
 file character set US ASCII
 xfer character set transparent
 remote name:  C:\TEMP\MUPEEN.TXT
 complete, size: 94033
Sending /usr/olga/oofa.txt
 as OOFA.TXT
 mode: text
 file character set US ASCII
 xfer character set transparent
 remote name:  C:\TEMP\OOFA.TXT
 complete, size: 95629
Transaction complete Fri Sep  6 23:23:05 1996
 files transferred      : 2
 total file characters  : 189662
 communication line in  : 811
 communication line out : 199533
 elapsed time (seconds) : 5
 effective data rate    : 37932
Transaction Log Closed
```

Summary

First-time Kermit users sometimes find the mechanics of file transfer confusing. But it's not very hard if you keep a few basic points in mind. First, establish a connection from the Kermit program on your local computer to the remote computer (or service, or server, or provider, or host, or BBS, etc; let's just call it a "computer") and, if necessary, log in.

Second, start the Kermit program on the remote computer. A file can't be transferred with Kermit protocol unless there is a Kermit program on each end of the connection. Now, just follow these three easy steps:

1. While still connected to the remote computer, tell the *remote* Kermit what to do: SEND or RECEIVE.

2. Return to your local Kermit program by typing its CONNECT-mode escape sequence, such as *Ctrl-\C* (usually) for C-Kermit or *Alt-X* for Kermit 95, OS/2 C-Kermit, or MS-DOS Kermit. Note that some communication software programs are always in "CONNECT mode," and therefore do not require you to escape back.

3. If your local program has a selection of protocols (such as Xmodem, Ymodem, Zmodem, and Kermit), choose Kermit. At your local Kermit's prompt, tell it what to do: RECEIVE or SEND, or select RECEIVE (or "download") or SEND (or "upload") from your local software's file transfer menu. This is the opposite of what you told the remote Kermit to do. If you told the remote Kermit to SEND, you should tell the local Kermit to RECEIVE, and vice versa.

When you are finished using the remote computer, remember to CONNECT back to it (if necessary) and log out. You can transfer groups of files by including wildcard characters in the SEND-command file specification (or by giving a list of files to the MSEND command), you can record the progress of your file transfers in a transaction log, you can use SET FILE commands to select text or binary transfers, the treatment of filenames, the handling of filename collisions, and the disposition of incomplete transfers, and you can use the RESEND and PSEND commands to resume interrupted transfers. Here is a quick summary of the SET FILE commands presented in this chapter:

SET FILE COLLISION
Options: APPEND, BACKUP, DISCARD, OVERWRTE, RENAME, UPDATE. Default: BACKUP. Function: Specifies action to be taken when a file arrives that has the same name as an existing file. Give this command to the file *receiver*.

SET TRANSFER DISPLAY
Options: CRT, FULLSCREEN, SERIAL, or NONE. Default: FULLSCREEN or CRT. Function: Selects format for file transfer display. For use when C-Kermit is in *local* mode.

SET FILE INCOMPLETE

Options: DISCARD, KEEP. Default: KEEP. Function: Tells what to do with a file incompletely received. Give this command to the file *receiver*.

SET FILE NAMES

Options: CONVERTED, LITERAL. Default: CONVERTED. Function: How to handle file names during transfer. Meaningful to both the file sender and the file receiver.

SET FILE TYPE

Options: TEXT or BINARY. Function: Selects text or binary file transfer. Give this command to the file *sender* and, if necessary, also to the file receiver.

SET TRANSFER MODE { AUTOMATIC, MANUAL }

Default: AUTOMATIC. Controls whether the transfer mode (FILE TYPE and FILE NAMES) should be switched automatically based upon recognition of system type.

SET { SEND, RECEIVE } PATHNAMES

Options: ON, OFF. Default: OFF. Function: Tells whether path (device, directory) information should be included in transmitted filenames.

Variables (explained in Chapter 17):

\v(cps)	Speed of most recent transfer, characters per second
\v(crc16)	16-bit cyclic redundancy check of most recent transfer
\v(download)	SET FILE DOWNLOAD-DIRECTORY value
\v(filespec)	File specification used in most recent transfer
\v(fsize)	Size of file most recently transferred
\v(ftype)	SET FILE TYPE value
\v(tfsize)	Total size of file group most recently transferred

PROBLEMS: If a file transfer fails, use the SET PARITY command and try again. If it still fails, read Chapter 10. If file transfer works but the transferred file has the wrong format, issue the appropriate SET FILE TYPE command and try again. If file transfers work but seem inefficient, read Chapter 12.

Use the SHOW FILE command to display C-Kermit's file type, collision action, file naming, incomplete file treatment, transaction log, initialization file name, and other file-related settings. Use SHOW PROTOCOL to display file-transfer protocol settings.

These are the ABCs of Kermit file transfer, suitable for use between any two Kermit programs. More advanced and simpler techniques, which you can use once you have mastered the basic techniques, are described in the following chapters. Capabilities, command names, user interface, and so on, are likely to be different in non-Columbia Kermit implementations; consult the appropriate documentation for details.

Chapter 10

Solving File Transfer Problems

○ ○ ○ ○

If you had no trouble transferring files using the basic techniques given in Chapter 9, please do not feel compelled to read this chapter. But don't tear these pages out of the book and rip them into tiny shreds; some day you might need them. For now, skip ahead to Chapter 11 on page 227, which shows you how to turn C-Kermit into a file server and how to use C-Kermit as a client of another C-Kermit server — much easier and more flexible than the SEND/RECEIVE style of operation you have been using up till now. Then go on to Chapter 12 to learn how to transfer files more efficiently.

Like people, computers have different languages, conflicting customs, competing ideologies, quirks, idiosyncracies, and bad habits. Telecommunications systems punch holes in our data. Sensible data on one computer becomes incomprehensible gibberish on another. To transfer files in a diverse, and sometimes hostile, computing and communications environment, Kermit software programs use the *Kermit protocol*, a set of rules and procedures for exchanging structured, error-checked messages with each other.

C-Kermit's default settings for all kinds of communications-, file-, and protocol-related items are based on pessimistic assumptions about the quality and capacity of the connection, and so should almost always work. But there are hundreds of different kinds of computers in the world with different styles of communication and different file formats, and there are many different ways to connect these computers. So you might encounter some situations where the defaults are not appropriate.

Figure 10-1 Character Formats

Because C-Kermit lets you control virtually every aspect of its operation, you can teach it to overcome computer-related incompatibilities and communications impediments, and you can help it achieve maximum efficiency under all sorts of conditions. Let's begin by looking at the effects of the communications environment on file transfer and how you can use the SET command to adapt C-Kermit to them.

Parity

The most common cause for file transfer failure is *parity*. Once again, with emphasis:

The most common cause for file transfer failure is parity.

Computers store characters in 8-bit "bytes." Some computers prefer to transmit these bytes as 7 bits of data plus one bit of error-checking information, called the parity bit. The parity bit *replaces* one of the data bits.[24] The parity bit is set to 0 or 1 based on the values of the remaining seven data bits. There are five kinds of parity: even, odd, mark, space, and none. Even parity sets the parity bit to make the overall number of 1-bits in the transmitted character even. Odd parity makes the overall number of 1-bits odd. Mark parity always sets the parity bit to 1, and space parity always sets it to 0.

Parity is an unpleasant fact of life in data communications. The receiver of a transmitted character can't tell from looking at it whether it has 7 data bits and 1 parity bit, or 8 data bits. (See Figure 10-1.) Can you? Parity prevents the transmission of 8-bit data bytes, such as we find in binary files or international character codes.

During terminal emulation, C-Kermit ignores parity unless you tell it otherwise, on the assumption that only 7-bit ASCII or ISO 646 characters are being transmitted and the 8th bit carries no useful information. That is, C-Kermit assumes parity is probably in effect without the user's knowledge.

---

[24]Other arrangements are possible but occur rarely in practice. In the most common case, and the one supported by Kermit, a byte is always transmitted as 8 bits: either 8 data bits and no parity bit, or 7 data bits and a parity bit.

During file transfer, most Kermit programs normally put the communication line into 8-bit no-parity mode so they can transmit 8-bit data, on the assumption that the other Kermit program can do the same. Most Kermit programs can. The major exception is (usually) IBM mainframe Kermit, due to limitations of the IBM mainframe communication architecture.

However, it can — and often does — happen that a network or communication device between C-Kermit and the other computer might be using parity, even when both computers are not. These devices are generally cannot be controlled or influenced by Kermit.

File transfers can fail when parity is in use but the Kermit programs do not know about it, because Kermit might misinterpret the parity bits as data bits, and/or because useful data bits have been chopped off.

Luckily, this situation is caught by Kermit's own error-checking procedure so parity will not cause files to be transferred incorrectly — it simply prevents them from being transferred at all. Usually the error message is something like "Failure to receive acknowledgement" or "Too many retries." If this happens to you, use the SET PARITY command to tell the Kermit program what the parity is:

SET PARITY { EVEN, ODD, MARK, SPACE, NONE }
> This command, when given with any of its options other than NONE, tells Kermit to actually add the selected type of parity bit to all characters it sends, during both CONNECT mode and file transfer, and to remove the 8th bit of incoming characters.

If you don't know which kind of parity to use, don't worry. Just pick one. EVEN is a good first choice for serial connections; try SPACE for TCP/IP TELNET or RLOGIN connections. Give matching SET PARITY commands to the two Kermit programs and file transfer should work smoothly:

```
C-Kermit>receive                    (Receive a file)
Alt-x                               (Escape back)
MS-Kermit>set file type binary     (Binary transfer mode)
MS-Kermit>send budget.wks          (Send a spreadsheet file)
                                   (Many retries, and then...)

?Too many retries

MS-Kermit>connect                  (Let's try it again)
C-Kermit>set parity even           (Once more, with parity)
C-Kermit>receive
Alt-x                              (Escape back again)
MS-Kermit>set parity even         (Here too)
MS-Kermit>send budget.wks         (Send it again)

   (The file is transferred)

Transfer complete.                (This time it works)
MS-Kermit>
```

If EVEN or SPACE parity doesn't do the trick, try MARK or ODD. MARK is used with some mainframes and X.25 networks. ODD is rarely, if ever, used in data communications.

When PARITY is used during file transfer, data characters whose 8th bit is 1 are transmitted as 2-character sequences: the data character itself has its 8th bit replaced by a parity bit, and the result is preceded by an ampersand (&) character, which also has the appropriate parity bit applied to it. The receiving Kermit removes the 8th bit from each arriving character and converts the special 2-character sequences back to a single 8-bit character. As you can imagine, this can add a lot of transmission overhead. But it does allow Kermit to transfer 8-bit data through a 7-bit connection, a claim that other protocols cannot make.

HINT: Some Kermit programs, including C-Kermit and MS-DOS Kermit, attempt to detect parity *automatically* during file transfer, so even if you forget to SET PARITY there is a chance the transfer will work correctly anyway. This technique is not totally dependable because there is no way to tell the difference between space parity and no parity at all. So it is still better to SET PARITY explicitly, on *both* ends of the transfer, if your connection does not allow 8-bit data to pass through. But in case you had your PARITY set to NONE and found it changed to, say, EVEN after a file transfer, now you know why.

Speed and Flow Control in the Full Duplex Environment

During file transfer, Kermit programs compose a packet (see page 245) and send it as a unit, all at once. But the receiving computer might not be able to swallow that many bytes in one gulp, in which case the file transfer could fail. Like when your sink backs up — the water doesn't go down the drain as fast as it comes out of the faucet and eventually it spills onto the floor. With computers, this condition is called a buffer overflow.

Buffer overflows rarely occur on network connections but are common on serial (direct or dialed) connections. One way to cope with buffer overflows is to connect the two computers at a lower transmission speed. The slower the data bytes arrive, the more time the computer has to process them. However, reducing transmission speed increases the time it takes to transfer a file, and therefore also your phone bill and your aggravation level.

If your serial transmission speed is too high, buffer overflows can result in lost characters, which cause packet retransmissions and reduced efficiency. If the speed is too low, transmission capacity is wasted. But there is no way to pick the perfect speed — speeds, like clothes, only come in certain sizes: 1200, 2400, 4800, . . . (those are speeds, not waist sizes). And conditions change: computers can slow down and speed up depending on what other tasks they are working on.

If you have a *full duplex* connection between your computers, you may be in luck. While one computer is sending a packet, the other computer can talk back to it: "Stop!"   "OK,

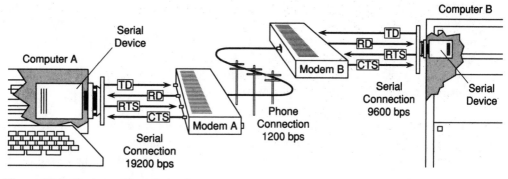

Figure 10-2 Hardware Flow Control

I'm caught up, continue." This is called flow control. It works if both computers know how to do it and are told in advance that they *should* do it. There are two major types of flow control:

Software flow control

> is accomplished by inserting special characters into the data stream. These characters are normally Ctrl-S (XOFF), and Ctrl-Q (Xon). The data receiver sends an Xoff to tell the sender to stop sending, and an Xon to tell it to resume sending.

Hardware flow control

> occurs between the computer and the device it is immediately connected to; for example, between a PC and a high-speed modem. It is accomplished using separate wires, normally the RS-232 Request To Send (RTS) and Clear To Send (CTS) circuits. When both devices are properly configured for the same type of hardware flow control, its effect is immediate.

To illustrate, Figure 10-2 shows a modem connection between two computers. Computer A is connected to its modem at 19200 bps, but the two modems are connected at only 1200 bps. Modem A takes care of the speed discrepancy with its speed buffering feature. But now Computer A can send data into Modem A much faster than Modem A can send it to Modem B. So Modem A stems the flow of data from Computer A by turning off its CTS signal, then turns it back on when it is ready for more data. This type of flow control is also used by error-correcting modems; if the telephone connection is noisy, the modems might be retransmitting data between themselves and therefore must block further data arriving from the computer.

Now let's turn the tables. Suppose Computer A isn't fast enough to keep up with the data coming in from Modem A. Computer A turns off its RTS signal to make the modem stop sending. But Computer B doesn't know about this, so it continues to send data. Somehow Modem A has to tell Modem B to stop sending, then Modem B has to tell Computer B. For all this to work, there must be some kind of higher-level protocol going on between the two modems (such as MNP or V.42), and local flow control of some kind must be enabled between Modem B and Computer B. Thus, for hardware flow control to function effectively, it must take place at every junction along the connection path and it should propagate rapidly from one end to the other.

When flow control is in effect and working properly, you can set the transmission speed to the highest value supported reliably by the physical connection, and you shouldn't have to worry about buffer overflows. Assuming the flow control signals are delivered promptly and correctly, the effective data rate will be as high as it could possibly be at any given moment, adjusting itself automatically to varying conditions of load on the two computers and the communication medium.

The command governing flow control is:

SET FLOW-CONTROL { AUTOMATIC, KEEP, NONE, RTS/CTS, XON/XOFF }
Selects the desired type of flow control: Xon/Xoff (software), RTS/CTS (hardware), no change (KEEP), or none at all (NONE). AUTOMATIC is the default, meaning that C-Kermit should pick the most appropriate type of flow control for the connection, the capabilities of the underlying operating system, and the type of modem you are using, if any. Use the question mark to see which options are offered by your version of C-Kermit:

```
C-Kermit>set flow ? One of the following:
  automatic    none      keep      rts/cts    xon/xoff
```

Xon/Xoff software flow control usually operates *end to end;* that is, between C-Kermit and the computer on the other end of the connection (but you can also configure your modem for local Xon/Xoff flow control). The Xon and Xoff characters are subject to delay and corruption, just like any other transmitted characters. If you have a long-delay connection, for example one where it takes a second or two for your characters to echo, software flow control probably will not be very effective.

Hardware flow control solves these problems and should be used when available. Even when C-Kermit's SET FLOW-CONTROL command does not offer it, you might still be able to use hardware flow control by issuing an operating system command before you start C-Kermit, or by using a special device name in the SET LINE command, in conjunction with C-Kermit's SET FLOW-CONTROL KEEP option. See the manual or appendix for your operating system.

On most network connections, particularly TCP/IP, it is usually beneficial to SET FLOW NONE. The network takes care of flow control itself, so Kermit (or the underlying operating system's terminal device driver) doesn't need to duplicate the effort, and this can make your file transfers go faster.

Half Duplex Communication

Half duplex communication should be familiar to anyone who has used CB radio but may seem unnatural to the rest of us who are accustomed to blurting out whatever comes into our heads. It works like CB: while you are talking, the other person can't talk until you release your talk button. When the direction of transmission is reversed, you have to wait until the other person is finished. If you talk out of turn, your partner can't hear you.

The talk button is the key to this process. When computers are connected with a half duplex communication channel, they too have a talk button. It is usually a special control character. A computer can send a message of any length at all, and the communication line cannot turn around until this character, called a *handshake*, is sent.

Certain kinds of mainframes communicate with their terminals in half duplex. The person at the terminal types a command and terminates it with the Enter key (which sends a carriage return character). The carriage return turns the communication channel over to the mainframe. The mainframe responds to the command, possibly sending many lines or screens full of who knows what, and when it is done sends its own handshake character, such as an Xon (Control-Q) character. The carriage return is the terminal's handshake, and the Xon is the mainframe's. Kermit's commands for half duplex communication are:

SET DUPLEX HALF
> Enables local echoing during terminal connection. This command does not affect file transfer, but is listed here for completeness. Synonyms: **SET LOCAL-ECHO ON**, **SET TERMINAL ECHO ON**.

SET FLOW-CONTROL NONE
> Disables full-duplex flow control. Xon or Xoff characters sent out of turn by C-Kermit on a half-duplex connection will probably be ignored, or they might interfere with successful communication. However, it might still be possible to use hardware flow control, such as RTS/CTS, for example, if you are using a high-speed modem that supports it.

SET HANDSHAKE *[{* **BELL, CR, ESC, LF, NONE, XOFF, XON, CODE** *number }]*
> During file transfer, C-Kermit should wait for the specified character after a packet has been received before sending the next packet, so as not to send the packet before the other Kermit program is prepared to read it. C-Kermit's default handshake is NONE. The most common handshake character on half duplex connections is Xon.

If you have made a connection to a remote computer and found that you had to SET DUPLEX HALF before you could see your characters echo during CONNECT mode, and then you found that file transfer didn't work and that SETting PARITY was not enough to cure the problem, try SET HANDSHAKE XON or one of the other HANDSHAKE options. For example, the following settings are typical for a linemode connection to an IBM mainframe:

```
C-Kermit>set parity mark        (Parity is mark)
C-Kermit>set duplex half        (Local echo is needed)
C-Kermit>set flow none          (No full-duplex flow control)
C-Kermit>set handshake xon      (Handshake is xon)
```

How do you know what the handshake character is? One way to find out is to use C-Kermit's session-debugging feature, which displays control characters on your screen in printable form during CONNECT mode. Here is an example in which we give a command to an IBM mainframe and then observe the last character it sends after executing the command. This is most likely the handshake character:

```
C-Kermit>set terminal debug on
C-Kermit>connect
.query time^J^M^@TIME IS 15:28:00 EST WEDNESDAY 02/08/95^M^J^@
Ready; T=0.01/0.01 15:28:01^M^J^@.^Q
```

The final character is "^Q" — Control-Q (XON, see the ASCII chart in Table VII-1)), and that's your handshake character: SET HANDSHAKE XON.

The Pause that Refreshes

There are situations in which neither flow control nor handshake are available to prevent one Kermit program from sending a packet before the other one is ready to receive it. Sometimes there is no remedy but to pause before sending each packet, to give the network or the other computer time to get ready for it. You can tell C-Kermit to do this with the command:

SET { SEND, RECEIVE } PAUSE *number*
   This command instructs Kermit to pause the indicated number of *milliseconds* (thousandths of seconds) before sending each packet. SET SEND PAUSE and SET RECEIVE PAUSE do exactly the same thing. Example, in which Kermit is given a one-and-a-half-second pause time:

```
C-Kermit>set send pause 1500
```

Noise and Interference

Once you have found a common "language" for the two computers, you still have no guarantee that they can communicate, any more than the fact that two people speak the same language guarantees they can talk at a party with loud music and other people shouting in their ears. If I ask you "Are you having fun?" and you respond "Lentils and pasta," I know you didn't receive my message correctly and I repeat my question.

Data signals are subject to distortion, interference, and loss as they travel through the wires. One of Kermit's most important jobs is to detect when this happens and retransmit any portions of your data that were damaged. Kermit does this by including a *block check* in each Kermit packet. The packet sender computes the block check when constructing the packet, and the packet receiver computes its own version when reading the packet. If the two don't agree, the packet is rejected by the receiver and retransmitted.

Block Check Options

C-Kermit supports all four types of block checks that are defined for the Kermit protocol. The strongest one is used by default, but is not necessarily supported by the other Kermit program[25]. The single-byte block check, however, is a required feature of all Kermit implementations, and will be used automatically if C-Kermit fails to negotiate a higher one with the other Kermit. In such cases, you might want to try an intermediate level. Therefore, and also because some non-Columbia Kermit programs flub the block check negotiation, C-Kermit lets you choose the among the various options explicitly:

SET BLOCK-CHECK 1

A single-character block check, the 8-bit sum of all the other characters in the packet, folded into 6 bits.

SET BLOCK-CHECK 2

A two-character block check, the 12-bit sum of all the other characters in the packet.

SET BLOCK-CHECK BLANK-FREE-2

A two-character block check, the 12-bit sum of all the other characters in the packet, exactly like type 2, except encoded in such a way that neither of the two characters can be a blank. For use on connections where "trailing blanks" might be stripped.

SET BLOCK-CHECK 3

A three-character block check, the 16-bit cyclic redundancy check (CRC) [56] of all the other characters in the packet. This is C-Kermit's default block check type.

Examples:

```
C-Kermit>set block-check 1
C-Kermit>set block 2
C-Kermit>set blo b
C-Kermit>set bl 3
```

The higher the block check number, the stronger the error detection. Block check type 3 is recommended for serial connections, especially when using long packets, transferring 8-bit data, or when the connection is noisy or prone to data loss, e.g. because there is no effective method of flow control. The penalty for using a higher-level block check is negligible, so it rarely hurts to use one unless the other Kermit does not implement it correctly.

---

[25]All four are supported by C-Kermit, MS-DOS Kermit, and IBM Mainframe Kermit.

The Retry Limit

Damaged packets are recovered by automatic retransmission. But there is a limit to the number of times each packet can be retransmitted. If the limit is exceeded, Kermit concludes that the connection is unusable and gives up with an error message like "Too many retries" or "Unable to receive acknowledgement". C-Kermit allows 10 retries per packet. You can use the SET RETRY command to change this number:

SET RETRY *number*

Specifies the maximum number of retransmissions allowed for each packet. Example:

```
C-Kermit>set retry 20
```

The purpose of the SET RETRY command is to help Kermit decide when a connection is unusable. Increase the retry limit if you know that the connection is very noisy and you want Kermit to make every effort to push the file through, even if the cost in retransmissions (and the size of your phone bill) is high. Reduce the number if you want Kermit to detect and give up on a bad connection quickly.

Timeouts

C-Kermit expects to receive each packet within a reasonable amount of time, the *timeout interval*. If the expected packet does not arrive within the timeout period, then depending on the direction of transfer, the most recent packet is retransmitted or a "negative acknowledgement" for the missing packet is sent to the other Kermit. This is supposed to get the transfer back on track.

Why would an expected packet fail to arrive? Either it was delayed in transit for some reason, or else it was destroyed completely or damaged so badly in transit that it could not be recognized as a packet at all. In the former case, a timeout will result in an unecessary retransmission, but in the latter a timeout is necessary to prevent a deadlock in which each Kermit program waits forever for the other to send something. Unfortunately, when the timeout interval has expired, there is no way to know what the reason is.

The trick is in setting the most appropriate timeout interval, so as to minimize both the time it takes to detect a missing packet *and* the number of unnecessary retransmissions. The time for a packet to arrive is determined by the length of the packet, the speed of the physical medium, the distance between the two computers, the speed of the two computers, the load on the two computers, the load on any communication or networking equipment the packet must go through, the load on the network itself if it is a network connection, or the quality of the modem connection. And many other factors, too. To complicate the situation, some of these factors can vary from one moment to the next: the load on a multiuser computer, the congestion on a network.

Modern Kermit programs (C-Kermit, Kermit 95, Kermit/2, MS-DOS Kermit, etc) manage their timeout values dynamically, using statistical methods based on the packet rate. The initial timeout is set conservatively, based on various factors including the packet length and (on serial connections) the serial-port speed; then after several packets have been exchanged the statistical methods kick in, and the timeout at any instant is (approximately) the average interval between packet arrivals, weighted to count recent history the most heavily, plus three standard deviations [61, 55]. You can watch this, and the packet round trip time (RTT), on the file transfer display (Figure 9-4 on page 184).

Other Kermit programs might have hardwired and/or constant timeout intervals, or no timeout capability at all. For example, IBM Mainframe Kermit cannot time out at all due to limitations of the underlying operating systems (VM/CMS, MVS/TSO, etc). Since it is sufficient for only one of the Kermit partners to time out, it is usually better to let C-Kermit do it. The commands for controlling timeouts are:

SET SEND TIMEOUT *number [{* **DYNAMIC** *[mininum [maximum]],* **FIXED** *}]*
If you do not specify DYNAMIC or FIXED, DYNAMIC is used. When SEND TIMEOUTs are DYNAMIC, the *number* of seconds is used as the initial timeout value (subject to adjustment upward based on packet length and so on). You can include maximum and minimum dynamic timeout values, or you can omit them and let Kermit pick its own. When FIXED, the given *number* of seconds is constant throughout the transfer. If you do not give this command at all, dynamic timeouts are used.

SET RECEIVE TIMEOUT *number*
Tells C-Kermit the timeout interval to request the other Kermit to use, in seconds. If you use 0, the other Kermit should not time out, thus allowing C-Kermit to control the timeouts, which is usually desirable. If you send a positive number, the other Kermit should use it unless it has been configured to do dynamic timeouts.

In most cases, you need not bother with either of these commands and C-Kermit will do the right thing: by default it uses dynamic timeouts, and tells the other Kermit to set a timeout interval that is so long it will be used only in case of disaster.

Transparency Problems

Kermit packets are normally framed by a Control-A character (Start of Header) at the beginning and Carriage Return (Control-M) at the end, as shown in Figure 12-1 on page 246. In between, there are no control characters at all (unless you have "unprefixed" them yourself; see Chapter 12). Control characters in your file data are encoded as printable character sequences (for example, Control-S is encoded as #S) to prevent their interception by devices or drivers along the communication pathway (this encoding is what allows Xon/Xoff flow control to work during file transfer).

But some computers or communication processors won't let even Control-A and Carriage Return to pass by unscathed. For example, we have heard of at least one modem that uses Control-A as its escape character: send your first Kermit packet and you're back talking to your modem dialer instead of to the other computer! For pathological cases like this, C-Kermit lets you adjust the framing of the packets:

SET { SEND, RECEIVE } START-OF-PACKET *control-character*

Changes the packet-start character from Control-A to something else, which can be any 7-bit ASCII character. A control character should be used unless the communication path refuses to allow any control characters at all to pass through. Give the numeric ASCII code for the character (see Table VII-1, page 557); for example, 2 for Ctrl-B, 5 for Ctrl-E. You must give corresponding commands to both Kermit programs:

```
MS-Kermit>set send start-of-packet 7   (PC sends Ctrl-G)
MS-Kermit>connect                      (Connect to remote)
C-Kermit>set receive start 7           (C-Kermit receives Ctrl-G)
C-Kermit>send oofa.txt                 (Start the transfer)
Alt-x                                  (Escape back to the PC)
MS-Kermit>receive                      (Receive the file)
```

Here we change the packet-start character only for the packets that are being sent by the PC to C-Kermit; Control-A is still used to start the packets send by C-Kermit to the PC. You can also change the packet-start character in the other direction or in both directions. Just remember to give the corresponding SET SEND START-OF-PACKET and SET RECEIVE START-OF-PACKET commands to both Kermit programs.

SET { SEND, RECEIVE } END-OF-PACKET *control-character*

Changes the packet-end character from Carriage Return to something else, which must be an ASCII 7-bit control character. Give corresponding commands to both Kermits, for example:

```
MS-Kermit>set send end-of-packet 10    (PC sends Ctrl-J)
MS-Kermit>connect                      (Connect to remote)
C-Kermit>set receive end 10            (C-Kermit looks for Ctrl-J)
C-Kermit>receive                       (Wait for files)
Alt-x                                  (Escape back to the PC)
MS-Kermit>send *.txt                   (Send some files)
```

This changes the packet terminator in the PC-to-C-Kermit direction.

In addition to changing the packet start and end characters, you can also tell C-Kermit to send additional characters *between* the packets:

SET { SEND, RECEIVE } PAD-CHARACTER *control-character*

Specifies an additional character to insert before the start-of-packet character. It must be different from the start-of-packet character. Pad characters are ignored by the Kermit protocol, but can be useful to give the receiving computer time to prepare to read the packet. There is at least one case where the pad character is used to put the packet receiver's front end into a special "transparency mode." Without this, the packet itself could not pass through. SET SEND PAD-CHARACTER tells C-Kermit which character to send for padding; SET RECEIVE PAD-CHARACTER tells C-Kermit to tell the other computer's Kermit program which character to *send* as padding.

SET { SEND, RECEIVE } PADDING *number*
This tells how many copies of the pad character to insert before each packet.

Here, for example, is the series of commands that allows C-Kermit to transfer files with a Cray supercomputer running the CTSS operating system and Cray Kermit:

```
C-Kermit>set parity even        (Even parity required)
C-Kermit>set send end 23        (Packet end is Ctrl-W)
C-Kermit>set send padding 1     (Use 1 pad character)
C-Kermit>set send pad-char 26   (Pad char is Ctrl-Z)
C-Kermit>send animation.dat     (Now send a file)
```

IBM Mainframe Linemode Communication

There are two types of connections to IBM mainframes: full-screen and linemode. A full-screen connection goes through a device that converts between IBM 3270 EBCDIC block-mode terminal and asynchronous ASCII character-mode terminal conventions, called a 3270 protocol converter. It masks all the peculiarities of IBM mainframe-style communication from the user and can be used (usually) with little extra effort.

IBM mainframe linemode connections, on the other hand, require Kermit to jump through more than a few hoops. Nearly every communication parameter — duplex, parity, flow control, handshake — is contrary to C-Kermit's defaults, and so must be set explicitly.

Even though IBM linemode sessions are infrequently used nowadays, it is nevertheless instructive to feel our way through one to illustrate some important concepts in data communications, neglected by more than a few popular communications software packages, to the point that they are nonfuctional in this kind of environment.

Figure 10-3 on the next page shows an example of a C-Kermit local-mode file transfer with an IBM mainframe running the VM/CMS operating system. To add a little spice, the modem intercepts the Ctrl-A character, so Kermit's packet-start character must be changed (the modem name is fictional, to avoid lawsuits).

To complicate matters further, the login process reveals the connection to be very noisy, so the user prudently adjusts communication parameters for extra noise resistance.

```
$ kermit                              (Start Kermit on UNIX)
C-Kermit 6.0.192 6 Sep 96, Solaris 2.5
Type ? or HELP for help
C-Kermit>set modem type xyz           (Specify modem type)
C-Kermit>set line /dev/ttyh8          (and communication device)
C-Kermit>set speed 19200              (and speed)
C-Kermit>set parity mark              (Mainframe needs mark parity)
C-Kermit>set duplex half              (Connection is half duplex)
C-Kermit>set flow none                (No full duplex flow control)
C-Kermit>set handshake xon            (Use XON for line turnaround)
C-Kermit>set send start 2             (Change out-packet start to ^B)
C-Kermit>dial 5551234                 (Dial the number)
Call complete.                        (The call is answered)
C-Kermit>connect                      (Connect to the mainframe)
VIRTUAL MAC~xINE/S{{TEM PRODU=T       (Notice the noisy herald)
.login olga                           (Log in)
Enter password:XXXXXXXX
LOGON AT 22:00:52 EDT TH~~{Y 08/02/96
CMS7 VM/ESA V1.1.0 PUT 9101
Ready; T=0.07/0.11 2~~{{:55
CMS
.kermit                               (Run Kermit on the mainframe)
Kermit-CMS Versi%x 4.3.2
Enter ? for a ~~st of valid commands

Kermit-CMS>set retry 20               (Allow many retries)
Kermit-CMS>set block 3                (Use strongest error checking)
Kermit-CMS>set receive start 2        (Change in-packet start to ^B)
Kermit-CMS>send profile exec          (Send a file)
Kermit-CMS ready to send.
Please escape to local Kermit now to RECEIVE the file(s).

KERMIT READY TO SEND...
Ctrl-\c                               (Escape back to C-Kermit)

C-Kermit>set xfer displ serial        (Display progress with dots)
C-Kermit>set retry 20                 (Allow many retries)
C-Kermit>receive                      (Tell it to receive the file)
SF
PROFILE.EXEC A Size: 18113
=> profile.exec ..N%N%..T%..N%..T%T%T%N%......T%..N%..Z [OK]
B
C-Kermit>connect                      (Connect back to the mainframe)

Kermit-CMS>exit                       (Leave mainframe Kermit)
Ready; T=0.02/0.08 22:01:37
.logoff                               (Log out)
Ctrl-\c                               (Escape back to C-Kermit)
C-Kermit>exit                         (Exit from C-Kermit)
$
```

Figure 10-3 IBM Mainframe Linemode Example

IBM Mainframe Full-Screen Communication

Full-screen Kermit connections to IBM mainframes go through 3270 protocol converters or through TCP/IP tn3270 software. These devices and programs translate between normal ASCII and the IBM EBCDIC character sets, they translate IBM 3270 screen directives into escape sequences for your terminal, and they generally fool the parties on either end of the connection into thinking they are dealing with their own familiar world.

The techniques used by C-Kermit to transfer files with an IBM mainframe through such connections depend on whether the connection can be put into transparent mode by IBM mainframe Kermit. Transparent means the protocol conversion functions are turned off and the device or program passes data through without modification. Some protocol converters allow this; others don't.

A connection to a protocol converter is just like a connection to a full-duplex computer host or service, except that even parity is usually a requirement. A connection through a tn3270 program is usually the same as your connection to the host or terminal server where the tn3270 software is running, except you might have to use space parity (in some cases, 8-bit transparency is possible — try it and see!).

File Transfer with Transparent Mode

Many 3270 protocol converters and software allow transparent-mode operation, which is preferred because it makes for simpler and more efficient file transfer. Common examples include the IBM Series/1, 7171, 4994, 3174 AEA, and 938x ASCII subsystem, as well as many non-IBM products, recent-model Cisco terminal servers, and some versions of the UNIX tn3270 program. Kermit-370 on the IBM mainframe attempts to detect transparent-mode capability automatically and use it. When automatic detection doesn't work, IBM mainframe Kermit's SET CONTROLLER command can be used to force a specific style of transparency when it is available. When the protocol converter can be put into transparent mode, file transfer works normally:

```
C-Kermit>set parity even
C-Kermit>show communications
 Line: ttx4, speed 19200, parity: even
 duplex: full, flow: xon/xoff, handshake: none, ...
C-Kermit>connect              (Connect to the mainframe)
.
. kermit                      (Start mainframe Kermit)
Kermit-CMS Version 4.3.2
Enter ? for a list of valid commands
Kermit-CMS>send maketape exec   (Send a file)
Please escape to local Kermit now to RECEIVE the file(s).

KERMIT READY TO SEND...
Ctrl-\c                       (Escape back)
C-Kermit>receive              (Receive the file)
```

If this example does not work for you, use IBM mainframe Kermit's SHOW CONTROLLER command to find out what kind of transparency, if any, is being used, and then try using different SET CONTROLLER commands to achieve transparency:

```
Kermit-CMS>set controller series1
Kermit-CMS>set controller graphics
Kermit-CMS>set controller aea
```

and try the file transfer again. If it still doesn't work, use shorter packets (for example, tell the receiving Kermit to SET RECEIVE PACKET-LENGTH 40). If nothing seems to work, consult the IBM mainframe Kermit documentation for further information or ask the IBM mainframe system administrators for help. If all else fails, you can access the mainframe in linemode (if that is possible at your site) rather than full-screen mode when you need to transfer files. Or you can use the non-transparent technique.

File Transfer without Transparent Mode

When the protocol converter can *not* be put into transparent mode, it is impossible to send a normal Kermit packet through it because *all* control characters are filtered out, including Kermit's packet-start and -end characters. Lines (packets) longer than the screen width are broken and wrapped, blanks might be discarded, the protocol converter can engage in screen optimizations that interfere with packets sent by the mainframe, and each packet sent to the mainframe can be echoed once, twice, or more by the protocol converter.

By switching to a slightly modified version of the Kermit protocol, in which there are no distinguished characters to mark the beginning and end of a packet, and with a special type of block check that never includes blanks, even these obstacles can be overcome. IBM mainframe Kermit version 4.2.3 or later is required.

The trick is to tell IBM mainframe Kermit to operate in fullscreen mode, rather than transparent mode, then set the packet-start character to be a printable ASCII character, avoid the use of handshake characters, and use the "blank-free-2" block check:

```
C-Kermit>set parity even          (Even parity)
C-Kermit>set send start 62        (Packet start is ">")
C-Kermit>set receive start 62     (in both directions)
C-Kermit>set block-check b        (Type B block check)
C-Kermit>set handshake none       (No handshake)
C-Kermit>connect                  (Now go to the mainframe)
. kermit                          (Start mainframe Kermit)
Kermit-CMS Version 4.3.2
Enter ? for a list of valid commands
Kermit-CMS>set controller fullscreen   (No transparent mode)
Kermit-CMS>set send start 62      (Packet start is ">")
Kermit-CMS>set receive start 62   (in both directions)
Kermit-CMS>set block-check b      (Type B block check)
Kermit-CMS>set handshake 0        (Do not send handshake)
Kermit-CMS>send data sas b        (Send a file...)
```

NOTE: All four start-of-packet characters must be the same.

The file is transferred more slowly than with transparent mode, but at least it can be done. Short packets are used automatically to avoid "formatting assistance" by the protocol converter, and various other trickery goes on behind the scenes. In some cases, mainframe Kermit's ASCII/EBCDIC translation tables might need to be altered, depending on the make, model, and configuration of the protocol converter. For detailed information about which protocol converters are transparent and which are not, and about file transfer through non-transparent 3270 protocol converters, consult the IBM mainframe Kermit documentation [19].

For X.25 Users Only

If you have connected to the remote computer through an X.25 network PAD, your connection is probably set up for character-mode interactive operation. In the normal setup, each character you type is sent to the remote computer in a separate X.25 packet so it can be processed and echoed immediately. You want this to happen when you are conducting an interactive session with the remote computer.

However, this mode of operation can be very inefficient during Kermit file transfer. Transfers can proceed much faster if you change your network connection to make Kermit packets correspond as much as possible with X.25 packets. A detailed discussion of X.25 networking is beyond the scope of this book,[26] but you might try escaping back to the PAD (normally by typing Ctrl-P) and issuing X.3 commands to put the PAD into a mode suitable for Kermit packet transmission:

```
Kermit-11>send report.txt              (Send file from remote Kermit)
Ctrl-P                                 (Escape back to the PAD)
@PAR?                                  (See your current PAD settings)
PAR1:1,2:1,3:0,4:80,5:0,6:1,7:0,8:0,9:0,10:80,11:3,12:0
@SET 2:0,3:0,4:0,5:1,6:0,10:0,12:1     (Change them)
@continue                              (Connect back to remote host)
Ctrl-\c                                (Escape back to C-Kermit)
C-Kermit>receive                       (Receive the file)
```

These commands tell the PAD not to echo, to forward characters sent by the terminal (that is, your local Kermit program) only after a carriage return (Kermit's normal packet termination character) has been received, to use no packet forwarding timeout, to enable Xon/Xoff flow control between the terminal and the PAD (rather than end-to-end), to suppress network messages that might interfere with the Kermit packets, and to do no line folding. If your local Kermit has built-in X.25 network support, you can use the corresponding SET PAD Kermit commands instead (see Chapter 3, page 129).

---

[26]Read the literature provided by your X.25 service provider, for example, *How to Use SprintNet Asynchronous Dial Service*, or consult references [13, 14, 15, 16].

When you connect back after the file transfer, your PAD connection will no longer be suitable for interactive use, so you must restore the original PAD parameters, as in the following example:

```
C-Kermit>connect                         (Connect back to remote)
Ctrl-P                                    (Escape back to the PAD)
@SET 2:1,3:2,4:80,5:0,6:1,10:80,12:0 (Restore old settings)
@continue                                 (Connect back to remote host)
Kermit-11>
```

Hint: After you read the chapters on macros and scripts, you will be able to write macro commands that make this procedure a lot easier and faster. *Another Hint:* Certain networks have built-in commands to condition your connection for file transfer, for example SprintNet's DTAPE command. See the literature from your network service provider.

If Files Are Corrupt after Transfer

Sometimes a file will appear to have been transferred correctly, but the copy on the receiving end will be incomplete or otherwise corrupted. The most common explanations are:

1. The file was not transferred completely, and Kermit's FILE INCOMPLETE setting was KEEP. Use Kermit's recovery features to continue the file transfer from the point of interruption (see Chapter 9).

2. The file was transferred in text mode when it should have been transferred in binary mode, or vice versa (see Chapter 9). Usually the file transfer mode is determined by the most recent SET FILE TYPE command given to the file sender, which automatically informs the receiver of the transfer mode, but in case the file receiver is not a modern Columbia University Kermit program, it might be necessary to give the appropriate corresponding SET FILE TYPE commands to *both* Kermit programs prior to transfer.

3. You are using some combination of C-Kermit 5A(190) or later, MS-DOS Kermit 3.14 or later, or IBM Mainframe Kermit 4.3.1 or later in client/server mode (explained in Chapter 11). In this case, it is the *client's* file type setting, rather than the file sender's, that prevails. Cure: tell the *client* to SET FILE TYPE BINARY, or to be extra sure, tell them both.

4. Some non-Columbia Kermit implementations simply do not work correctly, including the ones found in certain BBS software. Typical symptoms might include corruption of particular characters (e.g. letter Y becomes Ctrl-Y) or a change in the file size after binary-mode transfer). The cure is to replace the offending software with a real Kermit implementation from Columbia University.

5. You are sending files from VMS C-Kermit, which is unique among Kermit programs in its ability to automatically switch between text and binary mode based on each file's local characteristics, but the file's characteristics are inappropriate to its actual type (this happens commonly with ZIP files). Please read about the SET FILE TYPE IMAGE command in Appendix IV, page 535.

6. You are doing a text-mode transfer of a text file that contains accented or non-Roman characters, but you have not set up the character-set translations correctly. This is the topic of Chapter 16.

Finally, there is the possibility that the file was corrupt to begin with; perhaps uploaded incompletely or using an inappropriate transfer mode. For example, it might be a ZIP file that was transferred by FTP in text mode.

Collecting the Evidence

If you have file transfer problems:

1. Check your communications settings (espcially parity) with the SHOW COMMUNICATIONS command.

2. Check your file parameters (especially your FILE TYPE setting, text or binary) with the SHOW FILE command.

3. Check your Kermit protocol parameters with the SHOW PROTOCOL command.

Make any desired adjustments and try again. If all else fails, you can capture C-Kermit's (mis)behavior in two types of log files:

LOG PACKETS *[filename [{* **APPEND, NEW** *}]]*
Records Kermit's file transfer packets in the specified file. If you omit the FILENAME, PACKET.LOG is used. A new file is created unless you include the word APPEND at the end of the command, which means to add records to the end of the named file. Show the packet log to a Kermit guru or decode the packets yourself if you have a copy of *Kermit, A File Transfer Protocol* [21], which spells out the details of Kermit packet format and protocol rules.

LOG DEBUG *[filename [{* **APPEND, NEW** *}]]*
Records voluminous information about C-Kermit's inner workings in the specified file. For Kermit gurus only. Used for serious late-night marathon debugging sessions in combination with the C-Kermit source code and gallons of coffee. Knowledge of the C programming language [53] is a plus.

These log files are closed automatically when you EXIT from C-Kermit. You can also close them at any desired time with the CLOSE PACKETS or CLOSE DEBUG commands.

Chapter 11

Using a Kermit Server

By now you should be a wiz at Kermit file transfer. You can use SET commands to adapt Kermit programs to all sorts of different conditions and you can send files back and forth successfully. In this chapter, you'll learn an easier way to transfer files, in which you won't have to give commands to *both* Kermit programs. And you'll see that Kermit not only transfers files but can help you manage them, too.

In Kermit's basic mode of operation, you tell the remote Kermit what to do, then escape back to the local Kermit and tell the local Kermit what to do. If you are transferring only one file or one group of files, this is no major inconvenience — no more than, say, cooking a simple dinner for yourself at home. But if you want to upload some files, download some others, delete some, print some, and so on, repeated connecting and escaping back can become tiresome. This is more like hosting a dinner party. For such occasions, you might prefer to take your friends to a restaurant and eat out.

A *Kermit server* is a Kermit program running in a special way. You tell your local Kermit program what you want and it tells the Kermit server what to do, like the waiter gives your order to the chef. The server performs the required tasks silently, out of sight in the kitchen, and relays the results back to your local Kermit program, just as your waiter brings your dinner once the chef has prepared it.

The difference between using a Kermit server and eating in a restaurant is that with Kermit, before you can order anything you might have to visit the kitchen and install the chef. Once installed, your chef no longer talks to you directly, but only to the waiter, who translates your order into the colorful restaurant jargon that only the chef understands.

Before you can "eat out," you need two things: one Kermit program that can be a server (the chef) and another (the waiter) that can talk to the server. The computer jargon for the waiter is "client." The Kermit client is usually the local Kermit, and the server is usually on the remote end. But not always. C-Kermit can act as either a client or a server.

Configuring the Server

If you are in control of both ends of the connection — client and server — you can skip ahead to the next section. The commands described in this section are primarily for setting up a Kermit server for other people to use:

SET SERVER DISPLAY *{ ON, OFF }*
> If C-Kermit is in local mode and has been given a SERVER command, it normally produces a file transfer display of whatever style was specified in your most recent SET FILE DISPLAY command, if any, or else the default style. You can SET SERVER DISPLAY OFF to suppress it if desired.

SET SERVER GET-PATH *[directory [directory [. . .]]]*
> This command lets you tell C-Kermit where to look for files when the client gives a GET (or REGET) command, but does not specify a full pathname. Normally the server just looks in its current directory. There can be up to 64 directories in the SERVER GET-PATH. If you specify one or more directories in the SERVER GET-PATH, the server searches them in the order given. Example (for UNIX):

```
C-Kermit> set server get-path /usr/olga/ ~olaf /tmp
```

> If a SERVER GET-PATH is set, then it, and only it, is used for finding files whose names are not absolute. The filename from the GET request is appended to the first element in the GET-PATH and C-Kermit checks to see if the file exists. If not, the process is repeated for the second and subsequent GET-PATH element until the file is located or the GET-PATH is exhausted. If you want to include the current directory in the GET-PATH, you must mention it explicitly.

SET SERVER IDLE-TIMEOUT *number*
> This command, if it is available in your version of C-Kermit, restricts the amount of time the server will wait for a command from the client to the given number of seconds. The default *number* is 0, which tells the server to wait forever. If the number is greater than 0, and no commands are received from the client within that many seconds, C-Kermit exits from server mode.

SET SERVER LOGIN *[username [password [account]]]*
> If you give this command prior to putting C-Kermit in server mode, no client will be able to issue any commands to the server until it uses REMOTE LOGIN (explained later) to supply a username (and password, if you specified one) that exactly match those

from SET SERVER LOGIN. Logins and logouts are recorded in the transaction log. Only one username/password combination can be set up; there is no "password file" or user list by which the Kermit server supports multiple users. The account, if any is given, is recorded in the transaction log.

SET SERVER TIMEOUT *seconds*

When the server is not fulfilling a request it is waiting for a command from the client. Normally, the waiting is "silent" — the server does not send any characters at all to the client. You can use this command to make it time out and send NAK packets (see page 246) at periodic intervals while it is waiting for a command. This is useful if the client program is not capable of timing out. If a packet from a such a client is lost, the client will wait forever for the reply that never comes; having the server issue periodic NAKs will break this sort of deadlock. If *seconds* is 0, there are no timeouts during server command wait. The default SERVER TIMEOUT is 0. It is rarely necessary to use this command.

You can control access to the C-Kermit server's services on an individual basis with the DISABLE and ENABLE commands. All services are enabled by default.

DISABLE *service*

Instructs the server not to perform the named service.

ENABLE *service*

Reinstates a service that was previously disabled.

Here are the services that can be disabled and enabled; the services themselves are explained in the next section. The effect of disabling each service is described. Enabling a service removes all restrictions that were imposed when you DISABLEd it. If you want to disable certain functions, be sure to give the appropriate DISABLE commands *before* you give the SERVER command.

DISABLE ASSIGN

Don't allow the client to manipulate server variables.

DISABLE BYE

Ignore BYE commands; remain in server mode. Example:

```
C-Kermit>disable bye            (Don't let them log me out)
C-Kermit>server                 (Enter server mode)
Entering server mode, blah blah blah ...
Alt-x                           (Escape back)
MS-Kermit>bye                   (Try to log out the server)
Error: BYE disabled
MS-Kermit>
```

The server remains in server mode, ready to accept and execute any commands that have not been disabled.

DISABLE CD

Disallow changing of the default device and/or directory. Don't allow files to be transferred into or out of any but the current device/directory. Don't allow files outside the current directory to be listed, deleted, or typed.

DISABLE { COPY, DELETE, DIRECTORY }

Ignore the indicated REMOTE commands from the client.

DISABLE FINISH

Ignore FINISH commands; remain in server mode.

DISABLE GET

Ignore GET commands; don't send files.

DISABLE HOST

Do not execute host commands on behalf of the client.

DISABLE MAIL

Do not accept files to be delivered as mail.

DISABLE PRINT

Do not accept files for printing.

DISABLE QUERY

Don't allow the client to read server variables.

DISABLE RENAME

Ignore RENAME commands from the client.

DISABLE RETRIEVE

Do not let the client command the server to send and then delete files.

DISABLE SEND

Refuse to receive files when the client Kermit tries to send them.

DISABLE SET

Do not allow the client to change the server's settings.

DISABLE SPACE

Do not tell the client how much space is available.

DISABLE { TYPE, WHO }

Ignore these REMOTE commands from the client.

CAUTION: Some of these commands, including COPY, DELETE, DIRECTORY, RENAME, SPACE, TYPE, and WHO, might also be accessible via REMOTE HOST. If you want to prevent users from accessing these functions through the server, you must DISABLE HOST, too.

The SET SERVER and ENABLE/DISABLE settings are shown by the SHOW SERVER command:

```
C-Kermit>sho server
Function          Status:
 GET              enabled
 SEND             enabled
 REMOTE ASSIGN    enabled
 REMOTE CD/CWD    enabled
 REMOTE COPY      enabled
 REMOTE DELETE    enabled
 REMOTE DIRECTORY enabled
 REMOTE HOST      enabled
 REMOTE MAIL      enabled
 REMOTE PRINT     enabled
 REMOTE QUERY     enabled
 REMOTE RENAME    enabled
 REMOTE RETRIEVE  enabled
 REMOTE SET       enabled
 REMOTE SPACE     enabled
 REMOTE TYPE      enabled
 REMOTE WHO       enabled
 BYE              disabled
 FINISH           enabled
 ...
C-Kermit>
```

Starting the Server

After the server is configured the way you want it, start it with this command:

SERVER
> Tells the Kermit program to enter server mode using current communication and protocol settings. The prompt disappears, and all further communication takes place using Kermit protocol packets.

Here's an example in which your local computer is a PC running Kermit 95, and you start a C-Kermit server on a *remote* UNIX computer:

```
[D:\K95] K-95> connect              (Connect to the remote computer)
login: olga                         (Login if necessary)
Password: _____

$ kermit                            (Start Kermit)
C-Kermit>server                     (Put it in server mode)
Entering server mode.  If your local Kermit software is menu driven, use
the menus to send commands to the server.  Otherwise, enter the escape
sequence to return to your local Kermit prompt and issue commands from
there.  Use SEND and GET for file transfer.  Use REMOTE HELP for a list of
other available services.  Use BYE or FINISH to end server mode.

KERMIT READY TO SERVE...
Alt-X                               (Escape back to PC)
[D:\K95] K-95>
```

From this point, you may conduct all further business from your local Kermit's prompt. If you try typing commands before you escape back, nothing will happen: the characters you type are not likely to be valid Kermit packets, so the server ignores them. In an emergency, however, you can get back to the C-Kermit command prompt by typing three Ctrl-C's in a row, or whatever else your TRANSFER CANCELLATION setting calls for:

```
C-Kermit>server                        (Put C-Kermit in server mode)
Entering server mode.  If your local Kermit software is menu driven, use
the menus to send commands to the server.  Otherwise, enter the escape
sequence to return to your local Kermit prompt and issue commands from
there.  Use SEND and GET for file transfer.  Use REMOTE HELP for a list of
other available services.  Use BYE or FINISH to end server mode.

KERMIT READY TO SERVE...
Ctrl-C Ctrl-C Ctrl-C                    (Type Ctrl-C three times)
^C...
C-Kermit>                      .        (The prompt comes back)
```

To operate a Kermit server on a dialin or network port, so that others can make a connection to it and use it, you should put all the preparatory commands into a command file and then have C-Kermit TAKE the command file. A command file is needed because your SET HOST or ANSWER command waits until a connection comes in, and the SERVER command can't be given until it does, which could be minutes, hours, or days later. Here is a typical procedure for setting up a dialup server.

```
set take error on        ; Exit from command file upon any error
cd ~/public              ; Change to desired directory
set modem type telebit   ; Specify your modem type
set line /dev/cua        ; Communication port
set flow rts/cts         ; Flow control
set speed 57600          ; Speed
disable cd               ; Don't let them leave it
set server login username password  ; Require login with password

(Give any other desired SET SERVER or DISABLE commands here)

answer                   ; Wait for a call to come in
server                   ; Enter server mode
```

And for a TCP/IP connection:

```
set take error on        ; Exit from command file upon any error
cd /tmp                  ; Change to desired directory
disable cd               ; Don't let them leave it
disable send             ; Don't let them upload files
disable delete           ; Don't let them delete files
set server login username password  ; Require login with password

(Give any other desired SET SERVER or DISABLE commands here)

set host * 3000          ; Listen for a TCP connection on port 3000
server                   ; Enter server mode
```

Sending Commands to Kermit Servers

The previous section explained how to set up a server; this section explains how the client uses it. The first interactive Kermit command you learned was EXIT. The first command you should learn for controlling a Kermit server is the one that takes it out of server mode:

FINISH

Sends a command packet from a Kermit client to a Kermit server. This packet instructs the server to exit server mode and return to its interactive Kermit prompt, or to exit to the system prompt, depending on how it was started. Example:

```
MS-Kermit>finish          (Shut down the server)
MS-Kermit>connect         (Go back)
C-Kermit>                 (C-Kermit's prompt has returned)
```

A similar command makes the entire remote session just go away:

BYE

Tells the client Kermit program to send a command packet to a Kermit server. This packet tells the server to destroy itself and log out the session or job under which it is running and hang up the connection. It should be equivalent to FINISH, then exit from remote Kermit, then log out from remote session. On network connections, the BYE command also causes the *client* to close the connection.

Let's practice starting and stopping a remote C-Kermit server a few times from a PC:

```
MS-Kermit>connect          (Connect to the remote computer)
login: olga                (Log in)
Password: _____          (Supply your password)

$ kermit                   (Start Kermit)
C-Kermit>server            (Put it in server mode)
Entering server mode.  If your local Kermit software is menu driven, use
the menus to send commands to the server.  Otherwise, enter the escape
sequence to return to your local Kermit prompt and issue commands from
there.  Use SEND and GET for file transfer.  Use REMOTE HELP for a list of
other available services.  Use BYE or FINISH to end server mode.

KERMIT READY TO SERVE...
help                       (Type commands to the server)
exit                       (See how it ignores them)
Alt-X                      (Escape back to PC)
MS-Kermit>finish           (Shut down the server)
MS-Kermit>connect          (Connect again)
C-Kermit server done
C-Kermit>                  (The prompt is back)
C-Kermit>server            (Start the server again)

Entering server mode.  If your local Kermit software is menu driven, use
the menus to send commands to the server.  Otherwise, enter the escape
sequence to return to your local Kermit prompt and issue commands from
there.  Use SEND and GET for file transfer.  Use REMOTE HELP for a list of
other available services.  Use BYE or FINISH to end server mode.
```

```
KERMIT READY TO SERVE...
Ctrl-C Ctrl-C Ctrl-C                    (Type 3 Ctrl-C's)
^C...
C-Kermit>                               (Prompt reappears)
C-Kermit>server                         (Start the server again)
```

Entering server mode. If your local Kermit software is menu driven, use
the menus to send commands to the server. Otherwise, enter the escape
sequence to return to your local Kermit prompt and issue commands from
there. Use SEND and GET for file transfer. Use REMOTE HELP for a list of
other available services. Use BYE or FINISH to end server mode.

```
KERMIT READY TO SERVE...
Alt-X                                   (Escape back to PC)
MS-Kermit>bye                           (Terminate the remote session)
MS-Kermit>
```

All other client commands are sent to the server in the same way: by typing them at the
client Kermit program's prompt or, if the client Kermit program is menu driven or has a
graphical user interface (GUI), by selecting the desired items from the client/server menu.
Of course, client commands can also come from command files or macros.

Interrupting Server Operations

SEND, GET, and the other client commands can be interrupted the same way you would interrupt a file transfer: X to cancel a file, Z to cancel a group, and so on (see Chapter 9).
You can also CONNECT to the C-Kermit server and type three Ctrl-C's, or whatever other
sequence its TRANSFER CANCELLATION setting calls for.

Transferring Files with a Server

Now that you know how to start and stop the server, let's put it to work. Here are the
basic commands for transferring files, which you would give to your *local* client Kermit
program's prompt, *after* putting the *remote* Kermit program in server mode and escaping
back to the local Kermit program:

SEND *filespec [remote-filename]*

Sends the file or group of files named by *filespec* to the server (or, if no *filespec* is
given, then the files in the Send List, if any). This is exactly the same command that
you use to send files to a Kermit program that has been given the RECEIVE command
and it works the same way in every respect (see Chapter 9).

MOVE *filespec [remote-filename]*

Sends the file or group of files named by *filespec* to the server, and then deletes the
original (source) copy of each file that was sent successfully and completely.

MSEND *filespec [filespec [...]]*

You can also use the MSEND command to send a selected group of files to the server,
each under its own name.

MMOVE *filespec [filespec [. . .]]*

Like MSEND, but deletes each source file after it has been sent successfully.

SEND

You can also use the ADD SEND-LIST command to build a send list, and then SEND without a *filespec*, to send a mixed group of files, possibly in mixed transfer modes, with any desired assortment of "as-names," to a server.

GET *filespec [filespec [. . .]]*

Asks the Kermit server to send the file or file group specified by the *filespec*(s), which are given in the syntax of the server's computer.

REGET *filespec [filespec [. . .]]*

Asks the Kermit server to RESEND the specified file or file group using the file transfer recovery method described in Chapter 9. Works only for binary-mode transfers.

RETRIEVE *filespec [filespec [. . .]]*

Asks the Kermit server to send the given files and then delete each one that was sent successfully.

GET (and REGET, and RETRIEVE) are quite different from RECEIVE. Unlike RECEIVE, which passively waits for a file to arrive from another Kermit that has been given a SEND command, the GET command actively requests a particular file with a "please send me" protocol message containing the file name(s). If you give a RECEIVE command instead, the server doesn't know what file you want:

```
[D:\K95] K-95> receive            (Should have been "GET filespec")
Protocol Error: Did you say RECEIVE instead of GET?
[D:\K95] K-95>
```

A special form of the GET, REGET, and RETRIEVE commands lets you ask for a single file and then store it under a different name. Just type carriage return (press the key marked Return or Enter) immediately after the word GET (or REGET), and Kermit prompts you for the remote and local names separately:

```
[D:\K95] K-95> get
 Remote source file: foo bar b
 Local destination file: foo.bar
```

You can use wildcards in all the file transfer commands. Wildcards in the GET, REGET, and RETRIEVE commands must be written in the notation of the computer where the server is running.

When C-Kermit itself is the server, your GET, REGET, or RETRIEVE command can include a single filename, a wildcard filename, or a list of any mixture of these. The C-Kermit server sends all the requested files in a single operation:

```
MS-Kermit>get ck*.c *.h ~olga/oofa.doc
```

The file specifications are separated by spaces (not commas). If you need to include a space in a filename, use \32 (backslash followed by the ASCII code for space). In this example we ask a VMS C-Kermit server to send a file that resides on another DECnet node (more about this in Appendix IV):

```
MS-Kermit>get node"USER\32PASSWD"::dev:[dir]name.ext
```

If you need to include a backslash in the filename, you might need to use two of them, depending on the quoting rules of the Kermit client.

Choosing Text or Binary Transfer

As you learned in Chapter 9, the transfer mode — text or binary — in SEND/RECEIVE file transfers is determined by the file *sender*.

When using modern Kermit software in a client/server arrangement, however, the file transfer mode (SET FILE TYPE) and filename conversion (SET FILE NAMES) are controlled in a more convenient, if somewhat more complex, manner.

The precise method used by any Kermit client/server pair to determine the transfer mode is as follows:

1. If both client and server support the "whoami" feature (see Table 1-1 on page 10), by which they inform each other of their system type, and they determine that they are running on the same type of system, *and* SET TRANSFER MODE is AUTOMATIC, then both client and server switch automatically into BINARY transfer mode (in OS/2 and VMS they switch into LABELED transfer mode). Otherwise:

2. If both client and server support the "whatami" feature (again, see Table 1-1), by which the two Kermits inform each other of their client/server status, transfer mode, and file names setting, the *client's* settings take precedence. Otherwise:

3. If both client and server support Attribute packets (Table 1-1), by which the file sender informs the receiver of (among other things) the transfer mode, the *file sender's* settings dominate. Thus the client can change settings prior to sending files and all will work as expected. But when GETting files from the server, the server's settings dominate. In case the server does not have the desired modes, you can use REMOTE SET, explained later in this chapter, to change them.

4. If none of the above is true, then you must give the appropriate SET FILE TYPE and SET FILE NAMES commands to both client and server to ensure correct transfer.

To put it more simply: When using modern Kermit versions in client/server mode, and you have not gone out of your way to disable their features, you can control the transfer mode by giving commands to the client, without having to tell the server too.

The Client's REMOTE Command

So far, we've seen the Kermit server only as a new way of doing the same old thing — transferring files. But you can also use the server for remote file management, just as you can use C-Kermit for local file management by giving it DIRECTORY, DELETE, and similar commands. The difference is the word REMOTE. The REMOTE prefix lets you send commands to the remote Kermit server instead of executing them locally:

```
MS-Kermit>delete data.tmp          (Delete a local file)
MS-Kermit>remote delete data.tmp   (Delete a remote file)
```

The DELETE command deletes a file on your local computer; the REMOTE DELETE command asks the remote Kermit server to delete a file on *its* computer.

Most REMOTE commands send back their results to your screen, like the REMOTE HELP command shown on the next page. You can also redirect this material to a file or to another process using the following notation (shown with the REMOTE DIRECTORY command, but it works with any REMOTE command):

```
remote dir                         ; Displays on screen
remote dir > filename              ; Goes to a (new) file
remote dir >> filename             ; Appends to a file
remote dir | command               ; Piped into a command
remote dir | command > filename    ; .. whose output goes to a file
remote dir | command >> filename   ; .. or is appended to a file
```

The redirection indicators ">", ">>", and "|" are the familiar ones from UNIX and DOS. ">" means to create a new file of the given name, overwriting any existing file having the same name. ">>" means to append to (write to the end of) the named file if it exists, otherwise create a new file. "|" indicates a "pipe" to another program or to a system command; the Kermit material is sent as "standard input" to the indicated command.

The REMOTE commands are as follows. They are executed if the server understands them and they have not been disabled in the server.

REMOTE CD [directory]

Tells the client Kermit to ask the Kermit server to change its default (working) directory to the one given, expressed in the syntax of the server's file system. If none is given, the server changes to its home, login, or default directory. Examples:

```
MS-Kermit>remote cd /usr/include   (UNIX)
MS-Kermit>remote cd sys$system     (VMS)
MS-Kermit>remote cd                (Default directory)
```

REMOTE COPY filespec1 filespec2

Tells the client to ask the Kermit server to copy the file or files given by *filespec1* to the device, directory, or file(s) given by *filespec2*. The copy operation is performed on the server's computer. Write/create access is required for *filespec2*. Example:

```
C-Kermit>remote copy oofa.txt copy-of-oofa.txt
```

REMOTE DELETE *filespec*

Tells the client to ask the Kermit server to delete the specified file or files on the server's computer. Normal access restrictions apply — the server can't delete a file that you could not delete yourself. Example:

```
MS-Kermit>remo del *.tmp          (Delete all my .tmp files)
```

REMOTE DIRECTORY *[filespec]*

Tells the client to ask the server to send a directory listing of the specified file or files to your screen. The *filespec* is in the syntax of the Kermit server's operating system. If no *filespec* is given, the server sends a directory listing of all files in its current directory.

```
MS-Kermit>remo dir *.txt          (List all my .txt files)
MS-Kermit>rem dir                 (All files in current dir)
MS-Kermit>rem dir [ivan]          (A different directory)
```

REMOTE HELP

Tells the client to ask the remote server for a list of the services it offers. In this example, an MS-DOS Kermit client queries a UNIX C-Kermit server:

```
MS-Kermit>remote help
C-Kermit Server REMOTE Commands:

GET files          REMOTE CD [dir]        REMOTE HOST command
REGET files        REMOTE SPACE [dir]     REMOTE DIRECTORY [files]
RETRIEVE files     REMOTE DELETE files    REMOTE LOGIN user password
SEND files         REMOTE PRINT files     REMOTE SET parameter value
RESEND files       REMOTE TYPE files      REMOTE QUERY type variable
MAIL file user     REMOTE WHO [user]      REMOTE ASSIGN variable value
FINISH, BYE        REMOTE HELP
MS-Kermit>
```

If the client Kermit has these commands, the C-Kermit server can execute them. Other Kermit servers might have different menus.

REMOTE HOST *command*

Tells the client to ask the server to ask its host operating system to execute the given command or program and return the results to your screen. This command is described more fully on page 240.

REMOTE KERMIT *text*

Tells the client Kermit program to send the text to the server, which is to interpret it as if it were a Kermit command typed at its own Kermit prompt. C-Kermit can send this command as a client, but a C-Kermit server cannot respond to it (presently, this command is useful only when sent to an IBM Mainframe Kermit server).

REMOTE LOGIN *name [password [account]]*

Tells the client Kermit program to send user ID, password, and, optionally, account information to a Kermit server that has been set up to require login before it will execute any other commands.

REMOTE LOGOUT

Terminates your access rights with a Kermit server that you have previously accessed via REMOTE LOGIN.

REMOTE PRINT *filespec [options]*

Sends the specified local file to the Kermit server and asks the Kermit server to print it using the specified options, if any. The options are in the syntax of the server's host operating system. If no options are specified, the server system's defaults are used:

```
MS-Kermit>remote print oofa.txt /queue=laser /copies=3   (VMS)
MS-Kermit>remo prin oofa.txt -Plaser -#3                  (UNIX)
MS-Kermit>rem pri oofa.txt
```

Note: If you want to tell the server to print a file that is already resident on the server's computer, use a REMOTE HOST command, such as "remote host lpr oofa.txt" (UNIX) or "remote host print/copies=2 oofa.txt" (VMS).

REMOTE PWD

Tells the client Kermit program to ask the server to display its current directory ("pwd" means "print working directory"). Example:

```
C-Kermit>remo cd ~olga
C-Kermit>rem pwd
/users/olga
C-Kermit>
```

REMOTE RENAME *filename1 filename2*

Tells the client to ask the server to change the name of the file whose name is *filename1* to *filename2*. Example:

```
C-Kermit>remote rename oofa.txt newname-of-oofa.txt
```

REMOTE SPACE *[device-or-directory]*

Tells the client Kermit program to ask the Kermit server to give a brief report on space used or available on the given device or directory or, if none is given, in the server's current device or directory. Examples:

```
MS-Kermit>remot space /usr          (UNIX, /usr partition)
MS-Kermit>remo spac sys$login       (VMS, login disk)
MS-Kermit>rem spa a:                (Windows or OS/2, A: disk)
MS-Kermit>rem spa                   (Any, current disk)
```

REMOTE TYPE *filespec*

Tells the client Kermit program to ask the Kermit server to display the specified file on your screen. The file is assumed to be a text file. Example:

```
MS-Kermit>remote type oofa.txt
```

REMOTE WHO *[user]*

Tells the client Kermit program to ask the Kermit server to send information about a particular user of its computer or, if the computer is on a network, about any user on any computer on the network. If no user is specified, the server sends a list of all users who are currently logged in. Examples:

```
MS-Kermit>remote who                    (All logged-in users)
MS-Kermit>remote who olaf               (A particular user)
MS-Kermit>remote who kermit@watsun (A user on the network)
```

REMOTE commands are system-independent. They are translated by your local Kermit into standard protocol messages understood by all Kermit servers that support these commands. If you send a command that is not in the server's repertoire, the server responds with a message like "Unimplemented server command".

The REMOTE HOST Command

As noted in the previous section, the REMOTE HOST command lets the client program run a command or program on the server's host computer. This command differs from other REMOTE commands in several ways.

First, the syntax for redirection is a bit different. For example, does this:

```
remote host ls -lt > filename
```

mean the command "ls -lt" is to have its output sent to a file on the server's computer or on the client's? In cases like this, you can "disambiguate" redirectors using braces:

```
remote host blah blah > file              ; File on this end
remote host { blah blah } > file          ; File on this end
remote host { blah blah > file }          ; File on that end
remote host { blah blah > file } > file ; Files on both ends
```

So much for syntax. As for execution, the *command* must not require a dialog; it has to be the sort of command that you can give to your host operating system completely on one line and that responds by printing a message on your screen using ordinary characters — not graphics or pop-up windows — or by not printing anything, and then exits. Examples:

```
MS-Kermit>remote host ln -s oofa.old oofa.new
MS-Kermit>remo hos date                 (UNIX date and time)
Sat Jul  4 18:42:43 EDT 1996
MS-Kermit>rem ho show time              (VMS date and time)
   4-JUL-1996 18:42:43
MS-Kermit>remote host rmdir temp        (Delete UNIX directory)
MS-Kermit>remo ho delete/dir temp       (Delete VMS directory)
```

If you invoke any other kind of program with REMOTE HOST, the results are unpredictable, and probably not what you wanted. For example, if the server is running under MS-DOS and you give a command like "remote host format a:", your session will get stuck as DOS on the server end prompts the PC's real keyboard and screen to insert a diskette and press the Enter key when ready. Even if the REMOTE HOST *command* conforms to the rules, it might take a long time to execute. In case this causes problems for your client program, such as timing out and giving up, adjust your client program's timeout interval.

Sending E-Mail Through the Server

When the computer that the server is running on has a mail delivery system, you can send files to the server to be delivered as electronic mail. The client command is:

MAIL *filespec address*

Sends the specified local file(s) to the Kermit server, asking the server to deliver it/them as e-mail to the specified address(es) rather than storing it on disk. Examples:

```
MS-Kermit>mail oofa.txt olga, ivan
MS-Kermit>mail message.txt kermit@columbia.edu
MS-Kermit>mail message.* olaf
```

Changing the Server's Settings

If your server allows it and your local Kermit program has the commands for it (MS-DOS Kermit, Kermit 95, Kermit/2, and C-Kermit all can do both), you can change selected server settings from the client:

REMOTE SET *parameter value*

Tells the Kermit client to ask the remote Kermit server to set the given parameter to the specified value. The parameters include many of the same ones used in the SET command, like BLOCK-CHECK, FILE TYPE, and so forth. Issuing the REMOTE SET command to your local Kermit program is exactly like issuing the corresponding SET command to the remote Kermit program if it were in interactive command mode and (in cases where it makes a difference) also issuing the same command to your client program. Here is an example in which we switch a Kermit server from sending files in text mode to binary mode.

```
MS-Kermit>get *.txt                     (Get text files)
MS-Kermit>remote set file type binary
MS-Kermit>get *.bin                     (Get binary files)
```

(Note: This example works independently of the WHATAMI feature, because REMOTE SET FILE TYPE BINARY sets *both* the client's and the server's file transfer mode.)

To see a complete list of REMOTE SET commands supported by your client Kermit program, just type REMOTE SET followed by a space and a question mark; for example:

```
MS-Kermit>remote set ? One of the following:
 attributes   file    incomplete  block-check    receive   retry
 server          transfer  window-slots
MS-Kermit>remote set attributes date off
```

These are the REMOTE SET commands an MS-DOS Kermit client can send to a Kermit server. As with the local SET command, some of these commands have further options:

```
MS-Kermit>remote set receive ? One of the following:
 packet-length   timeout
MS-Kermit>remote set receive timeout 8
MS-Kermit>
```

When C-Kermit itself is the client, it can send the following REMOTE SET commands to a Kermit server:

```
C-Kermit>remote set ? One of the following:
 attributes    file          receive        server         window
 block-check   incomplete    retry          transfer
C-Kermit>
```

And when C-Kermit is the server, it also allows these commands to be sent to it. If you send a REMOTE SET command to a Kermit server that does not support this feature, it replies with an error message like "Unimplemented server function" or "Unknown REMOTE SET parameter".

Transmission of Variables

It is possible for the client to define, query, and in some cases change variables that reside in the server and the server's host operating system. We mention this now for completeness, but the topic of variables is not covered until Chapter 17, and so a complete treatment of transmission of variables between client and server is deferred until that chapter. Briefly, the commands are:

REMOTE ASSIGN *variable-name [value]*
> Tells the Kermit client to ask the Kermit server to assign the given value (if any) to the named variable. If no value is given, the server's variable is deleted.

REMOTE QUERY { KERMIT, SYSTEM, USER } *variable-name*
> Tells the client to ask the server to send the value of the variable of the given type that has the given name. If the query succeeds, the value is displayed on your screen and it is also stored in a local client variable, \v(query).

See Chapter 17 for details.

Turning the Tables

Now that you can control a remote Kermit server from your local computer, can you think of any reason why you might want to have the *remote* Kermit program act as a client to a Kermit server running on your *local* computer?

Suppose you want to send a mixture of text and binary files from a remote UNIX computer to MS-DOS Kermit on your local PC. (The remote UNIX computer has an old version of C-Kermit that does not support ADD SEND-LIST). Here is one way to do it. Connect and login to the remote computer from your local PC. Then use your UNIX text editor to create a *command file* for UNIX C-Kermit containing the necessary SET FILE TYPE and SEND commands, as in this example, called download.ksc:

```
echo Return to your local Kermit and give the SERVER command.
set delay 5              ; Allow time to escape back
set file type binary     ; Binary for object and executable files
msend *.o wermit
set file type text       ; Text for source files
msend *.c *.h
finish                   ; Return the PC to normal
```

The FINISH command makes MS-DOS Kermit's prompt reappear after all the files have been transferred.

Now start C-Kermit on the UNIX system, have it TAKE the command file, then escape back to the PC and put MS-DOS Kermit into server mode:

```
C-Kermit>take download.ksc          (TAKE the command file)
Return to your local Kermit and give the SERVER command.
Alt-x                                (Escape back to the PC)
MS-Kermit>serve                      (Put it in server mode)
```

And now go to lunch while all the files are being transferred.

An even better reason for a reverse client/server relationship is presented in Chapter 13. But first, Chapter 12 examines the performance of the Kermit protocol and shows you how to get the most out of it.

Command Summary

The following commands are used to configure and start a C-Kermit server:

```
SET SERVER DISPLAY { ON, OFF }
SET SERVER GET-PATH directory [ directory ... ]
SET SERVER IDLE-TIMEOUT number
SET SERVER LOGIN [ username [ password [ account ] ] ]
SET SERVER TIMEOUT seconds
DISABLE service
ENABLE service
SERVER
```

The following services can be ENABLEd and DISABLEd:

```
ASSIGN        QUERY
BYE           PRINT
CD            RENAME
COPY          RETRIEVE
DELETE        SEND
DIRECTORY     SET
FINISH        SPACE
GET           TYPE
HOST          WHO
MAIL
```

Use the SHOW SERVER command to display the server configuration and list which services are enabled and disabled.

Client Summary

To log in and out from the server, if required:

```
REMOTE LOGIN name [ password  [ account ] ]
REMOTE LOGOUT
```

To find out what services are available:

```
REMOTE HELP
```

To change the server's settings:

```
REMOTE SET parameter value
REMOTE KERMIT command
```

To access the server's variables:

```
REMOTE QUERY { KERMIT, SYSTEM, USER }
REMOTE ASSIGN variable-name [ value ]
```

To send files to the server:

```
SEND [ filespec [ remote-filename ] ]
MOVE filespec [ remote-filename ]
MSEND filespec [ filespec ... ]
MMOVE filespec [ filespec ... ]
MAIL filespec address
REMOTE PRINT filespec [ options ]
```

To get files from the server:

```
GET filespec [ filespec ... ]
REGET filespec [ filespec ... ]
RETRIEVE filespec [ filespec ... ]
```

For file and user access on the server:

```
REMOTE CD [ directory ]
REMOTE COPY filespec1 filespec2
REMOTE DELETE filespec
REMOTE DIRECTORY [ filespec ]
REMOTE PWD
REMOTE RENAME filename1 filename2
REMOTE SPACE  [ device/directory ]
REMOTE TYPE filespec
REMOTE WHO  [ user ]
```

To execute host commands on the server's computer:

```
REMOTE HOST command
```

To shut down the server:

```
FINISH
BYE
```

Chapter 12

High-Speed Kermit File Transfer

Not to wear out our pet analogy, but learning to use Kermit is like learning to drive a car. We stress safety first, performance later. If you have been following the chapters in sequence, you should be experiencing reliable transfers of all types of files between all manner of systems on all sorts of connections. But you might have noticed that the transfers were not particularly fast. This might be the cause of the persistent but unfounded rumor that Kermit protocol is intrinsically slow compared to other protocols like ZMODEM.

Safety first. You don't learn to drive at 120 miles per hour; first you master the basic skills at lower speeds. And no matter how skilled you are, you can't drive your car at high speed down a bumpy road through a traffic jam. But suppose the road is smooth, wide, and straight and you have it all to yourself. How fast can you go?

Here is an easy speed trial for those who are using any combination of C-Kermit, Kermit 95, Kermit/2, or MS-DOS Kermit. Fasten your seat belts! At the Kermit prompt of each Kermit program, type the command FAST prior to starting a file transfer; for example:

```
C-Kermit> fast                    (Make the remote Kermit fast)
C-Kermit> receive                 (Tell it to wait for a file)
Alt-x                             (Escape back)
MS-Kermit> set file type binary  (It's a binary file)
MS-Kermit> fast                   (Make the local Kermit fast)
MS-Kermit> send kermit.exe        (Send a file)
```

If the transfer worked at all, it should have been plenty fast. If it didn't, well... that's what the rest of this chapter is for, in which we take a look at the performance features of the Kermit protocol and how to harness them.

Overview of the Kermit Protocol

When you transfer a file, Kermit breaks it up into a series of messages called *packets*. Each packet consists of distinct start and end markers; a length field for framing; a sequence number for detection of missing, duplicated, or out-of-sequence packets; a packet type; maybe some data; and a checksum for error detection, as shown in Figure 12-1.

Except for the start and end markers (Control-A and Carriage Return, respectively), the packets are normally encoded by the sender as short, simple lines of printable text to survive even the most hostile communication environments, and decoded by the receiver into the appropriate form. Each control character (ASCII 0–31, 127–159, and 255) is encoded as a sequence of two printable characters; for example, Control-C (ASCII 3) is encoded as the two-character sequence "#C".

The file sender sends packets of various types, and the file receiver replies to each packet with an acknowledgement (ACK) to indicate that the packet was received correctly, or a negative acknowledgement (NAK) that tells the sender a packet was received in damaged condition — or not received at all — and therefore needs to be retransmitted.

Because the file sender waits for an acknowledgement before sending the next packet, the rate at which packets are exchanged is controlled by the receiver, which prevents a fast sender from overrunning a slower receiver. This style of packet exchange, called "stop and wait," is illustrated in Figure 12-2. Of course, the protocol does not stop and wait forever. If an expected packet does not arrive within a certain amount of time, there is an automatic timeout and retransmission to break the deadlock.

The packet exchange proceeds through the following phases, each of which is associated with a particular packet type, shown in parentheses (see Table 9-2 on page 186 for a more complete list of Kermit packet types):

1. (S) Send initation and feature negotiation. "I am sending one or more files to you and here are some facts about my features and configuration." This lets the two Kermits determine which features they have in common and agree to use them, and allows the newest, most full-featured version of Kermit to work automatically with even the oldest barest-bones version.

2. (F) The file sender sends the file name so the receiver can create the new file with the same name.

<START>	LEN	SEQ	TYP	DATA		CHK	<END>

Figure 12-1 Kermit Packet Format

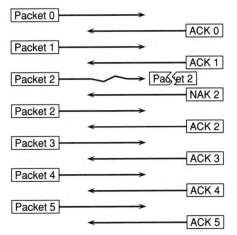

Figure 12-2 Stop-and-Wait Packet Exchange

3. (A) The file sender sends information about the file (file attributes) so the receiver can create the file with the appropriate attributes, including size, creation date, transfer mode (text or binary), character set, and so forth.

4. (D) The file sender sends the contents (data) of the file, usually requiring many packets. During the data phase of a text-mode transfer, the Kermit protocol accomplishes the necessary conversions by translating between the local computer's character codes and file formats and the standard ones specified by the protocol, so each computer needs to know only its own local conventions and the standard ones.

5. (Z) When all the file's data has been sent, the file sender sends an end-of-file packet so the receiving computer knows the file has been completely received and can close it.

   If there are more files to send, steps 2–5 are repeated for each file.

6. (B) When all the files have been sent, the file sender terminates the operation by sending a "Break" packet, causing each Kermit program to leave packet mode and return control to the user, with the local Kermit program notifying the user that the file has been completely transferred.

So, in short, the Kermit protocol breaks a file up into packets, encodes the data somehow, and sends messages back and forth in packet form. This tends to introduce some overhead and might be slower than (say) just blasting all of the file's bytes out the communication channel all at once without any kind of protocol at all. But it works better.

A Word about Efficiency

How do we measure the efficiency of a file transfer? It is the ratio of the speed at which the file was transferred to the speed of the connection. For example, suppose we have a 1200 bps (120 cps) serial connection and we transfer 36,000 bytes of information in 400 seconds. The speed of the transfer is therefore 90 cps, so we have used the connection at 90 / 120 = 75% efficiency. If we transferred the same data in 200 seconds, the efficiency would be 150%; this might occur with data compression.

But this assumes that we know the speed of the underlying connection, and that it remains constant. This might be the case on a direct serial connection, such as a null-modem cable between two computers. The capacity of the connection is simply the serial port speed. But the full capacity might not be used if one of the computers is slow or busy. A slow sender will exhibit gaps between characters; a slow receiver will exert flow control to throttle the sender. Nevertheless, one can measure the efficiency of a file transfer on such a connection. If neither computer is a bottleneck, then the efficiency number is also a good measure of the efficiency of the file-transfer protocol.

At the opposite end of the spectrum, network connections are entirely unpredictable. In the first place, we rarely know the "transmission speed" of the network, and if we did it would be irrelevant anyway, since the medium is shared by an unknown number of other connections, and the speed of the interface to the network might not be the same as the speed of the network transmission medium. In any event, the network load goes up and down depending on the number of connections and how busy they are; the worse the congestion, the longer each transmission must wait its turn. On a long-distance network connection, the load on each network segment and on the routers or switches that join them also must be considered. And of course, we still must take into account the speed of, and the load on, the two end systems that are using the network to communicate.

The speed of a modem connection depends on many factors: the modulation protocol, the modulation speed, the error correction and data compression protocols (if any), and the interface speeds on each end, which can be different from each other and from the modulation speed itself. If the connection is error-corrected, then noise on the telephone line slows down the data because the modems are retransmitting between themselves, invisibly. If data compression is active, its effectiveness is limited by the lower of the two interface speeds. If the modems have negotiated a mutually acceptable fallback and fallforward arrangement, as is common with V.34 modems, the modulation speed is likely to shift down and up throughout the connection. And the same constraints remain as on direct connections: the speed of and load on the end systems. And when a terminal server is involved, the speed of and load on the terminal server and the network that connects it to the remote system must also be factored in.

So in the modern world of high-speed modems and wide- and local-area networks, efficiency is an increasingly ephemeral concept. We can measure the data transfer rate, but what do we compare it with to calculate the efficiency? We could do this back in the days of direct serial connections and 1200 bps modems, but today efficiency calculations tend to be baseless and misleading.

Analyzing Kermit's Performance

Let's transfer a file on a 9600 bps direct serial connection, using all of C-Kermit's default and deliberately conservative protocol settings[27].

After a file transfer is finished, you can use the STATISTICS command to get information about its efficiency and what parameters were used:

```
C-Kermit>stat
Most recent transaction --
 files transferred:      : 6
 files not transferred:  : 0
 characters last file    : 109313
 total file characters   : 452992
 communication line in   : 25989
 communication line out  : 489226
 packets sent            : 5180
 packets received        : 5187
 damaged packets rec'd   : 4
 timeouts                : 2
 retransmissions         : 7
 parity                  : none
 control characters      : 28328 prefixed, 0 unprefixed.
 8th bit prefixing       : no
 locking shifts          : no
 window slots used       : 1 of 1
 packet length           : 94 (send), 94 (receive)
 compression             : yes [~] (79010)
 block check type used   : 1
 elapsed time            : 681 sec
 transmission rate       : 9600 bps
 effective data rate     : 665 cps (69%)
C-Kermit>
```

Let's take a brief look at this report. It contains all the information needed to tune Kermit's peformance.

---

[27]Kermit 95, Kermit/2, and perhaps some other Kermit versions might have "higher" defaults, so we explicitly set the relevant parameters back to their base values — use the ROBUST command to do this.

```
files transferred:       : 6
files not transferred:   : 0
characters last file     : 109313
total file characters    : 452992     (f)
```

This tells you how many files were transferred, how many were skipped, and how many characters were in the last file transferred and in all the files that were transferred. Let's call this last number f.

```
communication line in    : 25989      (p_i)
communication line out   : 489226     (p_o)
```

This tells you how many characters were received (p_i) and transmitted (p_o) on the communication device. The number of extra characters introduced by the Kermit protocol is:

$$p_i + p_o - f$$

The encoding efficiency is the ratio of the file size to the total number of characters sent and received:

$$\frac{f}{p_i + p_o}$$

which, in this case, comes out to $452992 / (25989 + 489226) = 0.88$. If this number is less than 1, there is a net expansion, and therefore a loss of efficiency. If it's greater than 1, the data must have been compressed more than enough to compensate for the packet overhead.

```
packets sent             : 5180
packets received         : 5187
damaged packets rec'd    : 4
timeouts                 : 2
retransmissions          : 7
```

This tells us how many packets were sent and received. The number of damaged packets is a good indicator of the quality of the connection. A perfectly clean and effectively flow-controlled connection should have none. Timeouts can indicate either a very poor connection (bad enough to make a packet indistinguishable from line noise), long delays, lost packets due to inadequate flow control, or a timeout value based on incorrect assumptions. The number of retransmissions is the number of times packets had to be sent again because of a timeout, because a NAK was received, or because a damaged packet was received.

```
parity                   : none
8th bit prefixing        : no
locking shifts           : no
```

These items tell whether C-Kermit is operating in 7-bit or 8-bit mode. If PARITY is not NONE, you have a 7-bit connection, and 8-bit data is transmitted using single shifts (8th-bit prefixing) or locking shifts (described later) if these features are successfully negotiated (see Table 1-1 on page 10). Both of these methods add additional overhead and should be avoided when possible. In other words, never set PARITY to EVEN, ODD, MARK, or SPACE unless file transfers don't work with PARITY set to NONE.

```
control characters   : 28328 prefixed, 0 unprefixed.
window slots used    : 1 of 1
packet length        : 94 (send), 94 (receive)
compression          : yes [~] (79010)
```

These are Kermit's performance boosters. Keep reading this chapter to find out how to use them.

```
elapsed time         : 681 sec        (t)
transmission rate    : 9600 bps       (r)
effective data rate  : 665 cps (69%) (e)
```

This is Kermit's report card: 69 percent efficiency. We'll improve our score shortly, but first let's see how it was calculated [22]:

$$e = \frac{f \times 10}{r \times t}$$

where:

e = efficiency, 1.00 is perfect
f = file size in characters
t = elapsed time in seconds
r = transmission rate, bits per second

That is, the ratio of total file bits actually transferred to the number of bits that could possibly be transferred in the elapsed time. In our example, this is:

$$\frac{452992 \times 10}{9600 \times 681} = 0.6929$$

or about 69 percent.[28]

Kermit's small packet size and stop-and-wait technique of exchanging packets tend to result in this kind of performance on direct or directly dialed connections, and worse performance than this on connections with noticeable round-trip delays. But this design lets Kermit protocol work on many types of connections where other protocols fail to work at all — half-duplex connections, 7-bit connections, connections that are not transparent to control characters, connections that have small buffers and/or inadequate flow control, and so on. Of course other factors must be considered in the performance too, such as the speed of the computers (CPU power, load on the system, disk access time, and so on), the quality of the connection (the number of retransmissions), the properties of the data communication devices (e.g. compressing versus non-compressing modems).

---

[28]The percent efficiency is reported by the STATISTICS command only on direct serial connections, with no modems involved, which is the only case in which C-Kermit knows the communication speed.

There are several ways to improve the performance of Kermit file transfer:

- Compress the data

- Increase the ratio of real data to packet overhead characters

- Reduce or eliminate the wait between packets

- On 7-bit connections, reduce the amount of 8th-bit prefixing

- Reduce the amount of control-character prefixing

In the next sections we present the tools you will need to accomplish each of these feats, one at a time or in any combination.

Data Compression

Whenever you initiate a file transfer, the sending Kermit asks the receiving Kermit if it can accept compressed data. If there is agreement, the file sender collapses repeated bytes into a sequence composed of a compression prefix character, a repeat count, and then the character itself. For example:

```
~@C
```

stands for 32 letter C's in a row (~ is the prefix character, @ is the encoded repeat count, and C is the letter C itself). Since the repeat count is a single printable ASCII character, the maximum number of repeated characters that can be represented by a repeat-count sequence is 94, the number of printable ASCII characters.

Text files containing long strings of blanks and binary files with repeated null characters turn out to be quite common. The average file — text or binary — is compressed about 15 percent during transmission using this simple method [21, pp. 248–250], which tends to offset most other types of overhead introduced by the Kermit protocol. As an extreme example, we transfer a Sun SPARC executable program ("Hello World"), 24576 bytes in length:

```
C-Kermit>set file type binary
C-Kermit>s hello
   . . .
C-Kermit>statistics
 total file characters    : 24576
 communication line out : 3032
 compression              : yes [~] (23504)
 elapsed time             : 4 sec
 transmission rate:       : 9600 bps
 effective data rate:     : 6144 cps  (647%)
```

"(23504)" means that 23504 file bytes were compressed.

Unfortunately, Kermit's compression feature is handled incorrectly by some shareware and BBS Kermit implementations, so sometimes we have to turn it off to compensate. The command is:

SET REPEAT COUNTS *{ ON, OFF }*

    Enables or disables repeat-count count compression during file transfer. By default, it is enabled.

Some people claim that if files are being transferred through a data-compressing modem, that Kermit's compression is not only redundant but adds unnecessary overhead, thus actually slowing down the transfer. If you are curious, you can compare results with SET REPEAT COUNTS ON and OFF, as we will do before concluding this chapter.

You can also change the repeat prefix character, although there is almost never a need to do this. One reason might be if you were sending a file that contained many tilde characters as data, which themselves could not be compressed. The worst-case file would be composed completely of non-tilde characters interspersed with tildes:

```
~A~B~C~D~E~F~G~H~I~J~K...
```

Each tilde would need to be "quoted" to distinguish it from a repeat prefix, and so the sequence above would be encoded as:

```
#~A#~B#~C#~D#~E#~F#~G#~H#~I#~J#~K...
```

The command to change the repeat prefix is:

SET REPEAT PREFIX *number*

    Changes the repeat prefix to the ASCII character whose code is *number*, which must be in the range 33–63 or 96–126. The default is 126 (tilde).

Before leaving the topic of compression, it is worth noting that the shortest run of repeated characters that results in a savings when compressed is four. However, Kermit compresses even when there are three characters in a row, for two reasons. First, since the compressed sequence is also three characters long, there is no gain in overhead. Second, and more important, this allows Kermit transfers to proceed through modems that return to command mode when they see three plus-signs (or other characters) in a row.[29] Thus, the deadly plus-plus-plus sequence:

```
+++
```

becomes, harmlessly:

```
~#+
```

and your connection does not mysteriously hang up.

---

[29]These are generally Hayes-compatible modems that do not implement a "guard time" around the escape sequence because use of a guard time requires payment of a license fee to the patent holder.

Long Packets

Kermit data packets can be any length between about 5 and 9000 characters.[30] Normal Kermit packets are 94 characters long, and most C-Kermit implementations use this length unless told otherwise. As Figure 12-1 shows, each packet has five control fields in addition to the data, and each packet must be acknowledged by another packet that includes five control fields of its own, but (usually) no data.

Kermit's packet length is a major factor in its performance. The longer the packet, the higher the proportion of actual data to protocol overhead characters, and the fewer acknowledgements required. In a typical trial, Kermit's file transfer efficiency was increased 800 percent just by using longer packets [22, page 13, Table 4]. The trick is to find the ideal packet length for a given connection. The command that governs Kermit's packet length is:

SET RECEIVE PACKET-LENGTH *number*

Give this command to the *file receiver* before the transfer starts. The file receiver gives permission to the file sender to send packets up to the given *number* of bytes (characters) in length. When you are using long packets, you should also stick with the default strong error-checking method (SET BLOCK 3), since the probability of undetected errors goes up with the packet length. Example:

```
C-Kermit>set rec pack 2000       (Set the packet length)
C-Kermit>receive                 (Receive a file)
Alt-x                            (Escape back to the PC)
MS-Kermit>set block-check 3      (Use strong error checking)
MS-Kermit>send oofa.txt          (Send a file)
```

The SET RECEIVE PACKET-LENGTH command works only when you give it to the *file receiver*. Of course, the file sender can decide to use shorter packets anyway, for example if its maximum packet length is less than what the receiver asked for or if it doesn't support long packets at all (see Table 1-1 on page 10). For that matter, you can even tell the file sender yourself:

SET SEND PACKET-LENGTH *number*

Give this command to the *file sender*. The maximum length packet used in the transfer is the smaller of the receiver's RECEIVE PACKET-LENGTH and the sender's SEND PACKET-LENGTH.

---

[30]The absolute limit is $95^2 - 1 = 9024$, but some Kermit programs have a lower limit because of memory or addressing limitations. Most non-Columbia Kermit implementations are limited to 94; lengths greater than 94 require the "long packet" protocol feature [21]. Use the SHOW PROTOCOL command to find the maximum packet length of your Kermit program.

Thus, it is impossible to force a Kermit program to send packets longer than the receiver asks for, but it is possible to force shorter ones.

To find the optimum packet length for a given connection, select a moderate-size file and transfer it using different packet lengths. Note the effective data rate reported by C-Kermit's STATISTICS command after each transfer. Use whatever packet length results in the highest performance. In this example, we use 2000-byte packets to transfer a 53,000-byte text file:

```
C-Kermit>set receive packet-len 2000     (Try 2000-byte packets)
C-Kermit>r                               (Receive a file)
Alt-x                                    (Escape back to PC)
MS-Kermit>set block 3                    (Use CRC error detection)
MS-Kermit>s test.txt                     (Send the file)

   (The file is transferred)

MS-Kermit>c                              (Connect back)
C-Kermit>stat                            (Get statistics)
 ...
 packet length          : 94 (send), 2000 (receive)
 elapsed time           : 61 sec
 transmission rate      : 9600 bps
 effective data rate    : 870 cps (90%) (Better than 69%!)
C-Kermit>
```

Dynamic Packet Length

In a perfect world, it would make sense to use the longest possible packets all the time, perhaps even to send the entire file — no matter how long — in one big packet. But this is the real world, where sometimes long packets can actually *reduce* the efficiency of a file transfer:

> *The longer a packet, the more likely it is to cause a buffer overflow or be damaged by noise and the longer it takes to retransmit.*

When C-Kermit is sending a file, it tries to compensate for noise on the communication line by reducing packet lengths automatically whenever a packet is damaged or a timeout occurs, and then slowly increasing it again for each packet that is transmitted successfully: the packet length adjusts to the noise level [18]. This trick is not foolproof, however. If a packet is absolutely, positively too long for the receiver's or network's buffers, it will never get through and the only remedy is to start again with a shorter maximum packet length.

C-Kermit tries to find the best packet length automatically, using a *slow start* technique. If the maximum negotiated packet length is greater than 500, the file sender begins by sending a 244-byte packet. If it is acknowledged, the packet length is increased, and so on up to the maximum negotiated length. Any errors reduce the size, but then it starts to grow back again. Throughout this process (which can repeat many times on a bad connection), Kermit keeps an eye out for the best length, and uses it as the length to grow back to when recovering from errors; this might or might not be the maximum negotiated length. The slow-start procedure is used unless you give instructions to the contrary:

SET TRANSFER SLOW-START *{ ON, OFF }*

Enable or disable the slow start procedure; it is enabled by default. If you turn it OFF, then the initial packets are sent at the maximum negotiated length. Use OFF if you are trying to set some kind of speed record.

This command does not affect packet-length reduction in response to errors.

Sliding Windows

On a clean direct or dialed connection, long packets are often all you need to achieve good performance. But suppose you have a long-distance connection through an X.25 network or an earth satellite, or you are using the Internet on a bad day. It might take a second or more for a packet to reach its destination and just as much time for an acknowledgement to make the return trip. Or suppose you have a connection that is noisy or in which there are buffer-size limitations, irrespective of delays. Kermit's *sliding window* feature is designed for these situations.

Kermit's normal packet protocol is: send packet number n, wait for an acknowledgement for packet n, then send packet $n+1$, and so on, as you saw in Figure 12-2. When the connection has a long round-trip delay, the waiting time destroys the efficiency of the protocol. For example, on a 9600 bps connection with 1 second delay, where one tenth of a second is required to transmit a 94-byte packet, the waiting time could have been used to transmit 9 more packets. Efficiency plummets to about 10 percent, as in this example, using the same 53K file as before:

```
C-Kermit>set rec pack 94        (No long packets)
C-Kermit>c                      (Receive a file)
Alt-x                           (Escape back to PC)
MS-Kermit>send test.txt         (Send a test file)

  (The file is transferred)

MS-Kermit>c                     (Connect back)
C-Kermit>stat                   (Get statistics)
  ...
 packet length         : 94 (send), 94 (receive)
 elapsed time          : 686 sec
 transmission rate     : 9600 bps
 effective data rate    : 77 cps (8%) (Terrible!)
C-Kermit>
```

That's 11 minutes to transfer the file at 8 percent efficiency, when you would expect to be able to transfer it in about a minute. If you are using an external modem, you can watch the receive and transmit lights to appreciate what's happening: the transmit light blinks on for a brief moment, then both lights go dark. After a long pause, you get a blip on the receive light, followed immediately by a blip on the transmit light, then another long pause. And so on. More than 90 percent of the time is wasted.

Let's try the same transfer again with 1000-character packets to see how much long packets might help. Here we show just the statistics:

```
C-Kermit>stat                     (Get statistics)
 ...
 packet length        : 94 (send), 1000 (receive)
 window slots used     : 1 of 1
 elapsed time          : 117 sec
 transmission rate     : 9600 bps
 effective data rate   : 451 cps (47%)
C-Kermit>
```

Much better, but still less than half the transmission speed. The same long intervals of dead air remain between each packet, only now we have fewer of them.

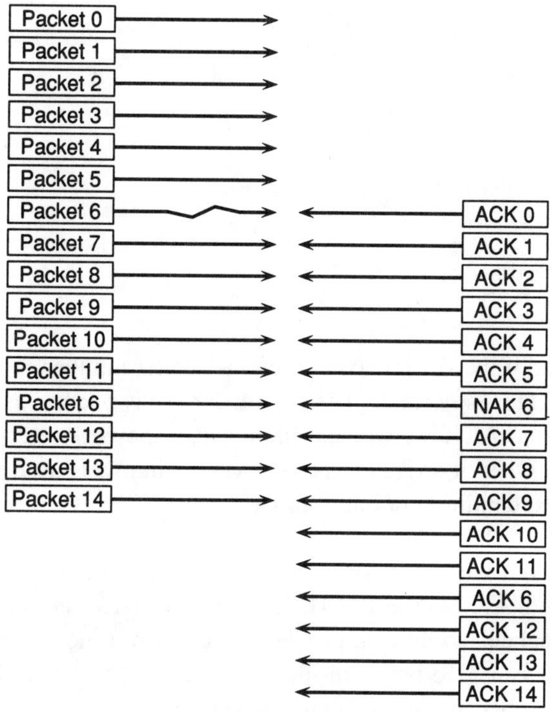

Figure 12-3 Sliding Windows

On full-duplex connections, the inter-packet waiting time can be eliminated if the normal stop-and-wait rule is relaxed to let Kermit send packet *n*+1 before packet *n*'s acknowledgement arrives. C-Kermit is so relaxed about this rule it can happily tolerate as many as 32 outstanding packets, using the sliding window technique [21] illustrated in Figure 12-3 on the previous page.

SET WINDOW *number*

> Specifies how many packets, 1 to 32, may be transmitted before acknowledgements arrive. With a sufficiently large window size, Kermit (usually) can transfer packets continuously. It is necessary to give a SET WINDOW command to *both* Kermit programs to make this feature work. If the window sizes differ, the smaller of the two is used. If the other Kermit does not support sliding windows at all, normal stop-and-wait packet exchange is used automatically, which is equivalent to using a window size of 1.

Let's see if we can pep up our connection with a combination of long packets and sliding windows. Here we transfer the same file again, over the same long-distance connection:

```
C-Kermit>set rec pack 500      (Packet-length is 500)
C-Kermit>set window 4          (Use four window slots)
C-Kermit>r                     (Receive a file)
Alt-x                          (Escape back to PC)
MS-Kermit>set window 4         (Select window size)
MS-Kermit>send test.txt        (Send the file)

  (The file is transferred)

MS-Kermit>c                    (Connect back)
C-Kermit>stat                  (Get statistics)
  ...
  packet length       : 94 (send), 500 (receive)
  window slots used   : 2 of 4
  elapsed time        : 65 sec
  transmission rate   : 9600 bps
  effective data rate : 816 cps (85%)
C-Kermit>
```

That's more like it! Don't be alarmed if the file receiver reports a smaller number of window slots used than the file sender. This is normal. The file sender sends packets as fast as it can until its window fills up or an ACK arrives; the file receiver, however, gets the packets in order and ACKs each one when it arrives. The receiver's window is used only when packets are received in damaged condition or out of order.

Sliding windows can be beneficial even when the connection has no delays at all. First, sliding windows eliminate the ACK/NAK overhead. The ACKs and NAKs are on the wire simultaneously with the data packets, so they don't take up any extra time. Second, sliding windows and shorter packets can give better results than stop-and-wait and long packets on noisy connections. Remember the rule for long packets: *The longer a packet, the more likely it is to be damaged and the longer it takes to retransmit.*

When sliding windows are in use and a packet is damaged or lost (perhaps it was stolen by a pick-packet?), the Kermit protocol recovers by *selective retransmission*, meaning that only the damaged packet is retransmitted, as with Packet 6 in Figure 12-3. If packets are short, they are *less* likely to be damaged and take *less* time to retransmit.

But when the connection is clean and unobstructed, we can use long packets and sliding windows together to obtain optimum results, as in this example with a window size of 4 and a packet length of 4000:

```
C-Kermit>stat
...
packet length         : 94 (send), 4000 (receive)
window slots used     : 4 of 4
elapsed time          : 57 sec
transmission rate     : 9600 bps
effective data rate   : 921 cps (96%)
C-Kermit>
```

To achieve this level on a particular connection, experiment with different combinations of packet length and window size.

Windows and Buffers

If sliding windows are so beneficial, perhaps you are wondering why the SET WINDOW command is necessary at all. Why not use a large window size all the time? First of all, many packets sent in a continuous stream could have the same ill effect as a very long packet when computers or networks have small buffers: fatal indigestion.

Second, many Kermit programs have limited memory for packet buffers. To use sliding windows, Kermit must keep all windowed packets in memory simultaneously so selected packets can be retransmitted and packets arriving out of sequence can be sorted before writing their contents to disk. If the total packet buffer memory available is less than the product of the maximum packet size and the maximum window size ($9024 \times 32 = 288768$ bytes plus some extra), the window size or the packet size must be reduced.

Most implementations of C-Kermit are set up to allow packet buffers to be allocated dynamically. You can increase the overall packet buffer size using the command:

SET BUFFERS *send-length* [*receive-length*]

Allocates the specified number of bytes of memory for send and receive packet buffers, respectively. If the *receive-length* is omitted from the command, it is set to the same value as the *send-length*, which is recommended because it avoids problems in environments where packets might be echoed back. Example:

```
C-Kermit>set receive packet-len 9000
C-Kermit>set window 31
 Adjusting receive packet-length to 286 for 31 window slots
```

```
C-Kermit>show protocol
 Receive packet-length: 286, Windows: 31, Buffers: 9065 9065
C-Kermit>set buffers 280000
C-Kermit>set rec pack 9000
C-Kermit>show protocol
 Receive Packet-length: 9000, Windows: 31, Buffers: 280015 280015
C-Kermit>
```

If Kermit can't find the memory you asked for, the command fails. If the SET BUFFERS command gives a syntax error, your version of C-Kermit does not support dynamic memory allocation, and you can't increase the packet buffer size:

```
C-Kermit>set buffers 280000 280000
?No keywords match - buffers
C-Kermit>check dynamic
 Not available
C-Kermit>
```

Now perhaps you are wondering why the SET BUFFERS command is necessary. Why not always allocate 288768 bytes of memory for each kind of buffer and be done with it? The answer is simple: different computers have different amounts of memory available, different memory allocation strategies, different strategies for paging and swapping, and so forth. On some computers (but not others), allocating a lot of memory for packet buffers can result in extremely poor performance: just the opposite of what you wanted, because (for example) the computer has a slow disk and is swapping itself to death. So once again the onus is on you to find the numbers that are *just right* for your computer. Note, however, that on some computers where we can expect big memories and high performance, the default buffer size is quite large.

Single and Locking Shifts

When Kermit transfers 8-bit data over a 7-bit connection, it uses a single-shift method. Each 8-bit character is preceded by a special prefix character, normally ampersand (&), that tells the receiving Kermit to put back the 8th bit. This 8-bit transparency technique is supported by virtually all Kermit versions (see Table 1-1 on page 10). It is negotiated automatically; C-Kermit bids to use this option if its PARITY is set to (or automatically sensed as) any value other than NONE, and agrees to use it whenever the other Kermit asks for it. Otherwise, the 8th bit of each data byte is preserved, which, of course, results in better performance. C-Kermit has no command, other than SET PARITY, to control the use of single shifts.

Since 8-bit characters occur either not at all, or else more or less randomly, in most types of files, this simple approach lets the data get through without too much extra overhead. The penalty is approximately zero for ASCII text, about 5 percent for text written in Western European languages, and 50 percent for non-textual binary files that contain a uniform distribution of 8-bit byte values.

Locking Shifts

Certain types of files can have long sequences of 8-bit bytes. The most common examples are text files written in a non-Roman alphabet and encoded in character sets like ISO Latin/Cyrillic, Latin/Greek, Latin/Hebrew, Latin/Arabic, and especially the EUC encoding for Japanese Kanji.[31] The penalty for single-shift encoding in typical Cyrillic text is about 80 percent, and for EUC Kanji it is very close to 100 percent. When you need to transfer this type of file over a 7-bit connection, C-Kermit uses locking shifts [37] as well as single shifts if the other Kermit program agrees. A locking shift is a special character, Ctrl-N (Shift-Out, SO), that means that all the following characters up to the next Ctrl-O (Shift-In, SI) are to have their 8th bits set to 1 upon receipt:[32]

```
Seven-bit-text<SO>Eight-bit-text<SI>Seven-bit-text
```

While encoding data to be sent, in each case C-Kermit decides whether it is more efficient to use a locking shift or single shift. The use of locking shifts is almost never bad. At worst, performance is about the same with it as without it (as with 7-bit text files and 8-bit binary files). In some cases (particularly for Kanji and Cyrillic text), it produces a dramatic increase in efficiency, as much as 100 percent. The use of locking shifts is controlled by a SET command:

SET TRANSFER LOCKING-SHIFT { OFF, ON, FORCED }

Specifies whether or how locking shifts should be used by Kermit for encoding and decoding packets. Synonym: **SET XFER LOCKING-SHIFT**. The options are:

ON: If PARITY is *not* NONE C-Kermit tries to negotiate the use of locking-shift protocol with the other Kermit, and uses it if the other Kermit agrees. If PARITY *is* NONE, locking shifts aren't used unless the other Kermit requests them.

OFF: Don't use locking shifts, regardless of the PARITY setting. If the other Kermit asks for locking shifts, C-Kermit refuses.

FORCED: Use locking shifts, regardless of the PARITY setting and negotiations. This command lets the file sender send shifted data to a receiver that doesn't understand locking shift protocol; the embedded SO and SI characters are stored in the received file, where they can be processed by terminals, printers, and other devices. And it makes the receiver treat SO and SI characters in the data as shift commands. This option automatically disables the use of single shifts.

To illustrate the effect of locking shifts, let's try transferring a Japanese Kanji text file through a 7-bit connection without them (notice how the STATISTICS command tells whether locking shifts were actually used):

---

[31]Character sets are discussed in Chapter 16.

[32]The Ctrl-N and Ctrl-O characters are, of course, encoded as printable characters, #N and #O, during packet transmission.

```
C-Kermit>set parity even
C-Kermit>set file character-set shift-jis
C-Kermit>set xfer character-set japanese
C-Kermit>set xfer locking-shift off
C-Kermit>send kanji.txt
  . . .
C-Kermit>statistics
 total file characters   : 29440
 communication line out  : 58451
 8th bit prefixing       : yes [&]
 locking shifts          : no
 elapsed time            : 61 sec (50%)
C-Kermit>
```

and with them (but otherwise the same settings as before):

```
C-Kermit>set xfer locking-shift on
C-Kermit>send kanji.txt
  . . .
C-Kermit>stat
 total file characters   : 29440
 communication line out  : 32404
 8th bit prefixing       : yes [&]
 locking shifts          : yes
 elapsed time            : 34 sec (90%)
C-Kermit>
```

Nearly twice as fast. So . . .

> When you're in Japan or the (ex)-USSR
> And your file transfers need a lift,
> Remember the old football cheer:
> Lock that Shift! Lock that Shift! Lock that Shift!

Control Character (Un)Prefixing

Binary files tend to contain a large number of bytes whose code values are in the control range, 0–31, 127–159, and 255. A compressed file tends to exhibit a uniform distribution of byte values, and so normally consists of about 26% control characters. So even if you have followed all the instructions in this chapter for maximizing your Kermit file transfer performance, and you are achieving 90–100% efficiency for text files, your efficiency for (say) ZIP-file transfer might still be in the neighborhood of 75%. This section shows you how you can squeeze out that additional 20-25% efficiency, but not without some risk.

First, let's set a goal for ourselves. Users of V.34/V.42/V.42*bis* modems regard 3200 cps as the target speed for transferring a ZIP file through a connection between two such modems, just as users of V.32*bis*/V.42/V.42*bis* modems set 1600 cps as their standard.

The V.34 modulation speed is 28800 bps, but since these modems use a synchronous mode of communication between themselves (8 bits per character rather than the 10 needed for asynchronous communication), and since the computer's interface speed is set higher than the modulation speed so as not to be a limiting factor, we obtain:

$$\frac{28800\,bits/sec}{8\,bits/char} = 3600\,chars/sec$$

from which must be deducted about 11% for the modem-to-modem LAPM protocol overhead[33], yielding a theoretical maximum throughput of about 3200 bps for data that has already been compressed enough that cannot be further compressed by the modems.

So can we achieve 3200 cps when transferring ZIP files through V.34 modems with Kermit? It would appear the only way to do this is to reduce the prefixing of control characters as much as possible. It must be emphasized that doing so will override many of Kermit's safety features. Sending any particular control character "bare" over certain kinds of connections is very likely to result in deadlocks, disconnections, or any of the other undesirable phenomena that the Kermit protocol was originally designed to avoid. Three common examples: a Ctrl-S could cause a flow-control deadlock at any point where Xon/Xoff flow control is in use; a Ctrl-P could "escape back" to an X.25 PAD; a Ctrl-Caret (^) could escape back to a Cisco terminal server.

The essence of the problem is that a Kermit program has no way of knowing which control characters are safe to send, because it does not know what lies between itself and the other Kermit program. So you, the user, have to tell it exactly which control characters can be "unprefixed", i.e. sent as-is. If you are wrong, the transfer will fail. Thus some trial and error is often required. Here are the relevent commands:

SET { SEND, RECEIVE } CONTROL-PREFIX *number*

Sets the control-character prefix that C-Kermit uses to the ASCII character whose code is the given *number*, which must be in the range 33–63 or 96–126. Normally it is 35 (#, number sign). The SEND CONTROL-PREFIX is the one that C-Kermit will use in the packets it is sending; the RECEIVE CONTROL-PREFIX should never be used, except to override some kind of protocol negotiation foulup with a buggy BBS or shareware Kermit implementation. Synonym: SET { SEND, RECEIVE } QUOTE.

SET CONTROL-CHARACTER UNPREFIXED { *number* ..., ALL }

This tells C-Kermit that you think it's safe to include the control character represented by *number* in packets that C-Kermit sends without prefixing. The *number* is the numeric ASCII code for a control character, 1-31, 127-159, or 255 (Table VII-1). For example, linefeed (code 10) is normally sent as two printable characters, #J. SET CON-

---

[33]Deduced empirically from measurements of V.42 data transfers on various brands of modems.

TROL UNPREFIXED 10 lets linefeed be sent literally. Include the word ALL to unprefix all control characters (except 0). Or you can specify a list of one or more numeric values, separated by spaces, e.g.:

```
C-Kermit> set control unprefixed 1 3 17 19 30
```

This command will not let you unprefix the NUL character (0), nor the following characters if C-Kermit's current FLOW-CONTROL setting is XON/XOFF: 17, 19, 145, 147. Nor can you unprefix character 255 on a TELNET connection (if C-Kermit *knows* it's a TELNET connection).

SET CONTROL-CHARACTER PREFIXED { number ..., ALL }

Says that the given control character(s) must be prefixed in Kermit packets. By default, all control characters, 0–31, 127–159, and 255, are prefixed.

SHOW CONTROL-PREFIXING

Displays the current control prefix and a table of all control-character values, showing 1 for each one that will be prefixed and 0 for each one that will not be prefixed.

The following command lets you select among four common prefixing arrangements without having to specify the ASCII codes for each character:

SET PREFIXING { ALL, CAUTIOUS, MINIMAL, NONE }

SET PREFIXING ALL is equivalent to SET CONTROL PREFIXED ALL. SET PREFIXING NONE is equivalent to SET CONTROL UNPREFIXED ALL (this one is *not* recommended). MINIMAL means to prefix only 0, 1, 13 and their 8-bit equivalents, plus 255, plus Xon and Xoff and their 8-bit equivalents if using Xon/Xoff flow control. CAUTIOUS adds several well-known problem characters to MINIMAL such as the escape characters used by widespread communication devices and software (most of those in Table 12-1 on the next page). CAUTIOUS is a good starting point for experimentation.

The purpose of the SET CONTROL UNPREFIX command is to *unilaterally* configure C-Kermit to skip prefixing and printable encoding of the specified control characters to achieve higher performance when sending files. This feature takes advantage of the fact that most Kermit programs will accept control characters within packet data-fields literally, provided they get through at all and provided they have no special meaning to the receiving Kermit program (as do the packet-start and packet-end characters).

There is no protocol negotiation between the two Kermit programs to determine a "safe set" of control characters, and in fact any such negotiation would be largely meaningless, because in most cases neither Kermit program has all the needed information. For example, a terminal server or PAD might be between them that is sensitive to a particular control character, even though the two Kermit programs are not.

If you unprefix any control characters that are unsafe, any of several things might happen:

1. Transfer of any file containing these characters will fail.

2. The receiving Kermit program might be interrupted or halted.

3. Your connection might become hung, stuck, or broken; for example, because a control character causes a PAD or terminal server to go from online mode to command mode.

The set of safe control characters depends on the two Kermit programs, their settings, the host operating systems and their configurations, the communication and flow control methods, and all the devices, drivers, and protocols that lie between the two Kermit programs. Therefore, this feature is recommended only for use on well-known and often-used connections, so the time invested in finding an optimal unprefixed control-character set will pay off over many file transfers. For troubleshooting, Table 12-1 lists control characters that are apt to cause trouble and therefore are likely candidates for prefixing. In particular, note that unprefixing of the packet-start character (normally Ctrl-A = 1) can cause big problems if the communication link is noisy, likely to lose characters, or has long delays.

Table 12-1   Dangerous Control Characters

```
set con p 0     ; Ctrl-@ = NUL, internal string terminator in C-Kermit.
                ;          Also, often discarded as padding.
set con p 1     ; Ctrl-A = Packet-start character.
set con p 3     ; Ctrl-C = Likely to cause interruptions on some systems.
set con p 13    ; Ctrl-M = Carriage return, packet-end character.
                ;          Always prefix on TELNET connections.
set con p 14    ; Ctrl-N = Shift Out
set con p 15    ; Ctrl-O = Shift In
set con p 16    ; Ctrl-P = Commonly-used X.25/X.3 PAD escape character
set con p 17    ; Ctrl-Q = XON, must be prefixed with Xon/Xoff flow control
set con p 19    ; Ctrl-S = XOFF, must be prefixed with Xon/Xoff flow control
set con p 27    ; Ctrl-[ = ESC, prefix if going through some kind of ANSI device
set con p 28    ; Ctrl-\ = CONNECT-mode escape for most C-Kermits
set con p 29    ; Ctrl-] = CONNECT-mode escape for some TELNETs and Kermits
set con p 30    ; Ctrl-^ = Cisco terminal server escape.
set con p 127   ; Ctrl-? = DEL, often discarded as padding.
                ;          Also becomes TELNET IAC if parity bit is added.
set con p 128   ; = NUL     + 128 (i.e. NUL + parity bit)
set con p 129   ; = Ctrl-A + 128
set con p 131   ; = Ctrl-C + 128
set con p 141   ; = CR      + 128
set con p 145   ; = XON     + 128
set con p 147   ; = XOFF    + 128
set con p 255   ; 255 = TELNET IAC, must be prefixed on TCP/IP TELNET connections
                       including  TELNET connections through terminal servers!
```

Case Study: Achieving the Best Transfer Rate

Many people believe the best way to judge the performance of a file transfer protocol is by transferring a fairly large amount of precompressed data. Good compression techniques such as the ones used by GZIP, UNIX compress, or PKWARE's PKZIP program, produce a result that can not be further compressed by other methods, including Kermit's own and the modem's, and that contain a relatively uniform distribution of all possible byte values, 0 through 255.

In this exercise, we download a 731K ZIP file in binary mode from a VAXstation 3100 running VMS C-Kermit to an HP-9000 workstation running UNIX C-Kermit over a V.34/V.42/V.42*bis* dialup connection through a Cisco terminal server, using the Cisco TELNET protocol (rather than, say RLOGIN or LAT) to access the VAX. Both computers, as well as the terminal server and the Ethernet that connects it to the VAX, are lightly loaded. The serial interface speed on both ends is 57600 bps, with RTS/CTS hardware flow control between the HP and the calling modem as well as between the answering modem and the terminal server. There is no appreciable delay in the connection; it is a directly dialed local call. The moon is in its first quarter.

Using all the protocol defaults — 1 window slot, 94-byte packets — we get a data rate of 424 cps, only 13% of our target speed. Now we set a window size of 31 by telling each Kermit program to:

```
C-Kermit>set buffers 300000
C-Kermit>set window 31
```

This should prevent any kind of round-trip delay. Then we transfer the file using various packet sizes. After each transfer, we note the elapsed time and effective throughput and look to see how many window slots were actually used by the sender. This gives us some indication of the channel characteristics of the modem connection and lets us find its optimal packet length and window size. Note:

1. Effective flow control is essential for top performance, especially when dealing with error-correcting, data-compressing modems. RTS/CTS hardware flow control is recommended.

2. This exercise applies only to this particular connection. The results might be different for other connections.

3. Before and after each file transfer, the modem (a US Robotics Sportster) was queried (ATI6) about the link speed to make sure it was at 28800 bps and had not dropped to a lower value due to line quality deterioration. If it had, the connection was redialed until a new 28800 bps connection was achieved and the transfer was repeated (this test is not foolproof, however, since the modulation speed might have fallen back and then recovered one or more times during the connection).

4. In all cases, no errors or retransmissions were reported by Kermit or the modem.

5. Remember, only the file sender can accurately report the window size that was actually used, since when there are no errors, the receiver never uses more than one window slot.

The results are shown as Trials 1 through 13 in Table 12-2.

Right away you can see how beneficial sliding windows are, even on a locally dialed connection. Without even increasing the packet size, we get an immediate doubling of throughput. Perhaps you are wondering why we do not enable this feature by default; after all, if the other Kermit program doesn't support sliding windows, the negotiation phase will ensure they are not used. The answer is that (a) neither Kermit program *knows* what sorts of devices, buffers, and flow control methods might lie along the communication path, and (b) some BBS and shareware Kermit implementations do not handle sliding windows correctly even after negotiating them.

Table 12-2 V.34 ZIP-File Transfer Performance

Trial	Window Size	Packet Length	Unprefixing	Repeat Counts	Time mm:ss	CPS	Efficiency
1	1/1	94	None	On	28:42	424	13%
2	31/31	94	None	On	11:33	1055	33%
3	31/31	250	None	On	6:33	1860	58%
4	31/31	500	None	On	4:56	2470	77%
5	13/31	1000	None	On	4:49	2529	79%
6	13/31	2000	None	On	4:47	2547	80%
7	8/31	3000	None	On	4:50	2521	79%
8	5/31	4000	None	On	4:51	2512	78%
9	4/31	5000	None	On	4:45	2565	80%
10	4/31	6000	None	On	4:47	2547	80%
11	3/31	7000	None	On	4:51	2512	78%
12	4/31	8000	None	On	4:53	2495	78%
13	3/31	9000	None	On	4:45	2556	80%
14	4/31	9000	All but 0	On	3:47	3221	101%
15	3/31	9000	All but 0	Off	3:43	3278	102%

The top thirteen entries in the table show that efficiency on this connection peaks and flattens out with packets of 1000 bytes or longer. We have also learned that, on this connection, it does no harm to set a high window size. So, with an eye toward achieving the highest possible throughput (rather than, say, toward prudence), we settle on a packet length of 9000 and let the protocol use whatever window size it needs (Trial 13). But at 2556 cps, we are still only at 80% of our target speed.

Now that we have settled on the packet length and window size, the next step is to look at what is *in* the packets. The STATISTICS command shows:

```
total file characters  : 731627
control characters      : 191718 prefixed, 0 unprefixed
compression             : yes [~] (2542)
```

So about 26% of all the bytes in the ZIP file were in the control range (as expected), and barely any bytes were compressed by Kermit (also expected). Therefore, we should be able to make up the lost efficiency by unprefixing as many control characters as possible. Optimistically, we tell VMS C-Kermit (the file sender) to:

```
C-Kermit>set control unprefix all
```

Fortunately, unprefixing *all* characters (except 0) works on this connection. (Don't expect this work on every connection!) Nevertheless, this simple command did exactly what was hoped, raising the effective throughput to 3221 cps (Trial 14), slightly above the target speed. The result is due to the unprefixing:

```
control characters  : 6933 prefixed, 184785 unprefixed
compression         : yes [~] (2542)
```

This means we have removed approximately 185,000 control prefix characters from the data stream, about 25% of the total characters.

Let's see if we can increase the speed by disabling Kermit's compression (SET REPEAT COUNTS OFF). The ZIP file happens to contain 5546 tilde characters (7- and 8-bit versions) accounting for about 0.7% of the file, and each of these tildes had to be prefixed to distinguish it from the compression prefix. Indeed our transfer rate rises by about that much to 3278 cps (shaving four seconds off the elapsed time, less than one percent), Trial 15 in the table. Disabling the modem's built-in V.42*bis* compression, however, made no difference at all in our tests.

Finally, as an experiment, let's see what happens if we disable the modem's V.42 error correction, which, since we've shown that V.42*bis* compression does not effect ZIP-file transfer performance, must impose its own performance penalty of about 11% (the difference between 3200 and 3600 cps). But now the modems must transmit 10 bits per character rather than 8, because we lose the synchronous modem-to-modem protocol when we disable error correction. Thus we would expect a throughput of approaching 2880 cps (28800 bps / 10).

The result with 9000-byte packets: 2583 cps, averaged over several trials; in each trial there were several retransmissions due to line noise that was not corrected by the modems. As you can see the retransmission penalty for 9000-byte packets is rather high! However, when dropping the packet length to 1000, we achieve 2765 cps, which is 96% of the 2880 bps V.34 modulation speed even with the same amount of noise.

Remember that ZIP-file transfer is a "worst-case scenario" as far as Kermit file transfer is concerned. Uncompressed files fare better. For example, on the same connection, using all the same settings as in Trial 14, we transferred 3.5 million bytes of netnews (text) in 11 minutes and 23 seconds, or 5059 characters per second.

How does control-character unprefixing affect uncompressed files? Text files, as Kermit transmits them, generally contain only about 4 or 5 percent control characters — carriage return and linefeed — which are risky to send bare. Carriage return, especially, should normally be prefixed, so unprefixing linefeed gains about 2 percent.

Uncompressed binary files, on the other hand, particularly executable program images, might contain a very large proportion of control characters, such as (for example) the un-stripped C-Kermit 5A binary for Solaris 2.4 on Intel platforms:

Size: 1563112
Control characters: 734598 = 47%

So there is a significant gain from control-character unprefixing, even more than with compressed files.

So what have we learned?

1. Use the biggest window size that works.

2. The performance gain from packets longer than 1000 is significant mainly to benchmarkers. While there might be a marginal improvement in using very long packets, it is outweighed by the retransmission penalty when errors occur.

3. The advantage gained from disabling Kermit's or the modem's compression is negli-gible when transferring precompressed files, but the performance gain when transfer-ring uncompressed binary data is considerable, so you should leave compression en-abled everywhere.

4. Control-character unprefixing can make a significant difference in speed when trans-ferring precompressed or binary files. But if a file transfer fails when you have con-trol characters — *any* control characters — unprefixed, you know where to look first!

Three simple commands — SET WINDOW, SET RECEIVE PACKET-LENGTH, and SET PREFIXING — let you pick any desired tradeoff between speed and safety, just as you do with the accelerator, transmission, and brake when driving a car; you know the road, so it's your choice.

Summary and Conclusion

The old debate about which protocol is faster, Kermit or *x* (where *x* is usually ZMODEM), is best settled by observing transfers of all types of files over different kinds of connections of varying quality between all combinations of computers. *When a transfer fails, the speed is 0.* When the connection is poor, how effective are the error recovery procedures? Kermit differs from most other protocols in offering you a full range of "personality" controls to adapt it to any type or quality of connection.

Given the kind of clean, clear, and totally transparent connection that ZMODEM was designed for, you can use these controls to — in effect — *turn* Kermit into ZMODEM[34]. But faced with a difficult connection — small buffers, noise, lack of transparency to the 8th bit or to control characters, lack of flow control, you name it — you can just as easily turn Kermit into a rugged and persistent off-the-road vehicle — a Jeep rather than a rocket sled — to transport your cargo over the roughest terrain.

Several common combinations of packet length, window size, and prefixing can be selected easily with the following commands:

FAST

> Equivalent to SET WINDOW 20, SET RECEIVE PACKET-LENGTH 4096, SET PREFIXING MINIMAL. The specific window size and packet length might be smaller in some C-Kermit versions where memory is at a premium.

CAUTIOUS

> = SET WINDOW 4, SET RECEIVE PACKET-LENGTH 1000, SET PREFIXING CAUTIOUS.

ROBUST

> = SET WINDOW 1, SET RECEIVE PACKET-LENGTH 90, SET PREFIXING ALL.

Several performance-related command-line options (Appendix I) are also available:

-v *n*   Set the window size to *n*.
-e *n*   Set the receive packet-length to *n*.
-Q   SET WINDOW 20, SET RECEIVE PACKET-LENGTH 4096, SET PREFIXING CAUTIOUS.

For example:

```
$ kermit -YQqD 0 -is oofa.zip
```

starts C-Kermit fast (-Y means "don't execute the initialization file") to send (-s) the `oofa.zip` file in binary mode (-i), with no delay (-D 0), quietly (-q) and quickly (-Q).

---

[34]But with better error recovery characterstics: "Kermit's windowing approach is faster than protocols such as XModem and YModem . . . What many people don't realize is that under less-than-ideal conditions, Kermit's windowing approach is significantly faster than ZModem, a protocol with a well-deserved reputation for fast transfers over good-quality lines" [55].

Several variables (Chapter 17) are performance related:

`\v(cps)`

> The speed of the most recent file transfer in characters per second.

`\v(packetlen)`

> The current RECEIVE PACKET-LENGTH setting.

`\v(window)`

> The current window size setting.

The SHOW PROTOCOL command lists C-Kermit's protocol-related settings:

```
C-Kermit>show protocol
Protocol Parameters:   Send   Receive
  Timeout:              10        7    Server Timeout:   0
  Padding:               0        0    Block Check:      3
  Pad Character:         0        0    Delay:            4
  Packet Start:          1        1    Max Retries:      10
  Packet End:           13       13    8th-bit Prefix:   '&'
  Packet Length:        90     1000    Repeat Prefix:    '~'
  Maximum Length:     9024     9024    Window Size:      2 set, 1 used
  Buffer Size:        9065     9065    Locking-Shift:    enabled, used

C-Kermit>
```

Table 12-3 summarizes the major Kermit protocol options, who controls them, and with what commands.

Table 12-3 Kermit File Transfer Feature Summary

Feature	Controlled By	Command
File collision	Receiver	SET FILE COLLISION to *receiving* Kermit
File type	Client/sender	SET FILE TYPE to *client* or *sending* Kermit
File character-set	Both	SET FILE CHARACTER-SET to *both* Kermits
Transfer character-set	Sender	SET XFER CHARACTER-SET to *sending* Kermit
Block check	Sender	SET BLOCK-CHECK to *sending* Kermit
Control prefixing	Sender	SET CONTROL [UN]PREFIX to sender
Single shifts	Either	SET PARITY to *either* Kermit, or automatic
Locking shifts	Either	SET PARITY, SET XFER LOCKING-SHIFT
Sliding windows	Both	SET WINDOW to *both* Kermits
Packet length	Receiver	SET RECEIVE PACKET-LENGTH to *receiving* Kermit
Slow start	Sender	SET XFER SLOW-START to sender
Compression	Automatic	Unless disabled by SET REPEAT COUNTS OFF
Attributes	Automatic	SET ATTRIBUTE . . . OFF to disable
Incomplete transfers	Receiver	SET FILE INCOMPLETE to *receiver*

## Chapter 13

Automatic File Transfer and Command Execution

Now that you know all about terminal emulation, file transfer, and server mode, and a fair amount about C-Kermit's command language, you are ready to use some of C-Kermit's automation features ("Now that you have learned to drive a stick-shift, you are ready to use an automatic transmission" :-)

Remote-Control File Transfer

In Chapter 9 you learned the classic, labor-intensive, manual method for transferring files when using a Kermit program as your terminal emulator: enter CONNECT mode, start Kermit on the remote computer, tell it to send (or receive) a file, escape back, tell the local Kermit to receive (or send); when the transfer is complete, CONNECT again so you can log out or continue your business there. So many steps! But remember, this is the universal and "safe" method that should work in any situation. So in case you encounter unwanted surprises with the automatic methods described in this chapter, or software that does not support the automatic methods, you always have the classic method to fall back on.

Now let's switch Kermit's transmission from manual to automatic:

```
C-Kermit> set terminal autodownload on
C-Kermit> connect
```

You can give these commands to C-Kermit (most versions), MS-DOS Kermit 3.15 or later, Kermit 95, or Kermit/2.

Only do this on your *local* computer. See the cautions and explanations back on page 162, which we would reproduce here if this book were not thick enough already.

Now that you are CONNECTed to the remote computer, start Kermit there and tell it to send a file. For example, if the remote computer has C-Kermit:

```
$ kermit -s testing.123
```

Here we use the shortcut for running C-Kermit to execute just one command, in this case SEND, which is written on the command line as "-s". (Command-line options are covered in Appendix I.) You could just as well have given a SEND, MSEND, MOVE, MMOVE, or RESEND command at the Kermit prompt; it doesn't matter how the send operation is started, nor does it matter whether you are sending one file or a group of them.

So what happened? If all went according to plan, the file-transfer screen should have popped up automatically, the file should have been received, and when the transfer was finished, you should have found yourself back in CONNECT mode and back at the UNIX prompt. So hurray, no more escaping back and reCONNECTing.

How did it work? The local Kermit program's terminal emulator saw a Kermit S (send) packet appear in its CONNECT screen, and so switched into Kermit RECEIVE mode automatically. And when the file transfer was finished, it remembered that it had entered RECEIVE mode automatically, and so automatically went back to CONNECT mode.

Automatic Uploading

The feature just described is commonly known as "autodownload," and you might also find it in other communication software where it works with ZMODEM protocol. But its opposite — "autoupload" — is a feature you don't often run across, except right here. To initiate an upload while in CONNECT mode, you have to tell the remote Kermit program to GET the desired file. Do this by giving a GET command (or REGET or RETRIEVE) at the Kermit prompt or by using the command-line GET option; e.g. for C-Kermit:

```
$ kermit -g oofa.txt
```

This tells the remote Kermit program to GET (-g) the file named OOFA.TXT. Your local Kermit program's terminal emulator sees an I (server information) packet and automatically enters server mode, then it receives further instructions ("send me the file called OOFA.TXT") from the remote Kermit program. This is the reverse client/server relationship we hinted at in the final section of Chapter 11, in action. To control the file transfer mode — text or binary — give the appropriate commands to the remote Kermit. For example, include the "-i" command-line option to select binary transfers when the remote Kermit is C-Kermit, or tell it to SET FILE TYPE BINARY at its prompt.

Automatic Uploading, Part Deux

Here we discover the "other side" of automatic uploading. Suppose you are at your local Kermit prompt and you gave a SEND command but forgot to start Kermit on the other end, or you did start it but you forgot to put it in RECEIVE or SERVER mode, so it's sitting at its prompt. In both cases, the local Kermit is sending packets, but the remote computer is expecting a command; two entirely different species! The result is a lot of error messages from the remote computer plus a lot of packet timeouts and retransmissions by the local one, while you scratch your head in bewilderment. Shouldn't this stuff just work???

Chances are it just does, and you might have wondered how. C-Kermit lets you specify a command to be sent automatically prior to uploading. By default it is:

```
kermit -r
```

followed by a carriage return. This is how you start C-Kermit to execute the RECEIVE command and then exit automatically when the transfer is done. It can be used with the UNIX, VMS, AOS/VS, VOS, or other host-resident C-Kermit versions.

If the host computer is at its system command (shell) prompt, and "`kermit -r`" works at its command prompt, then you should be able to send files this way, without bothering to start Kermit on the remote computer.

On the other hand, if C-Kermit on the remote computer is at its own command prompt, "`kermit -r`" is treated exactly like a RECEIVE command.

On the third hand, if the remote Kermit is already in RECEIVE mode or SERVER mode, the "`kermit -r`" string is harmlessly absorbed and ignored.

If your host computer has a different Kermit program, you can use the following command to adjust the "autoupload" command appropriately:

SET PROTOCOL KERMIT *[binary-mode-command text-mode-command]*

Tells C-Kermit the character string to be sent prior to uploading files in binary mode and text mode, respectively. A carriage return is automatically appended. If you omit the commands, the default ones are restored: "`kermit -ir`" and "`kermit -r`" respectively. If you want to disable the sending of autoupload strings, put pairs of empty braces in their places:

```
C-Kermit> set protocol kermit {} {}
```

Recall that in most modern Kermit programs, the file sender tells the file receiver what the transfer mode is, so in most cases the "i" in "`kermit -ir`" is not needed, but some older Kermit programs might not support the transfer-mode notification feature and so would need to be commanded explicitly into the appropriate mode.

IBM Mainframe Kermit-370 accepts interactive-mode commands on the command line, rather than short and cryptic UNIX-style command-line options. If there is to be more than one command on the Kermit-370 command line, they are separated by the "line end" character, such as "number sign" (#). So to set the automatic upload commands for sending files from C-Kermit to IBM Mainframes, use:

```
set proto k {kermit set file type binary # receive} {kermit receive}
```

Strictly speaking, the SET FILE TYPE BINARY command isn't needed, because any version of Kermit-370 since the 1980s should pick up the transfer mode automatically. But it doesn't hurt either.

Other Remote-Control Curiosities

Suppose you are using MS-DOS Kermit as your terminal emulator and you are CONNECTed to a VMS computer. You want to send a directory listing from the PC to VMS. The tedious method would be to run the DIR command in DOS, redirect its output to a file, and then upload the file. Here's an easier way (building on the material from Chapter 11); just start C-Kermit on VMS and give it a command like the following:

```
C-Kermit> remote dir > pcfiles.txt
```

This pops the local Kermit program into server mode and has it send a directory listing to the remote C-Kermit client, which in turn redirects the incoming directory listing to a file.

You can do the same with any REMOTE command. Suppose, for example, you want to print a host-resident text file on your PC's printer[35]. Just tell the remote Kermit to:

```
C-Kermit> remote print invoice.txt
```

and out comes the file on your local printer, error-free.

Some Things to Watch out For

Automation is a good thing when it makes difficult tasks easier, but by shielding us from complexity and "texture" it makes us more vulnerable to unpleasant surprises and baffles us when they occur.

Into this category falls the odd situation, alluded to in Chapter 8, when you have a multihop connection; two or more Kermit programs are in CONNECT mode simultaneously. If more than one of them has autodownload enabled, and a Kermit packet arrives, *all* of them go into RECEIVE or SERVER mode automatically at the same time. But only the most

---

[35]If your local Kermit program is MS-DOS Kermit, Kermit 95, or Kermit/2, you could use its terminal emulator's transparent printing feature for this, but the method discussed here applies to all Kermit programs that support the autodownload feature. It is also superior to transparent printing in that the file is transferred error-free, an important consideration on noisy connections.

distant one will actually receive the file. Your local Kermit will become very disappointed that no packets are arriving, and start to send NAK packets, which in turn are likely to confuse the middle Kermit to no end. So please remember:

> *When making multihop Kermit connections, be sure that autodownload is enabled in no more than one Kermit program.*

Here's something else to watch out for. Kermit packets might appear on your terminal screen for reasons other than file transfer. For example, suppose you followed the directions in Chapter 10 for recording a packet log to troubleshoot a failed download. Then, to take a look at it, you told the remote computer to "TYPE PACKET.LOG". Surprise, your local Kermit pops into RECEIVE mode. It's a bother, but you should have disabled autodownload before looking at the packet log:

```
C-Kermit> set term auto off
C-Kermit> connect
$ type packet.log
```

(Packets are shown, nothing bad happens...)

Should the file-transfer display screen pop up unexpectedly, you can always make it go away by cancelling the file transfer with Ctrl-C. Be sure to SET TERM AUTO OFF before returning to the remote host, where you will probably notice that a packet or two had been diagnosed by your system command processor as strange commands indeed.

Handy Aliases for Automatic File Transfer

In UNIX, VMS, and other operating systems, you can define aliases for commands and programs. When used with C-Kermit's command-line options (Appendix I), you can construct a little set of commands to use at the system (shell, DCL, CLI) prompt for downloading and uploading files in text and binary mode quickly and conveniently. Especially convenient when your terminal emulator supports Kermit autodown- and uploads.

Here, for example, are sample alias definitions for the UNIX K-Shell [5], which you could put into your ~/.env file, for use when C-Kermit is the remote Kermit:

```
alias "kts=kermit -YQqD 0 -Ts"        # Send in text mode
alias "kbs=kermit -YQqD 0 -is"        # Send in binary mode
alias "ktg=kermit -YQqD 0 -Tg"        # Get in text mode
alias "kbg=kermit -YQqD 0 -ig"        # Get in binary mode
```

The equivalent commands for VMS would go in your SYS$LOGIN:LOGIN.COM file:

```
kts :== "$kermit ""-YQqD"" 0 ""-Ts"""   ! Send in text mode
kbs :== "$kermit ""-YQqD"" 0 ""-is"""   ! Send in binary mode
ktg :== "$kermit ""-YQqD"" 0 ""-Tg"""   ! Get in text mode
kbg :== "$kermit ""-YQqD"" 0 ""-ig"""   ! Get in binary mode
```

Now just "kts oofa.txt" to send a text file and see how easy and fast it is.

Automatic Command Execution

The previous section showed how the remote Kermit could initiate Kermit protocol transactions — file transfer or client/server interactions — through the local Kermit's terminal emulator. This section presents a feature that lets any remote application (Kermit or otherwise) send commands to your local Kermit program through its terminal emulator.

While in CONNECT mode, C-Kermit for Windows 95 and NT, OS/2, UNIX, and VMS, as well as MS-DOS Kermit, are able to respond automatically to a special ANSI-format escape sequence called Application Program Command, or APC, which allows the host application to send commands to Kermit, through its terminal emulator, for execution. (The Windows and OS/2 versions, which have their own terminal emulators built in, recognize APC commands only when they are emulating an ANSI X3.64 [4] compatible terminal, such as VT100 or above, ANSI or one of its variants, Wyse 370, etc.) APC has obvious benefits in the area of automation, but it also carries some risks.

C-Kermit's response to APC sequences is controlled by the following command:

SET TERMINAL APC { ON, OFF, UNCHECKED }

The default setting is OFF, meaning that C-Kermit ignores APC sequences unless you tell it otherwise. In the Windows and OS/2 versions, APCs are harmlessly absorbed and not displayed. In the UNIX and VMS versions, they are passed through transparently, in case you want them acted on by your actual terminal or terminal emulator when C-Kermit is "in the middle." To activate the APC feature in a relatively safe way, use:

SET TERMINAL APC ON

This allows execution of all commands received in APC sequences except those considered dangerous, such as: PUSH, RUN, !, REDIRECT, DELETE, RENAME, OUTPUT, ENABLE, DISABLE, SCRIPT, and (of course) SET TERMINAL APC. With this setting, for example, it would not be possible for someone to send you a "letter bomb" or screen message that contained an APC sequence to execute a command on your computer (because RUN and ! are disabled). The commands allowed by SET TERMINAL APC ON are only the ones that affect Kermit itself, including the initiation of Kermit file transfers.

Should you want to enable APC execution of *all* commands, which can be dangerous and therefore is not recommended unless you know exactly what you are doing, you can use:

SET TERMINAL APC UNCHECKED

Use UNCHECKED at your own risk. Note, however, that even ON is not risk free. For example, the host application could send a file to your PC that replaces an existing file that you might not want replaced. So be sure to enable APC only when you are communicating in a trusted environment.

Sending APCs

The format of an APC sequence is:

```
<ESC>_text<ESC>\
```

where "<ESC>" is ASCII character 27 (Escape), and *text* is a Kermit command, or a list of Kermit commands separated by commas. (Note: don't confuse <ESC> with Kermit's CONNECT-mode escape character, which might or might not be <ESC>). On 8-bit connections, you can also use the 8-bit form:

```
<APC>text<ST>
```

Where <APC> (Application Program Command) and <ST> (String Terminator) are ISO 6429 [47] 8-bit control characters having decimal values of 159 and 155, respectively.

An APC operation has two "ends." Let's call the application that sends an APC escape sequence the "APC sender", and the application that receives it, and which is supposed to execute the commands it contains, the "APC receiver." Any host application (not just Kermit) can be an APC sender. To send an APC, all it needs to do is display the desired Kermit commands on your terminal screen, enclosed between <ESC>_ and <ESC>\.

C-Kermit (which can be a host application too) has a command for doing this:

APC *text*

> where the *text* is a command (or list of commands) for the APC receiver. Leading and trailing spaces are removed from the text unless it is enclosed in braces:

```
C-Kermit> apc { text }
```

> The *text* is evaluated for backslash codes and variables before being sent. If C-Kermit is in local mode, the APC text is sent out the communication connection rather than to your terminal screen.

Here's an example that sets local Kermit parameters from the remote C-Kermit's command line:

```
C-Kermit> apc set receive packet-length 2000, set window 4
```

This command causes C-Kermit to send the following characters:

```
<ESC>_set receive packet-length 2000, set window 4<ESC>\
```

The local Kermit recognizes the APC sequence, extracts the commands from it, and executes them automatically without ever leaving CONNECT mode.

We'll have more to say about APCs in Chapter 18, when we see how they can be used together with macros to achieve all sorts of interesting effects.

Chapter 14

Using External Protocols

○ ○ ○ ○
This chapter applies primarily to the UNIX version of C-Kermit. It does not
apply at all to Kermit 95 or Kermit/2, which include XMODEM, YMODEM, and
ZMODEM as built-in protocols.

C-Kermit gives you a way to use other protocols over the connections it makes, providing
the other protocols are available as programs that can be invoked with a simple command
line, and their input and output can be redirected. If your version of C-Kermit has this
feature, the command CHECK XYZMODEM will succeed:

```
C-Kermit> check xyzmodem
xyzmodem available
C-Kermit>
```

In C-Kermit versions that have this feature, SEND, RECEIVE, MSEND, MOVE, and similar
commands use the selected protocol. The command to select the protocol is:

SET PROTOCOL *name [s1 s2 [s3 s4 s5 s6]]*
Choose the protocol you want to use for transferring files, and specify the autoupload
strings (*s1* and *s2*) and, if the protocol is not Kermit, the commands for invoking the
external protocol, *s3* through *s6*.

The *name* can be KERMIT, XMODEM, YMODEM, YMODEM-g, ZMODEM, or OTHER. If the
SET PROTOCOL command ends with the protocol name, the protocol is selected with its
previous command list and all its previous protocol-specific settings. If you include anything after the protocol name, and the protocol name is not KERMIT, you have to include
all six fields.

The six command fields are:

s1 Autoupload command for sending files in binary mode
s2 Autoupload command for sending files in text mode
s3 Send command for binary mode
s4 Send command for text mode
s5 Receive command for binary mode
s6 Receive command for text mode

In each of these fields, you can include "%s" to be substituted by a filename, and if the field contains any spaces, you must enclose it in braces; for example:

```
set proto zmodem rz {rz -a} {sz %s} {sz -a %s} rz {rz -a}
```

To specify a blank field, use an empty pair of braces:

```
set proto zmodem {} {} {sz %s} {sz -a %s} rz {rz -a}
```

You don't need to (and shouldn't) put carriage returns or linefeeds on the ends of these strings — these are supplied automatically for you, based on the current connection type, terminal settings, and TELNET mode (if any). Note that when using XMODEM protocol, you must give the filename to both the sender and the receiver, and only one file can be sent at a time.

If you want to use an external protocol other than ZMODEM, YMODEM, YMODEM-G, or XMODEM, specify OTHER in your SET PROTOCOL command. For example, if you had a CompuServe B+ protocol program at hand called "bplus", you could use SET PROTOCOL OTHER, and include the appropriate "bplus" commands in the *s1*–*s6* commands.

The default values for each field are shown in Table 14-1. The name of the current protocol is available in the \v(protocol) variable; \v(ftype) is the current transfer mode. Use SHOW PROTOCOL to display *s1* through *s6* plus all the relevant settings for the currently selected protocol.

Table 14-1 SET PROTOCOL Command Defaults

		Kermit	*Zmodem*	*Ymodem*	*Ymodem-g*	*Xmodem*	*Other*
s1	Autoupload binary:	kermit -ir	rz	rb	rb	rx %s	*(none)*
s2	Autoupload text:	kermit -r	rz -a	rb -a	rb -a	rx %s	*(none)*
s3	Send binary:	*(n/a)*	sz %s	sb %s	sb %s	sx %s	*(none)*
s4	Send text:	*(n/a)*	sz -a %s	sb -a %s	sb -a %s	sx -a %s	*(none)*
s5	Receive binary:	*(n/a)*	rz	rb	rb	rx %s	*(none)*
s6	Receive text:	*(n/a)*	rz	rb	rb	rx %s	*(none)*

Sending Files

The autoupload command is sent to the remote computer when you give a SEND (or MOVE, or MSEND, etc) command. This spares you from having to type the command at the remote computer yourself. If the other computer is at its system prompt, this command should start the appropriate program to receive a file with the selected protocol. If the program is already started on the remote computer, the autoupload command should be absorbed harmlessly. In the example below, the autoupload command for binary ZMODEM transfers is "rz", and so when you give a SEND command to C-Kermit, it sends the "rz" command to the other computer before it starts sending. If C-Kermit's FILE TYPE were set to TEXT, it would send "rz -a".[36]

After sending the autoupload string, if any, C-Kermit uses the binary-mode or text-mode form of the protocol's send command to start the external protocol on the local computer to send the file. The file's name is substituted for the "%s", and the program's standard input/output is redirected (if the program allows this) over C-Kermit's communications connection. To illustrate:

```
C-Kermit> set proto z {rz} {rz -a} {sz %s} {sz -a %s} rz {rz -a}
C-Kermit> set file type binary
C-Kermit> send oofa.zip
```

This results in sending the command "rz" to the other computer, which starts the "Receive Zmodem" program and then, since Kermit's FILE TYPE is set to BINARY, runs the local command "sz oofa.zip" ("oofa.zip" replaces "%s").

While the file is being transferred, the external program takes over your screen, so the file transfer display (if any) is not Kermit's. When the transfer is completed, the C-Kermit> prompt reappears.

Receiving Files

This works like sending files, except the autoupload command is not used since we are not uploading. However, if the protocol is ZMODEM or Kermit and your version of C-Kermit has the autodownload feature, *and* if SET TERMINAL AUTODOWNLOAD is ON, then when C-Kermit is in CONNECT mode and you start a download from the remote computer, C-Kermit will automatically go into file-receive mode using the same protocol, Kermit or ZMODEM, regardless of your current protocol setting.

---

[36]The rz, sz, and similar commands shown as examples pertain to products of Omen Technology Inc., 17505-V NW Sauvie IS Road, Portland OR 97231 USA; Web: http://www.omen.com/, Phone: +1 (503) 621 3406.

Things to Watch Out for

C-Kermit's built-in external protocol support works only with programs that transfer files using "standard input" and "standard output." The standard input and output (I/O) channels are redirected to use C-Kermit's own connection. If C-Kermit is in remote mode, then standard I/O is used directly.

However, not all external protocol programs work this way. Some of them obtain explicit, non-standard-I/O file descriptors for the purpose of file transfer, and these cannot be redirected, and therefore these programs cannot be used as external protocols by Kermit.

Even if they can be successfully redirected, protocols such as XMODEM, YMODEM, and ZMODEM are likely to fail over TELNET connections because of transparency issues. The external protocol programs themselves are unaware that they have been redirected over a TELNET connection, and so even if they *would* know what to do in this case, they don't know they are supposed to do it. If your external protocol program has a command-line option to let you tell it to take precautions (certain ZMODEM implementations let you "escape" certain characters — carriage return and "all ones" are the ones to watch out for), use it.

The only C-Kermit setting that applies to external protocols is FILE TYPE (text or binary), and it is up to you to pass this setting along by assigning the appropriate commands to *s1* through *s6*. No other settings are conveyed to external protocols, since Kermit does not know their invocation syntax. But since *you* might know it, then you can easily write macros to translate Kermit settings into the appropriate command syntax for the selected protocol (after you have read Chapter 17).

Finally, the client/server operations described in Chapter 11 are unique to the Kermit protocol and so work only when C-Kermit's PROTOCOL is set to KERMIT. You can't use commands like GET, BYE, or FINISH, nor any of the REMOTE commands, except when your protocol is Kermit.

Command Summary

Commands:

```
SET PROTOCOL name [ s1 s2 [ s3 s4 s5 s6 ] ]
   names = KERMIT, XMODEM, YMODEM, YMODEM-G, ZMODEM, OTHER
   s1 = binary-mode autoupload command
   s2 = text-mode autoupload command
   s3 = external protocol binary-mode send command
   s4 = external protocol text-mode send command
   s5 = external protocol binary-mode receive command
   s6 = external protocol text-mode receive command
```

Variables: \v(protocol) \v(ftype)

## Chapter 15

Transferring Files without a Protocol

Not all computers have Kermit or XYZMODEM software available. For example, certain dialup data and typesetting services might not offer an error-correcting file transfer program. The same might be true of various types of data-taking and laboratory devices, as well as of certain application software, particularly electronic mail and text editors, found on the hosts or services that you access with C-Kermit.

In such situations, C-Kermit lets you transmit files to and capture files from computers, devices, services, or applications that don't support any better methods of file transfer. This is done *without error detection or correction of any kind*. Data transferred without error correction is subject to corruption, loss, interference, misinterpretation, duplication, and other types of damage.

In most cases, only textual data can be transferred using the methods described here, and often only 7-bit text. In general, these methods work only for a single file, not for a group of files. This method of data transfer is sometimes referred to as "ASCII protocol" or (when Xon/Xoff flow control is in effect) "Xon/Xoff protocol."

Before proceeding, consider the alternatives. Can you get Kermit or XYZMODEM software installed on the other computer? Is a network connection available with its own file transfer or sharing method? Is there some kind of removeable storage medium common to both computers — compatible diskettes or tapes? If none of these options is viable, read on.

Downloading to C-Kermit

Unguarded downloading is the act of capturing a file from a remote computer without its knowledge. It thinks it is simply displaying the file on your screen. You, however, are surreptitiously recording the screen characters on your disk during your C-Kermit CONNECT session. Here are the commands to use:

LOG SESSION *[filespec [{* **APPEND, NEW** *}]]*

The characters sent to C-Kermit during CONNECT mode are recorded in the specified file. The default filename is SESSION.LOG. All current communication settings are used, including duplex, flow control, shift-out/shift-in, and parity. RTX/CTS or Xon/Xoff flow control can be used to help prevent loss of data on serial connections. If parity is in use or the terminal bytesize is set to 7, the 8th bit of each character is discarded. Character-set translations implied by your TERMINAL CHARACTER-SET settings are performed (Chapter 16). A new session log file is created unless you include the APPEND option, which adds the recorded material to the end of the named file, if it exists, and otherwise creates a new one. When a new log is created, any previously existing file with the same name (on the same device, in the same directory, on the same computer) is destroyed, unless the underlying operating system supports multiple versions of the same file (as does VMS).

SET SESSION-LOG *{* **BINARY**, **TEXT** *}*

(UNIX, AOS/VS, and OS-9 only) Specifies the recording format for the session log. TEXT is the default, meaning that certain control characters are discarded, including Carriage Return (ASCII 13), Null (ASCII 0), and Delete (ASCII 127). BINARY means that every character that arrives is recorded. Character-set translations are done in both cases unless you use SET TERMINAL CHARACTER-SET TRANSPARENT to disable them. SET SESSION-LOG BINARY does *not* mean you can capture binary files such as executable programs in a session log.

To capture a remote file, display it on the other computer while logging your session with C-Kermit. The trick is to avoid capturing an excessive amount of extraneous data, such as commands, system prompts, and so forth. Here is an example in which you use C-Kermit to log in to a UNIX system and copy a coveted recipe. The SET FLOW, PARITY, and SESSION-LOG commands are included for emphasis; the settings shown are the defaults, so you won't need to give these commands unless you have previously changed the settings:

```
C-Kermit>set modem type microlink    (Select modem type)
C-Kermit>set line /dev/ttyh8         (Select communication device)
C-Kermit>set speed 57600             (and speed)
C-Kermit>set flow rts/cts            (and flow control)
C-Kermit>set parity even             (and parity)
C-Kermit>set session-log text        (and session log format)
C-Kermit>dial 7654321                (Dial the phone number)
Connection completed.
```

```
C-Kermit>connect                          (Begin terminal emulation)
BUON GIORNO!

login: garfield                           (Login)
Password: _____                           (Supply your password)
```

So far everything is normal. Now comes the tricky part. You must type the command to display the text file you want to capture, *but without the terminating carriage return* (for UNIX, the command is `cat` — what else? — for most other systems it is TYPE). Then escape back, turn on the session log, CONNECT again, and *then* type the carriage return. When the system's prompt reappears, escape back again, close the session log, and you've got the file, or at least as much of it as appeared on your screen, plus one system prompt at the end, which you can remove with a text editor.

```
$ cat lasagna.recipe                      (Don't press Return yet!)
Ctrl-\C                                   (Escape back)
C-Kermit>log sess lasagna.recipe          (Start the session log)
C-Kermit>connect                          (Go back)
<RETURN>                                   (and press carriage return)
Ingredients:                              (The characters that appear)
1 lb Moozarel'                            (on your screen are being)
1 lb Rigotha                              (recorded in the session log)
1 lb tiny meatballs
...                                       (etc etc)
$                                         (Prompt reappears)
Ctrl-\C                                   (Escape back again)
C-Kermit>close session                    (Close the session log)
C-Kermit>type lasagna.recipe              (Check it out)
Ingredients:                              (Looks good, mmmmmm!)
1 lb Moozarel'
1 lb Rigotha
1 lb tiny meatballs
...                                       (etc etc, good it worked)
$                                         (Notice the system prompt)
C-Kermit>
```

Now edit the file to remove or correct any unwanted material — system dialog, prompts, messages, noise interference, and so on.

To ensure that the captured file is as close to the original as possible, you should make sure the host is not sending any characters that are not part of the file. For example, you should take whatever measures the host allows to turn off services like line or word wrap, tab expansion, pausing at end of each screenful, and so on, as well as eliminating other possible sources of interference such as messages from other users, e-mail notifications, alarm clocks, or host-generated status lines.

HINT: This process includes quite a few routine steps that could be easily automated in a script program. Chapters 17–19 cover script programming.

Uploading from C-Kermit

How do you create a text file on a computer? You set up a process on the computer that copies your keystrokes to a disk file. This could be a simple copy process, or it could be a text editor. When you have finished entering characters into the file, you type a special key or sequence to tell the copy process or text editor to close the file. The simplest way to create a file in UNIX is like this:

```
$ cat > file.new                    (Start the copy process)
I am typing some characters.        (Type characters into the file)
They are being copied into
file.new.
Ctrl-D                              (Ctrl-D closes the file)
$                                   (and returns you to the prompt)
```

and in VMS it is:

```
$ create file.new                   (Start the copy process)
I am typing some characters.        (Type characters into the file)
They are being copied into
file.new.
Ctrl-Z                              (Ctrl-Z closes the file)
$                                   (and returns you to the prompt)
```

Other systems, of course, have other methods.

Now suppose you have a text file on your computer that you want to send to a remote computer that doesn't have a file transfer program. Instead of retyping the characters of the text file with your own fingers, you can set up the remote computer for creating a file, as shown in the previous examples, and then tell C-Kermit to imitate what you would do if you were typing the file at your keyboard. The remote computer will never know the difference. The command is:

TRANSMIT *filename*

> Sends the characters of the file out the current communication device, just as if you were typing them in CONNECT mode. The TRANSMIT command obeys all current (and relevant) communications and terminal settings, including echo, parity, flow control, and shift-out/shift-in. Unless you say otherwise, the TRANSMIT command also displays the transmitted data on your screen according to the current TERMINAL ECHO setting. Synonym: **XMIT**.

The most important factor affecting how the TRANSMIT command works is the current FILE TYPE setting:

SET FILE TYPE TEXT

> If the current file type is TEXT, the TRANSMIT command treats each line of the file as an individual record. It reads a line, strips off the line termination characters (such as LF for UNIX or AOS/VS, CRLF for VMS or OS/2, CR for OS-9 or MacOS), and

sends a single carriage return at the end of each line, just as you would do if you were typing the line yourself. Then it waits a certain amount of time for the remote system to echo a linefeed before sending the next line (so if your file contains long lines, be sure the remote host or service has been told not to wrap them). Characters are translated according to the current TERMINAL CHARACTER-SET setting (Chapter 16). If you want to avoid translation, SET TERMINAL CHARACTER-SET TRANSPARENT before giving the TRANSMIT command.

SET FILE TYPE BINARY

The file's bytes are sent exactly as they are stored on the disk with no conversion at all, and there is no synchronization between the two sides as there is with text file transmission. Use binary transmission with caution and skepticism.

The standard text and binary transmission procedures might not work in every case, so C-Kermit also offers you the customary selection of SET commands to modify their operation as needed:

SET TRANSMIT ECHO { OFF, ON }

Tells C-Kermit whether you want to see the transmitted characters echoed on your screen. The default setting is ON, in which case echoing is done according to the current TERMINAL ECHO (DUPLEX) setting. If the computer or device on the other end of the connection does not echo, you should SET TERMINAL ECHO ON (or SET DUPLEX HALF, same thing) if you want C-Kermit itself to display each character it sends, or SET TRANSMIT ECHO OFF if you don't want the characters displayed. No echoing is more efficient but less informative. Synonym: **SET XMIT ECHO**.[37]

SET TRANSMIT EOF [string]

Tells C-Kermit the character or characters to send after EOF (End Of File) is encountered, or when you type Ctrl-C to interrupt transmission. Normally, nothing is sent. To include control characters in the *string*, use backslash codes such as \4 for Ctrl-D or \26 for Ctrl-Z (see Table VII-2 on page 558). To cancel a previous TRANSMIT EOF setting, type this command without specifying a *string*. Examples:

```
C-Kermit>set transmit eof \4        (Send Ctrl-D on EOF)
C-Kermit>set transm eof \26         (Send Ctrl-Z on EOF)
C-Kermit>set xmit eof               (Send nothing on EOF)
```

The next example shows a typical sequence that might be sent to a text editor to exit from text insert mode, save the file, and exit:

```
C-Kermit>set xm eof \26save\13\exit\13
```

The TRANSMIT EOF setting applies to both text and binary file transmission.

---

[37] All the SET TRANSMIT commands can also be entered as SET XMIT.

SET TRANSMIT FILL *number*

The TRANSMIT command normally sends a blank line as a sequence of two carriage returns. Some computer text entry systems, however, treat two carriage returns in a row as an "end of file." This command lets you specify a single character to insert into each blank line so it won't be blank any more. The *number* is the code for the character, such as 32 for ASCII space (blank). This setting applies only in text mode. Examples:

```
C-Kermit>set transmit fill 32      (Add space to empty lines)
C-Kermit>set transm fill           (Don't fill empty lines)
```

SET TRANSMIT LINEFEED *{ OFF, ON }*

SET TRANSMIT LINEFEED ON tells C-Kermit to send both carriage return *and* linefeed at the end of each line, rather than just a carriage return. This command applies only in text mode. The default is OFF, meaning that only a carriage return is sent at the end of each line. Examples:

```
C-Kermit>set transmit linefeed on
C-Kermit>set xm li off
```

SET TRANSMIT LOCKING-SHIFT *{ OFF, ON }*

If you want to transmit 8-bit data over a 7-bit connection, and the remote computer or service supports Shift-Out and Shift-In (Ctrl-N and Ctrl-O) as a way of shifting between 7-bit data and 8-bit data, you can use SET TRANSMIT LOCKING-SHIFT ON to have Kermit provide the shifting. Use SET TRANSMIT LOCKING-SHIFT OFF to cancel a previous SET TRANSMIT LOCKING-SHIFT ON command. Applies only in text mode.

SET TRANSMIT PAUSE *number*

If the FILE TYPE is TEXT, this command tells C-Kermit to pause the given number of milliseconds (thousandths of a second) after sending each line. If the FILE TYPE is BINARY, the pause occurs between each character.

SET TRANSMIT PROMPT *number*

Use this command to tell C-Kermit to wait for some character other than linefeed as permission to send the next line. The *number* is the code for the character to wait for, such as 17 for Control-Q (Xon). A value of 0 tells C-Kermit not to wait at all, but to send all the characters of the file without waiting for any response, which is useful for transmitting text to devices that do not echo a suitable, unique character at the end of each line. This command applies only in text mode. In binary mode, the TRANSMIT command never waits for a response.

```
C-Kermit>set file type text        (Use text mode)
C-Kermit>set transmit prompt 17    (Wait for Xon)
C-Kermit>set transm pr 0           (Don't wait for anything)
```

You can examine SET TRANSMIT settings with the SHOW TRANSMIT (or SHOW XMIT) command:

```
C-Kermit>show xmit
 File type: text
 See SHOW CHARACTER-SETS for character-set info
 Terminal echo: remote
 Transmit EOF: none
 Transmit Fill: none
 Transmit Linefeed: off
 Transmit Prompt: 10 (host line end character)
 Transmit Echo: on
 Transmit Locking-Shift: off
 Transmit Pause: 0 milliseconds
C-Kermit>
```

TRANSMIT Examples

Now let's work through two examples. In the first, we upload a text file to a UNIX computer. On the UNIX end we simply `cat` (type) from the keyboard to a file. C-Kermit is told to transmit the file, followed by a Ctrl-D to close it.

```
$ kermit                            (Start Kermit)
C-Kermit>set modem type hayes       (Select modem type)
C-Kermit>set line /dev/ttyh8        (Select communication device)
C-Kermit>set speed 2400             (and speed)
C-Kermit>set flow xon/xoff          (and flow control)
C-Kermit>dial 7654321               (Dial the phone number)
C-Kermit>connect                    (Begin terminal emulation)
WELCOME TO THE HOLLYWOOD SCRIPT AGENCY

login: olga                         (Log in)
Password: _____

$ cat > stormy.txt                  (DO press Return/Enter here!)
Ctrl-\c                             (Escape back to C-Kermit)
C-Kermit>set transm eof \4          (Send Ctrl-D when done)
C-Kermit>transmit stormy.txt        (Transmit the file)
THE DARK AND STORMY NIGHT           (The lines are displayed)
```

It was a dark and stormy night in Plainville. Everyone was huddled inside their houses, safe and dry. In the old abandoned house on Main Street, a sinister light shone from the attic window...
etc etc

```
C-Kermit>                           (C-Kermit prompt returns)
C-Kermit>connect                    (Go back to the remote system)
$ cat stormy.txt                    (Look at the file)
THE DARK AND STORMY NIGHT
```

It was a dark and stormy night in Plainville. Everyone was huddled inside their houses, safe and dry. In the old abandoned house on Main Street, a sinister light shone from the attic window...
etc etc

```
$
$ exit                                      (Log out)
Communications disconnect.
C-Kermit>exit                               (All done)
$
```

This example was easy because C-Kermit's default settings are well suited for a direct
dialup connection to the remote UNIX system. The UNIX system has a simple mechanism for entering text from the keyboard into a file; it does not react adversely to blank
lines and it echoes a linefeed whenever it receives a carriage return to indicate it is ready
for another line.

Now let's see how far we can push C-Kermit by trying to upload the same file to an IBM
mainframe with the VM/CMS operating system, using a text editor on the mainframe.
The connection is linemode and half duplex, so we must wait for the editor's prompt
(which is a period followed by an Xon, or Ctrl-Q) before sending the next line or else data
will be lost. The text editor, Xedit, leaves text insertion mode if it gets a blank line and
therefore must have a fill character in case the file contains blank lines. The fill character
is chosen to be capital X (ASCII 88) because a printable character is required — blank
won't do. The EOF string is set to be a carriage return (\13), which sends a blank line,
putting the editor back into command mode, followed by the commands to save the file
(save\13) and exit (qq\13).

```
$ kermit                                    (Start C-Kermit)
C-Kermit>set modem hayes                    (Select modem type)
C-Kermit>set line /dev/ttyh8                (Select communication device)
C-Kermit>set speed 2400                     (and speed)
C-Kermit>set duplex half                    (Connection is half duplex)
C-Kermit>set flow none                      (No Xon/Xoff flow control)
C-Kermit>set parity mark                    (Mainframe uses MARK parity)
C-Kermit>dial 8765432                       (Dial the phone number)
Connection completed.
C-Kermit>connect                            (Begin terminal emulation)

VIRTUAL MACHINE/SYSTEM PRODUCT--CUVMB --PRESS BREAK KEY

Ctrl-\B                                     (Send BREAK)
!
.login olga                                 (Log in)

Enter password: XXXXXXXX                    (Half duplex; password echoes)

LOGON AT 23:23:23 EDT FRIDAY 09/06/96
VM/SP REL 5 04/19/88 19:39
.
CMS
.xedit stormy txt                           (Start the editor)
.i                                          (Put it in text input mode)
DMSXMD573I Input mode:
Ctrl-\C                                     (Escape back to C-Kermit)
```

```
C-Kermit>set transm fill 88      (Fill blank lines with X)
C-Kermit>set transm prompt \17   (Wait for Xon)
C-Kermit>set transm eof \13save\13qq\13
C-Kermit>transmit stormy.txt     (Send the file)
THE DARK AND STORMY NIGHT        (The echoed lines are displayed)
X
It was a dark and stormy night in Plainville. Everyone was huddled
inside their houses, safe and dry.  In the old abandoned house on
Main Street, a sinister light shone from the attic window...
etc etc

C-Kermit>                        (Prompt returns when done)
C-Kermit>connect                 (Return to the mainframe)
.
Ready; T=0.02/0.06 23:29:11
.lf stormy                       (Make sure file is there)
STORMY    TXT                    (It is)
Ready; T=0.01/0.01 23:29:16
.type stormy txt                 (Take a peek)
THE DARK AND STORMY NIGHT
X
It was a dark and stormy night in Plainville. Everyone was huddled
inside their houses, safe and dry.  In the old abandoned house on
Main Street, a sinister light shone from the attic window...
etc etc

Ready; T=0.01/0.01 23:29:20
.logout                          (Log out from the mainframe)
CONNECT= 00:01:11 VIRTCPU= 000:00.12 TOTCPU= 000:00.32
LOGOFF AT 23:29:25 EDT FRIDAY 09/06/96
Ctrl-\C                          (Escape back to C-Kermit)
C-Kermit>exit
$
```

The X's can be removed with a text editor (such as Xedit, the same editor that made you put them there in the first place).

Encoding 8-Bit Data Files for Transmission

Unguarded transfer of binary files is an iffy proposition at best. If even one byte is lost or corrupted, terrible damage could result. And it usually is not easy to repair a damaged binary file with a text editor, as you can do with a text file. It is often better to convert a binary file into simple short lines of printable ASCII text, then up- or download it in text mode, and then convert it back into its original form. The easiest, most reliable, and most portable format is called "hex" (hexadecimal), in which each 8-bit byte is translated into two printable hexadecimal digits taken from the set 0123456789ABCDEF. Short lines are formed, composed of only these characters. A file of this form is slightly more than twice the length of the original, but it is immune to any known translation or transparency problems. A pair of short C-language programs for hexifying and dehexifying is included in Appendix IX.

Other encoding methods might be more efficient. For example, a pair of programs, uuencode and uudecode, is available on most UNIX computers but not necessarily on other systems. The encoding is more efficient than hex but also uses a bigger alphabet that might cause transparency or translation problems; for example, with EBCDIC hosts.

Many other file encoding, compaction, and archiving techniques are available, too. Use whatever works best for you. The primary considerations are transparency (can the encoded data survive the passage to the other computer?) and portability (can you reconstruct and use the original data after transmitting to another computer?).

The latter consideration is particularly important when transmitting text files between computers that have different record formats, such as UNIX and DOS (or OS/2 or Windows). If you encode the file on UNIX, the UNIX single-character line terminator (linefeed) is kept in the file, and when when you decode in DOS, where carriage return *and* linefeed are used, the lines are no longer properly terminated and will not be recognized by most applications.

This type of problem is most severe when when using archive formats such as ZIP to collect a mixture of text and binary files into a single archive file. When unZIPping such a file on an unlike file system, even when the unZIP program has an option for record-format conversion, it cannot be used without also corrupting any binary files that are also in the archive.

Command Summary

The following commands are used for unguarded file capture and transmission:

LOG SESSION *[filespec [{* APPEND, NEW *}]]*
SET FILE TYPE *{* TEXT, BINARY *}*
SET SESSION-LOG *{* TEXT, BINARY *}*
SET TRANSMIT ECHO *{* OFF, ON *}*
SET TRANSMIT EOF *[string]*
SET TRANSMIT FILL *number*
SET TRANSMIT LINEFEED *{* OFF, ON *}*
SET TRANSMIT LOCKING-SHIFT *{* OFF, ON *}*
SET TRANSMIT PAUSE *number*
SET TRANSMIT PROMPT *number*
TRANSMIT *filename*

Synonyms:

XMIT = TRANSMIT
SET XMIT = SET TRANSMIT

## Chapter 16

International Character Sets

○ ○ ○ ○

If you have no need to transfer text files that contain accented or non-Roman characters and you never need to display these characters on your screen at C-Kermit command level or during CONNECT mode, skip ahead to Chapter 15 on page 285.

All the different computers and operating systems supported by C-Kermit use the ASCII character set: the American Standard Code for Information Interchange [1], listed in Table VII-1 on page 557.[38] C-Kermit's command and file names, messages and help text — all textual matter is encoded in ASCII.

ASCII contains uppercase and lowercase Roman letters, decimal digits, and punctuation marks sufficient for representing English text and most computer commands and programming languages. But it does not contain the accented or special letters needed for Italian, Norwegian, French, German, or other languages written using Roman-based alphabets, let alone the non-Roman characters of languages like Russian or Japanese.

Although C-Kermit's user interface is strictly English and ASCII, you can use C-Kermit to conduct terminal sessions and transfer files in a wide variety of Roman and non-Roman character sets. This chapter tells you how.

---

[38]ASCII is the United States version of ISO 646 [42].

Table 16-1 Decimal Character Codes for Accented Capital Letter A

Character		IBM PC CP 850	Macintosh Quickdraw	Data General DGI	DECstation DEC MCS	NeXTSTEP
A-Grave	À	183	231	193	192	129
A-Acute	Á	181	203	192	193	130
A-Circumflex	Â	182	229	194	194	131
A-Tilde	Ã	199	204	196	195	132
A-Diaeresis	Ä	142	128	195	196	133
A-Ring	Å	143	129	197	197	134

Proprietary Character Sets

There are thousands of different languages in the world, hundreds of different kinds of computers, and a potentially vast number of ways to represent the characters of each language on each computer. If we consider only the written languages based on the Roman alphabet, such as Italian, Portuguese, or Norwegian, we find that different computers, such as the IBM PC, the Apple Macintosh, the Data General MV system, the DECstation, and the NeXTstation represent the accented letters and other special symbols in completely different ways internally. Table 16-1 shows the codes for the uppercase letter A with various accents used by each of these computers.

CP850 is IBM's ASCII-based multilingual code page for PCs, Quickdraw is the character set most commonly used on Apple Macintosh computers, DGI is the Data General International character set, DEC MCS is DEC's Multinational Character Set, and the NeXT character set is used in NeXTSTEP (see Table VII-4 on page 560 for a fuller listing). These are just a few of the many proprietary character sets in current use.

Most modern equipment supports some form of national or international text. As long as you stick with a particular manufacturer's equipment — display, keyboard, printer — you can create, read, and print text in any language supported by your equipment. This is a great leap forward from the ASCII-only days. But what if you need to access a different kind of equipment from within your own computing environment? What if you need to exchange text with users of a different kind of equipment?

There are several ways to cope with this problem. The traditional solution has been to ban the use of accented Roman letters as well as all letters from languages like Russian or Hebrew that have non-Roman alphabets. Since computers everywhere support the letters A–Z, transportability of data is assured. But the nature of the data is severely limited, and non-English speaking computer users justifiably resent this approach.

At the other extreme, we could attempt to translate directly between each character set and all the others. This works adequately when the number of sets is small, but quickly becomes unwieldy and unmanageable as the number increases. If the number of character sets is n, the number of translations is $n \times (n-1)$ (the number of pairs chosen from a set of size n, sampling without replacement; see any statistics book, e.g. [61]).

So if we have two character sets, A and B, we need two translations, one from A to B and one from B to A. If we have three sets — A, B, and C — we need $3 \times 2 = 6$ translations: AB, BA, AC, CA, BC, and CB. And so on. Each translation is typically a pair of tables, 256 bytes in each. Now consider that as of 1990, IBM alone listed 276 different coded character set identifiers in its registry [41]. If we needed translations between every pair of IBM character sets, we would require 75,900 of them, or about 4 megabytes of tables. Now add in all the other companies and their character sets to appreciate the magnitude of the problem.

A more reasonable approach is to represent characters in a *standard* intermediate character set for purposes of transmission. The sender translates from its local codes to the standard ones, the receiver translates from the standard codes to its local ones. This cuts the problem down to a manageable size; each computer needs to know only its own character sets plus a handful of standard sets.

Standard Character Sets

Standard character sets come in 7-bit and 8-bit single-byte varieties, as well as multibyte sets such as those used for Chinese, Japanese, and Korean.

The 7-bit sets include US ASCII and other national sets provided for by ISO Standard 646 [42]. The more flexible 8-bit international standard character sets include ISO 8859 Latin Alphabets 1 and 2 for Western and Eastern European languages, respectively, and the ISO 8859-5 Latin/Cyrillic[39] Alphabet [45]. Multibyte character sets include the Chinese, Japanese, and Korean national standard sets, plus Unicode [63] and ISO 10646 [46].

ISO 646 is the international standard for 7-bit character sets. It is identical to ASCII except that 12 of its positions are set aside for the characters needed for each national language. In ASCII itself, the US version of ISO 646, these 12 positions are occupied by the familiar brackets, braces, bars, and so on, used in many programming languages. In other ISO 646 national versions, these character positions are occupied by national characters.

---

[39]"Cyrillic" refers to the family of alphabets used for Russian, Ukrainian, and other Slavic (and some non-Slavic) languages, created by Saints Cyril and Methodius in the 9th century A.D.

Table 16-2 7-Bit National Character Sets, Differences from ASCII

	2/03	4/00	5/11	5/12	5/13	5/14	5/15	6/00	7/11	7/12	7/13	7/14
decimal	35	64	91	92	93	94	95	96	123	124	125	126
US ASCII	#	@	[	\	]	^	_	`	{	|	}	~
British	£	@	[	\	]	^	_	`	{	|	}	~
Canadian-French	#	à	â	ç	ê	î	_	ô	é	ù	è	û
Chinese Roman	#	@	[	¥	]	^	_	`	{	|	}	‾
Danish	#	@	Æ	Ø	Å	^	_	`	æ	ø	å	~
Dutch	£	¾	ÿ	½	|	^	_	`	¨	ƒ	¼	'
Finnish	#	@	Ä	Ö	Å	Ü	_	é	ä	ö	å	ü
French	£	à	°	ç	§	^	_	µ	é	ù	è	¨
German	#	§	Ä	Ö	Ü	^	_	`	ä	ö	ü	ß
Hungarian	#	Á	É	Ö	Ü	^	_	ú	é	ö	ü	ʼʼ
Icelandic	#	Þ	Ð	\	Æ	Ö	_	þ	ð	|	æ	ö
Italian	£	§	°	ç	é	^	_	ù	à	ò	è	ì
Japanese Roman	#	@	[	¥	]	^	_	`	{	|	}	‾
Norwegian	§	@	Æ	Ø	Å	^	_	`	æ	ø	å	|
Portuguese	#	´	Ã	Ç	Õ	^	_	`	ã	ç	õ	~
Spanish	£	§	¡	Ñ	¿	^	_	`	°	ñ	ç	~
Swedish	#	É	Ä	Ö	Å	Ü	_	é	ä	ö	å	ü
Swiss	ù	à	é	ç	ê	î	è	ô	ä	ö	ü	û

For example, the character that occupies position 91, left bracket ([) in ASCII, is replaced by Æ in Danish, ÿ (ij) in Dutch, Ä in Finnish, É in Hungarian, Ð in Icelandic, and so on, as shown in Table 16-2.

The Latin alphabets are 8-bit, 256-character sets. As shown in Figure 16-1, the left half (first 128 characters) of each Latin alphabet is the same as ASCII. It includes 32 7-bit control characters (C0), the Space (SP) character, 94 7-bit graphic characters (GL), and the additional control character, DEL. The right half contains 32 8-bit (C1) control characters and 96 graphic characters (GR) for a particular group of languages. Table 16-3 lists the Latin alphabets. Note that when English is listed as a supported language, this means modern English — Old and Middle English have some additional letters like Eth (ð), Yogh (3), Ash (æ), and Thorn (þ) — plus any language that can be written in the 26-letter Roman alphabet without accents, including Latin, German (using alternative notation for Umlauts and ß), Dutch (with the "ij" digraph written as i and j), and so on.

Figure 16-1 Structure of an 8-Bit Latin Alphabet

	┌ C0 ┐		┌─── GL ───┐						┌ C1 ┐		┌─── GR ───┐					
	00	01	02	03	04	05	06	07	08	09	10	11	12	13	14	15
00	NUL	DLE	SP	0	@	P	`	p								
01	SOH	DC1	!	1	A	Q	a	q								
02	STX	DC2	"	2	B	R	b	r								
03	ETX	DC3	#	3	C	S	c	s								
04	EOT	DC4	$	4	D	T	d	t								
05	ENQ	NAK	%	5	E	U	e	u								
06	ACK	SYN	&	6	F	V	f	v								
07	BEL	ETB	'	7	G	W	g	w								
08	BS	CAN	(	8	H	X	h	x			*(Special Graphics)*					
09	HT	EM	)	9	I	Y	i	y								
10	LF	SUB	*	:	J	Z	j	z								
11	VT	ESC	+	;	K	[	k	{								
12	LF	FS	,	<	L	\	l										
13	CR	GS	–	=	M	]	m	}								
14	SO	RS	.	>	N	^	n	~								
15	SI	US	/	?	O	_	o	DEL								

└ C0 ┘ └─── GL ───┘ └ C1 ┘ └─── GR ───┘

Table 16-3 The ISO Latin Alphabets

Character Set	Standard	Languages
Latin-1	ISO 8859-1	Danish, Dutch, English, Faeroese, Finnish, French, German, Icelandic, Irish, Italian, Norwegian, Portuguese, Spanish, Swedish
Latin-2	ISO 8859-2	Albanian, Czech, English, German, Hungarian, Polish, Romanian, Serbocroatian (Croatian), Slovak, Slovene
Latin-3	ISO 8859-3	Afrikaans, Catalan, English, Esperanto, French, Galician, German, Italian, Maltese, and Turkish
Latin-4	ISO 8859-4	Danish, English, Estonian, Finnish, German, Greenlandic, Sami, Latvian, Lithuanian, Norwegian, and Swedish
Latin/Cyrillic	ISO 8859-5	Bulgarian, Belorussian, English, Macedonian, Russian, Serbocroatian (Serbian), Ukrainian, other former-SSR languages.
Latin/Arabic	ISO 8859-6	Arabic, English
Latin/Greek	ISO 8859-7	Greek, English
Latin/Hebrew	ISO 8859-8	Aramaic, Hebrew, Ladino, Yiddish, English
Latin-5	ISO 8859-9	Dutch, English, Faeroese, Finnish, French, German, Irish, Italian, Norwegian, Portuguese, Spanish, Swedish, Turkish
Latin-6	ISO 8859-10	English, Estonian, Finnish, Lithuanian, Sami, Swedish.

Table 16-4 Right Half of Latin Alphabet 1

	10	11	12	13	14	15
00		°	À	Ð	à	ð
01	¡	±	Á	Ñ	á	ñ
02	¢	²	Â	Ò	â	ò
03	£	³	Ã	Ó	ã	ó
04	¤	´	Ä	Ô	ä	ô
05	¥	µ	Å	Õ	å	õ
06	¦	¶	Æ	Ö	æ	ö
07	§	•	Ç	×	ç	÷
08	¨	,	È	Ø	è	ø
09	©	¹	É	Ù	é	ù
10	ª	º	Ê	Ú	ê	ú
11	«	»	Ë	Û	ë	û
12	¬	¼	Ì	Ü	ì	ü
13		½	Í	Ý	í	ý
14	®	¾	Î	Þ	î	þ
15	¯	¿	Ï	ß	ï	ÿ

Table 16-5 DEC Multinational Character Set

	10	11	12	13	14	15
00		°	À		à	
01	¡	±	Á	Ñ	á	ñ
02	¢	²	Â	Ò	â	ò
03	£	³	Ã	Ó	ã	ó
04			Ä	Ô	ä	ô
05	¥	µ	Å	Õ	å	õ
06		¶	Æ	Ö	æ	ö
07	§	•	Ç	Œ	ç	œ
08	¤		È	Ø	è	ø
09	©	¹	É	Ù	é	ù
10	ª	º	Ê	Ú	ê	ú
11	«	»	Ë	Û	ë	û
12		¼	Ì	Ü	ì	ü
13		½	Í	Ÿ	í	ÿ
14			Î		î	
15		¿	Ï	ß	ï	

Table 16-4 shows the graphic characters (columns 10–15) of the right half of Latin Alphabet 1. The DEC Multinational Character Set is very similar to Latin-1, as you can see by comparing Tables 16-4 and 16-5.

International Characters in Commands

If you have an 8-bit communication link (no parity) between your terminal (keyboard and screen) and C-Kermit, or if you are running C-Kermit on a PC or workstation, use the following command to tell C-Kermit to allow 8-bit characters in your commands:

SET COMMAND BYTESIZE { 7, 8 }

Specifies the character size, in bits, to be used in C-Kermit's commands and messages. The default is 8 in Kermit 95 and Kermit/2; 7 elsewhere.

For example, suppose you have a German keyboard and an 8-bit connection to C-Kermit. SET COMMAND BYTESIZE 8 lets you use German letters in your commands. Correct display of 8-bit characters depends, of course, on your terminal emulator or console driver.

```
C-Kermit>set command bytesize 8
C-Kermit>echo Grüße aus Köln!
Grüße aus Köln!
C-Kermit>
```

International Characters in Terminal Emulation

Host-resident versions of C-Kermit provide no particular kind of terminal emulation during CONNECT mode. Kermit just passes all characters received from the remote host along to your screen and passes your keystrokes to the remote host. The responsibility for most terminal-oriented functions — escape sequence interpretation, function keys, screen rollback, and so on — lies in your terminal, emulator, or workstation window.

Character-set translation is an exception to this rule. If the remote computer or service uses a character set different from your local computer and it is known to C-Kermit, you can ask C-Kermit to translate between the remote character set and the one used by your terminal or emulator so the characters sent by the remote computer will have the correct appearance on your screen and the characters you type will be translated into the remote computer's character set before being sent.

Choosing the Terminal Character Set

C-Kermit usually has no way of knowing which character sets are in use. You must tell it by giving the following command:

SET TERMINAL CHARACTER-SET *remote-cset [local-cset]*
> Specifies the character set used on the remote computer (*remote-cset*) and the character set used by your terminal or emulator (*local-cset*). If *local-cset* is not specified a suitable default, such as C-Kermit's current FILE CHARACTER-SET (explained on page 308), is used. To disable terminal character-set translation, use SET TERMINAL CHARACTER-SET TRANSPARENT, which is the default.

To find out which character sets are available, type a question mark in either one of the character-set name fields:

```
C-Kermit>set terminal character-set ?
remote terminal character-set, one of the following:
  ascii           danish              hp-roman8       portuguese
  british         dec-multinational   hungarian       short-koi
  canadian-french dg-international    italian         spanish
  cp437           dutch               koi8-cyrillic   swedish
  cp850           finnish             latin1-iso      swiss
  cp852           french              latin2-iso      transparent
  cp862-hebrew    german              macintosh-latin
  cp866-cyrillic  hebrew-7            next-multinational
  cyrillic-iso    hebrew-iso          norwegian
C-Kermit>set terminal character-set spanish
C-Kermit>
```

Table 16-7 on page 307 tells you which character sets these names refer to. The sets with "national" names, like French, Dutch, Finnish, and so on, are 7-bit ISO 646 national sets, shown in Table 16-2 on page 298. The Roman 8-bit sets (Latin-1, DEC Multinational, NeXT, etc.) are shown in Tables VII-4 and VII-5, the Cyrillic codes are listed in Table VII-6, and the Hebrew ones in Table VII-7. These tables begin on page 560.

Here is an example in which we CONNECT from C-Kermit on a PC running SCO UNIX and using PC Code Page 437 to a remote Mailbox (BBS) in Cologne, Germany, that uses the German ISO 646 set.

```
C-Kermit>connect
Gr}~e aus K|ln!
F}r Mailbox "gast" eingeben...
login:
```

If this does not look like German to you, it's because the remote computer is using a different character set than your local one. Let's try it again, but this time with C-Kermit providing the translation from German ISO 646 to CP437:

```
C-Kermit>set terminal char german cp437
C-Kermit>connect
Grüße aus Köln!
Für Mailbox "gast" eingeben...
login:
```

When terminal character-set translation is in effect, C-Kermit uses a standard character set (such as Latin-1), if necessary, as an intermediate step between the local and remote sets. Otherwise, C-Kermit's 33 terminal character sets would require 1056 translation functions! But by choosing an appropriate intermediate set for each pair, we have about 100, and these also happen to be the same ones we use for file transfer.

However, as a result of this ecologically sound design, we can lose characters that the local and remote character sets do not have in common with the intermediate set. For example, both the Macintosh and NeXT character sets have a Florin sign (f), but since Latin-1 doesn't have one (see Table 16-4), it is replaced by something else along the way, most likely a question mark.

Using a 7-Bit Terminal Character Set

If both the remote and local terminal character sets are 7-bit sets (ASCII, Short KOI, or one of the ISO 646 national sets like Italian, Portuguese, or Norwegian), you should be able to operate equally well in the 7-bit and 8-bit communication environments.

However, a word of warning is required. If the remote computer sends escape sequences to control the appearance of your screen, these sequences might contain 7-bit graphic characters that would normally be translated before they reach your screen. For example,

Table 16-6 ANSI Escape Sequence Formats

Introducer	Type	Terminator
ESC [	Control Sequence	64–126
ESC P	Device Control String	ESC \
ESC]	Operating System Command	ESC \
ESC ^	Privacy Message	ESC \
ESC _	Application Program Command	ESC \
ESC *other*	Escape Sequence	48–126

many ANSI and therefore VT100, VT200, and VT300 escape sequences [4] include the left bracket ([ ) character, as in:[40]

```
ESC [ 24 ; 40 H
```

which moves the cursor to column 40 of line 24 on the screen. But the left bracket is an ISO 646 national character and would be translated as shown in Table 16-2 on page 298, thus destroying the escape sequence and interfering with your screen display.

C-Kermit does its best to avoid this effect by skipping translation of ANSI escape sequences during CONNECT mode. ANSI escape sequences begin with the ESC (Escape) character, ASCII 27, and terminate under various conditions, depending on the character that follows the Escape, as shown in Table 16-6. Whenever C-Kermit sees an Escape character under these conditions, it reads the ensuing characters up to and including the final character or sequence, listed in the *Terminator* column in the table, and sends them to the screen without translation. In the example:

```
ESC [ 24 ; 40 H
```

ESC [is a Control Sequence Introducer, which means that the escape sequence continues until a terminating character in the range 64–126 appears. The first such character in the example is H (ASCII character 72).

This technique is used only when translation of a 7-bit character set is requested, and so 8-bit escape sequences are not, and don't need to be, recognized. Except in Kermit 95 and Kermit/2, C-Kermit makes no attempt to avoid unwanted translations in non-ANSI terminal control codes.

---

[40]ESC is the ASCII Escape character. Spaces are shown for clarity, but are not part of the escape sequence.

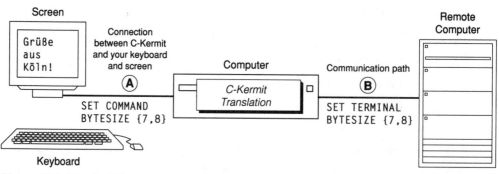

Figure 16-2 Terminal Character Set Translation

Using an 8-Bit Terminal Character Set

During C-Kermit CONNECT mode, there are two components to the connection between your desktop terminal or computer and the remote computer or service: the one between C-Kermit and your keyboard and screen, and the one between C-Kermit and the remote host or service. Each component can be either a 7-bit or an 8-bit connection. Most versions of C-Kermit treat both as 7-bit connections unless you say otherwise. This is to prevent parity from being mistaken for real data, a sensible default given the widespread use of parity and the equally widespread lack of awareness about it. But this default prevents the use of 8-bit character sets during a CONNECT session.

Figure 16-2 shows the two components of the CONNECT-mode connection. If the communication path between your terminal or emulator and C-Kermit (A in the figure) is truly 8-bits-no-parity, you can give the command SET COMMAND BYTESIZE 8 to tell C-Kermit not to strip the 8th bit from each character that comes in from your keyboard and goes out to your screen (not necessary in Kermit 95 and Kermit/2).

Similarly, if the path between C-Kermit and the remote host (B in the figure) is really 8 bits, give the commands SET TERMINAL BYTESIZE 8 and (if necessary) SET PARITY NONE to prevent Kermit from stripping the 8th bit of characters that go in to and out of the communication device.

If all components of the communication path are "8-bit clean," you can give all three of these commands and then use 8-bit terminal character sets with no further ado. You can also start C-Kermit with the command-line option "-8", which is equivalent to giving the same three commands.

Please note: These commands do not *make* the connection 8-bit clean, they merely tell C-Kermit that it *is* 8-bit clean.

Using an 8-Bit Terminal Character Set on a 7-Bit Connection

If the connection between C-Kermit and the remote host (B) is normally 7 bits but you need to transmit and receive 8-bit characters, you might still be able to do so. Explore the terminal- and communication-related commands of the remote host and any communication equipment or networks in between: SET TERMINAL /EIGHT in VMS, `stty pass8` or `stty -parity` on some UNIX systems, `rlogin -8` *host* when making "rlogin" connections from one UNIX system to another; check the configuration of your modem, terminal server, network PAD, or any other intermediate devices. Do whatever you can to achieve an 8-bit connection.

If all else fails, the C-Kermit CONNECT command supports a terminal-oriented protocol, known as shift-out/shift-in (SO/SI), that allows it to exchange 8-bit data over a 7-bit terminal connection. The remote host must also be using this protocol. It works like this: if an 8-bit character (a character with its 8th bit set to 1) must be sent on a 7-bit connection, an SO character (Shift-Out, Control-N, ASCII 14) is sent first, then the 8-bit character is sent with its 8th bit replaced by the required parity bit. When the receiver gets the SO, it knows to set the 8th bit of subsequently received characters to 1 before interpreting them. The next time a 7-bit character must be sent, an SI character (Shift-In, Control-O, ASCII character 15) is sent first. This tells the receiver to set the 8th bit of subsequently received characters to 0. Thus, SO applies to all subsequent characters until an SI is received, and vice versa. To illustrate, suppose we have the German phrase:

```
Grüße aus Köln!
```

encoded in Latin Alphabet 1. Using SO/SI, it would be transmitted like this:

```
Gr<SO>|_<SI>e aus K<SO>v<SI>ln!
```

where `<SO>` and `<SI>` represent the Shift-Out and Shift-In control characters. The "funny" characters are obtained by removing the 8th bit from the Latin-1 special characters, which is equivalent to subtracting 128 from their code values. For example, the Latin-1 code for ü is 252, minus 128 is 124, which is the code for vertical bar, |.

Here is the C-Kermit command that controls the use of Shift-out/shift-in during terminal connection:

SET TERMINAL LOCKING-SHIFT { OFF, ON }

This setting, which normally is OFF, applies to the portion of the connection between C-Kermit and the remote host. If you plan to use an 8-bit character set on the remote host, but you only have a 7-bit connection, *and* the remote host can use Shift-In and Shift-Out codes to switch between 7-bit and 8-bit characters, set this option to ON. When TERMINAL LOCKING-SHIFT is ON, C-Kermit interprets incoming characters according to the current shift state and automatically shifts the characters you type on your keyboard before sending them to the remote host.

If the remote host uses an 8-bit character set, but you can't get an 8-bit connection to it, and it does not support shift-out/shift-in, all is not necessarily lost. For example, on a remote UNIX host, you can pipe your 8-bit files through a shift-out/shift-in filter like the one listed in Appendix X:

```
$ cat latin1.txt | so | more
```

Key Mapping

C-Kermit translates each key you press into the remote host's character set before transmitting it, according to your most recent SET TERMINAL CHARACTER-SET command. These translations also apply to any key redefinitions you have made with the SET KEY command.

National or international characters in your key definitions should use the coding of your *local* character set, not the remote coding. This is the more natural arrangement and it allows you access to different remote computers that use different character sets without having to change your key mappings.

Transferring International Text Files

The Kermit protocol distinguishes between vendor-specific codes, used in storing and displaying files on each computer, and the codes used within Kermit's packets when transferring a file [36]. The vendor-specific file encoding is called the *file character-set*; the file character-sets known to C-Kermit are listed in Table 16-7. The code used during file transfer is called the *transfer character-set*. The Kermit protocol supports only a small number of transfer character-sets; namely, those that are well-established as international standards, such as ISO 8859 Latin Alphabets 1 and 2 or ISO 8859-5 Latin/Cyrillic.[41] The sender translates the file from its local code to the standard transfer code, and the receiver translates from the transfer code to its own local code, as shown in Figure 16-3.

Specifying Character Sets for File Transfer

If your computer supports international character sets at all, it probably does so only as an afterthought. Most computers and operating systems were designed to support only a single character code such as ASCII or EBCDIC, suitable only for representing English. As computer users in non-English-speaking countries began to demand support for their own languages, IBM, DEC, Apple, and other manufacturers introduced terminals, printers, and PCs capable of displaying French, German, Italian, Russian, Hebrew, Arabic,

---

[41]There is now a single standard multibyte encoding that encompasses most of the world's character sets, ISO 10646 [46], and its cousin, UNICODE [63], but it will take some time, maybe lots of it, for this "Universal Character Set" to catch on.

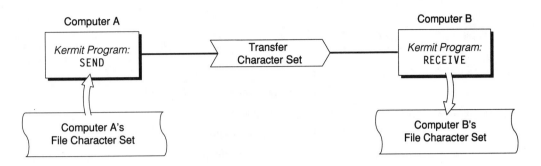

Figure 16-3 International Text File Transfer

Japanese, and other languages, but in most cases they did this without significantly changing the computers themselves. Text is still stored on the disk in undistinguished, anonymous 8-bit bytes, and the terminal or printer must be told how to interpret them. Files are stored on most computers without any indication of character set.

Table 16-7   C-Kermit File Character Sets

Name	Bits	Description
ascii	7	ISO 646 United States Version, ASCII, ANSI X3.4-1986 [1]
british	7	ISO 646, British Version, BSI 4730 [7]
canadian-french	7	French-Canadian NRC (DEC) [28]
cp437	8	PC Code Page 437, used on PCs [40]
cp850	8	PC Code Page 850, used on PCs [40]
cp852	8	PC Code Page 852 for Eastern Europe [40]
cp862	8	PC Code Page 862 Hebrew [40]
cp866	8	PC Code Page 866 Cyrillic, used on PCs [57]
cyrillic-iso	8	ISO 8859-5 Latin/Cyrillic Alphabet [45]
danish	7	(Same as Norwegian) [48]
dec-kanji	M	DEC multibyte Japanese Kanji
dec-multinational	8	DEC Multinational Character Set [28]
dg-international	8	Data General International Character Set [25]
dutch	7	Dutch NRC (DEC) [28]
finnish	7	Finnish NRC (DEC) [28]
french	7	ISO 646, French Version, NF Z 62010-1982 [48]

Table 16-7   C-Kermit File Character Sets (continued)

Name	Bits	Description
german	7	ISO 646, German Version, DIN 66083 [48]
hebrew-7	7	7-bit Hebrew and uppercase Roman
hebrew-iso	8	ISO 8859-8 Latin/Hebrew Alphabet 1 [45]
hp-roman8	8	Hewlett Packard Roman 8
hungarian	7	ISO 646, Hungarian Version, HS 7795/3 [48]
italian	7	ISO 646, Italian Version [48]
japanese-euc	M	Japanese Extended UNIX Code, JIS X 0201 + JIS X 0208
jis7-kanji	M	Japanese 7-bit JIS Encoding
koi8-cyrillic	8	"Old KOI-8" Cyrillic (GOST 19768-74) [58]
latin1-iso	8	ISO 8859-1 Latin Alphabet 1 [45]
latin2-iso	8	ISO 8859-2 Latin Alphabet 2 [45]
macintosh-latin	8	Apple Quickdraw extended
next-multinational	8	NeXTSTEP
norwegian	7	ISO 646, Norwegian Version, NS 4551 [48]
portuguese	7	ISO 646, Portuguese Version [48]
shift-jis-kanji	M	Code Page 932 Kanji, used on PCs
short-koi	7	7-bit Roman and Cyrillic, uppercase only [58]
spanish	7	ISO 646, Spanish Version [48]
swedish	7	ISO 646, Swedish Version, SEN 850200 [48]
swiss	7	Swiss NRC (DEC) [28]

To send or receive a file containing international characters, you must tell C-Kermit which character sets to use: which character set the original file is encoded in, which standard character set is to be used during transfer, and which character set is to be used in the new copy of the file. The first command you need is:

SET FILE CHARACTER-SET *name*
    Identifies the character set to be used for file input or output. The file sender translates from the file character set to the transfer character set, and the file receiver translates from the transfer character set to its own file character set. In most cases, the default file character-set is ASCII. In certain versions of C-Kermit, the local character set is known, so that is your default file character-set. For example, in NeXTSTEP, it is the NeXT character set; on AOS/VS systems, it is DG-International; in Windows or OS/2, it is your current PC code page.

Your version of C-Kermit does not necessarily support all of the file character-sets listed in Table 16-7. C-Kermit can be configured to omit one or more character-set families: East European, Cyrillic, or Japanese Kanji. You can use the SHOW FEATURES and CHECK commands to obtain configuration information:

```
C-Kermit>show features
...
 No Kanji character-set translation
C-Kermit>check latin2
 Available
C-Kermit>
```

To see the list of supported file character-sets, use a question mark in the SET FILE CHARACTER-SET command:

```
C-Kermit>set file char ? local file code, one of the following:
 ascii              danish            hebrew-iso        macintosh-latin
 british            dec-kanji         hp-roman8         next-multinational
 canadian-french    dec-multinational hungarian         norwegian
 cp437              dg-international   italian           portuguese
 cp850              dutch             japanese-euc      shift-jis-kanji
 cp852              finnish           jis7-kanji        short-koi
 cp862-hebrew       french            koi8-cyrillic     spanish
 cp866-cyrillic     german            latin1-iso        swedish
 cyrillic-iso       hebrew-7          latin2-iso        swiss
C-Kermit>set file char hungarian
```

This is the list you would see with a fully-configured C-Kermit program as of this writing; others are likely to be added as time goes on.

Choosing the appropriate file character-sets for the two computers solves two thirds of the puzzle. To complete the puzzle, you must choose the transfer character-set that is best capable of representing the characters in your file character-sets:

SET TRANSFER CHARACTER-SET *name*
> Identifies the intermediate character set to be used in Kermit-to-Kermit communication, that is, in Kermit's data packets. Synonym: **SET XFER CHARACTER-SET**.

The default transfer character-set is TRANSPARENT, meaning that no translation takes place during file transfer.

C-Kermit supports the following transfer character-sets:

LATIN1-ISO
> Is ISO 8859-1 Latin Alphabet 1 [45], or Latin-1 for short. This is the usual choice for Western European languages based on the Roman alphabet, such as Italian, Portuguese, Norwegian, French, and Spanish, because it is capable of representing all the characters used in about 15 of these languages (see Table 16-3). Latin Alphabet 1 is listed in Table VII-4.

LATIN2-ISO

Is ISO 8859-2 Latin Alphabet 2, or Latin-2 for short. This is the usual choice for Eastern European languages based on the Roman alphabet, such as Czech, Polish, Romanian, and Hungarian (see Table 16-3). Latin Alphabet 2 is listed in Table VII-5.

CYRILLIC-ISO

Is ISO 8859-5, the Latin/Cyrillic Alphabet [45], also known as ECMA-113 [31], which can represent Russian, Ukrainian, and other languages written in Cyrillic and (because it includes ASCII as its left half) also English. Listed in Table VII-6.

HEBREW-ISO

Is ISO 8859-8, the Latin/Hebrew Alphabet [45], also known as ECMA-121 [32], which can represent Hebrew, Yiddish, Ladino, Aramaic, and Judeo-Arabic, as well as English. Listed in Table VII-7.

JAPANESE-EUC

Should be used for Japanese text.

ASCII

Means to render each character as its closest ASCII equivalent, for example by removing diacritical marks from accented Roman vowels, or by converting Cyrillic characters "by sound." Use this option when your computer does not have a way to display the file's characters correctly (these conversions don't work for Japanese).

TRANSPARENT

Means that no character translation occurs; each code is sent as-is. This is the default transfer character-set. This option can also be used whenever both computers use the same character set.

Your version of C-Kermit might be configured differently. To find out which transfer character-sets are available to you:

```
C-Kermit>set transfer char ?
 ascii      latin1-iso        transparent
```

When you specify the file and transfer character-sets, Kermit picks the appropriate translation function and uses it as shown in Figure 16-4 on the next page, which illustrates what happens when you transfer an Italian language text file from a PC with MS-DOS Kermit to a Data General AViiON workstation with C-Kermit.

It's your job to use the SET FILE CHARACTER-SET and SET TRANSFER CHARACTER-SET commands to pick the translation you need. Kermit can't do this for you because it doesn't know what you are trying to accomplish. To illustrate this point, let's suppose you want to receive a French-language text file with C-Kermit on an SCO UNIX system running on an IBM or compatible PC. The TRANSFER CHARACTER-SET is LATIN1. Your PC uses Code Page 437. You can choose your FILE CHARACTER-SET to be:

```
MS-Kermit>set file char cp437
MS-Kermit>set transfer char latin1
MS-Kermit>send linguini.txt
```

```
C-Kermit>set file char dg
C-Kermit>set xfer char latin1
C-Kermit>receive
```

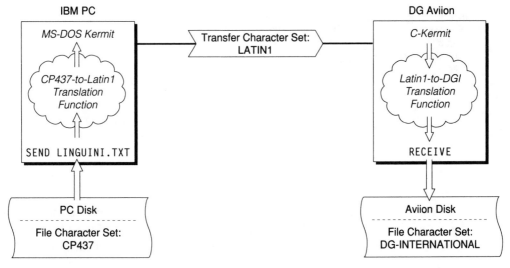

Figure 16-4 Linguini Transfer

- CP437 if you want the file to display correctly on your PC console screen

- CP850 if you want to copy the file to a tape cartridge for an IBM RS/6000

- LATIN1 if you want to keep the Latin-1 encoding intact for an application on your PC that requires Latin-1 rather than CP437

- FRENCH if you want to print the file on your PC printer, but your printer supports only the French ISO 646 character set

- ASCII if you want to convert the special characters to plain ASCII, for example because your PC-based e-mail system only supports ASCII

- NEXT if you want to copy the file to a DOS-format diskette to be read on a NeXT workstation

And so on.

Use the SHOW CHARACTER-SETS command to see C-Kermit's current terminal, file, and transfer character-sets:

```
C-Kermit>sho char
```

```
File Character-Set: US ASCII (7-bit)
Transfer Character-Set: Transparent
Unknown-Char-Set: Keep
Terminal character-set: transparent

   (Now change them...)

C-Kermit>set file char next
C-Kermit>set xfer char latin1
C-Kermit>set term char dg next
C-Kermit>set unkn discard
C-Kermit>sho char

 File Character-Set: NeXT Multinational (8-bit)
 Transfer Character-Set: LATIN1, ISO 8859-1
 Unknown-Char-Set: Discard
 Terminal character-sets:
   Remote: dg-international
   Local: next-multinational
   Via:   latin1-iso

C-Kermit>
```

The UNKNOWN-CHAR-SET setting tells C-Kermit what to do if a file arrives announcing itself with a character set that C-Kermit doesn't support. Normally the file is accepted (KEEP) without translation, but you can also instruct C-Kermit to reject such files:

```
C-Kermit>set unknown-char-set discard
```

The SET UNKNOWN-CHAR-SET command is effective only when given to the file receiver.

Transferring Roman Text

Let's try a simple example. Suppose we have a German-language file stored on an IBM PC using PC Code Page 437. The file is called modem.txt and it looks like this:

```
Wer ein Selbstwähl-Modem hat, muß zur Herstellung der Verbindung
mit dem anderen Rechner die Wählkommandos eintippen. Man kann zur
Kermit-Kommandoebene zurückgelangen durch Eintippen der
'Rückkehrsequenz'.
```

Let's transfer this file from the PC to a UNIX system that uses the 7-bit German character set. Assume we're already logged in. The Kermit program on *each* computer must be told which file character-set to use, but only the file sender has to be told the transfer character-set because the sender automatically informs the receiver in the attribute packet. First tell MS-DOS Kermit on the PC which character sets to use:

```
MS-Kermit>set file type text              (Use text mode)
MS-Kermit>set transfer mode manual        (Don't switch to binary)
MS-Kermit>set file character-set cp437
MS-Kermit>set transfer character-set latin1
```

Now go to the UNIX system, start C-Kermit, tell it which file character-set to use, then tell it to wait for the file:

```
MS-Kermit>connect
$ kermit
C-Kermit>set file character-set german
C-Kermit>receive
```

Now escape back to the PC and send the file. MS-DOS Kermit automatically tells C-Kermit that the transfer character-set is Latin-1.

```
Alt-X                              (Escape back)
MS-Kermit>send modem.txt           (Send the file)
   (The file is transferred...)
```

Now the file is stored on the UNIX system with German ISO 646 encoding. To check that it was transferred correctly, tell MS-DOS Kermit's terminal emulator about the character set, then connect back to UNIX and display the file on your screen:

```
MS-Kermit>set terminal character-set german
MS-Kermit>connect
C-Kermit>type modem.txt

Wer ein Selbstwähl-Modem hat, muß zur Herstellung der Verbindung
mit dem anderen Rechner die Wählkommandos eintippen. Man kann zur
Kermit-Kommandoebene zurückgelangen durch Eintippen der
'Rückkehrsequenz'.
$
```

As you can see, the file arrived with its special characters intact. Now let's transfer the same file from UNIX to another PC. But this time it is to be printed on a device that does not have German characters. Here we choose ASCII as the transfer character-set to translate the special characters to their closest ASCII equivalents, rather than into gibberish:

```
C-Kermit>set file type text        (Transfer in text mode)
C-Kermit>set xfer mode manual      (Don't switch to binary)
C-Kermit>set file char german      (Translate from this)
C-Kermit>set xfer char ascii       (to this)
C-Kermit>send modem.txt            (Send the file from UNIX)
alt<X>                             (Escape back)
MS-Kermit>receive                  (Wait for the file on the PC)
   (The file is transferred...)
MS-Kermit>type modem.txt           (Take a look...)

Wer ein Selbstwahl-Modem hat, mus zur Herstellung der Verbindung
mit dem anderen Rechner die Wahlkommandos eintippen. Man kann zur
Kermit-Kommandoebene zuruckgelangen durch Eintippen der
'Ruckkehrsequenz'.
$
```

Notice how ä has become simply a, ü has become u, and ß has become s. Without these translations, the text would have been printed like this:

```
Wer ein Selbstw{hl-Modem hat, mu~ zur Herstellung der Verbindung
mit dem anderen Rechner die W{hlkommandos eintippen. Man kann zur
Kermit-Kommandoebene zur}ckgelangen durch Eintippen der
'R}ckkehrsequenz'.
```

Transferring Cyrillic Text

Cyrillic text (Russian, Ukrainian, Belorussian, and so on) can be encoded using a variety of different and incompatible character sets, including at least the following:

- PC Code Page 866 [57], used on PCs, which, like other PC code pages, has ASCII in the left half and the special characters in the right. Supported by MS-DOS Kermit and C-Kermit.

- Alternative Cyrillic, a precursor to Code Page 866, developed for PCs in the Soviet Union by Bryabin, *et al.* [6].

- PC Code Page 855 for PCs [40]. Like Code Page 866, but with different encoding.

- KOI-8, also known as "Old KOI-8," an 8-bit Soviet government standard (GOST 19768-74) [58] character set consisting of full upper- and lowercase Latin and Cyrillic alphabets, in which the 8-bit Cyrillic letters run parallel to their 7-bit ASCII phonetic equivalents. KOI stands for Код для Обмена Информатсии — Kod dlia Obmiena Informatsii (Code for Information Interchange, like the CII in ASCII). Old KOI-8 corresponds to the 1974 first edition of ECMA-113 [30] and is still in wide use, as in the relcom.* newsgroups.

- Short KOI [58], a 7-bit code containing the uppercase Roman and Cyrillic letters, but no lowercase. The Roman letters are in ASCII order, and Cyrillic letters parallel the Roman letters phonetically.

- DKOI [58], similar to KOI-8, but with an EBCDIC-style layout, used on IBM compatible mainframes and supported by IBM mainframe Kermit [19].

- IBM Country Extended Code Page (CECP) 880 [40], IBM's EBCDIC-based Cyrillic Multilingual Code Page for IBM mainframes, totally different from DKOI, supported by IBM mainframe Kermit [19].

- IBM Country Extended Code Page 1025, a newer revision of CECP 880.

- ISO 8859-5 Latin/Cyrillic, similar to Latin-1, but with Cyrillic characters in the right half. Also known as "New KOI-8", this is the international standard Cyrillic character set; it corresponds to GOST 19768-87 and to the second edition of ECMA-113 [31].

Each of these sets is capable of representing both Roman and Cyrillic letters. The Kermit protocol uses ISO 8859-5 Latin/Cyrillic as the transfer character-set for Cyrillic text, supported, as of this writing, by MS-DOS Kermit, IBM mainframe Kermit, and C-Kermit. Use this command:

SET TRANSFER CHARACTER-SET CYRILLIC

to select the Latin/Cyrillic transfer character-set.

C-Kermit supports the following Cyrillic file character-sets:

SET FILE CHARACTER-SET CYRILLIC
ISO 8859-5 Latin/Cyrillic.

SET FILE CHARACTER-SET CP866
PC Code Page 866.

SET FILE CHARACTER-SET KOI8
(Old) KOI-8.

SET FILE CHARACTER-SET SHORT-KOI
Short KOI.

These character sets are listed in Table VII-6 on page 566. The method for transferring Cyrillic files is the same as for Roman text. You have to identify the file character-set to be used on each computer and you also must tell the file sender which transfer character-set to use. Here is an example in which we send a KOI-8 file from C-Kermit to an IBM-compatible mainframe, where it is to be stored using EBCDIC CECP 880:

```
Kermit-CMS>set file char cp880      (Translate to PC code page)
Kermit-CMS>receive                  (Receive the file)
Ctrl-\c                             (Escape back to C-Kermit)
C-Kermit>set file char koi8         (Identify the file character-set)
C-Kermit>set xfer char cyrillic     (Translate to Latin/Cyrillic)
C-Kermit>send icsti.txt             (Send the file)
```

C-Kermit tells IBM Mainframe Kermit that the transfer character-set is Latin/Cyrillic, and IBM Mainframe Kermit translates from this to Code Page 880.

Suppose you need to look at Cyrillic text on a computer that does not have a Cyrillic display device available. Use Short KOI, in which all Roman letters are converted to upper-case, and Cyrillic letters are converted to their lowercase Roman phonetic equivalents, listed in Table VII-6 on page 566. In this example, we send a copy of Pushkin's poem "Bronze Horseman" from a PC, where it is stored using CP866, to C-Kermit, where it is stored in Short KOI format.

```
MS-Kermit>type horseman.txt           (Read it in Russian)
   На берегу пустынных волн
Стоял он, дум великих полн,
И вдаль глядел. Пред ним широко
Река неслася; бедный чёлн
По ней стремился одиноко.
   . . .
MS-Kermit>connect                     (Go to UNIX)
C-Kermit>set file char short-koi      (Translate to Short KOI)
C-Kermit>receive                      (Wait for the file)
Alt-X                                 (Escape back)
```

```
MS-Kermit>set file char cp866          (Translate from this...)
MS-Kermit>set transf char cyr          (to this)
MS-Kermit>send horseman.txt            (Send the file)

  (The file is transferred...)

MS-Kermit>connect                      (Go back to UNIX)
C-Kermit>type horseman.txt             (Look at the result)

   na beregu pustynnyh woln            (You can almost read it aloud)
stoql on, dum welikih poln,
i wdalx glqdel.  pred nim {iroko
reka neslasq; bednyj ~eln
po nej stremilsq odinoko.
   ...
```

You can translate between 8-bit Roman-based and Cyrillic-based character sets during file transfer, but then you lose either the Cyrillic characters or the accented Roman ones. For example, if you translate from KOI-8 to Latin-1, the ASCII text survives, but the Cyrillic characters all become question marks (but see page 321 before giving up on this idea).

Similarly, if you translate from Latin-1 to Latin/Cyrillic, it is the same as translating from Latin-1 to ASCII. All accents and other diacritical marks are lost.

Transferring Hebrew Text

The Hebrew alphabet is approximately 2000 years old, and is used for writing Hebrew, Aramaic, Yiddish, Ladino, and Judeo-Arabic.

The Hebrew alphabet consists of 22 letters and five final forms, with no upper/lowercase case distinctions, as shown in Table VII-7 on page 570. Other characters (vowel points, digraphs or ligatures, cantillation marks, and special punctuation) are sometimes also used for certain purposes, but they are not included in the standard single-byte Hebrew computer character sets.

The Hebrew script is written right to left, but is commonly mixed with Arabic numerals and Roman text that is written left to right; therefore Hebrew is considered a bidirectional writing system.

Hebrew character sets include:

- Hebrew-7, a 7-bit code, constructed from ASCII, but with accent grave and the 26 lowercase letters a–z replaced by the 22 Hebrew letters and five final forms in normal Hebrew order; used on Hebrew-model DEC VT100-series terminals.

- PC Code Page 862, based on PC code page 437, but with the 27 Hebrew letters replacing many of the accented Roman characters. Includes all upper- and lowercase un-accented Roman letters.

- IBM CECP 424, the Hebrew EBCDIC Country Extended Code Page for IBM mainframes.

- ISO 8859-8 Latin/Hebrew, similar to Latin-1, but with Hebrew letters in the right half, rather than accented Roman ones, and with many open positions.

Hebrew-7, CP862, and ISO Latin/Hebrew are supported by C-Kermit and MS-DOS Kermit. CECP 424 is supported IBM Mainframe Kermit. The Kermit protocol uses ISO 8858-8 Latin/Hebrew as the transfer character set for Hebrew text:

SET TRANSFER CHARACTER-SET HEBREW-ISO

C-Kermit also supports the following Hebrew file character sets:

SET FILE CHARACTER-SET CP862
 PC code page 862.

SET FILE CHARACTER-SET HEBREW-7
 Hebrew-7.

SET FILE CHARACTER-SET HEBREW-ISO
 ISO 8859-8 Latin/Hebrew.

In the following example, we transfer a Hebrew text file from a PC, where it is encoded in CP862, to a UNIX server, translating to Latin/Hebrew in the process:

```
C-Kermit> set file character-set hebrew-iso
C-Kermit> set xfer character-set hebrew-iso
C-Kermit> receive
Ctrl-\c                                (Escape back to Kermit 95)
K-95> set file character-set cp862
K-95> set xfer char hebrew-iso
K-95> send hebrew.txt
```

Only the character code values are changed. Kermit protocol does nothing about the order in which the characters appear.

Transferring Japanese Text

Japanese writing combines several distinct elements:

- Kanji, ideograms similar to those used in China and Korea, with each ideogram standing for a word. More than 6000 Kanji symbols are in common use.

- Kana, a phonetic writing system, containing 50–60 characters, including punctuation and sound symbols. Kana comes in two major varieties, Katakana and Hiragana, the latter being a more cursive and stylized form.

- Roman letters, digits, and punctuation.

As you might expect, there is more than one character set commonly used for representing Japanese text:

- JIS (Japan Industrial Standard) X 0201 [49] combines Roman and Katakana in a Latin-alphabet-like 8-bit single-byte character set. It differs from a Latin alphabet in that the left half is not exactly ASCII (backslash is replaced by Yen sign, tilde by over-bar). The right half has some empty positions.

- JIS X 0208 [50] is a set of 6877 two-byte characters including Roman, Cyrillic, Greek, Katakana, Hiragana, and Kanji characters, plus special symbol and line-drawing characters.

- JIS X 0212 [51] is a newer revision of JIS X 0208.

- Japanese EUC (Extended UNIX Code) combines JIS X 0201 and 0208 into a single code in which single-byte Roman characters have their 8th bits set to 0, double-byte JIS X 0208 codes have their 8th bits set to 1, and single-byte JIS X 0201 Katakana codes are invoked via a single-shift mechanism.

- Shift-JIS (Code Page 932) is used on PCs and includes single-byte Roman and Katakana and 2-byte Kanji, but at different code points than the standard sets or EUC.

- DEC Kanji is used on VMS and OpenVMS and is equivalent to EUC, but without single-byte Katakana.

- Various "EBCDIC" Kanji codes are used on IBM, Hitachi, and Fujitsu mainframes, supported by IBM mainframe Kermit [19].

To complicate matters, we have 7-bit transmission media and e-mail to contend with. For this, a variation of EUC called JIS7 is used, in which all characters are represented by 7-bit bytes, and switching among JIS Roman, JIS Katakana, and JIS X 0208 is done by locking shifts [36, 43] imbedded in the data stream.

C-Kermit uses Japanese-EUC as the transfer character-set for Japanese text, since it ac-commodates the three major writing methods and still distinguishes between single- and double-width Roman and Katakana characters:

SET TRANSFER CHARACTER-SET JAPANESE-EUC

C-Kermit supports the following Japanese file character-sets:

SHIFT-JIS
Shift-JIS (CP932) on PCs.

DEC-KANJI
DEC Kanji, used primarily on VMS and OpenVMS.

JIS7-KANJI
The code most commonly used in electronic mail.

JAPANESE-EUC
Japanese Extended UNIX code itself, commonly found on UNIX computers.

Here we use MS-DOS Kermit on a PC in Kyoto (which uses Shift-JIS) to send a Kanji file to C-Kermit on a VAX in Tokyo (which uses DEC-Kanji). We also use the SET PROMPT command to distinguish between the two C-Kermit prompts:

```
MS-Kermit>set prompt Kyoto>      (Local PC Kermit prompt)
Kyoto>set file char shift-jis    (Translate from this...)
Kyoto>set xfer char japanese     (to this)
Kyoto>connect                    (Go to the VAX)

$ kermit                         (Start Kermit)

C-Kermit>set prompt Tokyo>       (Change the prompt)
Tokyo>set file char dec-kanji    (Translate to this)
Tokyo>r                          (Receive the file)

Ctrl-\c                          (Escape back)
Kyoto>send genji.txt             (Send the file)
```

There is no mechanism for translating Japanese into Roman characters or vice versa. C-Kermit lets you combine Japanese and non-Japanese transfer and file character-sets, but only the Roman letters are preserved. As of this writing, C-Kermit does not support Japanese character-set translation during terminal emulation (but MS-DOS Kermit does).

Language-Specific Translations

When C-Kermit is receiving a file encoded in the Latin-1 transfer character-set but has been told to store the file as ASCII, or when it is sending a file encoded in a national or international character set but has been told to use ASCII as its transfer character-set, it strips diacritical marks and stores or sends the bare letters; for example, *à côté* becomes *a cote* (French), *Füße* becomes *Fuse* (German). For most Romance languages (Italian, Spanish, etc.), not much else can be done.

Languages like Dutch, Norwegian, Danish, Swedish, and German, however, have conventions for changing accented or other special characters into the plain letters A–Z. These rules are shown in Table 16-8 (in which Scandinavian means Danish, Finnish, Norwegian, or Swedish). Since Kermit does not know what language a file is written in, you must tell it. Here's the command:

SET LANGUAGE *name*
Tells C-Kermit which language text files are written in so it can apply language-specific transliteration rules when converting between ASCII and a national or international character set. Type a question mark to see which languages are supported by your C-Kermit program, for example:

Table 16-8 Language-Specific Transliteration Rules

Character	Dutch	French	German	Icelandic	Scandinavian
Å	–	–	–	–	Aa
å	–	–	–	–	aa
Ä	–	–	Ae	–	Ae
ä	–	–	ae	–	ae
Æ	–	–	–	Ae	Ae
æ	–	–	–	ae	ae
Ö	–	–	Oe	Oe	Oe
ö	–	–	oe	oe	oe
Œ	–	Oe	–	–	–
œ	–	oe	–	–	–
Ø	–	–	–	–	Oe
ø	–	–	–	–	oe
Ü	–	–	Ue	–	Ue
ü	–	–	ue	–	ue
ÿ	ij	–	–	–	–
ß	–	–	ss	–	–
Ð	–	–	–	D	–
ð	–	–	–	d	–
Þ	–	–	–	Th	–
þ	–	–	–	th	–

```
C-Kermit>set language ? One of the following:
 danish      finnish    german     norwegian  russian    ukrainian
 dutch       french     icelandic  none       swedish
C-Kermit>set language finnish
```

NONE, which is the default, means that no special language rules should be applied.

If you SET LANGUAGE to DUTCH, FRENCH, GERMAN, ICELANDIC, or any of the Scandinavian languages DANISH, FINNISH, NORWEGIAN, or SWEDISH, you get the effects shown in Table 16-8 when translating into ASCII from an 8-bit character set or from a 7-bit ISO 646 national version, but *not* in the other direction. The language-specific translations are not invertible.

You can find out your current character sets and language with the SHOW FILE, SHOW LANGUAGES, or SHOW CHARACTER-SETS commands, for example:

```
C-Kermit>set xfer ch latin1
C-Kermit>show lang

  Language-specific translation rules: Icelandic
  File Character-Set: ASCII
  Transfer Character-Set: Latin-1

C-Kermit>
```

To illustrate the use of the SET LANGUAGE command, let's transfer our German file again, and suppose again that the file is to be printed on a device that does not have the German special characters. We can convert the German characters to ASCII without any loss of information by using our special language rules:

```
MS-Kermit>set file character-set cp437
MS-Kermit>set transfer character-set latin1
MS-Kermit>connect
$ kermit
C-Kermit>set file character-set ascii
C-Kermit>set language german
C-Kermit>receive
Alt-X
MS-Kermit>send modem.txt
MS-Kermit>connect
C-Kermit>type modem.txt
Wer ein Selbstwaehl-Modem hat, muss zur Herstellung der Verbindung
mit dem anderen Rechner die Waehlkommandos eintippen. Man kann zur
Kermit-Kommandoebene zurueckgelangen durch Eintippen der
'Rueckkehrsequenz'.
$
```

The umlaut-a's have become ae's, the umlaut-u's are now ue's, and the German double-s is two s's — perfectly acceptable and proper German. Note, however, that these rules can not be applied in the opposite direction. For example, if oe were always translated to ö, then *Kommandoebene* would be improperly written as *Kommandöbene* and *Rueckkehrse-quence* would become *Rückkehrseqünce*.

SET LANGUAGE RUSSIAN (or UKRAINIAN) has a special meaning. If C-Kermit's file character-set is one of the Cyrillic ones (KOI8, Cyrillic-ISO, etc.), but the transfer character-set is ASCII, C-Kermit uses Short KOI in place of ASCII in the Kermit packets. This lets you send, for example, a Latin-Cyrillic file in Short-KOI form, or receive a file in Short-KOI form and store it in a proper 8-bit Cyrillic character set. This is useful when the one of the two computers does not support Cyrillic characters. For example, here we send a short file composed of both Roman and Cyrillic characters from a Russian computer running C-Kermit to a CP/M microcomputer running Kermit-80:

```
C-Kermit>set file character-set koi8      (Translate from this)
C-Kermit>set xfer character-set ascii     (to this)
C-Kermit>set language russian             (using Short KOI)
```

```
C-Kermit>send kepmit.txt              (Send a file)
Ctrl-]C                               (Escape back to micro)
Kermit-80>receive                     (Receive the file)

   (The file is transferred)

Kermit-80>type kepmit.txt             (Take a look at it)
protokol pereda~i fajlow KERMIT.

ppf razrabotan w sootwetstwii so standartom ISO 7498 "|talonnaq
modelx wzaimodejstwiq otzayplh sistemy princip raboty ppf
zakl'~aetsq w obmene paketami KERMIT mevdu kompxywerami. format
paketow KERMIT:

+------+-----+-----+------+-- -- -- ---+-------+
? MARK ? LEN ? SEQ ? TYPE ?    DATA    ? CHECK ?
+------+-----+-----+------+-- -- -- ---+-------+

MARK        - marker paketow KERMIT;
LEN         - dlina paketa;
SEQ         - nomer paketa;
TYPE        - tip paketa;
DATA        - dannye;
CHECK       - kontrolxnaq summa.
Kermit-80>
```

In the Short-KOI result, uppercase words are English and lowercase words are Russian. Question marks indicate untranslatable characters. For example, the original text had vertical bars (|) in the diagram, but since vertical bar is the Short KOI notation for the Cyrillic letter Э (see Table VII-6), they can't also represent themselves.

Transferring 8-Bit Text Files in the 7-Bit Environment

The Japanese-EUC, Latin/Hebrew, and Latin/Cyrillic transfer character sets contain a preponderance of 8-bit characters. Does this mean that you must pay a heavy performance penalty when transferring Japanese, Hebrew, or Russian text across a 7-bit data connection?

As part of its international text transfer capability, the Kermit protocol has been fitted with an efficient locking shift mechanism, explained in Chapter 12, pages 260–262 and in Reference [37]. Rather than prefix each 8-bit byte with an additional character, Kermit shifts into and out of 8-bit character sequences much as you push the Caps Lock key on your keyboard, thus reducing the shifting overhead to per-word or per-sentence rather than per-character.

Locking shifts are used automatically whenever you have told Kermit to SET PARITY to anything but NONE and the other Kermit agrees to use them (see Table 1-1 on page 10).

When the other Kermit program does not implement locking-shift protocol, single shifts are used; thus the file is still transferred correctly, but probably (in the case of Russian, Hebrew, or Japanese) less efficiently.

Translating without Transferring

Since the facilities for translation are already in place for CONNECT sessions and file transfer, C-Kermit includes — at no extra cost — a command to translate a local file from one character set to another:

TRANSLATE *file1 cs1 cs2 [file2]*
  Translate the local file *file1* from the character set *cs1* into the character set *cs2*. Both character sets may be selected from C-Kermit's repertoire of file character sets. The result is stored in *file2* or (if *file2* is not specified) displayed on your screen.
  Synonym: **XLATE**.

As with terminal connection and file transfer, an intermediate standard character set is used in translation. If the target character-set (*cs2*) is Cyrillic (CP866, KOI8, Short KOI, etc.), Latin/Cyrillic is the intermediate set. If Hebrew, Latin/Hebrew is the intermediate set. Japanese EUC is used as the intermediate set if either one of the files is Japanese. If either one of the sets is Latin-2 or CP852, Latin-2 is used. Otherwise, Latin-1 is used.

Here's an example in which a Swedish-language electronic mail message has been received and then saved to disk as diab.msg. It is encoded in Swedish 7-bit ISO 646, but needs to be converted to HP-Roman8 for printing on a Hewlett Packard printer:

```
C-Kermit>xla diab.msg swedish hp-roman8 diab.hp8    (Translate)
C-Kermit>xla diab.hp8 hp-roman8 swedish             (Check it)
From: bl@diab.se (Benny Löfgren)
Subject: C-Kermit 5a(177)
Date: Thu, 30 Jan 92 12:55:58 MET

Är det annonserat någon nyare C-Kermit än 5A(177)? Jag har
kompilerat upp den med TCP/IP-stöd på DS90, och det verkar
fungera bra.  Kan lägga upp binären på klubben.  Följande
entry har jag lagt till i makefilen:
========= cut ========= cut ========= cut ======== cut =========
#DIAB DS90, DNIX 5.3 or later, with HDB UUCP, nap, rdchk, TCP/IP
dnix5r3net:
...
C-Kermit>print diab.lat          (Looks good, print it)
```

In case you are not lucky enough to have a printer with accented letters, you can use the SET LANGUAGE command with the TRANSLATE command the same way it is used in file transfer. Here we convert the Swedish message for printing on an ASCII-only printer:

```
C-Kermit>set language swedish
C-Kermit>xla diab.msg swedish ascii diab.asc    (Translate)
C-Kermit>type diab.lat                          (Check it)
From: bl@diab.se (Benny Loefgren)
Subject: C-Kermit 5a(177)
Date: Thu, 30 Jan 92 12:55:58 MET
```

```
Aer det annonserat naagon nyare C-Kermit aen 5A(177)? Jag har
kompilerat upp den med TCP/IP-stoed paa DS90, och det verkar
fungera bra.  Kan laegga upp binaeren paa klubben.  Foeljande
entry har jag lagt till i makefilen:
========= cut ========= cut ========= cut ======== cut =========
#DIAB DS90, DNIX 5.3 or later, with HDB UUCP, nap, rdchk, TCP/IP
dnix5r3net:
...
C-Kermit>print diab.asc          (Looks OK, print it)
```

See how the special characters were converted according to the rules listed in Table 16-8:
a-ring to aa, and so on.

One-Sided Translation

If the Kermit program on the other end of the connection does not support character-set
translation (most non-Columbia Kermits do not), that doesn't mean you can't use
C-Kermit's translation features with other Kermit programs that don't support this feature.
Whenever you send a file from C-Kermit to a non-internationalized Kermit on a computer
that happens to support one of Kermit's transfer character-sets, have C-Kermit translate
the file in the normal way, for example:

```
C-Kermit>set file char cp437
C-Kermit>set xfer char latin1
C-Kermit>sen oofa.txt
```

The other Kermit does no translating, but it doesn't have to.

If a local file is encoded in any character set that is also supported by the other computer,
you can use the TRANSPARENT transfer character-set to send it from C-Kermit, in which
case your current file character-set setting is ignored.

You can also use C-Kermit's TRANSLATE command to pre- and/or postprocess transferred
files. In this example, C-Kermit running on an Apple Macintosh with A/UX uploads an
Icelandic-language file to a bulletin board system (BBS) that has Kermit protocol built in,
but which does not support character-set translation. The BBS is on a PC that uses Code
Page 850. C-Kermit translates the file from Macintosh Latin to CP850 and then sends it
without further translation:

```
C-Kermit>type kermit.txt
```

```
Af hverju er Kermit svona vinsæll?  Hann er ódýr og góður.  Með
Kermit getur þú tengst tölvum, stórum eða litlum, nær og fjær.
Þú getur skiptst á upplýsingum, á þægilegan og öruggan hátt, við
næstum hvaða tölvu sem er.  Þú getur tengst fréttakerfum,
verslunum, póstkerfum, bönkum, verðbréfabönkum og sent og tekið á
móti skrám.  Þú getur skiptst á gögnum við vini og nágranna, þó
þeir eigi öðruvísi tölvu en þú.  Þú getur unnið heiman frá þér.
Kermit getur tengt þig við "netið."  Notið ímyndunaraflið.  Með
```

```
nútíma alþjóðlegu símakerfi og ört vaxandi tækni í síma
og tölvumálum eru ykkur engin takmörk sett.

C-Kermit>translate kermit.txt macintosh-latin cp850 kermit.850
C-Kermit>set transfer character-set transparent
C-Kermit>send kermit.850
```

When the remote computer supports only ASCII, C-Kermit can send files to it using ASCII as the transfer character-set, perhaps together with C-Kermit's SET LANGUAGE command for language-specific rules. In this example, we upload the same Icelandic text file to another BBS, but this BBS supports neither the Kermit protocol nor any 8-bit character sets, so we use the rules from Table 16-8 to transliterate the Icelandic letters to ASCII:

```
C-Kermit>set file char mac        (Macintosh-Latin)
C-Kermit>set xfer char asc        (ASCII)
C-Kermit>set lang icelandic       (Icelandic rules)
C-Kermit>transmit kermit.txt      (Unguarded upload)
```

```
Af hverju er Kermit svona vinsaell?  Hann er odyr og godur.  Med
Kermit getur thu tengst toelvum, storum eda litlum, naer og fjaer.
Thu getur skiptst a upplysingum, a thaegilegan og oeruggan hatt, vid
naestum hvada toelvu sem er.  Thu getur tengst frettakerfum,
verslunum, postkerfum, boenkum, verdbrefaboenkum og sent og tekid a
moti skram.  Thu getur skiptst a goegnum vid vini og nagranna, tho
their eigi oedruvisi toelvu en thu.  Thu getur unnid heiman fra ther.
Kermit getur tengt thig vid "netid."  Notid imyndunaraflid.  Med
nutima althjodlegu simakerfi og oert vaxandi taekni i sima
og toelvumalum eru ykkur engin takmoerk sett.

C-Kermit>
```

Finally, it is conceivable that a Kermit program attempts to perform character-set translation but does so incorrectly, or at least not according to your preferences. You can prevent two Kermit programs from negotiating automatic translation with each other by issuing the command SET ATTRIBUTES CHARACTER-SET OFF, which forces the transfer character-set to be TRANSPARENT.

Labor-Saving Devices

If you always work in a particular language and character-set environment, you can save yourself some work by putting the appropriate commands in your C-Kermit customization file so they will be in effect whenever you run C-Kermit. Say, for example, you always use the Italian character set on the computer where you run C-Kermit and you often transfer Italian-language text files from there to your MS-DOS PC, where they must be encoded in the PC's character set, CP437. Put the following commands in your Kermit customization file:

```
set file character-set italian
set transfer character-set latin1
```

If you add the corresponding commands to the customization file for Kermit on your PC:

```
set file character-set cp437
set transfer character-set latin1
set terminal character-set italian
```

you will never have to worry about character sets again and you can forget everything you have read in this chapter.

Command Summary

Character-set translation occurs during file transfer only when the transfer mode is text:

```
SET FILE TYPE TEXT
```

Remember that the transfer mode is controlled by the file sender or, in a client/server relationship, by the client. Also recall that two Kermit programs, even if they are *both* in text mode, might switch to binary (or labeled) mode automatically if they are the same type of system. So in case you need to transfer text files with character-set translation between like systems, also remember to:

```
SET TRANSFER MODE MANUAL
```

rather than AUTOMATIC, which is normally the default.

The commands affecting character-set display and transfer are:

Terminal emulation:

```
SET COMMAND BYTESIZE { 7, 8 }
SET TERMINAL BYTESIZE { 7, 8 }
SET PARITY { EVEN, ODD, MARK, NONE, SPACE }
SET TERMINAL CHARACTER-SET remote-cset [ local-cset ]
SET TERMINAL LOCKING-SHIFT { OFF, ON }
```

File transfer:

```
SET FILE CHARACTER-SET name
SET TRANSFER CHARACTER-SET name
SET TRANSFER LOCKING-SHIFT { ON, OFF, FORCED }
SET LANGUAGE name
```

Local translation:

```
TRANSLATE file1 cs1 cs2 [ file2 ]
```

The SET TRANSFER LOCKING-SHIFT command is important for efficient transfer of Japanese, Cyrillic, and Hebrew text files in the 7-bit communications environment; it is discussed in Chapter 12.

## Chapter 17

Command Files, Macros, and Variables

○ ○ ○ ○

If you have digested the material in the preceding chapters and applied the examples to your own connections, you should be comfortable using C-Kermit to accomplish your communication chores by hand. But manually operating communications software does not make the best use of your time. In these three chapters, you'll see how to automate all the procedures you have learned so far. By the end of Chapter 19 you will be able to create and use commands that make the connection for you, log you in, carry on scripted dialogs with remote hosts or services, and transfer data automatically, even when you are elsewhere.

This chapter shows you how to group commands together into command files and macros so you can execute many commands by issuing a single command. It also introduces the concept of *variables* and describes the kinds of variables offered by C-Kermit and what you can do with them.

Chapter 18 shows you how to program C-Kermit to make decisions, execute commands repeatedly in loops, read and write files, and so on, using C-Kermit commands similar to the ones you're already accustomed to. Finally, in Chapter 19 these somewhat abstract concepts are put to practical use, automating the making and using of connections and transfer of data. The remainder of the book is devoted to reference material.

Command Files Revisited

You first encountered command files back in Chapter 2. There you learned that you could put any Kermit commands at all in a file and then execute all of them, one after another, no matter how many, by giving a single command, TAKE *filename*, at the C-Kermit prompt. For purposes that will become clearer in Chapter 19, we will start using the terms "command file" and "script file" interchangeably. A *script* is a series of commands that has been recorded in some form.

A *script file* is a script recorded in a file. Kermit script files can have any name at all, but since it has become increasingly important in recent years for each application to have its own special "filetype" or "extension" (the part of the filename after the period) for files that it uses, we are recommending that you use "ksc" (Kermit Script) for Kermit script (command) files, and hopefully no other application will lay claim to this same filetype.

In this example we compose a very short script file on a VMS system, where the CREATE command is the easiest way to make a short text file. Of course you could also use any text editor or word processor that is capable of creating a plain-text file.

```
$ create escape.ksc          (Create a Kermit Script File)
set escape 29                (Enter text from the keyboard)
show escape
^Z                           (Ctrl-Z closes the file)
$                            (System prompt reappears)
```

Now we execute the command file by telling C-Kermit to TAKE it:

```
$ kermit                      (Start C-Kermit)
C-Kermit 6.0.192, 6 Sep 96, OpenVMS VAX
Type ? or HELP for help
C-Kermit>take escape.ksc
  Escape character: Ctrl-] (ASCII 29, GS)
C-Kermit>
```

If the command file is not in your current directory, you have to supply its complete file specification:

```
C-Kermit>take $disk1:[olga]escape.ksc   (VMS)
C-Kermit>take /usr/olga/escape.ksc      (UNIX or OS-9)
C-Kermit>take d:\olga\escape.ksc        (OS/2 or Windows)
C-Kermit>take d:/olga/escape.ksc        (Amiga)
C-Kermit>take :udd:olga:escape.ksc      (AOS/VS)
C-Kermit>take hd80:olga:escape.ksc      (Macintosh)
```

You can also have C-Kermit execute the command file by supplying its name as C-Kermit's first command-line argument:

```
$ kermit escape.ksc
```

A command (script) file can include as many C-Kermit commands as you like, including TAKE commands for other command files. The TAKE command normally executes all the commands in the file, from the beginning to the end, or up to the first command that tells it to stop, such as EXIT or QUIT. If a command has a syntax or execution error, C-Kermit prints an error message and goes on to the next command in the file. For example, if you executed a command file called TOAST.KSC that looked like this:

```
echo Making toast...          ; Valid command
set toaster dark              ; No such SET command
toast two slices              ; There is no TOAST command
mail toast                    ; Valid command but no "toast" file
echo The toast is in the mail. ; Valid command
```

The result would be:

```
C-Kermit>take toast.ksc
Making toast...
?No keywords match - toaster
Command file: toast.ksc, line 2
?Invalid: toast two slices
Command file: toast.ksc, line 3
?No files match - toast
Command file: toast.ksc, line 4
The toast is in the mail.
C-Kermit>
```

But you might not want C-Kermit to be so tolerant of failing commands, especially not if later commands depend on earlier ones succeeding. To illustrate, suppose you wanted to send a file to another computer and then delete the original after it is transferred[42]:

```
send oofa.txt
delete oofa.txt
```

In this case you would *not* want the file to be deleted if it was *not* transferred successfully.

An all-or-nothing approach to error handling is offerred by SET TAKE ERROR command:

SET TAKE ERROR { ON, OFF }

OFF, the normal and default setting, means that errors in command files do not cause termination of the command file. ON means that any command in the file that has a syntax or execution error terminates execution of the command file.

Execution errors occur when a command is syntactically (grammatically) correct but C-Kermit can't carry it out successfully; for example, if you tell C-Kermit to TAKE, TYPE, or SEND a file to which you don't have read access.

---

[42]And you didn't know about the MOVE command, which does exactly this.

When writing and debugging long script files, it can be helpful to watch them execute:

SET TAKE ECHO { ON, OFF }

> OFF means that lines from the script file are not displayed on your screen. This is the normal and default setting. ON means that each command is displayed on your screen at the time C-Kermit reads it from the file, together with its line number in the file, just prior to executing it.

Of course, you can put SET TAKE commands in the script files themselves to turn echoing on and off around interesting sections or to change the error handing.

Command File Example

To illustrate the usefulness of the TAKE command, suppose that on a certain day you need to upload and download an odd mixture of text and binary files totaling many millions of bytes in size. How much time are you willing to devote to this task? If you do it interactively, you'll have to sit and watch your screen constantly and enter new commands at the right times. It could take all day.

With a command file, each command is executed when the previous one completes, no sooner, no later; no time is wasted, and while all this is happening you can be off somewhere else doing something that *may* be more fun than watching Kermit's file transfer display. Here's a sample command file for the job; let's call it BIGJOB.KSC.

```
; BIGJOB.KSC - Kermit Script to send and get lots of files
set take error on                    ; Quit if there's an error
log transactions                     ; Keep a record of what happened

set file type text                   ; Transferring text files
send daily.*                         ; Upload daily reports
send weekly.*                        ; Upload weekly reports
send monthly.*                       ; Upload monthly reports
get orders.new                       ; Download new orders

set file type binary                 ; Switch to binary mode
send budget.wks                      ; Upload budget worksheet
send salary.wks                      ; Send salary worksheet

set file type text                   ; Back to text mode
mail ok.txt boss                     ; Send e-mail when done
bye                                  ; Logout remote job
```

After you've composed this file with a text editor and saved it on disk, you can start Kermit, make your connection to the remote computer, log in, start Kermit there, put it in server mode, escape back to C-Kermit, and TAKE the command file:

```
$ kermit                              (Start kermit)
Ready to dial...                      (Message from init file)
C-Kermit>dial 765-4321                (Dial the number)
C-Kermit>c                            (CONNECT to remote computer)
. login olga                          (Enter username)
Password: _____                 (Enter password)

. kermit                              (Start Kermit on remote computer)
Kermit-CMS>server                     (Put it in server mode)
Ctrl-\C                               (Escape back to C-Kermit)
C-Kermit>take bigjob.ksc              (TAKE the command file)
```

Later, when you come back from wherever you went, you can examine the transaction log to see what happened. Your electronic mail message (composed previously and stored in the file OK.TXT) is sent to the boss only if all the files were transferred successfully. The SET TAKE ERROR ON command ensures that any errors terminate the command file before the message is sent so you won't look like a fool.

Later, you will see how to automate the entire process, including making the connection and logging in, as well as a finer-grained method of error handling.

Nested Command Files

When a command file itself contains TAKE commands, the command files are said to be *nested,* one within the other. Any C-Kermit command is legal in a command file, including TAKE. In fact, one command file can TAKE another, which TAKEs yet another, which TAKEs still another, and so on, to any reasonable nesting depth. This feature lets you create building-block command files that can be pieced together in different ways, possibly saving you much duplication of effort over the years.

But there can be more down-to-earth, if less obvious, reasons for nesting command files. Suppose, for example, BIGJOB.KSC encountered an error. The command file would terminate immediately, the C-Kermit prompt would return, but the connection to the remote computer would not necessarily be broken. If your absence from the office was longer than expected, you might have run up a large phone bill for nothing. But if you invoke BIGJOB.KSC from a superior TAKE file, it would regain control as soon as BIGJOB.KSC completed — successfully or not. Such a "wrapper" file might look like this:

```
take bigjob.ksc                  ; TAKE the command file
hangup                           ; Hang up the phone when done
```

Call this two-line superior command file BIGGERJOB.KSC and start it like this:

```
C-Kermit>take biggerjob.ksc
```

Then, no matter how BIGJOB.KSC might terminate, C-Kermit hangs up the telephone without delay.

Macros

"Macro" usually means "big," but in computer jargon it means something small that stands for something bigger. Kermit macros are new commands that you create by combining existing commands (or even other macros). Like command files, macros give you a way to group commands together so you can execute a bunch of them with a single word. The command for making macros is:

DEFINE *name [text]*

This command creates a macro with the given *name*. The macro's definition is the *text*, if any, following its name. This is normally a list of C-Kermit commands (possibly including names of other macros), separated by commas, but it can be any text at all. Example:

```
define noconversion set file type binary, set file names literal
```

No interpretation, evaluation, or verification of the text is done; the definition is taken literally. If a macro of the given name already exists, its definition is replaced by the one given. If no text follows the macro name, the named macro (if it exists) is removed from C-Kermit's "macro dictionary" and becomes undefined.

UNDEFINE *name*

Removes the definition, if any, for the macro whose *name* is given. This just like DEFINE *name* when no *text* is given.

You can type these commands at the C-Kermit prompt, put them in command files, and even put them inside other macro definitions. Again, there is nothing magic about where commands are executed from.

If you have taken the trouble to construct a macro that you want to use frequently, the best place to put its definition is in your C-Kermit customization file so it will be defined for you automatically whenever you start C-Kermit in the normal way.

The macro name can be any reasonable character string that contains no spaces or control characters, up to about 64 characters in length. Uppercase and lowercase letters are treated equivalently. Remember that DEFINE is a command like any other and so has the same restriction on its length. The maximum length for a C-Kermit command is usually about 4000 characters, but can vary with the particular implementation (use SHOW COMMAND to see the limit in your version).

Here is an example you can try if you have C-Kermit running next to your bed:

```
define alarm echo Good night!, sleep 6:55:00, beep, echo Wake up!
```

The macro's name is:

```
alarm
```

The definition is:

```
echo Good night!, sleep 6:55:00, beep, echo Wake up!
```

The DEFINE command puts the ALARM macro in C-Kermit's macro dictionary, turning it into a new C-Kermit command:

```
C-Kermit>alarm
Good night.
```

And then at 6:55 the next morning:

```
<BEEP>Wake up!
C-Kermit>
```

The following command destroys the definition of the ALARM macro so you can't use it any more:

```
C-Kermit>undef alarm
```

(This is like throwing your alarm clock out the window.)

A common and straightforward use for macros is to group SET commands together to allow rapid switching among different kinds of connections, for example:

```
define vms set parity none, set duplex full,-
  set flow xon/xoff, set handshake none
def ibm-linemode set parity mark, set dupl half,-
  set handsh xon, set flow none
```

Here two macros are created, the first named VMS and the second IBM-LINEMODE.

Pay careful attention to punctuation: use commas to separate commands, and hyphen (dash) to continue a line. Remember, DEFINE, just like any other Kermit command, is *one line*, and, like other commands, it can be continued onto new lines by using hyphens as shown. The final line of the definition, of course, must *not* end with a hyphen. If you accidentally omit a hyphen, the next line is taken as a new command, rather than part of the macro definition.

If your macro definition is in a command file (including your customization file), you can add trailing comments to each line:

```
define vms -                    ; Macro for connecting to VMS
  set parity none,-             ; No parity
  set command byte 8,-          ; 8-bit data,
  set terminal byte 8,-         ; from end to end
  set terminal echo remote,-    ; The VAX echoes
  set flow xon/xoff,-           ; Use Xon/Xoff flow control
  set handshake none            ; No line turnaround handshake
```

When a line is continued, trailing comments must come *after* the continuation character, not before it, and must be preceded by at least one space or tab. If you put a hyphen at the end of a trailing comment, the next line becomes a continuation of the same comment.

You can find out the definition of a macro with the SHOW MACRO command:

```
C-Kermit>show macro ibm-linemode
ibm-linemode = set parity mark,-
  set dupl half,-
  set handsh xon,-
  set flow none
```

The definition is shown one command per line, with commas separating the commands, and hyphens showing line continuation.

If you type SHOW MACRO without giving the name of a macro, C-Kermit shows you all the currently defined macros and their definitions. Even if you haven't defined any macros, you will still see definitions for some of C-Kermit *predefined* macros, such as FAST, CAUTIOUS, and ROBUST.

Structured Notation for Macro Definitions

Macro definitions can be quite long, and when they are continued onto many lines, all the commas and hyphens can become quite confusing, unsightly, and a likely source of typographical errors that produce strange effects when the macro is executed.

A more natural and familiar notation can also be used for defining macros, resembling the block structure used in the C programming language. The rules are simple:

1. If a line (not counting any trailing comment) *ends* with an *opening* curly brace ("{"), this *begins* a "block".

2. If a line *begins* with a *closing* curly brace ("}"), this *ends* a block.

Lines are significant within a block. The end of each line (after stripping any trailing comment), is taken to be the end of a command (unless it ends with a hyphen); Kermit combines the lines and supplies commas between the commands. Example:

```
define COUNT {      ; optional comment
    echo one        ; optional comment
    echo two        ; optional comment
    echo three      ; optional comment
}                   ; optional comment
```

becomes:

```
define COUNT { echo one, echo two, echo three }
```

which is entirely equivalent to:

```
define COUNT echo one, echo two, echo three
```

The two notational styles can be mixed and matched in any desired manner, even within a macro definition, but the block-structured style is recommended for its increased readability and flexibility.

A block can contain blank lines and full-line comments, which can't included in macro definitions when using "comma-hyphen" notation:

```
define COUNT {
; This is a macro that prints "one", "two", and "three".
    echo one          ; This line prints "one"
    echo two          ; And so on ...
    echo three
}
```

Block structured notation can be used with any command, if you can think of a reason to do it. Just remember that it inserts a comma after each line line within the braces, e.g.:

```
echo {
    one
    two
    three
}
```

prints "one, two, three".

We will stick with block-structured notation in this text for clarity, but you can use the "comma-hyphen" style too.

Using Macros

Now that you know how to create macros, you might also want to know how to use them. There are two ways to use (invoke) a macro. The first and most natural way is simply to type its name at the C-Kermit prompt, either in full:

```
C-Kermit>ibm-linemode
```

or abbreviated unambiguously:

```
C-Kermit>ib
```

This way works as long as your macro does not have the same name as, and is not an abbreviation of, a built-in C-Kermit command.

The second way is with the DO command:

DO *macro-name*

Invokes the macro whose name is given. The macro name may be abbreviated to any length that still distinguishes it from the names of all other defined macros. Examples:

```
C-Kermit>do ibm-linemode
C-Kermit>do ibm
```

The DO command removes any possible confusion between macros and built-in commands because it looks only in the macro dictionary. If you type a question mark at the

C-Kermit prompt, the macro names are not listed. But if you type DO followed by a space and a question mark, the names of all the defined macros are listed:

```
C-Kermit>do ? macro, one of the following:
 ibm-linemode      vax
C-Kermit>
```

If you have defined a macro with the same name as a built-in command, the DO command is the only way to invoke it because C-Kermit gives priority to its built-in commands. If you always pick original names for your macros, there is no ambiguity and the DO command need not be used.

Macro execution can be controlled in the same ways as command file execution:

SET MACRO ECHO { OFF, ON }

> Controls whether commands from the macro definition are echoed on your screen as C-Kermit reads them. MACRO ECHO is normally OFF, meaning that the commands are not shown. You can use SET MACRO ECHO ON for debugging.

SET MACRO ERROR { OFF, ON }

> Controls whether an error — syntax or execution — in a command causes C-Kermit to terminate execution of the macro. Normally MACRO ERROR is OFF, meaning that even when a command fails, execution proceeds to the next command, if any, in the macro definition.

Execution of a macro can be interrupted at any time by typing Ctrl-C.

Macros That Invoke Macros

Like command files, macros can be nested to any reasonable level. Just as command files can TAKE other command files, macros can invoke other macros. For example:

```
define modem set modem type microlink, set speed 57600
define computer set parity even, set term char italian
define communication modem, computer
define protocol set window 4, set rec packet-len 2000, set block 3
define setup communication, protocol
```

After you have executed these definitions, invoking the SETUP macro will invoke the COMMUNICATION and PROTOCOL macros. The COMMUNICATION macro will, in turn, invoke the MODEM and COMPUTER macros.

Macros That Define Macros

Before proceeding, let's stop and ask ourselves the vital question: How can we define a macro that defines other macros? Suppose you use C-Kermit to access two different remote computers, one of them running the VMS operating system and the other running UNIX. Suppose also that on each computer you switch back and forth between Italian and Russian text.

But the two computers use different character sets for each of these languages. You want to have one set of macros called VMS and UNIX for switching between the two computer systems, and another set called ITALIAN and RUSSIAN for switching between the two languages appropriately for each machine.

To illustrate how to construct macros that define macros, let's make the VMS and UNIX macros each define their own appropriate ITALIAN and RUSSIAN macros.

But first we must solve a small syntax problem. In the command:

```
def unix def italian set xfer char latin1, set file char italian
```

which macro, UNIX or ITALIAN, does the SET FILE CHAR ITALIAN command belong to? (As written, it belongs to the UNIX macro; not what we intended.) We need a way of grouping commands inside a macro definition so Kermit can tell which definition each command belongs to. For this, we use curly braces around the definition to indicate grouping.

So using braces for both block structure and for grouping (and ignoring the question of how fonts are switched), we define the VMS macro as follows:

```
define VMS {
    set parity none              ; No parity
    set terminal bytesize 8      ; 8-bit characters
    set terminal type vt320      ; VT320 terminal emulation

    define ITALIAN {
        set terminal character-set dec-mcs
        set file character-set cp850
        set transfer character-set latin1
    }
    define RUSSIAN {
        set terminal character-set koi8 cp866
        set file character-set cp866
        set transfer character-set cyrillic
    }
}
```

Note the use of indentation, spacing, blank lines, comments, and capitalization to increase the readability of the macro definition. None of these elements are required, nor do they make any difference in the execution of the macro; they just make it more readable.

When you execute the VMS macro, it sets the parity and terminal parameters immediately and then defines ITALIAN and RUSSIAN macros for later use. The internal curly braces tell Kermit which commands are part of the VMS macro definition and which ones are part of the ITALIAN and RUSSIAN macro definitions.

The corresponding UNIX macro is written for a 7-bit communications environment, in which Italian is encoded in the 7-bit Italian version of ISO 646 and Russian is encoded in Short KOI:

```
define UNIX {
    set parity even
    set terminal bytesize 7
    set terminal type vt100

    define ITALIAN {
        set terminal character-set italian
        set file character-set cp850
        set transfer character-set latin1
    }
    define RUSSIAN {
        set terminal character-set short-koi cp866
        set file character-set cp866
        set transfer character-set cyrillic
    }
}
```

To use these macros, add their definitions to your C-Kermit customization file. Then, whenever you have started C-Kermit, you can type "VMS" or "UNIX", to specify which type of system you are accessing. And then you can type "ITALIAN" or "RUSSIAN" to set up or switch between the appropriate character sets for Italian or Russian, the same way on each system.

The On_Exit Macro

Just as C-Kermit has an initialization file for commands to be executed automatically every time the program starts, it also has a way to execute commands of your choice automatically when it exits.

If you have defined a macro called ON_EXIT, Kermit executes it when you give the EXIT or QUIT command, just before its final acts of cleaning up and self destruction. The ON_EXIT macro should be defined in your C-Kermit customization file. Here's a sample that can be used by someone who always uses C-Kermit to dial out with an external modem:

```
define on_exit hangup, echo Remember to turn off your modem!
```

To illustrate its use:

```
$ kermit                            (Start Kermit)

   (Transfer some files, etc...)

C-Kermit>exit                       (EXIT hangs up the phone)
Remember to turn off your modem!    (and prints a reminder)
$
```

Macros versus Command Files

Command files and macros can be mixed in every conceivable way. Macros can be (and typically are) DEFINEd in command files, macros can be invoked from command files, command files can be TAKEn from inside a macro, a macro can DEFINE another macro, and so on. What are the differences between command files and macros?

- A command file can be any length at all, whereas a macro definition is restricted to the length of C-Kermit's command buffer, as shown by SHOW COMMAND.

- Macros, once defined, are available at all times while C-Kermit is running and can be invoked simply by name, regardless of C-Kermit's current directory.

- Macro execution can be faster, because C-Kermit executes macros out of its own memory rather than by opening and reading a disk file.

- You can define all your macros in a single command file, which can be preferable to cluttering up your disk with lots of command files.

- Most important, macros can have *arguments*.

Macro Arguments

You can furnish a macro with additional information in the form of operands, or *arguments*, by including them after the macro name when you invoke it and separating each argument by whitespace (one or more spaces or tabs).

You can think of a macro as a verb to which you can give different objects, like "eat spaghetti," "eat corn," "eat salad." Eating is a routine operation, but it can be performed on a variety of foods.

Programmers can think of macros as "routines" in the programming sense: subroutines or functions that do a routine task on whatever data is fed to them.

Here is a simple example:

```
C-Kermit>define eat echo Thank you for the \%1. It tastes good.
C-Kermit>eat bread
Thank you for the bread. It tastes good.
C-Kermit>eat calzone
Thank you for the calzone. It tastes good.
C-Kermit>
```

The arguments are real data — words, numbers, filenames, and so on — that are plugged into special placeholders in the macro definition (\%1 in the previous example) before the commands in the macro are executed.

Here is a more complete, formal, and precise description of macro invocation:

[DO] macro-name [arg1 [arg2 [... [arg9]]]]

Sets the variable \%0 to the name of the macro. Copies the text of the arguments into the variables \%1, \%2, ..., \%9. Sets the variable \v(argc) (explained later in this chapter) to the number of arguments plus 1 and then executes the commands in the definition, substituting any occurrences of these variable names in the macro definition with the values just assigned.

Let's try that again in English. When you invoke a macro, you can also put some other stuff — up to nine "words" — after the macro's name. Each word is assigned to a *variable* that has a funny-looking name: backslash-percent-digit; for example, \%2. The digit tells the position of the word in the command you just typed: 0 for the name of the macro itself, 1 for the first word after its name (the first argument), 2 for the second word, and so on. If there are more than 9 arguments, the extra ones are ignored. If there are fewer than 9, the extra variables are given a null (empty) value. Argument variable names (\%0, \%1, etc.) that occur anywhere in your macro definition are replaced by the corresponding arguments when the commands in the macro are executed.

Maybe another example will help. Here is a macro definition that adds a command, TDIR (time-order directory) to the UNIX version of C-Kermit to display a directory listing in reverse chronological order (ls -lt), pausing at the end of each screenful (| more), by running the the corresponding UNIX commands:

```
C-Kermit>define tdir run ls -lt \%1 \%2 \%3 \%4 \%5 | more
```

Execute this macro by typing its name, followed by zero, one, two, up to five, filenames or wildcards:

```
C-Kermit>tdir                            (All files)
C-Kermit>tdir *.txt                      (All .txt files)
C-Kermit>tdir file1 file2 file3          (Three specific files)
C-Kermit>tdir oofa.txt /tmp/oofa.txt     (files in different places)
```

When the macro is executed, \%1 is replaced by the first file specification (if any), \%2 is replaced by the second one (if any), and so on. So the commands that Kermit actually executes are, respectively:

```
run ls -lt | more
run ls -lt *.txt | more
run ls -lt file1 file2 file3 | more
run ls -lt oofa.txt /tmp/oofa.txt | more
```

Kermit's argument-passing scheme should be crystal clear to you now — so clear that you put this book down between the last paragraph and this one, ran to your keyboard, added even more new commands, and then translated all of Kermit's built-in commands into Hungarian simply by defining macros for them. If you didn't do all that, go do it now.

Format of Macro Arguments

A macro argument is a string of printing characters surrounded by whitespace (spaces or tabs). The final macro argument can be either the final string of printing (non-whitespace) characters on the command line, or it can be followed by a trailing comment, which is ignored. To illustrate, we define a macro, ARGLIST, that prints its first four arguments, and then we invoke it in various ways:

```
C-Kermit>def arglist echo 1=(\%1) 2=(\%2) 3=(\%3) 4=(\%4)
C-Kermit>arglist amethyst blue red yellow green
1=(amethyst) 2=(blue) 3=(red) 4=(yellow)
C-Kermit>arglist one two
1=(one) 2=(two) 3=() 4=()
C-Kermit>arglist one two ; with a comment
1=(one) 2=(two) 3=() 4=()
C-Kermit>
```

If you want an argument to include (or be) spaces, enclose it in curly braces:

```
C-Kermit>arglist {this one has four words} { abc } { }
1=(this one has four words) 2=( abc ) 3=( ) 4=()
```

As you can see, the braces are removed. If you want the braces kept, use two pair:

```
C-Kermit>arglist {{abc xyz}} {{}}
1=({abc xyz}) 2=({}) 3=() 4=()
```

You can force an argument to be empty by using an empty pair of braces:

```
C-Kermit>arglist first second {} fourth
1=(first) 2=(second) 3=() 4=(fourth)
```

The command SHOW ARGUMENTS, given inside a macro, displays the macro's arguments:

```
C-Kermit>define shoargs show arguments
C-Kermit>shoargs one two {three and} four
Macro arguments at level 0
 \%0 = shoargs
 \%1 = one
 \%2 = two
 \%3 = three and
 \%4 = four
C-Kermit>
```

Scope of Macro Arguments

The argument variables \%0 through \%9 are created when the macro is invoked and are available to the macro throughout its execution. Arguments that are not specified are set to null (empty) values, as shown in the previous examples.

If macro A invokes macro B, macro B gets a whole new set of arguments \%0 through \%9, and it does not have access to macro A's arguments at all. When macro B terminates, macro A still has its own original copies of these variables. (In programming lingo, macro arguments are on the "macro call stack," but not inherited.) This process is replicated as deeply as macro invocations can be nested. To illustrate:

```
C-Kermit>def top show arg, middle Testing, show arg
C-Kermit>def middle show arg, bottom XXX, show arg
C-Kermit>def bottom show arg
C-Kermit>top Hello                 (Invoke TOP macro with arg "Hello")
Macro arguments at level 0         (Now we're in the TOP macro)
 \%0 = top                         (TOP macro shows its arguments)
 \%1 = Hello                       (This is what I typed)
Macro arguments at level 1         (TOP macro invokes MIDDLE macro)
 \%0 = middle                      (MIDDLE macro shows its name)
 \%1 = Testing                     (and its argument)
Macro arguments at level 2         (MIDDLE invokes BOTTOM)
 \%0 = bottom                      (BOTTOM macro shows its name)
 \%1 = XXX                         (and its argument)
Macro arguments at level 1         (Now back to MIDDLE macro)
 \%0 = middle                      (Its name is still the same)
 \%1 = Testing                     (and so is its argument)
Macro arguments at level 0         (Now back to TOP macro)
 \%0 = top                         (Its name is still the same)
 \%1 = Hello                       (and its argument is too)
C-Kermit>
```

If a macro definition happens to include a TAKE command, the macro's arguments are available to the command file, too (the macro call stack is unchanged). To illustrate, suppose the file HAYES.KSC contains:

```
set modem type hayes        ; Specify modem type
set line /dev/cua           ; Specify communication device
set speed 2400              ; Set the speed
dial \%1
```

Also suppose you define the following macro and then invoke it:

```
C-Kermit>define hayes take hayes.ksc
C-Kermit>hayes 7654321
```

C-Kermit executes the commands in the HAYES macro, replacing all the backslash-percent variables by the macro's actual arguments. Because the HAYES macro is still active while the command file is being executed, the \%1 variable is available in the command file, too, and so the command:

```
dial \%1
```

in HAYES.KSC becomes:

```
dial 7654321
```

before C-Kermit executes it.

So in case you wanted to create your own dialing method rather than using C-Kermit's built-in one, you could do it by writing a script such as this one, but replacing the DIAL command with a series of explicit interactions with the modem, using techniques presented in this and the following chapters.

A Macro Sampler

To bring the concepts of macros and arguments down to earth, here is a brief sampling of connection and file-transfer macros that real C-Kermit users actually use in everyday life.

Dialing Macros

Suppose you have a PC on your desk at work with communication port 1 (COM1) connected to your company's voice/data PBX, a Rolm Computerized Branch Exchange, and with COM2 connected to a US Robotics modem on a regular telephone line. It assumes you have left FLOW-CONTROL at its default setting, AUTO. Here is how you can define macros to let you make connections with one or the other:

```
; ROLM - All the steps needed for a Rolm data call in one command
define ROLM {
    set macro error on          ; Quit on failure
    set modem type rolm         ; Modem type
    set port com1               ; Device name
    set speed 19200             ; Speed
    set dial display on         ; Watch call progess reports
    dial =\%1                   ; Dial the "number" literally
    connect                     ; Only if the call is completed
}
```

The Rolm data communications module (DCM) uses "data group" names rather than phone numbers. Notice the equals sign (=) to force Kermit to treat the name literally.

Use this macro by typing its name followed by a data group name. Note that since MACRO ERROR is ON, the macro quits executing immediately any time there is an error so, for example, we don't go into CONNECT mode if the call is not completed:

```
C-Kermit>rolm accounting       ; A data group name
C-Kermit>rolm shipping         ; Another data group name
```

Add the DEFINE command to your C-Kermit customization file, and the ROLM macro will be available to you whenever you start C-Kermit.

Now let's make a similar macro for the US Robotics modem. It assumes country code, area code, dialing prefixes, etc, are already defined appropriately in your C-Kermit customization file:

```
; USR - All the steps needed for a USR modem call in one command
define USR {
    set macro error on          ; Quit on failure
    set modem type usr          ; Modem type
    set port com2               ; Device name
    set speed 57600             ; Speed
    set dial display on         ; Watch what happens
    dial \%1\%2\%3\%4\%5\%6     ; Dial the number
    connect                     ; Only if the call is completed
}
```

In this example, we do not include the equal sign because we want C-Kermit to use its dialing directory and handle area and country codes. And we list six macro arguments in the DIAL command to allow you to type telephone numbers with spaces in them:

```
C-Kermit>usr 18005551212          ; A telephone number
C-Kermit>usr +1 (800) 555 1212    ; This works too
C-Kermit>usr compuserve           ; A dialing directory entry
```

Here are sample macros that use ROLM and USR to place calls to specific departments or services:

```
define accounting rolm accounting           ; Rolm data group name
define shipping   rolm shipping             ; Rolm data group name
define compuserve usr  compuserve           ; Dialing directory name
define attmail    usr  attmail              ; Dialing directory name
define mcimail    usr  +1 (800) 456 6245    ; Actual phone number
```

You can use these macros to call a host or service by typing just the macro name at the C-Kermit prompt. You can even abbreviate the name:

```
C-Kermit>ship
C-Kermit>mci
```

Adapt these macros to your own setup and the hosts or services you use and put their definitions in your C-Kermit customization file. Then let *Kermit's* fingers do the walking!

Pager Macros

Refer to the discussion about how to dial numeric pagers on page 72. Now that you have a macro to dial your modem, you can build on that to send a numeric page:

```
define NPAGE {
    usr \%1@\%2#;
    clear dial-status
}
```

That's it. Remember, for most Hayes compatible modems @ means "wait for quiet answer" and the semicolon makes the modem return to command mode immediately after dialing, which makes Kermit sense that a "partial call" is in progress. The # terminates the message. CLEAR DIAL-STATUS clears the partial call status so subsequent DIAL commands will work normally.

The format for invocation is a bit more restrictive than for regular calls, since the macro must be able to distinguish the phone number from the message. So the first argument is the phone number and the second argument is the message. Recall that you can't include spaces within a macro argument (unless you surround it with braces). Examples:

```
C-Kermit>npage 5554321 7654321
C-Kermit>npage {555 4321} 7654321
```

Both examples call the phone number 5554321 and leave the numeric message 7654321. Alphanumeric pagers are covered in Chapter 19.

Network Macros

If you're a network user, you can add similar macros to your C-Kermit customization file for the network connections you commonly make. Here are macros to make the appropriate settings for TCP/IP and X.25 networks. The communications and file transfer parameters are samples only, and not necessarily optimal for all connections:

```
define TCP {
    set macro error on
    set flow none
    set parity none ; (or space)
    set receive packet-length 2000
    set window 4
    telnet \%1 \%2   ; \%2 is an optional service name or number
}
define X25 {
    set macro error on
    set net x.25
    set flow xon/xoff
    set parity mark ; (or space, even, or none)
    set receive packet-length 250
    set window 8
    set host \%1
    connect
}
```

And here are macros to make frequently used connections just by typing their names:

```
define chemsun tcp sun.chem.myu.edu ; Chemistry Department Sun
define catalog tcp locis.loc.gov    ; US Library of Congress
define weather tcp madlab.sprl.umich.edu 3000 ; Today's weather
define mcimail x25 1234567890        ; (Fictitious X.25 address)
```

Network Dialing Macros

Suppose your computer is on a local TCP/IP network with a "reverse terminal server," allowing users of the local net to Telnet to a special port (say, 2000) on the terminal server to reach, say, a Telebit modem that can be used for dialing out. This is another excellent use for a macro, since a number of commands must be issued in a specific order, which who can remember? In this example, let's say the IP hostname of the terminal server is `dialout.xyzcorp.com`:

```
define NETDIAL {
    set macro error on
    set network tcp/ip
    set host dialout.xyzcorp.com 2000
    set modem type telebit
    dial \%1\%2\%3\%4\%5\%6
    connect
}
```

Again, note that the macro quits immediately if any command fails. Thus we don't DIAL if we can't make a TCP connection to the desired port on the terminal server, and we don't CONNECT if the call was not completed.

File Transfer Macros

Here are two simple macros for selecting and initiating text or binary mode file transfer:

```
define bsend set file type binary, send \%1 \%2
define tsend set file type text, send \%1 \%2
```

The first argument, \%1, is the name a file to send; the second (optional), \%2, is a different name under which to send the file. (These macros work only with single files; for more general versions, see the standard C-Kermit initialization file.)

And here are macros for quickly switching among three different levels of file-transfer performance:

```
define robust set window 1, set receive packet 90, set prefixing all
define cautious set win 4, set rec pack 1000, set prefixing cautious
define fast set win 20, set rec pack 4000, set prefixing minimal
```

These macros are so useful that they are predefined in C-Kermit, which means they are *always* available, even if you don't execute DEFINE commands for them. Of course you can still undefine them or redefine them.

Where to Put Macro Definitions

Aside from C-Kermit's several predefined macros, a macro is *not* defined, and therefore is not available for use, until C-Kermit executes a DEFINE command for it. As you can see from some of the preceding examples, a macro can be rather long and complicated, so you certainly don't want to *type* its definition at the prompt every time you run C-Kermit. So instead, you should put the macro definition in a file. Which file?

We recommend that end users not modify the standard C-Kermit initialization file. Many of C-Kermit's services depend on macros that are defined there. So that leaves:

1. Your C-Kermit customization file. This is the best place to put definitions for macros that you *always* want to have available. Putting macro definitions here is like adding new, personalized commands to C-Kermit.

2. Some other file. If you record macro definitions in some other file, you have to tell C-Kermit to TAKE the file (or, equivalently, give the file's name as C-Kermit's first command-line argument) before you can use the macros defined in it. This is the natural approach for seldom-used, special-purpose, or one-shot macros.

If you try to execute a macro that isn't defined, C-Kermit complains "?No keywords match". You can get a list of all the defined macro names with "DO ?". You can find out how many macros are defined, and what the maximum number of macros is, with the SHOW COMMAND command. You can see the definition of a particular macro with SHOW MACRO *name-of-macro*.

Variables

Variables are things that stand for other things. At different times, the same variable might take on different values. Its value can *vary*, which is why it's called a variable, but its name always stays the same. Macro arguments are one type of C-Kermit variable, accessible only within their own macro. This section describes several other kinds of variables, which, unlike macro arguments, can be *global* — meaning they are accessible to all commands at all levels — or *local*, meaning they are accessible at the level at which they are defined, and below.

Letter Variables

Letter variables are like macro arguments, but spelled with (unaccented Roman) letters instead of digits: \%a, \%b, \%c, ..., \%z. The case of the letter doesn't matter; \%a is the same variable as \%A, so there are 26 letter variables available for your use. All of these variables have the null (empty) value until given a definition:

```
C-Kermit>define \%n Fred C. Dobbs
C-Kermit>defin \%d 1(212)555-1212
C-Kermit>def \%f oofa.txt
```

You can find out which letter variables are defined and what their values are with the SHOW GLOBALS command:

```
C-Kermit>show glob
Global variables:
 \%f = oofa.txt
 \%d = 1(212)555-1212
 \%n = Fred C. Dobbs
C-Kermit>
```

You can use a letter variable almost anywhere in any Kermit command. Simply place it where you want its value inserted:

```
C-Kermit>echo \%n calling \%d to transfer \%f...
Fred C. Dobbs calling 1(212)555-1212 to transfer oofa.txt...
C-Kermit>dial \%d                (dial 1(212)555-1212)
C-Kermit>send \%f                (send oofa.txt)
C-Kermit>
```

Evaluation of these variables is simply a matter of text substitution. Variables do not have types, like integer versus character versus string. Their values are substituted in place at the time the commands in which they appear are parsed. If the result is illegal, an error is diagnosed in the same way it would be you had typed the illegal value in directly. To illustrate:

```
C-Kermit>define \%x oofa          (A non-numeric value)
C-Kermit>set block-check \%x      (Use it in a numeric context)
?Invalid - set block oofa         (Kermit doesn't understand)
```

```
C-Kermit>define \%x 2            (Try a numeric value)
C-Kermit>set block-check \%x     (Use it in the same context)
C-Kermit>                        (No complaint)
```

If you want to use a variable name itself literally in a command, precede its name with a backslash:

```
C-Kermit>define \%a Hello again
C-Kermit>echo My name is "\\%a".  My value is "\%a".
My name is "\%a".  My value is "Hello again".
C-Kermit>
```

You should keep in mind one restriction on C-Kermit's text substitution. You can't place a variable that expands into multiple words in a command field that is required to be a single word. For example:

```
C-Kermit>def \%a file type binary
C-Kermit>set \%a
?More fields required
C-Kermit>
```

But:

```
C-Kermit>def \%b file            (Define each word separately)
C-Kermit>def \%c type
C-Kermit>def \%d binary
C-Kermit>set \%b \%c \%d
C-Kermit>                        (No complaint)
```

Assigning versus Defining

Variable definitions can be nested, meaning that the definition of one variable can contain the names of other variables:

```
C-Kermit>define \%a My name is \%b.
C-Kermit>define \%b not \%c
C-Kermit>define \%c Olga
C-Kermit>echo \%a
My name is not Olga.
C-Kermit>
```

This raises an interesting question: what happens if we define a variable in terms of itself?

```
C-Kermit>define \%a 5            (\%a is defined to be "5")
C-Kermit>define \%a -\%a         (\%a defined to be "-\%a")
C-Kermit>echo \%a               (What does this do?)
```

Luckily, you'll never know. This is called a circular definition and would result in the construction of an infinitely long string of dashes in front of the 5, quickly filling up the computer's memory if C-Kermit didn't notice and put a stop to it:

```
?Definition circular or too deep
C-Kermit>
```

But what if all we really wanted to do was replace the definition of \%a by itself with a dash in front of it, for example to turn a positive number into a negative one? We need a way to tell C-Kermit to copy the *values* of the variables in the definition, rather than their names. This capability is provided by the ASSIGN command:

ASSIGN *name* [*text*]

This command can be used to create or give new values to either macros or variables. Unlike DEFINE, it evaluates any variables in the *text* before making it the value of the variable or macro. Synonym: **ASG**. Example:

```
C-Kermit>define \%a 5
C-Kermit>assign \%a -\%a
C-Kermit>echo \%a
-5
C-Kermit>
```

The difference between DEFINE and ASSIGN is important when the definition contains variables whose values might change before they are used. DEFINE copies variable names literally, postponing their evaluation until a command actually refers to them, allowing future references to pick up the new values, whereas ASSIGN evaluates them at the time the assignment is made, preserving their *current* values.

Macros as Variables

Macros can be used as variables too. Define a macro in the normal way but, if you intend to use it as a variable rather than as a list of commands, it can contain any text at all:

```
C-Kermit>define phone-number 1(212)555-1212
```

You can refer to it using special notation: its name preceded by \m and enclosed in parentheses. C-Kermit replaces this construction with the macro's definition:

```
C-Kermit>echo \m(phone-number)
1(212)555-1212
C-Kermit>dial \m(phone-number)
```

These variables differ from letter and digit variables, like \%a and \%1, not only in the format of their names, but also in how they are evaluated. Letter and digit variables are evaluated *recursively*, meaning that if their values contain further variable references, then those, too, are evaluated and the process repeats until all variable references are resolved. The \m() operator, however, is replaced by the literal definition of the macro it references. To illustrate:

```
C-Kermit>define \%a PAINTBUCKET
C-Kermit>define \%b \%a
C-Kermit>define \%c \%b
C-Kermit>define foo \%a
C-Kermit>echo \m(foo) = \%c
\%a = PAINTBUCKET
C-Kermit>
```

This property is useful in dealing with DOS filenames, used not only in DOS, but also Windows and OS/2, where the backslash character is the directory separator.

```
C-Kermit>define \%a C:\WINDOWS\SYSTEM.INI
C-Kermit>define filename C:\WINDOWS\SYSTEM.INI
C-Kermit>echo \%a
C:WINDOWSSYSTEM.INI
C-Kermit>echo \m(filename)
C:\WINDOWS\SYSTEM.INI
C-Kermit>
```

Notice how backslashes are swallowed up by the evaluation of \%a, but are preserved when using the \m() form. Therefore you should use the \m() form for holding filenames or any other text that is likely to contain backslashes that are to be used literally.

Local Variables and Settings

Whenever a computer program becomes even moderately complex, the danger of variable-name conflicts arises. This is especially true in the Kermit language, in which there are only 26 distinct letter variables. Meanwhile, as the corpus of programs in a particular language grows, it becomes increasingly desirable to have a way to package up procedures in a portable and reusable way. We have said that macros (and to some extent, command files) are the "subroutines" of the Kermit language, but for subroutines to be portable, reusable, and safe, they must be self-contained and should execute without side effects. This can be accomplished, at least in part, by using local variables.

A *local variable* exists only in the context of the command level (macro or command file) that declares it, including any macros or command files invoked from the current command level, and so on. It is ceases to exist when the macro or command file in which it was declared exits. Thus it can have the same name as other variables outside of the macro or command file without causing any conflict or affecting their values. Local variables are defined by the LOCAL command:

LOCAL *name1 [name2 [...]]*
> Declares the variables whose names are listed to be local to the macro or command file in which the LOCAL command appears, and to its "children" and "descendents" The variables may be letter variables or macro names. This command does not create or define the variables; it merely reserves their names local use. Example:
>
> ```
> local \%a \%b \%x filename phone-number
> ```

Here is a simple demonstration how local variables work:

```
define TESTING {
    local \%a
    define \%a This is the local value.
    echo \%a
}
```

```
define \%a This is the original value.
print \%a
testing
print \%a
```

When you execute these commands, the result is:

```
This is the original value.
This is the local value.
This is the original value.
```

So you can see that defining the *local* copy of \%a in the TESTING macro does not affect the *global* copy of \%a. Declaring \%a to be LOCAL in the macro *hides* and *protects* the global value of \%a from the macro, and it hides the local value of \%a from the higher levels of the program.

Kermit's local variables are on the call stack. Unlike macro arguments, however, they *are* inherited; they are invisible at higher levels but visible at lower ones. Suppose variable \%x is defined globally. Then, if macro A declares variable \%x to be local and then invokes macro B, macro B can "see" variable \%x unless macro B itself declares a local variable of the same name, in which case a *third* copy of the variable is created, hiding and protecting the second one, and so on.

Just as local variables can go on the command stack, so do certain settings (for a complete list, see page 458). We have already seen some examples:

```
SET MACRO ERROR { ON, OFF }
SET TAKE ERROR { ON, OFF }
```

The SET MACRO ERROR command affects only the current macro and any macros it might invoke (and any macros they might invoke, and so on). When the macro that issued this command exits, the previous SET MACRO ERROR setting is restored. Thus the Kermit macro programmer is free to change MACRO ERROR settings without having to worry about how to restore them when the macro terminates — or for that matter, if it is interrupted. Similar comments apply to SET TAKE ERROR. We will see practical applications for local variables and "stackable" commands in subsequent chapters.

Arrays

An array is a global variable that has a list of values, each one with its own *index*, a number ranging from 0 to a maximum that you choose. An array name looks like a letter variable name, except with an ampersand instead of a percent sign: \&a, \&b, ..., \&z. As with other variable names, case doesn't matter: \&a is the same array as \&A.

The array index goes in square brackets appended to the name: \&a[0] is the "zeroth" element, \&a[1] is the first element, and so on.

Before you can use an array, you must DECLARE its size so Kermit can allocate the required amount of memory for it:

DECLARE *array-name*[*number*]

Creates an array of the given name, with *number* + 1 elements, 0 through *number*. For example, the command:

```
C-Kermit>declare \&x[200]
```

creates an array named \&x that has 201 elements, numbered 0 through 200.
Synonym: **DCL**.

Array elements, like any other variable, can be created with the DEFINE or ASSIGN command. An array index can be a constant or any type of variable, including another array element:

```
C-Kermit>dcl \&x[1000]         (Declare array \&x, size 1001)
C-Kermit>def \&x[100] HUNDRED  (Define 100th element of \&x)
C-Kermit>def \%i 100           (Define a global variable)
C-Kermit>ech \&x[\%i]          (Use it as an index)
HUNDRED
C-Kermit>asg \&x[99] \%i       (Define another array element)
C-Kermit>ech \&x[\&x[99]]      (Use it as an index)
HUNDRED
C-Kermit>
```

You can use arithmetic in array subscripts (\%i still has a value of 100):

```
C-Kermit>def \&x[99] NINETY-NINE   (Define 99th element of \&x)
C-Kermit>ech \&x[\%i-1]            (Arithmetic in index field)
NINETY-NINE
C-Kermit>def \&x[515] FIVE-FIFTEEN
C-Kermit>def \%j 5
C-Kermit>ech \&x[(\%i+2)*\%j+5]
FIVE-FIFTEEN
C-Kermit>
```

C-Kermit arrays are one-dimensional. That is, you cannot create or use an array that has more than one index. A declaration for an array that already exists destroys the previous array and allocates a new empty one with the same name and with the given size. A declaration with a size of zero destroys the array and releases its memory:

```
C-Kermit>declare \&x[0]
```

You can find out which arrays are declared with the SHOW ARRAYS command:

```
C-Kermit>sho arra
Declared arrays:
 \&@[4]
 \&a[3]
 \&x[200]
```

We'll see some uses for arrays in the coming chapters.

The C-Kermit Argument Vector Array

The array `\&@[]` is special. It is created automatically when Kermit starts up, and it contains the program's "argument vector" — the command you gave to start C-Kermit. For example, suppose you started C-Kermit by giving the following command at the UNIX shell prompt:[43]

```
$ kermit -l /dev/ttya
C-Kermit>echo \&@[0]
kermit
C-Kermit>echo \&@[1]
-l
C-Kermit>echo \&@[2]
/dev/ttya
C-Kermit>
```

Kermit does not let you change the values of the `\&@[]` array. They are read-only.

The Macro Argument Vector Array

The array `\&_[]` is also special. Whenever a macro is invoked, the elements of this array refer to the macro's arguments. Thus `\&_[0]` is `\%0` (the name of the macro), `\&_[1]` is `\%1` (the first argument), and so on. Each macro gets its own copy of this array, and so it too is on the call stack. You can use this array in a macro to access the arguments programmatically rather than by name, using the techniques presented in the next chapter.

Built-in Variables

C-Kermit offers a selection of built-in, read-only, named variables. Read-only means C-Kermit gives them their values; you can't DEFINE or ASSIGN them yourself, you can only use the values Kermit gives them. Built-in variables have names that look like this:

`\v(name)`

that is, a backslash, the letter v, and then the variable name in parentheses. Either upper- or lowercase letters can be used.

As an aside, perhaps you can see a pattern emerging in variable name format. The name of the variable begins with a backslash, and then the next character tells which type of variable it is, and then the character(s) after that identify the specific variable. When the identifier is more than one character long, as in `\m(name)` or `\v(name)`, the identifier is enclosed in parentheses so we know where it ends.

C-Kermit's built-in read-only variables are listed in Table 17-1 at the end of this chapter. The SHOW VARIABLES command gives you a complete list of C-Kermit's built in variables and their current values. In the following sections, we look at some of them in detail.

---

[43]Command-line arguments are explained in Appendix I.

The Command Environment

`\v(args)`

The number of "words" you typed when you invoked C-Kermit (the size of `\&@[]`):

```
$ kermit -p e -l /dev/acu -b 2400
C-Kermit>echo \v(args)
7
C-Kermit>
```

`\v(argc)`

The number of arguments to the current macro, including its name. Example:

```
C-Kermit>define countwords echo Arguments: \v(argc)
C-Kermit>countwords here are some words
Arguments: 5
C-Kermit>
```

When no macros are active, the value of `\v(argc)` is 0.

`\v(cmdlevel)`

Current command level; 0 means interactive. Anything greater than zero means C-Kermit is getting its commands from a command file or a macro definition.

`\v(cmdsource)`

The current source of commands: PROMPT (if interactive), FILE (if a command file), or MACRO (if a macro definition).

`\v(cmdfile)`

The name of the current command file, if any. Example:

```
Echo Greetings from \v(cmdfile)!
```

`\v(_line)`

The current line in the current command file, if any:

```
Echo Greetings from line \v(_line) of \v(cmdfile)!
```

`\v(macro)`

The name of the current macro, if any. Same as `\%0`.

`\v(exitstatus)`

The numeric return code that C-Kermit would give to your computer's host operating system if you gave it the EXIT command right now. This code indicates success or failure in various operations (explained on page 463).

`\v(version)`

The Kermit program's numeric version number. For example, version 6.0.192 is 600192. Use this to construct scripts that can take advantage of commands in new releases of C-Kermit that aren't present in old releases.

Computer Environment

`\v(directory)`

The current (default) directory. Example:

```
C-Kermit>assign \%d \v(dir)       (Save current directory in \%d)
C-Kermit>cd elsewhere             (Change current directory)
...
C-Kermit>cd \%d                   (Go back to previous directory)
C-Kermit>set prompt [\v(dir)] C-Kermit>
[/usr/olga] C-Kermit>cd correspondence
[/usr/olga/correspondence] C-Kermit>
```

`\v(home)`

Your home (login) directory. For UNIX, something like `/usr/olga/`. For VMS, something like `$DISK1:[OLGA]`. `\v(home)` is a portable construction suitable for concatenation with a filename without any intervening characters; a construction like `\v(home)oofa.txt` should work on all operating systems where C-Kermit runs.

`\v(host)`

The network host name, if any, of the computer where C-Kermit is running:

```
C-Kermit>set prompt \v(host):Kermit>
CHEMVAX:Kermit>
```

`\v(platform)`

The specific platform for which your version of C-Kermit was built, such as `AT&T_System_V_R4`. This is the same as the system type announced in C-Kermit's version herald, but with spaces replaced by underscores to make it one word.

`\v(program)`

The name of this program, C-Kermit, as distinct from (say) MS-DOS Kermit.

`\v(tmpdir)`

The name of a directory that can be used for creating temporary files.

Date and Time

`\v(date)`

The current date, for example `8 Aug 1996`. The month is the first three letters of the month's name. The date string contains imbedded spaces. Example:

```
C-Kermit>echo Today is \v(date).
Today is 8 Aug 1996.
C-Kermit>
```

`\v(ndate)`

The current date in numeric *yyyymmdd* format, e.g. 19960808, suitable for sorting, for numeric comparisons, or for making filenames. For example:

```
C-Kermit>log transactions \v(ndate).log
```

`\v(day)`

The day of the week, written as the first three letters of the weekday: Sun, Mon, ...,
Sat. Example:

```
C-Kermit>echo Today is \v(day), \v(date).
Today is Thu, 8 Aug 1996.
C-Kermit>
```

`\v(nday)`

The numeric value of the day of the week. 0 is Sunday, 1 is Monday, and so on until
Saturday, which is 6.

`\v(time)`

The current local time in 24-hour hh:mm:ss format. Example: 15:28:00.

`\v(ntime)`

Numeric time. The current time in seconds since midnight, local time. For example,
10:00 p.m. would be 79200.

Communications

`\v(connection)`

The current type of communications connection: REMOTE if C-Kermit is in remote
mode, SERIAL if it is a serial connection, TCP/IP if it is a TCP/IP connection, and so on.

`\v(line)`

The current communication line or device or network host name or number (the most
recent SET LINE, SET PORT, or SET HOST value).

`\v(modem)`

The current modem type. Also see Table 17-1 at the end of this chapter for numerous
modem and dialing related variables.

`\v(local)`

1 if Kermit is in local mode; that is, you have given a SET LINE, SET HOST, or TELNET
command to initiate a connection from the computer where C-Kermit is running to
another, remote computer. 0 otherwise.

`\v(parity)`

The current parity setting: even, odd, mark, space, or none.

`\v(speed)`

The current speed of the current SET LINE or SET PORT device, if any, otherwise -1.

`\v(ttyfd)`

The file descriptor of the communication device or connection selected in the most
recent SET LINE or SET HOST command. Use this to construct command lines to make
the communication connections device available to other programs via RUN command.

File Transfer

`\v(protocol)`

The current file transfer protocol: Kermit, ZMODEM, etc, as established in the most recent SET PROTOCOL command.

`\v(packetlen)`

The current SET RECEIVE PACKET-LENGTH value.

`\v(window)`

The current SET WINDOW value.

`\v(ftype)`

The current SET FILE TYPE value, such as "text" or "binary".

`\v(download)`

The current download directory, if any, as established in the most recent SET FILE DOWNLOAD-DIRECTORY command.

`\v(filespec)`

The file specification from your most recent file transfer. Useful for referring to the same group of files again for other purposes, for example:

```
C-Kermit>send x*.*
C-Kermit>echo \v(filespec)
x*.*
C-Kermit>remote dir \v(filespec)
```

`\v(fsize)`

The size of the file most recently transferred, in bytes.

`\v(tfsize)`

The total size of the file group most recently transferred, in bytes.

`\v(cps)`

The speed of the most recent file transfer in characters per second.

`\v(crc16)`

The 16-bit cyclic redundancy check of the file or file group most recently transferred.

Environment Variables

Environment variables are global variables that certain computer operating systems or application environments make available to application software (such as C-Kermit) at runtime. An environment variable has a name and a value. C-Kermit gives you access to your computer's environment variables (if it has any) with variables of the form:

`\$(name)`

that is, backslash and dollar sign followed by the name of the environment variable enclosed in parentheses. Which, if any, variables are available depends on your computer system and your own setup, which is entirely unknown to C-Kermit. Those commonly available on UNIX and VMS include:

\\$(HOME)   Your home directory

\\$(USER)   Your login username

\\$(TERM)   Your terminal type

Alphabetic case is usually significant in environment variable names. Example (with results shown for both UNIX and VMS):

```
C-Kermit>echo HOME=\$(HOME), USER=\$(USER), TERM=\$(TERM)
HOME=/usr/olga, USER=olga, TERM=vt320
HOME=$disk1:[olga], USER=OLGA, TERM=vt300-80
```

In UNIX, DOS, Windows, and OS/2, you can find out what environment variables are currently defined by issuing the command "set" at the shell prompt, or by using the C-Kermit command:

```
C-Kermit>run set
```

In UNIX, you can define an environment variable like this:

```
$ MYNAME=Olaf ; export MYNAME        (sh or ksh)
% setenv MYNAME Olaf                  (csh)
```

In VMS, C-Kermit treats logical names and symbols as environment variables:

```
C-Kermit>echo \$(SYS$SYSTEM)
SYS$SYSROOT:[SYSEXE]
```

You can list the defined logical names with the VMS SHOW LOGICALS or SHOW SYMBOL command, and you can define new ones with the VMS DEFINE command:

```
$ define MYNAME "Olaf"
$ show logical myname
   "MYNAME" = "Olaf" (LNM$PROCESS_TABLE)
$ kermit
C-Kermit>echo Hello there, \$(MYNAME).
Hello there, Olaf.
C-Kermit>
```

Defining versus Assigning Revisited

Some of C-Kermit's \v() variables change depending on conditions. For example, \v(directory) changes whenever you give a CD command; the \v(time) variable changes every second, all by itself. These variables serve nicely to illustrate the distinction between DEFINE and ASSIGN, in case it is still in doubt. Let's create a variable \%a that includes a reference to \v(time) in its value. First with the DEFINE command, which copies the *name* of the \v(time) variable into the definition of \%a:

```
C-Kermit>DEFINE \%a The time is \v(time)
C-Kermit>show globals                (Check the value of \%a)
 \%a = The time is \v(time)
C-Kermit>echo \%a                    (Evaluate it)
The time is 13:25:03
C-Kermit>sleep 60                    (Let one minute pass)
C-Kermit>echo \%a                    (Look again)
The time is 13:26:03                 (See how it changed)
```

And again, but with the ASSIGN command, which evaluates the \v(time) variable and copies its *value* into the \%a definition:

```
C-Kermit>ASSIGN \%a The time is \v(time)
C-Kermit>sho globals                 (Check the value)
 \%a = The time is 13:31:47          (No \v(time))
C-Kermit>echo \%a                    (Evaluate \%a)
The time is 13:31:47
C-Kermit>sleep 60                    (Sleep one minute)
C-Kermit>echo \%a                    (Check again)
The time is 13:31:47                 (Time stands still!)
```

So, once again, the rule is: use ASSIGN to get the current value of a variable whose value might change before you want to use it. Use DEFINE to ensure that whenever you reference a variable, you get its latest value. When the definition text does not contain variables, DEFINE and ASSIGN are equivalent.

Transmission of Variables between Client and Server

When two Kermit programs have a client/server relationship and both have variables, and both support this optional feature of the Kermit protocol, the client program can both set and query the values of the server's variables. As of this writing, MS-DOS Kermit and C-Kermit (including Kermit 95, Kermit/2, and Macintosh Kermit) support this feature. The commands are:

REMOTE QUERY { KERMIT, SYSTEM, USER } *variable-name*
Asks the server to send the value of the variable of the given type that has the given name. If the query succeeds, the value is displayed on the client's screen and it is also stored in the client's \v(query) variable. If the query fails, an error message is printed and the \v(query) variable is set to the empty string.

In C-Kermit and MS-DOS Kermit, KERMIT variables are the \v(*name*) kind, such as \v(time), \v(version), \v(date), as well as \f...() built-in functions, which are discussed in the next chapter. SYSTEM variables are DOS or UNIX environment variables, such as PATH, USER, HOME, or VMS logical names or symbols, or the equivalent, if any, on other operating systems. USER variables are everything else — the letter variables \%a–\%z, macro names, and even macro arguments (in case the SERVER command was executed from within a macro).

The name of a KERMIT or SYSTEM variable must be given in an implementation-independent format without special syntax, e.g. TIME, DATE, VERSION, PATH, USER, etc, rather than (say) \v(time), \$(PATH). Similarly for functions (discussed in the next chapter):

```
C-Kermit> remote query kermit files(oofa.*)
```

rather than:

```
C-Kermit> remote query \ffiles(oofa.*)
```

Alphabetic case might or might not be significant in system variables, depending on the system (in UNIX, for example, it makes a difference). The name of a USER variable is given in the syntax of the server's command language, e.g. \%a. Examples:

```
C-Kermit>remote query kermit time
13:25:18
C-Kermit>echo The server's time is: \v(query)
The server's time is: 13:25:18
C-Kermit>rem q k dir                (Note, abbreviations allowed)
/usr/olga/letters
C-Kermit>echo The server's current directory is: \v(query)
The server's current directory is: /usr/olga/letters
C-Kermit>rem q system USER
olga
C-Kermit>echo user = \v(query)
user = olga
C-Kermit>
```

The command with which the client defines or changes variables in the server is:

REMOTE ASSIGN *name [value]*

Asks the server to assign the given *value* to the remote USER variable denoted by *name*. The *value* is fully evaluated *locally* before being sent to the server. The maximum length for the value is governed by the maximum negotiated packet length, i.e. the server's RECEIVE PACKET-LENGTH. Synonym: **REMOTE ASG**.

Examples:

```
C-Kermit>rem asg myname Olga          (Define server's myname macro)
C-Kermit>remote query user myname     (Get its value)
Olga
C-Kermit>echo \v(query)
Olga
C-Kermit>remote assign \%a \v(time)   (Assign my time to server's \%a)
C-Kermit>remote query user \%a
13:41:18                              (This is the client's time)
C-Kermit>
```

To force a variable name to be sent literally, use two backslashes:

```
C-Kermit>remote assign \%a \\v(time)  (Assign "\v(time)" to server's \%a)
C-Kermit>remote query user \%a
13:41:18                              (This is the server's time)
C-Kermit>
```

You can disable and enable the server's handling of REMOTE QUERY and ASSIGN with the commands:

DISABLE QUERY	The server should not respond to REMOTE QUERY commands
DISABLE ASSIGN	The server should not respond to REMOTE ASSIGN commands
ENABLE QUERY	The server should respond to REMOTE QUERY commands
ENABLE ASSIGN	The server should respond to REMOTE ASSIGN commands

By default, like most other ENABLE/DISABLE items, the initial state is ENABLEd.

Here is a practical application in which we use the \v(crc16) variable to assure ourselves that a binary-mode file transfer succeeded. If it did succeed, the original and the transferred copy of the file (or files) should be identical. The CRC is a 16-bit number calculated from all the bytes in the file, which is extremely likely to be different for two files that are not identical, and which is the same for two files that *are* identical. The mathematics and statistics are explained in numerous references, such as [54, 56].

When you transfer a file between two Kermit programs that have a \v(crc16) variable, you can check its value on each end after the transfer. This is particularly easy in a client/ server setting:

```
C-Kermit> send kermit.exe
C-Kermit> echo \v(crc16)
22835
C-Kermit> remote query kermit crc16
22835
C-Kermit>
```

If the numbers don't agree, then you probably have transferred the file in text mode. Files are rarely identical after text-mode transfer, since its purpose is to furnish any required record-format or character-set conversions.

Summary of Built-in Variables

Table 17-1 lists C-Kermit's built-in \v(*name*) variables alphabetically.

Table 17-1   Built-in Variables

Variable	Description
\v(_line)	Line number in current command file
\v(apcactive)	1 if APC command active, otherwise 0
\v(argc)	Number of arguments to current macro, plus 1; 0 if no macro
\v(args)	Number of command-line arguments, plus 1

Table 17-1 Built-in Variables (continued)

Variable	Description
\v(charset)	Current file character-set
\v(cmdfile)	Name of current command file, if any
\v(cmdlevel)	Current command level, 0 = top level
\v(cmdsource)	"prompt", "macro", or "file"
\v(cols)	Number of columns on screen, or -1 if unknown
\v(connection)	Type of connection: "remote", "serial", "tcp/ip", "x.25", etc.
\v(count)	Current value of SET COUNT counter.
\v(cps)	Speed of most recent file transfer, characters per second.
\v(cpu)	Type of central processing unit in this computer, if known
\v(crc16)	16-bit Cyclic Redundancy Check of most recent file transfer
\v(d$ac)	SET DIAL AREA-CODE value
\v(d$cc)	SET DIAL COUNTRY-CODE value
\v(d$ip)	SET DIAL INTL-PREFIX value
\v(d$lp)	SET DIAL LD-PREFIX value
\v(date)	Current date, e.g. "6 Sep 1996"
\v(day)	Day of week, e.g. "Fri"
\v(dialnumber)	Number or name most recently given to DIAL command
\v(dialresult)	Dial result message or code from modem
\v(dialstatus)	Numeric code for result of most recent DIAL command, Table 5-3
\v(directory)	Current directory
\v(download)	Download directory
\v(errno)	System error number of most recent error
\v(errstring)	Error message associated with \v(errno)
\v(evaluate)	Result of most recent EVALUATE command
\v(exedir)	Directory where the Kermit executable resides
\v(exitstatus)	Current C-Kermit EXIT status
\v(filespec)	File specification from most recent file transfer
\v(fsize)	Size of file most recently transferred
\v(ftype)	SET FILE TYPE value, e.g. text or binary
\v(home)	Your home directory

Table 17-1   Built-in Variables (continued)

Variable	Description
\v(host)	Hostname, if any, of your computer
\v(input)	Current contents of the INPUT command buffer
\v(inchar)	Single-character INPUT value
\v(incount)	Count of characters processed by most recent INPUT command
\v(inidir)	Directory where the C-Kermit initialization file was found
\v(instatus)	Status of most recent INPUT command
\v(ipaddress)	IP address, if any, and if known, of your computer
\v(keyboard)	Keyboard type (Windows, OS/2)
\v(line)	SET LINE, SET PORT, or SET HOST value
\v(local)	1 if C-Kermit is in local mode, 0 if in remote mode
\v(macro)	Name of currently active macro, if any
\v(minput)	MINPUT command value indicating which item was matched
\v(modem)	SET MODEM TYPE value
\v(m_aa_off)	AUTOANSWER OFF command for current modem type
\v(m_aa_on)	AUTOANSWER ON command for current modem type
\v(m_dc_off)	COMPRESSION OFF command for current modem type
\v(m_dc_on)	COMPRESSION ON command for current modem type
\v(m_dial)	DIAL command for current modem type
\v(m_ec_off)	ERROR-CORRECTION OFF command for current modem type
\v(m_ec_on)	ERROR-CORRECTION ON command for current modem type
\v(m_fc_hw)	HARDWARE-FLOW command for current modem type
\v(m_fc_no)	NO-FLOW-CONTROL command for current modem type
\v(m_fc_sw)	SOFTWARE-FLOW command for current modem type
\v(m_hup)	HANGUP command for current modem type
\v(m_init)	INIT-STRING command for current modem type
\v(m_pulse)	PULSE command for current modem type
\v(m_tone)	TONE command for current modem type
\v(ndate)	Numeric date, *yyyymmdd*, e.g. 19960906
\v(nday)	Numeric day of the week, 0=Sunday, 1=Monday, . . . , 6=Saturday
\v(newline)	Line terminator used in text files on your computer

Table 17-1   Built-in Variables (continued)

Variable	Description
\v(ntime)	Numeric time of day, seconds since midnight
\v(packetlen)	SET RECEIVE PACKET-LENGTH value
\v(parity)	Current parity setting: none, even, space, mark, or odd
\v(password)	SET LOGIN PASSWORD value
\v(platform)	Specific operating system of your computer, e.g. Solaris
\v(program)	Always "C-Kermit"
\v(query)	Result of most recent REMOTE QUERY command
\v(prompt)	Current SET LOGIN PROMPT value
\v(protocol)	Current file transfer protocol: Kermit, ZMODEM, etc.
\v(return)	Value of most recent RETURN command
\v(rows)	Number of rows (lines) on your terminal
\v(speed)	Speed of current communications device, -1 if unknown or N/A.
\v(space)	Amount of free space on current disk
\v(startup)	C-Kermit's startup directory
\v(status)	Status of most recent command, 0=success, nonzero=failure.
\v(sysid)	Internal Kermit code for local operating system type
\v(system)	Generic operating system name, e.g. UNIX
\v(terminal)	Current terminal type
\v(tfsize)	Total size of file group most recently transferred
\v(time)	Current time hh:mm:ss, 24-hour notation
\v(tmpdir)	Pathname of a temporary directory
\v(ttyfd)	File descriptor of SET LINE/PORT/HOST device
\v(userid)	SET LOGIN USERID value
\v(version)	numeric C-Kermit version number, e.g. 600192
\v(window)	Current SET WINDOW value
\v(xversion)	Platform-specific C-Kermit version number

## Chapter 18

Programming Commands

Command files, macros, and variables are useful tools, but by themselves they are little more than conveniences. However, if they are used within the framework of a programming language, they can open up all sorts of new possibilities. *Programming language?* If you're not a programmer, don't be alarmed. The language we're talking about is nothing more than the Kermit commands you are already familiar with, plus a few additional ones for decision-making, for skipping other commands, for repeatedly executing groups of commands, for reading and writing file data, and for getting information from the user.

The IF Command

Let's begin by introducing Kermit's decision-making command.

IF *condition command*
> If the *condition* is true, the *command* is executed. If the condition is not true, the command is ignored and not executed.

IF NOT *condition command*
> If the *condition* is *not* true, the *command* is executed. If the condition is true, the command is ignored.

The *command* can be any C-Kermit command, including another IF command, but not an ELSE command (see page 367), and it can also be a macro invocation or a TAKE command. It is on the same line as the IF command, separated from it by one or more spaces, and without commas, braces, or other punctuation. The *condition* is a statement that can be true or false, consisting of one to four "words" separated by spaces. Example:

```
if equal {\%a} {Rumpelstiltskin} echo You guessed my name!
```

The *condition* is:

```
equal {\%a} {Rumpelstiltskin}
```

and the *command* is:

```
echo You guessed my name!
```

Note how \%a and Rumpelstiltskin are enclosed in braces. This is a trick to protect against the error that would occur if \%a were not defined, in which case there would be a missing field, or if "Rumpelstiltskin" had any spaces in it, in which case there would be extra fields. The braces force each field to be exactly one "word." The following sections describe C-Kermit's IF conditions.

Comparing Numbers

Let's begin with the IF commands that compare numbers. The numbers in the following IF conditions can be constants (literal numbers) or variables of any kind whose values are whole numbers, positive or negative. If these comparisons are used with nonnumeric values or numbers containing decimal points, they give a syntax error message and fail.

IF = *number1 number2 command*

If *number1* is equal to *number2*, the *command* is executed. Example:

```
C-Kermit>define \%a 2
C-Kermit>if = ? First number or variable name
C-Kermit>if = \%a ? Second number or variable name
C-Kermit>if = \%a 3 echo They are equal    (Nothing happens)
C-Kermit>if = \%a 2 echo They are equal    (Condition is true)
They are equal                             (Command is executed)
C-Kermit>
```

IF NOT = *number1 number2 command*

If *number1* is not equal to *number2*, the *command* is executed. Example:

```
C-Kermit>define \%a 2
C-Kermit>if not = \%a 2 echo Not equal    (Nothing happens)
C-Kermit>if not = \%a 3 echo Not equal    (Condition is true)
Not equal                                 (Command is executed)
C-Kermit>
```

IF < *number1 number2 command*

If *number1* is less than *number2*, the *command* is executed. Example:

```
C-Kermit>define \%a 2
C-Kermit>if < \%a -5 echo It's less       (Nothing happens)
C-Kermit>if < \%a 100 echo It's less      (Condition is true)
It's less                                 (Command is executed)
C-Kermit>
```

IF NOT < *number1 number2 command*

If *number1* is not less than (is greater than or equal to) *number2*, the *command* is executed. Example:

```
C-Kermit>define \%a 2
C-Kermit>if not < \%a 1 echo Not less    (Condition is true)
Not less                                 (Command is executed)
C-Kermit>if not < \%a 2 echo Not less    (Nothing happens)
C-Kermit>
```

IF > *number1 number2 command*

If *number1* is greater than *number2*, the *command* is executed. Example:

```
C-Kermit>define \%a 2
C-Kermit>if > \%a 1 echo Greater    (Condition is true)
Greater                             (Command is executed)
C-Kermit>if > \%a 2 echo Greater    (Nothing happens)
C-Kermit>
```

IF NOT > *number1 number2 command*

If *number1* is not greater than (is less than or equal to) *number2*, the *command* is executed. Example:

```
C-Kermit>define \%a 2
C-Kermit>if not > \%a 2 echo Not greater    (Condition is true)
Not greater                                 (Command is executed)
C-Kermit>if not > \%a 1 echo Not greater    (Nothing happens)
C-Kermit>
```

IF *number command*

Executes the *command* if the *number* is not 0, and does not execute the command if the *number* is 0. The *number* can, of course, be a variable that contains a number.

IF NOT *number command*

Executes the *command* if the *number* is zero, does not execute the command if the *number* is *not* zero.

The ELSE Command

The IF command can be followed on the next line by an ELSE command:

ELSE *command*

Executes the *command* if the preceding command was an IF command and its condition was not true.

Example:

```
C-Kermit>if = 1 2 echo 1 = 2          (Not true)
C-Kermit>else echo 1 is not 2         (So ELSE is executed)
1 is not 2
C-Kermit>
```

The ELSE command causes an error if it is executed after any command other than IF. IF and ELSE are separate commands, not two parts of the same command (a more flexible XIF-ELSE construction is described later in this chapter). They are intended primarily for use within command files and macros, but they can also be executed at the C-Kermit prompt, in which case you should not be alarmed if another prompt suddenly appears after the IF condition:

```
C-Kermit>if = 1 2 echo Strange...    (False, nothing happens)
C-Kermit>if = 1 1                     (True, new prompt appears)
C-Kermit>echo As expected...          (ECHO command is executed)
As expected...
C-Kermit>
```

When the condition is true, C-Kermit prompts you for a command to be executed. If the condition is not true, C-Kermit treats the rest of the IF command as a comment. Here is an example of using IF and ELSE in a macro:

```
C-Kermit>def add if = \%1 1 if = \%2 1 echo 2, else echo Too hard!
C-Kermit>add 1 1
2
C-Kermit>add 2 2
Too hard!
```

The comma separating the IF and ELSE commands is necessary because IF and ELSE are separate commands. This example also shows how an AND effect can be achieved by combining multiple IF commands on the same line.

Here is an example of a compound IF construction that obeys the rule that ELSE can only follow IF but the ELSE *command* can be any command at all, even another IF:

```
if < \v(ntime) 43200 define \%x morning      (Before noon)
else if < \v(ntime) 61200 def \%x afternoon   (Before 5)
else def \%x evening                          (After 5)
echo Good \%x!
```

String Comparisons

The following commands compare character strings just as the IF =, IF <, and IF > commands compare numbers, and you can use NOT in these commands the same way. Note that EQUAL does not equal =. For example, "1" and "01" are = but they are not EQUAL.

IF EQUAL *string1 string2 command*

Executes the *command* if the two character strings are equal, meaning they are the same length and contain the same characters in the same order. *string1* and *string2* may be literal strings or variables. Examples:

```
if equal \%1 secret echo You guessed the secret word!
if not equ \%1 secret echo Sorry, wrong again.
```

Remember the IF condition consists of three fields: the comparison operator (EQUAL in this case) and two strings. If one or both of the strings is undefined, there won't be enough fields, and the first word or two of the COMMAND will be misinterpreted as one or both of the comparison strings. On the other hand, if either of the strings contains (or evaluates to a string that contains) more than one word, there will be *too many* fields, again resulting in undesired effects. To guard against both situations, enclose both strings in braces:

```
C-Kermit>define \%a This is a string
C-Kermit>if equal {\%a} {This is a string} echo It's a string!
It's a string!
C-Kermit>
```

IF LLT *string1 string2 command*

Executes the *command* if *string1* is "lexically" less than (LLT) *string2*, in other words; if *string1* would be alphabetized before *string2* according to the ASCII collating sequence or, more precisely, according to the codes used to represent the characters in the string. Example:

```
if llt {\%a} {zyzzniak} echo It's less.
```

IF NOT LLT means "lexically greater than or equal to."

IF LGT *string1 string2 command*

Executes the *command* if *string1* is lexically greater than (LGT) *string2*. Example:

```
if lgt {\%a} {aardvark} echo It's greater.
```

IF NOT LGT means "lexically less than or equal to."

The treatment of alphabetic case in string comparisons is governed by the command:

SET CASE OFF

In all C-Kermit's string comparison and matching commands — IF and others still to come — causes uppercase and lowercase letters to be treated equivalently: "A" is the same as "a", "aardvark" equals "AARDVARK" equals "Aardvark", etc.

SET CASE ON

Causes upper- and lowercase to be treated as distinct: "A" and "a" are different characters. In the ASCII character set, the code for "A" (65), and other uppercase letters, is less than the code for "a" (97) and other lowercase letters. See Table VII-1.

SET CASE is a "stackable" command. That is, you can give this command in a command file or macro without affecting the SET CASE value at higher levels in the call stack.

Unless you tell Kermit otherwise, alphabetic case is ignored.

WARNING: caseless string comparisons, for example in the IF EQUAL, IF LLT, and IF LGT commands, work only for 7-bit ASCII characters. For international (accented and/or non-Roman) characters, you must use case-sensitive comparisons. Even then, there is no guarantee that IF LLT or IF LGT will work correctly (but IF EQUAL will).

Checking for Success and Failure

One of the most useful features of C-Kermit's programming language is the ability to take different actions depending on whether a command succeeded or failed. For example, if a command doesn't work as expected, you might want to print a message and stop or try a different command instead of going on to the next command or terminating the current script file or macro immediately. Every C-Kermit command except COMMENT and SHOW STATUS sets the SUCCESS/FAILURE indicator and the \v(status) variable when it completes; \v(status) is 0 if the most recent command succeeded, nonzero otherwise.

IF SUCCESS *command*

Executes the *command* if the previous command succeeded. Equivalent to IF NOT FAILURE. Synonym: **IF OK**. Example:

```
send oofa.txt
if success echo The SEND command succeeded.
else echo The SEND command failed.
```

You can inquire about the success or failure of the previous command with the SHOW STATUS command:

```
C-Kermit>type oofa.txt
?File not found - oofa.txt
C-Kermit>show status
 FAILURE
C-Kermit>set file type binary
C-Kermit>show status
 SUCCESS
C-Kermit>
```

IF FAILURE *command*

Executes the *command* if the previous command failed (i.e. if \v(status) is not 0). Equivalent to IF NOT SUCCESS. A command fails not only if it doesn't work, but also if it has a syntax error. Synonym: **IF ERROR**.

Checking Files and Directories

The following IF commands let you check whether files exist, or one file is newer than another, or whether a file is a directory:

IF EXIST *filename command*

Executes the *command* if a single, regular, readable file of the given name exists and it is not a directory or a wildcard file group specification. Here's an example in which we add the UNIX more command to the UNIX version of C-Kermit:

```
define MORE {
    if not def \%1 echo more what?     ; Make sure filename was given
    else if exist \%1 run more \%1     ; If file exists...
    else echo "\%1" not found          ; If file doesn't exist...
}
```

IF NEWER *filename1 filename1 command*

Executes the *command* if the file whose name is *filename1* is newer than the file whose name is *filename2*, according to the modification or creation dates of the two files. Both files must exist. Example:

```
if newer /usr/olga/\%f /usr/olaf/\%f send /usr/olga/\%f
else send /usr/olaf/\%f
```

IF DIRECTORY *filename command*

Executes the *command* if the *filename* refers to a directory. Here is an example showing how to ensure that a directory exists, creating it if it doesn't, and then making it the current directory:

```
if not directory \%d if not exist \%d mkdir \%d
if not directory \%d end 1 ERROR: \%d is not a directory
cd \%d
if fail end 1 Failure to change directory to \%d
```

(The END command is explained on page 375.)

Checking the Time

The SET ALARM and IF ALARM commands can be used to check whether a certain amount of time has elapsed or a specific time of day has passed:

SET ALARM *[{ number, hh:mm:ss }]*

Establishes a time in the future, either *number* seconds from now or the specific time given by *hh:mm:ss* (time of day in 24-hour time format), for use with subsequent IF ALARM statements. If the time-of-day format is used and the time is earlier than the current time, then it is taken to indicate the given time in the next day. If no time is given, then any pending alarm is cleared.

IF ALARM *command*

If the time established by the most recent SET ALARM command has passed, the *command* is executed. If the time is still in the future or if no alarm has been set, the COMMAND is not executed.

SHOW ALARM

Displays the date and time at which the current alarm, if any, expires.

Example:

```
echo Press any key to cancel - you have 10 seconds...
set alarm 10
pause 5
if fail end 1 Canceled
echo You have 5 more seconds...
pause 5
if not alarm end 1 Canceled
else echo Proceeding...
```

Other IF Commands

IF DEFINED *name command*

Executes the *command* if *name* is the name of a macro, a macro argument, a letter variable, a user-defined variable, a built-in variable, an environment variable, an invocation of a built-in function, or an array element that is defined and has a nonempty value. Example:

```
C-Kermit>define \%a foo              (Define a variable)
C-Kermit>if def \%a echo It's defined
It's defined
C-Kermit>undefine \%a               (Undefine it)
C-Kermit>if def \%a echo It's defined
C-Kermit>if not def \%a echo Not defined
Not defined
C-Kermit>
```

IF NUMERIC *name command*

Executes the *command* if *name* consists only of digits, or is a variable whose value consists only of digits, possibly with a leading plus or minus sign.

IF FOREGROUND *command*

(UNIX) Executes the *command* if Kermit is running in the foreground; that is, if its standard input is coming from the keyboard and its standard output is going to the screen. Example:

```
send oofa.txt
if success if foreground echo Transfer succeeded.
```

This command can be used to control whether messages are printed on the screen during execution of a command file or macro. If Kermit is running in the background, you probably don't want messages interfering with your foreground work.

IF BACKGROUND *command*

(UNIX) Executes the *command* if Kermit is running in the background, and/or with its standard input and/or output redirected. IF BACKGROUND is the same as IF NOT FOREGROUND.

IF COUNT *command*

This command is used for counted loops (explained later in this chapter). The COUNT variable may be referred to only as an IF condition, whereas the variable \v(count) can be used anywhere.

IF VERSION *number command*

Executes the *command* if C-Kermit's numeric version number is greater than or equal to the *number* given. The numeric version number is displayed by the VERSION command:

```
C-Kermit>version
C-Kermit 6.0.192, 6 Sep 96
 Numeric: 600192
C-Kermit>
```

The IF VERSION command gives C-Kermit command files and macros independence from the program version. For example, suppose a future release of C-Kermit — say, 710300 — has a new command SET BLOCK-CHECK 6 (the current release does not). If you guard new commands within IF VERSION statements, older releases of C-Kermit will not attempt to execute them:

```
if version 710300 set block-check 6
else set block-check 3
```

This would let the same script run on both newer and older versions of C-Kermit and select the highest available block check type without causing an error. You can refer to C-Kermit's numeric version in other contexts with the built-in variable \v(version):

```
if not < \v(version) 710300 set block-check 6
else echo No block-check 6 in version \v(version).
```

IF REMOTE-ONLY *command*
Executes the *command* if the "-R" (remote only) option was given on the command line or this version of C-Kermit can run only in remote mode. Used, for example, in initialization files to skip over sections that apply only to local mode, such as reading in the services directory. This allows C-Kermit to start faster when it is only going to be used in remote mode.

IF TRUE *command*
Always executes the *command*.

IF NOT TRUE *command*
Never executes the *command*.

IF FALSE *command*
Never executes the *command*.

IF NOT FALSE *command*
Always executes the *command*.

IF NOT NOT FALSE *command*
Never executes the *command*.

IF NOT NOT NOT FALSE *command*
Always executes the *command*.

And so on . . .

An EDIT Macro

Now we have all the tools we need to construct somewhat smart macros that are both useful and friendly. This one is called EDIT, and it lets you edit a file directly from C-Kermit command level with your favorite editor, returning you to the C-Kermit prompt when you are finished editing. The first time you use the EDIT macro, you must furnish the name of a file to edit. The next time, if you leave out the filename, the macro uses the same name as before. If you supply a new filename, the macro uses that one instead of the old one.

```
define myeditor emacs            (Name of my editor)
undefine myfile                  (No edit file specified yet)
define EDIT {                    (Define the EDIT macro)
    if > \v(argc) 2 echo WARNING: \%2 \%3 \%4 \%5 \%6... ignored
    if = \v(argc) 1 assign myfile \%1
    if not defined myfile echo Edit what?
    else run \m(myeditor) \m(myfile)
}
```

What's happening here? First, we defined a macro, MYEDITOR, to be the name of the system command that starts our favorite editor. If yours isn't EMACS, replace the word `emacs` with whatever you want. Then we ensured that the macro, MYFILE, is not defined.

Then we defined the EDIT macro itself, using block-structured style. If the argument count `\v(argc)` is greater than 2, we print a warning that extra arguments are ignored. If it is *at least* 2 — the macro name itself plus one argument — the argument `\%1` is taken as the name of a file to edit, and the value of this variable is assigned to the global macro MYFILE, which will hold our filename even after the EDIT macro completes. Next, we check to see if the MYFILE variable is defined. If it isn't, the user must have typed EDIT without giving the name of a file and had not specified a file name in any earlier EDIT command. So we just print a message and quit. But if MYFILE is defined, we execute the ELSE command, which runs our chosen editor on the file. Examples:

```
$ kermit                         (Start Kermit)
C-Kermit>edit                    (No previous filename)
Edit what?                       (Error message)
C-Kermit>edit oofa.txt

   (oofa.txt is edited...)

C-Kermit>edit                    (No filename given)

   (oofa.txt is edited, EDIT macro remembers last filename...)

C-Kermit>
```

Notice that we did not use IF EXIST to check if the argument was a real file. That was on purpose, to allow the EDIT command to create new files.

The STOP and END Commands

Macros and command files normally are terminated after C-Kermit reads and executes all their commands, or if they contain an EXIT or QUIT command, or if an error occurs and you have SET MACRO ERROR ON or SET TAKE ERROR ON. There are also two other ways to explicitly terminate execution of a macro or command file at any point:

STOP *[number [text]]*

This command returns you to the C-Kermit command prompt immediately from any level of command file or macro execution, no matter how deeply nested. When given at the C-Kermit prompt, the STOP command has no effect. If a *number* is given, it is used as a return code. If *text* is also given, it is printed on the screen. For example, here is a command file called TESTSTOP.KSC:

```
echo Testing the STOP command...
stop 1 This is an error message from the STOP command.
echo You shouldn't see this.
```

Now we execute it:

```
C-Kermit>take teststop.ksc
Testing the STOP command...
This is an error message from the STOP command.
C-Kermit>show status
  FAILURE
C-Kermit>
```

The number 1 in "STOP 1" is what caused the failure. STOP 0 would have resulted in success.

END *[number [text]]*

This command causes the current macro or command file to return immediately to the command level from which the current command file or macro was invoked. Thus it "returns" one level up the call stack, to its caller. The optional *number* is a return code, and the optional *text* is a message to be printed. Synonym: **POP**.

The default *number* is 0 (for success) for both commands. The *text* message cannot be printed unless a number is included before it.

The return code lets a macro or command file declare whether it succeeded or failed. For example, suppose you have defined a macro called SENDTWOFILES and you invoke it from inside a command file:

```
sendtwofiles
if success echo Macro succeeded.
```

The message will always appear, even if the macro failed, because the (implied) DO command itself succeeded. DO or TAKE commands fail only when the given macro or command file can't be found. To make the macro pass along a failure code, use the END or STOP command with a return code, as in this macro definition:

```
C-Kermit>take daily.tak
```

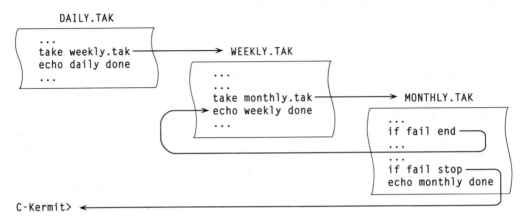

Figure 18-1 Returning from Nested Command Files

```
define SENDTWOFILES {
    set macro error off    ; This macro does its own error checking
    set file type text
    send oofa.txt
    if failure end 1 Can't send oofa.txt ; Return a failure status
    set file type binary
    send oofa.exe
    if fail end 1 Can't send oofa.exe   ; Return a failure status
    else end 0                          ; Return success
}
```

To illustrate the difference between STOP and END, suppose we have a command file called DAILY.KSC, which we run every day. This command file performs its daily tasks and then checks (using \v(day) or \v(nday)) to see if it is Friday. If so, it TAKEs another command file, WEEKLY.KSC, which in turn checks to see if it is the first week of the month,[44] and if so TAKEs MONTHLY.KSC. So our command files are nested 3 deep. Now suppose MONTHLY.KSC encountered an error and could not continue. If it gives the END command, WEEKLY.KSC will resume executing after its TAKE MONTHLY.KSC command. If MONTHLY.KSC gives the STOP command, C-Kermit will cancel all the command files and return to its prompt, as shown in Figure 18-1.

---

[44]By extracting the day of the month from \v(date) or \v(ndate). We'll learn about substrings later in this chapter.

The GOTO Command

So far we've used the decision-making capability of the IF statement in a very limited way: to execute or not execute a single command. But often, we would like to decide whether to execute whole groups of commands. There are two ways to do this. The way you know already is to group statements in macros or command files, because DO and TAKE count as single commands. Examples:

```
if equal \%a yes do this      ; "this" is a macro name
else take that.ksc            ; "that.ksc" is a command file
```

The new way is the GOTO command. It changes the order in which Kermit executes commands in a command file or a macro:

GOTO *label-name*

In a command file or a macro, go immediately to the first command after the first occurrence of the *label* in the current macro or command file and begin executing commands at that point. If the label is not found, return to the previous level (macro or command file) on the call stack and look there. Repeat this process until the label is found or the search fails. If the label is never found, C-Kermit returns to its prompt and issues an error message. In case of duplicate labels within a command file or macro, the first one is used.

The GOTO command has no effect as an interactive command or when piped into C-Kermit's command processor from standard input, except to cause an error message:

```
C-Kermit>goto sleep
?Sorry, GOTO only works in a command file or macro
C-Kermit>
```

A *label* is a character string of your choosing. It must begin with a colon (:), and it must be on a line by itself (but it can have a trailing comment). Here is an example of a command file that uses GOTO commands and labels to do what the MOVE command does, but with some additional messages:

```
set exit status 0             ; Clear any previous exit status
set file type text            ; Select text-mode transfers
send oofa.txt                 ; Send a text fail
if failure goto bad           ; Handle failure
delete oofa.txt               ; Worked OK - delete it
echo oofa.txt sent and deleted. ; Print message
goto done                     ; Skip around error handler
:BAD
echo oofa.txt was not sent.   ; Print error messages
echo Keeping oofa.txt.        ; and "fall through"
:DONE
end \v(exitstatus) Finished.  ; Return the transfer status
```

In this example, BAD and DONE are labels. If the file is sent successfully, it is deleted and the messages in the BAD section are skipped. If the file was not sent, it is not deleted and the messages in the BAD section are displayed. In both cases, the "Finished" message is displayed and the \v(exitstatus) variable, which becomes nonzero automatically if a file-transfer command fails, is used as the return code of the script.

Here is the same example converted to a macro that takes the filename as an argument:

```
define MYSEND {
    local rc                 ; Local variable for return code
    send \%1                 ; Send the file
    assign rc \v(status)     ; Remember the result
    if not \m(rc) goto bad
    delete \%1
    echo \%1 sent and deleted.
    goto done
  :BAD
    echo \%1 was not sent.
    echo Keeping \%1.
  :DONE
    end \m(rc) Finished.
}
```

You can use the MYSEND macro to send and delete any file:

```
C-Kermit>mysend oofa.txt
C-Kermit>mysend oofa.zip
```

The *label-name* by which the GOTO command refers to the label should be the same as the label, except that the colon can be omitted. Alphabetic case is always ignored when searching for labels. The following GOTO statements are all equivalent, meaning they all look for the same label, BEGIN:

```
goto begin
GoTo :begin
GOTO :BEGIN
```

GOTO label references can be (or contain) variables. This lets you execute different groups of commands depending on the value of a variable:

```
echo Setting parameters for \v(system)...
goto \v(system)
:UNIX
set parity even
set file character-set italian
end 0
:VMS
set parity none
set file character-set dec-mcs
end 0
; (and so on...)
```

Finally, here is an example that shows how Kermit peels back macro invocation levels to find the GOTO label:

```
define first :loop, echo \%0, do second
define second echo \%0, do third
define third echo \%0, goto loop
do first
```

If you put these commands into a command file and then TAKE it, you will soon see that it repeats forever: first, second, third, first, second, third, first, and so on. This is called a *loop*. Programmers call loops that go on forever *infinite loops*. You can terminate this infinite loop by typing Ctrl-C. But a way is also needed to terminate loops automatically, without human intervention.

But first, a brief note about performance. If you are writing a very long script — say, hundreds of lines — you should know that GOTO works by "rewinding" the current command file or macro and searching for the label from the beginning. This can slow down the execution of the script considerably under certain circumstances. But if you know that the target label is *ahead* of the GOTO, you can skip the rewinding:

FORWARD *label-name*
> Just like GOTO, but commences its search at the next command in the current command file or macro, rather than going back to the beginning.

Programming purists will find FORWARD an even greater atrocity than GOTO, and for good reason: if chunks of code are ever rearranged, they might easily stop working. Nevertheless, when performance is critical, this command can make a big difference. Later in this chapter, we'll present other mechanisms not only more structured but also more efficient than GOTO and FORWARD.

Counted Loops Using GOTOs

A somewhat more practical use of the GOTO command lets you repeat selected portions of a command file or macro a specified number of times. Before you can do this, you need a counting mechanism. C-Kermit offers several of these. The simplest one is the SET COUNT / IF COUNT construction:

SET COUNT *number*
> Sets the variable called COUNT to the given number, which must be greater than 0, for example:
>
> ```
> C-Kermit>set count 5
> ```

IF COUNT *command*
> Subtracts 1 from the COUNT variable. If the new value of COUNT is greater than 0, the *command* is executed.

The SET COUNT and IF COUNT commands can be combined with the GOTO command to form a counted loop:

```
set count 10
:loop
echo \v(count)
if count goto loop
echo Zero!
```

If you put these commands in a command file and TAKE the file, they print "10, 9, 8, 7, 6, 5, 4, 3, 2, 1, Zero!" You can do the same thing in a macro:

```
def COUNTDOWN -
  set count 10,:loop,echo \v(count),if count goto loop,echo Zero!
```

The COUNT "variable" is usable only as the condition of an IF statement. In other contexts, use the \v(count) variable, as shown. Referring to the \v(count) variable does not change its value; only IF COUNT does that.

Structured Programming

The SET COUNT / IF COUNT / GOTO mechanism is easy to use, but modern programming practice calls for a more structured approach. C-Kermit includes a selection of structured programming constructs, including a block-structured "extended" IF-ELSE command, a FOR loop, a WHILE loop, and SWITCH-CASE construction. Each of these allows groups of commands to be executed conditionally or repeatedly without the use of GOTOs.

The XIF Command

The XIF (extended IF) command lets you group multiple commands in the IF and ELSE parts, thus allowing groups of commands, rather than a single command, to be executed depending on the condition:

XIF *condition* { *command [, command . . .] }* [**ELSE** { *command [, command . . .] }]*
If the condition is true, execute the command or commands enclosed in the first set of curly braces. If an ELSE-part is provided, and the *condition* is not true, execute the commands inside the second set of curly braces. The conditions are the same as for the regular IF command. Examples:

```
xif < \%a \%b { echo \%a is less} else { echo \%b is less}

xif not exist oofa.txt { echo no oofa.txt!, stop } -
  else { send oofa.txt, echo oofa.txt sent ok. }
```

Note that whereas IF and ELSE are *separate* commands, the XIF-ELSE construction is a *single* command and therefore must be written on a single line or hyphenated for continuation as in the examples above.

You can also use block structure when writing XIF-ELSE commands. Here are the same XIF commands again, written in a more legible way and documented with comments:

```
xif < \%a \%b {             ; If \%a is less than \%b
    echo \%a is less        ; then print the value of \%a
} else {                    ; otherwise
    echo \%b is less        ; print the value of \%b
}

xif not exist oofa.txt {    ; If the file doesn't exist
    echo no oofa.txt!       ; print a message
    stop                    ; and stop
} else {                    ; otherwise
    send oofa.txt           ; transfer it
    echo oofa.txt sent ok   ; and print a message
}
```

When using block structure, remember the rules: a block *begins* when a left curly brace is the *last* non-comment, non-whitespace character on a line, and *ends* when a right curly brace is the *first* non-whitespace character on line. Thus:

```
} else {
```

both ends the previous block and begins the next one.

The commands within the blocks can be any commands at all, including other XIF commands. Here is a truly silly example of a macro that uses a nested, multipart XIF command to find the smallest of its three arguments:

```
def SMALLEST  {
    local result
    xif < \%1 \%2 {                          ; Compare first two args
        echo \%1 is less than \%2            ; First one is smaller
        xif < \%1 \%3 {                      ; Compare 1st with 3rd
            echo \%1 is less than \%3        ; The first is smaller
            asg result \%1                   ; Copy to result
        } else {                             ; 1st arg is not smaller
            echo \%1 is not less than \%3 ; Say so
            asg result \%3                   ; Copy to result
        }
    } else {                                 ; Otherwise
        echo \%1 is not less than \%2        ; The 2nd is smaller
        xif < \%2 \%3 {                      ; Compare it with 3rd
            echo \%2 is less than \%3        ; The 2nd is smaller
            asg result \%2                   ; Copy to result
        } else {                             ; The 3rd is smaller
            echo \%2 is not less than \%3
            asg result \%3                   ; Copy it to result
        }
    }
    echo So the smallest is \m(result).   ; Announce the winner
}
```

If you have stored this macro definition in a file called SMALLEST.KSC, you can issue a TAKE command to read the definition, and then you can try it out:

```
C-Kermit>take smallest.ksc      (This defines the macro)
C-Kermit>smallest 6 4 9         (Try it)
6 is not less than 4
4 is less than 9
So the smallest is 4.
C-Kermit>
```

FOR Loops

The FOR-loop construction lets you repeat one or more commands based on a counter, without using GOTOS, and also with a more flexible counter than the one used by SET COUNT / IF COUNT:

FOR *variable initial final increment* { *command [, command . . .]* }

Repeats the *commands* that are enclosed in braces a certain number of times, governed by the values of *initial, final,* and *increment,* which must all be numbers or variables with numeric values. First, the *initial* value is assigned to the *variable.* If the value has not passed the *final* value, the *commands* are executed. Then the *increment* is added to the *variable* and the process is repeated until the *variable* finally passes the *final* value. *Passes* means "becomes greater than" if the *increment* is positive, and it means "becomes less than" if the *increment* is negative. So the number of times the *commands* are executed is:

$$ n = \frac{final - initial}{increment} + 1 $$

If *n* is 0 or less, the commands are not executed at all.

Here are some simple examples:

```
for \%i 1 5 1 { echo hello }    ; Prints "hello" five times
```

You can read this as, "Counting from 1 to 5 by ones, echo the word hello."

```
for \%j 2 10 2 { echo \%j }     ; Counts to 10 by twos
```

Meaning: "Counting from 2 to 10 by twos, echo the counter." It prints 2, 4, 6, 8, and 10.

```
for \%k 10 0 -1 { echo \%k }    ; Counts backwards
```

This one means "Counting backwards from 10 to 0 by –1, print the counter." It prints 10, 9, 8, . . . , 0.

Here's an example in which we have an array `\&f[]` containing the names of files to be sent and then deleted, with appropriate messages printed. There are `\%n` filenames in the array. A file is deleted only if it is sent successfully. Since this loop is moderately long, we use block structure for ease of reading:

```
set file display none
for \%i 1 \%n 1 {
    echo Sending file \%i: \%f[\%i]...
    send \&f[\%i]
    xif success {
        echo OK - deleting \&f[\%i]
        delete \&f[\%i]
    } else {
        echo Failed - \&f[\%i] not deleted
    }
}
```

We use a "loop variable," \%i, to index the elements of an array; it increases by 1 (the increment) with each trip through the loop, thus accessing the next array element. We can use the same technique to print the command line and macro argument arrays. Recall that the array \&@[] contains the command-line arguments, and its highest element is one less than the value of the built-in variable \v(args); \&_[] is the macro argument array, highest element \v(argc) minus 1:

```
for \%k 0 \v(args)-1 1 { echo \\&@[\%k] = "\&@[\%k]" }
for \%k 0 \v(argc)-1 1 { echo \\%\%k = "\&_[\%k]" }
```

These examples show how arithmetic can be used on the loop variables.

FOR loops can contain many commands and can be nested. This example sorts the array \&x, which has \%n text elements, using the "Programming 101" bubble sort algorithm:

```
local \%i \%j \%t                     ; Local variables
for \%i 1 \%n-1 1 {                    ; Outer loop: i from 1 to n-1
    for \%j \%i \%n 1 {                ; Inner loop: j from i to n
        xif lgt \&x[\%i] \&x[\%j] {    ; Compare array elements
            asg \%t \&x[\%i]           ; If out of order,
            asg \&x[\%i] \&x[\%j]      ; exchange them
            asg \&x[\%j] \%t
        }
    }
}
for \%i 1 \%n 1 { echo \&x[\%i] }      ; All sorted - print them
```

WHILE Loops

The SET COUNT / IF COUNT and FOR-loop constructions let you execute groups of commands a certain number of times. But it is also sometimes desirable to loop until a certain condition is satisfied. That's what the WHILE loop is for:

WHILE *condition* { *command* [, *command*...] }
    Executes the *commands* as long as the *condition* is true.

The loop is entered only if the *condition* is true. Each time the end of the loop is reached, the WHILE command goes back to the top and evaluates the *condition* again and, if it is still true, executes the commands again, and so on until the condition becomes false or the loop is terminated some other way.

Here's how to print a message every minute, but only up until 11:00 p.m.:

```
while < \v(ntime) 82800 {
    echo The time is \v(time)
    sleep 60
}
```

And here is an example that uses C-Kermit's file transfer recovery feature to keep trying to send a file until it is completely transferred (we'll have a real-life example of this for you in the next chapter):

```
set file type binary      ; Transfer in binary mode
send bigfile.zip          ; Send this file
while failure {           ; If it failed
    resend bigfile.zip    ; Send the rest
}                         ; and so on until complete
```

Sometimes it is desirable to have an infinite loop. Suppose, for example, you want to have a Kermit receive files forever. That's where the TRUE condition comes in handy:

```
while true { receive }
```

In an XIF, FOR, or WHILE command, the part within the braces is called the *object command list*. In case you're curious, the XIF, FOR, and WHILE commands are implemented as Kermit macros (SHOW MACROS will display their definitions — don't try to understand them or you'll get a headache). The object command list is a single macro argument — so now you know why it's enclosed in braces.

Altering Loop Execution

The following commands let you exit from FOR or WHILE loops early or skip parts of them and go back to the top:

BREAK

Exits immediately from a SWITCH statement (next page) or a FOR or WHILE loop. The following example tries to send a file until it succeeds, up to 10 tries:

```
for \%i 1 10 1 { send bigfile.zip, if success break }
```

If loops are nested, BREAK exits from the innermost enclosing loop. BREAK is an illegal command if it is executed outside a SWITCH statement or a FOR or WHILE loop.

CONTINUE

Causes the next cycle of the enclosing FOR or WHILE loop to begin immediately, skipping any commands between the CONTINUE command and the end of the loop. Here's an example in which the array \&f[50] contains names of files, some of which might exist, others might not. This loop transfers the files that exist:

```
for \%i 1 50 1 { if not exist \&f[\%i] continue, send \&f[\%i] }
```

CONTINUE is illegal outside a FOR or WHILE loop.

The SWITCH Statement

The SWITCH statement is a convenient way to execute a specific group of commands based on the value of a variable, similar to the C-language `switch()` statement:

SWITCH *variable* { *case-list* }

The variable name must be the type that starts with a backslash, e.g. `\%a`, `\%1`, `\&a[1]`, `\m(foo)`, `\v(day)`, and so on. The *case-list* is a series of C-Kermit labels and commands. The SWITCH statement searches for a label in the case list that matches the value of the variable, and if it is found, executes all the statements after the label up to the first BREAK (or END, STOP, EXIT, etc) command, if any, or the end of the case list, whichever comes first. You may include a DEFAULT label for statements to be executed when no labels match the variable's value.

If you leave the BREAK command off the end of a case, Kermit "falls through" to the next case, as in case 2 in the following example, in which we print the name of the current day of the week in German:

```
switch \v(nday) {
    :0, echo Sonntag, break
    :1, echo Montag, break
    :2, echo Dienstag und zunächst kommt...
    :3, echo Mittwoch, break
    :4, echo Donnerstag, break
    :5, echo Freitag, break
    :6, echo Samstag, break
    :default, echo Invalid day - \v(nday)!
}
```

Like other structured programming commands, SWITCH statements may be nested. There should be no statements between SWITCH and first label — if there are, they will not be executed. The DEFAULT label, if any, should be last. Alphabetic case in matching the variable contents against the labels follows your INPUT CASE setting. Switch labels can be strings of any reasonable length, but they must be constants, not variables.

Like XIF, FOR, and WHILE, SWITCH is implemented internally as a macro. Therefore commas within the case list delimit commands (and labels). So be careful about using commas for other purposes, as in ECHO commands:

```
:default, echo Sorry, Invalid day - \v(nday)!
```

This makes Kermit complain about an invalid command called "Invalid". Instead use:

```
:default, echo {Sorry, Invalid day - \v(nday)!}
```

C-Kermit's structured programming constructs are intended for use within command files or macros and are not very handy to type interactively, but you can do it if you want to. You will find that question-mark help does not work on object commands, because they are just text passed as arguments to macros.

Built-in Functions

You're almost a full-fledged Kermit programmer. You have mastered decision making, GOTOs, loops, and structured programming. Next comes the *function call*. All programming languages offer a variety of built-in functions to perform operations on numbers or character strings, and C-Kermit's script language is no exception.

A function is a kind of "black box" into which you place some information and that returns a result based on that information. The items you give to the function are its *arguments*. There can be zero, one, two, or more arguments but only one result.

C-Kermit's built-in functions have names that look like this:

`\fname()`

That is, backslash, the letter *F*, the name of the function, and then a pair of parentheses to enclose its arguments. The F and the name can be upper- or lowercase. The name can be abbreviated to any length that distinguishes it from other built-in function names. The *arguments* are separated by commas, and can be constants or variables. For example, in:

`\fmax(\%a,100)`

the function's name is "max" and there are two arguments, `\%a` and `100`. The arguments are evaluated before the function is called; thus functions can not change the value of an argument variable.

The function reference is replaced by its return value. In this example, `\fmax()` is a function that returns the larger of its two arguments, which must be numeric:

```
C-Kermit>define \%a 333
C-Kermit>echo The maximum of \%a and 100 is "\fmax(\%a,100)".
The maximum of 333 and 100 is "333".
C-Kermit>
```

If the function call is illegal in any way, its result is null (empty):

```
C-Kermit>define \%a oofa
C-Kermit>echo The maximum of \%a and 333 is "\fmax(\%a,333)".
The maximum of oofa and 333 is "".
C-Kermit>
```

There is no other error indication, so in cases where there is some doubt whether an argument is legal, check it first:

```
if numeric \%a echo The maximum of \%a and 333 is "\fmax(\%a,333)"
else echo Error: "\%a" is not numeric
```

Function arguments can be literal strings of characters, variable names, macro arguments, array elements, backslash character codes, invocations of other functions, or any combination of these, but they are legal only if they represent the type of data required for the particular function argument.

Numeric arguments can be numbers like 0, -3, or 128, or they can be variables that have numeric values, or they can be arithmetic expressions containing any combination of numbers and variables. Examples:

```
C-Kermit>define \%x 7
C-Kermit>define \%y 8
C-Kermit>echo \fmax(7,8)
8
C-Kermit>echo \fmax(\%x,8)
8
C-Kermit>echo \fmax(\%x,\%y)
8
C-Kermit>echo \fmax(\fmax(\%x,55),\%x*\%y)
56
C-Kermit>echo \fmax(\%y+2,((\%x^2)/(\%y-1))+4)
11
C-Kermit>
```

The notation used in mathematical expressions is the natural one. The specific rules and notation are given later in this chapter, starting on page 394.

The function argument list normally should not contain spaces, but you can get away with it in contexts where the function reference is not in a single-word field:

```
C-Kermit>if = \fmax(8,7) 8 echo EQUAL
EQUAL
C-Kermit>if = \fmax(8, 7) ?Invalid: "if = \fmax(8,"
C-Kermit>echo The maximum of 8 and 7 is \fmax( 8, 7 ).
The maximum of 8 and 7 is 8.
C-Kermit>
```

Function arguments that contain commas, parentheses, or leading or trailing spaces must be enclosed in braces:

```
C-Kermit>echo "\fsubst({1, 2, 3,)4, 5},7,3)"
"3,)"
C-Kermit>
```

You can list of C-Kermit's built-in functions with the SHOW FUNCTIONS command:

```
C-Kermit>sho func

The following functions are available:

  \Fbasename()   \Fdate()        \Flength()    \Fpathname()  \Fspan()
  \Fbreak()      \Fdefinition()  \Fliteral()   \Frepeat()    \Fsubstring()
  \Fcapitalize() \Fevaluate()    \Flower()     \Freplace()   \Ftod2secs()
  \Fcharacter()  \Fexecute()     \Flpad()      \Freverse()   \Ftrim()
  \Fchecksum()   \Ffiles()       \Fltrim()     \Fright()     \Funhexify()
  \Fcode()       \Fhexify()      \Fmaximum()   \Frindex()    \Fupper()
  \Fcontents()   \Findex()       \Fminimim()   \Frpad()      \Fverify()
  \Fcrc16()      \Fipaddress()   \Fnextfile()  \Fsize()

C-Kermit>
```

Evaluation Functions

The following functions are used for evaluating their character-string arguments in specific ways:

`\Fliteral(arg)`

Copies its argument literally, preventing any evaluation of variables (or other functions) from taking place. Example:

```
C-Kermit>def \%a foo
C-Kermit>echo \flit(\%a) = \%a
\%a = foo
C-Kermit>
```

`\Fcontents(variable-name)`

Returns the current contents (definition) of a `\%` (letter or macro argument) variable. If the definition includes variable names or function references, these are copied literally, not replaced by their values. Thus, this function forces "1-level deep" evaluation of the kinds of variables that are usually evaluated "all the way down." Example:

```
C-Kermit>def \%a I like \%b.
C-Kermit>def \%b pizza
C-Kermit>echo \%a
I like pizza.
C-Kermit>echo \fcont(\%a)
I like \%b.
C-Kermit>
```

`\Fdefinition(macro-name)`

Returns the literal definition of the named macro. This is equivalent to the `\m()` notation for macro names. Example:

```
C-Kermit>define xxx echo \%1
C-Kermit>echo \fdef(xxx)
echo \%1
C-Kermit>echo \m(xxx)
echo \%1
C-Kermit>
```

Note how different degrees of textual replacement can be achieved by using (or not using) the `\fliteral()` and `\fcontents()` functions:

```
C-Kermit>def \%a foo              (\%a is "foo")
C-Kermit>def \%b I like \%ad.     (\%b includes \%a)
C-Kermit>echo \%b                 (Full replacement)
I like food.                      (Nested variables are handled)
C-Kermit>echo \fcont(\%b)         (Contents of \%b)
I like \%ad.                      (Nested variables not handled)
C-Kermit>echo \flit(\%b)          (Take it literally)
\%b                               (No replacement at all)
C-Kermit>
```

To force *full* evaluation of a macro, assign it to a letter variable and then use the letter variable wherever you want full evaluation to occur:

```
C-Kermit>define \%a Olga
C-Kermit>define whoiam My name is \%a.
C-Kermit>echo \fdef(whoiam)
My name is \%a.
C-Kermit>assign \%x \fdef(whoiam)
C-Kermit>echo \%x
My name is Olga.
```

Character Functions

The two functions in this category convert between single characters and their internal numeric representations:

\Fcharacter(*number*)

Returns the byte whose numeric code is given. The code must be in range 0–255. If you give a negative number or a number larger than 255, only the low-order 8 bits are used. Example:

```
C-Kermit>echo \fchar(79)\fchar(79)\fchar(70)\fchar(65)!
OOFA!
C-Kermit>
```

Characters in the range 128–255 depend on the character set. Here is a way to display your terminal's 8-bit character set (if you have an 8-bit connection to C-Kermit):

```
set command bytesize 8
for \%i 0 255 1 { echo \%i: [\fchar(\%i)] }
```

\Fcode(*character*)

Returns the numeric code of the given character, for example \fcode(A) is 65, the ASCII value of uppercase letter A. If the argument is longer than one character, the numeric code of the first character is returned. If there is no argument, an empty string is returned.

Note that \fcode(\fchar(\%a)) = \%a and \fchar(\fcode(\%b)) = \%b.

Character String Functions

The functions in this category are used for manipulating character strings. Their handling of alphabetic case is governed by the most recent SET CASE command. By default, alphabetic case is ignored.

\Fbreak(*text*,*string*)

Returns the given *text* up to the first occurrence of any character that is also in the given *string*. If no characters from the *string* also occur in the *text*, or the *string* is omitted, the entire *text* is returned. Examples:

```
C-Kermit>def digits 0123456789
```

```
C-Kermit>def \%a abcdefghijklmnop0123456789
C-Kermit>echo "\fbreak(\%a,d)"
"abc"
C-Kermit>echo "\fbreak(\%a,z)"
"abcdefghijklmnop123456789"
C-Kermit>echo "\fbreak(\%a,\m(digits))"
"abcdefghijklmnop"
C-Kermit>
```

Also see \fspan() and \fverify().

\Fcapitalize(*text*)

Returns the *text* with its initial letter uppercased and all subsequent letters lowercased. Synonym: \Fcaps(). Example:

```
C-Kermit>define \%a 1. this IS a LINE.
C-Kermit>echo "\fcaps(\%a)"
"1. This is a line."
C-Kermit>
```

This function is not guaranteed to work on accented or non-Roman letters.

\Fhexify(*text*)

Returns the hexadecimal representation of the given *text*. Example:

```
C-Kermit>echo "\fhex(Oofa!)"
4F6F666121
C-Kermit>
```

\Findex(*string1*,*string2* [,*number*])

Looks for a string, *string1*, in another string, *string2*, and tells its starting position:

```
C-Kermit>echo \find(ss,Mississippi)    (Find "ss" in Mississippi)
3
C-Kermit>
```

This means that the first occurrence of the string "ss" starts at position 3 in the string "Mississippi". You can also make this function start looking at a specified position in the string instead of starting from the beginning, by including the optional third argument, *number*, which must be a number or a variable that has a numeric value:

```
C-Kermit>echo \findex(ss,Mississippi,4)    (Find second "ss")
6
C-Kermit>
```

Character positions are numbered starting from 1. The first character is at position 1, the second character at position 2, and so on. If the string *string1* is not found in *string2*, the return value is zero:

```
C-Kermit>echo \findex(sss,Mississippi)
0
C-Kermit>
```

Any of the arguments can be variables of any kind (macro arguments, letter variables, array elements, or built-in variables), or even functions. In this example we find the position of the first "i" in "Mississippi" that comes after the first "s":

```
C-Kermit>def \%a Mississippi
C-Kermit>echo \findex(i,\%a,\findex(s,\%a)+1)
5
C-Kermit>
```

The example shows the \Findex function calling itself, which is permissible. For searching from the right, see \frindex(), "reverse index."

\Flength(*string*)

Returns the length of the argument string, after evaluation of any variables or functions it might contain. Example:

```
C-Kermit>def \%a oofa!        (Define a variable)
C-Kermit>echo \flen(\%a)      (Length of its value)
5                             (The length is 5)
C-Kermit>
```

\Flower(*text*)

Converts all uppercase letters in the *text* to lowercase, for example:

```
C-Kermit>define \%a FINE
C-Kermit>echo This is a \fLower(\%a Mess).
This is a fine mess.
C-Kermit>
```

\Flpad(*text*,*number*,*character*)

Left-pads the *text* to length *number* with *character*. If the *character* is omitted, blank (space) is used. Handy for lining things up. Examples:

```
C-Kermit>def xx echo \flpad(\%1,10)
C-Kermit>xx 20
        20
C-Kermit>xx 1996
      1996
C-Kermit>echo \flpad($50,10,*)
*******$50
C-Kermit>
```

Also see \frpad().

\Fltrim(*text*,*string*)

"Left trim." Returns the string that is obtained by removing all characters from the left of the *text* that are also in the *string*, stopping with the first character that is not in the *string*. If the *string* is omitted, spaces and tabs ("whitespace") are removed. Also see \Ftrim().

\Frepeat(*text*,*number*)

Repeats the first argument the number of times given by the second argument:

```
C-Kermit>echo \frepeat(=,10)
==========
C-Kermit>echo +\frep(-+,10)
+-+-+-+-+-+-+-+-+-+-+
```

`\Freplace(text,string1,string2)`

Returns the string obtained by replacing all occurrences of *string1* in the given *text* with *string2*. *string2* can be omitted, in which case all occurrences of *string1* are removed from the *text*. If *string1* is empty or omitted, the result is the *text* argument, unchanged. Examples:

```
C-Kermit>echo \freplace(oofa,o,O)
OOfa
C-Kermit>echo \freplace(oofa,o,oo)
oooofa
C-Kermit>echo \freplace(oofa,o)
fa
C-Kermit>echo \freplace(oofa,fa,ps)
oops
C-Kermit>echo \freplace(oofa)
oofa
C-Kermit>
```

or (more practically for DOS, Windows, and OS/2):

```
C-Kermit>echo \freplace(\v(cmdfile),\\,/)
c:/kermit/scripts/login.ksc
C-Kermit>echo \freplace(\v(cmdfile),\\,\\\\)
c:\\kermit\\scripts\\login.ksc
C-Kermit>
```

`\Freverse(text)`

Reverses the order of the characters in its text argument, for example:

`\frev(mupeen)` is neepum.

`\Fright(text,length)`

Is replaced by the rightmost *length* characters of the *text*, or the entire *text*, whichever is shorter. Example:

```
C-Kermit>echo "\fRight(kermit.exe,4)"
".exe"
C-Kermit>
```

`\Frindex( string1,string2 [ ,number ] )`

Right index. Searches for *string1* in *string2* starting from the right. If the optional *number* is included, the rightmost *number* characters of *string2* are skipped before commencing the search. Returns the 1-based position in *string2* of the string that was found or 0 if none was found. Also see `\findex()`.

`\Frpad(text,number,character)`

Right-pads the *text* to length *number* with *character*. If *character* is omitted, blank (space) is used. Also see `\flpad()`.

`\Fspan(text,string)`

Returns as much of the given *text*, starting from the left, that contains only characters that are also in the given *string*. Example:

```
C-Kermit>define digits 0123456789
C-Kermit>define \%a 73751 El Camino Real
C-Kermit>echo "\fspan(\%a,\m(digits))"
"73751"
C-Kermit>
```

Also see \fbreak().

\Fsubstring(*text*,*start*,*length*)

The result of this function is the portion of the *text* argument that starts at position *start* and is *length* characters long; *text* can be any text and can also be, or include, variable names, other functions, etc.; *start* and *length* must be numbers or variables or functions that have numeric values. The start position is 1 for the first character, 2 for the second, and so on. Example:

```
C-Kermit>echo "\fsubst(hello there,7,3)"
"the"
C-Kermit>
```

If the length argument is omitted, all of the characters from the starting position to the end are returned:

```
C-Kermit>def \%a 123456789
C-Kermit>ech \fsub(\%a,4)
456789
C-Kermit>
```

\Ftrim(*text*,*string*)

Returns the string that is obtained by removing all characters from the right of the *text* that are also in the *string*, stopping with the first character that is not in *string*. If the *string* is omitted, spaces and tabs ("whitespace") are removed. Also see \Fltrim().

\Funhexify(*hexadecimal-string*)

Returns the text obtained from decoding the *hexadecimal-string*. Example:

```
C-Kermit>echo "\funhex(4F6F666121)"
"Oofa!"
C-Kermit>
```

If the string contains any non-hex characters (i.e. other than 0–9, a–f, or A–F), or has an odd length, the empty string is returned. Also see \fhexify().

\Fupper(*text*)

Converts all lowercase letters in its text argument to uppercase. Also see \flower().

\Fverify(*string1*,*string2*,*number*)

Returns the 1-based position of the first character in *string2* that is not also in *string1*. If a *number* is given, the characters in *string2* at positions 1 through *number* are ignored. If no characters in *string2* are not also in *string1*, 0 is returned. Use this function for preverifying hexadecimal numbers, phone numbers, and so on:

```
if \fverify(01234567,\%a) echo "\%a" - not an octal number.
```

Integer Arithmetic Functions and Commands

These functions require numeric arguments — whole numbers, or variables or functions whose values are whole numbers — which can be positive or negative. If the arguments are illegal in any way, these functions return the null (empty) string.

\Fmax(*n1*,*n2*)

Returns the maximum of its two numeric arguments. Examples:

```
C-Kermit>define \%x 9
C-Kermit>echo \fmax(12,\%x)
12
```

\Fmin(*n1*,*n2*)

Returns the minimum of its two numeric arguments.

\Fmod(*n1*,*n2*)

Returns the *modulus* of the two arguments; that is, remainder after dividing *n1* by *n2*. Example:

```
C-Kermit>echo \fmod(\v(ntime),60)
27
C-Kermit>
```

\Fevaluate(*expression*)

Evaluates the given arithmetic expression. The precedence is the normal, intuitive algebraic (or programming) precedence, and can be altered by the use of parentheses, which have higher precedence than any other operator. Spaces may be used to separate operators from operands, but they are not required. Examples:

```
C-Kermit>def \%x 6
C-Kermit>def \%y 10

C-Kermit>echo \feval(\%x)
6
C-Kermit>echo \feval(\%x + 2)
8
C-Kermit>echo \feval((\%x+2) * \%y)
80
C-Kermit>echo \feval(\%x + (2*\%y))
26
```

Table 18-1 shows the mathematical operators accepted by \feval(). The heading marked *Fix* tells where the operator goes in relation to its operands. The choices are *in* (the operator goes in between its operands, for example 2+2); *pre* (it goes before its operand, for example −1, minus one); *post* (it goes after its operand, for example 3!, three factorial); or *circum* (it goes around its operands, for example (2+2), two plus two in parentheses). The Precedence column shows the precedence of the operator: the lower the number, the higher the precedence. For example, * has higher precedence than + so:

\feval(2 * 3 + 4 * 5)

is 26 because the multiplications are done before the addition (as you learned in school).

Table 18-1 \Feval() Operators

Operator	Fix	Precedence	Operation	Example	Result
\%a = 2,	\%b = -3,	\%c = 7,	\%d = 27		
( )	circum	1	Group	(\%a + 3) * (\%b-5)	-40
!	post	2	Factorial	\%c!	5040
~	pre	3	Logical NOT	~1	-2
-	pre	3	Negate	-\%a	-2
^	in	4	Raise to power	2^\%c	128
*	in	5	Multiply	\%c * 5	35
/	in	5	Divide	\%d / 5	5
%	in	5	Modulus	\%d % 5	2
&	in	5	Logical AND	\%d & 7	3
+	in	6	Add	\%a + \%c	9
-	in	6	Subtract	31 \%c	24
|	in	6	Logical OR	\%c | 4	4
#	in	6	Exclusive OR	\%d#7	28
@	in	6	Greatest Common Divisor	\%d @ 51	3

As you can see from the table, parentheses have the highest precedence of all, so you can use them to change the order of evaluation:

```
\feval(2 * (3 + 4) * 5)
```

This makes Kermit evaluate the expression in parentheses, (3+4), first, so the result is 70 rather than 26.

Only integer arithmetic is available: no fractions, no decimals, no scientific notation. The remainder of an integer division operation is discarded (except, of course, by the modulus operator, which discards the quotient).

Note that the # Exclusive OR operator is the same as one of Kermit's comment introducers, so you can't use it in an \feval() function unless you make sure it is not followed by a space:

```
C-Kermit>echo \feval(7 # 2)
?Invalid   echo \feval(7 #
C-Kermit>echo \feval(7#2)
5
```

See the rules for comments on page 32.

Several Kermit commands are also available to perform simple arithmetic on variables:

EVALUATE *expression*

This command evaluates the given *expression*, printing the result and also assigning it to the `\v(evaluate)` built-in variable. Examples:

```
C-Kermit>eval \v(ntime) / 3600
16
C-Kermit>echo Today is already \v(eval) hours long...
Today is already 16 hours long...
C-Kermit>
```

INCREMENT *name [value]*

Adds the *value* to the named variable. If the *value* is omitted, adds 1. If the variable does not have a numeric value, prints an error message and fails. Examples:

```
C-Kermit>def \%a 9
C-Kermit>increment \%a
C-Kermit>echo \%a
10
C-Kermit>incr \%a 5
C-Kermit>echo \%a
15
C-Kermit>incr \%a -20
C-Kermit>echo \%a
-5
C-Kermit>
```

DECREMENT *name [value]*

Subtracts the *value* from the named variable. If the *value* is omitted, subtracts 1. If the variable does not have a numeric value, prints an error message and fails. This example is a loop that counts down from 10 to 0:

```
def \%i 10
while not < \%i 0 { echo \%i, decr \%i }
```

The *value* given in the INCREMENT and DECREMENT commands need not be a constant. You can include variables:

```
C-Kermit>define \%n 1
C-Kermit>while < \%n 5000 { echo \%n, increment \%n \%n }
 1 2 4 8 16 32 64 128 256 512 1024 2048 4096
C-Kermit>
```

And you can use any other item that C-Kermit can evaluate into a number: backslash character codes, array references, function invocations, environment variables, or built-in variables, even expressions:

```
C-Kermit>define \%x 24
C-Kermit>decrement \%x (\v(ntime)+1800)/3600
C-Kermit>echo { Hours remaining till midnight: \%x}
 Hours remaining till midnight: 8
C-Kermit>
```

File Functions

C-Kermit offers the following functions for expanding "wildcard" file-group notation into lists of files and for obtaining information about files:

\Ffiles(*filespec*)

Returns the number of files that match the given file specification, for example:

```
C-Kermit>echo \ffiles(ck*.c)
37
C-Kermit>
```

If no files match, the result is 0. If too many files match, the result is –1.

\Fnextfile()

Returns the next filename that matches the \Ffiles() file specification, until none are left, or you use \Ffiles() again, or you execute any command (such as SEND, TYPE, or OPEN) that parses a filename. \Ffiles() and \Fnextfile let you write loops that process a selected group of files.

\Fpathname(*filespec*)

Returns the full pathname of the given file specification. The *filespec* can be wild, and it can refer to a file that does not exist. Example:

```
C-Kermit>pwd
/usr/olga/budget
C-Kermit>echo \fpathname(fy9697.wks)
/usr/olga/budget/fy9697.wks
C-Kermit>
```

\Fbasename(*filespec*)

Returns the filename portion of the file specification; directory, device, and other fields are removed; opposite of \fpathname().

\Fdate(*filename*)

Returns the creation or modification date of the file in *yyyymmdd hh:mm:ss* format:

```
C-Kermit>echo \fdate(oofa.txt)
19960906 23:23:00
C-Kermit>
```

\Fsize(*filename*)

Returns the size in bytes of the given file:

```
C-Kermit>echo \fsize(oofa.txt)
162
C-Kermit>
```

Here's an example showing how to make a do-it-yourself MYDIRECTORY command, that produces a nice lined-up listing with totals at the end:

```
define MYDIRECTORY {
    local \%f \%n \%x size               ; Local variables
    echo Directory of \fpathname(\%1): ; Print heading
    assign size 0                        ; Initialize total size
    assign \%n \ffiles(\%1)              ; How many files match
    for \%i 1 \%n 1 {                    ; Loop for each file
        asg \%f \fnextfile()             ; Get next file
        asg \%x \fsize(\%f)
        echo \frpad(\%f,16) \flpad(\%x,8) \fdate(\%f)
        increment size \%x
    }
    echo {Total files: \%n, Total bytes: \m(size)}
}
```

The next example defines a macro called AUTOSEND that you can use to send a wildcard group of files to a Kermit server, switching between text and binary modes automatically for each file. In this case, binary mode is used if the last four characters of the file's name are .exe.

```
define AUTOSEND {
    local \%n
    assign \%n \ffiles(\%1)                    ; How many files match
    echo files = \%n                           ; Print a message
    declare \&f[\%n]                           ; Make an array for names
    for \%i 1 \%n 1 {                          ; Copy names into array
        asg \&f[\%i] \fnextfile()
    }
    for \%i 1 \%n 1 {                          ; Loop for each file
        if eq {.exe} {\fright(\&f[\%i],4)} {   ; If suffix is .exe
            set file type binary,              ; use binary mode
            echo Sending \&f[\%i] (binary)     ; print a message
        } else {                               ; Otherwise
            set file type text                 ; use text mode
            echo Sending \&f[\%i] (text)       ; print a message
        }
        send \&f[\%i]                          ; and send the file
    }
}
```

Invoke this macro with a command like:

```
C-Kermit>autosend oofa.*
```

Replace oofa.* with the file specification of your choice. Of course, this example depends on the receiving Kermit's ability to switch automatically between text and binary mode based on the Attribute packet sent by C-Kermit (see Table 1-1).

Miscellaneous Functions

`\Fipaddress(`*`string,number`*`)`

> Returns the first IP address found in the *string*, searching from the left, starting at position *number*, or from the beginning if the *number* is omitted. Useful for getting your IP address from a SLIP server's message. Typically used on the `\v(input)` variable after an INPUT command, explained in the next chapter.

`\Ftod2secs(`*`hh:mm:ss`*`)`

> Converts a time of day in hours:minutes:seconds format into seconds since midnight and returns the result.

User-Defined Functions

A user-defined function is a macro that returns a value, invoked as if it were a built-in function. To return a value, a new command is needed:

RETURN *[value]*

> Terminates the execution of the current macro and makes the *value* available to the caller (that is, the command level from which the macro was invoked). If the RETURN command is used in a command file, it can not return a value; only macros may return values. If the RETURN command is given without a value, an empty (null) value is returned, in which case it is equivalent to the END 0 command.

To illustrate, here is a simple function that returns the first character of its argument:

```
define first return \fsubstr(\%1,1,1)
```

Its return value is made available in the built-in variable `\v(return)`:

```
C-Kermit>first oofa
C-Kermit>echo The first character of "oofa" is "\v(return)".
The first character of "oofa" is "o".
C-Kermit>
```

But, more usefully, it also becomes the return value of the `\fexecute()` function:

`\Fexecute(`*`macro[,arguments...]`*`)`

> Executes the *macro* whose name is given, with the given arguments, if any, and returns the macro's RETURN value, or the empty string if the macro does not return a value. The macro name and arguments are separated by commas or spaces. Example:
>
> ```
> C-Kermit>echo The first character of \%a is "\fexec(first,\%a)".
> The first character of oofa is "o".
> C-Kermit>define paste return (\%1)(\%2)(\%3)
> C-Kermit>echo "\fexec(paste,One,Two,{Three,Four,Five})"
> "(One)(Two)(Three,Four,Five)"
> C-Kermit>
> ```

The last one shows how to use braces to protect commas *within* macro arguments from being taken for the commas that *separate* macro arguments.

Functions that Call Themselves

"In order to understand recursion, first we must understand recursion." – anon.

A user-defined function can call upon built-in functions and other user-defined functions, and it can even call upon itself. Here, for example, is a function that adds all the numbers from 1 up to and including its argument:[45]

```
def SUM {
    if not def \%1 return      ; Make sure there is an argument
    if not numeric \%1 return  ; Make sure argument is numeric
    if not > \%1 0 return      ; Make sure argument is positive
    if = \%1 1 return 1        ; If argument is 1, the sum is 1
    else return \feval(\%1+\fexec(sum,\feval(\%1-1)))
}
```

Translated into English, it reads something like this: If you ask me to add up all the numbers from 1 to 1, I can tell you right away the answer is 1. If the number is larger than 1, the answer is the number you gave me plus the sum of all the numbers less than that. The process repeats to get the sum of "all the numbers less than that," until we reach 1, and then the results are returned up the call stack and accumulated along the way. This process is called *recursion*. To give yourself a better idea how it works, try working through the SUM function for the number 4.

You can write a simple macro to call the SUM function and print its value:

```
C-Kermit>def addemup echo sum = \fexec(sum,\%1)
C-Kermit>addemup 6
sum = 21
C-Kermit>addem 11
sum = 66
C-Kermit>
```

This is just an illustration of how recursion works and is not intended for practical applications. Recursion depth is limited to the size of C-Kermit's macro call stack (as revealed by SHOW COMMAND), so if you need a version of SUM that works satisfactorily for larger numbers, do it Carl's way:

```
define SUM return \feval(\%1*(\%1+1)/2)
```

One final note about user-defined functions: any Kermit action commands (like SEND, CONNECT, etc) are ignored by \fexecute(). This is because the \fexecute() function is parsed and executed in the middle of another command, and affairs would become quite confused if a file transfer display or terminal emulation screen suddenly popped up before the command containing the \fexecute() was finished.

---

[45]Of course, we all know there is a closed solution to this problem: $n \times (n + 1) / 2$, compliments of the 7-year-old Carl Friedrich Gauss (1777–1855).

Can We Talk?

You can already carry on a dialog with C-Kermit. It prompts you for a command, you type a command, it prompts you for another one, and so on. You can do this because you know what C-Kermit's commands are. But suppose you want to set up a procedure for someone who is not familiar with Kermit. Here are the commands you can use to issue prompts on the screen and read responses from the keyboard:

ASK *variable [text]*

> Prints the text on the screen and reads what the user types in response, up to a carriage return. Stores what the user types in the named variable, without the carriage return. The variable can be a letter variable (\%a-z), a macro argument (\%1-9), an array element (\&a-z[]), or a macro name. The user's characters echo on the screen as they are typed.

ASKQ *variable [text]*

> "Ask Quietly." Just like ASK, but does not echo what the user types. Use ASKQ to read passwords or other sensitive information.

Example:

```
C-Kermit>ask name   What is your name\?
What is your name?Olaf
C-Kermit>askq \%p Hello, \m(name), what's your password\?
Hello Olaf, what's your password?_____
C-Kermit>
```

As you can see, Kermit strips leading and trailing blanks from the ASK and ASKQ prompts, and it requires you to quote any question marks in the prompt with backslash (an unquoted question mark gives a help message at top level, but not in command files or macros). If you want to have leading or trailing spaces in the prompt, enclose it in curly braces:

```
C-Kermit>ask name {   What is your name\? }
   What is your name? Olaf you idiot
C-Kermit>askq \%p {   Hello, \m(name), what's your password\? }
   Hello Olaf you idiot, what's your password? _____
C-Kermit>
```

When the user responds to the prompt, all of Kermit's special command editing keys are active: Delete, Backspace, Ctrl-W, Ctrl-U, Ctrl-R, etc., so the user doesn't have to worry about not making mistakes.

In an interactive dialog with a user, it is common to ask a question that requires a Yes or No answer. A friendly program does not care if the user spells these words out in full or abbreviates them, or about their alphabetic case. And neither does C-Kermit's GETOK command:

GETOK *[text]*

Asks the user a yes-or-no question. The *text* is the question. If you omit the text, Kermit supplies the question "Yes or no?" The user can answer by typing Yes, No, or OK in upper or lowercase, abbreviated or in full. Any other answer results in an error message and a repetition of the question. The GETOK command succeeds if the user gives an affirmative answer and fails if the answer is negative. Here is an example in which the user is asked whether temporary files should be deleted, and then the files are deleted or not according to the answer:

```
getok Should I delete your temporary files\?
xif success {
    echo Deleting temporary files *.tmp...
    delete *.tmp
} else {
    echo OK, I won't.
}
```

To include leading or trailing blanks, enclose the question text in curly braces:

```
C-Kermit>getok \%a { OK to proceed\? }
 OK to proceed? ok
C-Kermit>sho status
 SUCCESS
C-Kermit>
```

You can also prompt the user for a single character:

GETC *variable [text]*

Prints the *text*, waits for the user to type a character, and stores the character in the given *variable*. The character is not echoed. Example:

```
getc \%a Press any key to continue:
```

Calculators and Adding Machines

Here is a macro you can use to have Kermit evaluate arithmetic expressions for you interactively. Kermit's answer to the pocket calculator:

```
define CALC {
    echo Press Return to exit        ; Say how to exit
    def \%1 1                         ; Initial condition for loop
    while defined \%1 {               ; Loop until they want to exit
        ask \%1 { expression: }       ; Ask for an expression
        echo \flpad(\feval(\%1),10)   ; Evaluate and print answer
    }
    echo Back to...                   ; All done
}
```

To use the calculator, first execute this macro definition.[46] Then just type CALC at any

---

[46]You'll find a copy in the command demonstration file, CKEDEMO.KSC, that is distributed with C-Kermit.

time at the C-Kermit prompt. You can type any kind of arithmetic expression listed in Table 18-1, and the operands can be either integer constants or variables that have integer values.

```
$ kermit                                  (Start Kermit)
C-Kermit 6.0.192, 6 Sep 96
Type ? or HELP for help
C-Kermit>def \%a 7                        (Define some variables)
C-Kermit>def \%b 9
C-Kermit>calc                             (Start the calculator)
Press Return to exit

 expression: 1+1                          (Add 1 and 1)
          2
 expression: 6!                           (6 factorial)
        720
 expression: 2^16                         (2 to the 16th power)
      65536
 expression: (\%a + 3) * (\%b    5)       (Expression with variables)
         40
 expression:                              (Press Return to exit)

Back to...
C-Kermit>
```

Here is a small interactive program that imitates an adding machine, illustrating the use of ASKQ along with functions that line things up, WHILE loops, and other items you learned in this chapter. But first, let's learn one more command:

XECHO *[text]*

Just like ECHO, but does not supply a carriage return and linefeed at the end of the *text*. For use only in scripts; if you use it at the prompt, the next prompt is likely to overwrite whatever you just XECHOed. Synonym: **WRITE SCREEN**.

Now here's the adding machine, in which we use XECHO to avoid cluttering up the screen with blank lines:

```
define ADDINGMACHINE {
    local \%s
    echo Adding machine.
    echo Type numbers or press Return to quit...
    assign \%s 0                              ; Initialize the sum
    while true {                              ; Loop till done
        askq \%1                              ; Wait for a number
        if not def \%1 break                  ; Return quits loop
        increment \%s \%1                     ; Add it to the sum
        xecho \flpad(\%1,10)\flpad(\%s,10)    ; Print results
    }
    echo Total\flpad(\%s,15,.)
}
```

Once this macro is defined (for example, by TAKEing the C-Kermit demo file) you can add up a column of numbers any time you want (integers only, positive or negative): just type ADDINGMACHINE at the C-Kermit prompt.

Using Escape Sequences

When commands like ECHO and ASK print your text on the screen, they evaluate all variables and other backslash codes first. This lets you achieve special effects on the screen. For example, you can send escape sequences for clearing the screen, positioning the cursor, highlighting text, changing colors, and so on. Kermit itself has no built-in knowledge of terminal control sequences, so you're on your own for this. A common terminal type is the DEC VT100 series [27], and some useful escape sequences (which also apply to the VT200, 300, and higher series) are listed in Table 18-2. For other types of terminals, see your terminal manual.

Several of the entries in the table require you to insert specific values. The escape sequence to position the cursor to a specific row and column needs the row and column number, separated by a semicolon (;). The rows and columns are numbered from 1. So, to position the cursor in the upper left corner of the screen:

```
xecho \27[1;1H
```

and to put it in row 17, column 53:

```
xecho \27[17;53H
```

To "home" the cursor and clear the screen:

```
xecho \27[1;1H\27[2J
```

The escape sequence for setting the scrolling region requires the row numbers of the top and bottom lines; for example, to use lines 7 through 24:

```
xecho \27[7;24r
```

To make the whole screen the scrolling region, use:

```
xecho \27[r
```

The escape sequences for setting foreground and background color are from ANSI X3.64 [4] and usable with most terminal emulators in ANSI or VT terminal mode. The x in the escape sequence is replaced by a digit between 0 and 7 to select the color (0 = black, 1 = red, 2 = green, 3 = orange, 4 = blue, 5 = amethyst, 6 = turquoise, 7 = white), for example:

```
xecho \27[36m\27[45m
```

results in turquoise characters on an amethyst background.

Here is an example for you to try. If you have a color-capable ANSI or VT terminal emulator (such as MS-DOS Kermit, Kermit 95, or Kermit/2), the results will be in technicolor. Put these commands in a file and TAKE the file from C-Kermit:[47]

---

[47]A copy of this file is distributed with C-Kermit as CKEVT.KSC so you don't have to type it in.

Table 18-2 Selected VT100 Escape Sequences

Escape Sequence	Kermit Notation	Description
Ctrl-H	\8	Backspace cursor
Ctrl-I	\9	Horizontal tab
ESC # 3	\27#3	Double height/width line, top half
ESC # 4	\27#4	Double height/width line, bottom half
ESC # 6	\27#6	Double width line
ESC D	\27D	Moves cursor down one line
ESC M	\27M	Moves cursor up one line
ESC [r ; c H	\27[r;cH	Moves cursor to row r, column c
ESC [t ; b r	\27[t;br	Sets scrolling region from row t to row b
ESC [0 J	\27[0J	Erases from cursor to end of screen
ESC [1 J	\27[1J	Erases from start of screen to cursor
ESC [2 J	\27[2J	Erases entire screen
ESC [0 K	\27[0K	Erases from cursor to end of line
ESC [1 K	\27[1K	Erases from start of line to cursor
ESC [2 K	\27[1K	Erases entire line
ESC [? 5 h	\27[\?5h	Reverse video, whole screen
ESC [? 5 l	\27[\?5l	Normal video, whole screen
ESC [0 i	\27[0i	Prints current screen
ESC [4 i	\27[4i	Stops transparent printing
ESC [5 i	\27[5i	Starts transparent printing
ESC [0 m	\27[0m	Regular characters
ESC [1 m	\27[1m	Bold characters
ESC [2 m	\27[2m	Underscored characters
ESC [5 m	\27[5m	Blinking characters
ESC [7 m	\27[7m	Reverse-video characters
ESC [3x m	\27[3xm	Selects foreground color ($x = 0$ through 7)
ESC [4x m	\27[4xm	Selects background color ($x = 0$ through 7)
ESC Z	\27Z	Terminal type query (host to terminal)
ESC [? 1 c	\27[\?1c	VT100 terminal ID (terminal to host)
ESC [? 6 c	\27[\?6c	VT102 terminal ID (terminal to host)
ESC [? 62 c	\27[\?62c	VT200 terminal ID (terminal to host)
ESC [? 63 c	\27[\?63c	VT300 terminal ID (terminal to host)
ESC _ *text* ESC \	\27_*text*\27\	Application Program Command

```
define on_exit echo \27[r\27[0m\27[1;1H\27[2JGoodbye!
define \%g \27[0m\27[32m\27[7m\frepeat(=,80)\27[0m\27[34m
echo \27[1;1H\27[2J\%g\27[47m
ask \%n { What is your name\? \27[30m\27[7m}
echo \%g
echo \27[35m\27[5m Welcome to Kermit, \27[30m\27[5m\%n\13\10\%g
echo \13\10\27[0J\27[7;24r\27[22;1H
set prompt {\%g\13\10 \27[33mWhat is your command\? \27[34m}
```

Without giving away any secrets, it can be observed that this program does some unusual things to VT-series terminals. Note the use of the ON_EXIT macro to put the terminal back to normal when C-Kermit exits.

PC Printing

Here is a simpler but perhaps more practical use for escape sequences. It lets C-Kermit print a file on your local printer if you have a VT100-series terminal (VT102 or higher), or a PC running a VT terminal emulator, with a printer attached. We define a macro, VTPRINT, to send the escape sequence to turn on "transparent printing," then display the file, which should cause your terminal or emulator to send the text to the printer instead of the screen, and then send the escape sequence to turn off transparent printing:

```
define VTPRINT xecho \27[5i, type \%1, xecho \27[4i
```

Execute this macro definition, and then print files on your local printer like this:

```
C-Kermit>vtprint oofa.txt
```

Some printers might require a formfeed (ASCII 12) at the end to force the last or only page out of the printer. In that case:

```
define vtprint xecho \27[5i, type \%1, xecho \12\27[4i
```

Sending APC Commands

Recall from Chapters 8 and 13 that Application Program Command escape sequences can be used to send commands to Kermit programs through their terminal emulators (if you, the user of the local Kermit program, have enabled APCs with SET TERMINAL APC ON). This opens the door to all sorts of interesting possibilities. For example, any application can customize the local Kermit program's key map.

Suppose, for example, the application is C-Kermit, and the terminal emulator is MS-DOS Kermit. C-Kermit can assign shortcuts to PC hot keys (note the double backslashes; remember, use two backslashes to when you need to refer to one backslash literally):

```
define mykeys apc {set key \\4424 \\2, set key \\4432 \\14}
def on_exit apc {set key \\4424 \\kpuparr, set key \\4432 \\kpdnarr}
```

In this example, C-Kermit sets the PC's gray up- and down-arrow keys to send Ctrl-B and Ctrl-N, respectively, which are C-Kermit's command recall keys. And by defining the ON_EXIT macro appropriately, it also ensures that when C-Kermit exits it restores the normal definitions for these keys.

Some software vendors distribute files with hundreds of SET KEY commands, to be used by the Kermit terminal emulator when accessing the vendor's application. When the vendor's application starts, it issues an APC sequence containing a TAKE command for its keymap file, rather than issuing hundreds of SET KEY commands inside of APC sequences.

APCs are seeing increasing use by "system integrators," who write automated scripts allowing users to perform specific tasks without having to type (or know) any Kermit commands. A question that is frequently asked by these script writers is, "How can I make Kermit return from CONNECT mode automatically?"

CLEAR APC

An APC is a macro sent to the terminal emulator to be executed, with automatic return to CONNECT mode. The CLEAR APC command clears the APC status of the macro, so when it finishes executing, it does not reCONNECT, but rather, executes the next command from its current command source (command file, macro, or prompt).

APCs can be used to initiate file transfers, but it's easier to rely on the emulator's autodown/upload capability (see Chapters 8 and 13). Nevertheless, for illustrative purposes, here is a pair of macros to let C-Kermit initiate transfers automatically with any local Kermit program whose emulator supports APCs, and has them enabled:

```
COMMENT - PCSEND macro.  Arguments:
; \%1 = Name of file to send, \%2 = Optional name to send it with.
;
def PCSEND {
    local \%n
    asg \%n \ffiles(\%1)          ; See how many files match
    if not \%n -                  ; If none match
      end 1 {\%1 - not found}     ; give message and fail
    apc receive                   ; Tell local Kermit to receive
    if = 1 \%n send \%1 \%2       ; Single file with as-name
    else send \%1                 ; or wildcard with no as-name
}
COMMENT - PCGET macro.  Arguments:
; \%1 = Name of file to get, \%2 = Optional name to store it under.
;
def PCGET {
    local tmp
    apc server                    ; Put local Kermit in server mode
    xif def \%2 {                 ; If we have an "as-name"
        get, \%1, \%2             ; use multiline GET
    } else {                      ; Otherwise
        get \%1                   ; use regular GET
    }
    asg tmp \v(status)            ; Remember status
    finish                        ; FINISH the server
    end \m(tmp)                   ; Return status from GET command
}
```

Once C-Kermit has these macros defined, e.g. by reading their definitions from its initialization file, the user can initiate file transfers from the `C-Kermit>` prompt without having to escape back, type commands, or re-CONNECT:

```
C-Kermit>pcsend oofa.txt              (Single file)
C-Kermit>pcsend oofa.txt x.txt        (Single file with as-name)
C-Kermit>pcsend oofa.*                (Multiple files)
C-Kermit>pcget oofa.txt               (Single file)
C-Kermit>pcget oofa.*                 (Multiple files)
C-Kermit>pcget oofa.txt x.txt         (Single file with as-name)
```

Reading and Writing Files and Commands

Like any conventional programming language, C-Kermit lets you open, read, write, and close files. Computer people call this I/O (Input/Output). The commands, not surprisingly, are OPEN, READ, WRITE, and CLOSE.

OPEN { READ, WRITE, APPEND } *filename*

Opens the given file in READ, WRITE, or APPEND mode. A READ file must already exist and is opened for reading only. A WRITE file is created as a new file, overwriting any existing file of the same name. An APPEND file, if it already exists, will have new information added to the end of it. If it does not exist, it is created as a new file.

```
open read oofa.txt          ; Read from the file oofa.txt
open write oofa.new         ; Create the file oofa.new
open append oofa.log        ; Write to end of oofa.log
```

These commands fail if the file can't be found or can't be opened in the desired mode, for example if a file is protected against you.

OPEN { !READ, !WRITE } *command*

You also can open files that aren't files at all, but system commands or programs, and then read from their output or write to their input. Here's an example for use in VMS:

```
open !read dir /except=(*.doc,*.hlp) /after=yesterday ck*.*
```

This causes VMS to produce a list of all the files in the current directory whose names start with CK, except the ones with filetypes of .DOC or .HLP, created since yesterday. C-Kermit can read this list and use it, for example, to send the selected files.

The next example shows how Kermit can write lines of text to the UNIX, OS/2, or Windows SORT utilities directing the sorted output to the file `alpha.txt`:

```
open !write sort > alpha.txt
```

Only one READ or !READ file can be open at once, and only one WRITE, !WRITE, or APPEND file can be open at once. Reading from and writing to subprocesses works only with operating systems that support straightforward methods of input and output redirection.

Now that we know how to open files and processes for reading and writing, we also need to get data into and out of them. For this, we use the READ and WRITE commands:

READ *variable-name*

Reads the next line of text from the current OPEN READ or OPEN !READ file and makes the line of text, without its line terminator, the value of the named variable, for example:

```
read line
```

If no more lines remain in the file, the command fails and the file is closed automatically. Here is an example that reads and displays an entire file:

```
open read oofa.txt
if fail stop 1 Can't open oofa.txt
read line
while success { echo \m(line), read \m(line) }
```

WRITE *file text*

Writes the *text* to the indicated log or file. The *text* can include backslash codes, variables, etc., which are fully evaluated before the text is written. The *text* is not terminated by a line terminator in the output file unless you include one explicitly, for example:

```
write debug-log { Here is where the trouble starts...\13\10}
```

For portability, however, you should not include literal line terminators in your scripts, so you can use the \v(newline) variable instead; its value is the appropriate text-file line terminator for whatever platform C-Kermit is running on:

```
write debug { Here is where the trouble starts...\v(newline)}
```

For the common case, in which a line is to be written, rather than a fragment of a line, you can use:

WRITE-LINE *file text*

Writes the *text* to the indicated file, and supplies the appropriate line terminator at the end. Pascalisches Synonym: **WRITELN**. Example:

```
writeln debug-log { Here is where the trouble starts...}
```

The *file* can be any of the following files or logs, which must already be open:

DEBUG-LOG

The C-Kermit debugging log (opened with LOG DEBUG).

FILE

The currently open WRITE, !WRITE, or APPEND file.

PACKET-LOG

C-Kermit's packet log (opened with LOG PACKETS).

SCREEN

Your screen. WRITE SCREEN is the same as XECHO; WRITELN SCREEN is just like ECHO. The SCREEN "file" is always open, so C-Kermit does not give you a command to open or close it.

ERROR

Just like SCREEN, but uses standard error rather than standard output. Useful on systems like UNIX that separate the two, especially when output redirection has been done on one but not the other.

SESSION-LOG

C-Kermit's session log (opened with LOG SESSION).

TRANSACTION-LOG

C-Kermit's file transfer transaction log (opened with LOG TRANSACTIONS).

When you are finished reading or writing a file (or process), you should close it. The command is:

CLOSE *name*

Closes the named file: DEBUG-LOG, PACKET-LOG, SESSION-LOG, TRANSACTION-LOG, READ, or WRITE. A READ or !READ file is closed automatically when end-of-file (EOF) is encountered during a READ operation, but it does no harm to close it again. WRITE, !WRITE, and APPEND files should be closed explicitly with CLOSE WRITE. All files are closed automatically when you EXIT or QUIT from C-Kermit.

Here is a C-Kermit program that reads lines from one file, OOFA.TXT, and writes them into another file, NUMBERED.TXT, with line numbers added:

```
local \%c line
set take error off                    ; So EOF can be handled
open read oofa.txt                    ; Open input file "oofa.txt"
if fail end 1 Failure to open input file
open write numbered.txt               ; Open output file "numbered.txt"
if fail end 1 Failure to open output file
define \%c 0                          ; Start line counter at 0
while true {                          ; Loop to read all lines
    read line                         ; Read one line into "line"
    xif fail {                        ; End of file
        close write                   ; Close the files
        end 0 Lines copied: \%c.  ; Print a message
    }
    increment \%c                     ; Count the line
    writeln file \flpad(\%c,3). \m(line)  ; Format and write it
}
```

A Mass Mailing

In this example we use C-Kermit's file input/output feature on a UNIX computer to send annual review letters to our employees via electronic mail — the personal touch! These are form letters that look like this:

```
Dear \m(name),
You have done a \m(word) job this year.
Keep up the \m(word) work.
```

This is called a *boilerplate*, and we have stored it in a file called BOILER. It contains C-Kermit variables to be filled in by our program for each employee, based on records in another file, EMPLOYEES, that look like this:

```
name address comment
```

In each record, *name* is the employee's name, *address* is the employee's electronic mail address, and *comment* is a word characterizing the employee's performance for the year, for example:

```
Olga ole great
Olaf oop swell
Ivan itt terrible
```

Figure 18-2 on page 412 lists the program that reads and processes the records, sending personalized mail to each employee. Store it in a file and then TAKE the file.

Now you have fulfilled your managerial responsibilities, spending mere seconds on a task that normally takes weeks. While your employees are contemplating their review letters, you can go back to playing video games on your PC.

Programming Considerations

C-Kermit's programming language is the result of a series of additions to its original command language, each with an eye toward backward compatibility and also compatibility with MS-DOS Kermit. Thus command files written for MS-DOS Kermit or C-Kermit as far back as the mid-1980s should still work with little or no alteration.

The tradeoff is a certain awkwardness that is not present in real programming languages like C, Pascal, or Algol. This is also true for most other scripting languages, in which items such as variables and looping constructs are grafted on top of an existing command language, as in the UNIX shell. The advantage of a scripting language is that it is *the same* as the command language, and therefore relatively approachable and easy to learn; the disadvantage is its sometimes awkward appearance and quoting rules.

GOTOs were first implemented in MS-DOS Kermit many years ago. Even though they were "considered harmful" [29], GOTOS (when used in combination with IF) transformed

```
; File REVIEWS.KSC
; A Kermit Script to send personalized review letters to the staff.

local \%d \%i \%m \%n line   ; Local variables
local name user word split   ; More local variables
define \%d 100               ; Maximum lines in a letter
declare \&z[\%d]             ; Array for lines
set take error off           ; Catch errors ourselves

def SPLIT {                  ; SPLIT macro assigns words in its
   asg name \%1              ; argument to separate variables
   asg user \%2
   asg word \%3
}
open read boiler             ; Open the boilerplate file
if fail stop 1 Can't open boilerplate file

; Loop to read each line of boilerplate file.
;
for \%n 1 \%d 1 {            ; \%n is the line number
   read \&z[\%n]             ; Store this line in the array
   if fail break            ; Stop at end of file
}
if = \%n \%d -              ; If too many lines before end of file,
   end 1 Your letter is too long ; stop here

; Read employee records
;
def \%m 0                    ; Employee counter
open read employees          ; Open the employee file
if fail -                    ; Handle failure
   end 1 Can't open employee file
while true {                 ; Loop for each employee
   read line                 ; Read a record
   if fail break             ; Failure means we're done
   increment \%m             ; Got a record, count the employee

   split \m(line)            ; Get name, address, and comment

 ; Write boilerplate lines to mail program, making substitutions

   open !write mail \m(user) ; Start the mail program
   for \%i 1 \%n 1 {         ; Write lines 1 through \%n
      writeln file \&z[\%i]  ; to the mail program "file"
   }
   close write               ; Close the mail program
}
echo Done, letters: \%m      ; Print completion message
```

Figure 18-2 Mass Mailing Script

the strictly linear command language into a programming language. We carry them forward for compatibility with older releases of MS-DOS Kermit, but they can almost always be avoided by using XIF-ELSE, FOR, WHILE, or SWITCH.

Structured statements should be used in preference to GOTO (and its even more evil twin, FORWARD) if for no other reason than because they execute more quickly. Suppose the following fragment appears toward the bottom of a long command file:

```
assign \%i 1
:loop
read \&a[\%i]
if fail goto done
increment \%i
if not > \%i \%n goto loop
:done
```

Each GOTO LOOP "rewinds" the command file to the beginning and searches line by line until it finds the LOOP label. If you recode the loop as follows:

```
for \%i 1 \%n 1 {
    read \&a[\%i]
    if fail break
}
```

it goes *much* faster, it's shorter, it's easier to read, and best of all, it's politically correct. Any sort of loop can usually be recoded in this manner. Should block contents become too big, portions of the block can be extracted into a macro that can be called with negligible extra expense from within the block. This has the side benefit of making the program more readable and modular.

Summary of Built-in Functions

Table 18-3 lists C-Kermit's built-in functions alphabetically, showing their arguments and the type of value returned.

Table 18-3   Built-in Functions

Name	Returns	Description
\Fbasename(*filespec*)	*text*	Filename extracted from *filespec*
\Fbreak(*s1,s2*)	*text*	*s1* up to first character that is in *s2*
\Fcapitalize(*s1*)	*text*	*s1* with first letter capitalized
\Fcharacter(*n*)	*character*	Character whose numeric code is given
\Fchecksum(*s1*)	*number*	Checksum of text *s1*

Table 18-3   Built-in Functions (continued)

Name	Returns	Description
\Fcode(c)	number	Numeric code value of character c
\Fcontents(variable)	text	Value of variable, unevaluated
\Fcrc16(text)	number	CRC-16 of text s1
\Fdate(file)	text	Creation or modification date of file
\Fdefinition(macro)	text	Definition of macro
\Fevaluate(expression)	number	Value of arithmetic expression
\Fexecute(macro args)	any	Return value of macro execution
\Ffiles(filespec)	number	Number of files that match filespec
\Fhexify(s1)	hex-string	s1 encoded in hexadecimal
\Findex(s1,s2,n)	number	Position of leftmost s1 in s2 starting at n
\Fipaddress(s1,n)	ip-address	Extracts first IP address from s1 starting at n
\Flength(s1)	number	Length of s1
\Fliteral(s1)	text	Literal s1, no evaluation
\Flower(s1)	text	Letters in s1 converted to lowercase
\Flpad(s1,n,c)	text	s1 left-padded to length n with char c
\Fltrim(s1,s2)	text	s1 with all characters from s2 trimmed from left
\Fmaximum(n1,n2)	number	Larger of the two numbers
\Fminimum(n1,n2)	number	Smaller of the two numbers
\Fmodulus(n1,n2)	number	n1 modulus n2
\Fnextfile()	filename	Next filename from \Ffiles() list
\Fpathname(file)	filename	Full pathname of file
\Frepeat(text,n)	text	n repetitions of text
\Freverse(text)	text	text reversed
\Fright(text,n)	text	Rightmost n characters of text
\Frindex(s1,s2,n)	number	Position of rightmost s1 in s2 starting at n
\Frpad(text,n,c)	text	text right-padded to length n with character c
\Fsize(file)	number	Size in bytes of file
\Fspan(s1,s2)	text	s1 up to 1st char that is not in s2
\Fsubstring(text,n1,n2)	text	Substring of text starting at n1, length n2
\Ftod2secs(hh:mm:ss)	number	Converts time of day to seconds since midnight
\Ftrim(s1,s2)	text	s1 with all chars from s2 trimmed from the right.
\Fupper(s1)	text	Letters in s1 converted to uppercase
\Fverify(s1,s2,n)	number	Pos of 1st char in s2 starting at n that's not also in s1

Chapter 19

Script Programming

You're probably wondering what Chapters 17 and 18 have to do with data communications and file transfer. On the surface, not much. But the programming techniques introduced there — repetitive loops, decision making, and so on — resemble the things you do yourself when you are interacting with a computer. In this chapter, you will use these techniques to teach C-Kermit to do automatically exactly what you do when you use it by hand to connect to, log in to, and use a remote computer or service. You'll even see how to do things you couldn't have done by hand.

Anything you do with Kermit — whether at the command prompt or in CONNECT mode — in a routine and repetitive way is a good candidate for automation. A certain sequence of commands is always required for dialing out or for making a network connection. A certain dialog is required for logging in to a particular remote computer or service. Automating these routine procedures has all sorts of benefits. It makes them easier and more robust, it makes them easily accessible to the computer-shy, and it lets computers talk to each other even when no humans are around: late at night when phone rates are lowest, the computers can call each other up and exchange data automatically.

○ ○ ○ ○

The material in this chapter is primarily for those who use C-Kermit in *local mode*; that is, for dialing out or making network connections from C-Kermit to remote computers or services. If you will be using C-Kermit only in *remote mode*, skip ahead to the appendices starting on page 461 and skim through them to see the types of reference material that are available to you.

415

Automated Connection Establishment

Before you can use a remote computer or service, you must establish a connection to it from your local computer. C-Kermit supports three primary types of connections: direct, network, and dialed, all described in Chapter 3, plus the network dialing method described in Chapter 6.

Let's write macros to automate the connection task, one for each type of connection. First we'll handle direct serial connections. For this kind of connection, Kermit only needs to know the device name and the connection speed. Let's define a macro that takes these two items as arguments, issues the appropriate commands, and checks to make sure the commands were successful:

```
COMMENT - SERIAL macro.   Arguments:
; \%1 = device name
; \%2 = speed
;
define SERIAL {
    if < \v(argc) 3 end 1 Usage: SERIAL device speed
    set line \%1                            ; OK, try to SET LINE
    if failure end 1 Can't open device: \%1 ; Failed
    set speed \%2                           ; Try to set the speed
    if fail end 1 Unsupported speed: \%2    ; Failed
    end 0 Connection successful.            ; Succeeded
}
```

\%1 is the device name and \%2 is the connection speed in bits per second. Both are required; there are no defaults; if you omit them, the macro gives a helpful usage message and fails. Use the SERIAL macro like this:

```
C-Kermit>serial /dev/tty01 9600        (UNIX)
C-Kermit>serial txa5 2400              (VMS)
C-Kermit>serial com1 19200             (Windows or OS/2)
Connection successful.
C-Kermit>
```

Now let's define a NET macro for making network connections. The required items are the network type (such as TCP/IP or X.25) and the network host name or address:

```
COMMENT - NET macro.   Arguments:
; \%1 = network type
; \%2 = host name or address
;
define NET {
    if < \v(argc) 3 end 1 Usage: NET network host
    set network \%1                       ; Set network type
    if fail end 1 unsupported network: \%1 ; Failed
    set host \%2                          ; Make the connection
    if fail end 1 can't reach host: \%2   ; Failed
    end 0 Connection successful.          ; Succeeded
}
```

For TCP/IP connections, the second argument can include a service port name or number, attached with a colon. You can use the NET macro like this:

```
C-Kermit>net tcp/ip oofacorp.com              (Internet)
C-Kermit>net tcp/ip oofacorp.com:3000         (Internet with port)
C-Kermit>net x.25 31182120010300              (X.25)
Connection successful.
C-Kermit>
```

For dialed connections, Kermit needs to know the modem type, the name of the device the modem is connected to, the speed for dialing, and the phone number. If the phone number is busy or doesn't answer, the call is redialed according to your SET DIAL RETRIES and SET DIAL INTERVAL settings[48]. Here is our CALL macro:

```
COMMENT - CALL macro.   Arguments:
; \%1 = modem type
; \%2 = device name
; \%3 = speed
; \%4 = phone number
;
define CALL {
    if < \v(argc) 5 -            ; All arguments present?
      end 1 Usage: CALL modem device speed number
    set modem \%1                ; Set modem type
    if fail end 1 unknown modem type: \%1
    set line \%2                 ; Communication device
    if fail end 1 can't open device: \%2
    set speed \%3                ; Communication speed
    if fail end 1 unsupported speed: \%3
    set dial retries 10          ; Try up to 10 times
    dial \%4                     ; Dial the number
    if fail end 1 Can't place call: \%4
    end 0 Connection successful.
}
```

Again, all arguments are required:

```
C-Kermit>call
Usage: CALL modem device speed number
C-Kermit>call telebit /dev/acu 38400 555-9876
Connection successful.
C-Kermit>
```

The macro issues the DIAL-related commands in the proper order, verifies that each command was executed successfully, and then places the call. If the call completes successfully within your DIAL RETRIES limit, the macro issues the "Connection successful" message and exits successfully, otherwise it fails.

---

[48]Set these in your C-Kermit customization file according to your own needs and local laws and regulations. Note that the phone number can also be a dialing directory entry.

How about dialing out with a network-resident "reverse terminal server?" Here we combine network access with modem dialing by making a TCP/IP connection to a specific port on a terminal server that is on the local network. Most terminal servers can be configured to provide this kind of service, which is on a specific TCP port. If you make a TCP connection to that port, you get a dialout modem in command mode. This technique was explained back in Chapter 6 on page 126. Here we construct a TCPCALL macro to place the call.

```
COMMENT - TCPCALL macro.  Arguments:
;
; \%1 = server:port
; \%2 = modem type
; \%3 = phone number
;
def TCPCALL {
    if < \v(argc) 4 -         ; All arguments present?
      end 1 Usage: TCPCALL server[:port] modem number
    set net tcp/ip            ; Which network to use
    if fail end 1 unsupported network: tcp/ip
    set host \%1              ; Access server and port
    if fail end 1 can't access server \%1
    set modem \%2             ; Set modem type
    if fail end 1 unknown modem type: \%2
    dial \%3                  ; Dial the number
    if fail end 1 Can't place call: \%3
    end 0 Connection successful.
}
```

The port number, if any, must be concatenated with the terminal server hostname, separated by a colon (:). For example, if you have a terminal server whose hostname is DIALOUT and the TCP service port is 2000:

```
C-Kermit>tcpcall dialout:2000 telebit 7654321
```

These four macros, which are included in the standard C-Kermit initialization file, let you make different kinds of connections without having to remember which commands are needed and in what order — which is especially important for modem dialing, where the order can make all the difference.

When you give a SERIAL, NET, CALL, or TCPCALL command and receive the "Connection successful" message in return, Kermit is ready to communicate. Now you can give a CONNECT command and go through your normal login procedure.

Or you can have Kermit log in for you automatically.

Synchronization Commands

The connection-establishment macros are useful in their own right, but they are only the first step in automating online access. Now let's take the next step and automate the login procedure, in which you get the remote computer's attention and identify yourself to it. The method differs for each type of computer or service, but each time you connect to a particular one, you usually perform the same steps.

How do you know what to put in a login script? The best way to construct a successful script is to go through the connection and login procedure once by hand, observing exactly which characters are sent and received, in what order, and with what timing.

To illustrate, let's use our new CALL macro to dial a VMS computer, then CONNECT to it and log in:

```
C-Kermit>call hayes /dev/cua 2400 7654321
Connection successful.          (Get confirmation message)
C-Kermit>connect                (Connect to the VMS system)
<CR>                            (Type a carriage return)
Welcome to the Complaint Department
The more you complain, the longer you get to live.

Username: olga                  (See prompt, type username)
Password: _____                 (See prompt, type password)

Welcome to VMS V5.5-1

Last interactive login on Wednesday, 6-SEP-1996 23:23
Last non-interactive login on Thursday, 8-FEB-1996 20:02

$                               (See system prompt)
```

Observe what you type and what VMS sends back in return. The VMS system sends two types of text to your terminal: informational or greeting messages, and prompts that you should reply to. In this example, the prompts are:

```
Username:
```

and:

```
Password:
```

The login process is complete when you see the system prompt:

```
$
```

That's a dollar sign, followed by a space, on the left margin (\13$\32).

How can we automate this procedure? Let's clear up one misconception right away. You can't use the CONNECT command to send precomposed text to the remote computer. The CONNECT command always reads from the keyboard, never from a file. To illustrate, the following command file:

```
set line /dev/ttyh8
set speed 9600
connect
olga
secret
```

does *NOT* log the user Olga in to the remote computer. It does *not* send the strings "olga" and "secret" out the communication device. When you put a CONNECT command in a command file or macro, it does exactly what it does when you issue it interactively: it connects your keyboard and screen to the remote computer. The previous example will do just that; then when you escape back from CONNECT mode, Kermit will try to execute the commands "olga" and "secret," which are not C-Kermit commands at all.

We can't simply blast text at the remote computer, expecting it to be processed correctly and at the right time. We have no guarantee this will happen, and practically every assurance that it won't. Instead, we want Kermit to do what we do: look for a particular prompt, send the appropriate text, look for the next prompt, and so on, ignoring (just as we do) all the informational and greeting messages. We should *synchronize* our responses with the remote computer's prompts; we should *not* send text to the remote computer until it has issued a prompt for it.

Synchronization is important for many reasons. For example, you must not send characters on a half-duplex connection until the remote system has given you permission by sending you its line turnaround character, such as Ctrl-Q (Xon). If you (or Kermit) do not wait for the Xon, the characters sent prematurely are lost.

Even on full duplex connections there might be times when "typeahead" is not allowed. When you log in to UNIX, for example, the login program clears the input buffer of typeahead after issuing the "Password:" prompt and before reading your password, as a security measure; any part of your password that you send before the prompt appears is lost and your login fails.

So before we can write our login scripts, we must learn how to synchronize Kermit's responses with the prompts and actions of the remote computer.

The OUTPUT and INPUT Commands

A script program is a lot like a movie script containing a dialog between two actors. In a C-Kermit script, the actors are the two computers, and their lines are spoken and read, respectively, by C-Kermit's OUTPUT and INPUT commands. These commands do what you would do if you were interacting manually with the other computer during a CONNECT session: CONNECT requires a person at the controls, whereas INPUT and OUTPUT work on automatic pilot. OUTPUT "types" what you would type and INPUT reads the computer's responses:

```
output \13              (Send a carriage return)
input 5 login:          (Wait 5 seconds for login prompt)
output olaf\13          (Send my user ID and <CR>)
input 5 Password:       (Wait for password prompt)
```

OUTPUT *text*

Sends the text out the current communication path (serial port, modem, network, or if C-Kermit is in remote mode, its controlling terminal). Example:

```
C-Kermit>output I am not really typing this text.
```

The text may contain any of the backslash codes, variables, or functions described in Chapters 2 and 17–18, e.g.:

```
C-Kermit>out The local time is \v(time).\13
```

It can also include the special codes \B, which means to send a BREAK signal (the letter B can be upper- or lowercase); \L (upper- or lowercase) to send a Long BREAK signal;[49] or \N (upper or lower) to send a NUL (ASCII 0):

```
C-Kermit>output \b               (Send a BREAK signal)
```

If you want to include leading or trailing spaces in the text, enclose it within curly braces:

```
C-Kermit>output { hello }
```

The enclosing braces are removed by C-Kermit's command processor, so the command just shown sends the word *hello* with a leading blank and a trailing blank.

If you want to output text that actually begins and ends with curly braces, use two of each:

```
C-Kermit>output {{ hello }}    (sends "{ hello }")
```

If you need to output a literal backslash, use two of them:

```
C-Kermit>output AT\\Q3\13         (sends "AT\Q3<CR>")
```

Kermit does not add a carriage return or linefeed to the end of the OUTPUT text. You must include the appropriate backslash code for any control characters that you would have typed, for example:

```
C-Kermit>output hello\13          (Include a carriage return)
```

The OUTPUT command succeeds unless there is a device output error, for example if the connection was broken.

---

[49]On a serial connection, a BREAK is a 0.275-second spacing (0) condition and a Long BREAK is a 1.5-second spacing condition. On a TCP/IP TELNET connection, both \B and \L send the TELNET BREAK command to the remote TELNET server.

In some cases, the device you are OUTPUTting characters to might break if the characters arrive too close to each other. In such cases, you can slow down the rate at which OUTPUT sends its text:

SET OUTPUT PACING *number*

This tells Kermit to pause for the given number of milliseconds (thousandths of a second) between each character in the *text* of subsequent OUTPUT commands. The default OUTPUT PACING is 0, i.e. no pauses. Example:

```
set output pacing 500
output ATZ\13
```

Note: to OUTPUT a relatively large volume of characters all at once, put them in a file and use TRANSMIT to send it in either binary or text mode, as appropriate; see Chapter 15.

INPUT *number [text]*

Waits up to the given *number* seconds for the specified *text* to arrive on the communication connection or, if C-Kermit is in remote mode, from the keyboard. The *text* may contain backslash codes, variables, or functions, which are evaluated before the arriving characters are scanned, but it may not include NUL (ASCII 0) characters, which serve only to terminate the text. To include leading or trailing spaces in the text, or if the text ends with a hyphen (-), enclose the text in curly braces. Alphabetic case in the text is ignored unless you have SET CASE ON.

The 8th bit of each character is ignored if your current PARITY setting is anything but NONE (NONE is the default) or if your TERMINAL (if in local mode) or COMMAND (remote mode) BYTESIZE is set to 7. If the text arrives within the specified interval, the command succeeds. If the specified number of seconds passes without the text arriving, the command terminates automatically and fails. Here is an example of how to test whether INPUT succeeds or fails:

```
input 10 login:                    ; Wait for login prompt
if failure end 1 No login prompt
```

If you omit the *text* from the INPUT command, it waits the given interval for any character at all, including NUL:

```
input 10                           ; Wait for any character
if failure end 1 No input
```

The last character that was read by the INPUT command, whether it succeeded or not, is available in the \v(inchar) variable. The number of characters read by the most recent INPUT command is given by the \v(incount) variable.

If C-Kermit is in local mode, you can interrupt an INPUT command in progress by typing any character (such as space), which causes INPUT to fail and, if a script is active, to proceed to the next command in the script. You can also interrupt it, like all other commands, by typing Ctrl-C, which returns C-Kermit directly to its prompt.

You can also get additional details about the most recent INPUT command from the \v(instatus) variable\v(return), whose values are:

-1 No INPUT command given yet
 0 Succeeded
 1 Timed out
 2 Interrupted by user
 3 Internal error
 4 I/O error or connection lost

The INPUT and OUTPUT commands are hooked into the session log. If you have given a LOG SESSION command, all characters processed by INPUT and OUTPUT are recorded in the session log, just as if they had been captured during CONNECT mode, except that no conversions take place (character-set translation, removal of linefeeds, and so on).

When you combine the INPUT and OUTPUT commands with the decision-making powers of the IF command, you can make Kermit imitate your own behavior: it "types" what you would have typed, it reads the responses, and makes the same decisions you would make.

Using the INPUT Buffer

Characters that are read by the INPUT command are copied to the INPUT buffer, which you can refer to at any time using the built-in variable \v(input), and you can also look at text accumulated by recent INPUT commands with the REINPUT command:

REINPUT *number text*

Works like INPUT except that it scans the INPUT buffer for the text rather than reading new characters from the connection. If the requested text is present, REINPUT succeeds immediately, otherwise it fails immediately. The timeout interval is ignored.

Here's a small script program in which Kermit dials a Hayes 2400 bps modem, reads the modem's response, and takes various actions depending on the response. The modem's response is a string of characters surrounded by linefeed characters (\10).

```
set speed 2400                    ; Use 2400 bps
output atdt7654321\13             ; Dial the number
input 40 \10                      ; Wait 40 sec for first linefeed
if failure end 1 No response      ; Timed out, quit
input 20 \10                      ; Wait 20 sec for next linefeed
if failure end 1 Timed out        ; It didn't come
reinput 0 BUSY                    ; Got response, was it "BUSY"?
if success end 1 Line is busy     ; Quit with message
reinput 0 CONNECT                 ; Was it "CONNECT"?
if failure end 1 No CONNECT       ; No, give up
reinput 0 CONNECT 1200            ; Yes, did modem speed change?
if success set speed 1200         ; Yes, change Kermit's too
```

(This example is illustrative only, since you would normally use C-Kermit's DIAL command for this, and also because the modem has many other responses not shown here.)

The example shows that a script program can contain any Kermit commands at all, not just INPUT, REINPUT, IF, OUTPUT, and ECHO; for example, the SET SPEED command used to change the computer's interface speed in response to advice from the modem.

The INPUT buffer has a certain size, 256 characters unless you change it. Each INPUT command adds new material where the last INPUT command left off. When the end of the buffer is reached, new material wraps around to the beginning, overwriting what was there before (computer folks call this a *circular buffer*). Thus, the words or phrases you are looking for might have wrapped around too. The INPUT and REINPUT commands know how to cope with this situation, but if you are searching the \v(input) variable yourself with \findex(), you can use a trick like this:

```
assign myipaddress \fipaddress(\v(input)\v(input))
if def myipaddress echo My IP address is \m(myipaddress).
else echo IP address not found
```

To handle the possibility that the item we are searching for, in this case an IP address (such as might be printed by a terminal server before entering SLIP mode), wrapped around, we concatenate the input buffer to itself. This pastes the beginning of the possibly broken address at the end of the buffer to the end of the address at the beginning of the buffer, in case it is split in half (clear?).

Speaking of clear, you can erase the entire INPUT buffer with the CLEAR command:

CLEAR *[{* **INPUT-BUFFER, DEVICE-BUFFER, BOTH** *}]*
> The CLEAR command erases the contents of the INPUT command buffer, the communications device input buffer, or both (the default is BOTH).

In the following example, the CLEAR INPUT command ensures that each line that is INPUT from the communication device starts at the beginning of the input buffer, so it can be processed as a line of text (in this case, simply displayed) without any extraneous characters before or after it. The loop stops if a line starts with "$".

```
set input echo off              ; Echo lines ourselves
while true {                    ; Loop for each line
    clear input                 ; Clear INPUT buffer
    input 5 \10                 ; Read a line
    if eq \fsubstr(\v(input),1,1) $ break
    xecho \v(input)             ; Display the line
}
```

The MINPUT Command

As in our Hayes-modem dialing example, it is sometimes necessary to look for several possible responses, not just one. When dialing a modem, for example, there can be many different result messages: CONNECT, BUSY, NO DIALTONE, and so on. To look for several strings at once, use the MINPUT command:

MINPUT *number [text1 [text2 [text2 [...]]]]*

> Waits up to the given *number* of seconds for any of the *text* strings to arrive. If any of them does arrive within the time limit, the command succeeds and sets the variable \v(minput) to 1 if it was *text1*, 2 if it was *text2*, and so on. If none of the strings arrives within the time limit, the command fails and \v(minput) is set to 0. The strings are constants or variables, separated by spaces (*not* commas). Strings containing spaces must be enclosed in braces. Example:

```
define \%a CONNECT
define \%b NO CARRIER
minput 20 \%a {\%b} BUSY {NO DIALTONE}
```

> The \v(input), \v(inchar), \v(incount), and \v(instatus) variables are set by MINPUT in the same way they are set by INPUT.

Let's recode our Hayes dialing script using MINPUT and SWITCH:

```
define \%x 0
set speed 2400
output atdt7654321\13
clear input
minput 40 BUSY {CONNECT 1200} {CONNECT 2400} {NO CARRIER}
switch \v(minput) {
    :0, echo {No response from modem}, break
    :1, echo {Line is busy, try again later}, break
    :2, set speed 1200
    :3, def \%x 1, break
    :4, echo {No carrier, try again later}, break
    :default, echo {Unexpected response: \v(input)}
}
xif \%x { echo SUCCESS } else { echo FAILURE }
```

Is this a bit clearer? When the SWITCH statement is finished, the variable \%x is 0 if the call failed and 1 if it succeeded. This can be used to decide what to do next. Notice the trick at case 2 (CONNECT 1200); we change Kermit's speed to 1200 and "fall through" to case 3 (CONNECT 2400, where we don't need to change the speed). It's just a trick; case 2 could just as easily (but more redundantly) have been written as:

```
:2, def \%x 1, set speed 1200, break
```

If a command file or macro is terminated automatically because of an INPUT failure when TAKE (or MACRO) ERROR was ON, the TAKE or (implied) DO command also fails.

Controlling the INPUT Command

You can use the SET INPUT command to control how the INPUT, MINPUT, and REINPUT commands match character sequences, display their progress, and so forth:

SET INPUT BUFFER-LENGTH *number*

Changes the size of the INPUT buffer to the given *number* of bytes. This might be needed for REINPUT, in case the items you are looking for are so widely separated that they do not fit into the regular 256-byte buffer.

SET INPUT CASE { IGNORE, OBSERVE }

Tells whether the INPUT command should pay attention to alphabetic case when comparing its text to the characters that arrive from the communication device. The default is IGNORE. Caseless comparison is possible only for unaccented Roman letters (A–Z = a–z). Synonym: **SET CASE { OFF, ON }**.

SET INPUT ECHO { OFF, ON }

Tells whether the INPUT command should display the characters from the communication device on your screen as it receives them. The default is ON, meaning that arriving characters are displayed.

SET INPUT SILENCE *number*

Tells C-Kermit the longest interval of silence, in seconds, that will be tolerated by the INPUT command. If *number* is less than the timeout interval given in the INPUT command, and if *number* seconds pass without any characters at all arriving during the INPUT timeout interval, the INPUT command fails. If *number* is 0, which is the default, there is no silence constraint and only the INPUT timeout interval applies. Silence is broken by the arrival of any character at all, including NUL.

SET INPUT TIMEOUT-ACTION { PROCEED, QUIT }

Tells whether a failure of the INPUT command to match its text within the specified timeout interval should cause the current macro or command file to be terminated automatically. SET INPUT TIMEOUT QUIT is equivalent to following every INPUT command with IF FAILURE END 1. The default is PROCEED, so you can use IF SUCCESS or IF FAILURE to decide what to do after each INPUT command.

International Character Sets

Character set translation is *not* done by INPUT, REINPUT, and OUTPUT commands. If you want to OUTPUT a non-ASCII character, include a backslash code with the appropriate numeric value in the OUTPUT command, for example "output Gr\252\233e\13", to send *Grüße* and a carriage return to a host that uses the Latin-1 alphabet. Similarly, if you need to match international characters from the remote host in an INPUT command, you should also use backslash codes to express their values in the character set used on the remote host. See Tables VII-4–VII-7 for the character code values.

The PAUSE and WAIT Commands

Kermit scripts are often used to navigate through a series of devices until a final destination is reached. For example, a number is dialed; the call is answered by a port selector that, after a dialog, connects to a terminal server for another dialog, and from there to a front end, more dialog, and finally the desired host. Switching from device to device can take time; if Kermit sends characters before the switching is finished, they might be lost. You can use the PAUSE and WAIT commands to get past these periods of transition:

PAUSE *[{ number, hh:mm:ss }]*

Does absolutely nothing for the specified number of seconds, or until the given time. If no *number* or time is given, PAUSE pauses for 1 second. If a time of day is given that is earlier than the current time, it is taken to be tomorrow's time. Synonym: **SLEEP**. Examples:

```
C-Kermit>pause 10          (Pause 10 seconds)
C-Kermit>pause 14:30:00    (Until 2:30 pm)
C-Kermit>paus \%s          (Use value of variable)
C-Kermit>pau               (Pause 1 second)
```

The PAUSE command can be interrupted by typing any character on your keyboard. Interruptions can be detected by an IF FAILURE command:

```
echo Please wait for 20 seconds...
pause 20
if failure end 1 Please don't touch the keyboard!
else echo Thank you for your patience.
```

The PAUSE command turns out to be surprisingly useful. Many a nonfunctioning script can be made to work by inserting PAUSEs at strategic locations.

MSLEEP *[{ number, hh:mm:ss }]*

Sleeps (pauses) for the given number of *milliseconds* (thousandths of seconds), or until the given time of day. Synonym: **MPAUSE**.

WAIT *[{ number, hh:mm:ss }] [{ CD, CTS, DSR } ...]]*

Waits up to the specified number of seconds or until the given time of day for all of the given modem signals to appear on the currently selected (SET LINE) serial communication device. If no modem signals are included, WAIT is equivalent to PAUSE. If all the specified modem signals don't appear within the prescribed interval, or if there is an interruption from the keyboard, the WAIT command fails. Examples:

```
wait 45 cd
if fail end 1 No carrier
wait 5 dsr cts
if fail end 1 Modem not ready
```

When given with modem signals, the WAIT command fails immediately if C-Kermit is in remote mode, or the communication device is not a serial device, or the underlying operating system is not capable of reporting modem signal status, or a system error occurs while trying to obtain the modem signals.

Constructing a Login Script for VMS

Let's look again at the procedure for logging in to a VMS computer:

```
C-Kermit>call hayes /dev/cua 2400 9876543
Connection successful.          (Get confirmation message)
C-Kermit>connect                (Connect to VMS)
<CR>                            (Type a carriage return)
Welcome to the Complaint Department
The more you complain, the longer you get to live.

Username: olga                  (See prompt, type username)
Password: _____                (See prompt, type password)

Welcome to VMS V5.5-1

Last interactive login on Wednesday, 6-SEP-1996 23:23
Last non-interactive login on Thursday, 8-FEB-1996 20:02

$                               (See system prompt)
```

Now let's see if we can use the INPUT and OUTPUT commands to automate the process. We'll begin by writing a C-Kermit command file called VMS.KSC:

```
set input timeout quit      ; INPUT failures are fatal
set input echo off          ; Work quietly
output \13                  ; Send a carriage return
input 10 Username:          ; Wait 10 sec for username prompt
output olga\13              ; Send username and carriage return
input 5 Password:           ; Wait 5 sec for password prompt
pause                       ; Don't send password too soon
output secret\13            ; Send password and carriage return
input 100 {\13$ }           ; Wait 100 sec for system prompt
```

This is a straightforward translation of our actions and decisions into a Kermit script program. We don't know yet whether it actually works, but even on the surface it has one *extremely serious* flaw: the user's password is stored in the command file.

Never store a password in a file!

This is easy to fix. Just have the script program prompt for the password

```
askq \%p Password:          ; Make the user type the password
```

and then use this variable when it is needed:

```
input 5 Password:           ; Wait 5 sec for password prompt
output \%p\13              ; Send password and carriage return
```

Now let's run our script and see what happens:

```
C-Kermit>call hayes /dev/cua 2400 987-6543
Connection successful.
C-Kermit>take vms.ksc
Password:_____
?Input timed out
```

It didn't work. Why not?

The first step in debugging a script program is to SET INPUT ECHO ON so we can watch it in action. Since there was a SET INPUT ECHO OFF command in the VMS.KSC file, we simply remove it and TAKE the file again:

```
C-Kermit>call hayes /dev/cua 2400 987-6543
Connection successful.
C-Kermit>take vms.ksc
Password:_____
Welcome to the Complaint Department
The more you complain, the longer you get to live.

Username: olga
Password:

Welcome to VMS V5.5-1

Last interactive login on Wednesday, 6-SEP-1996 23:23
Last non-interactive login on Thursday, 8-FEB-1996 20:02

?Input timed out
C-Kermit>
```

It looks like the script program logged us in correctly, but we never got the system prompt. Don't panic. Scripts like this usually work. The failure of this one gives us a chance to track down and fix a subtle problem. In this case, there was an *invisible conversation* between VMS and your terminal, using control characters and escape sequences that did not appear on your screen when you logged in by hand.

To view these elusive fragments, use Kermit's SET TERMINAL DEBUG ON command to display control characters in ^X notation rather than passing them along literally to your terminal emulator. In this example, we log in to a VMS computer again:

```
C-Kermit>set line /dev/ttyb
C-Kermit>set terminal debug on
C-Kermit>connect
(Debugging Display...)
^M^J^G^M^J^M^JWelcome to the Complaint Department^M^JThe more
 you complain, the longer you get to live.^M^J^M^JUsername: O
LGA^M^J^MPassword:_____^M^JYou again? Welcome to VMS V5.5
-1^M^J^M^JLast interactive login on Wednesday,  6-SEP-1996 23
:23^M^JLast non-interactive login on Thursday, 8-FEB-1996 20:
02^M^J^[Z^[[c^[[0c^M^J%SET-W-NOTSET, error modifying TWA26:^M
^J-SET-I-UNKTERM, unknown terminal type^M^J^M$ Ctrl-\C
(Back at Local System)
C-Kermit>
```

^M represents Carriage Return, ^J is Linefeed, and ^[is Escape (see Table VII-1 on page 557). The user typed in her username and password, and then after the "last login" messages were printed, the characters ^[Z appeared on the screen: Escape followed by the letter Z, which is VMS's terminal identification query. Normally, you don't see this; your terminal or terminal emulator intercepts it and replies automatically with its ID (see Table 18-2 on page 405). But your terminal did not respond this time because the Escape character was translated by Kermit's debugging display to ^[(Circumflex and Left Bracket), so VMS timed out after several seconds and sent additional terminal ID requests in different formats. Finally VMS gave up and complained that your terminal type was unknown. The same thing happens when using the INPUT command, and this prompts us to state a very important rule:

The terminal emulator is not active during an INPUT command.

Therefore, *any* escape sequences that arrive do not have their normal and intended effects. These include not only terminal identification queries, but possibly also terminal status report requests (like "how big is your screen?"), setting of tabs, colors, and so forth. Now having stated this very important rule, we must state the equally important exception:

Except when the Kermit program includes its own terminal emulator.

So, for example, Kermit/2 and Kermit 95 users can ignore the talk about escape sequences during scripts. But let's continue for the benefit of those who use the UNIX, VMS, and other non-terminal-emulating versions. Why should we have to write the script differently depending on which version of C-Kermit we have? We don't:

IF EMULATION *command*

Executes the *command* only if this version of C-Kermit has emulation active during the execution of scripts. And, obviously, IF NOT EMULATION executes the command if a terminal emulator is not active.

So the debugging display has shown us all we needed to know to correct our script program and automate our VMS logins. The new VMS.KSC file handles the terminal ID request and includes several other improvements. For example, it tries three times to get the VMS Username: prompt in case there was noise on the communication line.

```
COMMENT - C-Kermit command file VMS.KSC.
;
; Log in to a VMS system
;
local \%i \%p                       ; Local variables
askq \%p Password:                  ; Make user type in password
for \%i 1 3 1 {                     ; Allow 3 tries to log in
    output \13                      ; Send a carriage return
    input 5 Username:               ; Wait for login prompt
    if fail continue                ; Try again
}
```

```
if > \%1 3 end 1 No login prompt
output olga\13                           ; Send my username
input 5 Password:                        ; Wait for password prompt
if fail end 1 No password prompt
msleep 500                               ; Not so fast!
output \%p\13                            ; Send password, carriage return
xif not emulation {                      ; No emulator built in?
    minput 10 {\27Z} {\27[c} {\27[0c} ; Get terminal ID query
    if success output \27[?1c        ; Send VT100 terminal ID
}
input 200 {\13$ }                        ; Wait for system prompt
echo Login successful.
```

This command file should work. Let's try it:

```
C-Kermit>call hayes /dev/cua 2400 987-6543
Connection successful.
C-Kermit>take vms.ksc
Password:_____
Login successful.
C-Kermit>
```

It works, but it still has some shortcomings. First, it works only for user Olga. Each user would have to edit this file to substitute the appropriate username. And then there is the fact that the script is a command file. Suppose you change your default directory and try to run it again:

```
C-Kermit>cd articles
C-Kermit>call hayes /dev/cua 2400 987-6543
Connection successful.
C-Kermit>take vms.ksc
?No files match - vms.ksc
C-Kermit>
```

Kermit can't find it. You could solve this problem by giving the full pathname of the command file in your TAKE command. Or you could define a macro to do it:

```
define govms take ~olga/kermit/vms.ksc        ; (UNIX)
define govms take [olga.kermit]:vms.ksc       ; (VMS or OpenVMS)
define govms take c:\\kermit\\vms.ksc         ; (OS/2)
define govms take :udd:olga:kermit:vms.ksc    ; (AOS/VS)
etc...
```

But now you need different definitions of the GOVMS macro depending on which operating system you are running it from. If you keep the file in your home (login) directory, you can use C-Kermit's portable notation:

```
define govms take \v(home)vms.ksc     ; (All systems)
```

This statement should work on any computer that C-Kermit runs on.

But you can fix the problems with this command file even more simply by rewriting it as a macro and putting its definition in your C-Kermit initialization file. That way, it is always ready for use, and the username and password can be passed to it as macro arguments. The complete, real-life, production quality VMSLOGIN macro is listed in Figure 19-1. Let's dissect it. The first command:

```
if < \v(argc) 2 -
    end 1 Usage: \%0 userid [ password [ prompt ] ]
```

checks to make sure you specified a user ID. If not, it gives you a usage message and fails. The next command is a short WHILE loop:

```
while not defined \%2 {
    askq \%2 { \%1's password: }
}
```

If the \%2 password variable is not already defined, C-Kermit prompts for a password and reads it from the keyboard into the \%2 variable without echoing it. A WHILE loop is used here rather than a simple IF command to make sure the user actually types in a password. If the user just hits the Return (Enter) key, the password prompt comes back, and the process repeats until some nonblank characters have been entered. The next section:

```
set parity none              ; Set communication parameters
set duplex full
set handshake none
```

establishes the appropriate communication parameters. Some of them happen to be identical to C-Kermit's defaults, but we set them here deliberately to ensure the right settings in case they have been changed. Now we can start to send and read characters. The following section:

```
in 5 Username:               ; Is prompt already there?
xif fail {                   ; No
    for \%i 1 3 1 {          ; Try 3 times to get it.
        out \13             ; Send carriage return
        in 5 Username:      ; Look for prompt
        if success break    ; Success, go log in
    }
    if > \%i 3 end 1 No Username prompt
}
```

looks first to see if the prompt is already waiting for us, as normally would be the case on a network connection. If not, the script sends a carriage return and waits 5 seconds for the Username: prompt. If the prompt does not appear within the 5-second time limit, the process repeats up to 3 times. If the prompt does not appear after 3 tries, the VMSLOGIN macro fails (END 1).

If the prompt does appear, we proceed to the next section:

```
out \%1\13                   ; Send username, carriage return
inp 5 Password:              ; Wait 5 sec for this prompt
if fail end 1 No password prompt
pause                        ; Wait a sec
out \%2\13                   ; Send password
```

```
COMMENT - VMSLOGIN macro.  Arguments:
; \%1 = VMS user ID
; \%2 = Password.  If password not supplied, it is prompted for.
; \%3 = System prompt.  If omitted a default is supplied.
;
define VMSLOGIN {
    if < \v(argc) 2 -
      end 1 Usage: \%0 userid [ password [ prompt ] ]
    while not defined \%2 {
        askq \%2 { \%1's password: }
    }
    set parity none                 ; Set communication parameters
    set duplex full
    set handshake none
    set input timeout proceed       ; Handle timeouts ourselves
    in 5 Username:                   ; Is prompt already there?
    xif fail {                      ; No.
        for \%i 1 3 1 {             ; Try 3 times to get it.
            out \13                ; Send carriage return
            in 5 Username:          ; Look for prompt
            if success break        ; Success, go log in
        }
        if > \%i 3 end 1 No Username prompt
    }
    out \%1\13                      ; Send username, carriage return
    inp 5 Password:                 ; Wait 5 sec for this prompt
    if fail end 1 No password prompt
    pause                           ; Wait a sec
    out \%2\13                      ; Send password
    xif not emulation {             ; No emulator built in?
        set input echo off          ; Protect terminal from this
        minput 10 {\27Z} {\27[c} {\27[0c} ; Get terminal ID query
        xif success {               ; Got one
            output \27[\?1c         ; Send VT100 terminal ID
            in 2 \27[6n             ; Screen size query?
            if succ out \27[\v(rows);\v(cols)R ; Send dimensions
        }
        set input echo on           ; Echo input again
    }
    if not def \%3 -                ; If we were not given a prompt
      asg \%3 {\v(prompt)}          ; use the SET LOGIN PROMPT value
    if not def \%3 -                ; If we still don't have a value
      asg \%3 {\13$\32}             ; use this one as the default.
    reinp 0 \%3                     ; INPUT got the prompt already?
    if fail inp 60 \%3              ; No, look now.
    end 0 Login successful.
}
```

Figure 19-1 The VMSLOGIN Macro

which sends the user ID and a carriage return (\%1 is the user ID and \13 is the carriage return), waits five seconds for the Password: prompt, waits another second in case the VMS system clears its input buffer after giving its password prompt, and then sends the password (\%2).

Next comes the tricky bit:

```
xif not emulation {              ; No emulator built in?
    set input echo off           ; Protect terminal from this
    minput 10 {\27Z} {\27[c} {\27[0c} ; Get terminal ID query
    xif success {                ; Got one
        output \27[\?1c          ; Send VT100 terminal ID
        in 2 \27[6n              ; Screen size query?
        if succ out \27[\v(rows);\v(cols)R ; Send dimensions
    }
    set input echo on            ; Echo input again
}
```

If this version of C-Kermit does *not* have a built-in emulator to handle escape sequences that arrive during execution of this script, the script must handle them itself. We wait up to 10 seconds for any of several possible terminal-type queries to arrive. If one of them does, then we respond with the escape sequence that identifies a VT100 (*exercise for the reader:* use the \v(terminal) variable and SWITCH command to select a more appropriate response), and *then* we wait to see if the VMS system will also send <ESC>[6n, which requests the terminal to send its dimensions (newer versions of VMS are likely to send this query; older ones do not). We respond with an escape sequence constructed from our built-in \v(rows) and \v(cols) variables. INPUT ECHO is turned off during this period to prevent your terminal from seeing the terminal type query, in which case it too might respond and matters would become very confused indeed.

Finally, regardless of whether we have handled the escape sequences ourselves or the emulator handled them for us, we wait for the system prompt:

```
if not def \%3 -                 ; If we were not given a prompt
    asg \%3 {\v(prompt)}         ; use the SET LOGIN PROMPT value
if not def \%3 -                 ; If we still don't have a value
    asg \%3 {\13$\32}            ; use this one as the default
reinp 0 \%3                      ; INPUT got the prompt already?
if fail inp 60 \%3               ; No, look now.
end 0 Login successful.
```

If the caller did not provide a special prompt when invoking VMSLOGIN, then if a \v(prompt) value has been set by SET LOGIN PROMPT, we use that; otherwise we supply a default: dollar sign on the left margin followed by a space ({\13$\32}).[50]

---

[50]This default was arrived at by experimentation with many versions of VMS on many types of connections, but might still need adjustment — if you have trouble with it, use the session debugging technique described on page 429 to reveal the cause. If you see NUL characters (^@), ignore them, because so does C-Kermit's INPUT command.

We check to see if the prompt is already in our INPUT buffer, which could happen in the previous section if we were waiting for an escape sequence that did not arrive. If it's not there, then we wait for it to come. If it does, the VMSLOGIN macro completes successfully (END 0). If not, it completes at the end of the timeout interval and returns a failure code (but your connection is still there). If the 60-second wait does not allow ample time for system messages to be displayed and your login command procedure to be executed, use a longer timeout interval.

And so we have constructed our first login script. If the process seemed difficult to you, don't worry — we picked a hard case on purpose. The others will be easier. But before writing more login scripts, let's reflect on how they fit into the big picture. The only prerequisite for VMSLOGIN is that the connection is already there. VMSLOGIN doesn't care what kind of connection it is. Once you have defined this macro (normally by executing your C-Kermit initialization file), you can use it after any of the connection-establishment macros, SERIAL, NET, TCPCALL, or CALL:

```
C-Kermit>serial /dev/ttyh8 19200
Connection successful.
C-Kermit>vmslogin ivan
 ivan's password: _____
Login successful.
C-Kermit>
```

If the login script succeeds, it does not enter CONNECT mode; instead, it leaves C-Kermit waiting for the next command. This is to allow you to use your login scripts not just as an easy way to log in, but also as a lead-in for further automated tasks, such as uploading or downloading files.

When using VMSLOGIN in a script, test it for success and then proceed as desired:

```
call hayes /dev/cua 2400 987-6543
if fail end 1 Call failed
vmslogin olga
if fail end 1 Can't log in
connect
```

Replace CONNECT with any other desired commands, such as the following, which upload a file and then log out, leaving a record of the results in a transaction log.

```
log transactions         ; Keep a record of what happened
output kermit -Qr\13     ; Start Kermit on the other computer
input 5 READY TO RECEIVE... ; Wait for READY message
fast                     ; Use fast transfer settings
binary                   ; Transfer in binary mode
send oofa.zip            ; Send a file
output logout\13         ; Log out when finished
exit                     ; Exit from C-Kermit
```

In the next few sections, we will write login scripts for several other kinds of computers and services. When we are done, we will have a versatile set of building blocks, allowing us to make many kinds of connections to many kinds of computers and services, and they will be completely portable among all implementations of C-Kermit and for the most part, also to MS-DOS Kermit.

Then we will see what we can build with these blocks. But first let's look at how to log in to a few more common computers and services.

A UNIX Login Script

Logging in to UNIX is just like logging in to VMS, except without the escape sequence complications. So without further ado, here is our UNIXLOGIN macro:

```
COMMENT - UNIXLOGIN macro.  Arguments:
; \%1 = UNIX user ID
; \%2 = Password.  If password not supplied, it is prompted for.
; \%3 = System prompt.  If omitted a default is supplied.
;
define UNIXLOGIN {
    if < \v(argc) 2 -
      end 1 Usage: \%0 userid [ password [ prompt ] ]
    while not defined \%2 {
        askq \%2 { \%1's password: }
    }
    set parity none               ; Set communication parameters
    set duplex full
    set handshake none
    set input timeout proceed     ; Handle timeouts ourselves
    set case on                   ; Case is important in UNIX
    in 5 login:                   ; Is the prompt already there?
    xif fail {                    ; No
        for \%i 1 3 1 {           ; Try 3 times to get it
            out \B\13             ; Send BREAK and CR
            in 5 login:           ; Look for prompt
            if success break      ; Success, go log in
        }
        if > \%i 3 end 1 No login prompt
    }
    if not def \%3 -              ; If we were not given a prompt
      asg \%3 {\v(prompt)}        ; use the SET LOGIN PROMPT value
    if not def \%3 -              ; If we still don't have a value
      asg \%3 {\10$ }             ; use this one as the default
    reinp 0 \%3                   ; Prompt was INPUT already?
    if fail inp 60 \%3            ; No, look now
    end 0 Login successful.
}
```

Like the VMSLOGIN macro, the UNIXLOGIN macro can be used after any of the connection-establishment macros: SERIAL, NET, TCPCALL, or CALL.

An IBM Mainframe Linemode Login Script

This example shows an interactive login to an IBM mainframe running the VM/CMS operating system over a half-duplex line-at-a-time connection:

```
VIRTUAL MACHINE/SYSTEM PRODUCT--CUVMB     --PRESS BREAK KEY
!(Press BREAK key here)
 Enter one of the following commands:
   LOGON userid                 (Example:  LOGON VMUSER1)
   DIAL userid                  (Example:  DIAL VMUSER2)
   LOGOFF
.<Ctrl-Q>logon olaf
Enter password:
 **************<CR>HHHHHHHHHHHHHH<CR>SSSSSSSSSSSSSS
.<Ctrl-Q>_____
```

In response to the message PRESS BREAK KEY, you have to send a BREAK signal. Then at the dot prompt (which happens to be followed by a Ctrl-Q line turnaround character, which you can verify using SET TERM DEBUG ON) you enter your user ID. Then you are given a password prompt, which includes a lot of overprinted asterisks, H's, and S's to cover your password (in case you are logging in from a hardcopy terminal), followed by the dot prompt and Ctrl-Q. Once you have supplied a correct password, greeting messages are printed and you must type a Carriage Return in response to the system prompt two times before you can begin to do any work. (At least, that's how our local VM/CMS system operates.) Here is a VMLINELOGIN macro that takes care of all this:

```
COMMENT - VMLINELOGIN macro.  Arguments:
; \%1 = User ID
; \%2 = Password
;
define VMLINELOGIN {
    if < \v(argc) 2 -
      end 1 Usage: \%0 userid [ password ]
    while not defined \%2 {
        askq \%2 { \%1's password: }
    }
    set parity mark              ; Set communication parameters
    set flow none
    set handshake xon
    set duplex half
    set input timeout quit       ; Don't bother with IF FAILURE
    input 10 BREAK KEY           ; Look for BREAK KEY prompt
    pause 1                      ; Wait a second
    output \B                    ; Send BREAK
    input 10 .\17, output logon \%1\13    ; Now log in
    input 10 .\17, output \%2\13          ; Send password
    input 10 .\17, output \13             ; Send carriage return
    input 10 .\17, output \13             ; Send another one
    echo Login successful.
}
```

Once we have made sure we have the user ID and password, we set the IBM mainframe linemode communication parameters, which are very different from Kermit's defaults. Then we send the BREAK signal and the required material in response to each of four identical prompts (period followed by Control-Q).

For variety as well as compactness, we have omitted the IF FAILURE commands after each INPUT command. Instead, we have simply SET INPUT TIMEOUT QUIT to force the entire macro to fail automatically if any of its INPUT commands failed, in which case the FAILURE status is returned. And we also omitted the business about the custom prompt, since, to our knowledge, it is always period. If your mainframe is different, you should be able to alter the script without difficulty. Like the other login macros, the VMLINELOGIN macro can be used in conjunction with any of the connection-establishment macros.

An IBM Mainframe Fullscreen Login Script

The more popular style of communication with IBM mainframes is called *block mode* or *full screen*, in which the IBM mainframe believes it is connected to a 3270-style terminal, but in reality the connection goes through a *protocol converter* (such as an IBM 7171 or 3174 AEA) that converts the 3270 screens to your ASCII terminal type, such as VT100. Protocol converters generally use full duplex communication, Xon/Xoff flow control, and even parity.

For the screen to be painted correctly, the protocol emulator must know your terminal type. In general the procedure is to type a carriage return (for speed recognition); in response, the protocol emulator prompts you for a terminal type with a message like this:

```
ENTER TERMINAL TYPE:
```

and you respond with a terminal type, such as:

```
ENTER TERMINAL TYPE: vt-100
```

Then a login screen like the one in Figure 19-2 is displayed. The mainframe login screen contains fields for the ID and password, which you must fill in. You should send this information only after the screen is completely painted and the mainframe is waiting for input. This is indicated by the word RUNNING somewhere near the lower right corner, as shown in the figure.

When the RUNNING message appears in the lower right, you may type your user ID and password, separated by a tab character. As in the linemode example, a couple of carriage returns are needed after that. The VMFULLOGIN macro that automates the process appears on the next page.

```
VIRTUAL MACHINE/SYSTEM PRODUCT


               CCCCCC   UU      UU VV      VV MM        MM BBBBBB
               CCCCCCCC UU      UU VV      VV MMM      MMM BBBBBBB
               CC    CC UU      UU VV      VV MMMM   MMMM BB    BB
               CC      UU      UU VV      VV MM MMMM MM BB    BB
               CC      UU      UU VV      VV MM  MM   MM BBBBBB
               CC      UU      UU VV      VV MM        MM BB    BB
               CC    CC UU      UU  VV    VV  MM        MM BB    BB
               CCCCCCCC UUUUUUUU    VVVV    MM        MM BBBBBBB
               CCCCCC   UUUUUU       VV     MM        MM BBBBBB


              C O L U M B I A     U N I V E R S I T Y
                  Center for Computing Activities



Fill in your USERID and PASSWORD and press ENTER
(Your password will not appear when you type it)
USERID   ===>
PASSWORD ===>

COMMAND  ===>
                                                     RUNNING   CUVMB
```

Figure 19-2 Sample IBM 3270 Login Screen


```
COMMENT - VMFULLOGIN macro.  Arguments:
; \%1 = User ID
; \%2 = Password
;
define VMFULLOGIN {
    if < \v(argc) 2 -
      end 1 Usage: \%0 userid [ password ]
    while not defined \%2 {
        askq \%2 { \%1's password: }
    }
    set input timeout quit        ; Quit if INPUT fails
    set parity even               ; Set communication parameters
    set duplex full
    set handshake none
    set flow xon/xoff
    out \13                       ; Send carriage return
    inp 5 TERMINAL TYPE:          ; Get terminal-type prompt
    out vt-100\13                 ; Just send "vt-100"
    inp 20 RUNNING                ; Get RUNNING message
    pau 1                         ; Wait 1 second
    out \%1\9\%2\13               ; Send user ID, tab, password
    out \13\13                    ; Two more carriage returns
    echo Login successful.
}
```

Login Scripts for Commercial Data Services

A common use of communication software is to log in to commercial information services like CompuServe, MCI Mail, or Dow Jones News/Retrieval. In many cases, the connection and login procedure is similar to that for UNIX: dial the phone number, type a carriage return, and then supply your user ID and password in response to the prompts. For example, a CompuServe login might look like this:

```
C-Kermit>set modem hayes
C-Kermit>set line /dev/ttya
C-Kermit>set speed 1200
C-Kermit>dial 5551212
Connection completed.
C-Kermit>connect
Type CR here
  01NMS

Host Name:  CIS
User ID: 00000,0000
Password: _____
```

and then you get a greeting, a menu, and the prompt, ending with:

```
CompuServe Information Service
```

The login script is straightforward:

```
COMMENT - CISLOGIN macro.  Arguments:
; \%1 = CompuServe User ID
; \%2 = Password
; \%3 = Prompt
;
define CISLOGIN {
    if < \v(argc) 2 -
        end 1 Usage: \%0 userid [ password [ prompt ] ]
    while not defined \%2 {
        askq \%2 { \%1's password: }
    }

    set terminal byteszie 7      ; No 8-bit characters
    set input timeout quit       ; Skip the IF FAILUREs
    output \13                   ; Send initial carriage return
    input 5 Host Name:           ; Look for Host Name prompt
    output cis\13                ; Send "cis" and carriage return
    input 5 User ID:             ; Look for User ID prompt
    output \%1\13                ; Send ID and carriage return
    input Password:              ; Look for Password prompt
    output \%2\13                ; Send password and CR
    if not def \%3 asg \%3 \v(prompt)
    if not def \%3 asg \%3 {CompuServe Information Service}
    input 30 \%3
    echo
    echo Login successful.
}
```

Sometimes it is preferable to go through a public data network to access the desired service, rather than dialing it directly. In the following example, we dial a SprintNet node and tell it to connect us to Dow Jones News/Retrieval.

```
C-Kermit>set modem type hayes     (Choose modem type)
C-Kermit>set line /dev/ttya       (Communication device)
C-Kermit>set speed 1200           (Communication speed)
C-Kermit>dial 5551212             (Dial the fake number)
Connection completed.             (Call is answered)
C-Kermit>connect                  (Connect to SprintNet)
Type CR here
Type CR here
TELENET                           (SprintNet greeting)
212 517A

TERMINAL=D1                       (Enter terminal type)
@c dow                            (Connect to Dow)

DOW CONNECTED                     (Dow greeting)

WHAT SERVICE PLEASE????           (Dow service prompt)
djnr                              (Enter "djnr")
ENTER PASSWORD                    (Password prompt)
WWWWWWWWW<CR>MMMMMMMMM<CR>@@@@@@@@@ <Ctrl-Q>    <Ctrl-Q>
```

As you can see, the procedure is to type two carriage returns, get a greeting and the TERMINAL= prompt, enter D1, then get the SprintNet @ prompt. At this point, you tell it to connect (c) you to "dow". Once you have been put through, Dow asks you which service you want. You reply "djnr" (Dow Jones News/Retrieval) and then supply your password in response to a rather tricky prompt, which ends with two Ctrl-Q's separated by some spaces. This is quite different from our other examples, because we have to make what amounts to *two* calls, rather than one. The first call is to SprintNet, and the second call is from SprintNet to DJNR. Naturally, you can also call other hosts and services from SprintNet, and it is conceivable that DJNR can also be reached in other ways in addition to SprintNet. So let's separate the two functions. First, we write the macro that asks SprintNet to call a given service:

```
COMMENT - SPRINT macro.  Arguments:
; \%1 = Service name or address
;
define SPRINT {
    if < \v(argc) 2 end 1 Usage: \%0 service
    set input timeout proceed           ; Use IF FAILURE
    output \13\13                        ; Send two CRs
    input 10 TERMINAL=                   ; Get TERMINAL= prompt
    if fail end 1 No terminal prompt     ; Fail if it doesn't come
    out D1\13                            ; Send terminal type, CR
    inp 10 @                             ; Look for at-sign prompt
    if fail end 1 No atsign prompt       ; Fail if it doesn't come
    output c \%1\13                      ; Connect to  service
    input 10 CONNECTED                   ; Look for confirmation
    if fail end 1 Can't access \%1 from SprintNet
}
```

Here is the Dow login macro, which can be used after the service has been reached, independent of the communication method:

```
COMMENT - DOWLOGIN macro.  Arguments:
; \%1 = Dow Jones Password
;
define DOWLOGIN {
    while not defined \%1 {              ; Get password
        askq \%1 { Dow Jones password: }
    }
    set input timeout proceed
    input 20 SERVICE PLEASE\?\?\?\?      ; Look for Dow prompt
    if fail end 1 No service prompt
    out djnr\13                         ; Select DJNR
    input 10 @@@@                       ; Get password prompt
    if fail end 1 No password prompt
    pause 1                             ; Wait a second, then...
    output \%1\13                       ; send password and CR
    if not def \%3 asg \%3 \v(prompt)
    if not def \%3 asg \%3 ENTER QUERY
    input 30 \%3                        ; Get DJNR query prompt
    if fail end 1 No main query prompt
    pause 1
    echo Login successful.
}
```

The PAUSE commands toward the end of the script allow time for the invisible characters (control characters and spaces) to arrive before the password is sent.

Here is how we use our macros to access DJNR via dialup:

```
C-Kermit>call hayes /dev/tty01 2400 7418100
C-Kermit>sprint dow
C-Kermit>dowlogin
 Dow Jones password: _____
```

But suppose you want to use only one macro for logging in to Dow Jones through Sprint-Net, rather than two. Easy. Add this definition to your C-Kermit initialization file:

```
define DJNRSPRINT sprint dow, if success dowlogin
```

Finally, let's consider hosts or services that don't require any login at all. For these, we define a special macro that does nothing:

```
COMMENT - NOLOGIN macro.
;
define NOLOGIN comment
```

What were these last two items for? Keep reading.

A Directory of Services

○ ○ ○ ○

The material in this section might be coals-to-Newcastle for users of Kermit 95,
Kermit/2, or other Kermit programs that have graphical connections databases.
But still worth reading by serious script writers (lighthearted ones too), since the
principles and examples here can also be applied elsewhere.

C-Kermit's services directory is described in Chapter 7, where we confess it is implemented entirely by macros, and promise to show you how it's done. So here goes.
Let's look again at our sample services directory file:

```
XXVMA         vmlinelogin olaf      serial /dev/ttyh8 9600
XXVMB         vmfullogin  olaf      call hayes /dev/cua 2400 765-4321
CUMIN         vmslogin    olaf      net  tcp/ip cumin
WATSUN        unixlogin   olaf      net  tcp/ip watsun.cc.columbia.edu
COMPUSERVE    cislogin    000,0000  call hayes /dev/cua 2400 876-5432
DJNR          djnrsprint  xxxx      call hayes /dev/cua 2400 741-8100
GEOGRAPHY     nologin     xxxx      net  tcp/ip 141.212.99.9:3000
CONGRESS      nologin     xxxx      net  tcp/ip dra.com
```

The file has one line for each service, and each line contains four items:

1. The name of the computer or service

2. The name of the macro used to log in to it

3. Your user ID on the computer or service

4. The name of the macro used to establish a connection to the computer or service, followed by its arguments

The items in each line are separated by one or more spaces or tabs. Whenever you want to
add, delete, or modify a service, just use a text editor to make the changes. Our job now is
to design a macro that lets you access any of these services by name. We will call it
ACCESS and use it like this:

```
C-Kermit>access compuserve
C-Kermit>access watsun
C-Kermit>access djnrsprint
```

How might the ACCESS macro work? The straightforward, but less efficient, way would
be for it to read the services file every time you use it, searching for the service name.
Let's try a slightly more complicated but more efficient approach. We will read the services file only once, copying it to an internal array that can be searched more quickly.
First we add the following commands to the C-Kermit initialization file. These commands
tell Kermit to read the services directory file into an array \&d[] whenever you start

C-Kermit. Let us assume that the C-Kermit initialization file has already assigned the file specification of the services directory to the _servicedir variable:

```
xif not exist \m(_servicedir) forward connection
echo { Services directory is \m(_servicedir)}

def MAX_SVCS 200                 ; Adjust this if necessary
define _sd 0                     ; Assume no services directory
open read \m(_servicedir)        ; Try to open services directory
xif success {
    declare \&d[\m(MAX_SVCS)]    ; Open - declare directory array
    for \%i 1 \m(MAX_SVCS) 1 {   ; Read the lines into the array
        read \&d[\%i]
        if fail break
    }
    close read
    xif > \%i  \m(MAX_SVCS) {
        echo Too many entries in services directory
        echo { Maximum is \m(MAX_SVCS).  To allow more,}
        echo { change definition of MAX_SVCS in \v(cmdfile).}
        echo { Services directory disabled.}
    } else {
        asg \&d[0] \feval(\%i - 1)
        define _sd 1
    }
}
```

In this example, we're allowing up to 200 entries. If you want to have more, just change 200 to a larger number in the MAX_SVCS definition. Notice that the number of entries actually found in the directory is stored in the "zeroth" element of the array, \&d[0].

Next, we define a macro, called LIST, to list the services directory. In the simple form shown here, it prints all the entries. A somewhat more flexible version, which also accepts a service name and lists only that entry, appears in the standard CKERMIT.INI file. Here is the simple version:

```
define LIST {
  echo \&d[0] items in directory:
  for \%i 1 \&d[0] 1 { echo \&d[\%i] }
```

Which you can use like this:

```
C-Kermit>list
8 items in directory:
XXVMA       vmlinelogin olaf        serial /dev/ttyh8 9600
XXVMB       vmfullogin  olaf        call hayes /dev/cua 2400 765-4321
CUMIN       vmslogin    olaf        net  tcp/ip cumin
WATSUN      unixlogin   olaf        net  tcp/ip watsun.cc.columbia.edu
COMPUSERVE  cislogin    000,0000    call hayes /dev/cua 2400 876-5432
DJNR        djnrsprint  xxxx        call hayes /dev/cua 2400 741-8100
GEOGRAPHY   nologin     xxxx        net  tcp/ip 141.212.99.9:3000
CONGRESS    nologin     xxxx        net  tcp/ip dra.com
```

Now we define the ACCESS macro. Its two arguments are a service name and a password:

```
COMMENT - ACCESS macro.  Arguments:
; 1 = service name
; 2 = password (optional)
;
def ACCESS {
    if not defined \%1 end 1 access what?       ; Check service
    find \%1                                     ; Look it up
    if success doaccess {\%2} \v(return)         ; OK, try it
    else end 1 "\%1" not in services directory   ; Not found
    if fail end 1                                ; DOACCESS failed
    xif eq \v(cmdlevel) 1 {
        echo
        echo ACCESS: Login succeeded - CONNECTing...
        show escape
        output \13
        connect /quietly
    }
}
```

The ACCESS macro uses two other macros, which we define in a moment. The FIND macro looks up the service name in the service directory. If it is found, the entire directory entry — that is, the line that starts with the desired name — is returned and the DOACCESS macro is invoked with the password and the directory entry. Otherwise the ACCESS macro fails (END 1).

For security reasons, the service directory does not contain passwords. The ACCESS macro is designed to accept a password as a second argument after the service name:

```
C-Kermit>access compuserve mypassword
C-Kermit>acces djnr mypassword
C-Kermit>acc watsun mypassword
```

Notice that the service names can be abbreviated and that passwords echo when you type them on the ACCESS command line. You can also omit your password:

```
C-Kermit>access compu
C-Kermit>acces djnr
C-Kermit>acc wat
```

If you omit the password, the LOGIN macro prompts you for it and it does not echo when you type it:

```
C-Kermit>access watsun
 olaf's password: _____
```

When you omit the password, the \%2 argument is undefined, but that's OK because Kermit lets an argument be passed with a null (empty) value by enclosing it in braces.

```
    if success doaccess {\%2} \v(return)
```

The second argument, \v(return), is expanded *before* it is passed to DOACCESS, so although it looks like one argument here, DOACCESS sees a separate argument for each word in the directory entry.

Here is the FIND macro. It searches the `\&d[]` array, which contains the services directory, one line per array element, and returns the first matching line, or if no matches are found, the null (empty) string:

```
COMMENT - FIND macro.  Argument:
; \%1 = Service name to look for in services directory
;
def FIND {
    set case off
    for \%i 1 \&d[0] 1 {
        if eq {\%1} {\fsubstr(\&d[\%i],1,\flen(\%1))} break
    }
    if not > \%i \&d[0] return \&d[\%i]
}
```

The command:

```
if eq {\%1} {\fsubstr(\&d[\%i],1,\flen(\%1))} break
```

compares the name that you typed with a substring of each services-directory entry, starting at the first character, with the same number of characters as you typed. If they are equal (except for the case of the letters), the BREAK command terminates the FOR loop and FIND RETURNs the entire line of text from the directory.

Finally, here is DOACCESS. Its purpose is simply to pick apart the words from the services directory entry into separate macro parameters and call the connection establishment and login macros with them. It is called with a password followed by the services directory entry, so the password is argument `\%1`, the service name is `\%2`, the login macro name is `\%3`, the user ID is `\%4`, the connection-establishment macro name is `\%5`, and the connection-establishment macro arguments are `\%6` through `\%9`:

```
def SPLIT asg _word1 \%1, asg _word2 \%2

def DOACCESS {                  ; (Used internally by ACCESS macro)
    do \%5 \%6 \%7 \%8 \%9      ; Do the connection macro
    if fail end 1
    split \%3                   ; Get words from \%3
    asg \%3 \m(_word1)          ; Login macro name
    asg \%2 \m(_word2)          ; Prompt
    do \%3 \%4 {\%1} \%2        ; Macro, userid, password, prompt
}
```

The first command:

```
    do \%5 \%6 \%7 \%8 \%9
```

executes the connection-establishment macro from the services directory entry, together with its arguments. `\%5` is the name of the macro, and the rest are the arguments.

The next part is a bit tricky. Recall from Chapter 7 that you can "bundle" a prompt with the service name by enclosing the two in braces. This allows you to specify (or not specify) a nonstandard prompt for a particular service. Now you know what the curly braces do: they make the two words into a single macro argument, \%3 in this case. The easiest way to pick a string apart into its component words is to call a macro using the variable containing the string as its argument. We use the SPLIT macro for this. Now we have all the arguments needed for the login macro, so we can finally call it:

```
do \%3 \%4 {\%1} \%2
```

\%3 is the macro name and the others are its arguments: (\%4) is the user name and \%1 is the password, if any. The password argument is enclosed in braces in case there is no password, in which case the login macro prompts you for it. In the DO command above, if \%1 were empty and there were no braces around it, the next argument, \%2 (if any), would slide to the left and become the password, and we don't want that!

So much for automated connection establishment — now on to data transfer.

Unattended File Transfer

Establishing the connection and logging in is just the beginning of the story. Once logged in to a remote computer or service, you can program Kermit to do automatically just about anything that you would do by hand. For example, let's dial up a remote VMS computer, start Kermit there, send a file to it, then log out and hang up. We can easily construct a command file out of the building blocks from previous sections.

```
access cumin               ; Access a VMS computer
set input timeout quit
output kermit\13           ; Run C-Kermit on VMS
input 5 C-Kermit>          ; Get its prompt
out server\13              ; Put it in server mode
input 5 READY TO SERVE...  ; Get READY message
send oofa.txt              ; Send the file
bye                        ; Log out the VMS job
exit                       ; Finished
```

The first line makes the connection and logs you in. The ACCESS macro prompts you for the password since one was not supplied as an argument.

Nightly Polling

Let's construct a more ambitious example, in which we call up all our franchises at night, get their daily reports and inventories, and send them our new recipes. Using the building blocks we have already constructed, this is a relatively simple matter. We'll use our services directory for this purpose, which has already been read into memory by the C-Kermit initialization file. The list of franchises to be accessed is in another file, which we will call FRANCHISES.TXT, and which might look like this:

```
Anaheim
Boston
Milano
```

```
Moscow
Nashville
Paris
Stuttgart
Tokyo
```

Each name in this list corresponds to a services directory entry, for example:

```
Anaheim   vmslogin  hq  call hayes    /dev/cua  2400 1-213-555-0123
Boston    unixlogin hq  call telebit /dev/cub 19200 1-617-555-1234
```

Here is the script program, written as a command file. Let's name it NIGHTLY.KSC:

```
open read franchises.txt             ; Open the list of franchises
if error   end 1 Can't open franchises.txt
open write nightly.log               ; Keep a record of what happens
if error   end 1 Can't open nightly.log
write file  Polling franchises: \v(date) \v(time)

while true {                         ; Loop for each franchise
    read line                        ; Read a franchise name
    if fail break                    ; No more left, we're done
    write file \v(time): calling line
    access line                      ; Access the franchise
    xif fail {                       ; Check for failure
        write file Can't access \m(line).
        continue
    }
    output kermit\13                 ; Start Kermit there
    input 10 >                       ; Get its prompt
    output server\13                 ; Put it in server mode
    pause 2                          ; Give it time to get ready
    get inventory                    ; Get the inventory file
    xif success {
        rename inventory inventory.\m(line)
        writeln file \v(time): got inventory.\m(line)
    } else {
        writeln file \v(time): can't get inventory
    }
    send recipes                     ; Send the new recipes
    if fail writeln file \v(time): can't send recipes
    else writeln file \v(time): sent recipes ok
    bye                              ; Log out from the franchise
}
writeln file \v(time): done          ; Make final log entry
close write                          ; Close the log
end 0                                ; Succeeded
```

To poll the franchises, just start C-Kermit and tell it to TAKE this file:

```
$ kermit                             (Start Kermit)
C-Kermit>take nightly.ksc            (TAKE the command file)
```

Passwords and Security versus Automation

The problem with NIGHTLY.KSC is that it prompts you for the password of each franchise when the franchise is dialed, which could keep you sitting at the terminal all night! This difficulty could be solved easily by including all of the franchise passwords in the FRANCHISES.TXT file, along with the franchise names. But passwords in files pose an unacceptable security risk.

There is no perfect solution to this problem. One approach would be for NIGHTLY.KSC to read the entire FRANCHISES.TXT file into an array before it begins calling the franchises. As part of this process, it prompts you for each franchise's password and stores it in a parallel array, as in this example (which allows up to 50 franchises):

```
open read franchises.txt              ; The list of franchises
if error end 1 Can't open franchises.txt
define n_franchises 50                ; Change if you need more
declare \&f[\m(n_franchises)]         ; Array for franchise names
declare \&p[\m(n_franchises)]         ; Array for passwords
for \%i 1 \m(n_franchises) 1 {
    read \&f[\%i]
    if fail break
    askq \&p[\%i] Password for \&f[\%i]:
}
close read                            ; Close the file
decrement \%i                         ; Number of entries
assign \&f[0] \%i                     ; Record it here
```

Notice the use of ASKQ to request the passwords without echoing them. It is unsafe to echo passwords; someone might be looking over your shoulder.

Now you can change the main loop of NIGHTLY.KSC into a counted loop, from 1 to \&f[0], and when you ACCESS a franchise, you can provide both the service name and the password:

```
access \&f[\%i] \&p[\%i]
```

There are drawbacks to this approach. First, you still have to type the whole list of passwords every night, a tedious and error-prone process, especially when they don't echo! If you make a typographical error in a franchise password, NIGHTLY.KSC will not be able to access the franchise and your business can suffer.

Second, we have not really removed the security risk. The passwords are in an array in Kermit's memory for as long as NIGHTLY.KSC is running. A computer-literate burglar could break in after you leave, interrupt Kermit, and have it display the two arrays with a few simple keystrokes:

```
Ctrl-C ^C...
C-Kermit>for \%i 1 \&f[0] 1 { echo \&f[\%i]: \&p[\%i] }
```

Encryption

A second method is to store the franchise names and passwords together in the FRANCHISES.TXT file, but to encrypt the file with an encryption key known only to you. First, create the file in plain text. Each line has the name of a franchise (corresponding to a name in your services directory) and the password, separated by one or more spaces. Suppose your FRANCHISES.TXT file now looks like this:

```
Anaheim      goofy
Boston       beans
Milano       bongiorno
Moscow       priwjet
Nashville    howdy
Paris        pernod
Stuttgart    gruessgott
Tokyo        saki
```

If it does, you're already in trouble! Before you start worrying about how to make your C-Kermit script more secure, rush to the phone, call up your franchises, and have them fix their passwords to be harder to guess. Random combinations of upper- and lowercase letters and digits are recommended, as well as punctuation marks if the system allows them.

The rest of this section is aimed at UNIX users. We'd have said this earlier, but we wanted you to read about passwords first. This is (still) the 90s!

Now that your passwords are not easily guessable, encrypt the FRANCHISES.TXT file with the UNIX crypt program and then remove the plain-text version:

```
$ crypt keyword < franchises.txt > franchises.x
$ rm franchises.txt              (Delete the original)
$ mv franchises.x franchises.txt   (Rename)
```

The *keyword* is your encryption key, a string of characters that, like a password, should not be easily guessable. If you want to decrypt the file, just give the same crypt command again with the same keyword. For example, to view the file on your screen:

```
$ crypt keyword < franchises.txt
```

Now modify NIGHTLY.KSC to prompt you for the encryption key and then read the encrypted file through the crypt program. Now you have to type in only one password instead of many. This mitigates the consequences of both error and theft. Note that the key stays in Kermit's memory for only a brief instant, presumably while you are still present and *en garde:*

```
local key
askq key Encryption key:                      ; Ask for key
open !read crypt \m(key) < franchises.txt ; Read file through crypt
if fail end 1 Can't decrypt franchises.txt
undefine key                                  ; Erase key from memory
```

But what if you make a typographical error when entering the key? The entire nightly polling run would be wasted. You can avoid this by adding commands to check the key by displaying the first few lines of the FRANCHISES.TXT file:

```
while true {
    askq key { Encryption key: }                ; Ask for key
    run crypt \m(key) < franchises.txt | head ; Display some lines
    getok { Is this correct\? }                 ; Make sure key is correct
    if success break                            ; If not ask for key again
}
```

We get past this loop only when a working encryption key has been entered.

Next we modify NIGHTLY.KSC to make it as secure as possible. All the commands that deal with login passwords are moved into a macro, and we keep the login password in a temporary variable local to the macro. Should burglars interrupt C-Kermit, all local temporary variables are automatically erased from memory before the prompt returns.

Here is the secure version of the NIGHTLY.KSC file, for UNIX only.

```
COMMENT - File NIGHTLY.KSC: nightly franchise-polling program.

local franchise line key          ; Local variables

define WLOG -                      ; Macro for timestamped log entry
   writeln file \v(date) \v(time): \%1

define GETNAME -                   ; Macro to extract service name
   assign franchise \%1           ; from franchises.txt entry

open write \v(ndate).log                      ; Start a log file
if fail end 1 Can't write \v(ndate).log

while true {
    askq key { Encryption key: }               ; Ask for key
    if not def key continue                    ; Must be nonempty
    run crypt \m(key) < franchises.txt | head ; Display some lines
    getok { Is this correct\? }                ; Do they look OK?
    if success break                           ; Or get key again
}
; We have the encryption key.  Open and read the franchises file.
;
open !read crypt \m(key) < franchises.txt  ; Read & decrypt file
assign key \v(status)                         ; Get status, erase key
xif \m(key) {                                 ; Check status
  wlog Can't read franchises.txt
  end 1 Can't read franchises.txt
}
wlog Polling franchises: \v(date)  ; OK - proceed
```

```
while true {                            ; Loop for each franchise
    read line                           ; Read a line
    if fail break                       ; No more - done
    getname \m(line)                    ; Get the service name
    wlog {calling \m(franchise)}        ; Make a log entry
    access \m(line)                     ; ACCESS name password
    xif fail {                          ; Failed - make log entry
        wlog {Can't access \m(franchise)}
        continue                        ; Go on to next one
    }
    output kermit\13                    ; Start Kermit there
    input 10 Kermit>                    ; Get its prompt
    output server\13                    ; Put it in server mode
    pause 2                             ; Give it time to get ready
    get inventory                       ; Get the inventory file
    xif success { -
        rename inventory inventory.\m(franchise)
        wlog {got inventory.\m(franchise)}
    } else {
        wlog {can't get inventory from \m(franchise)}
    }
    send recipes                        ; Send the new recipes
    if fail wlog {recipes NOT sent to \m(franchise)}
    else wlog {recipes sent to \m(franchise)}
    bye                                 ; Log out from the franchise
}
wlog Done                               ; Make final log entry
close write                             ; Close the log
end 0                                   ; Succeeded
```

To run this secure version of NIGHTLY.KSC:

```
C-Kermit>take nightly.ksc
 Encryption key: _____
Anaheim u03gxz2p
Boston n2yU_6et9J
...
 Is this correct? yes
```

Remember, no computer program is totally secure; not our script program, not C-Kermit itself, not the underlying operating system or its utilities, and certainly not the communications path. While it is always better to take precautions like those we have used here, it is also wise not to have too much faith in them.

Nevertheless, look what we've accomplished: we have a table-driven, consistent, simple, automatic way of contacting a series of sites, *independent* of their location, the communication method, or the type of computer and operating system at each site. Milano might be an IBM mainframe contacted by dialing up a 7171 protocol converter; Tokyo might be a UNIX server on the Internet; Stuttgart could be a VMS system reached via X.25. The services directory smooths over all the differences and hides the details; it codifies the methods and procedures for each kind of connection to each kind of host for a net gain in both convenience *and* reliability.

Automatic File Transfer Recovery

As a practical example of how to use our script building blocks, let's write a script that really, *really* sends a file. If the connection is broken before the transfer is complete, we make the connection again and resume the transfer from the point of failure, using the RESEND command described in Chapter 9.

```
COMMENT - DELIVER macro:
;   \%1 = service name
;   \%2 = filename (can be wild)
;   \%3 = Maximum tries allowed (default = 1000)

define DELIVER {
    local \%i \%p              ; Local variables
    set input timeout proceed
    if not def \%3 def \%3 1000
    while not def \%p {
        askq \%p { Password for \%1 }
    }
    set file type binary      ; Transfer mode must be binary
    for \%i 1 \%3 1 {
        if > \%1 1 {           ; If not the first try
            hangup            ; hang up and print message
            echo CONNECTION BROKEN.
            Echo Reconnecting...
        }
        access \%1 \%p         ; Make the connection and log in
        if fail continue      ; Keep trying
        out kermit\13         ; Start Kermit on remote system
        input 10 >            ; Wait for prompt
        out receive\13        ; Tell it to RECEIVE
        input 10 KERMIT READY ; Wait for READY message
        pause 1               ; Plus a second for safety
        resend \%2            ; RESEND the file(s)
        if success break
    }
    if > \%1 \%3 -
        end 1 FAILED after \%3 tries.
    output logout\13          ; Success, log out
    pause 5                   ; Give it time...
    hangup                    ; Hang up
    end 0 \%2 delivered after \%i tries
}
```

The script might need a minor adjustments in the the syntax for running Kermit on the remote system and logging out from it, but in most cases it should work "out of the box." Since it's written as a macro, you can use it for all different hosts, files, and connection methods:

```
C-Kermit>deliver school homework.zip
C-Kermit>deliver tokyo slideshow.gif
```

Calling an Alphanumeric Pager

We have said that you can write a C-Kermit script to do anything that you would have done with C-Kermit by hand. In our final example, we show how to write a script to do something that very few people could do by hand: execute a simple protocol involving framed and checksummed messages. We do this in the ultimately practical framework of one of our most frequently asked questions: "How do I use Kermit to send a message to an alphanumeric pager?" (Numeric pagers are much simpler; see page 344).

Alphanumeric pagers differ from numeric ones by using computer character codes rather than DTMF touch-tones to represent data, and requiring a dialog between your computer and the paging station. The dialog follows prearranged sequences and formats, such as the Telocator Alphanumeric Protocol (TAP)[51].

In this example, we implement a useful TAP subset for sending a single-line message. Our TAPMSG macro is like our login macros; it expects the connection to already be complete. Following the TAP specification, we send carriage returns (CR, ASCII 13) until we get an "ID=" prompt, then we request an "automatic-mode" session by sending an Escape (ESC, ASCII 27) and then "PG1" and then a carriage return (\13). In response, we can receive an acknowledgement (ACK, ASCII 6), a negative acknowledgement (NAK, ASCII 21), or an error message terminated by ESC and end-of-text (EOT, ASCII 3), which terminates the session. If a NAK comes, we retransmit our message.

Once we have an ACK, we wait for the message go-ahead signal, ESC [p. Then we send the message, which consists of Start-of-text (STX, ASCII 2), the pager ID of the destination pager, a carriage return, the message itself, another carriage return, then ETX, then a checksum of all the preceding characters in the message, and finally a carriage return. The checksum is simply the sum of the ASCII values of all the characters in the message, which is easily obtained by using C-Kermit's built-in \fchecksum() function, broken into three 4-bit segments and changed into printable characters by adding 48 to each segment, producing ASCII characters in the range 48-63 (see Table VII-1).

Then we wait for the response to our message, one of the same ones described previously, handled in the same way. If we get an ACK, we "sign off" by sending End-of-Text (EOT, ASCII 4), wait for a confirmation, and then both sides hang up. All messages (ACK, NAK, EOT, etc.) have a carriage return added to them. A very simple protocol.

---

[51]The TAP specification is available from PCIA, the Personal Communications Industry Association, 500 Montgomery Street, Suite 700, Alexandria, VA 22314-1561, USA; phone +1 (703) 739-0300; Web: http://www.pcia.com/.

Our TAPMSG macro is shown in Figure 19-3 on page 456. It works as we have described, and also handles all sorts of errors, avoids infinite loops, and in general illustrates many of the programming constructions and techniques we have discussed in the past hundred pages or so.

To use the TAPMSG macro, place a call to your paging service using the communications parameters it specifies, then invoke TAPMSG with two arguments: the pager ID and the message. The pager ID (according to most vendor recommendations) should contain no punctuation or spaces. The message should fit on one line and must be enclosed in braces if it contains any spaces. Example:

```
C-Kermit>call usr com1 2400 5554321
Call complete.
C-Kermit>set parity even
C-Kermit>tapmsg 12345678 {Please call 9876543 - Urgent!}
C-Kermit>
```

If you always use the same paging service, port, modem, etc, then of course you can turn the entire process into a macro:

```
define APAGE {
    set modem type usr        ; I have a USR modem
    set port com1             ; on COM1
    set speed 2400            ; Must use 2400 bps
    set parity even           ; and even parity
    set flow xon/xoff         ; and Xon/Xoff flow control
    set modem flow none       ; end-to-end, not local
    set dial retries 10       ; Allow 10 redials
    dial 5554321              ; Call the pager service
    if success -              ; If the call is answered
       tapmsg \%1 {\%2}       ; Send the page
    else end 1 Page failed.   ; otherwise fail
}
```

If you forget to put braces around the text message, only the first word is sent. You can get around this, if you are willing to limit the message to 8 words. In the APAGE macro definition, change:

```
tapmsg \%1 {\%2}
```

to:

```
assign \%2 \%2 \%3 \%4 \%5 \%6 \%7 \%8 \%9
tapmsg \%1 {\ftrim(\%2)}
```

Here we redefine the \%2 argument to be all of the arguments from \%2 to \%9, separated by spaces. Then when we send the text, we trim any trailing spaces from the end, in case there were fewer than 8 words of text:

```
C-Kermit>apage 87654321 Go to Thirty-Third and Third
```

```
COMMENT- TAPMSG - Send a one-line alpha page using TAP
;    \%1 = Pager ID
;    \%2 = Message
;
def TAPMSG {
    local \%i \%m \%s block      ; Local variables
    asg \%m \2\%1\13\%2\13\3    ; <STX>ID<CR>msg<CR><ETX>
    asg \%s \fchecksum(\%m)      ; Get checksum and make block
    asg block \%m\fchar(\fmod(\%s/256,16)+48)-
\fchar(\fmod(\%s/16,16)+48)-
\fchar(\fmod(\%s,16)+48)\13      ; Checksummed TAP block

    for \%i 1 3 1 {              ; Try 3 times to get prompt
        output \13               ; Send <CR>
        input 3 ID=              ; Wait for "ID="
        if success break
    }
    if > \%i 3 end 1 No prompt
    for \%i 1 3 1 {              ; Send <ESC>PG1, get <ACK>
        msleep 500
        output \{27}PG1\13
        minput 3 {\6\13} {\21\13} {\27\4\13}
        switch \v(minput) {
           :0, continue                ; Timeout
           :1, break                   ; <ACK>
           :2, continue                ; <NAK>
           :3, end 1 Forced disconnect ; Fatal error
        }
        break
    }
    if > \%i 3 end 1 Timed out or unknown response
    input 5 \27[p\13                    ; Wait for go-ahead
    if fail end 1 No go-ahead           ; Didn't get it
    for \%i 1 3 1 {                     ; Try three times
        msleep 500
        output \m(block)                ; Send block
        minput 5 {\6\13} {\21\13} {\13\27\4\13} {\30\13}
        switch \v(minput) {             ; Get response
           :0, continue                 ; Timeout
           :1, break                    ; <ACK> - success
           :2, continue                 ; <NAK>
           :3, end 1 Forced disconnect
           :4, end 1 Illegal message
        }
        output \4\13                    ; Sign off with <EOT>
        input 5 \27\4\13                ; Get <ESC><EOT> back
        break                           ; But ignore timeout
    }
    if > \%i 3 end 1 Timed out or unknown response
    end 0
}
```

Figure 19-3 The TAPMSG Macro

Some Things We Didn't Tell You

This section lists some odds and ends that did not fit conveniently elsewhere, most of them of interest only to the most advanced script programmers. We begin with several invisible commands (i.e. commands that do not show up when you type question mark at the prompt) that are used in the interal macro definitions that execute the FOR, WHILE, XIF, and SWITCH commands. Note that all of their names begin with the underscore character:

_ASSIGN *variable [text]*

Just like ASSIGN, except the variable name is constructed from other variables, rather than taken literally. For example:

```
assign \%a 2
_assign x\%a \v(time)
```

assigns the current time to a variable named x2. Synonym: **_ASG**.

_DEFINE *variable [text]*

Just like DEFINE, except that, as with _ASSIGN, the variable name constructed, rather than taken literally.

_FORWARD *label*

Just like FORWARD except that if the label is not found at the current command level (macro or command file), the command stack is not popped. Furthermore, unlike the regular FORWARD and GOTO commands, alphabetic case *is* signigicant in the label if CASE is ON. This command is used internally by SWITCH for selecting the right case.

_GETARGS

Retrieves the macro arguments from two levels up the macro stack. For example, if A calls B and B calls C, and _GETARGS is executed in C, then C's copies of \%0 through \%9 are replaced by A's.

_PUTARGS

Sets the macro argument variables of the macro two levels up from the macro arguments at the current level. If A calls B and B calls C, and _PUTARGS is executed in C, then A's copies of \%0 through \%9 are replaced by C's.

The primary intention of all these commands is to allow the creation of macros that are *nestable*, e.g. FOR-loops within FOR-loops within FOR-loops. We use constructions like:

```
_assign _for\v(cmdlevel) { _getargs, ..., _putargs }
do _for\v(cmdlevel)
```

where ... is replaced by the loop variable tests and the commands that go inside the loop. So if we have three nested FOR-loops, they are named (e.g.) _FOR1, _FOR2, and _FOR3. A FOR-loop is actually implemented as a macro that defines the _FOR*x* macro for and then executes it; thus it is a macro within a macro, and that is why _GETARGS and _PUTARGS operate two levels up.

We have mentioned in various spots that certain commands are "stackable;" that is, their effects are felt only at the current command level and are inherited by lower levels, but not at higher levels. This lets you use these commands in macros and command files without worrying about them having any wider effects. Here is the complete list:

IF COUNT, SET COUNT

The COUNT variable is on the call stack. Thus any command files or macros that are invoked from within SET COUNT / IF COUNT loops can contain their own SET COUNT / IF COUNT loops without interfering with the ones at higher levels. But note that you can *not* nest these loops at the same command level (but you *can* nest FOR loops to achieve the same effect).

SET [INPUT] CASE

Whether alphabetic case is significant in string comparisons.

SET INPUT TIMEOUT-ACTION

Whether the current macro or command file ENDs if an INPUT command times out.

SET MACRO ERROR

Whether the current macro ENDs if there is any kind of error.

SET TAKE ERROR

Whether the current command file ENDs if there is any kind of error.

Finally, there are lots of macros and scripts we would have liked to include but did not for lack of space. Instead, we'll leave them as exercises for the interested reader :-)

- Rule sets for different dialing locales. See Chapter 5 for a few examples.

- A GETOK command substitute in the language of your choice, that has and displays a default answer, e.g.: Alle Dateien löschen? (Ja/Nein) [Nein]:

- Switching X.25 PADs between terminal mode and file-transfer mode (Chapter 10).

- A convenient way to capture files with LOG SESSION (Chapter 15).

- Getting your dynamically assigned IP address from a terminal server (*hint:* use \fipaddr(\v(input))) and then starting SLIP on your computer to use it.

- Call up a computer that calls you back using a secure dialback system (*hint:* use the HANGUP and ANSWER commands).

- Host mode — create a secure user ID and mini file system for multiple users, let people log in to your computer, give them a menu or command shell, let them send and receive messages, upload and download files within a restricted area, and so on. (If you have Kermit 95, no fair peeking at SCRIPTS\HOST.KSC.)

The SCRIPT Command

The SCRIPT command is shorthand for a series of INPUT and OUTPUT commands, allowing an entire login script to be executed in a single short (but cryptic) command. Strictly speaking, the SCRIPT command is not needed. There is nothing it can do that cannot be done by the methods already described. The SCRIPT command has been a part of C-Kermit since 1985 and is carried forward for compatibility with previous releases.

A SCRIPT command consists of a series of *expect* and *send* strings, separated by spaces. Kermit waits for the first *expect* string; when it comes Kermit sends its first *send* string and then waits for its next *expect* string, and so on:

SCRIPT *expect send [expect send [. . .]]*
> Executes the given series of *expect* and *send* strings. If an *expect* string does not arrive, the command fails. If all the *expect* strings arrive, the command succeeds.

The *send* and *expect* strings can contain special sequences prefixed by tilde (~), listed in Table 19-1 on the next page. Most of these can also be adequately represented by Kermit's normal backslash codes.

Kermit automatically includes a carriage return at the end of each *send* string unless it ends with ~c. Only the last seven characters in each *expect* are matched. A null *expect*, ~0 or two adjacent dashes, causes a short delay before proceeding to the next *send* sequence. A null *expect* always succeeds.

If there is a chance that an *expect* sequence might not arrive, you can express conditional sequences in the form:

```
-send-expect[-send-expect[...]]
```

where dashed sequences are followed until an *expect* succeeds. For example, on a noisy connection:

```
script ~0 login\32olaf-ssword:-login\32olaf-ssword:
```

sends "login olaf" followed by a carriage return. If the Password: prompt does not arrive within the default timeout interval, "login olaf" is sent again.

expect-send transactions can be debugged by logging transactions (LOG TRANSACTIONS). This records all exchanges, both expected and actual. The script execution is also logged in the session log, if that is activated.

Script execution can be interrupted by typing your interrupt character, normally Ctrl-C.

Table 19-1 Notation for SCRIPT Command

Notation	Description
~b	Backspace (you can also use \8)
~s	Space (= \32)
~q	Question mark (= \?)
~n	Linefeed (= \10)
~r	Carriage return (= \13)
~t	Tab (= \9)
~~	Tilde (= \126)
~x	XON (Control-Q) (= \17)
~c	Don't append a carriage return to a send string.
~n[n[n]]	Octal representation of an ASCII character code (= \onnn)
~0	(zero) When used as an *expect* string, this means "expect nothing" and proceed immediately to the next *send* string. When used by itself as a *send* string, it means to send nothing followed by a carriage return.
~d	Delay approximately 1/3 second during send.
~w[d[d]]	Wait the specified number of seconds during expect, then time out. The default waiting interval is 15 seconds.

The progress of a SCRIPT command is normally displayed on your screen, but you can control the display with the following command:

SET SCRIPT ECHO { ON, OFF }

Controls whether the characters sent and received during script execution are to be echoed on your screen. The default, ON, echoes the characters.

Here is an example in which the SCRIPT command is used to log in to a VMS computer, similar to our VMSLOGIN macro from page 433:

```
script ~0 ~0 name:--name: \%1 word: \%2 \27Z \27[\?1c $--$--$
```

In this example, we expect nothing, then send a carriage return, then wait for name: from the Username: prompt. If we don't get it, we send another carriage return and wait for it again. If we get it, we send our username (which is contained in the variable \%1), then wait for the Password: prompt. If it comes, we send our password \%2, wait for the terminal ID query, send a VT100 terminal ID, then wait for the VMS dollar sign prompt. If it doesn't come, we send a carriage return and wait again, and so on. The example demonstrates how a single SCRIPT command can replace a long series of OUTPUT, INPUT, and IF SUCCESS commands, accomplishing the same actions in a more compact (and more cryptic) form. The SCRIPT command does not allow intermixture of *expect-send* items with regular Kermit commands such as SET PARITY, SEND, RECEIVE, and so on, but SCRIPT commands themselves can be intermixed with any other C-Kermit commands.

Starting and Stopping C-Kermit

The command with which you start C-Kermit is called the command line. Items included after the program's name are interpreted by C-Kermit as filenames or commands. For example, if your system prompt is $, and you start C-Kermit by typing "kermit", then you could also start it like this:

```
$ kermit -s oofa.txt
```

which tells C-Kermit to do just one thing: send the file oofa.txt, and then exit. The complete format of the C-Kermit command line is:

kermit [filename] [options] [redirectors]

where:

kermit
> Is the command used to start C-Kermit, usually just "kermit".

filename
> Is the name of a script program file to execute (optional).

options
> Is a list of one or more command-line options (optional).

redirectors
> Are system-dependent indicators for redirection of standard input and output, such as "*< filename*", "*> filename*", and/or "*| command*" in UNIX (optional).

Command-line options are listed later in this appendix, starting on page 465.

The command to start C-Kermit depends on your computer and operating system, and how C-Kermit is installed. Usually it's just "kermit". In Windows 95 and NT, it's "k95"; in OS/2 it's "k2". If C-Kermit is not installed in your "path" or as a system command, you might need to type its full file specification, or prefix it by your system's "RUN" command (such as RUN in VMS, X in AOS/VS, etc). If you type the name alone, not followed by other material, you should see a greeting and then a C-Kermit> prompt, indicating that C-Kermit is ready for you to type commands.

If you include the name of an existing file immediately after the C-Kermit program name, this indicates a C-Kermit "application file" containing commands to be executed by C-Kermit. If you want C-Kermit to exit when execution of the application file is complete, you must include an EXIT command in the application file itself.

You can also start C-Kermit with its standard input piped from another command or program, on systems that support this notion; for example, in UNIX:

```
$ sort < commandfile | kermit
```

if you can think of any good reason to do this.

When C-Kermit starts, it executes its commands in the following order:

1. The -d (debug) command-line option, if any.

2. The commands in the initialization file, if any. If -Y (uppercase) was used, the initialization file is skipped. If -y (lowercase) was used to specify an alternative initialization file, it is executed instead of the standard one.

3. If a filename was given as the first command-line option, the commands in that file.

4. Command-line options (except -y and -C), if any.

5. The command list given in the -C command-line option, if any.

6. Interactive commands if no action commands were given on the command line, or if action commands were given and the -S option was included on the command line.

The interactive commands in (6) include commands piped in or redirected from files, in which case Kermit exits at the end of the file or pipe. When standard input is not redirected and no command files or macros are active, C-Kermit is said to be at top level and commands must be typed at the keyboard; C-Kermit keeps prompting you until it encounters an EXIT or QUIT command.

Note that standard input can be accessed only in a sequential manner, so GOTO and similar commands have no effect in the standard input stream, even if it happens to come from a file. In other words, GOTO and other forms of transfer of control can be used only in command files that are executed with the TAKE command, or in macros.

Program Termination

Normal termination occurs in the following ways:

1. The "action options," if any, given on the command line are completed. This is explained in the next section.

2. An EXIT command is executed.

3. The -E or -J options were given on the command line and the connection is lost or closed.

4. The program is interrupted while executing its initialization file or command-line action options.

When C-Kermit exits, it returns a numeric code that can be tested by batch programs, shell scripts, etc. A return code of 0 indicates overall success. A nonzero return code indicates a specific type of failure; it can can be the sum of any combination of one or more failure codes shown in Table I-1. For example, a code of 6 (= 4 + 2) means both a SEND command and a RECEIVE command failed.

The EXIT command can be used at the prompt, in a macro, or in a command file to terminate C-Kermit:

EXIT *[number]*

Closes all open files and devices, hangs up any dialed or network connection, restores the command terminal to its normal state, executes the macro named ON_EXIT if one is defined, and returns to the system. If a *number* is included, it becomes C-Kermit's exit status code, otherwise C-Kermit returns the status code given in the most recent SET EXIT STATUS command, if any; otherwise a code whose format depends on the host operating system, but which summarizes the overall success of its file transfer operations a shown in Table I-1. Synonym: **QUIT**.

If SET EXIT WARNING is ALWAYS, or a connection is open and SET EXIT WARNING is not OFF, C-Kermit warns you before exiting and gives you a chance to change your mind.

Table I-1 C-Kermit Return Codes

Code	Meaning
0	Overall success
1	A program error occurred
2	A SEND command failed
4	A RECEIVE command failed
8	A REMOTE command failed

To emphasize: when C-Kermit exits, *all files and devices that it opened are closed*. There is no way to have C-Kermit exit and leave a device or file open for use by other programs. This is not a C-Kermit feature; it is a feature of UNIX, VMS, OS/2, VOS, AOS/VS, Windows, and all the other operating systems where C-Kermit runs.

Note, however, that it is possible for C-Kermit to pass the file descriptor of an *open* communication device to an inferior program, by using the \v(ttyfd) variable. Similarly, it is possible for another program to invoke C-Kermit and pass it a numeric file descriptor in place of a device name in the "-l", "-F", or "-z" command-line options.

Several considerations affecting how, when, and whether C-Kermit exits are governed by the SET EXIT command and can be displayed with SHOW EXIT:

SET EXIT ON-DISCONNECT { ON, OFF }

When ON, C-Kermit exits when it senses that a local-mode connection has been closed, broken, or hung up; for example when you log out of a remote host or service. This is generally reliable on network connections, but on serial connections depends on the underlying device drivers, the physical aspects of the connection, and the CARRIER-WATCH setting. The default is OFF.

SET EXIT STATUS *number*

Tells C-Kermit the exit status to return when it exits. The *number* is used in all cases except when an EXIT *number* command is given. You can use the SET EXIT STATUS command to "build up" an exit status throughout execution of script, for example, by ORing various values into an exit status variable:

```
assign exit_status 0
...
assign exit_status \feval(\m(exit_status)|16)
```

SET EXIT WARNING { ON, OFF, ALWAYS }

Tells C-Kermit to warn you if you try to exit and a connection is still open, in which case it asks you whether you really want to exit:

```
C-Kermit> set exit warning on
C-Kermit> set host oofa.com
C-Kermit> exit
 A network connection to oofa.com might still be active.
OK to exit? no
C-Kermit> exit
 A network connection to oofa.com might still be active.
OK to exit? yes
$
```

SET EXIT WARNING ALWAYS means always ask. OFF means never ask. EXIT WARNING is ON by default, meaning ask only if a connection is (or appears to be) open. As with SET EXIT ON-DISCONNECT, the effectiveness of EXIT WARNING ON when used on serial connections depends on serial port drivers, wires, modems, etc.

Abnormal termination of C-Kermit occurs when:

- The program is terminated from another process; for example, by a "kill" command in UNIX or a STOP command in VMS, or a system shutdown procedure.

- The program crashes. It shouldn't happen, but anything's possible.

- The computer itself crashes, or other acts of nature.

When C-Kermit terminates abnormally, the results depend on the operating system and, of course, the manner of termination. Usually, any open files are closed in whatever their current state might be. Devices are closed. The most unnerving aspect of abnormal termination comes in UNIX, where the login terminal might be left in an unusable state (more about this in Appendix III) and a large core file might be left on disk. VMS might display a long "traceback" on the screen (if you can capture one of these, feel free to send it in to kermit-support@columbia.edu for analysis).

Command-Line Options

A selection of C-Kermit commands is available on the command line in environments that support passing command-line options to programs through the C-language "argv, argc" mechanism [53], provided that Kermit has been configured to use them. Command-line options can be useful for various reasons:

1. For a one-shot deal like sending a file, it is faster and easier to use C-Kermit this way — especially handy for autoup- and downloading.

2. You might want to use Kermit in a command pipeline, sending files from standard input or receiving them to standard output; for example, to transfer a file in compressed and/or encrypted form between two UNIX systems.

3. You might want to change Kermit's normal startup actions, for example specifying a different initialization file or no initialization file at all.

4. You might be using C-Kermit as a "helper" for a Web browser or other application, from which it can be invoked only with command-line options.

5. Some stripped-down versions of C-Kermit might be built for command-line operation only, without an interactive command parser.

Using command-line options, you can define convenient shortcuts. For example, using the UNIX K-Shell [5], you could define aliases like these in your .env file:

```
alias "kr=kermit -r"    # to receive files, just type 'kr'
alias "ks=kermit -s"    # to send text files, type 'ks filename'
alias "kb=kermit -is"   # to send binary files, type 'kb filename'
```

In VMS, Kermit must be installed as a foreign command so VMS will make the command line options available to Kermit, for example:

```
KERMIT :== $SYS$SYSTEM:KERMIT.EXE
```

If it is not installed this way, you must use the VMS RUN command to start it and you can't pass command-line options to it. But you can still put a command like the one above into your LOGIN.COM file as a workaround.

C-Kermit's command-line options conform to UNIX conventions [39]:

- Command names (like "kermit") must be between 2 and 9 characters long.

- Command names must include lowercase letters (in UNIX) and digits only.

- An option name is a single character.

- Options are delimited by " -", for example " -q -z".

- Options with no arguments may be grouped (bundled) behind one delimiter, for example " -s oofa.txt -qt".

- Option-arguments cannot be optional.

- A group of bundled options may end with an option that has an argument, for example " -qzs oofa.txt".

- Arguments immediately follow options, separated by whitespace.

- The order of options does not matter.

- "-" preceded and followed by whitespace means standard input.

C-Kermit's command-line options are summarized in Table I-2 on page 476 and described in the following sections.

Option List

C-Kermit has two kinds of command-line options: action options and non-action options. If you give one or more action options on the command line, C-Kermit exits after performing them, returning an appropriate exit status code to your system's command processor (shell, DCL, etc.), *unless* you also specified the -S (uppercase) "Stay" option. If the command line includes no action options, C-Kermit issues its prompt after executing the command-line options. The action options are primarily for entering CONNECT mode and for transferring files. The non-action options correspond mostly to SET commands. In VMS, uppercase options must be enclosed in doublequotes to prevent them from being converted to lowercase before C-Kermit sees them.

Program Management Options

The first group of options is concerned with program management:

-h Help. Action option. Displays a brief synopsis of the command line options, then exits. Example:

```
$ kermit -h
```

-y *filename*

Executes commands from the specified file instead of the standard initialization file. Applies to only interactive versions. Examples:

```
% kermit -y /usr/olga/special.ini      (UNIX)
$ kermit -y sys$login:special.ini      (VMS)
F:\>k95 -y c:\kermit\special.ini       (Windows 95 or NT)
C:\>k2 -y c:\kermit\special.ini        (OS/2)
```

-Y (uppercase Y) Do not read or execute any initialization file. Applies only to interactive versions. Examples:

```
$ kermit "-Y"                          (VMS - Note doublequotes)
% kermit -Y                            (Elsewhere)
```

filename

If the first item on C-Kermit's command line is a filename, C-Kermit executes commands from the named file after it finishes the initialization file, if any. Applies only to interactive versions. Example:

```
% kermit sendmyfiles
```

In UNIX only, C-Kermit command files can be constructed to be run as if they were programs, starting C-Kermit automatically. To do this, include a line like the following as the first line of the command file:

```
#!/usr/local/bin/kermit
```

where /usr/local/bin/kermit is the full pathname of the Kermit program on your computer. Add execute permission to the command file:

```
% chmod +x sendmyfiles
```

and then you can run it as if it were any other UNIX command, program, or shell script:

```
% sendmyfiles
```

In VMS, you can define convenient aliases to run Kermit easily with different command files by defining symbols for them; for example:

```
$ compuserve :== $sys$system:kermit.exe sys$login:compuserve.ksc
$ sprintnet :== $sys$system:kermit.exe sys$login:sprintnet.ksc
```

-C *"command, command, ..."*

(uppercase C) Executes the interactive-mode commands after the initialization file (if any), the other command-line options (if any), and the command file (if any). Applies to interactive versions only. The command list must be enclosed in doublequotes, with commands separated by commas. Examples:

```
$ kermit "-C" "set block-check b, send oofa.txt"   (VMS)
$ kermit -C "set block-check b, send oofa.txt"    (Elsewhere)
```

This option lets you give any commands at all to C-Kermit from the command line. The maximum length of the command line is your operating system's command line buffer size. The maximum length for the command-list is implementation dependent, usually either 1024 or 4072.

When you use the -C option, the command list is assigned to a macro called CL_COMMANDS (command-line commands), so you can also execute these commands later during your session simply by typing the name of this macro:

```
C-Kermit>cl_commands
```

The -C option is not considered an action option, even if the command list contains action commands. So if no action options are on the command-line, the C-Kermit prompt appears when the last command in the list has finished executing. To force C-Kermit to exit when finished executing the -C command list, include EXIT as its last command, as in this example, which uses all the power of C-Kermit to clear a VT100 terminal screen:

```
kermit -YHC "xecho \27[H\27[2J, exit"
```

-q Quiet. Suppresses screen messages during local-mode file transfer as well as most other screen writing. This option is used to allow a file transfer to take place in the background. It is equivalent to the interactive-mode command SET QUIET ON.

-H No Herald. Suppresses display of C-Kermit's program herald and greeting when C-Kermit starts.

-z Force foreground operation (UNIX). Even if Kermit thinks it is running in the background, it should behave as if it were in the foreground, issuing its normal prompts and messages, and so on. You can use this option whenever you start C-Kermit in some unusual way and its prompt fails to appear. It is equivalent to the interactive-mode command SET BACKGROUND OFF.

-E (uppercase E) Exit on disconnect. Exit automatically when the remote host or service hangs up or closes the connection. Normally C-Kermit returns to its prompt when this happens if it was not invoked with action options.

-d Debug. Equivalent to the LOG DEBUG command. Records debugging information in the file DEBUG.LOG in the current directory. Use this option if you believe Kermit is misbehaving, and show the resulting log file to your local Kermit maintainer.

-R (uppercase R) Remote-only. This tells C-Kermit that you intend to use it only in remote mode and causes the IF REMOTE test to succeed; useful in the initialization file for skipping the connection-establishment macro definitions that will not be used.

-M *username*

(uppercase M) My user name. Sets the internal \v(user) variable. Equivalent to the SET LOGIN USERNAME command.

-S (uppercase S) Stay. This option tells C-Kermit to issue its prompt and enter inter-active command mode even if the command line included action options. Examples:

```
$ kermit -s oofa.txt "-S"        (VMS)
$ kermit -r -a oofa.txt -S       (Elsewhere)
```

= *text*

Tells C-Kermit to ignore all command-line options that follow but (in an interactive version of C-Kermit that includes the script programming feature) make them avail-able, along with all the other items from the command line, in the array \&@[]. In VMS, this option must be enclosed in doublequotes if it is the first option. Examples:

```
$ kermit -z = this is some text (Anywhere)
$ kermit "=" this is some text  (VMS)
$ kermit = this is some text     (Elsewhere)
```

Communications Options

These are the options for selecting and configuring your communication device, and are therefore useful mainly in local mode.

-8 Eight-bit-clean. This tells C-Kermit it is safe to use 8-bit input and output on the com-munication device and on its own console terminal. Equivalent to SET PARITY NONE, SET COMMAND BYTESIZE 8, SET TERMINAL BYTESIZE 8

-l *device*

Specifies a serial communication device to use for file transfer and terminal connec-tion. Equivalent to the SET LINE command (see page 58). Examples:

```
% kermit -l /dev/ttyi5          (UNIX)
$ kermit -l txa5:               (VMS)
) kermit -l @con5               (AOS/VS)
C:\>kermit -l com1              (OS/2 or Windows)
```

You can also give a numeric file descriptor for a serial port that is already open:

```
$ kermit -l 6
```

This can be used for starting C-Kermit from some other communication software that already has opened the device, provided the other software gives you a way to put the file descriptor on the C-Kermit command line. In C-Kermit itself, for example:

```
C-Kermit> kermit -l \v(ttyfd)
```

When a serial communication device is being used, you also need some additional options for successful communication:

-b *number*

Bits per second. Specifies the transmission speed in bits per second ("baud rate") for the serial communication device given in the -1 option, as in:

```
$ kermit -l /dev/ttyi5 -b 38400
```

This option, equivalent to the SET SPEED command (p. 59), should always be included with the -1 option since the speed of a device when it is opened is not necessarily what you expect.

-p *letter*

Parity. Selects the type of parity for use on the selected communication device. The argument is a single letter, e, o, m, s, or n, identifying the type of parity: even, odd, mark, space, or none, respectively. The default is n, none. Equivalent to SET PARITY (page 158).

-t Specifies local echoing during CONNECT mode and half-duplex line turnaround with XON as the handshake character during file transfer. Used for communicating with IBM mainframes in linemode. Equivalent to SET TERMINAL ECHO ON (page 158) and SET HANDSHAKE XON (page 213).

-m *name*

Modem type: Hayes, Telebit, USR, etc. (see Table 3-2 on page 68). Use this option in conjunction with the -1 and -b options if you want to use C-Kermit to dial out. If you don't specify a modem type, and the modem is not asserting the carrier signal, Kermit might not be able to open the device given in the -1 option. The modem name can be abbreviated, e.g. "hay" for "Hayes." Equivalent to SET MODEM TYPE (page 66). Example:

```
$ kermit -m telebit -l /dev/cub -b 19200
```

You can also use the -C option to include a dialing command:

```
$ kermit -m telebit -l /dev/cub -b 19200 -C "dial 7654321"
```

If you want to use a network connection (pages 117–139) rather than a serial terminal device for communication, use the following options rather than -1, -b, and -m. Parity is usually not required. The speed (-b) option has no effect on network connections.

-j *host*

Host. Specifies a TCP/IP network host. Equivalent to the SET NETWORK TCP/IP and SET HOST commands. The *host* can be the name of an entry in your networks directory (if you have one), an IP host name, an IP host number (containing dots), or either one of these followed by a colon or a space and then a TCP service name or number (the default service is 23, which is TELNET). If you have a network directory, the *host* is looked up there unless you begin the hostname with an equals sign (=), in which case the part after the equals sign is used literally with no lookup. The following examples all connect to the TCP TELNET port on the same host:

```
$ kermit -j kermit.columbia.edu
$ kermit -j kermit.columbia.edu:23
$ kermit -j kermit.columbia.edu 23
$ kermit -j kermit.columbia.edu:telnet
$ kermit -j kermit.columbia.edu telnet
$ kermit -j 128.59.39.2
$ kermit -j 128.59.39.2:23
$ kermit -j 128.59.39.2 23
$ kermit -j 128.59.39.2:telnet
$ kermit -j 128.59.39.2 telnet
```

If you get a message like:

```
?Invalid argument, type 'kermit -h' for help
```

it means your Kermit version does not include TCP/IP network support.

The following example connects to a non-TELNET information server:

```
$ kermit -j martini.eecs.umich.edu:3000
```

This one starts an RLOGIN connection:

```
$ kermit -j unix.cmgcorp.com:513 -M olga
```

−F *number*

TCP/IP network file descriptor number; the file descriptor for an open TCP/IP TELNET connection:

```
$ kermit -j 4
```

−J *host*

(uppercase J) Like −j, but instructs C-Kermit to act like a TELNET program: enter CONNECT mode automatically, allow the user to escape back and reconnect repeatedly (e.g. to transfer files), and exit automatically when the connection is broken (e.g. when you log out from the remote host). You can use "kermit −J" anywhere that you would use "telnet"; the commands should be interchangeable. This allows you to specify C-Kermit as your Telnet program to other applications, such as a Web browser.

For X.25 connections only, you have four additional options:

−X *address*

(uppercase X) X.25 address. Specifies an X.25 network address.

−Z *number*

(uppercase Z) X.25 file descriptor. Specifies a file descriptor for an X.25 connection that is already open.

-o *index*
X.25 closed user group call.

-u X.25 reverse-charge call.

Here are C-Kermit's terminal connection options:

-c Establishes a terminal connection over the communication device before any Kermit protocol activity takes place. Get back to your local computer by typing the escape character (normally Control-Backslash) followed by the letter *C*. A communication device must also be specified. Equivalent to the CONNECT command (page 148). Examples:

```
% kermit -l /dev/ttya1 -b 2400 -c       (UNIX)
$ kermit -l txa4: -b 19200 -c           (VMS)
C:\>kermit -l com2 -b 57600 -c          (Windows or OS/2)
$ kermit -j watsun.cc.columbia.edu -c   (Network)
```

-n Like -c, but *after* Kermit protocol activity; -c and -n may both be used in the same command line. For example, the -c option lets you connect to the other computer, log in, and start a file transfer, and the -n option connects you back after the file transfer so you can log out.

File Transfer Options

The following command-line options are available to perform C-Kermit's basic text and binary file transfer operations, described fully in Chapters 9–12:

-s *filespec [filespec [filespec . . .]]*
Send. Action option. Sends the specified file or files to a Kermit program that is in RECEIVE or SERVER mode or, if your terminal emulator supports it, starts an autodownload of one or more files. In UNIX, if *filespec* contains wildcard (meta) characters, the UNIX shell expands it into a list of filenames. The *filespec* can also be a list of files, as in:

```
kermit -s ckcmai.c ckuker.h *.txt
```

Thus, this option is equivalent to the interactive-mode command MSEND. If the *filename* is - (a hyphen), Kermit sends from its standard input, which may come from a file:

```
kermit -s - < foo.bar
```

or piped in from a process:

```
ls -l | grep Tokyo | kermit -s -
```

But you can't use this mechanism to send characters from your keyboard. If you want to send a file whose actual name is -, you can precede it with a path name, as in:

```
kermit -s ./-
```

To use standard input as a source for sending files in VMS, you must redefine SYS$INPUT to be the desired file, for example:

```
$ define /user sys$input login.com
$ kermit -s "-"
```

Note that the final hyphen must be quoted; otherwise VMS interprets it as a DCL command-continuation character.

-r Receive. Action option. Waits passively for files to arrive from another Kermit program, which must be told to send the file(s). This option is equivalent to the RECEIVE command.

-k Receive to standard output. Action option. Receives a file or files from another Kermit, which must be told to send the file(s), and writes them to standard output. This option can be used in several ways:

```
kermit -k
```
Displays the incoming files on your screen; to be used only in local mode.

```
kermit -k > filename
```
(UNIX and other operating systems that support standard-output redirection via the > operator) Sends the incoming file or files to the named file, *filename*. If more than one file arrives, all are concatenated together into the single file, *filename*.

```
kermit -k | command
```
(UNIX and other operating systems that support command pipelines via |) Pipes the incoming file or files to the indicated command, as in:

```
kermit -k | sort > sorted.stuff
```

-a *filename*
As-name. When used with -s this tells the name to be sent to the other Kermit in place of the file's real name. When used with -g (next page) or -r, it tells the name to give to the arriving file, rather than storing it under the name it was sent with. If more than one file is sent or arrives, -a applies only to the first one. Example:

```
kermit -s foo -a bar
```

sends the file foo, telling the receiver that its name is bar ("send foo as bar"). When using -a with -g or -r, you may also give a device and/or directory name, without a filename. In that case, *all* arriving files are stored in the indicated device/directory. Example:

```
kermit -g oofa.* -a /tmp/
```

-x Server. Action option. Become a Kermit server. This is equivalent to the SERVER command.

Here are the options for sending commands to Kermit servers:

-g *remote-filename*

Get. Action option. Actively requests a Kermit server to send the named file or files; *remote-filename* is a file specification in the remote host's own syntax. In UNIX, if *remote-filename* happens to contain any special shell characters, like space, *, [, ~, etc., these must be quoted using the UNIX shell's quoting mechanisms, as in:

```
kermit -g x\*.\?
```

or:

```
kermit -g "profile exec"
```

The -g option is equivalent to the GET command. Use "kermit -g" to initiate an autoupload if your terminal emulator supports Kermit autouploads.

-f Finish. Action option. Sends a FINISH command to a remote server, equivalent to the FINISH command.

The command line may contain no more than one protocol action option; that is, only one of these: s, r, x, g, f, or k.

The following modifier options can be included with file-transfer action options:

-i Binary mode; equivalent to the SET FILE TYPE BINARY command. Specifies that files should be sent or received with no conversions. See Chapter 9.

-T Text mode; equivalent to the SET FILE TYPE TEXT command. Specifies that files should be sent or received with record format and possibly character-set conversions. See Chapters 9 and 16.

-w Writeover. If an incoming file has the same name as an existing file, it replaces the existing file. This changes the default behavior, which is to preserve the old file by changing the name of the existing file before creating the new one. Equivalent to SET FILE COLLISION OVERWRITE.

-e *number*

Receive packet-length. Specifies that C-Kermit is allowed to receive packets up to the specified length, between 10 and some large number, like 1000 or 2000, or even 9000, depending on the C-Kermit version. The default maximum length for received packets is 94. Packets longer than 94 are used only if the other Kermit supports and agrees to use the long packet protocol extension. This command is equivalent to SET RECEIVE PACKET-LENGTH.

-v *number*

Window size. Specifies that C-Kermit is allowed to send and receive files using a window size up to the given number. Window sizes greater than 1 speed up transfers in most situations, especially long-distance network connections. The default window size is 1, the maximum is 32. Sizes greater than 1 work only if the other Kermit supports this option and has been told to use it. Equivalent to the SET WINDOW command.

-Q Quick transfer options. Equivalent to SET RECEIVE PACKET-LENGTH 4096, SET WINDOW 20, SET PREFIXING CAUTIOUS.

-D *number*

Used in remote mode with -s. Equivalant to SET DELAY; how many seconds to wait before starting to send. Use 0 for no delay at all, which is useful when your terminal emulator supports Kermit autodownloads. Otherwise specify sufficient seconds to allow you do whatever is needed to instruct your terminal program to receive a file using Kermit protocol.

Command-Line Examples

`kermit -l /dev/ttyi5 -b 38400 -rcn`

Connects you (the c in -rcn) to another computer through the `ttyi5` device at 38400 bps, where you presumably log in, run Kermit, and give it a SEND command. After you escape back, C-Kermit waits for a file (or files) to arrive (the r in -rcn). When the file transfer is complete, you are reconnected (the n in -rcn) to the remote system so you can logout. This example illustrates the principles that the order of options does not matter and that options with no arguments can be grouped.

`kermit -l /dev/ttyi5 -b 38400 -cntp m -r -a foo`

Like the preceding command, except the remote system in this case uses half-duplex communication (the t in -cntp) with mark parity (-...p m). This illustrates how the final option (p) in an option bundle -cntp can take an argument. The first file that arrives is stored under the name foo (-a foo).

`kermit -ix`

Starts up C-Kermit as a server (note the bundling of the options -i and -x). Files are sent in binary mode.

`kermit -l /dev/ttyi6 -b 19200`

Sets the communication line and speed. No action is specified, so C-Kermit issues a prompt and enters an interactive dialog with you with these settings in effect unless you give commands to change them.

`kermit`

Starts up Kermit interactively with all default settings.

The next example shows how UNIX C-Kermit might be used to send an entire directory tree from one UNIX system to another, using the *tar* (tape archive) program as Kermit's standard input and output. On the originating system, in this case the remote, type (for instance):

```
tar cf - /usr/olga | kermit -is -
```

This causes tar to send the directory /usr/olga (and all its files and all its subdirectories and all their files...) to standard output rather than to a tape; C-Kermit receives this as standard input and sends it as a binary file. On the receiving system, in this case the local one, type (for instance):

```
kermit -il /dev/ttya -b 9600 -k | tar xf -
```

Kermit receives the tape archive and sends it via standard output to its own copy of tar, which extracts from it a replica of the original directory tree.

This example shows how the UNIX compression utility might be used to speed up Kermit file transfers between two UNIX computers:

```
kermit -cnikl /dev/cua -b 9600 | uncompress > foo (Local receiver)
compress < file | kermit -is -                     (Remote sender)
```

And the final example combines the previous two to give you the fastest serial line backup ever:

```
kermit -Qcnil /dev/ttya -b 9600 -k | uncompress | tar xf -
tar cf - /usr/olga | compress | kermit -Qis -
```

Table I-2 below and on the next page summarizes C-Kermit's command-line options.

Table I-2   C-Kermit Command-Line Options

Option	Argument	Action	Description
=		N	Ignore the rest of the command line
8		N	8-bit clean communications
-a	*filename*	N	As-name for transferred file
-b	*number*	N	Transmission rate, bits per second
-C	*"command-list"*	N	Interactive-mode Kermit commands to execute
-c		Y	CONNECT before file transfer
-D	*number*	N	Delay *number* seconds before sending file(s)
-d		N	Create a debugging log file, DEBUG.LOG

Table I-2   C-Kermit Command-Line Options (continued)

Option	Argument	Action	Description
-E		N	Exit on disconnect
-e	*number*	N	Set receive packet-length
-F	*number*	N	Numeric file descriptor for TCP/IP connection
-f		Y	Send a FINISH command to a Kermit server
-g	*filespec*	Y	Send a GET command to a Kermit server
-H		N	Don't print herald or greeting on startup
-h		Y	Print a help message listing the command-line arguments
-i		N	Transfer files in binary mode
-J	*host*	N	Like "telnet *host*"
-j	*host*	N	TCP/IP host name or address
-k		Y	Receive to standard output
-l	*device-name*	N	SET LINE to specified serial device
-M	*user*	N	My username = SET LOGIN USERNAME
-m	*modem-type*	N	SET MODEM to specified modem type
-N	*number*	N	NETBIOS adapter number
-n		Y	CONNECT after file transfer
-o	*number*	N	X.25 closed user group number
-p	*letter*	N	Parity: e(ven), o(dd), m(ark), s(pace), or n(one)
-Q		N	Quick file transfer settings
-q		N	Quiet mode, suppress messages and file transfer display
-R		N	Remote-only advisory
-r		Y	RECEIVE files
-S		N	Stay, enter command mode even if action options specified
-s	*filespec*	Y	SEND files
-T		N	Transfer files in text mode
-t		N	Local echo, XON handshake for file transfer
-U	*text*	N	Specify X.25 call user data
-u		N	Specify X.25 reverse-charge call
-v	*number*	N	Specify file transfer sliding window size
-w		N	Incoming files write over existing files with same name
-X	*number*	N	Specify an X.25 host (X.121) address
-x		Y	Enter server mode
-Y		N	Do not execute the initialization file
-y	*filename*	N	Execute *filename* instead of the normal initialization file
-Z	*number*	N	Specify the file descriptor of an open X.25 connection
-z		N	Force foreground operation (UNIX)

Environment Variables

C-Kermit can pick up various operating parameters from "environment variables" in systems that offer them, including UNIX, Windows, OS/2, and VMS (in VMS they are called logical names or symbols). In most cases, environment variables are used only as a last resort, in the absence of better information. For example, if C-Kermit needs to know the local area code to execute a DIAL command, but you have not given a SET DIAL AREA-CODE command, it uses the value of the K_AREACODE variable if one is defined. In other cases, they are used to override built-in defaults, such as the name or location of the initialization file. Table I-3 lists the environment variables meaningful to C-Kermit. Consult product-specific documentation (e.g. for Kermit 95) for others. You can access any environment variable from within C-Kermit by using the \$ (*name*) construction.

Table I-3 Environment Variables Meaningful to C-Kermit

Variable	Description
CKERMIT_INI	Initialization file directory (VMS)
CKERMIT_INIT	Pathname of initialization file (VMS)
CKERMOD	Pathname of customization file (overrides default)
COMSPEC	Preferred command shell (OS/2, Windows)
EDITOR	Preferred text editor
HOME	Home directory
KSTR	Pathname of strings file (2.xBSD)
K_AREACODE	Area code of this location
K_COUNTRYCODE	Country code of this location
K_DIAL_DIRECTORY	Dialing directory list
K_INTL_PREFIX	International dialing prefix from this location
K_LD_PREFIX	Long-distance dialing prefix from this location
K_NET_DIRECTORY	Pathname of networks directory
K_PBX_ICP	PBX internal call prefix
K_PBX_OCP	PBX external call prefix
K_PBX_XCH	Exchange of PBX at this location
K_SERVICE_DIRECTORY	Pathname of services directory
K_TF_AREACODE	Toll-free area code(s)
K_TF_PREFIX	Toll-free dialing prefix from this location
SHELL	Preferred command shell (UNIX)
TEMP *or* TMP	Pathname of temporary directory
TERM	Terminal type
USER	Username

A Condensed Guide to Serial Data Communications

Communication between two computers requires not only a physical connection, but also an agreement about how the computers will use it. When you establish the connection yourself, for example by dialing up or installing your own cable, you need to understand the elements that must agree. Otherwise a working connection is an unlikely stroke of good fortune.

Character Format and Parity

A byte, or character, is generally made up of 8 bits. Textual data is represented by a specific code, such as ASCII or ISO Latin-1. ASCII and other 7-bit codes leave one of the 8 bits unused, so in many applications this spare bit is dedicated to a rudimentary kind of error detection called *parity*. The extra bit, or *parity bit*, is set to 0 or 1 to make the overall number of 1 bits even (or odd). For reasons lost in antiquity, or perhaps simply for completeness, there also exist "mark parity" (in which the parity bit is always 1), and "space parity" (in which the parity bit is always 0). Thus there are five possibilities for parity: even, odd, mark, space, and none. Parity is commonly used with 7-bit character codes. Figure II-1 on the next page shows a 7-bit character with even parity and an 8-bit character with no parity.

The devices on both ends of a data connection should agree on their parity settings, otherwise data can be misinterpreted. For example, 11000101 is Latin-1 A-ring on an 8-bit connection, uppercase E on a 7-bit connection with even or mark parity, and it's an illegal bit combination on a 7-bit connection with odd or space parity (see Figure II-1).

ASCII Capital Letter A

| 0 | 1 | 0 | 0 | 0 | 0 | 0 | 1 |

↑
Even Parity Bit

Latin-1 Capital A with Ring (Å)

| 1 | 1 | 0 | 0 | 0 | 1 | 0 | 1 |

No Parity

Figure II-1 Character Formats

Serial Asynchronous Transmission

Characters are transmitted over short distances using digital signals: small discrete voltages representing the binary digits (bits) 0 and 1, such as +12V for 0 and –12V for 1, transmitted through copper wires. The electrical characteristics and distance limitations are spelled out in a venerable industry standard, EIA RS-232 [33] (or ITU-T V.24 [9], its international counterpart) followed by practically every computer manufacturer. In the terminology of RS-232 and V.24, a computer or terminal is *data terminal equipment*, DTE for short. The word *terminal* designates a device that is at the end of a connection, which is often, indeed, a terminal; that is, a device with a keyboard, a screen, and a communications interface.

The bits within a character are transmitted in series, one after the other, in a specified order [2] through a wire connecting the two devices. This method of transmission, referred to as *serial* transmission, is preferred for all but very short distances over the more expensive parallel method, which requires one wire for each of the 8 bits in a character.

When a terminal is connected to a computer, the computer cannot predict when the person at the terminal will strike a key; the terminal and the computer are not synchronized. During serial transmission in this environment, characters are delimited using a "start bit" (0) and a "stop bit" (1) so the receiver knows where each character begins and ends [3], as shown in Figure II-2. The stop bit lasts until the next character comes. This mode of serial communication is said to be *asynchronous*.

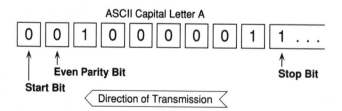

ASCII Capital Letter A

| 0 | 0 | 1 | 0 | 0 | 0 | 0 | 0 | 1 | 1 | ... |

↑   ↑
    Even Parity Bit   ↑
                                    Stop Bit
Start Bit

⟨ Direction of Transmission ⟨

Figure II-2 Asynchronous Character Transmission Format

Transmission Speed

Even in asynchronous communication, however, two DTEs are not entirely unsynchronized. The transmitters and receivers of each computer must be running at the same *speed* for the receiving computer to recognize each bit correctly, based on how long a bit "lasts." The transmission speed is expressed in bits per second (bps), sometimes called *baud* (but not by purists). Speeds commonly used in asynchronous serial data communication are 75, 110, 150, 300, 600, 1200, 2400, 4800, 9600, 19200, 38400, 57600, and 115200 bps.[52] If the speeds of the two devices do not agree, successful communication can not occur. Please note that not all computers are capable of handling the higher speeds supported by their serial devices. This is especially true when the serial device does not have its own built-in buffer and therefore must interrupt the computer every time a character arrives. Buffered serial devices (such as the 16550AFN UART[53] for PCs) are recommended over non-buffered ones (such as 8250 or 16450 UARTs).

Ten bits are required to transmit a character: the 8 bits of the character itself plus the start and stop bits. Therefore, 10 bits per second (bps) is the same as one character per second (cps) if characters are transmitted without gaps (long stop bits) between them.

It is possible, and common in some parts of the world, for the receiver and transmitter to run at different speeds. For example, a terminal sends characters at 75 bps and the computer receives them at 75 bps, but the computer sends and the terminal receives at 1200 bps. This is called *split speed* operation.

"Plex"

An asynchronous serial connection between two DTEs can be characterized by how the data flows. If data may go in one direction only, the connection is said to be *simplex*, or *one-way*. If data can go in both directions, the connection is *duplex*, or *two-way*.[54]

A duplex connection can be made using a single data wire or channel if the data goes in one direction at a time; this mode of transmission is called *half duplex* or *two-way alternate*. A special signal, called a *handshake*, is required to turn the direction around. Single-wire connections are rare, but half duplex communication is still common in mainframe computing environments. On a half duplex connection between a terminal and a computer, the terminal must *echo* each character you type. This is called *local echoing*.

---

[52]RS-232 is not designed to work at speeds beyond about 20000 bps, but many modern communication boards offer higher speeds. Speeds in excess of 19200 require very short direct connections, perhaps using special shielded and/or low capacitance cables, or a modem.

[53]Universal Asynchronous Receiver / Transmitter; the part numbers are for National Semiconductor models.

[54]Notice the dual terminology. The first term is the one used in US data communications literature, and the second term is the one used by international standards.

Today, most asynchronous serial communication takes place over two data wires, one for each direction. Data can go in both directions at once; this is called *full duplex* or *two-way simultaneous*. A full-duplex connection lets you type characters at the same time as received characters are being displayed on your screen, and it allows a computer to control the appearance of your screen by echoing characters selectively.

Flow Control

Whenever Computer A is sending data to Computer B, there is always the chance that Computer A's data will arrive faster than Computer B can process it. On a full duplex connection, where characters can travel in both directions at once, Computer B can tell Computer A to stop sending data even while the data is arriving. This gives Computer B a chance to "catch up"; when it has finished processing the characters that have accumulated, it tells Computer A to resume sending.

This process is called *flow control*. It is most commonly accomplished using the control characters Ctrl-S (ASCII DC3) to stop the flow of data, and Ctrl-Q (ASCII DC1) to resume it. In the context of flow control, these characters are called XON and XOFF, respectively. Flow control accomplished by mixing special characters with the data itself is called "in-band" or "software" flow control. Xon/Xoff flow control works when the computers have a full-duplex connection, both computers observe this convention, the connection between them is clean enough not to damage these special characters during transmission, and there is not a long transmission delay.

Hardware flow control is accomplished using separate wires, most commonly the RS-232 RTS and CTS circuits, and therefore is "out of band." It is much more reliable and responsive than software flow control, but can generally be used only over short distances, such as between a computer and the modem it is directly connected to.

Modems

The maximum distance allowed by RS-232 is 50 feet or 15 meters. To connect two DTEs over longer distances requires special *data communications equipment*, or DCEs. These are usually powered devices that boost the data's signal strength and modulate its form to allow it to travel greater distances. A *modem*[55] is a DCE that translates between the digital representation of computer data and the type of analog signaling that is used by traditional voice telephones. Modems are commonly used to connect distant computers to each other over the switched telephone network by placing a telephone call. Modems let any two computers in the world communicate with each other when a phone call can be placed between them and the modulation techniques of the two modems are compatible.

---

[55]The word *modem* is derived from the words *modulator* and *demodulator*.

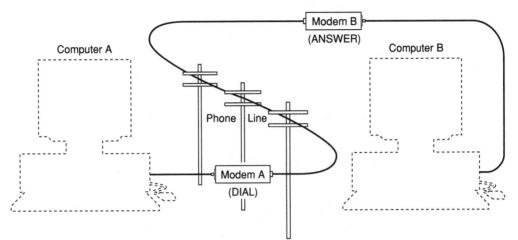

Figure II-3 Computers Connected by Modems

In a dialup modem connection, the modem actually replaces the telephone. It does what the telephone does, but instead of converting between human voice and analog electronic signals on the phone wire, it converts between the computer's digital signals and the analog phone signals.

Each computer must have its own modem, as shown in Figure II-3. The computer placing the call tells the modem to dial the number; it takes the phone off hook, listens for dial-tone, and dials the given number by simulating the clicks or beeps of the telephone it is mimicking. When the other modem answers the call, the originating modem sends a con-stant tone at a certain (originating) frequency. The answering modem recognizes this tone and replies with its own tone at a different (answering) frequency. When the two modems recognize each other's tones, the connection is complete and ready to use. These tones are called the *carrier* signal, and remain active throughout the connection. Transmitted data is impressed upon the carrier signals to alter their frequency, amplitude, or phase.

Modem Signals

Computers communicating through modems must be able to monitor and control them, just as people can monitor and control a phone call. For example, if you hear a click and a dialtone in the middle of a telephone conversation, you have good cause to suspect you've been disconnected and you can hang up your phone. This means you don't have to wait forever for the other party to finish a sentence. This sounds silly, but it's the kind of thing a computer might do if it couldn't tell when a connection is broken.

Modems handle such problems quite nicely, using special circuits defined by RS-232 and V.24 for signaling between the modem and the computer. The 10 circuits used in

Table II-1 RS-232 / V.24 Modem Signals and Pins

Circuit	V.24	Name	Direction	DB25	DB9	Description
FG		Frame Ground		1	–	Electrical safety
TD	103	Transmitted Data	To DCE	2	3	Data from computer
RD	104	Received Data	To DTE	3	2	Data to computer
RTS	105	Request To Send	To DCE	4	7	Hardware Flow Control
RTR	105	Ready To Receive	To DCE	4	7	*Same as RTS*
CTS	106	Clear To Send	To DTE	5	8	Hardware Flow Control
DSR	107	Data Set Ready	To DTE	6	6	DCE on and in data mode
SG	102	Signal Ground		7	5	Voltage measurement reference
CD	109	Carrier Detect	To DTE	8	1	Modems are communicating
DCD	109	Data Carrier Detect	To DTE	8	1	*Same as CD*
RLSI	109	Received Line Signal Indicator	To DTE	8	1	*Same as CD*
DTR	108	Data Terminal Ready	To DCE	20	4	DTE on and in data mode
RI	125	Ring Indicator	To DTE	22	9	Phone is ringing

asynchronous serial communication are listed in Table II-1. The *Circuit* column shows the RS-232 name for the circuit; the V.24 column shows the ITU-T V.24 circuit number. The DB-25 column shows the pin assignments for a standard RS-232 25-pin connector; the DB-9 column shows the pin assignments for the 9-pin connector originally used on the IBM PC/AT.

A modem call from computer A to computer B progresses something like this, as seen from the point of view of computer A (the originator of the call):

1. Computer A checks to see that Modem A's DSR signal is on. If not, the computer concludes that the modem is not connected or not turned on, and the call fails.

2. Computer A turns on its DTR signal to let the modem know that it wants to begin communicating.

3. Computer A gives Modem A the command to dial a phone number.

4. Modem A takes the phone "off hook" and listens for dialtone; if there is none, the process stops here. Otherwise, Modem A dials the number and waits for an answer.

5. If there is no answer within a prescribed amount of time, Modem A reports failure to the computer, and the process stops here.

6. When the other modem answers, Modem A sends its originate-frequency tone to it and waits for an answer-frequency tone. If none appears within a certain time, the process fails and stops here.

7. When the originating modem hears the answering modem's tone, it turns on its CD circuit, perhaps after some negotiations, so the computer knows it may exchange data with the other computer.

8. If Computer A turns off its DTR signal at any time during the connection, Modem A hangs up the phone. If Modem A stops hearing Modem B's carrier tone at any time during the connection, it turns off its CD signal.

The situation on the answering end (B) is similar. Modem B "hears" the phone ring and turns on its RI signal. Computer B sees RI come on, prepares itself to communicate, and then turns on its DTR signal. Modem B sees DTR and starts sending its carrier tone to the other modem. The two modems attempt to settle on a modulation technique (explained on page 488) and, if they succeed, both modems turns on their CD signals and communication between Computers A and B commences.

Detecting Failures Automatically

During the connection between computers A and B, at least five different components can fail: Computers A and B, Modems A and B, and the dialed connection itself. Using only two modem signals, CD and DTR, all components of the connection can detect a failure anywhere in the communication path and shut down gracefully in the event of any failure so computer data can be preserved and the telephone connection hung up:

- If Computer A dies suddenly, its DTR signal goes off. Modem A notices this and stops sending its carrier tone and hangs up the phone. This makes Modem B turn off its CD signal, which makes Computer B turn off its DTR signal, which makes Modem B hang up its end of the phone connection. The same thing happens in the other direction if Computer B dies.

- If Modem A suddenly stops working (because, for example, you tripped over the power cord and pulled it out of the receptacle), then Computer A no longer receives the CD or DSR signals and knows the connection is broken. Meanwhile, Modem B notices the absence of carrier and turns off CD and hangs up its end of the phone connection. The same thing happens if Modem B dies — just exchange A and B in all the sentences in this paragraph (except this one).

- If the connection itself is broken, both modems notice the loss of carrier and both turn off CD, so both computers know the connection is broken. Of course, the computers also turn off their DTR signals to make the modems hang up the phone, but since the connection is broken already, who cares?

Automatic Dialing

Most modern modems contain a little computer that accepts commands from the terminal or PC in the form of characters and reports the results back, also in character form. Although an international standard [10] specifies the repertoire and format of these commands and responses, it is not widely followed. In most parts of the world, modem dialing languages are defined by the modem makers, and there are many such languages. Perhaps the most popular dialing language is the Hayes AT command set, partially listed in Table II-2 on the next page. Most modern modems claim to be "Hayes compatible," but compatibility tends to stop after the basic command set shown in the table. Commands for selecting and controlling advanced and specialized features are usually different for each modem make and model.

In Hayes language, commands begin with the two letters AT. When you type (or the communication software sends) the letters AT, the modem uses them to recognize and adjust to your interface speed. Different modems recognize different sets of speeds, so if your AT commands do not echo or result in a response, then try a different speed. The normal response to a valid AT command is "OK" or "0".

The command to dial a phone number is ATD followed by the phone number and then a carriage return (press the Return or Enter key). The modem dials the number, waits for a response, and then reports the results using either a numeric code or a descriptive English word or phrase like CONNECT, CONNECT 1200, CONNECT 2400, BUSY, NO ANSWER, NO DIALTONE, or NO CARRIER [38]. Some useful Hayes commands are listed in Table II-2; each command must be terminated by a carriage return. Computer programs are easily written to feed commands to an autodial modem and interpret the results. People can also do this by hand using a terminal or emulator.

According to RS-232 and V.24, there should be no Carrier Detect (CD) signal from the modem during the dialing process. Carrier appears only after the connection is complete. Therefore, computer software like Kermit that controls modems must be prepared to ignore CD during the dialing process but pay attention to it after the connection is complete.

However, some computer systems (such as Data General AOS/VS) do not allow serial communication to occur at all in the absence of CD, so the modem (or the cable connecting it to the computer) must be configured to assert CD all the time. This robs the computer of the ability to detect a broken connection. Similarly, some computers do not turn on their DTR signals properly, so the modem must be configured to ignore DTR. But in general, a modem should be configured to:

- Pay attention to DTR from the computer. If DTR goes off, hang up the phone.

- Turn on Carrier Detect only when the two modems have carrier.

Table II-2 Selected Hayes Smartmodem 2400 Commands

Command	Action
AT	No action. Modem responds "OK" if it is in command state.
AT&C1	CD signal tracks carrier (recommended). AT&C0 keeps CD on always.
AT&D2	Modem hangs up and returns to command state if PC turns off DTR (recommended). AT&D0 makes modem ignore DTR signal from PC.
ATE1	Enables echoing of modem commands (recommended). ATE0 disables echoing.
ATM0	Turns off speaker. ATM1 turns on speaker while dialing.
ATQ0V1	Selects verbal result codes (OK, CONNECT) rather than numeric.
ATX0	Enables OK, CONNECT, RING, and NO CARRIER result codes.
ATX1	Enables OK, CONNECT, RING, NO CARRIER, ERROR, CONNECT 1200, and CONNECT 2400 result codes.
ATX4	Enables OK, CONNECT, RING, NO CARRIER, ERROR, CONNECT 1200, NO DIALTONE, BUSY, CONNECT, and CONNECT 2400 result codes (usually the factory setting).
ATDT*nnnnnnn*	Dials the phone number *nnnnnnn* (simulate Touch-Tone dialing). The phone number may contain digits, spaces, parentheses, and hyphens, which are ignored. A comma in the dial string causes the modem to pause (normally 2 seconds, specified in register S8). The letter W means wait up to 30 seconds (limit specified in register S7) for dial tone. An exclamation mark (!) means "hook flash" — hang up the phone for half a second, then reconnect. An at-sign (@) means to wait for the phone to stop ringing. Semicolon (;) means return to command state. Dollar sign ($) means wait for "bong."
ATDP*nnnnnnn*	Dials the phone number, like ATDT, but with pulse (rotary) dialing.
ATD*nnnnnnn*	Dials the phone number using the modem's default dialing method (Touch-Tone or Pulse).
ATH0	Hangs up the phone.
+++	Returns to command state without dropping the connection. This is the modem's escape sequence. Except in TIES modems (see page 593) it is ignored unless a full second of silence precedes and follows it, to prevent consecutive plus signs in your data from interfering with communication.
ATO	(Letter O) Returns to online state from command state.
ATZ	Initialize: Restores normal configuration.
ATS0=1	Enters answer mode (waits for a call). 0 means don't answer calls.
ATS7=*nnn*	Waits up to *nnn* seconds for carrier. Default depends on modem model.
ATS8=*nnn*	Duration of comma dial modifier. Default is 2 seconds.
ATS10=*nnn*	Delay between carrier loss and hangup, 10ths of seconds.
ATS25=*nnn*	DTR change detect time, 100ths of seconds.
ATI*n*	Might display some useful information about the modem model and configuration. Try different values of n — 0, 1, 2, 3, . . .

Modulation, Error Correction, and Compression

Modems communicate with each other using an ever-expanding variety of modulation techniques, such as the ones listed in Table II-3. Most modern modems support more than one such technique. For two modems to communicate, they must have at least one modulation technique in common and they also need a mutually acceptable negotiation method to find it.

When you place a call, the modem begins with a particular modulation technique. The technique is chosen according to the interface speed between your computer and the modem or according to the modem's configuration. For example, a V.32 modem might try to connect to the remote modem using V.32 if your interface speed is 9600, V.22*bis* if it is 2400, V.22 if it is 1200, and V.21 or Bell 103 if it is 300.

Suppose your modem tries to connect using V.32. If the other modem responds with a V.32 carrier signal, the modems recognize each other immediately and your modem raises its CD signal and tells you the connection is complete. If, however, the other modem does not support V.32, your modem will execute its *fallback* procedure. The fallback procedure is what allows modems of differing capabilities to find a common language. In this case your modem might fall back to V.22*bis* and, if that doesn't work, to V.22, and so on.

Modems that implement different fallback strategies might not be able to connect to each other automatically, even if they *do* have a modulation technique in common. In such

Table II-3 Modem Modulation Techniques

Designation	Year	Description
ITU-T V.34	1994	28800, 26400, 24000, 21600, 19200, 16800, 14400 bps; full duplex
ITU-T V.32*bis*	1991	14400, 12000, 9600, 7200 bps; full duplex
ITU-T V.32	1984-88	9600, 4800, 2400 bps; full duplex
ITU-T V.29	1976-84	9600 bps; for leased lines, but used by MNP Class 6
ITU-T V.26*ter*	1984-88	2400 bps; full duplex
ITU-T V.26*bis*	1972-84	2400, 1200 bps; half duplex with 75 bps back channel
ITU-T V.22*bis*	1984-88	2400, full duplex
ITU-T V.22	1980-84	1200 bps, full duplex
Bell 212A	1977	1200 bps, half duplex
Vadic VA3400	1973	1200 bps, full duplex
ITU-T V.23	1972-84	600, 1200 bps, half duplex with 75 bps back channel
ITU-T V.21	1964-84	(Europe) 300 bps, full duplex, incompatible with Bell 103
Bell 103	?	(USA) 110, 150, 300 bps, full duplex, incompatible with V.21

cases, it is your job to configure your modem to change its initial modulation technique, its fallback scheme, or both. Consult your modem manual.

Speed Buffering

Note the difference between *modulation speed* — the speed between the two modems — and the *interface speed* — the speed used on the RS-232 digital interface between the modem and the computer.

In most early low-speed modem models, the modulation speed and the interface speed had to be the same. As new modulations were added, modulation fallback always meant a drop in interface speed. So, for example, a call placed at 2400 bps on a Hayes 2400 Smartmodem that was answered by a 1200 bps modem would cause the originating modem to report CONNECT 1200 and then drop its interface speed to 1200. The communication software would have change the computer's interface speed to 1200 to match or else the speeds would be mismatched.

Modern high-speed modems have a feature called speed buffering, in which the interface speed is independent of the modulation speed, and can remain constant. This is important not only because of modulation fallback, but also because V.34 modems can change modulation speed up and down in response to changing line conditions during a connection, often to speeds (such as 21600 bps) not necessarily supported by the serial interface. The CONNECT message from a speed buffering modem can report either the modulation speed or the interface speed, depending on the modem's configuration.

Error Correction

Error-correcting modems are designed to overcome transmission errors caused by noisy telephone connections. Error correction, when it is effective, occurs only on the connection between the two modems, and *not* on the connection between each modem and its computer or terminal, where errors can still occur for all sorts of reasons, including loose connectors, data overruns, noisy buses, or interrupt conflicts.

Error correction requires a communications protocol, similar to Kermit's, between the two modems. Data sent by each modem is packaged with framing and checksum information; the other modem receives these structured messages, checks them for damage, and requests retransmission if necessary or else extracts the original data and passes it along to the receiving computer.

Several techniques are commonly used for error correction. Some of them are listed in Table II-4. To achieve an error-free connection, two modems must share at least one error correction technique. The error-correction method is settled after carrier has been established; that is, after the two modems have found a common modulation technique. Now that the modems can communicate with one another, they send messages attempting to negotiate an error-correction protocol.

Table II-4 Modem Error Correction and Compression Techniques

Designation	Description
MNP Class 1	Error Correction: Asynchronous byte-oriented half duplex ARQ
MNP Class 2	Error Correction: Asynchronous byte-oriented full duplex ARQ
MNP Class 3	Error Correction: Synchronous bit-oriented full duplex ARQ
MNP Class 4	Error Correction: MNP Class 3 plus dynamic packet size
MNP Class 5	Data Compression: Used in conjunction with MNP Class 4
MNP Class 6	MNP Class 5 plus Universal Link Negotiation and Statistical Duplexing
MNP Class 7	Enhanced Data Compression: used in conjunction with MNP Class 4
MNP Class 9	MNP Class 7 combined with V.32 modulation
MNP Class 10	MNP Class 4 error control adapted to cellular calls
PEP	Telebit Packet Ensemble Protocol, a combination of modulation, error control, and compression
HST	US Robotics High Speed Technology.
ITU-T V.42	Error Correction: Link Access Protocol for Modems (LAPM), the international standard error correction technique for modems
ITU-T V.42*bis*	Data Compression: The international standard compression technique for modems

Suppose, for example, you are dialing with a V.42 modem. Once carrier is established, your modem sends a message to the other modem requesting V.42 error correction. If the other modem is capable of V.42, it agrees. If it does not support V.42, but it is capable of a MNP class 4 or lower MNP level of error control, it notifies your modem and your modem falls back to the agreed-upon MNP level.

However, if the other modem does not support any level of error control, it is likely to pass your modem's negotiation message through to the remote computer or service, which can result in incorrect speed recognition, a failed login, or a hung-up connection.

Most modern modems can be configured to use or skip error correction, and to employ various fallback schemes in negotiating the error-correction method with the other modem. If you have trouble establishing a connection from an error-correcting modem, try turning off its error-correction feature, choosing a different error-correction method, or altering the modem's error-correction fallback scheme.

After you have made a successful error-corrected connection between two modems, your troubles are still not over. Suppose, for example, you have told the remote host to display a long file. Suddenly there is a period of severe noise on the telephone connection, causing many retransmissions between the two modems. The remote modem is so busy retransmitting previous data that it is unable to accept new data from the remote computer, yet the remote computer continues to send it. The modem needs a way to tell the computer to stop sending data for a while; that is, an effective flow control method. Without one, data will be lost.

Similarly, you need effective flow control between your own computer and modem, otherwise the modem might deliver data to your computer faster than the computer can handle it, or vice versa.

Finally, beware of certain types of modems that claim to provide error correction, but require that this be done by the communications software or external drivers. Such modems might (or might not) have the designation "RPI" or "Controllerless" on the box. These modems can be used effectively only with certain proprietary drivers or communications software packages on selected platforms (typically only Windows). When shopping for an error-correcting modem, be sure that error correction is done by the modem itself and does not require any external software to do it.

Data Compression

Above your modem's modulation and error-correction techniques, there can be still another layer of protocol between the two modems: data compression. As with modulation and error correction, various compression techniques are available, some of which are listed in Table II-4, and the same cautions about negotiation, fallback, and flow control hold true.

Flow control is absolutely essential when compression is operational. In theory, data cannot come out of modem B faster than it went in to modem A. In practice, however, it is common that the interface speeds of the two modems are different, and therefore the data sent to the slower modem by the faster one must be flow-controlled by the slower modem's computer. If you do not have an effective method of flow control — preferably RTS/CTS — you should disable your modem's compression feature.

To get maximum benefit from a data-compressing modem, lock its interface speed, if possible, at *four times* the modulation speed. For example, a 14400-bps V.32*bis* connection should use an interface speed of 57600 bps. Otherwise, the modem's compression capacity could be wasted.

A glance at Tables II-3 and II-4 gives you an idea of the many possible combinations of modulation, error-correction, and compression techniques offered by modern modems. Each modem manufacturer offers a different selection, different default configurations, different fallback schemes, and different ways to control all of these. New techniques are developed with alarming frequency and hit the marketplace with little delay. When you buy a new, full-featured modem, be prepared to spend long hours studying the manual and experimenting with its configuration and settings.

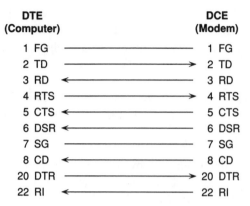

DTE
(Computer)

DCE
(Modem)

1 FG	————————	1 FG
2 TD	———————→	2 TD
3 RD	←————————	3 RD
4 RTS	———————→	4 RTS
5 CTS	←————————	5 CTS
6 DSR	←————————	6 DSR
7 SG	————————	7 SG
8 CD	←————————	8 CD
20 DTR	———————→	20 DTR
22 RI	←————————	22 RI

Figure II-4 Asynchronous Modem Cable Schematic

Beware of modems that claim to provide data compression, but in fact require external software or drivers to do it. These modems can be used effectively only with certain proprietary communications software packages or drivers on selected platforms (Windows). When shopping for a data-compressing modem, be sure that data compression is done by the modem itself and does not require external software to do it. (If this paragraph sounds remarkably similar to the final paragraph of the preceding section, it's no mistake.)

Cables and Connectors

The cable that connects a computer to a modem — that is, a DTE to a DCE — is called a *modem cable*. It includes at least the circuits listed in Table II-1 on page 484, and illustrated in Figure II-4, which also shows the direction of the signal and the connector pin numbers for standard 25-pin connectors.

In a modem cable, the wires go "straight through," connecting DTR on one side to DTR on the other, CD on one side to CD on the other, and so on, for each circuit. The cable terminates in *connectors* on each end.

Gender

A connector is either *female* or *male*, like the ones shown in Figure II-5 on the next page. Male connectors have pins sticking out, female connectors have holes to plug the pins into. By convention, DTEs have male connectors, DCEs female.[56]

---

[56]But conventions are made to be broken. When a connector is the wrong gender, an inexpensive adapter called a *gender changer* can be employed to make the needed connection.

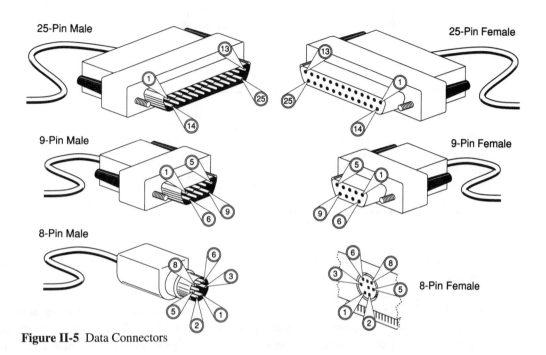

Figure II-5 Data Connectors

Number of Pins

The most common type of connector has 25 pins (or holes), one for each of the 25 RS-232 circuits; this is called a DB-25 connector. The assignment of connector pins to RS-232 circuits is specified by the RS-232 standard. 9-pin (DB-9) and 8-pin (Din-8) varieties are becoming increasingly common, but vendors don't follow a particular standard in assigning circuits to pins; each pin is numbered and assigned a circuit arbitrarily.

Case

The pins or holes are joined to the wires and housed inside a compact case, as shown in the figure, for protection and ease of handling. So, like Latin nouns, data connectors have *gender*, *number*, and *case*.

Null Modems

It is possible to connect two DTEs (such as two computers, or a terminal and a computer) directly to each other with no intervening modems. This is done using a *null modem* cable, or a small null modem adapter (or *modem eliminator*), that turns a modem cable into a null modem cable. The wires in a null modem cable do not go straight through, but are cross-connected in various ways as shown in Figure II-6 on the next page, which also shows the DB-25 pin numbers. The computers are tricked into believing they are connected to real modems. With the "fakeout" model (A), the two computers can transmit

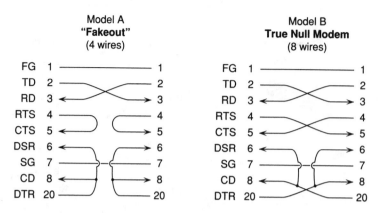

Model A
"Fakeout"
(4 wires)

FG	1	———————	1	
TD	2		2	
RD	3		3	
RTS	4		4	
CTS	5		5	
DSR	6		6	
SG	7		7	
CD	8		8	
DTR	20		20	

Model B
True Null Modem
(8 wires)

FG	1	———————	1	
TD	2		2	
RD	3		3	
RTS	4		4	
CTS	5		5	
DSR	6		6	
SG	7		7	
CD	8		8	
DTR	20		20	

Figure II-6 Asynchronous Null Modem Schematics

data but cannot signal each other in any other way. With a true null modem (B), each computer can detect when the other computer crashes or otherwise stops communicating.

In UNIX and VMS computer systems, the system administrator may define serial communication devices as either modem-controlled or direct lines. On a modem-controlled line, the operating system insists on receiving the CD signal, and possibly also DSR and CTS. If carrier drops, the next attempt to read a character from the device will result in a "device error," unless the device is opened in a special mode (such as the CLOCAL mode in UNIX).

On a direct line, modem signals are ignored. A direct line is typically used for a terminal, PC, or printer connected directly to a computer serial communication device with a short RS-232 null modem cable containing as few as three or four wires (sometimes the frame ground wire is omitted, but this is not recommended).

External and Internal Modems

An external modem is a separate device that connects to your computer's serial port with a data cable, and connects to the telephone jack with a telephone cable. An internal modem plugs directly into your computer's bus or backplane and takes the place of a serial port, allowing direct connection of your computer to the telephone jack. Your computer does not know it is a modem; it appears to the computer to be a serial port.

Even though they are usually more expensive, external modems are recommended over internal ones because you can use them on different kinds of computers, they are easier to support and configure and less likely to cause problems (like interrupt conflicts), and they have status lights that can be helpful in troubleshooting problem connections. And also because you can unplug an external modem from your serial port and use the port for other things, including diagnostic devices.

DB-25 versus Miniature Connectors

In the neverending quest for miniaturization, computer manufacturers continue to find new ways to shrink the serial connector. The original DB-25 RS-232 connector, approximately 3.5 by 0.6 cm and very well standardized, appeared in a 9-pin variety on the PC/AT, only 1.5 by 0.6 cm, a substantial savings in space on the back of the computer, an increasingly important consideration as computers become smaller, and especially important for laptops. The pin assignments are as shown in Table II-1. The reduction in the number of pins was possible because the pins that were eliminated were used only in synchronous communication, e.g. on leased-line computer-to-computer connections.

Meanwhile the original Macintosh also used a DB-9 connector for its serial port, but not only were the pin assignments different, so was the communication method: RS-423 [34] instead of RS-232. RS-423 uses four wires for data, rather than two, and does not include all the modem signals of RS-232. To use RS-423 with an RS-232 device (such as modem), a special wiring configuration is used in which certain of the circuits are cross-connected or grounded out.

The next generation of Macintosh reduced the size of the connector again, this time to the Mini-Din8 configuration shown in Figure II-5, appoximately 0.75 cm in diameter (the diagrams in the figure are roughly to scale). This reduction was possible because one of the wires in the RS-423 DB-9 was not used.

Since then, Mini-Din8 connectors have found their way onto numerous laptops and workstations. Unfortunately, the pin assignments differ from one implementation to the next, even though the connectors are identical. Thus different cables might be required to connect a modem to the Mini-Din8 on one computer than to the Mini-Din8 on another.

Furthermore, since RS-423 offers only a limited complement of control signals, you must choose between a cable that uses the CD and DTR circuits to allow the modem and the computer to detect a broken connection, and a cable that uses the RTS and CTS circuits for hardware flow control. You can't have both.

So, for example, if you have a hardware flow-control cable, you can't hang up the phone by lowering DTR — there *is* no DTR. Similarly, you can't tell if the other computer has hung up the connection by monitoring CD, because there is no CD either. You must configure your modem to ignore the DTR signal, and you must configure your communications software to ignore the CD signal. On the other hand, if you use a CD / DTR cable, you are likely to lose data because you don't have local flow control with the modem, and you must configure your modem to ignore the CTS signal and your software to ignore the RTS signal.

When purchasing a Mini-Din8 modem cable, you must specify not only whether you want a hardware-flow-control or a CD / DTR model, but also exactly which kind of computer it is for (Macintosh, SGI, NeXT, etc). Luckily most external modems still have female DB-25 connectors, so at least there are only two variables in the equation, not three.

Summary

It is not practical to list specific cabling and connector requirements for every kind of computer that C-Kermit runs on. Such a list would be very long indeed and obsolete by the time it was printed. Instead, please consult the technical documentation for your computer and/or modem, plus any supplementary material that comes with your specific version of C-Kermit. Meanwhile, a few general tips might smooth the way:

- For modem connections, use whatever modem cable is supplied or recommended by your computer manufacturer.

- For direct connections between two computers, use the supplied or recommended modem cable for each computer and interconnect the two modem cables with a female-female DB-25 modem eliminator.

- If your connections suffer from electrical interference, *shielded* cables and connectors (which are more expensive) might help.

Use hardware flow control if it is available. Enable it at each point along the connection; e.g. computer A, modem A, modem B, and computer B. And if you have an error-correcting, data-compressing modem, fix its interface speed at two to four times its maximum modulation speed for best performance.

Detailed debugging of cables and modem signals can be accomplished with a device called an RS-232 breakout box, available in computer supply catalogs. Another handy tool is the loopback connector, which can be used to test integrity at various points along the connection. Organizations that are large enough to have data communications or networking departments might also have a line analyzer or "data scope" available, that lets you view both modem signals and data going in both directions, often complete with history buffers and printouts.

Declarations that modems have reached the upper limits of telephone network capacity always prove premature. While many recently believed that V.34 was "as fast as you can go," we are already seeing (nonstandard) "V.34+" modems with a modulation speed of 33600 bps, and we are hearing talk of experimental models communicating at 512K bps. But whatever the speed, the general notions described here should apply for some time to come, or at least until today's telephone / modem combinations are made obsolete by ISDN, ADSL, cable modems, or who-knows-what.

UNIX C-Kermit

This appendix explains how to configure and use C-Kermit on a computer with the UNIX operating system. For an up-to-date list of limitations and restrictions in the UNIX version of C-Kermit, also read the files `ckcker.bwr` and `ckuker.bwr`.

UNIX has become a generic term, referring to a large family of operating systems whose members include AIX, BSD, DG/UX, Digital UNIX, DNIX, FreeBSD, HP-UX, IRIX, Linux, NetBSD, ODT, OSF/1, POSIX, QNX, Solaris, SunOS, System V, ULTRIX, XENIX, and many more. Each of these products differs from the others in numerous ways and each product goes through numerous releases. An important goal in the design of C-Kermit has been portability among the many releases of the many UNIX products on the market (see page 16 for a list) and easy adaptibility to future products and releases; see the files `ckcplm.doc`, `ckccfg.doc`, and `ckuins.doc` for details.

Installation

○ ○ ○ ○
Detailed instructions for building and installing UNIX C-Kermit are given in the file `ckuins.doc` in the C-Kermit software distribution and in the UNIX C-Kermit makefile itself. This section discusses the thorny issues of dialout device access that are of interest not only to the C-Kermit installer but all too often to the C-Kermit user too. Skip ahead to page 504 if you do not need to use C-Kermit for dialing out, or if C-Kermit is already configured correctly for dialing out on your UNIX computer.

Configuring tty Devices for Dialing Out

A device appears to the UNIX user as a file, usually in the /dev area. Here are some samples from a Sun computer (ls -l /dev/*):

```
crw-rw-rw-  1 root   13,   0 Jun 26 11:33 /dev/mouse  (A Mouse)
crw-rw-rw-  1 root    3,   2 Feb 14 13:44 /dev/null   (The null device)
crw-rw-rw-  1 root   30,   0 Feb  8 12:38 /dev/rmt0   (A magnetic tape)
crw-rw-rw-  1 root    2,   0 Aug  8 14:24 /dev/tty    (Controlling tty)
crw-rw-rw-  1 root   44,   0 Jun 11 12:03 /dev/ttyh0  (Specific ttys)
crw--w--w-  1 root   44,   1 Jun 11 15:03 /dev/ttyh1
crw--w----  1 cmg    44,   2 Aug  8 15:00 /dev/ttyh2
crw--w----  1 fdc    44,   3 Jun 11 05:09 /dev/ttyh3
```

The tty devices are the ones we're interested in. Different UNIX systems have different names for them, but they are generally of the form /dev/tty followed by two characters, such as 00 or h2 (/dev/tty by itself is a special generic device that refers to the user's controlling terminal, or console). Other commonly used forms include /dev/acu, /dev/cua, /dev/cub, etc. (cu stands for "calling unit," acu for "automatic calling unit"), or more complex forms such as /dev/term/b or /dev/cua0p0. Write permission (w) does not allow users to delete the file, but it does allow them to write to the associated device.

A UNIX terminal device is inbound, outbound, or both. An *inbound* terminal is for people to use as the controlling terminal of an interactive UNIX session. Each inbound terminal on the computer is being watched by a process called "getty," which waits for a connection to appear, and then issues the login prompt. *Outbound* terminals are not watched by getty, and cannot be logged in to. These are used for dialing out to other computers. Some UNIX systems allow terminal devices to be *bidirectional*, meaning they can be used for both logging in and dialing out.

The system administrator (superuser) configures each terminal device as inbound, outbound, or bidirectional. The method varies from system to system. You must consult your UNIX system administration manual for the relevant method. Traditionally, tty configuration is done by editing a file called /etc/ttys, which contains entries that look like this:

```
12console
02ttya
12ttyb
02ttyh0
12ttyh1
12ttyh2
12ttyh3
```

This file is read by the *init* process at system startup time. Two digits precede the tty name; you are concerned with the first digit: 0 means the line is outbound (no getty), 1 means the line is inbound (has getty).

Some UNIX systems have a more generalized way of defining terminals to the init process. For example, SunOS uses the file /etc/ttytab, which includes information about the terminal speed and type as well as whether getty is on or off:

```
ttyh0   "/usr/etc/getty std.9600"    vt100      off
ttyh1   "/usr/etc/getty std.19200"   vt100      on
ttyh2   "/usr/etc/getty std.9600"    vt100      on
ttyh3   "/usr/etc/getty std.9600"    vt100      on
```

Dialout lines must be configured with getty off, or if your system allows it, as bidirectional lines.

It is normally not necessary to shut down and restart your UNIX system in order to reconfigure a terminal device. Rather, you can edit the appropriate tty configuration file and then restart the init process, which is always process number 1:

```
$ kill -1 1
```

This operation, of course, requires superuser (root) privilege.

Once the tty device is configured to allow dialout, its permissions must also be set to let users access it in read and write mode:

```
$ ls -l /dev/ttyh4
crw--w----  1 root      44,   2 Aug  8 15:00 /dev/ttyh4
$ chmod go+rw /dev/ttyh4
$ ls -l /dev/ttyh4
crw-rw-rw-  1 root      44,   2 Aug  8 15:00 /dev/ttyh4
```

The chmod command adds read and write (rw) permission to ttyh4 for members of its group (g) and all others (o).

Finally, on certain workstations, it might be necessary to configure the terminal driver for dialing out. For example, Sun SPARCstations might come with serial ports that are *not* set up for use with a modem. To configure the serial port for dialout use, follow the directions in your system installation or network manager's guide. This might involve changing jumpers on your serial port board, reconfiguring the serial device driver, or both.

Ensuring Exclusive Access

Most operating systems allow serial devices such as terminals and magnetic tapes to be opened by only one job at a time. Any attempt to open the same device by another job results in an error like "exclusive access denied" or "device assigned by another user."

UNIX devices, however, can be shared by all users who have access to them based on their permissions. So if user A has a dialout connection over /dev/ttyh4, UNIX does not prevent user B from using /dev/ttyh4 at the same time, even though there is no conceivable reason to allow this. The result of multiple users reading from the same serial device is that the incoming characters are fanned out to them, as if they were hands of poker — nobody sees the whole deck. And of course, if multiple users write to the same device, then who- or whatever is on the other end will receive only a confused jumble of characters, impossible to sort out.

Before there was Kermit, there was UUCP, the UNIX-to-UNIX Copy Program [62]. UUCP was developed at AT&T Bell Laboratories by Mike Lesk in 1976, and publicly distributed for the first time with Version 7 of UNIX. It soon became the basis of Usenet, a loose voluntary confederation of UNIX computers that call each other up at night and exchange files, news, and electronic mail. It was not long until someone discovered that running two copies of UUCP at the same time on the same dialout line resulted in no useful exchange of data. The solution was, and remains to this day, the UUCP lock file.

UUCP and every other program on the computer that might be using a dialout line, including kermit, cu, and tip, are expected to observe a special convention: if the program wants to use a particular dialout tty device, first it checks to see if a file with a certain name exists in a certain directory, and if so the program does not attempt to use the tty device. If the file does not exist, the program must create it before starting to use the device and must destroy the file when it is finished. This file is called the UUCP lock file; its name is based on the tty device name.

Within a particular UNIX vendor's software offerings, this convention tends to work — uucp, cu, and tip are produced in the vendor's controlled proprietary environment. Unfortunately, the situation is not so controlled for Kermit, which needs to run on UNIX platforms from many manufacturers:

- The directory that contains the UUCP lock files is different on different systems: `/usr/spool/uucp`, `/usr/spool/locks`, `/var/spool/locks`, many others.

- The directory that contains the lock file might or might not be publicly readable and/or writable.

- The format of the lock file name can vary from system to system: `ttyh4`, `LCK..ttyh4`, and so on.

- Although the lock file name includes the device name, it might be subtly modified; for example, in SCO Xenix, the lock file for `/dev/tty1A` is `LCK..tty1a` (lowercase *a*).

- The same physical device might have multiple names, such as `/dev/tty0p0`, `/dev/ttyd0p0`, `/dev/cua0p0`, `/dev/cul0p0` in HP-UX 10.0.

- There might be more than one lock file; certain versions of IBM AIX require two lock files, one named (for example) `LCK..tty0`, and the other simply `tty0` (in fact, the second is a link to the first).

- The lock file itself may or may not be publicly readable and/or writable.

- The creation date and time of the lock file may or may not be significant.

- The contents of the lock file may or may not be significant. Some versions of UUCP require that the lock file contain the process ID (pid) of the process that created it.

- The format of the contents of the lock file can vary from system to system: the pid may be a binary integer (or other data type, such as short or long), or an integer in ASCII string format, with or without various numbers of leading spaces or zeros.

- Even on the same computer, lock file conventions can change from one UNIX release to the next, e.g. from SunOS 4.0 to SunOS 4.1, from AT&T System V R3 to R4.

- Recent UNIX standards like POSIX don't even try to address this issue.

Therefore, you must determine what lock file conventions are in use on your system and build Kermit to correspond to them; this is not always an easy task, because this information tends to be missing from vendor documentation. Each C-Kermit "make" option takes a best guess, but for Kermit to fit in properly with uucp, cu, and tip, you should make certain that this guess is correct. Here is one way to check:

1. Get a directory listing (`ls -lg`) from each of the possible lock file directories: `/usr/spool/uucp`, `/usr/spool/locks`, `/var/spool/locks`, `/etc/locks` (this is not necessarily a complete list).

2. Run one of your vendor-supplied UUCP-family communication programs, such as cu, giving the name of your dialout device (you might first have to find and edit the UUCP "`Devices`" file). Example:

```
$ cu -l /dev/ttya
```

This procedure assumes you are using cu (syntax can vary from system to system; check the "man" (manual) page for cu on your computer for details).

3. Escape from cu back to your local shell by typing carriage return, then tilde (~), then exclamation mark (!).

4. At the shell prompt, repeat step 1.

5. Exit from the inferior shell, exit from cu (carriage return, tilde, period).

6. Compare the directory listings to see which files, in what format, with what permissions, in which directories were created by cu.

In recent years, UNIX vendors have been converting to a new and somewhat more standardized version of UUCP called Honey DanBer (after its authors, Peter Honeyman, David A. Nowitz, and Brian E. Redman, who rewrote the original UUCP in 1983). If this trend continues, some of the confusion can be eliminated.

Installing Kermit without Privileges

If you are the sole user of a UNIX workstation, you don't have to worry about other users abusing their privileges or interfering with your work, so you need not be concerned with the material in this section unless you use UUCP.

If you are the manager of a multiuser UNIX system where all the users trust each other, and you trust them, you can make access to your tty devices and lock file directory unrestricted. For example, if your lock file directory is /usr/spool/uucp and your dialout device is ttyh4, give the following commands from superuser command level:

```
su% chmod 777 /usr/spool/uucp
su% chmod 666 /dev/ttyh4
```

The risk here is a free-for-all in the lock file directory; users can store any file there at all, and delete any file as well. They can even remove each others' lock files, despite the fact that the lock files are created with 444 (read-only) permission. Deletion is possible because the *directory* has write permission, which is required for people to create their lock files in the first place. And there is also some risk of one user interfering with another's use of the tty device.

To make your tty devices available only to a selected group of users, put those users in the uucp group (or whatever other group is used by uucp, tip, and cu). The method for doing this varies from system to system, but generally involves editing the /etc/group file to add these users to the uucp entry in that file. You don't have to make the Kermit program setuid or setgid, or give it any particular owner or group, but you do have to ensure that the uucp lock directory and the appropriate tty devices are members of the uucp group, and have the appropriate permissions in the group field:

```
su% chgrp uucp /usr/spool/uucp
su% chmod 770 /usr/spool/uucp
su% chgrp uucp /dev/ttyh4
su% chmod 660 /dev/ttyh4
```

Installing Kermit with Privileges

On multiuser UNIX systems where access to the uucp directory or to tty devices is a security issue, it is possible to restrict access to the lock file directory and the dialout tty devices, then give the Kermit program privileges to override these restrictions, and some or all users the ability to run the privileged Kermit. This prevents users from circumventing the lock file conventions built into Kermit (and uucp, cu, and tip), and therefore from accessing a tty device that somebody else is already using.

Despite the attractions of this setup, there are also serious risks. Any program that runs in privileged mode poses a tremendous security threat to your system, much greater than the possible inconveniences of open lock directories and tty devices. Although every effort has been made to ensure C-Kermit contains no loopholes, the slightest bug or oversight on the part of the authors or anyone who has modified or customized the source code — not to speak of the damage that could be done intentionally — could open doors for intruders. This warning is not particular to Kermit: it applies to *all* UNIX programs.

If you *really want* to make Kermit a privileged program, first make sure you have built it correctly for your system. There are several important compile-time options that must be considered, and that vary from system to system. The most important of these is whether your version of UNIX supports the "saved original setuid" feature. If it does not, then Kermit will not work right as a privileged program — it should not pose a security risk, but it won't be able to access protected files or tty devices either. For details, read the files `ckuins.doc` (the installation instructions), `ckuker.bwr` (the "beware" file), and `ckcplm.doc` (the program logic manual).

To install Kermit as a privileged program, make the owner of the Kermit program the same as the owner of the lock file directory and the tty device, and set the setuid bit in the Kermit program's permissions, so that while running Kermit, the user has the privileges of user uucp. For example:

```
su% chown uucp kermit                   (kermit's owner is uucp)
su% chmod u=srwx,g=rx,o=rx kermit        (Turn setuid bit on)
su% chown uucp /usr/spool/uucp           (Lock directory owned by uucp)
su% chmod 700 /usr/spool/uucp            (Can be accessed only by owner)
su% chown uucp /dev/ttyh4                (Dialout device owned by uucp)
su% chmod 600 /dev/ttyh4                 (Can be accessed only by owner)
```

The UNIX version of C-Kermit includes special code to turn off these privileges as soon as it starts up, and to turn them on only when it is manipulating lock files or opening the tty device, so that files are accessed and subprocesses are run with the user's own identity and access rights, but this code cannot be guaranteed to work correctly for every release of every variation of UNIX.

Caveat Installator!

For the lock file mechanism to achieve its desired purpose — prevention of access to the same tty device by more than one process at a time — *all* programs on a given computer that open, read or write, and close tty devices (kermit, uucp, cu, tip, and so on) must use the *same* lock file conventions.

Be alert to changes in new releases of your UNIX operating system. The installation procedure might change the permissions on your lock file directories and tty devices. What's more, it is quite common these days for new UNIX releases to change their lock file conventions; the new versions of uucp, tip, and cu will follow the new conventions, but Kermit and other communication programs that are not distributed by your UNIX vendor will still be using the old ones until you reconfigure (or reprogram!) them.

Using UNIX C-Kermit

UNIX operating systems are available for computers ranging from small desktop systems to large mainframes and supercomputers. To accommodate smaller computers that have restrictions on physical memory, address space, disk space, or compiler or linker capacity, C-Kermit can be built in reduced configurations. This is required primarily for UNIX versions running on DEC PDP-11s and on 8088, 8086, 80186, or 80286 PCs, and generally is not necessary elsewhere. The three major C-Kermit configurations are:

1. Fully configured, but perhaps without networking, Kanji character sets, and/or fullscreen display. In most cases, these features can be added by simple changes to the build procedure (see the files ckccfg.doc and ckuins.doc for instructions).

2. Minimum interactive. The C-Kermit prompt appears and a minimum set of commands is available for terminal connection and file transfer. There is no character-set translation, script programming language, or built-in HELP text.

3. Command-line only. This configuration has no prompt, no interactive dialog, and no initialization file. It is controlled exclusively with the command-line options listed in Appendix I, with the exception of -y, -Y, -C, -S, and any others that imply the availability of interactive commands.

See the file ckccfg.doc for detailed information about C-Kermit configuration options.

If you have an interactive version of C-Kermit, you can use the SHOW FEATURES command to find out exactly which features are included and excluded. If the SHOW FEATURES command itself is missing, you can use the CHECK command, which is included in all interactive configurations, for example:

```
C-Kermit>check kanji
 Not available
C-Kermit>
```

Preparing UNIX for C-Kermit

To make effective use of C-Kermit in the UNIX environment and, for that matter, to use UNIX itself to best advantage, you should ensure that your UNIX session is speaking the same language as the terminal or emulator that you are using to access it.

Establishing Your Terminal Type

Before starting C-Kermit, you should tell the UNIX system what kind of terminal you have so C-Kermit's FULLSCREEN file transfer display (if available) will work correctly.

To identify your terminal to UNIX, try one of the methods from Table III-1, which uses the DEC VT300-series terminal as an example. The actual method used depends not only

Table III-1 Setting Your Terminal Type in UNIX

Shell	Command
Bourne shell (sh)	`TERM=vt320 ; export TERM`
Korn shell (ksh)	`export TERM=vt320`
C-shell (csh)	`setenv TERM vt320`

on your shell, but on the site- or vendor-dependent peculiarities of your UNIX system. For example, some UNIX systems use a program called `term` or `tset`; others might prompt you for a terminal type when you log in.

To test whether your terminal type is set correctly, try a command that changes the appearance of your screen, such as "clear" (Berkeley UNIX) or "tput clear" (AT&T UNIX) to erase the terminal screen, or start a screen-oriented editor like VI or GNU EMACS. If your screen does not respond as expected, try another terminal type. In most cases, lower-case letters are required in the terminal name.

If you use a speaking or Braille device to read the screen to you, tell UNIX that you have a simple hardcopy terminal, such as a Teletype Model 33. Most UNIX systems support this under the name "tty" or "tty33." Also use this terminal type if you are logging in from a real hardcopy terminal, such as an ASCII TDD (Telecommunication Device for the Deaf).

UNIX Control Characters

The UNIX operating system and many UNIX applications support the use of control characters (and sometimes also printable characters) for editing or interrupting commands. The repertoire of functions available, and the characters assigned to them, can be discovered by using the `stty` command:

`% stty all`

(or `stty -a`, or `stty everything`).

In response, you should see a report that includes the following information (specific appearance may vary):

```
erase kill werase rprnt flush lnext susp    intr  quit stop    eof
^?    ^U   ^W     ^R    ^O    ^V    ^Z/^Y   ^C    ^\   ^S/^Q   ^D
```

These are the "significant characters" in your UNIX login session. Their meanings are listed in Table III-2. Control characters are shown in circumflex notation; ^U means Control-U, ^\ means Control-Backslash, and ^? means Delete. (For a complete listing of circumflex notation, see Table VII-2 on page 558.)

Table III-2 UNIX Terminal Control Characters

Notation	Meaning
eof	The character that generates an end of file condition at the terminal
erase	The character that erases the rightmost character from the current line
flush	The character that starts or stops discarding screen output
intr	The character that interrupts the current foreground process
kill	The character that erases the current line
lnext	The character that quotes the next character
quit	The character that terminates a process and creates a "core dump" file
rprnt	The character that reprints the current line to show the effects of any editing
stop	The software flow control stop and start characters
susp	The character that suspends the current foreground process
werase	The character that erases the rightmost word from the current line

You can change the interrupt character or any of the others in the list with the UNIX stty command. Normally, the method is to give the name of the terminal function you want to change, followed by the character you want to change it to, written in circumflex notation. For example, to change your interrupt character to Ctrl-B, enter:

```
% stty intr ^B
```

(that's circumflex followed by the letter B, not a real Ctrl-B). To disable a function altogether, use (depending on your UNIX version) undef or ^- (circumflex hyphen):

```
% stty quit undef   or   stty quit ^-
```

For details about the use of the stty command on your system, type man stty.

Flow Control

In your terminal session with the UNIX system, before you start C-Kermit, you should ensure that your UNIX login terminal device is using the same kind of flow control as your local terminal or emulator. For example, if your local terminal is using Xon/Xoff software flow control, then your UNIX session should be using it too. This can help prevent loss of data and fractured screens during your terminal session. Use the stty command to check whether Xon/Xoff flow control is enabled for your UNIX session. The Xon/Xoff characters are shown in the "stop" field of the stty report. If they are missing, you can enable them with a command like:

```
$ stty ixon ixoff
```

Consult man stty for details specific to your UNIX system.

If you are entering UNIX through a terminal server, you might find that Xon/Xoff flow control does not work promptly enough to prevent loss of data. In that case, you can enable it at the terminal server rather than at your UNIX session. For example, at the prompt of a Cisco terminal server, use:

```
ts>terminal flowcontrol software in out
```

However, this prevents transmission of Ctrl-S and Ctrl-Q characters as data, as required by certain UNIX applications such as the EMACS editor.

Some UNIX systems also support hardware flow control, most commonly RTS/CTS, but in most cases it won't be used unless you request it. In certain UNIX versions, like Dell System V Release 4, a login terminal must be permanently configured by the system manager for hardware flow control. In others, you can enable or disable hardware flow control by giving a UNIX command after you have logged in. Consult your system's "man pages" to find out the proper incantation. Here are some examples:

```
$ stty crtscts           (SunOS 4.0 or later)
$ stty rtsxoff ctsxon    (System V R4, some versions)
```

If you are entering UNIX through a terminal server, you might be able to enable hardware flow control there if it is not already enabled. On a Cisco terminal server, for example, the command is:

```
ts>terminal flowcontrol hardware in out
```

When C-Kermit is active, it attempts to use the type of flow control you have specified in your most recent SET FLOW command (Xon/Xoff by default). Hardware flow control, however, is often available only through the use of tricks that C-Kermit might not know about, for example `stty` commands like the ones just shown, special device names such as `/dev/tty00h` instead of `/dev/tty00`, or `/dev/cufa` instead of `/dev/cua`. Once again, consult your system documentation for details.

It can't be stressed enough that terminal connection and file transfer work best when an effective flow control method is active. Hardware flow control, if available, should be used in preference to software flow control.

Using International Characters in UNIX

Even though C-Kermit has extensive facilities for handling and converting character sets, you can't depend on UNIX itself for any help in this area. Older versions of UNIX do not support 8-bit no-parity terminal connections. They give you 7-bit terminal connections with even parity, restricting you to using only ASCII or a 7-bit national character set during your UNIX terminal session. UNIX terminal drivers make no provision, such as Shift-In/Shift-Out, for use of 8-bit characters in the 7-bit communications environment.

There is, however, a movement afoot to make newer versions of UNIX "8-bit clean" so 8-bit character sets such as the ISO Latin alphabets can be used. 8-bit cleanliness is a standard feature of many recent UNIX releases. In others, it is available upon request; for example in SunOS 4.1 and ULTRIX 4.0, where it is enabled by the command:

```
$ stty pass8
```

Other UNIX systems might or might not be 8-bit clean. Try `stty pass8`, `stty -parenb cs8`, or `stty -parity`. Check your UNIX system manuals or `man stty` for details. If you are accessing UNIX from a terminal or emulator, make sure that it is also set up for 8 data bits and no parity, as well as for the character set you want to use. If you are coming into UNIX through a terminal server or network connection, make sure that it is set up for 8-bit transparency too; for example, use `rlogin -8` rather than `rlogin`.

Program Control

C-Kermit is a character-mode application designed to be used from a terminal. If you are accessing your UNIX system from a terminal or terminal emulator, you can start the Kermit program in the normal way; that is, by typing its name possibly followed by command-line arguments. Then you can have an interactive dialog with it, using your keyboard and screen in the traditional manner.

If you have a desktop UNIX workstation with a mouse-and-window-oriented graphical user interface (GUI) such as Motif, NeXTstep, SunView, DECwindows, AIX Windows, and the like, you might find that clicking on C-Kermit in the File Browser, File Viewer, or whatever else it might be called in your windowing environment, does not work well. Some workstations complain that C-Kermit is not a *(name-of-GUI)* application. Others might automatically create a terminal window for C-Kermit, but one that does not have all the features of a UNIX terminal device, in which case C-Kermit will not work correctly.

The best way to start Kermit in a GUI environment is first to open a terminal emulation window that gives you the UNIX shell prompt, then start Kermit in the normal way from the shell prompt. On some systems you can write a shell script to do this, then you can click on the shell script in your GUI environment. See the `ckuker.bwr` file for ideas.

Starting C-Kermit

To start C-Kermit, just type "kermit" at the shell prompt:

```
$ kermit
C-Kermit 6.0.192 6 Sep 96, SCO OpenServer R5
Type ? or HELP for help
C-Kermit>
```

If you get a message like "not found" rather than C-Kermit's herald and prompt, it means that C-Kermit's directory is not in your PATH (in which case you should change the PATH definition in your login profile to include it), or it is called by some other name (such as "wermit" or "ckermit"), or it isn't there at all. If you get a message like "cannot execute" or "permission denied," C-Kermit is installed incorrectly. Review the installation instructions in the file ckuins.doc, or show them to whoever is responsible.

Initialization File

UNIX C-Kermit's initialization file is called .kermrc. Because the name begins with a period, it is a hidden file and normally does not show up in directory listings, and it is normally immune from rm * operations. The .kermrc file must be located in your home (login) directory. We recommend that you use the standard C-Kermit initialization file; create a separate file called .mykermrc to make any desired personal customizations. Your dialing directory file, if any, should be called .kdd, your network directory .knd, and your services directory .ksd, all in your home directory.

Redirection of Input and Output

C-Kermit reads its interactive-mode commands from the standard input device, normally your keyboard, and prints its messages on the standard output device, your screen. To redirect Kermit's standard input to come from a file, use the < operator on the UNIX command line:

```
$ kermit < commandfile
```

In this example, the file commandfile contains Kermit commands. Kermit executes them, one after the other, until it comes to the end of the file (or to a QUIT or EXIT command), and then it exits back to the system prompt.

You can also redirect Kermit's screen output to a file using similar mechanisms:

```
$ kermit > kermit.log
```

Of course, redirecting Kermit's screen output without also redirecting its input doesn't make much sense, because then you'll be typing Kermit commands to a blank screen. To redirect both input and output:

```
$ kermit < kermit.tak > kermit.log
```

You can even feed commands to Kermit from another process, if your mind is agile enough to conceive of a reason to do this:

```
$ grep ^send commandfile | sort | kermit
```

But note that Kermit does not have any way to jump around in the standard input stream; therefore commands fed to Kermit via redirection can not include GOTO.

Background Operation

If you're using Kermit in local mode, you can have it transfer files in the background while you do other work in the foreground. This can be accomplished by redirecting Kermit's standard input and output to command and log files and terminating the shell command that invokes Kermit with an ampersand:

```
$ kermit < cmdfile > logfile &
```

C-Kermit makes various system-dependent tests to see if it is running in the background. If it concludes that it is, prompts and most messages are not issued. If you start Kermit interactively but get no prompt after the greeting is printed, that means your operating system is reporting the symptoms of background operation even though Kermit is in the foreground. In such cases, you can force Kermit to behave as though it were in the foreground by including the –z command-line option:

```
$ kermit -z
C-Kermit 6.0.192 6 Sep 96, MIPS RISC/OS
Type ? or HELP for help
C-Kermit>
```

Don't use the –z option if you really *are* starting C-Kermit in the foreground.

Running C-Kermit in cron Jobs

cron is the UNIX way of scheduling and running tasks automatically without human intervention ("man cron" for details). Kermit jobs can be run this way too. Your crontab entry would normally look something like this:

```
0 0,6,12,18 * * * (cd /someplace; kermit cmdfile > kermit.log)
```

in which the material on the left is scheduling information, and the parentheses contain a list of commands to execute. Typically, you would change to a specific directory and then start Kermit, directing it to execute commands from a particular file (remember, if the first item on the C-Kermit command line is a filename, it is treated as a command file), and redirecting its output (messages, etc) to a log file.

A typical command file might be a login script with some file transfer commands. For neatness in the log file, you would probably want to include SET FILE DISPLAY NONE.

Interrupting C-Kermit

C-Kermit can be interrupted at its prompt, while typing a command, during execution of any command except CONNECT or remote-mode file transfer, and during local-mode file transfer by typing the interrupt character, which is normally Ctrl-C. The interrupt character should echo as ^C... and it should return you to the C-Kermit prompt immediately if you were running C-Kermit interactively, or back to the system prompt if you started C-Kermit with command-line action options (Appendix I).

If Ctrl-C does not interrupt C-Kermit, use the UNIX `stty` command as described on page 505 to find out what your UNIX `intr` character is. Use that character instead or change your interrupt character to Ctrl-C.

If you type the interrupt character while C-Kermit is executing its initialization file or command-line options, it exits.

To interrupt C-Kermit during remote-mode file transfer, type three Ctrl-C characters in a row (or whatever has been declared in the most recent SET TRANSFER CANCELLATION command).

To interrupt C-Kermit during CONNECT mode, use the CONNECT-mode escape character, followed by the letter C to get back to the prompt, or any of the other escape-level commands described in Chapter 8.

Suspending C-Kermit

On UNIX systems with job control (generally those that are based on Berkeley UNIX, AT&T UNIX System V R4, or POSIX), you can suspend Kermit by typing Ctrl-Z or whatever your suspend character is (you can find out by using the `stty` command as described on page 505; your suspend character is listed under `susp`):

```
C-Kermit>^Z
[4] + Stopped (signal) kermit
$
```

You can suspend C-Kermit this way at any time except when it is in CONNECT mode or engaged in remote-mode file transfer. When at C-Kermit prompt level, you can also suspend Kermit by using the SUSPEND command:

SUSPEND

> Suspends C-Kermit. Stops C-Kermit and returns to the system prompt, but does not remove C-Kermit from memory. Synonym: **Z**.

SET SUSPEND { ON, OFF }

> ON, the normal setting, means C-Kermit handles SUSPEND signals if it was built in an environment that supports them. OFF means C-Kermit ignores SUSPEND signals, and can not be suspended.

After you have suspended C-Kermit, you can get back to it by using the UNIX `fg` (foreground) command with Kermit's job number (as shown when you suspended Kermit, and also shown by the shell's `jobs` command) preceded by a percent sign:

```
$ fg %4
C-Kermit>
```

or its process ID number (as shown by the UNIX `ps` command). If Kermit was executing a command, it should resume where it left off. If it was at the prompt, you should get a new prompt. If you type "kermit" again, instead of "fg", you will start a new copy of Kermit; the old one will still be sitting in the background.

> **WARNING:** The UNIX version of C-Kermit allows itself to be suspended and continued if the underlying operating system supports this feature. But (and this is a *Big But*), you should not attempt to suspend Kermit or any other program if your UNIX shell does not also support this feature (Kermit cannot tell). Most C-Shells and K-Shells do, but most Bourne shells do not.[57] If you suspend C-Kermit in an environment that does not properly support job control, your session might become hopelessly hung. Your login session must be killed from another terminal (use the UNIX ps and kill commands).

There are three ways to deal with this problem:

1. Use a shell that supports job control. At most sites, you can use the chsh command to choose a different shell. For example, to use the C-Shell (csh):

   `$ chsh csh`

   Type man chsh for further information.

2. Give C-Kermit the command SET SUSPEND OFF to make C-Kermit ignore the suspend signal:

   `C-Kermit>set suspend off`

3. Disable the suspend signal before starting C-Kermit:

   `% stty susp undef`

Fixing Your UNIX Login Terminal Modes

If C-Kermit exits abnormally, for example because it was halted from another terminal, your login terminal might not function normally. In particular, it might not echo the characters you type and it might not recognize the Return or Enter key as a command terminator. In such cases, you should be able to restore your terminal to normal operation by issuing the reset or stty sane command (depending on your UNIX version). Type Ctrl-J, then the characters of the command, and terminate with another Ctrl-J (not Return or Enter); for example:

`$ <Ctrl-J>reset<Ctrl-J>`

---

[57]An exception is the Bourne shell distributed with AT&T System V Release 4.

UNIX C-Kermit Command Procedures

When creating a shell script program in UNIX, you can specify which shell (such as sh, csh, or ksh) is to execute the program by including a special type of "comment" as the first line, for example:

```
#!/bin/ksh
```

The # character is the shell comment introducer, and the second character, !, tells the shell that the rest of the line gives the name of the program that should be run to execute the shell script. The example tells your current shell to start /bin/ksh and to feed the file into ksh's standard input.

C-Kermit follows the same convention, which is possible because the # character is not only a UNIX shell comment introducer but also, by happy coincidence, a C-Kermit comment introducer. If you put a line like this:

```
#!/usr/local/bin/kermit
```

at the beginning of a C-Kermit command file and you also give execute permission to the file, you can run the file simply by typing its name at the system prompt, just as you would run a shell script. But in this case, the shell feeds the file to Kermit rather than to a UNIX shell. Of course, you can also use C-Kermit's TAKE command to execute the same file, in which case the #! line is ignored.

On your own UNIX system, substitute the actual pathname of the Kermit program if it is not /usr/local/bin/kermit. To give execute permission to the command file, use the chmod +x command at the UNIX shell prompt:

```
$ chmod +x cmdfile
```

The commands in the file are executed *after* your initialization file has been completely processed, but *before* the C-Kermit prompt appears. If you want the command file to exit to the system without issuing the C-Kermit prompt, include an EXIT command at the end.

You can also include C-Kermit command-line options in the command file invocation:

```
$ cmdfile -p e -l /dev/ttyh8
```

or, to have C-Kermit skip its initialization-file processing:

```
$ cmdfile -Y
```

When you start Kermit from a command file, the UNIX shell constructs a command of this form:

```
kermit-path-name command-file-name options
```

so you can also invoke Kermit like this yourself, for example:

```
$ kermit cmdfile -p e -l /dev/ttyh8
```

Terminal Connection

In the UNIX version of C-Kermit, terminal emulation is provided by your console driver, workstation terminal window, terminal emulator, or terminal. C-Kermit does not, itself, provide any particular type of terminal emulation beyond what is described in Chapter 8.

The CONNECT-Mode Escape Character

UNIX C-Kermit's default CONNECT-mode escape character is Ctrl-\ (Control-Backslash) except on certain workstations (such as the NeXT) that cannot generate this character from the keyboard, in which case Ctrl-] (Control-Rightbracket) is used. Use SHOW ESCAPE to find out what your escape character is, and SET ESCAPE to change it.

Key Mapping

C-Kermit's SET KEY command is effective only with keys that generate single-byte 7-bit or 8-bit codes. 7-bit keycodes are supported by C-Kermit for all UNIX versions, provided C-Kermit was configured with the key-mapping feature. 8-bit codes can be used if you have a keyboard capable of generating them, if C-Kermit has a clean 8-bit path to the keyboard, and if you have told C-Kermit to SET COMMAND BYTESIZE 8.

Suspending C-Kermit While in CONNECT Mode

During terminal connection, you can follow the CONNECT-mode escape character by the letter Z to suspend Kermit. This stops Kermit without breaking the connection and returns you to the same UNIX shell that you started Kermit from. Unlike the ! option, the z option lets you get at any other jobs (text editors, mail programs, etc.) that you might be running in parallel with Kermit. Use the UNIX fg command to continue Kermit's CONNECT session, as in this example:

```
C-Kermit>connect                          (CONNECT to remote host)
%                                         (Remote system prompt is %)
% ^\z                                     (Suspend Kermit)
[3] + Stopped (signal)    kermit
$                                         (Back at local system, prompt is $)
$ jobs                                    (List my jobs)

[3] + Stopped (signal)    kermit
[2] - Stopped             emacs
[1]   Stopped (signal)    mm

  (Here you can run other programs,
   continue your background jobs, etc.)
$
$ fg %3                                   (Restart C-Kermit)
%                                         (Connect session continues)
%
```

The usual cautions apply here. Don't try to suspend C-Kermit if it was invoked from a shell that does not support job control.

File Transfer

UNIX C-Kermit offers the full range of file transfer features, including text and binary transfers, file groups, attributes, recover, and the FULLSCREEN file transfer display if it has been configured in your version (use the CHECK FULLSCREEN command to find out). For text files, UNIX record format (lines terminated by LF) is automatically converted to Kermit's standard intermediate form (CRLF) during file transfer.

C-Kermit's packet buffers are a certain size, depending on the specific build options. Use SHOW PROTOCOL to find out what the buffer size is. The product of the window size and packet length can not be greater than the buffer size. If your version of UNIX C-Kermit was built with the DYNAMIC compilation option (use CHECK DYNAMIC to find out), you can use the SET BUFFERS command to increase the buffer size to allow more window slots or longer packets, for example:

```
C-Kermit>set buffers 80000
C-Kermit>set window 20
C-Kermit>set receive packet-length 4000
```

If your C-Kermit was built without the DYNAMIC feature, the buffer size can't be changed.

Interruption of Local-Mode File Transfer

In most C-Kermit versions, you can interrupt a local-mode file transfer by typing single letters like X, Z, or E (see Chapter 9). In C-Kermit versions based on AT&T System V UNIX or in POSIX, however, you might have to type the CONNECT-mode escape character (normally Ctrl-Backslash) before you type the interruption key.[58] C-Kermit's message at the start of file transfer gives you the information you need. Example:

```
C-Kermit>s oofa.txt
SF
Type escape character (^\) followed by:
X to cancel file,  CR to resend current packet
Z to cancel group, A for status report
E to send Error packet, Ctrl-C to quit immediately:
A
Sending: oofa.txt => OOFA.TXT
Size: 20659, Type: text
.........Ctrl-\X
Cancelling File  [interrupted]
ZB
C-Kermit>
```

In this case the escape character was Control-Backslash, so the user typed Ctrl-\ followed by the letter X to interrupt the file transfer.

---

[58]The control-character prefix is required because of limitations in the System V and POSIX terminal drivers. Nevertheless, your version of C-Kermit might include a workaround, so also try entering the interruption characters without the control-character prefix.

Background File Transfer

On UNIX systems with job control, you can type your suspend character (normally Ctrl-Z) to suspend Kermit during local-mode file transfer. This stops Kermit so you can talk to your shell or run other programs. Later (but not too much later) you can bring it back in the foreground (using the UNIX `fg` command); the file transfer resumes where it left off, provided the other Kermit has not timed out.

```
C-Kermit>s order.log
SF
Sending: order.log => ORDER.LOG
Size: 3712745, Type: text
X to cancel file,  CR to resend current packet
Z to cancel group, A for status report
E to send Error packet, Ctrl-C to quit immediately: A
........Ctrl-Z
[3] + Stopped (signal)  kermit
$ fortune                       (Quick, I need a fortune)
The moon is full.  Today is your lucky day.  You are very hungry.

$ fg %3                         (Resume Kermit)
kermit
N%....................... [OK]
ZB<BEEP>
C-Kermit>exit
```

You can also continue the file transfer in the background, leaving your terminal free for other work in the meantime:

```
.....Ctrl(Z)
[3] + Stopped (signal)  kermit
$ bg %3                         (Continue Kermit in the background)
[3] kermit&
$ jobs
[3] + Running           kermit
[2] - Stopped           emacs
[1]   Stopped (signal)  mm
```

Eventually, your shell will give you a message that the job has stopped because it wants "tty input," which means the transfer has completed. At that point you can put Kermit back in the foreground:

```
[3] + Stopped (tty input) kermit
$ fg %3                         (Back to the foreground)
C-Kermit>                       (Prompt reappears)
```

Sending Files

C-Kermit processes wildcard characters (metacharacters) in the SEND and related commands, and the C-Kermit server also processes them when it receives a GET command.

UNIX C-Kermit offers two options for processing wildcards: its own internal wildcard expander and that of your shell. Select the desired expansion method with this command:

SET WILDCARD-EXPANSION { KERMIT, SHELL }

Unless you say otherwise, Kermit expands wildcards itself. In this case, three special characters are recognized and expanded:

~ (Tilde) (at the beginning of a filename only) is translated into your login directory name (if followed immediately by a slash) or into the login directory of the user whose username immediately follows the tilde:

```
C-Kermit>send ~/.profile          (My own .profile file)
C-Kermit>send ~jrd/mskermit.ini   (JRD's mskermit.ini file)
```

* (asterisk) Matches zero or more characters within a file or directory name. The asterisk does not match the slash (/) character; that is, it does not work across directory separators.

```
C-Kermit>send *               (All files in current directory)
C-Kermit>send ~/*/*.ini       (.ini's in all subdirectories)
C-Kermit>send o*a             (o-anything-a)
```

In UNIX, "hidden" files (whose names begin with a period character), such as .login, are not sent unless the *filespec* also begins with a period:[59]

```
C-Kermit>send *               (All nonhidden files)
C-Kermit>send .*              (All hidden files)
C-Kermit>msend * .*           (All files)
```

? (question mark) Matches any single character except a directory separator (slash) or the leading period of a hidden file. You must quote the question mark with a backslash to override its normal help-giving function:

```
C-Kermit>send ckcker.\?       (ckcker.1-character)
C-Kermit>send ckcker.\?\?\?   (ckcker.3-characters)
C-Kermit>send ~kermit/\?*     (~kermit/-at-least-1-character)
```

If you don't quote the question mark, you get a list of matching filenames, and then you are reprompted with what you have typed so far:

```
C-Kermit>send ckcmai.? File(s) to send, one of the following:
 ckcmai.c           ckcmai.o
C-Kermit>send ckcmai.
```

The UNIX shells csh, ksh, and bash, but not the original Bourne shell, provide additional filename-matching wildcard characters. If you SET WILD SHELL, Kermit uses the shell whose file specification is given in the SHELL environment variable:

```
$ echo $SHELL
/bin/ksh
```

---

[59]This is compatible with the file matching of the UNIX shell and the ls command.

or if that fails, it uses your login shell (as recorded in the etc/passwd file). Internally, Kermit uses the specified shell's echo command to expand metacharacters. Exactly which metacharacters are available depends on your shell and its echo command. The following are generally available in addition to those listed; consult your shell's "man page" for further information.

[abc]

(csh, ksh, bash) Matches any single character that appears within the brackets:

C-Kermit>send ck[cuw]*.[cwh]   *(The UNIX Kermit source files)*

[a-z]

(csh, ksh, bash) Matches any single character in the range indicated in the brackets, in this case a through z. The characters in the range are determined by the internal numeric codes for the characters (for example their ASCII values):

C-Kermit>send x[0-9][0-9].log   *(x00.log thru x99.log)*
C-Kermit>send [Ff][Ii][Ll][Ee]   *("file" in any case)*

{aaa,bbb}

(csh, bash) Matches any of the comma-separated character strings within the braces:

C-Kermit>send ckcker.{upd,bwr}
C-Kermit>send {oofa.txt,hex.c}
C-Kermit>send ck[cuw]*.{[cwh],doc,bwr,nr}

As you can see, shell expansion can be more flexible than Kermit's own, and it is consistent with your own use of your preferred shell. But it also has several possible drawbacks:

- It might be difficult or impossible to refer to files whose names contain shell metacharacters. (Try quoting such characters with a backslash or two, or enclosing the filename in doublequotes, but this might not always work.)

- The same Kermit file transfer command might behave differently depending on what your current shell is. This is a particularly important consideration for command files. Kermit's internal expansion, on the other hand, works consistently.

- The echo command of certain shells (notably csh) might print not only filenames, but other words. For example, in the C-Shell:

```
$ echo foo*
echo: no match
```

In this case, if you happen to have files called echo:, no, or match, Kermit might try to transfer them.

- The echo command has an option -n. If you try to refer to a file whose name is -n, you must prefix it with a directory specification (for example, ./-n) to prevent echo from interpreting its name as a command option.

When you give the -s option on the C-Kermit command line, the file specification that follows can include any wildcard notation understood by your shell, regardless of C-Kermit's WILDCARD-EXPANSION setting. The shell expands wildcards into a list of files that is provided to Kermit via the "argv" mechanism. For example:

```
$ kermit -s *.txt
```

The shell, not Kermit, expands *.txt into a list of all the files in your current directory whose names end with ".txt". If any of the files actually contains a wildcard character as part of its name, C-Kermit makes no attempt to expand it further.

Receiving Files

Incoming files are stored in the current directory unless you told the RECEIVE command otherwise, or if the incoming file header packet includes a pathname and you have SET RECEIVE PATHNAMES ON, or if you have specified a FILE DOWNLOAD-DIRECTORY. A file can be created only if you have write access to the directory where the file is to be stored. If a file of the same name already exists in the target directory and C-Kermit's FILE COLLISION is set to BACKUP or OVERWRITE, you must also have write access to the previously existing file. C-Kermit will not create or delete files for you that you could not otherwise create or delete yourself.

Files are stored with the permissions of the containing directory combined with your "umask" (see the "man page" for your shell for further information). In other words, C-Kermit creates files with exactly the same permissions they would have if you created them any other way; for example, with the `cat` command or with a text editor.

C-Kermit does not set execute permission on incoming files. If you are using C-Kermit to receive shell scripts, executable binary programs, or other types of files that require execute permission, use `chmod +x` after the transfer.

If a UNIX file must be renamed because of your FILE COLLISION setting, C-Kermit appends a pseudo-version-number to the end of the file's name:

```
oofa.~n~
```

where oofa is the name the two files share and . ~n~ is a version number, for example:

```
oofa.~8~
```

If oofa exists, the new file is called oofa.~1~. If oofa and oofa.~1~ exist, the new file is oofa.~2~, and so on. If the new name would be longer than the maximum length for a filename on your UNIX system, then characters are deleted from the end first. For instance, `thelongestname` on a system with a limit of 14 characters would become `thelongest.~1~`. This scheme is compatible with the backup mechanism used by GNU EMACS on UNIX, and in fact the renamed files are recognized as backup files by EMACS, which can be used to clean up excessive numbers of them.

UNIX-to-UNIX Transfers

When using C-Kermit 6.0 or later to transfer files between two UNIX systems, each Kermit recognizes that the other system is UNIX, and the two programs switch to binary transfer mode and literal filenames automatically, regardless of your current FILE TYPE and FILE NAMES settings. This switching, however, does not affect your global settings, which are restored once the transfer is finished.

Should you wish to defeat this effect, you can use the command:

SET TRANSFER MODE MANUAL

(as opposed to AUTOMATIC, which is the default). In most cases automatic mode-switching is appropriate and desirable, but an exception would be if you wanted to use text transfer mode to force record-format or character-set conversion.

Command Summary

Here is a quick reference list of C-Kermit commands peculiar to or related to UNIX.

```
CHECK feature-name
SET SUSPEND { ON, OFF }
SET TRANSFER MODE { AUTOMATIC, MANUAL }
SET WILDCARD-EXPANSION { KERMIT, SHELL }
SHOW FEATURES
SUSPEND
```

UNIX shell commands useful with C-Kermit:

```
bg process-id
chgrp group file...
chmod permissions file...
chown user file...
chsh shell
cu
echo text
fg process-id
kill process-id
man command
stty
```

VMS C-Kermit

○ ○ ○ ○

This appendix explains how to use C-Kermit on a Digital Equipment Corporation VAX or Alpha computer with the VMS or OpenVMS operating system. For a current list of limitations and restrictions of VMS C-Kermit, also read the files CKCKER.BWR and CKVKER.BWR provided with the VMS C-Kermit distribution files. Prior to installing VMS C-Kermit, be sure to read the installation instructions in the file CKVINS.DOC.

VMS (Virtual Memory System) is the operating system for Digital Equipment Corporation (DEC) 32-bit VAX (Virtual Address Extended) computers, a product line ranging from desktop workstations to minicomputers to large mainframes. VMS is a multiuser, multitasking operating system. OpenVMS is the new name for the VMS operating system; OpenVMS runs on both VAX and 64-bit Alpha processors. C-Kermit runs under both VMS and OpenVMS, on both VAX and Alpha. In this book, the term VMS includes OpenVMS on both VAX and Alpha architectures.

Preparing Your VMS Session for C-Kermit

Before starting C-Kermit, make sure that VMS knows what kind of terminal you have so C-Kermit's FULLSCREEN file transfer display will work correctly. VMS C-Kermit (like VMS itself) supports only Digital Equipment Corporation terminal types for formatted screen display functions. If you are using C-Kermit on a terminal that is not compatible with these terminals, you should not use Kermit's FULLSCREEN file transfer display.

When you log in, most VMS systems send a special DEC-specific "What Are You?" query (<ESC>Z or <ESC>[0c to the terminal. All DEC terminals respond automatically with a character sequence indicating the terminal model — LA36, VT52, VT100, VT200, VT300, VT400, etc. If you are using a VT or compatible terminal, or a PC with a correctly functioning VT terminal emulator, such as Kermit 95, Kermit/2, or MS-DOS Kermit, your VMS terminal type is set automatically. Otherwise, there is a lengthy pause while VMS waits for a valid reply, doesn't get one, and then sets your terminal type to UNKNOWN.

You can find out what terminal types are supported by your VMS system by issuing the VMS command HELP SET TERMINAL/DEVICE. If your terminal appears on this list, you can give a VMS command to set your terminal type correspondingly, like:

```
$ set terminal /device=vt100
```

You can find out your VMS terminal characteristics with the SHOW TERMINAL command.

If you are using a speaking device or an ASCII TDD (Telecommunication Device for the Deaf), you should choose a hardcopy terminal type, such as LA36.

7-Bit versus 8-Bit Connections

If the communication channel between you and the VMS system permits transmission of 8-bit data, you should ensure that VMS itself is set up to allow 8-bit communication. Otherwise you will not be able to use 8-bit character sets (such as Latin-1 or DEC MCS) during your session, nor can you use the more efficient 8-bit form of the DEC terminal escape sequences. Conversely, if you have a 7-bit connection, but VMS believes your connection is 8 bits, 8-bit characters and escape sequences will be corrupted and your VMS session will consist mainly of gibberish.

VMS decides whether you have an 8-bit data path or not based upon your terminal type: for VT200-series and above, VMS assumes 8 bits, for VT173 and below, it assumes 7 bits. After logging in, use the VMS SHOW TERMINAL command to discover its idea of your terminal type and byte size. In the listing, "No Eightbit" means 7 bits, and "Eightbit" means 8 bits. To change its mind, if necessary:

```
$ set terminal /noparity /eight_bit    ! Tell VMS to use 8 bits
$ set terminal /noeight_bit             ! Tell VMS to use 7 bits
```

If you can't obtain an 8-bit connection, you are restricted to a 7-bit character code during terminal operations. This code may be ASCII or any other 7-bit code supported by your terminal or terminal emulator, such as an ISO 646 national character set.

Using VMS C-Kermit

VMS users might find C-Kermit's command processing to be somewhat unfamiliar. It lacks certain VMS features (such as arrow-key editing) and has some others (such as context-sensitive help menus, file menus, completion, and macros) that you will soon wish VMS had. C-Kermit's "user interface" is intended to be compatible with other Kermit programs, rather than with a particular operating system. Once you have learned to control one Kermit program, you will also be conversant with most others.

Program Control

VMS C-Kermit is a character-mode application designed to be used from a terminal. If you are accessing your VMS system from a terminal or terminal emulator, you can start the Kermit program in the normal way, that is, by typing its name possibly followed by command line arguments.[60] Then you can have an interactive dialog with C-Kermit, using your keyboard and screen:

```
$ kermit
C-Kermit 6.0.192 6 Sep 96, OpenVMS VAX
Type ? or HELP for help
C-Kermit>
```

If you have a desktop VMS workstation with a mouse-and-window-oriented graphical user interface (GUI) such as DECwindows, you should run C-Kermit in a VT terminal emulation window, also known as a DECterm.

Command-line options are converted to lowercase before C-Kermit sees them, which can interfere with important case distinctions, for example between the -y and -Y or -c and -C options. To include an uppercase option on the VMS C-Kermit command line, enclose it in doublequotes:

```
$ kermit "-Y"
```

The C-Kermit Initialization File

VMS C-Kermit identifies its initialization file by the following steps:

1. The file CKERMIT.INI, if it exists, in the directory designated by the system-wide logical name CKERMIT_INI:, if it is defined. You can override the system-wide definition, if any, by redefining this logical name, e.g. in your LOGIN.COM file.

2. The file designated by the logical name CKERMIT_INIT, if it is defined.

3. The file CKERMIT.INI in your login (home) directory.

---

[60]Or, if Kermit has not been installed as a system command, use the RUN command. The RUN command, however, does not permit command-line arguments.

If the CKERMIT_INI logical name does not exist, or does not turn up a CKERMIT.INI file, then the search proceeds down the list.

The system manager can install the standard C-Kermit initialization file in a central location and define the system-wide logical name CKERMIT_INI to identify the directory where this file is. To institute site-wide customizations, a C-Kermit command file called CKERMIT.SYS can be placed in the same directory as the system-wide CKERMIT.INI file.

The standard initialization file automatically executes the user's own customization file, CKERMOD.INI, if it exists in the user's home directory, so each user can create a personalized C-Kermit environment without having to duplicate the common material from the standard initialization file.

Users can further customize C-Kermit to use different settings when started from different directories. For example, you can put a different CKERMIT.INI file in each of your subdirectories. Then include the following as the last line in your login directory's CKERMOD.INI file:

```
if not equal \v(home) \v(dir) -
  if exist []ckermit.ini take []ckermit.ini
```

If you have a services directory file, it should installed in your login directory as CKERMIT.KSD. Dialing or network directory files go in the same place under the names CKERMIT.KDD and CKERMIT.KND, respectively. Of course, you can specify different, more, or fewer names by including the appropriate SET DIAL DIRECTORY or SET NETWORK DIRECTORY commands in your CKERMOD.INI file.

Interrupting C-Kermit

C-Kermit can be interrupted at its prompt, in the middle of typing a command, during execution of any command except CONNECT or remote-mode file transfer, and during local-mode file transfer by typing either one of the VMS interrupt characters, Ctrl-C or Ctrl-Y. Both should have the same effect.

The interrupt character should echo as ^C... and return you to the C-Kermit prompt immediately (if you were running C-Kermit interactively), or else back to the system prompt if you started C-Kermit with command-line action options (Appendix I).

To interrupt C-Kermit during remote-mode file transfer, type three consecutive Ctrl-C characters. This should return you to the C-Kermit prompt or, if you started C-Kermit with command-line action options, to the VMS system prompt.

To interrupt C-Kermit during CONNECT mode, use the CONNECT-mode escape character, followed by C to get back to the prompt, or any of the other escape-level commands described in Chapter 8.

Redirection of Input and Output

C-Kermit reads its interactive-mode commands from the standard input device, normally your keyboard, and prints its messages on the standard output device, which is normally your screen. To redirect Kermit's standard input to come from a file, redefine the SYS$INPUT logical name:

```
$ define /user_mode sys$input kermit.ksc
$ kermit
```

In these examples, the file KERMIT.KSC contains C-Kermit commands. C-Kermit executes them, one after the other, until it comes to the end of the file (or to an EXIT, STOP, or similar command), and then it exits back to the system prompt.

You can also redirect C-Kermit's screen output to a file by redefining the SYS$OUTPUT logical name before starting C-Kermit:

```
$ define /user_mode sys$output kermit.log
$ kermit
```

But if you redirect Kermit's screen output without also redirecting its input, you'll be typing Kermit commands to a blank screen. To redirect both input and output:

```
$ define /user_mode sys$input kermit.ksc
$ define /user_mode sys$output kermit.log
$ kermit
```

Background operation in VMS can be accomplished with the SPAWN/NOWAIT command:

```
$ spawn /nowait /input=kermit.ksc /output=kermit.log kermit
```

or by running Kermit in a batch job, using the VMS SUBMIT command.

Running C-Kermit in DCL Command Procedures

In a DCL .COM file, lines beginning with dollar sign are commands that you would type at the VMS system prompt; all others are input for a program. The following example shows how to construct a DCL command file that feeds interactive-mode commands to C-Kermit. The first two lines are DCL commands, the next three are C-Kermit commands, and the last line is another DCL command:

```
$ write sys$output "Starting Kermit..."
$ kermit
set file type binary
receive
exit
$ write sys$output "Kermit finished."
```

To make VMS C-Kermit read its commands from your keyboard when invoked from a DCL command procedure, include the following redefinition of the SYS$COMMAND logical name:

```
$ write sys$output "Starting Kermit..."
$ define /user_mode sys$input sys$command
$ kermit
$ write sys$output "Kermit finished."
```

DCL command procedures can pass their command-line arguments along to C-Kermit. For example, the following DCL command file, KSEND.COM, sends up to eight files (or groups of files) from a remote VMS system to the user's local Kermit program:

```
$ kermit -s 'p1' 'p2' 'p3' 'p4' 'p5' 'p6' 'p7' 'p8'
```

The p's in single quotes are DCL variables, similar to Kermit's macro argument variables. They are used here to pass command-line arguments from the DCL command procedure to C-Kermit. To use this command procedure, type (for example):

```
$ @ksend ckvker.mak ck*.h ck*.c
```

This example assumes the KSEND.COM file is in your current directory.

You can also define convenient aliases to run Kermit with different command files, by using VMS's DEFINE command, for example:

```
$ define compuserve $sys$system:kermit.exe sys$login:compuserve.ini
$ define sprintnet  $sys$system:kermit.exe sys$login:sprintnet.ini
```

Put these definitions in your VMS LOGIN.COM file.

Using C-Kermit in Batch Jobs

Kermit procedures that require no interaction with the user can be run as batch jobs, perhaps scheduled for execution at a later time. Batch jobs are simply DCL command procedures (that is, .COM files) are executed using the VMS SUBMIT command, rather than with @. Here is a sample batch job showing the various controls that are available; lines beginning with dollar sign ($) are DCL commands, other lines are executed by Kermit. The line numbers are for discussion and should not be included in the .COM file.

```
1. $ write sys$output "Hello from DCL"
2. $ set default [myuserid.mysubdirectory]
3. $ kermit
4. set prompt {}
5. echo Hello from C-Kermit
6. @ write sys$output "Hello from DCL from inside C-Kermit"
7. take update.ksc
8. exit
9. $ write sys$output "All done."
```

Lines 1–3 are DCL commands. Line 3 starts C-Kermit. Lines 4–8 are C-Kermit commands. Line 4 shows how to set C-Kermit's prompt to nothing to reduce clutter in the batch log, should you desire. Line 5 shows how to enter messages in the batch log. Line 6 shows how to run DCL commands from within Kermit (you can use @ (at-sign), ! (exclamation mark), or the word RUN — all of them are synonyms — followed by a DCL command). Line 8 exits from C-Kermit back to DCL. In line 7, C-Kermit is told to execute a script program from another file, UPDATE.KSC. Script programs to be run during the batch session are best kept in separate C-Kermit command files because certain commands, such as GOTO, do not work when entered in the batch command stream. Include SET TAKE ECHO ON in your script file if you want the commands from the script file to be written to the batch log.

Suppose the batch file name is UPDATE.COM and it's in your default directory. To execute it immediately, give the following command to VMS:

```
$ submit update
```

Include the /NOTIFY switch to have VMS send you a message when it's done:

```
$ submit /notify update
```

The log file UPDATE.LOG is created in your login directory. To execute the job later, and specify a particular name and place for the log file:

```
$ submit /after="7-Aug-1996 23:59:59" /log=[olga]hhb.log update
```

Use the VMS HELP SUBMIT command or see the appropriate VMS manuals for more information about batch jobs.

Exit Status

VMS C-Kermit does not provide program status codes in the normal VMS manner. Rather, it returns the codes listed in Table I-1 on page 463, by assigning them to the symbol CKERMIT_STATUS. For example, if a RECEIVE operation failed:

```
$ show symbol ckermit_status
  CKERMIT_STATUS == "4"
$
```

Arguments supplied to the EXIT (or QUIT) commands take precedence:

```
C-Kermit> exit 1234
$ show symbol ckermit_status
  CKERMIT_STATUS == "1234"
$
```

If C-Kermit encounters no execution errors, and EXIT (QUIT) is given without an operand, then:

```
C-Kermit> exit
$ show symbol ckermit_status
  CKERMIT_STATUS == "0"
$
```

You can use the CKERMIT_STATUS symbol as in this DCL example:

```
$ kermit "-C" "take inventory.ksc"
$ if ckermit_status .eq. 0 then goto ok
```

Terminal Connection

VMS C-Kermit's default CONNECT-mode escape character is Ctrl-\ (Control-Backslash). Terminal emulation is provided by your console driver, workstation terminal window, terminal emulator, or terminal. VMS C-Kermit recognizes keystrokes as single 7- or 8-bit bytes. 8-bit codes can be used if you have a keyboard capable of generating them, if C-Kermit has a clean 8-bit path to the keyboard, if you have told C-Kermit to SET COMMAND and TERMINAL BYTESIZE 8, *and* if your VMS terminal has the EIGHTBIT characteristic, as shown by the VMS SHOW TERMINAL command.

File Transfer

VMS C-Kermit sends most common types of files in the correct manner automatically, with no SET FILE TYPE commands required, and supports the full range of VMS wildcard characters for file group selection.

Wildcards

VMS lets you refer to groups of files in a single file specification by using wildcard characters. VMS wildcard characters are asterisk (*) and percent (%). Asterisk matches all or part of a directory name, file name, or file type. It can also be used to stand for all version numbers, but it cannot be used to match part of a version number. In the directory field, the asterisk does not operate across the periods that separate directory names. Percent sign matches any single character in a directory name, file name, or file type, but it cannot be used in the version number field. The following command:

```
$ directory [kermit.*]a*.%%%;0
```

lists the names of the most recent versions (;0) of all files whose names start with the letter *A* (alphabetic case does not matter in VMS filenames) and that have a three-character filetype, in all subdirectories of the [KERMIT] top-level directory of the current disk.

There are also two special wildcards for use with directory names. The ellipsis (...) means "from here all the way down," and hyphen (-) means "one level up." Two hyphens means two levels up, and so on.

Here are some sample wildcard file specifications:

```
$ dir [*]
```
All files in all top-level directories

```
$ dir [.*]
```
All files in all directories immediately below the current directory (one level down)

```
$ dir [...]
```
All files in the current directory and all directories below it

```
$ dir [OLGA.PROGRAMS...]
```
All files in OLGA.PROGRAMS and all directories below it

```
$ dir [-]
```
All files in the directory immediately above the current directory (one level up)

```
$ dir [--]
```
All files in the directory two levels up

```
$ dir [000000]
```
All files in the root directory of the current disk (if you have access)

Sending Files from VMS

When you are sending files from VMS C-Kermit and its FILE TYPE is set to TEXT or BINARY, it chooses the mode of transfer automatically. The rules are:

1. If the record format is Undefined, BINARY mode is used.

2. If the record format is Fixed *and* the file has no record attributes (the VMS DIRECTORY/FULL command reports "Record attributes: None"), BINARY mode is used.

3. If the record format is Fixed and the file has any record attributes (for example, Carriage Return Carriage Control), TEXT mode is used.

4. In all other cases, including Stream and Variable record formats, TEXT mode is used.

VMS C-Kermit automatically tells the receiving Kermit the transfer mode, text or binary, in an Attribute packet. This lets receiving Kermit interpret and store the file in the correct mode automatically if it understands Attribute packets (most modern Kermit programs do; see Table 1-1 on page 10). It also allows transfer of a mixture of text and binary files in a single SEND command. For example, you can send the C-language (text) source file OOFA.C and the (binary) executable OOFA.EXE together with one command:

```
C-Kermit>send oofa.*
```

When sending text files, C-Kermit handles all combinations of record format and carriage control, including Fortran (ANSI) and Print, converting each into Kermit standard ASCII/CRLF stream format. It also translates the file's character set according to any SET FILE CHARACTER-SET and SET TRANSFER CHARACTER-SET commands you have given.

When sending a binary file, VMS C-Kermit does no interpretation, translation, or reformatting of the file's data. Record-length and carriage control fields are discarded, and no characters are inserted at record boundaries or at the end of the file.

VMS C-Kermit also sends the file's size and creation date and time in the Attribute packet. This allows the receiving Kermit program to reject the file if it is too big for available storage and to set the file's creation date to match the original or to take file collision actions based on the date. The reported size of a text file might differ from the actual size due to record format conversions.

VMS C-Kermit also lets you include DECnet node names in filenames:

```
C-Kermit>send netlab::$disk1:[jrd.kermit]msvibm.boo
C-Kermit>receive kervax::lpt:
C-Kermit>send {spcvxa"TERRY PASSWORD"::kermit:ckvcvt.c}
```

The first example sends a publicly readable file from node NETLAB. The second example receives a file to a publicly accessible line printer on DECnet node KERVAX and then prints it.

The third example sends a file that is not publicly readable from node SPCVXA, so a valid user ID and password for that node must be included as part of the node name. These must be given in uppercase. Since the file specification includes a space, it must be enclosed in curly braces to prevent C-Kermit from thinking that the space introduces the next field of the command. Alternatively, the space can be represented as \32:

```
C-Kermit>send spcvxa"TERRY\32PASSWORD"::kermit:ckvcvt.c
```

If you invoke VMS C-Kermit with the command-line option to send files (-s, see Appendix I), wildcard characters are expanded internally by C-Kermit, using underlying VMS operating system services:

```
$ kermit -s a*.* login.com ckermit.ini [.*]*.com
```

This example sends all files in the current directory whose names start with A, plus LOGIN.COM and CKERMIT.INI from the current directory, plus all .COM files from all immediate subdirectories of the current directory.

VMS C-Kermit sends the most recent version of each file unless you include a specific version number:

```
C-Kermit>send [olaf]paper.txt        (Most recent version only)
C-Kermit>sen [olaf]stone.txt;3       (A specific version)
C-Kermit>s [olaf]scissors.txt;*      (All versions)
```

Receiving Files

When receiving files, VMS C-Kermit chooses between text and binary mode as follows:

1. If the Kermit program that is sending the file to C-Kermit includes an Attribute packet specifying the file type (text or binary), C-Kermit uses the given type.

2. If there is no Attribute packet, if the Attribute packet does not mention a file type, or if you have given the command SET ATTRIBUTE TYPE OFF, C-Kermit uses its current FILE TYPE setting.

VMS C-Kermit checks for sufficient free disk space if the remote Kermit supplies file size information. If there isn't enough space on the disk, the file is rejected. User quotas are not checked. If the device for the received file is not a disk (for example, the system lineprinter) the file is assumed to fit. To defeat space checking, give the command SET ATTRIBUTE LENGTH OFF.

Received text files are stored in "Sequential variable, carriage-return carriage control" format, with each line (record) terminated by carriage return and linefeed (CRLF). Lone carriage returns or linefeeds are stored within the record.

Files received in binary mode are stored by C-Kermit in fixed 512-byte records. If the last record does not end on a 512-byte boundary, the exact end of the file is marked using the RMS "first free byte" construct.

If there is valid date and time information in the incoming Attribute packet, C-Kermit sets the new file's creation date and time accordingly. The file is also marked as being revised once (initial creation) on the *current* date and time to ensure that the file is backed up on the next BACKUP run.

When the Automatic Methods Don't Work

○ ○ ○ ○

If you can successfully transfer both text and binary files to and from VMS with C-Kermit, feel free to skip the rest of this appendix, which presents special methods for transferring the kinds of VMS files that C-Kermit does not handle automatically.

VMS supports a wide variety of file formats. Information about each file is recorded in the file's directory entry and, in most cases, also in the file itself. Most other computers have simpler file systems, with no natural way to record or represent VMS's file types and attributes. When a complicated type of file is sent from VMS to, say, UNIX or MS-DOS, much of the VMS-specific information can be lost. When the file is sent back to VMS, it is no longer in its original format and might be unusable. Even when a file is transferred from VMS to VMS the results can be less than satisfactory if the transfer program can't convey all the descriptive information along with its contents.

Each VMS application defines its own data file formats. Everyday text-oriented applications like the CREATE command and the editors EDT and EVE use ordinary text files: stream files with lines terminated by carriage return and line feed, the same as Kermit's default for text files. The VMS operating system requires its executable program images to be in fixed 512-byte record format, the same as Kermit's default for binary files.

But the VMS linker requires its (binary) object files to have variable length records. A BACKUP saveset must have fixed-length records with a record length of at least 2048 bytes. A database file might have indexed or relative organization, rather than sequential. Some applications deliberately coerce their files into unusual formats to make it difficult for other applications to use them. File attributes such as record format and length can't be handled by other operating systems like Microsoft Windows, MS-DOS, OS/2, UNIX, or CP/M, so these files need special handling when you transfer them.

You can find out the particulars of a VMS file with the DIR/FULL command, for example:

```
$ dir /full oofa.obj

Directory $DISK1:[OLGA]

OOFA.OBJ;2                       File ID:   (3201,349,0)
Size:            37/38          Owner:     [USER,OLGA]
Created:     8-FEB-1996 14:20:55.17
Revised:     8-FEB-1996 14:21:48.47 (1)
Expires:     <None specified>
Backup:     14-FEB-1996 09:19:47.43
File organization:   Sequential
File attributes:     Allocation:38, Extend:10, Global buffercount:0
                     No version limit
Record format:       Variable length, maximum 512 bytes
Record attributes:   None
RMS attributes:      None
Journaling enabled:  None
File protection:     System:RWED, Owner:RWED, Group:RE, World:
Access Cntrl List:   None

Total of 1 file, 37/38 blocks.
```

VMS C-Kermit lets you store incoming binary files with any record length you like in either fixed or undefined format, and it offers you two VMS-specific file types for transferring VMS files that don't fit the normal mold.

Selecting the Record Length for Incoming Files

When VMS C-Kermit receives a text file, it stores it on disk using variable-length records, one record per line, using carriage return and linefeed to delimit the lines. The maximum length for a line is 65,534 characters. If you try to send VMS C-Kermit a line of text longer than this, the file transfer will fail with the message "Error writing data."[61]

Binary files, however, do not have lines and there is no automatic way for C-Kermit to sense record boundaries in arriving binary files. So unless you say otherwise, C-Kermit

---

[61]This is a limitation of the VMS file system. If you *really* have a text file with lines longer than 64K, you can send it in binary mode.

stores incoming binary files using fixed-length 512-byte records. When an incoming binary file, such as a BACKUP saveset, must be stored using some other record length, you can use the following command:

SET FILE RECORD-LENGTH *number*

Specifies the record length used by VMS C-Kermit to store an incoming file of type BINARY or IMAGE. The number can be up to 65534.

The record length setting is ignored when sending files; VMS C-Kermit uses the file's record length from its VMS directory entry. The record-length setting is also ignored when receiving text files.

To illustrate, let's create a BACKUP saveset on disk and transfer it to a PC. Remember to take careful note of the file's record length:

```
$ backup oofa.* /interchange testing.bck /save
$ dir /full testing.bck
...
Record format:  Fixed length 32256 byte records
...
$ kermit
C-Kermit>send testing.bck          (Send the file)
Alt-x                              (Escape back to the PC)
MS-Kermit>receive                  (Receive the file)
```

Note that no SET commands were necessary. VMS C-Kermit recognizes the file as binary because it has fixed-length records and automatically tells MS-DOS Kermit that the file-transfer mode is binary.

Now let's send the BACKUP saveset from the PC to a different VMS system and restore the files from it. The connection is already made and VMS C-Kermit is already started. The trick here is to tell VMS C-Kermit what record length to use when storing the file and to tell MS-DOS Kermit to send the file in binary mode, which also causes MS-DOS Kermit to tell C-Kermit that it is a binary file:

```
C-Kermit>set file record-length 32256 (Use the same number!)
C-Kermit>receive                      (Wait for the file)
Alt-x                                 (Escape back to the PC)
MS-Kermit>set file type binary        (Use binary mode)
MS-Kermit>send testing.bck            (Send the file)

    (The file is transferred)

MS-Kermit>connect                     (Go back to VMS)
C-Kermit>exit                         (Quit from C-Kermit)
$ backup testing.bck/save/log *.*     (Restore the files)
%BACKUP-S-CREATED, created OOFA.C;12
%BACKUP-S-CREATED, created OOFA.H;3
%BACKUP-S-CREATED, created OOFA.EXE;8
%BACKUP-S-CREATED, created OOFA.OBJ;11
$
```

If the record length had not been set correctly, BACKUP would have become very upset when you tried to restore the files:

```
%BACKUP-E-READERR, error reading TESTING.BCK
-BACKUP-E-BLOCKCRC, software block CRC error
%BACKUP-E-INVBLKSIZE, invalid block size in save set
%BACKUP-E-INVRECSIZ, invalid record size in save set
%BACKUP-E-INVRECSIZ, invalid record size in save set
%BACKUP-E-READERRS, excessive error rate reading TESTING.BCK
-BACKUP-I-HDRCRC, software header CRC error
%BACKUP-I-OPERSPEC
%BACKUP-I-OPERASSIST, operator assistance has been requested
```

Not only has BACKUP flooded your screen with complaints, it has also reported your misbehavior to the system operator!

Odd Record Lengths

When sending binary files that have an odd record length, note that these files are actually stored with an even record length on disk. For example, suppose DIR/FULL X.VDM says "fixed-length records, record length 17". On disk, the file really has 18-byte records; each 17-byte record is padded with a NUL (0) byte to make its length even; this is revealed by the VMS DUMP command.

C-Kermit sends the raw records, *including the padding*. Thus, if you send such a file to (say) DOS or UNIX for actual use, your DOS or UNIX application must be coded to account for this — if the record length is odd, add 1 to it. If you send the file back to VMS, just tell VMS C-Kermit to SET FILE RECORD-LENGTH to the original odd length, and the resulting file will be identical to the original one.

Storing Incoming Binary Files in Undefined Format

We have said that VMS C-Kermit detects the transfer mode of an incoming file automatically if the Attribute packet information is given. If an incoming file is announced as binary, C-Kermit normally stores it in Fixed format. But certain applications (such as Concept Omega Thoroughbred BASIC) require their files to be in Undefined format. VMS C-Kermit's SET FILE TYPE BINARY command has an optional trailing field to let you specify whether incoming binary files should be stored in Fixed or Undefined format. Here is a complete description of the SET FILE TYPE BINARY command for VMS:

SET FILE TYPE BINARY *[{ FIXED, UNDEFINED }]*

Incoming files are to be processed in binary mode unless they are accompanied by an Attribute packet identifying their type as text. When receiving a binary file, C-Kermit stores it using fixed-length records (no length fields), with the record length specified in the most recent SET FILE RECORD-LENGTH command, 512 by default, and uses the RMS "first free byte" attribute to record the precise end of file. By default, the record format of the incoming file is set to Fixed. If you SET FILE TYPE BINARY UNDEFINED, the record format of the incoming file is set to Undefined instead of Fixed. Only the directory entry is affected by your choice of Fixed or Undefined, not the storage format of the data itself.

RMS, the VMS Record Management System, cannot deal with undefined-format files, so only use BINARY UNDEFINED if you have an application that requires it. Here is an example in which a Thoroughbred BASIC file is transferred from a PC to a VAX:

```
$ kermit                          (Start Kermit on the VAX)
C-Kermit 6.0.192 6 Sep 96, VAX/VMS
Type ? or HELP for help
C-Kermit>set file type binary undef
C-Kermit>receive
Alt-x                             (Escape back to the PC)
MS-Kermit>set file type binary    (PC uses binary mode)
MS-Kermit>send schedule.bas       (Send the file)

  (The file is transferred)

MS-Kermit>connect                 (Let's go back and take a look)
C-Kermit>dir /full schedule.bas
  ...
Record format:      Undefined, maximum 512 bytes
  ...
C-Kermit>
```

When C-Kermit is sending files from VMS, it recognizes Undefined-format files and sends them correctly in binary mode.

The *SET FILE TYPE IMAGE* Command

IMAGE mode is a kind of "super-binary" mode, in which raw disk blocks are transmitted. Use it when SET FILE TYPE BINARY doesn't work.

SET FILE TYPE IMAGE

This command might better be called "binary, and this time I mean it!" When receiving a file, this mode is equivalent to SET FILE TYPE BINARY, except that it overrides the incoming Type attribute, if any. When sending a file, C-Kermit declares the file to be of type Binary in the Attribute packet and the blocks of the file are sent exactly as stored on disk, including any imbedded record-length fields and excluding any formatting characters (such as line terminators) that would normally be supplied by RMS based on the file's carriage-control attributes. Use SET FILE TYPE IMAGE to send files that have inappropriate or unusual file characteristics, such as a binary file that is stored in Stream LF format. Synonym: **SET FILE TYPE BLOCK**.

Here's an example. You have Lotus 1-2-3 on your PC and a version of Lotus 1-2-3 running on your VMS system. You can send a PC Lotus spreadsheet file to VMS using SET FILE TYPE BINARY, and VMS Lotus reads it perfectly and without complaint. But when you try to send a VMS Lotus spreadsheet to the PC in the same way, PC Lotus can't read it at all. Why not? Because VMS Lotus creates its spreadsheet files with carriage return carriage control, which makes C-Kermit send carriage return and line feed at the end of each record, resulting in an invalid format for PC Lotus. Use SET FILE TYPE IMAGE to circumvent the problem:

```
C-Kermit>set file type image      (The important command)
C-Kermit>send budget.wks          (Send the file)
Alt-x                             (Escape back to the PC)
MS-Kermit>receive                 (Receive the file)
```

Another case where IMAGE mode is required is for files created by the VMS version of UNZIP, a dearchiving program, from VMS-resident ZIP files. Even when these are binary files, the VMS ZIP program creates them with a "Stream_LF" record format, which C-Kermit treats as text unless you tell it otherwise. Use IMAGE for sending. BINARY works for receiving.

The same goes for any other VMS application that always creates Stream_LF files, regardless of the actual purpose of the file. This includes the Lynx Web browser, LHARC programs, and even DEC's own PATHWORKS file service.

VMS Labeled File Transfer

We've seen how to coax VMS C-Kermit into transferring simple types of sequential files whose record size or format might not match C-Kermit's defaults. But there still remain certain types of VMS files that defy all normal means of transfer — databases with indexed or relative organization, binary files with variable length records, and so on. Yes, you can transfer them, but when you bring them back to VMS, they are unusable. You can't even transfer them directly from one VMS system to another.

To illustrate, let's look at VMS object files. These are the files created by language compilers like Macro, Fortran, Pascal, and C, with names that end in .OBJ. For example, the command:

```
$ macro ckvhex
```

runs the Macro assembler on a source file called CKVHEX.MAR and produces an object file called CKVHEX.OBJ. This object file is composed of variable length records, like a text file, but it is binary. You can't use text mode to transfer it because the format of the record boundaries would be changed (carriage returns and linefeeds would be added), and you can't use binary mode because the record boundaries would be lost altogether. Image mode doesn't work either; the record boundaries are preserved but the record format information is lost from the directory entry.

For situations like this, you need a way of sending not only the contents of the file, but its entire directory entry along with it. To do this, C-Kermit offers a fourth file type, called

LABELED. Labeled mode is used to preserve all the characteristics of the file after transfer, including its directory entry, internal record layout, RMS attributes, and so forth. It can be used directly between two VMS systems, in which case all kinds of files arrive and are stored with all their proper characteristics.

Labeled mode transfers can also be done between VMS and any other kind of computer. A VMS file sent in labeled form to a non-VMS computer is unusable on the other computer. A labeled file sent *to* a VMS computer is recreated in its original form.

Thus labeled mode is suitable for both VMS-to-VMS transfers and archiving VMS files on non-VMS systems. A labeled file can float from one computer to another until it finally finds its way back to a VMS system, where it is reincarnated. The command to select labeled file transfers is:

SET FILE TYPE LABELED

When sending a file, C-Kermit sends an Attribute packet declaring the file to be of type Binary, then transmits all of the file's characteristics in a specially coded heading as part of the file data. The file data itself is transmitted in Image mode.

When C-Kermit's FILE TYPE is LABELED, incoming files (which must be sent in binary mode) are treated as LABELED if the Type Attribute says the file is binary, or if there is no Attribute packet at all. If C-Kermit's file type is LABELED and the incoming attribute says the file is Text, C-Kermit rejects the file. Once having agreed to accept a file in labeled mode, VMS C-Kermit interprets the labeling information and attempts to use it to create the transferred file with all the same characteristics as the original, but with the version number set in the normal way.

Labeled files carry with them certain information that you will want to use in certain circumstances and not in others. C-Kermit always includes this information when sending files in labeled format. Use the SET FILE LABEL command to say what it should do with this information when receiving files:

SET FILE LABEL NAME { OFF, ON }

The labeled file contains the file's full VMS file specification. The default is ON, meaning C-Kermit attempts to store the incoming file with its original name rather than the name that the other Kermit sent it with. Use SET FILE LABEL OFF to have it stored under the name it was sent with or any alternate name you may have given in the RECEIVE command.

SET FILE LABEL PATH { OFF, ON }

The labeled file also includes the file's original disk and directory name. Normally C-Kermit stores an incoming labeled file in the current disk and directory. Use SET FILE LABEL PATH ON to have C-Kermit attempt to store the file in the disk and directory recorded within the labeled file itself. If FILE LABEL PATH is OFF, the path is ignored.

SET FILE LABEL ACL *{ OFF, ON }*

The labeled file includes the file's original ACL (access control list), which contains information that would normally be useful only on the computer where the file originated. For example, VMS records access lists as binary numbers; restoring them on a different computer could wind up granting access to a random collection of users. Normally this data is ignored. SET FILE LABEL ACL ON to use it.

This command also governs the RMS Journaling, RMS Statistics, DDIF, PATHWORKS, and other file ACL entries. Note that you can create ACL entries that you can't see with DIR/FULL unless you have VMS Security privilege (but you should still be able to view — but not modify — them with EDIT/ACL). Unprivileged users can not delete or modify incorrect ACL entries without deleting the file itself. Even when FILE LABEL ACL is ON, RMS Journaling is not enabled for a received file.

SET FILE LABEL BACKUP *{ OFF, ON }*

Tells C-Kermit whether to preserve the file's backup date, if one was included. OFF, which is the default, means that C-Kermit should ignore the backup date in the incoming labeled file and store the new file so it will be backed up. ON means to keep the labeled file's backup date.

SET FILE LABEL OWNER *{ OFF, ON }*

C-Kermit normally makes you the owner of the incoming file. SET FILE LABEL OWNER ON if you want C-Kermit to preserve the file's original owner (privileges required).

SET FILE TYPE LABELED can be used for all VMS-to-VMS transfers, as long as character set translation is not required and C-Kermit is running on both ends. It is the only mode of transmission that works for all kinds of VMS files. The SET FILE TYPE LABELED command must be given to *both* VMS C-Kermit programs.

To send a VMS file to another kind of computer (UNIX or MS-DOS, for example) for archival, just give the SET FILE TYPE LABELED command to VMS C-Kermit before sending the file and make sure the other Kermit receives it in binary mode (it will do so automatically if it understands Attribute packets):

```
C-Kermit>set file type labeled    (Archival format)
C-Kermit>send oofa.x              (Send any kind of file)
Alt-x                             (Escape back to PC)
MS-Kermit>r                       (Receive the file)

  (The file is transferred)
```

The resulting file contains all the necessary information to reconstruct it on a VMS system, no matter where it may travel in the meanwhile, as long as all its travels are in binary mode. When the time eventually comes for it to return to VMS, make sure to send it in binary mode and to tell VMS C-Kermit to SET FILE TYPE LABELED:

```
C-Kermit>set file type labeled    (Archival format)
C-Kermit>r                        (Wait for the file)
Alt-x                             (Escape back to PC)
MS-Kermit>set file type binary    (Use binary mode)
MS-Kermit>send oofa.x             (Send the file)
   (The file is transferred)
```

You can easily identify a labeled file. Its first 20 characters are "KERMIT LABELED FILE:". If one of these files should happen to find its way back to VMS without being decoded by Kermit, you can use a separate program distributed with C-Kermit, called CKVCVT, to decode it into its original form, just as C-Kermit would have done if it had received the file with SET FILE TYPE LABELED in effect:

```
$ ckvcvt oofa.x
Creating OOFA.X...
...done.
$
```

A labeled file stored on your VMS disk can even be mistakenly sent in labeled mode to another computer, and then brought back to VMS in this form: labels within labels! The CKVCVT program can be used to peel away excessive layers of labeling. When transferring files in LABELED mode, the file transfer display will show the name the file was sent as, not the "true" name within the labeled file. Also, note that a transfer may fail with an obscure error (can't create output file) if there is something incorrect with the label information (for example, if you specified that the file should be restored to the original directory and you don't have privilege to write to that directory on this system).

VMS-to-VMS File Transfer

When two modern Kermit programs initiate a file transfer, they identify their underlying operating systems to each other. This allows them to skip certain conversions (such as file name or data record format) if they see each other as "kin." When two VMS C-Kermit programs recognize each other, they automatically switch to labeled transfer mode to ensure that *all* files, no matter how complex in structure, are transferred correctly. Under certain circumstances, however, you might wish to override this feature:

- There is a high probability that the transfer will be interrupted, in which case you want to be able to recover the transfer from the point of failure. Recovery does not work for partial files transferred in labeled mode.

- If the process on the receiving computer lacks privileges that might be required to manipulate the incoming file's directory structure. In this case, you can also give SET FILE LABEL commands to the file receiver to work around the trouble areas.

To inhibit automatic switching to labeled mode during VMS-to-VMS transfers, tell one or both of the C-Kermit programs to SET TRANSFER MODE MANUAL.

VMS C-Kermit Summary

Important filenames:

`CKERMIT.INI`

>The standard initialization file. It can be in your home (login) directory, or in a central shared location designated by the system-wide logical name CKERMIT_INI.

`CKERMIT.SYS`

>The system-wide customization file, used to augment or override the definitions made in the standard initialization file on a system-wide basis. VMS C-Kermit executes this file if it can be found in the directory denoted by the CKERMIT_INI logical name.

`CKERMOD.INI`

>Your personal customization file, used to augment or override the definitions made in the standard initialization file. Must be stored in your home directory.

`CKERMIT.KDD, CKERMIT.KND`

>Your dialing and network directories, stored in your home directory.

`CKERMIT.KSD`

>Your services directory, stored in your home directory.

VMS C-Kermit has the unique ability to send a mixture of text and binary files in the same SEND or MSEND command. Any other Kermit program that supports Attribute packets (see Table 1-1 on page 10) can accept such a mixture.

All VMS-to-VMS transfers are done in labeled mode unless you use SET TRANSFER MODE MANUAL.

Table IV-1 summarizes the interaction of the various file types, the SEND and RECEIVE commands, and Attribute (A) packets in VMS C-Kermit.

Table IV-1 VMS Kermit SET FILE Commands

SET FILE Command	Send	Receive
RECORD-LENGTH	Ignored	Used for Binary and Image, but not Text, transfers
TYPE TEXT	Ignored	Used unless overridden by A-packet
TYPE BINARY	Ignored	Used unless overridden by A-packet
TYPE IMAGE	Used	Used, overrides A-packet
TYPE LABELED	Used	Used if A-packet does not say the file is text and if the file is in legitimate Labeled format.

Table IV-2 shows the types and record lengths to be used for transferring selected types of files between VMS C-Kermit and various PC-based Kermits. The same settings should apply for other non-VMS Kermits, such as C-Kermit for UNIX or IBM mainframe Kermit. You can fill in the bottom of the table with any others that you encounter.

Table IV-2 PC – VMS File Transfer

Application	VMS File Type	PC File Type	VMS Record Length	Comments
VMS EDT, EVE, etc.	TEXT	TEXT	N/A	Files created with text editors
VMS FORTRAN	TEXT	TEXT	N/A	Fortran CC becomes CRLF
DCL-created	TEXT	TEXT	N/A	VFC files become stream
VMS LOTUS	IMAGE	BINARY	512	Can be used on VMS and PC
PC LOTUS	IMAGE	BINARY	512	Can be used on VMS and PC
VMS .EXE	BINARY	BINARY	512	Cannot be executed on PC
VMS .OBJ	LABELED	BINARY	N/A	Object files
VMS .OLB	BINARY	BINARY	512	Object libraries
BACKUP Saveset	BINARY	BINARY	≥ 2048	Use same record length as original
PC .EXE	BINARY	BINARY	512	Cannot be executed on VMS
SPSS Export	TEXT	TEXT	80	Can be used on VMS and PC
Thoroughbred BASIC	BINARY UNDEFINED	BINARY	N/A	A closed, non-RMS application
VMS .ZIP	IMAGE	BINARY	512	Can be used on both VMS and PC
VMS .LZH	IMAGE	BINARY	512	Can be used on both VMS and PC
VMS Lynx	IMAGE	BINARY	512	Can be used on both VMS and PC
PC .ZIP	BINARY	BINARY	512	Can be used on both VMS and PC
VMS Indexed	LABELED	BINARY	N/A	Archive only - not usable on PC
VMS Relative	LABELED	BINARY	N/A	Archive only - not usable on PC

Add others:

Command Summary

Here is a quick reference list of C-Kermit commands specific to VMS:

SET FILE LABEL ACL { OFF, ON }
SET FILE LABEL BACKUP { OFF, ON }
SET FILE LABEL NAME { OFF, ON }
SET FILE LABEL OWNER { OFF, ON }
SET FILE LABEL PATH { OFF, ON }
SET FILE RECORD-LENGTH *number*
SET FILE TYPE BINARY [{ FIXED, UNDEFINED }]
SET FILE TYPE IMAGE
SET FILE TYPE LABELED

The following VMS DCL commands were discussed in this chapter:

BACKUP *source-files* /INTERCHANGE *backup-file* /SAVE
BACKUP *backup-file* /SAVE/LOG *.*
DEFINE [/USER_MODE] *name value*
DIRECTORY [/FULL] [*filespec*]
DUMP *filename*
SET TERMINAL { /DEVICE=*name*, /NOPARITY, /[NO]EIGHT_BIT }
SHOW SYMBOL *name*
SPAWN [/NOWAIT] *program*
SUBMIT [{ /NOTIFY, /AFTER=*time* }] *filename*
WRITE SYS$OUTPUT [TEXT]

For more information about VMS commands, use the VMS HELP command, for example HELP SET TERMINAL or HELP SET TERMINAL /DEVICE. Or consult the VMS User's Manual.

AOS/VS C-Kermit

○ ○ ○ ○
This appendix lists the particulars of using C-Kermit on Data General MV-series computers with the AOS/VS and AOS/VS-II operating systems. For a current list of limitations and restrictions of C-Kermit for AOS/VS, also read the files CKCKER.BWR and CKDKER.BWR that were provided with the C-Kermit distribution.

AOS/VS (Advanced Operating System/Virtual System) is the operating system for the Data General Eclipse MV family of minicomputers. It is a multiuser, multitasking operating system that comes in two basic varieties: AOS/VS "Classic" and an enhanced version called AOS/VS II. Outgoing TCP/IP TELNET connections can be established only on AOS/VS II systems configured with TCP/IP II.

C-Kermit runs on both AOS/VS and AOS/VS II. As of this writing, the current revisions are 7.71x for AOS/VS and 3.20x for AOS/VS II, where the x in the revision number signifies a minor update, and appears as a single digit, 0–9. In this book, the term AOS/VS (or simply VS) refers to both operating systems, unless explicitly noted otherwise.

See reference [23] for a general introduction to AOS/VS. Reference [26] is the Command Language Interface (CLI) manual. Reference [24] describes the structure and functions of the AOS/VS operating system. For information about using AOS/VS CLI commands, you can also give the HELP command.

C-Kermit must be installed by the AOS/VS system manager. Refer to the file CKDINS.DOC for detailed instructions for installing C-Kermit under AOS/VS and configuring MV system communication devices (particularly serial ports and modems) appropriately.

Using C-Kermit in AOS/VS

C-Kermit for AOS/VS includes support for serial connections, both direct and dialed, as well as for TCP/IP TELNET connections.

Preparing Your AOS/VS Session for Kermit

AOS/VS systems are normally accessed via Data General DASHER terminals or emulators. When you log in to AOS/VS, it automatically sends a DASHER-specific "Read Model ID" escape sequence to your terminal. If you have a DASHER terminal or emulator (such as MS-DOS Kermit, Kermit/2, or Kermit 95), it responds appropriately and your terminal type is set automatically.

AOS/VS also supports DEC VT-100, 200, and 300 series terminals to a limited extent. To identify this type of terminal to AOS/VS, you must issue the command:

) characteristics/on/nas/xlt

where NAS and XLT are defined as follows:

NAS

When ON, NAS specifies a non-ANSI standard terminal. On input, this causes a carriage return to be converted to a carriage return and a line feed, and a linefeed to be converted to a carriage return. On output, it causes a linefeed to be converted to a carriage return and a linefeed.

XLT

When ON, XLT enables support for the VT100-compatible family of terminals. Support for VT100-compatible terminals must have been specified by the system manager in advance during system generation. If you turn on XLT, but still have problems with the backspace key, check with the system manager.

If you are using a speaking device or hardcopy terminal, you can inform AOS/VS with the following command:

) characteristics/hardcopy

You should also be sure that your terminal has the BMOB characteristic:

) characteristics/break=bmob

This ensures that if C-Kermit ever gets stuck, you can interrupt it by typing CMD-BRK[62] followed by Ctrl-C and Ctrl-B, which is the normal AOS/VS method for interrupting a process.

To enable Xon/Xoff software flow control on your login terminal, give this command:

```
) characteristics/on/ifc/ofc
```

and you can enable RTS/CTS hardware flow control as follows:

```
) characteristics/on/hifc/hofc
```

To use international character sets, you must issue the following command:

```
) char/on/8bt
```

which causes all 8 bits of each character to be treated as data. You can also use /16BT (and, for VT terminals, /XLT/KVT) to enable 16-bit character sets, such as for Japanese Kanji. The 8-bit text character set most commonly used in the AOS/VS environment is Data General International (DGI, see Table VII-4 on page 560).

The changes you make to your console's characteristics via the CHARACTERISTICS command are in effect only for the current session. To have them take effect in all of your terminal sessions, you can include the CHARACTERISTICS command that sets them to the desired values in your login macro, normally called LOGON.CLI. Check with your system manager for more information.

Starting C-Kermit in AOS/VS

The name of the C-Kermit executable image is KERMIT.PR. To see if it exists on your system, issue the following command:

```
) pathname kermit.pr
```

If the system returns an indication that it found KERMIT.PR, then you should check its revision number by issuing a REVISION command:

```
) rev/v kermit.pr
```

The revision should be 00.06.192.00, or greater. If it is not, it might lack some of the capabilities described in this book; consult your system manager. Otherwise, check to see if the KERMIT.CLI macro exists:

```
) pathname kermit.cli
```

---

[62]This is the DASHER key combination to send a BREAK signal; hold down CMD and press BRK/ESC. On other terminals or emulators, use the normal method for sending a BREAK, such as Alt-B in MS-DOS Kermit, Kermit/2, or Kermit 95.

You can use this macro to start C-Kermit:

```
) kermit
```

Otherwise, you can start KERMIT.PR directly by typing:

```
) x kermit
```

C-Kermit can also be run with redirected input and output. Suppose you have a file called INPUT.TEST containing C-Kermit commands:

```
echo Hello from Kermit.
exit
```

and you also have a file called OUTPUT.TEST, which is empty, but it has to exist. If you start C-Kermit like this:

```
) process/block/default/input=input.test/output=output.test kermit
```

then, after C-Kermit exits, OUTPUT.TEST has the following contents:

```
C-Kermit 6.0.192, 6 Sep 96, Data General AOS/VS
Type ? or HELP for help
C-Kermit>Hello from Kermit.
C-Kermit>
```

Initialization File

AOS/VS C-Kermit uses the standard initialization file, CKERMIT.INI. If a file with this name exists in your home directory, it is used. Otherwise, if a file of this name exists in the UTIL: directory, it is used. The file CKERMOD.INI, if it exists in your home directory, is executed after CKERMIT.INI. You can use SED or another text editor to create or modify your CKERMOD.INI file (type X SED *filename* to start the SED editor, then issue the HELP command for instructions on how to use it).

Interrupting C-Kermit

Most C-Kermit commands can be interrupted by typing Ctrl-C. C-Kermit commands, such as DIRECTORY or WHO, that work by running the AOS/VS command processor (CLI) as an inferior process, must be interrupted with the CLI interrupt sequence, BREAK followed by Ctrl-C and then Ctrl-A. To interrupt C-Kermit during remote-mode file transfer, type three Ctrl-C characters in a row (or whatever other sequence you have chosen with the SET TRANSFER CANCELLATION command):

```
C-Kermit>send oofa.txt            (Send a file)
...
^A0 Sz* @-#Y1~*   yE              (A packet appears)
^C^C                              (Type two Ctrl-C's)
^C...                             (Ctrl-C is echoed by C-Kermit)
C-Kermit>                         (The prompt returns)
```

To interrupt C-Kermit during CONNECT mode, use the CONNECT-mode escape character, followed by the letter *C* to get back to the prompt, or any of the other escape-level commands described in Chapter 8. In an emergency, the C-Kermit process itself can be interrupted by sending a BREAK signal and then typing Ctrl-C and Ctrl-B.

Terminal Emulation

C-Kermit's CONNECT command and associated features work in AOS/VS as described in Chapter 8. The default CONNECT-mode escape character is Ctrl-Backslash, which is entered on DASHER terminals by holding down the CTRL key and pressing the backslash (\\) key. The default local terminal character-set is DG-International. If this agrees with your terminal or emulator, you need specify only the remote set when selecting your terminal character-set, for example:

```
C-Kermit>set term char latin1
```

Otherwise you must specify the appropriate local set too, for example:

```
C-Kermit>set term char latin1 spanish
```

File Transfer

C-Kermit for AOS/VS offers the full range of file transfer features. For text files, AOS/VS record format (lines terminated by the single character, linefeed) is automatically converted to Kermit's standard intermediate form during file transfer. As in other C-Kermit versions, character-set translation is available. The default file character-set is DG-International, so to enable translation the only command you need to give is:

```
set transfer character-set latin1
```

Sending Files

In outbound AOS/VS filenames, dollar sign ($) and question mark (?) are converted to the letter X unless you have SET FILE NAMES LITERAL. You can use AOS/VS templates to specify a group of files in any of C-Kermit's commands that accept wildcard file specifications, as well as in GET commands sent to an AOS/VS C-Kermit server. AOS/VS template characters are listed in Table V-1.

Receiving Files

Incoming files are stored in the current directory unless you specified a different directory in the RECEIVE command, or the incoming file header packet includes a pathname, or you have designated a FILE DOWNLOAD-DIRECTORY, in which case C-Kermit attempts to store the file in the specified directory (and fails if the directory does not exist or is not writable).

A file can be created only if you have write access to the directory where the file is to be stored. The file is created using your default access control list (ACL), which, unless you

Table V-1 AOS/VS Template Characters

Character	Meaning
+	(plus sign) Matches any character string.
*	(asterisk) Matches any single filename character except a period (.). Example: FIG* matches FIG1 and FIG2, but not FIG. or FIGURE.
–	(dash) Matches any series of filename characters that does not contain a period. Example: TEST– matches TEST1 and TESTING, but not TEST.1.
\	(backslash) Omits the specified series of characters from the search. Example: +.DOC\KERMIT+ matches all files ending in .DOC except for files that start with the string KERMIT. Because backslash is also C-Kermit's command-quote character, you must enter two copies of it.
^	(circumflex) Causes the action to be applied to the parent directory instead of the current one. Example: ^+.DOC matches all files in the parent directory whose names end in .DOC.
#	(number sign) Causes the action to be applied to all directories beneath the current one. Example: #+.DOC matches all files in all inferior directories with names ending in .DOC.

have changed it with the AOS/VS DEFACL command, grants the site-dependent default access control list.

If a file of the same name already exists in the target directory and C-Kermit's FILE COLLISION is set to BACKUP or OVERWRITE, you must also have write access to the previously existing file. C-Kermit will not create, rename, or delete files for you that you could not otherwise create, rename, or delete yourself.

When AOS/VS C-Kermit receives a file that has the same name as an existing file, it might rename the existing file or the incoming file, according to your FILE COLLISION setting. The new name is the old name with a period and a version number appended. For example, OOFA.TXT would become OOFA.TXT.1. If both OOFA.TXT and OOFA.TXT.1 existed, an OOFA.TXT.2 would be created, and so on.

Dash (–) characters in incoming filenames are converted to underscores (_) unless you have SET FILE NAMES LITERAL.

It has been widely observed that, although AOS/VS C-Kermit can send files using large packet lengths and window sizes, the reverse is not generally true. If you have trouble sending files *to* AOS/VS C-Kermit, try reducing the packet and/or window size. This advice holds for both serial and Telnet connections.

Other C-Kermit Versions

C-Kermit is also available for several other computers and operating systems, including Stratus VOS, the Apple Macintosh, the Commodore Amiga, the Atari ST, Microware OS-9, and perhaps others by the time you read this. Consult the CKCKER.UPD file for news.

Amiga C-Kermit

○ ○ ○ ○

This section describes the Commodore Amiga version of C-Kermit. For further information, refer to the files CKCKER.BWR and CKIKER.BWR.

The Commodore Amiga is a desktop workstation with a graphical user interface called Intuition. Its multiprocessing operating system, AmigaDOS, gives you multiple windows selectable by mouse. You may create one or more character-oriented Command Line Interpreter (CLI) or Shell windows in which to type AmigaDOS commands. Commonly-used commands include LIST to display a list of files, DELETE to delete a file or files, TYPE to display the contents of a file, CD to change directory, INFO to display information about system usage, and STATUS to display process status. CLI and Shell are not case-sensitive; commands may be entered in uppercase, lowercase, or any mixture.

AmigaDOS has a hierarchical file system similar to OS/2. File specifications can optionally begin with a device name terminated by a colon (:). The directory specification shows the path through the directory tree from its root on the given device; the directory separator is slash (/), as in UNIX. Upper- and lowercase letters are not distinguished in Amiga file specifications. File specifications that do not begin with a device name are on the current device. File specifications that do not have a slash at the beginning (or immediately after the device name) are relative to the current directory.

Install the KERMIT program in your C: directory or another directory along your PATH, and place your initialization file CKERMIT.INI, your customization file CKERMOD.INI, and your services directory CKERMIT.KSD in the S: directory. If desired, you can create an icon for C-Kermit by using the Icon Editor; create a script file containing the two commands:

```
stack 10000
Kermit
```

and save it. Then use the Icon Editor to create a Project icon whose "default tool" is C:IconX for this file.

You can start C-Kermit from the desktop by clicking on its icon (if you made one) or from a CLI or Shell window by typing KERMIT or RUN KERMIT. In both cases, C-Kermit creates a new window for itself. Before starting C-Kermit in a CLI or Shell window, allocate a stack size of at least 10000 with the AmigaDOS STACK command as shown above.

When starting C-Kermit in a CLI or Shell window, you can include command-line options (see Appendix I). If any of these are action options, C-Kermit exits automatically when they are complete. If you want to run C-Kermit in this manner without having it create a new window, include the -q (quiet) command-line option.

During interactive operation, Amiga C-Kermit can be interrupted by typing Ctrl-C (hold down the Ctrl key and press the C key). A requestor window pops up to let you choose whether to quit C-Kermit or continue it.

Communications and Terminal Emulation

The default communication device is serial.device/0. Other devices can be specified using the same form: type.device/unit-number. You can configure the communication device in the Preferences window, including (for a serial device) its speed and flow control. Both software (Xon/Xoff) and hardware (RTS/CTS) flow control options are available.

Network connections, including TCP/IP and DECnet, can be accomplished by running a serial.device emulator over the network link, provided you have the underlying network hardware, software, and connection, and a suitable serial.device emulator.

The CONNECT command creates an AmigaDOS console device window. Using the default Preferences setting, this gives a 23-row by 77-column screen. In AmigaDOS 2.0 and later, you can increase the screen size in Preferences. In AmigaDOS releases prior to 2.0, the MoreRows program allows you to increase the size of the Workbench window beyond the 640 by 200 default size; increasing the number of rows by 8 and the number of columns by 16 allows a 24-row by 80-column Kermit window.

The Amiga console driver provides ANSI [4] (similar to VT100) terminal emulation; C-Kermit CONNECT mode uses the console driver, and does not provide any particular terminal emulation of its own.

The default CONNECT-mode escape character is Control-Backslash (*Ctrl-*). You can use *Ctrl-\H* to close the serial device and exit CONNECT mode; this turns the DTR signal off, causing most modems to hang up the phone line. In addition to the normal CONNECT-mode commands, extra session-logging control is available. If a session log file is open, the *Ctrl-\Q* sequence lets you temporarily suspend logging and the *Ctrl-\R* sequence resumes logging if it has been suspended.

Character-set translation is not available during CONNECT mode. The Amiga's native character set is ISO 8859 Latin Alphabet 1, and it is used during CONNECT mode if PARITY is NONE and you SET COMMAND BYTESIZE 8. Special characters are entered according to your keymap, configurable in Preferences, normally using "dead keys."

File Transfer

Amiga C-Kermit supports most of the file transfer features described in this book, including character-set translation (Latin-1 is the normal file character-set), the FULLSCREEN file transfer display, and the full range of file collision options.

When sending files, Amiga C-Kermit internally expands wildcards in SEND and similar commands, as well as in GET commands sent to an Amiga C-Kermit server. Asterisk (*) stands for any sequence of characters and question mark (?) matches any single character. When you use ? in a command, it must be preceded by backslash (\) to suppress its normal function of displaying a file menu:

```
C-Kermit>send cki*.\?
```

If the use of Attribute (A) packets has been successfully negotiated, Amiga C-Kermit includes an A-packet with each file it sends, containing the file's length, creation date, and transfer mode (text or binary).

When receiving files, Amiga C-Kermit reads the incoming A-packet (if any), sets the transfer mode (text or binary) accordingly, and sets the incoming file's creation date from the A-packet if a date is given and ATTRIBUTE DATE is ON. If an incoming file has the same name as an existing file, the selected FILE COLLISION action is taken. Files that must be renamed because of collision have a tilde (~) and a number appended; for example, oofa.txt becomes oofa.txt~1; oofa.txt~1 becomes oofa.txt~2, and so on.

OS-9 C-Kermit

○ ○ ○ ○
This section describes the OS-9 version of C-Kermit. For further information, refer to the files CKCKER.BWR and CK9KER.BWR.

OS-9/68000 is a multiuser, multitasking operating system designed to run on all Motorola 68000-family processors. A related operating system, OS-9000, is more portable; for example, to Intel as well as to various RISC processors. However, OS-9 C-Kermit has not, as of this writing, been tested under OS-9000. For news about this, as well as further information about C-Kermit under OS-9, please read the file CK9KER.BWR.

OS-9's 100% ROM-able, fast, compact code in conjunction with its real-time capabilities make OS-9/68000 ideal for ROM-based systems used in measuring and control systems in scientific and industrial spheres. Yet, a full disk-based OS-9 system offers a program development environment similar to UNIX, including limited UNIX software compatibility at the C source-code level and conformance to the UNIX input/output and task models as well as a UNIX-like shell and networking environment.

The basic commands of OS-9 are somewhat different from their UNIX counterparts:

DEL   Deletes a file

DELDIR   Deletes a directory

MAKDIR   Creates a directory

DIR   Displays a directory listing

PROCS   Shows processes currently running

LIST   Displays the contents of a text file

CWD   Changes working directory

PD   Prints working directory

Command references (like all references to names on OS-9/68000) are case-independent. All commands can be given a -? switch, which displays a brief (usually sufficient) help message.

OS-9 allows redirection of standard input, standard output, and standard error, just like UNIX, and supports command pipelines as well as background execution of programs and commands.

The OS-9 File System

All devices (terminal lines, networks, disks) can have arbitrary names but the usual conventions are:

Terminal devices:
term	The console terminal
t1	Terminal line number 1
t*n*	Terminal line number *n*

Hard disks:
h0	Hard disk number 0
h1	Hard disk number 1
h*n*	Hard disk number *n*

Diskettes:
d0	Diskette drive number 0
d1	Diskette drive number 1
d*n*	Diskette drive number *n*

Directories are hierarchical, as in UNIX, MS-DOS, and OS/2. The directory separator is slash (/). A pathname (file specification) starting with a slash must always include a device name as the first field. Pathnames that do not start with a slash are relative to the current device and directory.

OS-9/68000 files are sequential streams of 8-bit bytes, just like in UNIX, except that carriage return (CR, ASCII 13) is the line terminator, rather than linefeed (LF, ASCII 10). Binary files are simply streams of arbitrary 8-bit bytes. The OS-9 operating system and utilities are "8-bit clean," so text files can use any character set that is compatible with your display and data entry devices, for example ISO 8859-1 Latin Alphabet 1.

The OS-9 Console

The console terminal is either a real terminal, or the screen and keyboard of a workstation such as a Macintosh, Amiga, or Atari ST that is running OS-9. Terminal emulation is not done by OS-9 C-Kermit, but rather by the real terminal or the workstation console driver. This includes the capability to display national and international characters. As with other C-Kermit versions, you must SET COMMAND BYTESIZE 8 in order to enter and view 8-bit characters.

Using OS-9 C-Kermit

The C-Kermit program should be installed somewhere in your OS-9 PATH. Start it simply by typing its name, *kermit*. It reads its initialization, dialing directory, and services directory files from your home directory.

The OS-9 version of C-Kermit is very similar to the UNIX version. The primary differences between OS-9 and UNIX are the names of the common system commands and the line terminator used in text files.

If you start OS-9 C-Kermit with command-line action options (see Appendix I), C-Kermit executes the given commands and exits. The shell expands any unquoted wildcards on the command line, for example in the -s option. The available wildcard characters are *, which matches any sequence of characters of any length, and ?, which matches any single character.

If you start C-Kermit without command-line action options, it issues its prompt and runs interactively. C-Kermit's interruption character is Control-C. C-Kermit also expands wildcards itself, using the same notation as the OS-9 shell, for example:

```
C-Kermit>send ck*.\?
```

Note that the question mark must be prefixed by backslash to override its normal function of giving a help message.

When receiving files, OS-9 C-Kermit handles the full range of file collision options. When C-Kermit renames a file because of a collision, it appends an underscore and a digit to the file name:

```
oofa.txt
```

becomes:

```
oofa.txt_1
```

`oofa.txt_1` becomes `oofa.txt_2`, and so on.

The commands and operation of OS-9 C-Kermit should be identical to those of UNIX C-Kermit, with the exceptions noted above and in the "beware file," CK9KER.BWR.

Others

For documentation on other versions of C-Kermit, including Stratus VOS, the Atari ST, and the Apple Macintosh, please read the online files that are included with the software.

For Windows 95 and NT and OS/2, be sure to read the appropriate user manuals.

Character Set Tables

The standard structure for character sets is specified in ISO Standard 4873 [44] and illustrated in Figure VII-1 on the next page.

A standard 7-bit character set consists of 32 control characters (C0), 94 graphic (printing) characters (GL = Graphics Left), plus the characters Space (SP) and Delete (DEL), for a total of 128 characters, as shown in the left half of the figure.

The left half of a standard 8-bit character set is the 7-bit 128-character set known as the International Reference Version of ISO 646 [42], which happens to be identical to ASCII [1] and which is listed in greater detail in Tables VII-1 and VII-2 on pages 557–558. Many nonstandard 8-bit character sets, such as PC code pages, also use ASCII as their left halves.

The right half of a standard 8-bit character set has a similar structure to the left half. There is a second control region (C1) with 32 additional control characters and a second graphic region (GR = Graphics Right) with 94 or 96 additional graphic characters. The best-known standard 8-bit character sets are those specified by ISO Standard 8859 [45]: the Latin Alphabets. The blank GR area in the figure can have any of the various Latin Alphabets plugged into it: Latin-1, Latin-2, Latin/Greek, Latin/Arabic, Latin/Hebrew, Latin/Cyrillic, and so on. The blank C1 area is most commonly used for the control characters specified by ISO Standard 6429 [47]. A 94-character graphics set does not use the 10/0 and 15/15 positions, shown gray in the figure. A 96-character set does use them.

	CO		GL						C1		GR					
	00	01	02	03	04	05	06	07	08	09	10	11	12	13	14	15
00	NUL	DLE	SP	0	@	P	`	p								
01	SOH	DC1	!	1	A	Q	a	q								
02	STX	DC2	"	2	B	R	b	r								
03	ETX	DC3	#	3	C	S	c	s								
04	EOT	DC4	$	4	D	T	d	t								
05	ENQ	NAK	%	5	E	U	e	u								
06	ACK	SYN	&	6	F	V	f	v								
07	BEL	ETB	'	7	G	W	g	w			*(Special Graphics)*					
08	BS	CAN	(	8	H	X	h	x								
09	HT	EM	)	9	I	Y	i	y								
10	LF	SUB	*	:	J	Z	j	z								
11	VT	ESC	+	;	K	[	k	{								
12	LF	FS	,	<	L	\	l	|								
13	CR	GS	–	=	M	]	m	}								
14	SO	RS	.	>	N	^	n	~								
15	SI	US	/	?	O	_	o	DEL								

Figure VII-1 Structure of a Standard 8-Bit Character Set

Nonstandard 8-bit character sets, such as PC code pages or the Macintosh and NeXT character sets, use C1 and sometimes even C0 for graphic characters.

Each character in an 8-bit character set is represented internally by a number in the range 0–255. This can be a simple decimal number, like 65 for uppercase letter A, the hexadecimal (base 16) or octal (base 8) equivalent, or the column and row position from the table, for example 04/01 for uppercase letter A, where the value (code) of a character is 16 times the column number plus the row number ($16 \times 4 + 1 = 65$).

Rules for designation and invocation of character sets during data transmission are specified in ISO Standard 2022 [43]. In the 8-bit communications environment, a character with its 8th (high order) bit set to 0 denotes a character from the left half and a character with its 8th bit set to 1 denotes a right-half character. The rules for transmission of 8-bit characters in the 7-bit communication environment are, predictably, somewhat more complicated and are spelled out in the standard.

The ASCII and ISO 646 IRV Character Set

Key: *Dec* = decimal value, *Hex* = hexadecimal value, ^X = Ctrl-X.

Table VII-1 Character Codes of ASCII and ISO 646 IRV

Dec Hex	Name	Char	Dec Hex	Char	Dec Hex	Char	Dec Hex	Char
000 00	NUL	^@	032 20	SP	064 40	@	096 60	`
001 01	SOH	^A	033 21	!	065 41	A	097 61	a
002 02	STX	^B	034 22	"	066 42	B	098 62	b
003 03	ETX	^C	035 23	#	067 43	C	099 63	c
004 04	EOT	^D	036 24	$	068 44	D	100 64	d
005 05	ENQ	^E	037 25	%	069 45	E	101 65	e
006 06	ACK	^F	038 26	&	070 46	F	102 66	f
007 07	BEL	^G	039 27	'	071 47	G	103 67	g
008 08	BS	^H	040 28	(	072 48	H	104 68	h
009 09	HT	^I	041 29	)	073 49	I	105 69	i
010 0A	LF	^J	042 2A	*	074 4A	J	106 6A	j
011 0B	VT	^K	043 2B	+	075 4B	K	107 6B	k
012 0C	FF	^L	044 2C	,	076 4C	L	108 6C	l
013 0D	CR	^M	045 2D	-	077 4D	M	109 6D	m
014 0E	SO	^N	046 2E	.	078 4E	N	110 6E	n
015 0F	SI	^O	047 2F	/	079 4F	O	111 6F	o
016 10	DLE	^P	048 30	0	080 50	P	112 70	p
017 11	CD1	^Q	049 31	1	081 51	Q	113 71	q
018 12	DC2	^R	050 32	2	082 52	R	114 72	r
019 13	DC3	^S	051 33	3	083 53	S	115 73	s
020 14	DC4	^T	052 34	4	084 54	T	116 74	t
021 15	NAK	^U	053 35	5	085 55	U	117 75	u
022 16	SYN	^V	054 36	6	086 56	V	118 76	v
023 17	ETB	^W	055 37	7	087 57	W	119 77	w
024 18	CAN	^X	056 38	8	088 58	X	120 78	x
025 19	EM	^Y	057 39	9	089 59	Y	121 79	y
026 1A	SUB	^Z	058 3A	:	090 5A	Z	122 7A	z
027 1B	ESC	^[	059 3B	;	091 5B	[	123 7B	{
028 1C	FS	^\	060 3C	<	092 5C	\	124 7C		
029 1D	GS	^]	061 3D	=	093 5D	]	125 7D	}
030 1E	RS	^^	062 3E	>	094 5E	^	126 7E	~
031 1F	US	^_	063 3F	?	095 5F	_	127 7F	DEL

7-Bit Control Characters

Table VII-2 lists the 7-bit control characters used in the ASCII ISO 646 IRV character sets and in character sets based upon them, including the ISO 646 national sets and the ISO 8859 international sets as well as IBM code pages and other private sets. The official abbreviation and full name of each character is shown, along with the control-key combination normally used to produce each character on a US keyboard.

The code for each character is 16 times the column heading plus the row heading; for example, DC3 is in column 01, row 03, so its code is 19.

Table VII-2 7-Bit C0 Control Characters

	00		01		07
00	NUL ^@	Null	DLE ^P	Data Link Escape	
01	SOH ^A	Start of Heading	DC1 ^Q	Device Control 1	
02	STX ^B	Start of Text	DC2 ^R	Device Control 2	
03	ETX ^C	End of Text	DC3 ^S	Device Control 3	
04	EOT ^D	End of Transmission	DC4 ^T	Device Control 4	
05	ENQ ^E	Enquiry	NAK ^U	Negative Acknowledge	
06	ACK ^F	Acknowledge	SYN ^V	Synchronous Idle	
07	BEL ^G	Bell	ETB ^W	End of Transmission Block	
08	BS ^H	Backspace	CAN ^X	Cancel	
09	HT ^I	Horizontal Tab	EM ^Y	End of Medium	
10	LF ^J	Line Feed	SUB ^Z	Substitute	
11	VT ^K	Vertical Tab	ESC ^[	Escape	
12	FF ^L	Form Feed	FS ^\	File Separator	
13	CR ^M	Carriage Return	GS ^]	Group Separator	
14	SO ^N	Shift Out	RS ^^	Record Separator	
15	SI ^O	Shift In	US ^_	Unit Separator	DEL ^? Delete

7-Bit Roman Character Sets

Table VII-3 shows the 7-bit character sets used by C-Kermit. These sets are identical to ASCII (Table VII-1) except in the positions shown in this table. ASCII is United States ANSI X3.4-1986, which is the same as the ISO 646 International Reference Version. British, French, German, Hungarian, Italian, Japanese Roman, Norwegian, Portuguese, Spanish, and Swedish are ISO 646 national versions registered in the ISO International Register of Coded Character Sets. The others are taken from DEC VT terminal manuals and other sources. The Icelandic 7-bit set, rarely used any more, also includes two-character sequences to represent vowels with acute accents, not shown in the table.

Table VII-3 7-Bit National Character Sets, Differences from ASCII

Row/Column	2/03	4/00	5/11	5/12	5/13	5/14	5/15	6/00	7/11	7/12	7/13	7/14
Decimal	35	64	91	92	93	94	95	96	123	124	125	126
Hexadecimal	23	40	5B	5C	5D	5E	5F	60	7B	7C	7D	7E
ASCII	#	@	[	\	]	^	_	`	{	|	}	~
British	£	@	[	\	]	^	_	`	{	|	}	~
Chinese Roman	#	@	[	¥	]	^	_	`	{	|	}	‾
Danish	#	@	Æ	Ø	Å	^	_	`	æ	ø	å	~
Dutch	£	¾	ÿ	½	|	^	_	`	¨	ƒ	¼	'
Finnish	#	@	Ä	Ö	Å	Ü	_	é	ä	ö	å	ü
French	£	à	°	ç	§	^	_	μ	é	ù	è	¨
Fr-Canadian	#	à	â	ç	ê	î	_	ô	é	ù	è	û
German	#	§	Ä	Ö	Ü	^	_	`	ä	ö	ü	ß
Hungarian	#	Á	É	Ö	Ü	^	_	ú	é	ö	ü	″
Icelandic	#	Þ	Ð	\	Æ	Ö	_	þ	ð	|	æ	ö
Italian	£	§	°	ç	é	^	_	ù	à	ò	è	ì
Japanese Roman	#	@	[	¥	]	^	_	`	{	|	}	‾
Norwegian	§	@	Æ	Ø	Å	^	_	`	æ	ø	å	|
Portuguese	#	′	Ã	Ç	Õ	^	_	`	ã	ç	õ	~
Spanish	£	§	¡	Ñ	¿	^	_	`	°	ñ	ç	~
Swedish	#	É	Ä	Ö	Å	Ü	_	é	ä	ö	å	ü
Swiss	ù	à	é	ç	ê	î	è	ô	ä	ö	ü	û

West European Character Sets

Table VII-4 shows the graphic characters of the right half of ISO 8859-1 Latin Alphabet 1, which is supported as both a transfer character-set and a file character-set by C-Kermit, along with the code values in Latin-1, the DEC Multinational Character Set (MCS), the Data General International Character Set (DGI), Kermit's Macintosh Extended Latin character set (MAC), the NeXT workstation character set, and PC code pages 437 and 850. Characters shown in italics in the MAC column differ from the US version of the Apple Quickdraw character set. Characters that are not present in Latin-1 cannot be translated by Kermit.

Table VII-4   West European Character Sets

Character Name	Latin-1 dec hex	MCS dec hex	DGI dec hex	MAC dec hex	NeXT dec hex	CP437 dec hex	CP850 dec hex
No-break space	160 A0	160 A0	160 A0	202 CA	128 80	255 FF	255 FF
¡ Inverted exclamation	161 A1	161 A1	171 AB	193 C1	161 A1	173 AD	173 AD
¢ Cent sign	162 A2	162 A2	167 A7	162 A2	162 A2	155 9B	189 8B
£ Pound sign	163 A3	163 A3	168 A8	163 A3	163 A3	156 9C	156 9C
¤ Currency sign	164 A4	168 A8	166 A6	219 DB	168 A8		207 CF
¥ Yen sign	165 A5	165 A5	181 B5	180 B4	165 A5	157 9D	190 BE
¦ Broken bar	166 A6			201 C9	181 B5		221 DD
§ Paragraph sign	167 A7	167 A7	187 BB	164 A4	167 A7	021 15	021 15
¨ Diaeresis	168 A8		189 BD	172 AC	200 C8		249 F9
© Copyright sign	169 A9	169 A9	173 AD	169 A9	160 A0		184 B8
ª Feminine ordinal	170 AA	170 AA	170 AA	187 BB	227 E3	166 A6	166 A6
« Left angle quotation	171 AB	171 AB	176 B0	199 C7	171 AB	174 AE	174 AE
¬ Not sign	172 AC		161 A1	194 C2	190 BE	170 AA	170 AA
- Soft hyphen	173 AD	173 AD		*208 D0*			240 F0
® Registered trade mark	174 AE		174 AE	168 A8	176 B0		169 A9
¯ Macron	175 AF			248 F8	197 C5		238 EE
° Degree sign, ring	176 B0	176 B0	188 BC	161 A1	248 F8		248 F8
± Plus-minus sign	177 B1	177 B1	182 B6	177 B1	209 D1	241 F1	241 F1
² Superscript two	178 B2	178 B2	164 A4	*170 AA*	201 C9	253 FD	253 FD

Table VII-4   West European Character Sets (continued)

Character / Name	Latin-1 dec hex	MCS dec hex	DGI dec hex	MAC dec hex	NeXT dec hex	CP437 dec hex	CP850 dec hex
³ Superscript three	179 B3	179 B3	165 A5	*173 AD*	204 CC		252 FC
´ Acute accent	180 B4	180 B4	190 BE	171 AB	194 C2		239 EF
µ Micro sign	181 B5	181 B5	163 A3	181 B5	157 9D	230 E6	230 E6
¶ Pilcrow sign	182 B6	182 B6	178 B2	166 A6	182 B6	020 14	244 F4
• Middle dot	183 B7	183 B7	185 B9	165 A5	180 B4	250 FA	250 FA
¸ Cedilla	184 B8	184 B8		252 FC	184 B8		247 F7
¹ Superscript one	185 B9	185 B9		*176 B0*	192 C0		251 FB
º Masculine ordinal	186 BA	186 BA	169 A9	188 BC	235 EB	167 A7	167 A7
» Right angle quotation	187 BB	187 BB	177 B1	200 C8	187 BB	175 AF	175 AF
¼ One quarter	188 BC	188 BC		*178 B2*	210 D2	172 AC	172 AC
½ One half	189 BD	189 BD	162 A2	*179 B3*	211 D3	171 AB	171 AB
¾ Three quarters	190 BE			*186 BA*	212 D4		243 F3
¿ Inverted question mark	191 BF	191 BF	172 AC	192 C0	191 BF	168 A8	168 A8
À A grave	192 C0	192 C0	193 C1	203 CB	129 81		183 B7
Á A acute	193 C1	193 C1	192 C0	231 E7	130 82		181 B5
Â A circumflex	194 C2	194 C2	194 C2	229 E5	131 83		182 B6
Ã A tilde	195 C3	195 C3	196 C4	204 CC	132 84		199 C7
Ä A diaeresis	196 C4	196 C4	195 C3	128 80	133 85	142 8E	142 8E
Å A ring above	197 C5	197 C5	197 C5	129 81	134 86	143 8F	143 8F
Æ A with E digraph	198 C6	198 C6	198 C6	174 AE	225 E1	146 92	146 92
Ç C Cedilla	199 C7	199 C7	199 C7	130 82	135 87	128 80	128 80
È E grave	200 C8	200 C8	201 C9	233 E9	136 88		212 D4
É E acute	201 C9	201 C9	200 C8	131 83	137 89	144 90	144 90
Ê E circumflex	202 CA	202 CA	202 CA	230 E6	138 8A		210 D2
Ë E diaeresis	203 CB	203 CB	203 CB	232 E8	139 8B		211 D3
Ì I grave	204 CC	204 CC	205 CD	237 ED	140 8C		222 DE
Í I acute	205 CD	205 CD	204 CC	234 EA	141 8D		214 D6
Î I circumflex	206 CE	206 CE	206 CE	235 EB	142 8E		215 D7
Ï I diaeresis	207 CF	207 CF	207 CF	236 EC	143 8F		216 D8

Table VII-4 West European Character Sets (continued)

Character	Name	Latin-1 dec hex	MCS dec hex	DGI dec hex	MAC dec hex	NeXT dec hex	CP437 dec hex	CP850 dec hex
Ð	Icelandic Eth	208 D0			*220 DC*	144 90		209 D1
Ñ	N tilde	209 D1	209 D1	208 D0	132 84	145 91	165 A5	165 A5
Ò	O grave	210 D2	210 D2	210 D2	241 F1	146 92		227 E3
Ó	O acute	211 D3	211 D3	209 D1	238 EE	147 93		224 E0
Ô	O circumflex	212 D4	212 D4	211 D3	239 EF	148 94		226 E2
Õ	O tilde	213 D5	213 D5	213 D5	205 CD	149 95		229 E5
Ö	O diaeresis	214 D6	214 D6	212 D4	133 85	150 96	153 99	153 99
×	Multiplication sign	215 D7			*165 A5*	158 9E		158 9E
Ø	O oblique stroke	216 D8	216 D8	214 D6	175 AF	233 E9		157 9D
Ù	U grave	217 D9	217 D9	217 D9	244 F4	151 97		235 EB
Ú	U acute	218 DA	218 DA	216 D8	242 F2	152 98		233 E9
Û	U circumflex	219 DB	219 DB	218 DA	243 F3	153 99		234 EA
Ü	U diaeresis	220 DC	220 DC	219 DB	134 86	154 9A	154 9A	154 9A
Ý	Y acute	221 DD	221 DD		*160 A0*	155 9B		237 ED
Þ	Icelandic Thorn	222 DE			*222 DE*	156 9C		231 E7
ß	German sharp s	223 DF	223 DF	252 FC	167 A7	251 FB	225 E1	225 E1
à	a grave	224 E0	224 E0	225 E1	136 88	213 D5	133 85	133 85
á	a acute	225 E1	225 E1	224 E0	135 87	214 D6	160 A0	160 A0
â	a circumflex	226 E2	226 E2	226 E2	137 89	215 D7	131 83	131 83
ã	a tilde	227 E3	227 E3	228 E4	139 8B	216 D8		198 C6
ä	a diaeresis	228 E4	228 E4	227 E3	138 8A	217 D9	132 84	132 84
å	a ring above	229 E5	229 E5	229 E5	140 8C	218 DA	134 86	134 86
æ	a with e digraph	230 E6	230 E6	230 E6	190 BE	241 F1	145 91	145 91
ç	c cedilla	231 E7	231 E7	231 E7	141 8D	219 DB	135 87	135 87
è	e grave	232 E8	232 E8	233 E9	143 8F	220 DC	138 8A	138 8A
é	e acute	233 E9	233 E9	232 E8	142 8E	221 DD	130 82	130 82
ê	e circumflex	234 EA	234 EA	234 EA	144 90	222 DE	136 88	136 88
ë	e diaeresis	235 EB	235 EB	235 EB	145 91	223 DF	137 89	137 89
ì	i grave	236 EC	236 EC	237 ED	147 93	224 E0	141 8D	141 8D

Table VII-4   West European Character Sets (continued)

Character Name	Latin-1 dec hex	MCS dec hex	DGI dec hex	MAC dec hex	NeXT dec hex	CP437 dec hex	CP850 dec hex
í i acute	237 ED	237 ED	236 EC	146 92	226 E2	161 A1	161 A1
î i circumflex	238 EE	238 EE	238 EE	148 94	228 E4	140 8C	140 8C
ï i diaeresis	239 EF	239 EF	239 EF	149 95	229 E5	139 8B	139 8B
ð Icelandic eth	240 F0			*221 DD*	230 E6		208 D0
ñ n tilde	241 F1	241 F1	240 F0	150 96	231 E7	164 A4	164 A4
ò o grave	242 F2	242 F2	242 F2	152 98	236 EC	149 95	149 95
ó o acute	243 F3	243 F3	241 F1	151 97	237 ED	162 A2	162 A2
ô o circumflex	244 F4	244 F4	243 F3	153 99	238 EE	147 93	147 93
õ o tilde	245 F5	245 F5	245 F5	155 9B	239 EF		228 E4
ö o diaeresis	246 F6	246 F6	244 F4	154 9A	240 F0	148 94	148 94
÷ Division sign	247 F7			*214 D6*	159 9F	246 F6	246 F6
ø o oblique stroke	248 F8	248 F8	246 F6	191 BF	249 F9		155 9B
ù u grave	249 F9	249 F9	249 F9	157 9D	242 F2	151 97	151 97
ú u acute	250 FA	250 FA	248 F8	156 9C	243 F3	163 A3	163 A3
û u circumflex	251 FB	251 FB	250 FA	158 9E	244 F4	150 96	150 96
ü u diaeresis	252 FC	252 FC	251 FB	159 9F	246 F6	129 81	129 81
ý y acute	253 FD			224 E0	247 F7		236 EC
þ Icelandic thorn	254 FE			*223 DF*	252 FC		231 E7
ÿ y diaeresis	255 FF	255 FF	253 FD	216 D8	253 F3	152 98	152 98
ı Dotless i				245 F5	245 F5		213 D5
Ł L with stroke		195 C3		*195 C3*	232 E8		
ł l with stroke		212 D4		*212 D4*	248 F8		
Œ O with E digraph		215 D7	215 D7	206 CE	234 EA		
œ o with e digraph		247 F7	247 F7	207 CF	250 FA		
Ÿ Y diaeresis		221 DD	221 DD	216 D8			
ƒ Florin sign			180 B4	196 D4	166 A6	159 9F	159 9F

East European Character Sets

Table VII-5 shows the graphic characters of the right half of ISO 8859 Latin Alphabet 2 for East European languages, which is supported as both a transfer character-set and a file character-set by C-Kermit, along with the code values in Latin-2 and PC code page 852.

Table VII-5
East European Character Sets

Character	Name	Latin-2 dec hex	CP852 dec hex
	No-break space	160 A0	255 FF
Ą	A ogonek	161 A1	164 A4
˘	Breve	162 A2	244 F4
Ł	L with stroke	163 A3	157 9D
¤	Currency sign	164 A4	207 CF
Ľ	L caron	165 A5	149 95
Ś	S acute	166 A6	151 97
§	Paragraph sign	167 A7	245 F5
¨	Diaeresis	168 A8	249 F9
Š	S caron	169 A9	230 E6
Ş	S cedilla	170 AA	184 B8
Ť	T caron	171 AB	155 9B
Ź	Z acute	172 AC	141 8D
	Soft hyphen	173 AD	170 AA
Ž	Z caron	174 AE	166 A6
Ż	Z dot above	175 AF	189 BD
°	Degree sign, ring	176 B0	248 F8
ą	a ogonek	177 B1	165 A5
˛	Ogonek	178 B2	242 F2
ł	l with stroke	179 B3	136 88
´	Acute accent	180 B4	239 EF
ľ	l caron	181 B5	150 96

Table VII-5
East European Sets (continued)

Character	Name	Latin-2 dec hex	CP852 dec hex
ś	s acute	182 B6	152 98
ˇ	Caron	183 B7	243 F3
¸	Cedilla	184 B8	247 F7
š	s caron	185 B9	231 E7
ş	s cedilla	186 BA	173 AD
ť	t caron	187 BB	156 9C
ź	z acute	188 BC	171 AB
˝	Double acute	189 BD	241 F1
ž	z caron	190 BE	167 A7
ż	z dot above	191 BF	190 BE
Ŕ	R acute	192 C0	232 E8
Á	A acute	193 C1	181 B5
Â	A circumflex	194 C2	182 B6
Ă	A breve	195 C3	198 C6
Ä	A diaeresis	196 C4	142 8E
Ĺ	L acute	197 C5	145 91
Ć	C acute	198 C6	143 8F
Ç	C cedilla	199 C7	128 80
Č	C caron	200 C8	172 AC
É	E acute	201 C9	144 90
Ę	E ogonek	202 CA	168 A8
Ë	E diaeresis	203 CB	211 D3

Table VII-5
East European Sets (continued)

Character Name	Latin-2 dec hex	CP852 dec hex
Ě E caron	204 CC	183 B7
Í I acute	205 CD	214 D6
Î I circumflex	206 CE	215 D7
Ď D caron	207 CF	210 D2
Đ D stroke	208 D0	209 D1
Ń N acute	209 D1	227 E3
Ň N caron	210 D2	213 D5
Ó O acute	211 D3	224 E0
Ô O circumflex	212 D4	226 E2
Ő O double acute	213 D5	138 8A
Ö O diaeresis	214 D6	153 99
× Multiplication sign	215 D7	158 9E
Ř R caron	216 D8	252 FC
Ů U ring	217 D9	222 DE
Ú U acute	218 DA	233 E9
Ű U double acute	219 DB	235 EB
Ü U diaeresis	220 DC	154 9A
Ý Y acute	221 DD	237 ED
Ţ T cedilla	222 DE	221 DD
ß German sharp s	223 DF	225 E1
ŕ r acute	224 E0	234 EA
á a acute	225 E1	160 A0
â a circumflex	226 E2	131 83
ă a breve	227 E3	199 C7
ä a diaeresis	228 E4	132 84
ĺ l acute	229 E5	146 92
ć c acute	230 E6	134 86
ç c cedilla	231 E7	135 87

Table VII-5
East European Sets (continued)

Character Name	Latin-2 dec hex	CP852 dec hex
č c caron	232 E8	159 9F
é e acute	233 E9	130 82
ę e ogonek	234 EA	169 A9
ë e diaeresis	235 EB	137 89
ě e caron	236 EC	216 D8
í i acute	237 ED	161 A1
î i circumflex	238 EE	140 8C
ď d caron	239 EF	212 D4
đ d stroke	240 F0	208 D0
ń n acute	241 F1	228 E4
ň n caron	242 F2	229 E5
ó o acute	243 F3	162 A2
ô o circumflex	244 F4	147 93
ő o double acute	245 F5	139 8B
ö o diaeresis	246 F6	148 94
÷ Division sign	247 F7	246 F6
ř r caron	248 F8	253 FD
ů u ring	249 F9	133 85
ú u acute	250 FA	163 A3
ű u double acute	251 FB	251 FB
ü u diaeresis	252 FC	129 81
ý y acute	253 FD	236 EC
ţ t cedilla	254 FE	238 EE
˙ Dot above	255 FF	250 FA

Cyrillic Character Sets

Table VII-6 shows the characters of the ISO 8859-5 Latin/Cyrillic Alphabet (also known as ECMA-113), Microsoft Code Page 866, Old KOI-8, and the Short KOI equivalents that are used for displaying Russian words on ASCII devices by showing Cyrillic letters as lowercase ASCII and Roman letters as uppercase ASCII; for example, "Протокол Передачи Файлов Kermit" is written protokol pereda~i fajlow KERMIT.

The character names are taken from ISO Standard 8859-5, modified to show upper- or lowercase typographically rather than spelling out UPPERCASE and LOWERCASE for each letter. Unfortunately, the same name is used by ISO for two different characters: Cyrillic I (1) is the one that looks like a backwards Roman letter N, and Cyrillic I (2) looks like a Roman letter I.

CP866 and the KOI character sets lack the Macedonian and Serbocroatian letters, as well as the old Cyrillic letters and one of the Ukrainian letters, found in ISO 8859-5. The CP866 characters B0 through DF (hex) are identical to the line- and box-drawing characters of IBM CP437. The 8-bit ISO, KOI-8, and CP866 sets all include ASCII (ISO 646 IRV) as their first 128 characters (except $ is replaced by ¤ in KOI-8).

Table VII-6   Cyrillic Character Sets

Character	Name	ISO Dec Hex	CP866 Dec Hex	KOI-8 Dec Hex	Short KOI
А	Cyrillic A	176 B0	128 80	225 E1	a
а	Cyrillic a	208 D0	160 A0	193 C1	a
Б	Cyrillic Be	177 B1	129 81	226 E2	b
б	Cyrillic be	209 D1	161 A1	194 C2	b
В	Cyrillic Ve	178 B2	130 82	247 F7	w
в	Cyrillic ve	210 D2	162 A2	215 D7	w
Г	Cyrillic Ghe	179 B3	131 83	231 E7	g
г	Cyrillic ghe	211 D3	163 A3	199 C7	g
Д	Cyrillic De	180 B4	132 84	228 E4	d
д	Cyrillic de	212 D4	164 A4	196 C4	d
Е	Cyrillic Ie	181 B5	133 85	229 E5	e
е	Cyrillic ie	213 D5	165 A5	197 C5	e

Table VII-6 Cyrillic Character Sets (continued)

Character	Name	ISO Dec Hex	CP866 Dec Hex	KOI-8 Dec Hex	Short KOI
Ё	Cyrillic Io	161 A1	240 F0		e
ё	Cyrillic io	241 F1	241 F1		e
Ж	Cyrillic Zhe	182 B6	134 86	246 F6	v
ж	Cyrillic zhe	214 D6	166 A6	214 D6	v
З	Cyrillic Ze	183 B7	135 87	250 FA	z
з	Cyrillic ze	215 D7	167 A7	218 DA	z
И	Cyrillic I (1)	184 B8	136 88	233 E9	i
и	Cyrillic i (1)	216 D8	168 A8	201 C9	i
Й	Cyrillic Short I	185 B9	137 89	234 EA	j
й	Cyrillic Short i	217 D9	169 A9	202 CA	j
К	Cyrillic Ka	186 BA	138 8A	235 EB	k
к	Cyrillic ka	218 DA	170 AA	203 CB	k
Л	Cyrillic El	187 BB	139 8B	236 EC	l
л	Cyrillic el	219 DB	171 AB	204 CC	l
М	Cyrillic Em	188 BC	140 8C	237 ED	m
м	Cyrillic em	220 DC	172 AC	205 CD	m
Н	Cyrillic En	189 BD	141 8D	238 EE	n
н	Cyrillic en	221 DD	173 AD	206 CE	n
О	Cyrillic O	190 BE	142 8E	239 EF	o
о	Cyrillic o	222 DE	174 AE	207 CF	o
П	Cyrillic Pe	191 BF	143 8F	240 F0	p
п	Cyrillic pe	223 DF	175 AF	208 D0	p
Р	Cyrillic Er	192 C0	144 90	242 F2	r
р	Cyrillic er	224 E0	224 E0	210 D2	r
С	Cyrillic Es	193 C1	145 91	243 F3	s
с	Cyrillic es	225 E1	225 E1	211 D3	s
Т	Cyrillic Te	194 C2	146 92	244 F4	t
т	Cyrillic te	226 E2	226 E2	212 D4	t
У	Cyrillic U	195 C3	147 93	245 F5	u

Table VII-6 Cyrillic Character Sets (continued)

Character	Name	ISO Dec Hex	CP866 Dec Hex	KOI-8 Dec Hex	Short KOI
у	Cyrillic u	227 E3	227 E3	213 D5	y
Ф	Cyrillic Ef	196 C4	148 94	230 E6	f
ф	Cyrillic ef	228 E4	228 E4	198 C6	f
Х	Cyrillic Ha	197 C5	149 95	232 E8	h
х	Cyrillic ha	229 E5	229 E5	200 C8	h
Ц	Cyrillic Tse	198 C6	150 96	227 E3	c
ц	Cyrillic tse	230 E6	230 E6	195 C3	c
Ч	Cyrillic Che	199 C7	151 97	254 FE	~
ч	Cyrillic che	231 E7	231 E7	222 DE	~
Ш	Cyrillic Sha	200 C8	152 98	251 FB	{
ш	Cyrillic sha	232 E8	232 E8	219 DB	{
Щ	Cyrillic Shcha	201 C9	153 99	253 FD	}
щ	Cyrillic shcha	233 E9	233 E9	221 DD	}
Ъ	Cyrillic Hard Sign	202 CA	154 9A		
ъ	Cyrillic hard sign	234 EA	234 EA	207 CF	
Ы	Cyrillic Yeri	203 CB	155 9B	249 F9	y
ы	Cyrillic yeri	235 EB	235 EB	217 D9	y
Ь	Cyrillic Soft Sign	204 CC	156 9C	248 F8	x
ь	Cyrillic soft sign	236 EC	236 EC	216 D8	x
Э	Cyrillic E	205 CD	157 9D	252 FC	l
э	Cyrillic e	237 ED	237 ED	220 DC	l
Ю	Cyrillic Yu	206 CE	158 9E	224 E0	@
ю	Cyrillic yu	238 EE	238 EE	192 C0	@
Я	Cyrillic Ya	207 CF	159 9F	241 F1	q
я	Cyrillic ya	239 EF	239 EF	209 D1	q
Ѕ	Cyrillic Dze	175 AF			
ѕ	Cyrillic dze	255 FF			
І	Cyrillic I (2)	166 A6			
і	Cyrillic i (2)	246 F6			

Table VII-6 Cyrillic Character Sets (continued)

Character	Name	ISO Dec Hex	CP866 Dec Hex	KOI-8 Dec Hex	Short KOI
Ј	Cyrillic Je	168 A8	244 F4		
ј	Cyrillic je	248 F8	245 F5		
Љ	Cyrillic Lje	169 A9			
љ	Cyrillic lje	249 F9			
Њ	Cyrillic Nje	170 AA			
њ	Cyrillic nje	250 FA			
Ў	Belorussian Short U	174 AE	246 F6		
ў	Belorussian short u	254 FE	247 F7		
Ѕ	Macedonian Dze	165 A5			
ѕ	Macedonian dze	245 F5			
Ѓ	Macedonian Gje	163 A3			
ѓ	Macedonian gje	243 F3			
Ќ	Macedonian Kje	172 AC			
ќ	Macedonian kje	252 FC			
Ђ	Serbocroatian Dje	162 A2			
ђ	Serbocroatian dje	242 F2			
Ћ	Serbocroatian Chje	171 AB			
ћ	Serbocroatian chje	251 FB			
Є	Ukrainian Ie	164 A4	242 F2		
є	Ukrainian ie	244 F4	243 F3		
Ї	Ukrainian Yi	167 A7			
ї	Ukrainian yi	247 F7			
	No-break space	160 A0	255 FF		
№	Number Acronym	240 F0	252 FC		
§	Paragraph sign	253 FD			
	Soft hyphen	173 AD			

Hebrew Character Sets

Table VII-7 shows the characters of the ISO 8859-8 Latin/Hebrew Alphabet (ECMA-121), PC Code Page 862, and DEC Hebrew-7. Character names are taken from the ISO Standard [45]. Hebrew-7 is a form of ASCII (Table VII-1) in which characters 96 through 122 (accent grave and the lowercase letters a–z) are replaced by Hebrew letters; the Hebrew-7 column shows not only the character codes, but the equivalent ASCII character, for convenience of typing (or reading).

Latin/Hebrew and CP862 include ASCII as their "lower half." Note that Hebrew letters do not have upper- and lowercase forms. None of these character sets includes vowel points, cantillation marks, special Hebrew punctuation marks, or Yiddish digraphs.

Table VII-7   Hebrew Character Sets

Character	Name	ISO Dec Hex	CP862 Dec Hex	Hebrew-7 Dec Hex
	No-Break space	160 A0	255 FF	
¢	Cent sign	162 A2	155 9B	
£	Pound sign	163 A3	156 9C	
¤	Currency sign	164 A4		
¥	Yen sign	165 2A	157 9D	
¦	Broken bar	166 A6		
§	Paragraph sign	167 A7		
¨	Diaeresis	168 A8		
©	Copyright sign	169 A9		
ª	Feminine ordinal	170 AA	166 A6	
«	Left angle quotation	171 AB	174 AE	
¬	Not sign	172 AC	170 AA	
	Soft hyphen	173 AD		
®	Registered trade mark	174 AE		
¯	Macron	175 AF		
°	Degree sign, ring above	176 B0	248 F8	
±	Plus-minus sign	177 B1	241 F1	

Table VII-7   Hebrew Character Sets (continued)

Character	Name	ISO Dec Hex	CP862 Dec Hex	Hebrew-7 Dec Hex	
²	Superscript two	178 B2	253 FD		
³	Superscript three	179 B3			
´	Acute accent	180 B4			
µ	Micro sign	181 B5	230 E6		
¶	Pilcrow sign	182 B6			
•	Middle dot	183 B7			
¸	Cedilla	184 B8			
¹	Superscript one	185 B9			
º	Masculine ordinal	186 BA	167 A7		
»	Right angle quotation	187 BB	175 AF		
¼	One quarter	188 BC	172 AC		
½	One half	189 BD	171 AB		
¾	Three quarters	190 BE			
=	Double lowline	223 DF	202 CA		
א	Hebrew letter Aleph	224 E0	128 80	96 60	`
ב	Hebrew letter Bet	225 E1	129 81	97 61	a
ג	Hebrew letter Gimel	226 E2	130 82	98 62	b
ד	Hebrew letter Dalet	227 E3	131 83	99 63	c
ה	Hebrew letter He	228 E4	132 84	100 64	d
ו	Hebrew letter Waw	229 E5	133 85	101 65	e
ז	Hebrew letter Zain	230 E6	134 86	102 66	f
ח	Hebrew letter Chet	231 E7	135 87	103 67	g
ט	Hebrew letter Tet	232 E8	136 88	104 68	h
י	Hebrew letter Yod	233 E9	137 89	105 69	i
ך	Hebrew letter terminal Kaph	234 EA	138 8A	106 6A	j
כ	Hebrew letter Kaph	235 EB	139 8B	107 6B	k
ל	Hebrew letter Lamed	236 EC	140 8C	108 6C	l
ם	Hebrew letter terminal Mem	237 ED	141 8D	109 6D	m

Table VII-7   Hebrew Character Sets (continued)

Character	Name	ISO Dec Hex	CP862 Dec Hex	Hebrew-7 Dec Hex	
מ	Hebrew letter Mem	238 EE	142 8E	110 6E	n
ן	Hebrew letter terminal Nun	239 EF	143 8F	111 6F	o
נ	Hebrew letter Nun	240 F0	144 90	112 70	p
ס	Hebrew letter Samech	241 F1	145 91	113 71	q
ע	Hebrew letter Ayin	242 F2	146 92	114 72	r
ף	Hebrew letter terminal Pe	243 F3	147 93	115 73	s
פ	Hebrew letter Pe	244 F4	148 94	116 74	t
ץ	Hebrew letter terminal Zade	245 F5	149 95	117 75	u
צ	Hebrew letter Zade	246 F6	150 96	118 76	v
ק	Hebrew letter Qoph	247 F7	151 97	119 77	w
ר	Hebrew letter Resh	248 F8	152 98	120 78	x
ש	Hebrew letter Shin	249 F9	153 99	121 79	y
ת	Hebrew letter Taw	250 FA	154 9A	122 7A	z

Appendix VIII

Country Codes

Table VIII-1   Country Codes

Country	Code
Afghanistan	+93
Albania	+355
Algeria	+213
American Samoa	+684
Andorra	+376
Angola	+244
Anguilla	+1
Antigua & Barbuda	+1
Argentina	+54
Armenia	+374
Aruba	+297
Ascension	+247
Australia	+61
Australian External Territories	+672
Austria	+43
Azerbaijan	+994
Azores	+351
Bahamas	+1
Bahrain	+973
Bangladesh	+880
Barbados	+1
Belarus	+375

Table VIII-1 Country Codes (cont'd)

Country	Code
Belgium	+32
Belize	+501
Benin	+229
Bermuda	+1
Bhutan	+975
Bolivia	+591
Bosnia-Herzegovina	+387
Botswana	+267
Brazil	+55
Brunei	+673
Bulgaria	+359
Burkina Faso	+226
Burundi	+257
Cambodia (Kampuchea)	+855
Cameroon	+237
Canada	+1
Canary Islands	+34
Cape Verde Islands	+238
Cayman Islands	+1
Central African Republic	+236
Chad	+235
Chile	+56

Table VIII-1 Country Codes (cont'd)

Country	Code
China, People's Republic of	+86
China, Republic of	+866/+886
Colombia	+57
Congo	+242
Cook Islands	+682
Costa Rica	+506
Croatia	+385
Cuba	+53
Cyprus	+357
Czech Republic	+42
Denmark	+45
Diego Garcia	+246
Djibouti	+253
Dominica	+1
Dominican Republic	+1
Ecuador	+593
Egypt	+20
El Salvador	+503
Equatorial Guinea	+240
Eritrea	+291
Estonia	+372
Ethiopia	+251
Færoe Islands	+298
Falkland Islands	+500
Fiji	+679
Finland	+358
France	+33
French Polynesia	+689
Gabon	+241
Gambia	+220
Georgia	+995
Germany	+49
Ghana	+233
Gibraltar	+350
Greece	+30
Greenland	+299
Grenada	+1
Grenadines	+1
Guadeloupe	+590
Guam	+671/+1
Guatemala	+502
Guiana, French	+594
Guinea	+224
Guinea-Bissau	+245
Guyana	+592
Haiti	+509
Honduras	+504
Hong Kong	+852

Table VIII-1 Country Codes (cont'd)

Country	Code
Hungary	+36
Iceland	+354
India	+91
Indonesia	+62
Iran	+98
Iraq	+964
Ireland	+353
Ireland, Northern	+44
Israel	+972
Italy	+39
Ivory Coast (Côte d'Ivoire)	+225
Jamaica	+1
Japan	+81
Jordan	+962
Kazakstan	+7
Kenya	+254
Kiribati Republic	+686
Korea, Democratic P.R.	+850
Korea, Republic of	+82
Kuwait	+965
Kyrgyzstan	+7/+996
Laos	+856
Latvia	+371
Lebanon	+961
Lesotho	+266
Liberia	+231
Libya	+218
Liechtenstein	+41
Lithuania	+370
Luxembourg	+352
Macau	+853
Macedonia	+389
Madagascar	+261
Madeira	+351
Malawi	+265
Malaysia	+60
Maldives	+960
Mali	+223
Malta	+356
Mariana Islands	+670
Marshall Islands	+692
Martinique	+596
Mauritania	+222
Mauritius	+230
Moyotte	+269
Mexico	+52
Micronesia	+691
Moldova	+373

Table VIII-1 Country Codes (cont'd)

Table VIII-1 Country Codes (cont'd)

Country	Code
Monaco	+377
Mongolia	+976
Montserrat	+1
Morocco	+212
Mozambique	+258
Myanmar	+95
Namibia	+264
Nauru	+674
Nepal	+977
Netherlands	+31
Netherlands Antilles	+599
Nevis	+1
New Caledonia	+687
New Zealand	+64
Nicaragua	+505
Niger	+227
Nigeria	+234
Niue	+683
Northern Marianas	+670
Norway	+47
Oman	+968
Pakistan	+92
Palau	+680
Panama	+507
Papua New Guinea	+675
Paraguay	+595
Peru	+51
Philippines	+63
Poland	+48
Portugal	+351
Puerto Rico	+1
Qatar	+974
Reunion	+262
Romania	+40
Russian Federation	+7
Rwanda	+250
Saint Helena	+290
Saint Kitts & Nevis	+1
Saint Lucia	+1
Saint Pierre & Miquelon	+508
Saint Vincent & Grenadines	+1
Samoa, Western	+685
San Marino	+378
São Tome and Principe	+239
Saudi Arabia	+966
Senegal	+221
Serbia-Montenegro	+381
Seychelles	+248

Country	Code
Sierra Leone	+232
Singapore	+65
Slovak Republic	+42
Slovenia	+386
Solomon Islands	+677
Somalia	+252
South Africa	+27
Spain	+34
Sri Lanka	+94
Sudan	+249
Suriname	+597
Swaziland	+268
Sweden	+46
Switzerland	+41
Syria	+963
Tahiti	+689
Tajikistan	+7
Tanzania	+255
Thailand	+66
Togo	+228
Tokelau	+690
Tonga	+676
Trinidad & Tobago	+1
Tunisia	+216
Turkey	+90
Turkmenistan	+7/+993
Turks & Caicos Islands	+1
Tuvalu	+688
Uganda	+256
Ukraine	+380
United Arab Emirates	+971
United Kingdom	+44
United States of America	+1
Uruguay	+598
Uzbekistan	+7/+998
Vanuatu	+678
Vatican City State	+39/+379
Venezuela	+58
Viet Nam	+84
Virgin Islands	+1
Wallis & Futuna	+681
Western Samoa	+685
Yemen	+967
Zaire	+243
Zambia	+260
Zanzibar	+255/+259
Zimbabwe	+263

Hexification Programs

The C programs `hex.c` and `unhex.c` translate between 8-bit binary files and straight hex files, in which every pair of hexadecimal digits corresponds to a single 8-bit byte. The `hex.c` program translates the standard input into hexadecimal notation and sends the result to standard output. Usage on UNIX, DOS, Windows, OS/2:

```
hex < binaryfile > hexfile
```

```c
#include <stdio.h>              /* For EOF symbol */
#ifdef MSDOS                    /* Or Windows or OS/2 */
#include <fcntl.h>              /* For MS-DOS O_BINARY symbol */
#endif /* MSDOS */

unsigned int c; int count = 0; char a, b; char h[16] = {
 '0','1','2','3','4','5','6','7','8','9','A','B','C','D','E','F'};
main() {
#ifdef MSDOS
    setmode(fileno(stdin),O_BINARY);   /* Avoid DOS conversions */
#endif /* MSDOS */
    while ((c = getchar()) != EOF) {   /* For each file char */
        b = c & 0xF;                   /* Get low 4 bits */
        a = (c >> 4) & 0xF;            /* and high 4 bits */
        putchar(h[a]);                 /* Hexify & output them */
        putchar(h[b]);
        if (++count == 36) {           /* 72 chars per line */
            putchar('\n'); count = 0;
        }
    }
    putchar('\n');                     /* Terminate final line */
}
```

The unhex program converts a hex file back into its original binary format. Usage on UNIX or MS-DOS:

```
unhex < hexfile > binaryfile
```

```c
#include <stdio.h>                      /* Include this for EOF symbol */
#ifdef MSDOS
#include <fcntl.h>                      /* For MS-DOS setmode() symbol */
#endif

unsigned char a, b;                     /* High and low parts of byte */
unsigned int c;                         /* Char to translate them into */
unsigned char decode();                 /* Function to decode them    */
main() {
#ifdef MSDOS
    setmode(fileno(stdout),O_BINARY);   /* Avoid DOS conversions */
#endif /* MSDOS */
    while ((c = getchar()) != EOF) {    /* Read first hex digit */
        a = c;                          /* Convert to character */
        if (a == '\n' || a == '\r') {   /* Ignore line ends */
            continue;
        }
        if ((c = getchar()) == EOF) {   /* Read second hex digit */
            fprintf(stderr,"File ends prematurely\n");
            exit(1);
        }
        b = c;                          /* Convert to character */
        putchar( ((decode(a) * 16) & 0xF0) + (decode(b) & 0xF) );
    }
    exit(0);                            /* Done */
}

/* Function to decode a hex char */
unsigned char
decode(x) char x; {
    if (x >= '0' && x <= '9')           /* 0-9 offset by hex 30 */
      return (x - 0x30);
    else if (x >= 'A' && x <= 'F')      /* A-F offset by hex 37 */
      return(x - 0x37);
    else {                              /* All others illegal */
        fprintf(stderr,"\nInput is not in legal hex format\n");
        exit(1);
    }
}
```

Shift-Out/Shift-In Filter

Use this program, `so.c`, to display 8-bit text on your screen when your connection to the host is 7 bits. Usage examples:

```
$ so < german.txt
$ kermit -z | so
```

```
#include <stdio.h>                          /* Standard i/o library */
main() {                                    /* Main routine */
    int x = 0, shift = 0;                   /* Declarations */
    unsigned char c;

    while ((x = getchar()) != EOF) {        /* Read a character */
        c = x;                              /* Convert int to char */
        if (c > 127) {                      /* 8-bit character */
            if (shift == 0) {               /* Shifted already? */
                putchar('\16');             /* No, output SO (^N) */
                shift = 1;                  /* Remember shift */
            }
        } else {                            /* 7-bit character */
            if (shift == 1) {               /* Shifted? */
                putchar('\17');             /* Yes, output SI (^O) */
                shift = 0;                  /* Remember */
            }
        }
        putchar(c & 0x7F);                  /* Output the character */
    }
    putchar('\17');                         /* Return to normal */
}
```

Acronyms and Abbreviations

3270

A type of block-mode terminal used with IBM 370-series mainframes.

ACK

Acknowledgement.

ACL

Access Control List, a property of the VMS, OpenVMS, and AOS/VS file systems.

ACS

Asynchronous Communication Server. A device on a PC network that houses one or more serial ports that can be shared by all the PCs on the network.

ACU

Automatic Calling Unit. A modem that includes a dialer.

ADSL

Asymmetric Digital Subscriber Line.

Alt

The key that you hold down while pressing another key in order to produce an Alt character, on keyboards that have an Alt (or Alternate) key. For example, `Alt-X` is produced by holding down Alt and pressing X.

ANSI

The American National Standards Institute, which issues standards such as ASCII.

AOS/VS
Advanced Operating System / Virtual System, the operating system for Data General Eclipse MV-series computers.

APC
Application Program Command.

API
Application Program Interface.

ARQ
Automatic Repeat (or Retransmission) Request. Applies to a communications protocol in which retransmission of damaged messages can be requested.

ASCII
American Standard Code for Information Interchange, ANSI X3.4-1986. A 128-character code widely used by computers for representing and transmitting character data, in which each character corresponds to a number between 0 and 127. Listed in Table VII-1.

AXP
The Digital Equipment Corporation 64-bit computer architecture, now called Alpha.

BBS
Bulletin board system. A dialup computer service that lets you exchange messages with other users of the same BBS, read news on various topics, and upload and download software and files.

bis
[L] "twice" (used with ITU-T standards).

bps
Bits per second (transmission speed).

C
The programming language used predominantly on UNIX systems, and in which C-Kermit is written.

C0
(C Zero) A set of 32 7-bit control characters.

C1
(C One) A set of 32 8-bit control characters.

CB
Citizens Band.

CCITT

The International Telegraph and Telephone Consultative Committee of the International Telecommunications Union, which issues standards called Recommendations, such as CCITT Recommendations V.24, X.25 (*q.v.*). Renamed to ITU-T (*q.v.*) in 1993.

CD

Carrier Detect. The signal from a modem indicating it is connected to another modem. Also called Data Carrier Detect (DCD), Receive Line Signal Indicator (RLSI).

cd

Change Directory. The command used in UNIX, MS-DOS, OS/2, and several other operating systems to change your current (default) directory.

CECP

Country Extended Code Page. An EBCDIC-based national or international character set used on IBM mainframes.

CK

Filename prefix for C-Kermit files.

CLI

Command Line Interpreter (AOS/VS and Commodore Amiga).

CP

Code page, a character set used on PCs or IBM mainframes.

CPS

Characters per second, usually equivalent to 10 bits per second in asynchronous transmission, 8 bits per second in synchronous or network transmission.

CPU

Central processing unit. The "brain" of a computer.

CR

Carriage return (ASCII 13, Control-M).

CRC

Cyclic redundancy check, an error-checking mechanism, the remainder after dividing a message, viewed as a base-2 polynomial, by another base-2 polynomial.

CRLF

Carriage return and linefeed, the sequence of ASCII characters (codes 13 and 10) used by MS-DOS, OS/2, and other file systems to delimit lines in a text file.

CRT

Cathode ray tube. Commonly used to mean a video terminal.

csh

The C-Shell, the command interpreter supplied with Berkeley UNIX.

CTERM

The DECnet virtual terminal protocol used by the DECnet SET HOST command.

Ctrl

Control. The key you hold down while pressing another key (a letter or certain others) to produce a control character. For example, $Ctrl-C$ is produced by holding down Ctrl and pressing C.

CTS

Clear To Send. The RS-232 signal that indicates the DCE's readiness to accept data from the DTE.

DC

(informal) data compression.

DCC

Data Country Code (part of an X.121 address).

DCD

Data Carrier Detect. Same as CD, *q.v.*

DCE

Data Communications Equipment, such as a modem.

DCL

DIGITAL Command Language. A command interpreter as well as a language for writing command procedures on Digital Equipment Corporation computers.

DCM

Data Communications Module (Rolm).

DG

Data General Corporation.

DGI

Data General International (character set).

DEC

Digital Equipment Corporation.

DMA

Direct Memory Access.

DNIC

Data Network Identification Code (part of an X.121 address).

DOS

Disk Operating System. A computer operating system that uses a magnetic disk as its principal medium of permanent storage. Also, short for MS-DOS or PC-DOS.

DSR

Data Set Ready. A signal from a DCE to a DTE that says the DCE is turned on and in data mode.

DTE

Data Terminal Equipment, such as a computer or a terminal.

DTMF

Dual Tone Multi Frequency (touch tone).

DTR

Data Terminal Ready. A signal from a DTE to a DCE that says the DTE is turned on and ready to communicate.

EBCDIC

Extended Binary Coded Decimal Interchange Code. The 8-bit character code used on IBM mainframes. Many variations exist, described in reference [41].

EC

(informal) error correction.

ECMA

European Computer Manufacturers Association.

e.g.

[L] *exempli gratia* (for example).

EIA

The Electronic Industries Association, sponsor of RS-232.

EISA

Extended Industry Standard Architecture, a 32-bit extension to the 16-bit ISA bus architecture used by the IBM PC/AT and compatibles.

EOF

End Of File.

ESC

Escape, ASCII character 27, Control–[.

EU

European Union.

EUC

Extended UNIX Code.

FAQ

Frequently Asked Question.

FAT

File Allocation Table. The MS-DOS file system that is also supported by OS/2 and Windows, in which file names are limited to 8.3 format (eight characters before the dot, three after).

FTP

File Transfer Protocol. As a proper name, the file transfer protocol of the Internet, and the program of the same name that implements it.

G0

(G Zero) A set of 94 graphic characters, normally the graphic characters of ASCII (ISO 646 International Reference Version).

G1

(G One) A set of 94 or 96 graphic characters.

G2

(G Two) A set of 94 or 96 graphic characters.

G3

(G Three) A set of 94 or 96 graphic characters.

GL

Graphics Left. The set of graphic characters selected by a 7-bit character whose encoding is in the range 33–126.

GNU

GNU is Not UNIX. An effort to develop, collect, and distribute free software, mostly for UNIX, by the Free Software Foundation.

GOST

The (former) USSR State Committee on Standards. Now GOSSTANDART RF in Russia, UzGOST in Uzbekistan, SARM in Armenia, etc.

GR

Graphics Right. The set of graphic characters selected by an 8-bit character whose encoding is in the range 160–255 (96-character sets) or 161–254 (94-character sets).

GUI

Graphical User Interface.

HD

High Density, such as the recording format of a diskette.

HPFS

The OS/2 High Performance File System, which supports long filenames.

HST

US Robotics High Speed Technology, a proprietary modem-to-modem protocol.

IBM

International Business Machines Corporation.

i.e.

[L] *id est* (that is).

I/O

Input/Output.

IAC

Interpret As Command, the TELNET protocol negotiation lead-in byte, value 255 decimal.

ICSTI

International Centre for Scientific and Technical Information, Moscow (МЦНТИ).

IETF

Internet Engineering Task Force, the standards body of the Internet.

IP

Internet Protocol. The routing protocol and addressing conventions used in the Internet.

IRV

International Reference Version (of ISO 646).

ISA

Industry Standard Architecture, referring to the 16-bit bus used by the IBM PC/AT and compatibles.

ISDN

Integrated Services Data Network. The basis for a digital telephone network with combined voice and data capability.

ISO

International Organization for Standardization. A voluntary international group of national standards organizations that issues standards in a number of areas, including computers, information processing, and character sets.

ISO 646

The ISO standard for country-specific 7-bit character sets.

ISO 8859

The ISO standard for international 8-bit character sets.

ISO 10646

The ISO universal character-set standard, covering potentially all of the world's writing systems.

ITU

International Telecommunications Union.

ITU-T

Telecommunications Standardization Sector of the ITU, formerly CCITT (*q.v.*).

JIS

Japan Industrial Standard.

JIS X 0201

The Japanese standard single-byte code for Roman and Katakana characters.

JIS X 0208

The Japanese standard two-byte code for Kanji characters, including also Katakana, Roman, Cyrillic, Greek, and others.

K

Kilo, meaning either 1,000 or 1,024.

KDD

Kermit Dialing Directory.

KND

Kermit Network Directory.

KOI

(КОИ) Russian abbreviation for Код для Обмена Информатсией — Kod dlia Obmiena Informaciyey (Code for Information Interchange).

KSC

Kermit Script. The recommended filetype for Kermit script files.

KSD

Kermit Services Directory.

ksh

The K-Shell, or Korn shell [5]. An alternative command interpreter supplied with some versions of UNIX.

LAN

Local area network.

LAPM

Link Access Procedure for Modems, specified in ITU-T V.42 [11].

LAT

Local Area Transport protocol, used by DEC Ethernet terminal servers.

LDM

Limited Distance Modem.

LF

Linefeed, ASCII character 10.

LU

Logical Unit.

LZW

Lempel, Ziv, Welch data compression. Used, for example, in V.42*bis* [12].

M

Mega, meaning either one million or 1,048,576.

MNP

Microcom Networking Protocol, used by modems for error correction and data compression. Levels 1 through 4 provide error correction. Levels 5 and above also provide compression.

MS-DOS

Microsoft's Disk Operating System for microcomputers based on the Intel 8086 CPU family.

NANP

North American Numbering Plan, the system used for telephone numbers in the USA, Canada, and various Carribean and Pacific islands.

NAK

Negative Acknowledgement.

NFS

Network File System.

NIC

Network Information Center.

NRC

National Replacement Character set. A 7-bit character set, usually, but not always, an ISO 646 national version (DEC).

NTFS

The Microsoft Windows NT File System, which supports long filenames.

NTN

Network Terminal Number (part of an X.121 address).

NUL

ASCII character number 0, as distinct from the number 0 or the ASCII character digit 0 (ASCII 48). Also, the OS/2, Windows, and DOS null device [59].

NVT

Network Virtual Terminal, the base definition for a TELNET terminal.

OS

Operating system.

PAD

Packet Assembler and Disassembler, the terminal interface to an X.25 network, specified in ITU-T X.3 [13].

PBX

Private Branch Exchange. A telephone system that serves the internal needs of an organization and provides connections to the external telephone network. Some PBX's can be used for data as well as voice transmission within the organization.

PC

Personal computer.

PCIA

Personal Communications Industry Association.

PDN

Public data network, usually using X.25 protocols.

PEP

Telebit's Packet Ensemble Protocol, used between Telebit modems.

pid

Process identification number.

PM

Presentation Manager. The OS/2 graphical user interface.

PRN

The DOS, Windows, and OS/2 default printer device.

PSN

Packet switched network.

q.v.

[L] *quod vide* (which see).

REXX

Procedures Language/2 for OS/2 and other operating systems such as VM/CMS and AmigaDOS. A flexible language for writing system command procedures.

RFC

Request For Comments. Internet standards, maintained by the IETF, *q.v.*

RI

Ring Indicator, RS-232 signal with which the modem tells the computer that the telephone is ringing.

RLSI

Received Line Signal Indicator. Same as CD, *q.v.*

RMS

Record Management System. The file system interface for (Open)VMS and other DEC operating systems.

ROM

Read-Only Memory.

RPI

Rockwell Protocol Interface. Designation for a type of modem, which might be made or marketed by any manufacturer at all under any brand, that requires external software or drivers in order to perform error correction and data compression.

RS-232

An Electronic Industries Association (EIA) standard that gives the electrical and functional specification for serial binary digital data transmission. The most commonly used interface between DTEs and DCEs. The USA equivalent of ITU-T Recommendation V.24 [9].

RTR

Ready to Receive. New name for Request To Send (RTS), *q.v.*

RTS

Request To Send. A signal used by a DTE to regulate the flow of data from a DCE. When the DTE turns RTS on, the DCE is not supposed to send data. When the DTE turns RTS off, the DCE is allowed to send data.

RTS/CTS

A form of full-duplex flow control or half-duplex line access control that uses the RTS and CTS signals. Works between the PC and the device it is directly connected to, such as a high-speed modem. *Also see* RTS and CTS.

RTT

Round Trip Time.

sh

The standard UNIX shell, also known as the Bourne shell.

SLIP

Serial Line Internet Protocol.

SNA

Systems Network Architecture, an IBM mainframe networking method.

SO/SI

Shift-Out/Shift-In, a method for shifting between 7- and 8-bit characters on 7-bit connections.

TAP

Telocator Alphanumeric Protocol, PCIA standard for alphanumeric pagers.

TAPI

The Microsoft Telephony Application Programming Interface.

tar

Tape archive (UNIX).

TCP

Transmission Control Protocol. The transport layer of the TCP/IP protocol.

TCP/IP

A network protocol in widespread use for both local and wide area networking. The protocol of the worldwide Internet.

TDD

Telecommunication Devices for the Deaf. Usually a Teletype or other hardcopy terminal with a built-in modem. Original TDDs communicate at a very slow speed using a special modulation technique and a limited 5-bit character code called Baudot; ASCII TDDs are compatible with modern modems and character sets.

ter

[L] "thrice" (used with ITU-T standards).

TIES

Time Independent Escape Sequence. A trick used on Hayes compatible modems made by some manufacturers to avoid the Hayes-patented one-second guard time around the escape sequence.

TTY

Teletype, an abbreviation used to designate a terminal or a computer terminal port.

UART

Universal Asynchronous Receiver/Transmitter. An asynchronous communication port.

UNIX

A popular operating system originally developed at AT&T Bell Laboratories and noted for its portability.

URL

Uniform Resource Locator.

UUCP

UNIX-to-UNIX Copy Program.

V.22

ITU-T standard for 1200 bps full-duplex modems.

V.22*bis*

ITU-T standard for 2400 bps full-duplex modems.

V.23

ITU-T standard for 600 and 1200 bps half-duplex modems with 75 bps back channel (split-speed modems).

V.24

ITU-T standard that gives the electrical and functional specification for serial binary digital data transmission; the European equivalent of RS-232.

V.25*bis*

ITU-T standard modem dialing language.

V.32

ITU-T standard for 9600 bps modem connection.

V.32*bis*

ITU-T standard for 14400 bps modem connection.

V.34

ITU-T standard for 28800 bps modem connection.

V.42

ITU-T standard error correction for modems, also called LAPM.

V.42*bis*

The ITU-T data compression standard.

VAX

Virtual Address Extended. The Digital Equipment Corporation 32-bit computer architecture.

VMS

Virtual Memory System, the operating system for DEC VAX computers. Renamed to OpenVMS in later releases for both VAX and Alpha architectures.

WWW

The World Wide Web, a graphical / hypertext way of accessing the Internet.

X.3

The protocol specifying the interface between a terminal and an X.25 network, specified by ITU-T Recommendation X.3, used on public data networks.

X.25

A networking method, specified by ITU-T Recommendation X.25, used on public data networks.

X.121

An addressing method used on X.25 networks.

Xon/Xoff

The most common full-duplex flow control method, in which the receiver sends an Xoff character when its input buffer is close to filling up and an Xon when it has made room for more data to arrive. Also called software flow control, to distinguish it from hardware flow control methods such as RTS/CTS.

References

[1]   *ANSI X3.4-1986, Code for Information Interchange*
      American National Standards Institute, 1986.
      The ASCII character-set specification; the US version of ISO 646.

[2]   *ANSI X3.15-1976, Bit Sequencing of ASCII in Serial-By-Bit Data Transmission*
      American National Standards Institute, 1976.
      The standard that specifies how characters are transmitted on a serial connection.

[3]   *ANSI 3.16-1976, Character Structure and Character Parity Sense for
      Serial-By-Bit Data Communication in ASCII*
      American National Standards Institute, 1976.
      The standard that specifies the transmission format for ASCII characters.

[4]   *ANSI X3.64-1979, Additional Controls for Use with the American National Stan-
      dard Code for Information Interchange*
      American National Standards Institute, 1979.
      Control sequences for video terminals and peripherals.

[5]   Bolsky, Morris I., and David G. Korn.
      The Kornshell.
      Prentice-Hall, Englewood Cliffs, NJ, 1989.

[6]   Bryabin, V.M., et al.
      О Системе Кодирования для Персональных ЭВМ.
      Микропроцессорные Средства и Системы (4), 1986.
      The article in which the "Alternative Cyrillic" character set for PCs was first
          proposed, which became the basis for CP866.

[7]   *British Standard BS 4730, The Set of Graphic Characters of the United Kingdom*
        7-Bit Data Code
        British Standards Institution, 1975.

[8]   *CCITT Recommendation E.123, Notation for National and International*
        Telephone Numbers
        CCITT, Geneva, 1988.

[9]   *CCITT V.24, List of Definitions for Interchange Circuits between Data Terminal*
        Equipment and Data Circuit-Terminating Equipment
        CCITT, Geneva, 1984.
        The European equivalent of RS-232.

[10]   *CCITT V.25bis, Automatic Calling and/or Answering Equipment on the General*
        Switched Telephone Network (GSTN) Using the 100-Series Interchange Circuits
        CCITT, Geneva, 1984, 1988.

[11]   *CCITT Recommendation V.42, Error-Correcting Procedures for DCEs Using*
        Asynchronous-to-Synchronous Conversion
        CCITT, Geneva, 1988.

[12]   *CCITT Recommendation V.42 bis, Data Compression Procedures for Data Circuit*
        Terminating Equipment (DCE) Using Error Correcting Procedures
        CCITT, Geneva, 1990.

[13]   *CCITT Recommendation X.3, Packet Assembly Disassembly Facility (PAD) in a*
        Public Data Network
        CCITT, Geneva, 1988.

[14]   *CCITT Recommendation X.25, Interface between Data Terminal Equipment (DTE)*
        and Data Circuit-Terminating Equipment (DCE) for Terminals Operating in the
        Packet Mode and Connected to Public Data Networks by Dedicated Circuit
        CCITT, Geneva, 1989.

[15]   *CCITT X.28, DTE/DCE Interface for a Start-Stop Mode Data Terminal Equipment*
        Accessing the Packet Assembly/Disassembly Facility (PAD) in a Public Data Net-
        work Situated in the Same Country
        CCITT, Geneva, 1977.

[16]   *CCITT X.29, Procedures for the Exchange of Control Information and User Data*
        Between a Packet Mode DTE and a Packet Assembly/Disassembly Facility (PAD)
        CCITT, Geneva, 1977.

[17]   *CCITT Recommendation X.121, International Numbering Plan for Public Data*
        Networks
        CCITT, Geneva, 1988.

[18]   Chandler, John.
        Dynamic Packet Size Control.
        Kermit News 3(1), June, 1988.

[19]   Chandler, John.
        IBM System/370 Kermit User's Guide
        Columbia University Academic Information Systems, 1993.

[20]   Comer, Douglas and David L. Stevens.
        Internetworking with TCP/IP.
        Prentice-Hall, Englewood Cliffs, NJ, 1991.

[21]   da Cruz, Frank.
        Kermit, A File Transfer Protocol.
        Digital Press, Newton, MA, 1987.

[22]   da Cruz, Frank, and Christine Gianone.
        How Efficient Is Kermit?
        Kermit News (4), June, 1990.

[23]   Data General.
        Learning to Use Your AOS/VS System
        Data General, Westboro, MA, 1986.
        093-000031-02.

[24]   Data General.
        AOS/VS System Concepts
        Data General, Westboro, MA, 1986.
        093-000335-01.

[25]   Data General.
        Programming the Display Terminal: Models D217, D413, and D463
        Data General, Westboro, MA, 1991.
        014-002111-00.

[26]   Data General.
        Using the CLI (AOS/VS and AOS/VS II)
        Data General, Westboro, MA, 1991.
        093-000646-01.

[27]   Digital Equipment Corporation.
        VT102 Video Terminal User Guide
        Digital Equipment Corporation, Maynard, MA, 1982.
        EK-VT102-UG-003.

[28]   Digital Equipment Corporation.
        VT330/340 Programmer Reference Manual, Volume 1: Text Programming
        Digital Equipment Corporation, Maynard, MA, 1987.
        EK-VT3XX-GP-001.

[29]   Dijkstra, Edsgar W.
        Go To Statement Considered Harmful.
        Communications of the ACM 11(3), March, 1968.

[30]   ECMA.
*Standard ECMA-113, 8-Bit Single-Byte Coded Graphic Character Sets,
  Latin/Cyrillic Alphabet*
1st edition, European Computer Manufacturers Association, 1974.
KOI-8, equivalent to GOST 19768-1974.

[31]   ECMA.
*Standard ECMA-113, 8-Bit Single-Byte Coded Graphic Character Sets,
  Latin/Cyrillic Alphabet*
2nd edition, European Computer Manufacturers Association, 1988.
Equivalent to ISO 8859-5 Latin/Cyrillic and GOST 19768-1987.

[32]   ECMA.
*Standard ECMA-121, 8-Bit Single-Byte Coded Graphic Character Sets,
  Latin/Hebrew Alphabet*
European Computer Manufacturers Association, July 1987.
Equivalent to ISO 8859-8 Latin/Hebrew.

[33]   *EIA Standard RS-232-C, Interface Between Data Terminal Equipment and Data
Communication Equipment Employing Serial Binary Data Interchange*
Electronic Industries Association, 2001 Eye Street N.W., Washington, DC 20006,
  1969 (Reaffirmed 1981).
Recently supplanted by RS-232-D, which defined several of RS-232-C's unused
  circuits, and changed some terminology.

[34]   *EIA Standard RS-423-A, Electrical Characteristics of Unbalanced Voltage Digital
Interface Circuits*
Electronic Industries Association, 2001 Eye Street N.W., Washington, DC 20006,
  1979.

[35]   Gianone, Christine M.
Using MS-DOS Kermit.
Digital Press, Newton, MA, 1992.

[36]   Gianone, Christine M., and Frank da Cruz.
A Kermit Protocol Extension for International Character Sets.
Technical Report, Columbia University, 1990.

[37]   Gianone, Christine M. and Frank da Cruz.
A Locking Shift Mechanism for the Kermit File Transfer Protocol.
Technical Report, Columbia University, 1991.

[38]   *Hayes Smartmodem 2400 User's Guide*
Hayes Microcomputer Products, Inc., 1986.

[39]   Hemenway, Kathy, and Helene Armitage.
Proposed Syntax Standards for UNIX System Commands.
UNIX/WORLD 1(3), 1984.

[40]   *IBM National Language Support Reference Manual*
        IBM Canada Ltd., National Language Technical Centre, Ontario, 1990.
        SE09-8002-01.

[41]   *IBM Character Data Representation Architecture, Level 1 Registry*
        IBM Canada Ltd., National Language Technical Centre, Ontario, 1990.
        SC09-1391-00.

[42]   *ISO Standard 646, 7-Bit Coded Character Set for Information Processing
        Interchange*
        Second edition, International Organization for Standardization, 1983.
        Also available as ECMA-6, and similar to CCITT T.50.

[43]   *ISO International Standard 2022, Information processing — ISO 7-bit and 8-bit
        coded character sets — Code extension techniques*
        Third edition, International Organization for Standardization, 1986.
        Also available as ECMA-35.

[44]   *ISO International Standard 4873, Information processing — ISO 8-bit code for
        information interchange — Structure and rules for implementation*
        Second edition, International Organization for Standardization, 1986.
        Also available as ECMA-43.

[45]   *ISO International Standard 8859 Parts 1 through 10, Information
        Processing—8-Bit Single-Byte Coded Graphic Character Sets*
        International Organization for Standardization, 1987–1995.

[46]   *ISO/IEC 10646-1, International Standard 10646, Information
        Processing—Multiple-Octet Coded Character Set*
        ISO/IEC JTC1, 1993.

[47]   *ISO International Standard 6429, Information processing — C1 Control Charac-
        ter Set of ISO 6429*
        International Organization for Standardization, 1983.

[48]   *ISO International Register of Coded Characters to Be Used with Escape
        Sequences*
        European Computer Manufacturers Association (ECMA), 1990, updated
        periodically.

[49]   *JIS X 0201, The Japanese Katakana and Roman Set of Characters*
        Japan Industrial Standards Committee, 1969.

[50]   *JIS X 0208, The Japanese Graphic Character Set for Information Interchange*
        Japan Industrial Standards Committee, 1983, revised 1995.

[51]   *JIS X 0212, Supplementary Japanese Graphic Character Set for Information
        Interchange*
        Japan National Committee on ISO/IEC JTC1/SC2, 1991.

[52] B. Kantor.
      RFC 1282: BSD Rlogin.
      Technical Report, Network Working Group, December, 1991.

[53] Kernighan, Brian W., and Dennis M. Ritchie.
      Prentice-Hall Software Series: *The C Programming Language.*
      Prentice-Hall, Englewood Cliffs, NJ, 1988.

[54] Kientzle, Tim.
      The Working Programmer's Guide to Serial Protocols.
      Coriolis Group Books, Scottsdale, AZ, 1995.

[55] Kientzle, Tim.
      Improving Kermit Performance.
      Dr. Dobbs Journal :28–38, February, 1996.

[56] McNamara, John E.
      Technical Aspects of Data Communication.
      Digital Press, Newton, MA, 1988.

[57] *Microsoft MS-DOS Version 4.01 in Russian, Product Description*
      Microsoft Corporation, Unterschleißheim, Germany, 1989–1990.

[58] Пакеты Прекладных Программ Телеобработки Данных на МикроЭВМ
      International Center for Scientific and Technical Information (ICSTI), Moscow,
            1987.
      A Russian Kermit User Guide, including character tables for several Cyrillic
            character sets.

[59] Postel, J., and Reynolds, J.
      RFC 854: TELNET Protocol Specification.
      Technical Report, Network Working Group, May, 1983.

[60] Rasmussen, Bob.
      Who Is Kermit and Why Is He in My Computer?
      NCR Monthly , March, 1990.

[61] Snedecor, George W. and William G. Cochran.
      Statistical Methods.
      Iowa State University Press, Ames, 1989.

[62] Todino, Grace, and Dale Dougherty.
      Nutshell Handbook: *Using UUCP and Usenet.*
      O'Reilly & Associates, Inc., Newton, MA, 1987.

[63] The Unicode Consortium.
      The Unicode Standard, Version 2.0.
      Addison-Wesley Developers Press, July 1996.

Trademarks and Copyrights

The Telnet Song by Guy Steele on pages 169–170 appeared in Communications of the ACM, Volume 27, Number 4, April 1984, Copyright © 1984 by the Association for Computing Machinery, Inc, and is reprinted with permission of the author and of the Association for Computing Machinery, who asked us to say, "Permission to make digital or hard copies of part or all of this work for personal or classroom use is granted without fee provided that copies are not made or distributed for profit or commercial advantage and that copies bear this notice and the full citation on the first page. Copyrights for components of this work owned by others than ACM must be honored. Abstracting with credit is permitted. To copy otherwise, to republish, to post on servers, or to redistribute to lists, requires prior specific permission and/or a fee. Request permissions from Publications Dept, ACM Inc., fax +1 (212) 869-0481, or permissions@acm.org."

The products and services that are referred to in this book, including but not limited to the ones that follow, may be either trademarks and/or registered trademarks of their respective owners. The publisher and authors make no claim to these trademarks.

Adobe Systems Incorporated, Mountain View, CA: PostScript
Alliant: Alliant, Concentrix
Altos Computer Systems: Altos
Amdahl: UTS
Apollo: Aegis, Domain, SR10
Apple Computer, Cupertino, CA: Apple, Apple II, Macintosh, Lisa, LaserWriter, A/UX
AT&T, New York, NY: Touch-Tone
AT&T Information Systems, Morristown, NJ: StarLAN, StarGROUP, AT&T 6300, AT&T 6300 PLUS, UNIX PC, 3B2, 3B20

Atari, Sunnyvale, CA: Atari, ST, GEM, GEMDOS

Berkeley Software Design, Inc., Falls Church, VA: BSDI/386

Charles River Data Systems, Inc., Framingham, MA: UNOS

Chrysler Corporation: Jeep

Cisco Systems, Inc., Menlo Park, CA: cisco, Cisco, AGS, AGS+

Commodore Business Machines, West Chester, PA: Amiga, AmigaDOS, Amiga Workbench, Amiga 2000, Amiga 3000, Amiga 3000UX, Commodore 64, Commodore 128, Intuition

CompuServe, Inc. (an H&R Block Company), Columbus, OH: CompuServe

Concept Omega Corporation, Somerset, NJ: Thoroughbred BASIC

Concurrent, Oceanport, NJ: Concurrent, MASSCOMP, RTU, Xelos

Consensys Corporation, Universal City, TX: Consensys

Control Data Corporation: CDC, Cyber

Convergent Technologies, Inc., Santa Clara, CA: Convergent Technologies, Convergent, MegaFrame Computer System, MiniFrame Computer System, CTIX, CTOS

Convex: Convex, ConvexOS

Cray Research, Eagen, MN: Cray X/MP, Y/MP, C90, UNICOS

Data General Corporation, Westboro, MA: AOS/VS, AViiON, CEO, DASHER, DG/UX, ECLIPSE MV, MV/UX, RDOS, DESKTOP GENERATION

Dell Computer Corporation: Dell, Dell System

Diab Data AB, a Bull company, Tdby, Sweden: DIAB, DNIX

Dialog Information Services, Inc., Palo Alto, CA: DIALOG

Digital Equipment Corporation, Maynard, MA: The Digital logo, DEC, PDP-8, OS/8, OS/278, PDP-11, RSTS/E, RSX-11, RT-11, IAX, PDP-12, OS/12, VAX, AXP, Alpha, VMS, OpenVMS, VT52, VT100, VT102, VT220, VT320, Rainbow, VAXmate, DECmate, DECserver, DECstation, DEC-SYSTEM, DECsystem, TOPS-10, TOPS-20, VAXstation, MicroVAX, PATHWORKS, ULTRIX

Digital Equipment Corporation, Intel Corporation, Xerox Corporation: Ethernet

Digitel S/A Indústria Eletrônica, Porto Alegre, Brazil: Digitel DT-22

Dow Jones and Company, Princeton, NJ: Dow-Jones News/Retrieval Service

Encore Computer: Multimax, Umax

ESIX Computer, Inc., Santa Ana, CA: ESIX

EXABYTE Corporation, Boulder, CO: EXABYTE, EXATAPE

Fortune Systems, Redwood City, CA: For:Pro

Fujitsu, Japan: Fujitsu

Groupe Bull, France: Honeywell, VIP

Harris Corporation, Fort Lauderdale, FL: Night Hawk, CX/UX

Hayes Microcomputer Products, Inc., Atlanta, GA: Hayes Smartmodem 1200 and 2400

Heath Company, Benton Harbor, MI: Heath-19

Henson Associates, Inc., New York, NY: Kermit. The Kermit protocol was named after Kermit the Frog, star of THE MUPPET SHOW television series. The name "Kermit" is used by permission of Henson Associates, Inc., New York.

Hewlett-Packard Co., Palo Alto, CA: HP-9000, HP-UX

Insignia Solutions, Inc., Mountain View, CA: SoftPC

Integrated Computer Solutions, Cambridge, MA: ICS, ISI, VS8

Intel Corp., Santa Clara, CA: Intel 8080, 8086, 8088, 80286, 80386, 80486, i286, i386, i486, OpenNET

INTERACTIVE Systems Corporation, Division of SunSoft, Santa Monica, CA: INTERACTIVE UNIX

International Business Machines Corp., Armonk, NY: IBM, Series/1, VM/CMS, MVS/TSO, PC-DOS, Operating System/2, OS/2, Presentation Manager, 3270, 3705, 3725, System/370, IBM PC, IBM PC/XT, IBM PC/AT, IBM PC*jr*, IBM RT PC, PS/1, PS/2, IBM 7171, Token Ring, NETBIOS, CGA, MCGA, EGA, VGA, XGA, RS/6000, RISC System/6000, AIX, AIX Windows, ACIS, Micro Channel, REXX, Procedures Language/2

Linotype AG: Times

Lotus Development Corporation, Cambridge, MA: Lotus 1-2-3

Mark Williams Company, Chicago, IL: COHERENT

Massachusetts General Hospital: MUMPS

Massachusetts Institute of Technology: X-Window System

Masscomp, Framingham, MA: RTU

MCI Communication Corporation, Piscataway, NJ: MCI Mail

Meridian Technology Corporation, Chesterfield, MO: SuperLAT

Microcom, Inc., Norwood, MA: Microcom Networking Protocol, MNP, Universal Link Negotiation, Statistical Duplexing

Microport: Microport

Microsoft Corporation, Redmond, WA: Microsoft, MS, MS-DOS, Win32, Win32s, Windows, Windows NT

Microware Systems Corporation, Des Moines, IA: OS-9, OS-9000, OS-9/68000

MIPS Computer Systems, Inc., Sunnyvale, CA: MIPS, RISC/OS, UMIPS

Modular Computer Systems, Inc., Fort Lauderdale, FL: Modcomp: REAL/IX

Motorola, Inc., Tempe, AZ: Motorola, System V/68, System V/88, Motorola Delta Series

Motorola Semiconductors, Inc., Austin, TX: Motorola, 68000, 68010, 68020, 68030, 68040

MT XINU, Inc., Berkeley, CA: Mach^{386}

NCR Corporation, Dayton, OH: NCR, Tower

NeXT Computer, Inc, Redwood City, CA: NeXT, NeXTstep, NeXTcube, NeXTstation

Nippon Electric Corporation, Japan: NEC, NEC PC9801

Novell, Inc., Provo, UT: Novell, NetWare, NetWare 286, NetWare 386, LAN Workplace for DOS, Excelan

Ing. C. Olivetti & C., S.p.A., Ivrea, Italy: Olivetti, LSX, X/OS

Open Software Foundation, Cambridge, MA: Motif, OSF, OSF/1

Penril DataComm, Ltd, Hampshire, UK: Penril, Alliance

PKWARE, Inc., Brown Deer, WI: PKZIP

Plexus, San Jose, CA: Plexus

Prime Computer, Natick, MA: PRIME, PRIMOS, PRIMIX

Pyramid Technology Corp., Mountain View, CA: Pyramid

Racal-Vadic, Milpitas, CA: Vadic, VA3400

Regents of the University of California: Berkeley Software Distribution, BSD

Ridge Computers: Ridge 32

Santa Cruz Operation, Santa Cruz, CA: SCO Xenix, SCO UNIX, Open Desktop, ODT

Sequent Computer Systems, Inc., Beaverton, OR: Sequent, Balance, Symmetry, DYNIX, ptx, DYNIX/ptx

Silicon Graphics, Inc., Mountain View, CA: Silicon Graphics, IRIS, IRIS Indigo, IRIX

Solbourne Computer, Longmont, CO: Solbourne, OS/MP

Sony, Japan: Sony NEWS

SPARC International, Inc.: SPARC, SPARCstation

Sun Microsystems, Inc., Mountain View, CA: Sun Microsystems, Sun Workstation, Sun, Sun-3, Sun-4, SunOS, NFS, SunLink, SunSoft, SunView, Solaris

Tandy Corporation, Fort Worth, TX: Radio Shack, Tandy 16/6000

Andrew S. Tanenbaum: MINIX

Tektronix, Inc., Wilsonville, OR: Tektronix, UTek

Telebit Corporation, Sunnyvale, CA: Telebit, TrailBlazer, QBlazer, WorldBlazer, PEP

Telecom Canada, Ottawa, ON, Canada: Datapac

Teletype Corporation, Skokie, IL: Teletype

TGV, Inc., Santa Cruz, CA: MultiNet

3Com Corporation, Santa Clara, CA: 3Com, Bridge Applications Programmer Interface (BAPI)

Tri Star: Flash Cache

TYMNET, Inc., San Jose, CA: TYMNET

UNISYS Corporation, Blue Bell, PA: Unisys, PW2, PC/IT, Uniservo, CustomCare, Sperry, Burroughs, U6000/65, MightyFrame, S/Series, CTIX, BTOS

UNIX System Laboratories, Inc., Summit, NJ: UNIX, System III, System V, OPEN LOOK

US Robotics: Courier

US Sprint Communications Company Limited Partnership, Shawnee Mission, KS: US Sprint, SprintNet, Telenet

The Wollongong Group, Inc., Palo Alto, CA: WIN/TCP, WIN/ROUTE

WordPerfect Corporation, Orem, UT: WordPerfect

Xerox Corporation, Stamford, CT: Ethernet

Zenith Data Systems, Glenview, IL: Zenith-19 Terminal

Zilog, Campbell, CA: Zilog, ZEUS

Other brands or product names are trademarks or registered trademarks of their respective holders.

Colophon

The text of this book was entered using MS-DOS Kermit, Kermit 95, and/or Kermit/2 on PCs and C-Kermit 6.0 on NeXTstations into GNU EMACS on a SunOS UNIX system. The text was formatted for PostScript using the Scribe document preparation system on the Sun and set in Times Roman augmented by the Cyrillic Gothic font designed by Jay Sekora of Princeton University and the Jerusalem font from Hebrew University in Jerusalem, with much time-saving assistance from Trey Matteson's PostScript File Previewer on the NeXTSCRIBE TEXT FORMATTER.

MS-DOS Kermit, Kermit 95, Kermit/2, and C-Kermit are products of the Kermit Project, Columbia University, 612 West 115th Street, New York, NY 10025-7799, USA. GNU EMACS is a product of the Free Software Foundation, 675 Massachusetts Avenue, Cambridge, MA 02139, USA. Scribe is a commercial product of Cygnet Publishing Technologies, Inc., 355 Fifth Avenue, Suite 1515, Pittsburgh, PA 15222-2407, USA.

Index

For discounted media-only rates on C-Kermit software media, return this form; *the original, not a copy. TWO PRICES* are shown for each item. The first price applies in the USA, Canada, and Mexico. The second price applies to all other countries. All prices are in US dollars.

C-KERMIT DISTRIBUTION ON MAGNETIC MEDIA OR CD-ROM

Each includes all C-Kermit files: UNIX and VMS source code, installation files and instructions, help files, beware files, initialization files, plus selected binaries:

☐	ISO-format CD-ROM:	$15 / $20
☐	4mm DAT cartridge, UNIX tar format:	$150 / $185
☐	Quarter-inch tape cartridge (QIC), UNIX tar format:	$150 / $185
☐	8mm EXABYTE tape cartridge, UNIX tar format:	$150 / $185
☐	TK50 cartridge, VMS / OpenVMS BACKUP format:	$150 / $185
☐	4mm DAT cartridge, VMS / OpenVMS BACKUP format:	$150 / $185
☐	9-track 1600 BPI magnetic tape, ANSI format:	$100 / $135
☐	9-track 1600 BPI magnetic tape, UNIX tar format:	$100 / $135

Subtotal: $_____

BINARIES ON 3.5-INCH DOS-FORMAT DISKETTES

Includes the binary executable C-Kermit program for the system indicated, plus all relevant installation, initialization, demo, help, and beware files:

☐	C-Kermit for AIX 4.1/PowerPC:	$15 / $20
☐	C-Kermit for Linux:	$15 / $20
☐	C-Kermit for OS-9/68000:	$15 / $20
☐	C-Kermit for QNX 4.2x:	$15 / $20
☐	C-Kermit for SCO OpenServer R5:	$15 / $20
☐	C-Kermit for Solaris/Intel:	$15 / $20
☐	C-Kermit for Solaris/SPARC:	$15 / $20
☐	C-Kermit for UnixWare:	$15 / $20
	Others: Contact us for availability.	

Subtotal: $_____

ADDITIONAL KERMIT BOOKS

☐	*Using C-Kermit:*	$39.95 / $50
☐	*Using MS-DOS Kermit* (includes diskette):	$39.95 / $50
☐	*Kermit MS-DOS Mode d'Emploi* (in French):	$39.95 / $50
☐	*Kermit, A File Transfer Protocol*:	$34.95 / $45
☐	Any two of these books + software CD-ROM:	$75 / $100
☐	Any three of these books + software CD-ROM:	$100 / $140

Subtotal: $_____

TOTAL SOFTWARE AND BOOKS: $_____

(Please turn over . . .)

Prepayment is required. Shipping by post or parcel service is included in the price. Allow 2-8 weeks for delivery depending on location. Please do not add sales tax. You may pay by CREDIT CARD or by CHECK. Please complete ONE of the following three sections and mail this form, NOT A COPY, to the address shown on the bottom of the page.

1. PAYMENT BY CREDIT CARD, ALL COUNTRIES

❏ MasterCard ❏ Visa   AMOUNT OF PAYMENT: $_____

Card Number _____   Expires _____

Signature _____   Date _____

2. PAYMENT BY CHECK, USA ONLY   Please enclose a check payable to:

Columbia University Kermit Project

TOTAL AMOUNT OF YOUR CHECK: $_____

3. PAYMENT BY CHECK, ALL OTHER COUNTRIES

Please enclose a check for the total amount payable in US dollars. PLEASE DO NOT USE ELECTRONIC BANK TRANSFERS OR INTERNATIONAL POSTAL COUPONS. Make your check payable to:

Columbia University Kermit Project

If your check is *not* drawn on a US bank, please add a $35 check-cashing fee:

❏ Check-cashing fee: _____   TOTAL AMOUNT OF YOUR CHECK: $_____

SHIP TO:

Name:_____ Phone:_____

Organization:_____

Address:_____

City:_____ State or Province:_____

Country:_____ Zip or Postal Code:_____

MAIL YOUR COMPLETED ORDER FORM WITH PAYMENT TO

The Kermit Project, Dept CKB
Columbia University
612 West 115th Street
New York, NY 10025-7799 USA

Thank you!

Using C-Kermit, Second Edition

PROOF OF PURCHASE

Return this coupon — <u>the original</u>, not a
copy — to obtain discounts on *Kermit 95,
Kermit/2,* or other Kermit software, as
indicated on the appropriate order forms
available at the Kermit Web site:

`http://www.columbia.edu/kermit/k95.html`